•THE FIRST 100•

THE FIRST 100

Portraits of the Men and Women
Who Shaped Las Vegas

HUNTINGTON PRESS • LAS VEGAS

Huntington Press
3687 South Procyon Avenue
Las Vegas, Nevada 89103
(702) 252-0655 Phone
(702) 252-0675 Fax

The First 100
Copyright ©1999, Huntington Press

Printing History
1st Edition—November 1999

Dedicated to the memories of K.J. Evans and W.V. Wright,
kindred spirits in their love for Nevada and its history.

•CONTENTS•

·CONTENTS·

•CONTENTS•

Introduction

The First 100 was originally published as a three-part package in the *Las Vegas Review-Journal*, marking the approaching end of the century in which Las Vegas was born.

Sherman R. Frederick, publisher of the *Review-Journal*, conceived the project as a means of capturing memories of the community's formative years and founders while those memories were still relatively fresh.

"Las Vegas is unusual in that it was created entirely in the 20th century," Frederick pointed out in announcing the project in March 1998. "Many of those who made the important decisions remain alive, while immediate relatives and close acquaintances of others still survive. This gives the *Review-Journal* a special opportunity to portray them and their accomplishments with authentic detail, which newspapers and historians in other cities would envy."

The strategy adopted in this book is to tell the community's story through the lives of 100 people who played significant roles in it. Historians, journalists, and the newspaper's readers were invited to nominate people who should be profiled in *The First 100*. More than 300 people were nominated, and most would have made interesting and historically significant stories. But since time and resources limited the number of profiles to 100, editors had to make hard choices about which to leave out.

Because such choices were necessary, the *Review-Journal* has never represented that the 100 chosen are the most important who could have been selected; the newspaper does, however, represent that all are significant and interesting people. Nor did the editors attempt to rank the relative importance of the 100 people chosen. Instead, they are presented in a logical order, approximating the chronology of their contributions.

Condensing the stories into a hardbound book for permanent addition to the libraries and homes of Las Vegas was not an afterthought, but part of Frederick's original intention. Huntington Press was the writers' first choice as publisher, because of its track record for producing quality books about Las Vegas, chosen and edited by people who understand the city.

Special Projects Editor A.D. Hopkins and writer K.J. Evans worked full time on the project for more than 17 months. Both had been editors of *Nevadan*, a Sunday magazine

"Ol' Blue Eyes" himself, Frank Sinatra

Downtown's Vegas Vic is one of Young Electric Sign Company's (Yesco) best-known creations, with its Marlboro-like visage that stands above Fremont Street.
(Courtesy Yesco)

Introduction Continued ...

formerly published by the *Review-Journal,* which specialized in historical pieces and in-depth profiles. Hopkins also asked certain local historians and some of the *Review-Journal's* star writers to contribute stories.

Historical consultants for the project were Robert Faiss, former city editor of the *Las Vegas Sun* and now an attorney specializing in gaming law; Michael Green, a history professor at Community College of Southern Nevada; Eugene Moehring, a history professor at the University of Nevada-Las Vegas and the author of a respected history of Las Vegas; Frank Wright, curator at the Nevada State Museum and Historical Society; and W.V. "Bill" Wright, former chairman of the museum's board.

W.V. Wright, who was also the former general manager of the *Review-Journal* before his retirement in 1981, died in August 1998 after a short illness. He continued his involvement with *The First 100* until a few weeks prior to his death. Kenneth J. Evans died on September 10, 1999, the day the authors turned over the last story to Huntington Press.

Others greatly helpful to the project include the staffs of UNLV Special Collections and the Nevada State Museum and Historical Society; historian Elizabeth Warren; and Joanne L. Goodwin, an oral history teacher at UNLV.

The original *First 100* three-part series published in the *Las Vegas Review-Journal* would not have been possible without the sponsorship of the following: MGM Grand Hotel and Casino, Mirage Resorts, Del Webb Corporation, Howard Hughes Corporation, Park Towers at Hughes Center, the A.G. Spanos Companies, Palm Mortuary Inc., the Buzard Eye Institute, JHC Health Center, American Pacific Corp., Harrison Door Company, Imperial Palace Hotel and Casino, Jim Marsh Jeep Eagle Mazda Volvo, Mission Industries, Nest Featherings Interior Decorating, Sam's Town Hotel and Casino, Southwest Gas Corp., Sunrise Hospital, and Walker Furniture.

Yesco's neon creations, like the one for the Mint, became the trademark for Las Vegas, and their glare could be spotted by astronauts orbiting the Earth.
(Courtesy Yesco)

In 1931, when nearly everybody had given up on Prohibition, even Las Vegas' elite were unafraid to be photographed in the Meadows speakeasy.
(UNLV Special Collections)

Editors and Authors

A.D. Hopkins is a 30-year resident of Las Vegas and for 12 years edited *Nevadan*, the Sunday magazine formerly published by the *Las Vegas Review-Journal*. As special projects editor for the *Review-Journal*, Hopkins directed the newspaper's original *First 100* project, the forerunner of this book.

A lifelong Nevadan, Kenneth J. Evans was a reporter and editor for several Nevada newspapers, including the *Las Vegas Review-Journal*, before being appointed media relations manager for the Nevada Commission on Tourism in 1992. Returning to the *Review-Journal* in 1998 to work on *The First 100*, Evans died on September 10, 1999, shortly after the project was completed.

Alan Balboni teaches at the Community College of Southern Nevada, where his subjects include American immigration history and American government. Balboni's book, *Beyond the Mafia: Italian Americans and the Development of Las Vegas*, was published by the University of Nevada Press in 1996.

Dick Benoit is a publicity coordinator and speech instructor at the University of Nevada-Las Vegas. A 26-year U.S. Navy and Air Force veteran, he served as the public-affairs officer for Nellis Air Force Base from 1984 to 1987. Also a freelance writer, Benoit was a regular contributor to the *Review-Journal's* former Sunday magazine, *Nevadan*.

Dave Berns has been with the *Las Vegas Review-Journal* since 1994 and has written about the casino industry for the past three years. A graduate of the University of Oregon, Berns previously worked as a reporter for the *Statesman-Journal* in Salem, Oregon.

A business writer for the *Review-Journal*, John G. Edwards is currently working on a book about investing in casino operating companies. His free-lance articles have appeared in the *New York Times*, the *New York Daily News*, the *Chicago Tribune*, and the *Dallas Morning News*.

Dennis McBride is a Boulder City writer who specializes in local history. His published books include *Boulder City: How it Began* and *Hard Work and Far From Home: The Civilian Conservation Corps at Lake Mead*.

Award-winning entertainment columnist Michael Paskevich joined the *Review-Journal* in 1989 and is considered Las Vegas' toughest entertainment critic. A graduate of the University of California-Berkeley (MA 1976), Paskevich worked nearly two decades for California newspapers before moving to Las

To eye pictures of Yesco's oldest offerings, such as the sign for the now-defunct Thunderbird, is akin to scanning the pages of a scrapbook.
(Courtesy Yesco)

Editors and Authors Continued ...

Vegas where, in addition to his *R-J* columns, he is writing a book about the oddities of covering "the entertainment capital of the world."

Review-Journal columnist John L. Smith is a native Nevadan with family roots dating back to 1881. His most recent books are *Las Vegas Boulevard*, a column collection, and *The Animal in Hollywood*, a biography of Mafia figure Anthony Fiato. In 1998, Smith was honored for column writing by the National Headliner Awards and also was named "Out-

standing Journalist" by the Nevada Press Association.

Robert L. Stoldal is general manager of Las Vegas One, a 24-hour television news source, and was news director at KLAS-TV, Channel 8, during the late 1970s and early 1980s, when the station consistently led local newscasts in the Nielsen ratings. Stoldal has been a student of Southern Nevada history since his family moved here in 1957.

Ed Vogel has been with the *Las Vegas Review-Journal* for 22 years and has served as the newspaper's capital bureau chief in Carson City since 1985. He is a graduate of the University of Michigan.

A graduate of the University of Missouri, Mike Weatherford has been an entertainment reporter for the *Las Vegas Review-Journal* since November 1987. Weatherford's love of the "old Vegas" led to his upcoming book *Cult Vegas*, to be published by Huntington Press in

the spring of 2000.

A 13-year resident of Las Vegas, Joan Whitely earned a master's degree in journalism from Northwestern University in 1982. She currently writes for the "Living" section of the *Review-Journal* and has won a coveted "Best in the West" award for feature writing.

Liberace at practice in Montreal, late 1940s
(Liberace Museum)

The statue of Benny Binion stands at the corner of Second Street and Ogden Avenue.
(Review-Journal files)

THE FIRST 100

PART I:

The Early Years

John C. Fremont (1813–1890)

While other scouts and adventurers may have come through the valley first, a son of scandal is noted for pointing travelers toward the future Sin City. BY A.D. HOPKINS

"After a day's journey of 18 miles, in a northeasterly direction, we encamped in the midst of another very large basin, at a camping ground called Las Vegas—a term which the Spaniards use to signify fertile or marshy plains."

—John C. Fremont, May 3, 1844

Discoveries are rarely the work of one person, and no case shows this more clearly than the debate over who "discovered" Las Vegas for settlers of European ancestry.

There was Antonio Armijo, a New Mexico merchant who in the winter of 1829–1830 organized a trading expedition to California. There was Rafael Rivera, Armijo's scout, who probably camped in the valley before his commander. But it was John C. Fremont who literally put Las Vegas on the map. And because more than 20,000 copies of his map were immediately published and distributed to anybody who wanted one, Las Vegas became an important stop on the way West.

Elizabeth Warren, a Las Vegas historian who wrote her thesis on exploration of the region, thinks Fremont had the greatest impact, but adds that others should share the credit. "Trade was already a fact of life before European settlers came," noted Warren.

Greg Seymour, archaeologist at the Harry Reid Center for Environmental Studies, said the Anasazi, more usually associated with New Mexico and Arizona, the Patayan of the lower Colorado River, and the Southern Paiute all used the valley. "The Southern Paiute call the Old Spanish Trail the Paiute Trail, and believe it was in use even before them."

Mountain man Jedediah Smith probably never saw the Las Vegas Valley, yet his explorations may have brought others here. Hoping to export Rocky Mountain fur from some Pacific port, the trapper twice led expeditions to Spanish California via Nevada's Virgin River and northern Arizona, crossing the Colorado River near today's Laughlin. Both times Spanish authorities imprisoned the Americans, and on the second trip, formerly friendly Mojaves killed 10 of his men.

But one survivor of a Smith expedition, named Black, settled in Northern New Mexico. "He must have talked about that trip," figures Warren. Or word might have circulated from the mountain men's annual rendezvous.

"So when Armijo mounts his expedition in '29, he leaves with the secure knowledge it can be done. You can't otherwise account for 60 men and maybe 100 mules. This would reflect a joint venture by more than one investor; nobody has enough money to hire 60 men for a year." The caravan was laden with trade goods.

"By the time Armijo leaves in 1829, there has been 100 years of trading with the Utes, so there were known trading trails as far as Utah." Armijo took these for some distance, and proceeded down the Virgin River to its confluence with the Muddy.

On Christmas Day, a detachment of scouts left the party, returning on December 31. On New Year's Day, Armijo noted in his diary, "One man was missing from yesterday's detachment … citizen Rafael Rivera."

Rivera rejoined the group January 7. Following his lead, the party moved into some part of the Las Vegas Valley. Warren thinks they came up the Las Vegas Wash to Duck Creek, followed the creek to about the location of today's Paradise Spa, and left the valley via the low pass to the south. Their next camp was at a dry lake, probably near today's Jean.

Fremont in Southern Nevada

POP.*	DECADE
**	pre-1900
n/a	1900
30	1900
945	1910
2,686	1920
5,952	1930
13,937	1940
45,577	1950
123,667	1960
273,288	1970
463,087	1980
715,587	1990

■ Time spent in Southern Nev.
* - Population figures are for greater Las Vegas area (*Source: Nevada State Data Center*).
** - Fremont actually spent just three days in Southern Nevada in 1844.

John C. Fremont (seated) recognized Kit Carson for the unlettered genius he must have been after their first chance meeting on a steamer. Both men played key roles in the exploring accident that put Las Vegas on the map.

(UNLV Special Collections)

Armijo inspired other caravans, but they lasted only until about 1850. And most bypassed the Las Vegas Valley.

It is an accident of history that the Las Vegas route became famous as "The Old Spanish Trail." The accident involves one of the most remarkable adventurers of Western history—John C. Fremont.

Fremont was the son of Anne Beverly Whiting, a Virginia aristocrat whose family married her off at 17 to a rich man of 62. In 1808, when Anne was 29 and her husband 74, she fell in love with a Frenchman who taught languages and fencing. They fled Richmond together in 1810 and had a son, Fremont, in 1813. He became a brilliant scholar, yet was so often truant that he was expelled from college.

In 1837 the federal government decided to survey the Cherokee country of Georgia and the Carolinas. Here Fremont learned to camp and to pack a mule. He then was appointed to the U.S. Topographical Corps, and was a member of Joseph Nicolas Nicollet's expedition to map the country between the upper Mississippi and Missouri rivers.

Back in Washington by 1840, Fremont traded his stories of adventure for invitations and introductions, including an introduction to Senator Thomas Hart Benton. Fremont fell in love with Benton's 16-year-old daughter, Jessie, and she married him in October 1841.

Benton was a leading exponent of opening the West. He knew more about it than almost anybody in Washington. Fremont, however, had the charisma and courage to put Benton's dream into practice. And Fremont had the timing. The United States was ready to finance an expedition to map the Oregon Trail. In the spring of 1842, Fremont made his way to St. Louis and began assembling the first expedition that would bear his name.

On a chance meeting with Christopher "Kit" Carson, Fremont realized there was a remarkable man beneath the buckskins. Carson, at 33, had not yet learned to read nor write. Yet he spoke French, Spanish, English, and several Indian tongues, and was proficient in the sign language of the plains.

Carson guided Fremont's first expedition into the Wind River Valley, then swung south on his own trapping expedition. Fremont was back in Washington by October to write his report. Poetically phrased—most believe by the articulate Jessie—his reports were instant fodder for the newspapers.

In May 1843, Fremont's second expedition was to map the area between the Rockies and the Pacific Ocean. The men carried breechloading rifles—advanced weapons for the time—and also dragged along a small howitzer. Fremont pushed through what is now Utah and into Oregon. Then he turned south seeking the Rio Buenaventura, Klamath Lake, and Mary's Lake, all "described" by earlier explorers. He found Klamath Lake but the other two, it turned out, do not exist.

By January 1844, Fremont had abandoned the howitzer in heavy snowdrifts in Northern Nevada. History buffs and treasure hunters have been looking for the "Fremont Cannon" ever since. Today, a replica of it is a revolving trophy for football games between UNLV and UNR.

The expedition beat its way across the Sierra Nevada to Sutter's Fort, arriving with only 33 of the 67 horses and mules that started the trek. Fremont then headed south to strike the Spanish Trail toward Santa Fe.

Fremont described the march in his memoirs: "Forced on south by a desert on one hand, and a mountain range on the other; guided by a civilized Indian, attended by two wild ones from the Sierra; a Chinook from the Columbia; and our own mixture of American, French, German—all armed; four or five languages heard at once; above a hundred horses and mules, half wild; American, Spanish, and Indian dresses and equipments intermingle—such was our composition. Our march was a sort of procession. Scouts ahead, and on the flanks; a front and rear division; the pack animals, baggage, and horned cattle in the centre; and the whole stretching a quarter of a mile along our dreary path."

They made their way down the Mojave River, which runs only intermittently, and the cattle were growing weak from want of water and grazing. On April 24, Fremont stopped to slaughter three and dry the meat.

"In the afternoon we were surprised by the sudden appearance in the camp of two Mexicans—a man and a boy. The name of the man was Andreas Fuentes; and that of the boy (a handsome lad, 11 years old) Pablo Hernandez. They belonged to a party consisting of six persons, the remaining four being the wife of Fuentes, the father and mother of Pablo, and Santiago Giacome, a resident of New Mexico."

The group had been herding horses from Los Angeles toward Santa Fe when it was attacked by perhaps 100 Indians, said the fugitives. "The Indians charged down into their camp, shouting as they advanced, and discharging flights of arrows. ... Fuentes drove the animals over and through the assailants, in spite of their arrows; and, abandoning the rest to their fate, carried them off at speed across the plain."

Fuentes guided Fremont back over his own route. On April 29, Fremont's group

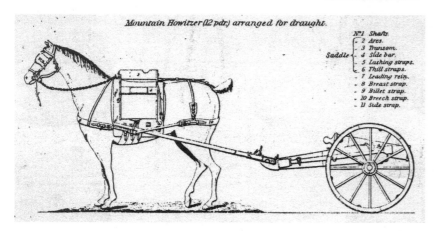

A 12-pounder brass howitzer, like the one shown in this drawing from the mountain artillery manual for the piece, was issued to John C. Fremont. The gun and carriage weighed 515 pounds, and special halters and shafts for drawing them, plus a full chest of ammunition, would have brought the total weight to more than 700 pounds. Fremont abandoned the gun somewhere west of Walker River.
(U.S. Army)

A reproduction of the Fremont Cannon is fired to salute touchdowns at University of Nevada-Reno football games.
(Courtesy UNR)

reached the spring where Fuentes' party had been attacked—near today's Tecopa, on the California-Nevada border.

"The dead silence of the place was ominous," wrote Fremont, "and galloping rapidly up, we found only the corpses of the two men; everything else was gone. They were naked, mutilated, and pierced with arrows. ... Of the women no trace could be found, and it was evident they had been carried off captive. A little lap-dog, which had belonged to Pablo's mother, remained with the dead bodies, and was frantic with joy at seeing Pablo; he, poor child, was frantic with grief, and filled the air with lamentations for his father and mother. Mi padre! mi madre! was his incessant cry."

Pablo Hernandez was adopted by Benton's family. Fuentes became a good explorer and would accompany Fremont on another expedition.

Now that Fremont was far off the main route to New Mexico, Fuentes guided him along the alternate. The camp Fremont's diary described on May 1 was probably today's Mountain Spring. They made but 12 miles the next day, camping in the region of Blue Diamond or Oak Creek Canyon.

And on May 3: "After a day's journey of 18 miles, in a northeasterly direction, we encamped in the midst of another very large basin, at a camping ground called Las Vegas—a term which the Spaniards use to signify fertile or marshy plains. … Two narrow streams of clear water, four or five feet deep, gush suddenly with a quick current, from two singularly large springs; these, and other waters of the basin, pass out in a gap to the eastward. The taste of the water is good, but rather too warm to be agreeable; the temperature being 71 in the one and 73 in the other. They, however,

afford a delightful bathing place."

Fremont wrote little more about the future Sin City.

His departure route, to the northeast, was difficult and dangerous. "Skeletons of horses ... between 50 and 60 miles without a drop of water," he noted. "We ate occasionally the [barrel cactus] and moistened our mouths with the acid of the sour dock."

On the Muddy River, Paiutes spotted Fremont, suspected he was raiding for slaves, and made a show of force. "They were barefooted and nearly naked; their hair gathered up in a knot behind, and with his bow, each man carried a quiver with thirty or forty arrows partially drawn out. Besides these, each held in his hand two or three arrows for instant service," he wrote. Fremont negotiated peace here, but on the Virgin River, a day's march farther northeast, one man fell behind and was never seen again.

Yet for all its dangers, the route through Las Vegas became well-traveled, simply because it became well-known. Congress printed 20,000 copies of Fremont's 1845 report of this trip and its map. "This meant anybody who wanted one could have it," said Warren. "It became so important that if a group of emigrants did *not* have one, that fact would be mentioned in diaries."

Of course, Fremont would be remembered for a good deal more. For instance, he helped provoke the Bear Flag Rebellion, which culminated in the United States' acquisition of California in the Mexican War.

Arriving in California in 1846, on what was supposed to be another scientific expedition, he was ordered to leave by the Mexican government. Instead, he took up a position on a hilltop, daring the Mexicans to attack. Fremont instigated several attacks by armed settlers and then took command of Sutter's Fort.

California would soon fall. Fremont was court-martialed for incidents growing out of his high-handed conduct. President James Polk canceled his dismissal from the Army, but Fremont resigned anyway and continued to explore with

private backing.

Leading Democrats offered to back him if he sought the party's nomination for president in 1856. But Fremont refused to endorse the Fugitive Slave Act, which said that slaves who had managed to escape to free-soil states could be forced back into slavery. Thus he became, instead, the first candidate fielded by the new Republican Party.

Against such a hero, Democrats leveled every gun. They fairly brought up his conduct in California and his unsuccessful business deals. Unfairly, they called him a drunk; he was very nearly a teetotaler. They accused him of being Catholic, which was also untrue, but Fremont refused to offend Catholics by denying it.

Buchanan carried 19 states to Fremont's 11. Millard Fillmore, who ran under the Know-Nothing banner, carried one state.

During the Civil War, President Abraham Lincoln made Fremont a general commanding the Department of the West. Fremont promptly issued his own emancipation proclamation in August 1861. It applied only in Missouri, but the threat of such a proclamation was the strongest hole card Lincoln held in trying to end the war, and he didn't appreciate Fremont playing it without asking him. He watered down Fremont's order and eventually transferred him East.

Fremont had become wealthy by purchasing real estate in California's early days, but by 1870 he had lost it all in litigation over mining rights and a failed railroad venture. The family's poverty was relieved somewhat by Jessie's emergence as a popular author. Fremont was appointed governor of the Arizona Territory from 1878 until 1881. His last home was in Los Angeles.

On a visit to New York City in July 1890, Fremont fell ill with peritonitis, possibly resulting from a ruptured appendix, and quickly died of it. At his own orders he was buried in a plain coffin and a civilian suit.

History adopted as his epitaph one short phrase attributed to Benton: "From the ashes of his campfire have sprung cities." ◢

William Bringhurst (1818–1883)

A group of missionaries braved the desert heat, built a fort, and founded the Las Vegas Mission of the Mormon Church in an effort to convert the area's Indians. **BY A.D. HOPKINS**

By 1855, travelers already knew the harshness of the Mojave Desert. They knew that the 52-mile jornada from the Muddy River to Las Vegas was best attempted in winter. Yet on June 13, perhaps 15 young men broke camp, filled every keg, bucket, and fruit jar with water, cracked their bullwhips, and headed southwest on a day one called the hottest he had ever seen. Men and oxen plodded all night, following a trail marked by bones.

It was 3 p.m. on the 14th before they reached the good water and grass of Las Vegas. "Their teams and their wagons were pretty well used up," remarked their historian. Even so, some men dumped their other cargo, refilled water barrels, and headed back into the desert to help another party of 15 who were driving weaker teams and had started the hard journey 24 hours later. It was June 15 before the last stragglers made it into camp.

What drove men into the desert summer was not a matter of life and death, but of eternal life. Once assigned to teach their Mormon faith to the Indians of the Las Vegas Val-

ley, they did not wait on a better season, but left almost at once.

None would strive harder to complete the mission than its president, William A. Bringhurst. So committed was he that when the mission's purpose was changed, he defied even the will of his church's leader, Brigham Young.

Born in Philadelphia in 1818, Bringhurst married Ann Dillworth in 1845 and traveled to Utah with the John Taylor Company, arriving in 1847. But for nearly two years, beginning in 1855, the diaries of others paint his efforts to colonize, civilize, and proselytize Las Vegas and its native inhabitants.

Las Vegas was targeted for several reasons. The main road through Las Vegas, mislabeled as the "Old Spanish Trail" when John C. Fremont mapped it in 1844, became so important to Utah colonists that it also was called the "Mormon Road."

Up that road came cuttings of California fruit trees, destined to bloom in Utah. Mormon converts from abroad landed at Pacific ports and traveled up the road to Utah. As early as 1851, church authorities en-

visioned a line of settlements, between the ports of the Pacific and Utah's southern counties, to provide travelers with food, fodder, and blacksmith services. The way stations also were to protect travelers and the mails from hostile Indians, and there may have been some hope of finding and exploiting minerals.

Some historians have denied any relation between the Las Vegas Mission and the Mormons' fear of military confrontation with the United States. Yet an alliance with desert Indians was clearly on the mind of colonist John Steele, when he wrote: "We can have 1,000 brave warriors on hand in a short time to help quell the eruption that might take place." Brigham Young, himself, in a meeting with departing missionaries that spring, said of the Indians, "By and by they will be the Lord's battle ax in good earnest." Ultimately, the differences were settled without war.

The missionaries were supposed to teach the Las Vegas Paiutes, who were hunters and gatherers, how to farm. But in the eyes of many, notably Bringhurst, the main purpose was religious. Mormons believed American Indians, or Lamanites, were descendants of the people of ancient Israel, and it was the responsibility of Mormons to convert Lamanites to their religion.

Though the missionaries hoped to live peaceably among the Indians, laying out a fort was almost their first step, commenced on June 18, only

Bringhurst in Southern Nevada

POP.*	DECADE
n/a	pre-1900
30	1900
945	1910
2,686	1920
5,952	1930
13,937	1940
45,577	1950
123,667	1960
273,288	1970
463,087	1980
715,587	1990

■ Time spent in Southern Nev.
* - Population figures are for greater Las Vegas area (*Source: Nevada State Data Center*).
** - Bringhurst was active in Southern Nevada in 1855 and 1856.

William Bringhurst, president of the Las Vegas Mission of the Church of Jesus Christ of Latter-day Saints. This photo is believed to date from the 1850s, when the mission was founded.
(UNLV Special Collections)

the second working day after their arrival. Part of this fort still stands at Las Vegas Boulevard and Washington Avenue. The location is three miles from Big Springs, but Las Vegas Creek flowed down a hillside, allowing for a small water-powered mill.

An uprising in central Utah in 1853 had prompted Brigham Young to advise that forts be built in all new settlements, and as many as 35 were accordingly built by Mormons. The one in Las Vegas was large and well-designed by frontier standards, and those who saw it in its heyday wondered how farmers and missionaries came to build in such a military manner. Research by James Hinds, a Las Vegas military historian, found the probable answer.

The Mormons' buildings and irrigation trenches, though unable to support 100 missionaries, did support ranchers who took them over later. The Mormon Fort was the seed of European-style civilization in Las Vegas.

Steele, the fort's designer, had served in the Mormon Battalion during the Mexican War. The war carried him to Pueblo, in what is now Colorado, where he presumably had the chance to study nearby Bent's Fort, built by traders. Irish born, Steele also had lived in Scotland, where he would have had other opportunities to view fortifications.

The main material for the fort was adobe brick, made on the spot. Foundations were stone. Walls were 14 feet high, 2 feet thick for the first 8 feet of height, and a foot thick above that. The fort's east wall doubled as the wall of "mess houses," or dwellings for families or groups of men who shared cooking and housekeeping chores. These were built inside the fort and faced out into the courtyard. Hinds discovered that the messes were two stories high, and he suggests that the first floor must have been made of dirt and the second of rough wood planks. Wood was used sparingly, for the closest timber lay many miles away in the Spring Mountains. Nails also were in short supply, so rawhide thongs or wooden pegs would have been used to attach the planks to

beams. There were holes in the wall for shooting at attackers, and two corners of the fort had bastions, protruding structures from which defenders might fire along the walls.

Garden plots and farmland were apportioned to each man, and the fields were fenced with branches of thorny mesquite. The missionaries planted "grain of all sorts," and at first the crops grew well; in July Bringhurst remarked in a letter that the corn grew an inch and one-half in 24 hours.

But the soil proved too alkaline for many crops. By October, Steele wrote to a friend, "I planted three acres of corn, oats, peas, beans, etc., and my oats came up most beautiful; and so did everything else, but ... the saleratus killed it, and I will not have three bushels of corn on it."

Relations with the Indians began auspi-

ciously. In July Bringhurst wrote the *Deseret News*: "Shortly after we arrived here, we assembled all the chiefs, and made an agreement [treaty] with them for permission to make a settlement on their lands. We agreed to treat them well, and they were to observe the same conduct towards us, and with all white men."

The mission's recorder, George Washington Bean, had learned the Ute tongue years before. He found the Paiute language different but could make himself understood. Bean wrote that the Indians "helped us grub the land, make adobes, attend the mason, and especially to herd the stock." The Paiutes' favorite unit of exchange was the squash, and they didn't expect many for a day's work.

In the spring of 1856, the missionaries laid out a farm for the Indians about a mile and a half north of the mission, plowed it, and showed the Indians how to plant it. Trying to teach Paiutes to farm was not culturally hopeless, as some have depicted. Paiutes to the northeast had been farming for at least 80 years.

Mormon fort ruins as depicted by Thaddeus Kenderdine in a book published in 1888, years after his visit. It is known that he made at least one mistake; there were bastions at two corners instead of at all four. But his is the best picture of the fort when it was still much as the Mormons left it.
(UNLV Special Collections)

The missionaries, however, found they could not grow enough food to feed themselves and all the Paiutes. Colonists estimated that at least 1,000 Indians lived in the Las Vegas Valley or near it; there were never more than 103 members of the Las Vegas Mission, and some of those were children too young to work.

In the fall of 1856, the mission was 4,000 to 5,000 pounds short of the amount of flour required to sustain it until the next harvest. Bringhurst called upon men skilled with carpenter tools to go to California and work for the flour.

That same year, some missionaries reported, a drought also hurt the Paiutes' traditional supplies of wild foods. Thefts became a problem. In July the mission books record: "Brother Bringhurst being informed that the Lamanites had been committing serious depredation upon the grain, melons, etc., by coming into the fields in the night time, he called up Chief Joshua [Patsearump, a Paiute leader who had been baptized and thus had a Christian name also] and gave him to understand that such things must be stopped immediately. ... Joshua pleaded his inability to govern his people when they were hungry, but his intentions were always good and friendly toward the brethren."

In early August, at the Paiutes' request, Mormon riflemen brought their better weapons and joined them in a hunt, but no game was found. The mission log records: "Sunday, Aug. 17. At night the brethren were watching in the corn field and caught an Indian boy stealing corn. Several others were with him, but ran away before they could be gotten hold of. Prest. Bringhurst ordered the boy chained up in the fort all night to see if it would have a salutary influence upon him and the others."

"Monday, Aug. 18. In the morning the chief

> *"Things began to change. The same old-fashioned sermons was preached and arses threatened to be kicked if men did not do what was wanted of them. ... [I thought] that more mild treatment would do just as well."*
>
> **—John Steele, designer of the Mormon Fort, on mounting tensions during a drought in 1856**

and some of the Indians came into camp, feeling perfectly friendly. They said it was alright to punish the boy, although some wanted to retaliate upon the cattle and horses, but the chief talked peace, saying that if they did not want to be tied up they must quit stealing. The boy was released early in the morning and sent to his camp."

An ox was driven off but recovered. A calf was killed. Tensions grew among the missionaries themselves. Steele wrote, "Things began to change. The same old-fashioned sermons was preached and arses threatened to be kicked if men did not do what was wanted of them. ... [I thought] that more mild treatment would do just as well."

The discovery of lead nearby, at what is now called Mount Potosi, also caused problems within the mission. In May 1856, Nathaniel V. Jones arrived in Las Vegas bearing orders from Young and claiming authority to take men from the mission to work the mines. Steele related, "Jones presented his letter of instruction to President Bringhurst and there was a great storm between them calling each other anything but gentlemen."

Bringhurst refused to accept Jones' authority. When food grew short, Bringhurst refused supplies to Jones' mining party, encamped southwest of Las Vegas at the location that would later be named Potosi. He refused to send the mission blacksmith to the mines.

Jones traveled to Salt Lake City to buy suitable material for an ore smelter. Returning December 4, he bore a letter from Brigham Young, notifying Bringhurst that he had been "dropped from the mission and disfellowshipped from the Church." One week later, Bringhurst started for California.

Getting the lead out proved to be even more challenging than harvesting a corn crop. The ore

proved complex, and could not be profitably mined by smelting alone, yet there was insufficient water at the site for other processes. In January 1857, the Jones group abandoned the mines. The Las Vegas missionaries were allowed to leave the mission in March, though a few remained voluntarily.

The final blow to the Mormon settlement came in the fall of 1858, when Indians who had not yet accepted the Mormons' teachings swept down from the mountains and stole the harvest from the fields. At a special conference in Santa Clara, Utah, church authorities officially abandoned the Las Vegas Mission.

Yet the mission was not such a failure as it might appear. The local Indians' relations with whites improved immediately upon the Mormons' arrival, and remained better after their departure than in much of the desert West. Las Vegas Paiutes retained their identity and also part of their original home territory near the fort. They regained more of their territory in recent years—the Snow Mountain reservation.

The Mormons' buildings and irrigation trenches, though unable to support 100 missionaries, did support ranchers who took them over later. The Mormon Fort was the seed of European-style civilization in Las Vegas.

Bringhurst would soon regain good standing in the church. He served several years as bishop of the ward at Springville, Utah, and Young selected him as one of the six founding trustees for Brigham Young Academy (now Brigham Young University). He died in February 1883.

Standard directories of Utah pioneers, and a biography provided by the BYU public information office, do not mention Bringhurst's service at the Las Vegas Mission, though it consumed nearly two years of his life. ◢

Nathaniel V. Jones was sent to Las Vegas to operate a lead mine at nearby Mount Potosi. Conflict between Jones and Bringhurst, over goals of mission work versus mining, hastened the mission's demise.
(UNLV Special Collections)

O.D. Gass (1827-1924)

Gold, fame, and fortune eluded O.D. Gass throughout his lifetime, part of which was spent in the portion of the Arizona Territory now known as Clark County. **BY K.J. EVANS**

Octavius Decatur Gass was a month too late to qualify as a Forty-Niner when he arrived in the San Francisco Bay area in early 1850. It was to be the story of his life. Almost at the right place at the right time, but never exactly. Opportunity knocked at his door regularly, but he was always in the bathtub.

Born in Richland County, Ohio, in 1827, Gass was of Scotch-Irish descent and was driven by the same urges that had sent other young men swarming around Cape Horn to the wild Sierra Nevada foothills of California. He wanted to dig up a fortune, perhaps dabble in politics, and live luxuriously ever after.

Frustrated in mining, Gass forsook El Dorado County, California, for Eldorado Canyon, in what was then the newly-created territory of Arizona. By 1863, Gass was zealously staking claims there. But his enthusiasm waned as the blisters on his hands grew and his fortune didn't. He wandered to San Bernardino, California, then headed for St. Thomas on the Muddy River. On his way, he had a look at the recently abandoned Mormon Fort at Las Vegas.

The original settlement had been developed in 1855 by 30 missionaries dispatched from Salt Lake City by Brigham Young. In 1857, political infighting among the mission leadership ended the venture.

By 1865, Gass had finally discovered that supplying boomers and travelers could be as lucrative as beating on rocks. He transformed the fort into a ranch and a way station for travelers, and supplied fresh food to settlements like those in Eldorado Canyon and along the Muddy River.

The 640-acre ranch produced grain, vegetables, and Mexican pink beans, which Gass used to pay his Indian ranch hands. Local Indians were accustomed to a diet heavy with mesquite beans and regarded the plump pink beans as a rare delicacy. Gass' orchards produced apples, peaches, figs, and apricots, and his vineyard produced the raw material for wine, which was one of the ranch's main attractions for thirsty travelers. He also raised horses and cattle, which were driven to Eldorado Canyon where fresh beef fetched a good price. And, as he had hoped, the ranch became a way station on the road from Southern California to Salt Lake City. Here travelers could rest, bathe, repair wagons at the ranch's blacksmith shop, and socialize around a 20-foot table over the culinary creations of the ranch cook, a Chinese man named Lee.

In 1864, the federal government halved New Mexico Territory and created Arizona Territory. During the first territorial legislature, the new solons created four counties, including Mohave County, the territory's northwest corner. Gass stood for election to the assembly. Being one of the few prosperous landowners in the region, he was elected. In 1865, he convinced the legislature to create Pah-Ute County, which included much of Nevada's present Clark County.

Gass excelled at politics and was regarded as a competent fellow. A tall, handsome man with a wavy 10-inch beard and a gentle manner, he had presence and personality, too. But during his second session, his freak luck intervened. He was not to be a politician, either.

On May 5, 1866, at the urging of Nevada Senators James W. Nye and William M. Stewart and Representative Delos R. Ashley, Congress made Pah-Ute County part of Lincoln County, Nevada. Gass blasted the bill as "the Nevada project of stealing us from Arizona." In fact, he ignored the legislation and continued to represent Pah-Ute County in the Arizona Territorial Legislature until 1869.

For Gass personally, the change meant real financial trouble. Nevada demanded two years' back taxes from him. Many Mormons in the Muddy River country—some of his best customers—refused to pay Nevada taxes and moved back to Utah.

Love came to the Gass Ranch in 1872, when Gass married Mary Virginia Simpson, a niece of

By the age of 50, Gass had all the trappings of a successful rancher. He owned 960 acres and employed more than 30 hired hands, including a veterinarian, a blacksmith, a barnkeeper, a carpenter, several Indian women to handle laundry, and Lee the cook.

Octavius Decatur Gass, 1860s
(UNLV Special Collections)

Ulysses S. Grant. Mary Gass settled into the ranch life well, and the couple had six children.

Gass generally regarded the native Paiutes as a nuisance—except, of course, for those he hired to work for him. However, he and his wife did take the trouble to learn their language, and there were few instances of outright hostility. The Paiutes called him "Pe-No-Kab," meaning "long back," in reference to his broad shoulders.

But there were occasional incidents. One of the more terrifying happened in 1878, when word came to the ranch that a war party of Mojaves were coming into the valley to engage their old foes, the Paiutes. Gass loaded his family, which included two children with whooping cough and a pregnant wife, into a wagon and made a 40-mile dash for Ivanpah, California, where the family lodged with friends.

As a Lincoln County justice of the peace, he was called upon to preside over a case in which one Paiute shot another. The suspect was brought before Gass, along with witnesses. Gass, knowing that any judgment would bring trouble from one Paiute faction or the other, ordered everyone to adjourn to the house for dinner. He left one Indian to guard the prisoner. As they dined, a gunshot was heard. Everyone ran outside to discover the defendant dead and the guard standing with a smoking gun. He had tried to escape, the guard explained. Gass was surprisingly calm about the incident.

He was even less concerned with the Indians' threatened insurrection. A half-breed had managed to convince a few of his colleagues that Gass was cheating them and owed them better compensation. The half-breed and two armed warriors went to the ranch house to demand their due. Both O.D. and Mary Gass made it clear that they were ready for a fight, and the confrontation ended with Gass giving the leader a couple of head of livestock. The Paiutes themselves were embarrassed and annoyed by the incident. They forced the ringleader to wear a dress and work in the fields, with the women, as punishment.

By the age of 50, Gass had all the trappings of

Local Paiutes were the main source of labor on the Gass Ranch. Many camped there, as did this family.
(UNLV Special Collections)

a successful rancher. He owned 960 acres and employed more than 30 hired hands, including a veterinarian, a blacksmith, a barnkeeper, a carpenter, several Indian women to handle laundry, and Lee the cook.

But he was heavily in debt and had been attempting to sell "The Las Vegas Rancho" since 1868. In 1879, he borrowed $5,000 in gold at 2.5 percent interest from Archibald Stewart, a prosperous rancher who operated a place north of Pioche. Gass had expected a bumper harvest to pay off the debt, but bad weather destroyed much of his crop and Gass found himself in default. Stewart foreclosed, and Gass was out of the ranching business.

It may be that Gass' financial plight was contrived. After all, he had been unable to sell the ranch, but had been able to hock it. He may never have intended to pay Stewart back.

Another concern, one Gass shared with his wife, was the lack of education for their children. He left the ranch in 1881 with his family, their personal possessions, and 1,500 head of cattle. They stopped first in Pomona, California, then tried unsuccessfully to raise grapes in the Yucaipa Valley. His mining fever never cooled, though, and he continued to prospect, going as far south as Baja California.

In 1900 and in his 70s, Gass finally joined his son, Fenton, in Bryn Mawr, near Redlands, California, where he tended a small garden and helped in the orange groves. He died after a fall on December 10, 1924, and was buried in the Masonic Plot at the Hillside Cemetery in Redlands.

Ironically, the man who first settled Las Vegas is memorialized only in a downtown street that bears his name. And it is probably just as well. Gass really never cared very much for Nevada, anyway. ✍

Gass in Southern Nevada

POP.*		DECADE
	**	pre-
n/a		1900
30		1900
945		1910
2,686		1920
5,952		1930
13,937		1940
45,577		1950
123,667		1960
273,288		1970
463,087		1980
715,587		1990

■ Time spent in Southern Nev.
* - Population figures are for greater Las Vegas area (*Source: Nevada State Data Center*).
** - Gass was in Southern Nevada between 1863 and 1881.

Ute Warren Perkins (1849–1903)

Living in the Muddy River country was difficult, but one man was up to the task, and took to task anyone who got in his way. BY K.J. EVANS

"I can whip any man this side of Salt Lake City," brayed the miner. Ute Warren Perkins stepped up to answer the challenge. Fists flew, facial features underwent modifications, and the men fought until both were exhausted. It was a draw. The Irishman wearily got to his feet and made another announcement: "I can whip any man this side of Salt Lake City except Ute Perkins," he croaked.

In 1880, Elizabeth Whitemore of St. George, Utah, and her young son, Brigham, were in the vanguard of the second Mormon colonization of Nevada's Muddy River country. She was a widow, and needed to hire a stout and fearless man to assist and protect her.

The toughest man in St. George was Ute Warren Perkins. He had proved it often. Grandson Orville Perkins told of an incident when Ute Warren encountered an Irish miner full of whiskey-fueled ferocity.

"I can whip any man this side of Salt Lake City," brayed the miner. Ute Warren Perkins stepped up to disagree. Fists flew, facial features underwent modifications, and the men fought to a draw. The Irishman wearily got to his feet and made another announcement: "I can whip any man this side of Salt Lake City except Ute Perkins," he croaked.

Whitemore purchased what is now virtually the entire Overton townsite for $4,000, then set her sturdy new hired hand, Perkins, to clearing mesquite, digging irrigation ditches, handling livestock, and fending off human predators.

Perkins was born in Council Bluffs, Iowa, in 1849. He came to Utah with his parents as an infant, and the family settled in St. George, where he later married Sarah Laub.

The Mormons had originally been called by Brigham Young to colonize the Muddy River area in 1865. With their policy of total self-sufficiency, they needed a warm place where cotton would grow. On January 8, 1865, Thomas Smith was named to preside over the first settlement on the Muddy, which was named after him—St. Thomas. The first crop of settlers consisted of 11 men and three women.

Living conditions were wretched. The river, which had its headwaters at geothermal springs in the upper valley, was warm and the water had an unpleasant taste that sickened some settlers. Malaria and dysentery were rampant. The constant theft of livestock taxed the patience of the Mormons, who normally treated the Indians with respect and charity.

Ute Warren Perkins as a young man
(UNLV Special Collections)

In 1863, the Muddy River country was part of the Arizona Territory, but the Mormons insisted it was in Utah. In 1864, Nevada was admitted to the Union and, in 1870, commissioned a survey that proved the colonies were in Nevada. The state demanded they pay their taxes "in U.S. gold and silver coin," retroactive to 1864. It was an impossible demand. Brigham Young, who had been disgusted by the place when he had made a brief visit, gave the colonists permission to leave.

So, in February 1871, 600 colonists packed their wagons and headed for St. George, leaving behind 150 homes, 500 acres of cleared land, about 8,000 bushels of wheat in the fields, and an irrigation system valued at about $100,000. Others quickly claimed those assets.

In 1881, Martha Cox was hired by the state of Nevada to be the valley's first schoolteacher. She didn't think much of her new neighbors. In her autobiography, she wrote: "The class of men who lived on the Muddy was of a low type. Old '49ers from the California gold fields, unsuccessful prospectors … these had wandered into the valley on their way and settled down on the fields the pioneers left, and lived in their houses."

The upper Moapa Valley belonged to the indigenous people, the Southern Paiute or Nuwuvi. They had farmed the upper Moapa Valley before the white man, and were happy to take over the newly cleared farmlands the Mormons left behind. But, as usual, whites still grabbed the best lands and the lion's share of the water.

Perkins in Southern Nevada

POP.*	DECADE
n/a	pre-1900
30	1900
945	1910
2,686	1920
5,592	1930
13,937	1940
45,577	1950
123,667	1960
273,288	1970
463,087	1980
715,587	1990

■ Time spent in Southern Nev.
* - Population figures are for greater Las Vegas area (*Source: Nevada State Data Center*).
** - Perkins arrived in Southern Nevada in 1880.

"Only three kinds of people live here. White people, Indians, and Perkinses."
Common saying in Muddy Valley (now Moapa Valley)

One of the white settlers in the area was Jack Longstreet, who came in 1882 and opened a drugstore and saloon, "a combination of enterprises that promised to cure what ailed a man either one way or the other," observed Sally Zanjani in her seminal work, *Jack Longstreet: Last of the Desert Frontiersmen.*

Longstreet, then in his 40s, was married to an Indian woman, spoke the language, and liked to join the Indians in their gambling games. He was known as a man quick with the gun, and with a checkered past. He is supposed to have been one of a gang of rustlers captured in Texas. His cohorts were hanged, but Longstreet, because of his youth, had one ear cropped. Until the end of his life, he wore his hair long to hide the rustler's shame.

In 1883, he gave up the booze business and homesteaded a tract of land a few miles south of the Moapa Indian Reservation. Being a naturally quarrelsome sort, it was inevitable that Longstreet would eventually get into a disagreement with his sole white neighbor, Alexander Dry. According to Orville Perkins, in his book *Hooky Beans and Willows,* Longstreet and Dry quarreled over water rights. Zanjani believes there were latent hard feelings over $1,000 Longstreet had lost to Dry on a horse race.

One afternoon, after a few friendly rounds of tonsil wash in St. Thomas, Dry and Longstreet departed north for their ranches, apparently harboring no ill will toward each other. As Perkins tells it, Dry was riding alone, when a bullet knocked him from his saddle. Dry tried to draw his weapon, but Longstreet lunged from his hiding place and finished him off with two more .44 slugs. Longstreet claimed self-defense, which was hard to argue since Dry's weapon was found unholstered.

On and around the land that Elizabeth Whitemore had purchased, Ute Warren Perkins had planted and rebuilt to prepare for the return of the Mormons. He turned out to be a natural leader, not just because of his martial skills—which prompted Lincoln County officials to depu-

tize him—but also because of his organizational skills and capacity for hard work.

The second colonization was much more successful than the first. The mines in Eldorado Canyon and Pioche were booming, and the Muddy Valley farmers had a market for their produce and livestock. The railroads from Salt Lake City had reached Milford, Utah, only 70 miles away. Civilization was moving toward the settlers, but there were still some of the old bad guys lurking about.

A famed horse thief named Black Jack Kellett headed a gang that passed through the Muddy Valley about once a year. They would steal horses in Idaho and drive them south at a breakneck speed to outrun the law, eventually arriving in the Muddy Valley—where they carefully avoided touching any local livestock. They would then alter brands, break broncs, and prepare the animals for sale in Arizona and New Mexico.

But neither Black Jack Kellett nor Jack Longstreet nor any other outlaw misbehaved on Ute Warren Perkins' turf. In fact, when Jack

Longstreet left the area, it is probable that he did so because he felt sure he would eventually get into a tangle with Perkins.

In the spring of 1903, Ute Warren Perkins was stricken with Bright's disease, a form of kidney failure. He was taken to a hospital in Salt Lake City, where he died in April of that year. His body was brought back to Overton for burial. Sarah Perkins survived for 35 more years, and died at age 88.

In addition to making the Muddy Valley a fit and safe place for their people to reclaim, Ute Warren and Sarah Laub Perkins did their part to repopulate the valley, parenting 13 children, plus caring for an adopted Indian boy.

Today, the Perkins family descendants number in the hundreds, as evidenced by the enormous family reunion held in Overton in 1980, the 100th anniversary of Ute Warren Perkins' arrival in the valley. In fact, in the old days, there was a common local saying in the Muddy Valley: "Only three kinds of people live here. White people, Indians, and Perkinses." ✍

Ute Warren and Sarah Laub Perkins. They were married in 1868.
(UNLV Special Collections)

The Perkins family, all descended from Ute Warren and Sarah, gathered for a family reunion in Valley of Fire State Park, early 1960s.
(UNLV Special Collections)

Ute Warren and Sarah Laub Perkins did their part to repopulate the valley, parenting 13 children, plus caring for an adopted Indian boy.

Helen J. Stewart (1854–1926)

Longing for a city with social graces, a young mother—who soon became a widow—
gracefully accepted her role as grand dame of Southern Nevada. **BY K.J. EVANS**

Hot, sore, and covered in dust, Archie Stewart pulled the freight wagon into the shade of the cottonwood trees on that blistering July day in 1884. He had been away from the Las Vegas Ranch for several days, delivering produce and livestock to miners in Eldorado Canyon. A couple of his hired men approached and began to unhitch the tired team. Stewart jumped down, slapped the dust off his pants legs, wiped his face and neck with his bandana, and walked toward the house.

His wife, Helen, was inside, still trying to decide how to tell her husband about the unsettling incident that had occurred a few days earlier. A ranch hand, Schyler Henry, had announced he was quitting and demanded his wages from Helen Stewart. She explained that she did not know how much he was owed, and that he would have to wait until her husband returned. Henry blustered, threatened, and insulted Helen, but she held firm.

It is unknown exactly what Schyler Henry said to Helen Stewart. She never repeated it, except to remark that the ranch hand owned a "black-hearted slanderer's tongue." But it was sufficiently provocative that Archibald Stewart saddled a horse, put his rifle in its scabbard, and rode off for the Kiel Ranch, near the present location of Carey Avenue and Losee Road in North Las Vegas. Operated by Conrad Kiel and his son, Edwin, the ranch had a well-deserved reputation

as a haven and hangout for various badmen, outlaws, and scoundrels, men like Hank Parrish and Jack Longstreet.

When Archie Stewart arrived at the ranch, he tied his horse to a tree behind a growth of grapevines and walked slowly to the back of the house. He evidently fired the first shot, and missed. A short firefight ensued, and when it was over, Stewart was dead with wounds in the chest and head. Schyler Henry received two flesh wounds.

At first, the killing was credited solely to Hank Parrish, who promptly disappeared. Conrad Kiel and Schyler Henry were hauled before a grand jury in Pioche. The jury declined to indict. As for Parrish, he was later tried and hanged in Ely for the last in a long line of murders.

The case remains unsolved to this day. But Helen Stewart believed for the rest of her life that the Kiels, Henry, and Parrish all had a part in her husband's death, and that the whole drama between her and Henry had been a ruse concocted to lure her husband to the ranch and kill him.

Helen Stewart also believed that the con-

spiracy was hatched by Parrish. A year before Archie Stewart was killed, somebody stole two of his horses. He followed and recovered the horses, but the thief escaped. Stewart also found some stolen cattle belonging to an acquaintance in Pahranagat Valley. Parrish, the supposed thief, sent word to Stewart that he would kill him.

No sooner had the smoke cleared from the shootout than Conrad Kiel dispatched a rider with a rude note for Helen Stewart: "Mrs. Sturd send a team and take Mr. Sturd away he is dead. C. Kiel." Helen went to the ranch herself and helped to load her husband's body. Archibald Stewart was buried the next day, the first of seven people who would be interred in a four-acre family plot.

And Helen Stewart was then on her own. She had four minor children, another on the way, a crop of peaches that needed to be picked, and travelers arriving each day in need of food, water, and rest. She would shortly face major le-

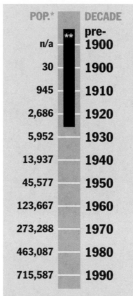
Helen J. Stewart as a young girl
(UNLV Special Collections)

gal problems because Archie had failed to leave a will.

The woman who became known as "The First Lady of Las Vegas" was born Helen Jane Wiser on April 16, 1854, in Springfield, Illinois. When she was 9, her parents took their five children west, to Sacramento, California. At age 18, she married 38-year-old Archibald Stewart. The newlyweds were then off for Lincoln County, where Archie had been running a freighting business since 1868. He also had a ranch near Pioche, where he raised cattle and vegetables. He had wisely combined his ranching and freighting operations, so when the inevitable boom and bust cycles rolled through the Pioche mines, he was able to prosper by hauling his goods as far north as Eureka and as far south as Eldorado Canyon.

By 1876, the Stewarts, now with sons William James and Hiram Richard, had moved into Pioche, much to the delight of Helen Stewart, who yearned for a social life. In 1879, Archibald Stewart purchased another local ranch, and he also made a loan that changed the course of Nevada history.

Octavius Decatur Gass had developed a mar-ginally successful ranching and farming operation around the abandoned Mormon Fort that had been built in 1855 near what is today the intersection of Las Vegas Boulevard North and Washington Avenue. In August 1879, he persuaded Stewart to loan him $5,000 in gold at 2.5 percent interest per month, payable in one year. Gass had been trying to sell the place since 1868, and he took the money and ran. Which is how, in 1880, Stewart acquired the 960-acre ranch and set about doing what no one had done before—making it profitable.

He told Helen he planned to move the family to Las Vegas. She was horrified. She was pregnant and frightened at the prospect of having the child without another woman in attendance, and was concerned about the lack of educational opportunities for her sons. Archie soothed her, saying it was to be only a temporary move.

The Stewarts' trip, in 1882, took nearly a week, and there was plenty to do when they arrived. Helen gave birth to her second daughter, Evaline La Vega, who derived her middle name from her place of birth. Helen seems to have found life at the ranch less isolated and lonely than at the Pioche place, mostly because of the nonstop flow of travelers. In her biography of Helen Stewart, published in the *Nevada Historical Society Quarterly,* Carrie Miller Townley noted, "When the arriving group contained women, Helen Stewart was especially happy, as she hungered for feminine companionship."

The ranch, with its cool creek and huge, shady cottonwood trees, was a resort for heat-weary miners from Eldorado Canyon. In a good year, the ranch's vines could produce as much as 600 gallons of serviceable wine, and the Stewarts sold it cheap. A writer in 1883 reported that many of the prospectors in Eldorado Canyon had "all quit work for some time and are rusticating up at the Vegas Ranch, having a jolly time drinking wine. Whenever any of them get drunk, they are placed in the works of the roots of a tree and made to sit there until sobered."

In 1885, the probate of Archie's estate was fi-nalized, and Helen Stewart wound up owning half the ranch. The other half was divided among the five children—Will, Hiram, Eliza (Tiza), Evaline, and the baby, Archibald. As administratrix of her children's affairs, Helen sought permission from the court to sell the entire ranch, arguing that if the children were forced to grow up there, they would be deprived of proper education. The request was granted. Prospective buyers came to look at the ranch in 1887 and 1889. But even though Archibald Stewart had turned down $11,000 for the place a couple of years after acquiring it, his wife had no such luck.

In 1886, Frank Roger Stewart, no relation to Archibald, arrived from Sandy Valley, where he and a partner had operated a store and post office. He proved an unusually valuable ranch hand. He was also a convivial host, and visitors observed that he spent a great deal of time in the wine cellar, entertaining travelers with wine and wit. Helen Stewart and Frank Stewart had a close relationship, based originally on his value as an employee. But the relationship evolved into something deeper and, by 1903, into marriage.

Because of its location, the Las Vegas Ranch had long been a message center for the region, and in June 1893, Helen Stewart was named postmaster of the "Los Vegas" post office. Authorities insisted on the incorrect spelling for fear of confusing the office with Las Vegas, New Mexico.

Stewart decided that the best way to ensure a quality education for her two daughters and her youngest boy, little Archibald, would be to pack them off to boarding school in California. Will and Hiram, having reached adulthood, split the ranch duties. Hiram handled most of the livestock and married the new schoolteacher at the ranch in 1896. Will tended to the crops and became in-

Helen Stewart as a member of early Las Vegas society
(UNLV Special Collections)

Helen Stewart (left) displays her basket collection, one of the finest and most complete in the country.
(UNLV Special Collections)

volved in civic duties.

In July 1899, young Archie was chasing wild horses at the ranch. He fell from his own horse, and was killed. His mother took the news harder than she had taken even the news of her husband's death.

Talk of a railroad through the valley had been circulating since 1889, and in 1902, Stewart signed a contract that became the de facto birth certificate for the city of Las Vegas. The contract was with Senator William A. Clark of Montana, and spelled out the terms for the sale of the Stewart Ranch to the San Pedro, Los Angeles, and Salt Lake Railroad. The price was $55,000, and did not include the "Four Acres" family cemetery or a small allotment of water from Las Vegas Creek. The four remaining Stewart children deeded their shares of the ranch to their mother for $1 "and love and affection," though Hiram, who knew only the ranching life, gave up his interest reluctantly.

In 1902, Helen J. Stewart and family were out of the ranching business in Southern Nevada, though knowing of the railroad's plans for her ranch and the surrounding land, she snatched up another 924 acres, including a 40-acre plot adja-

> *"If any woman ever tackled the world by herself, that woman was Helen J. Stewart."*
> —Carrie Miller Townley, in the *Nevada Historical Society Quarterly*

cent to the "Four Acres," where she lived for the rest of her life. First, however, the family took a trip to Los Angeles.

It was there that Hiram Stewart, only two months after the sale, caught a cold after going swimming and died when it escalated into pneumonia. He was embalmed and shipped back to Las Vegas, where he was buried in the "Four Acres" between his younger brother Archie and an Indian girl known as Nipe.

Will Stewart came back to Las Vegas in 1903 to supervise the building of the new house across the street from the old ranch. In 1905, the railroad auctioned 1,200 lots, creating the downtown core of Las Vegas which, of course, included a Stewart Street. Helen wrote: "Following the trail of the trapper and of the trail blazer, and the pioneer, came the iron horse, that great annihilator of time and distance, bringing all the modern ideas of advanced civilization in our midst and we awoke as if in a dream and found all the comforts of an advanced civilization with us. The hardships were no more."

Although Las Vegas in the first decade of the 20th century was hardly "an advanced civilization," it was all Helen Stewart had hoped for. Suddenly, there were other women in the new town. There was society, of sorts, and Stewart soon became immersed in the social and cultural life of the fledgling town. She steadily acquired local artifacts ranging from old Spanish coins and jewelry to Indian crafts. Her basket collection was the finest in the state.

When Jeanne Elizabeth Weir, founder of the Nevada Historical Society, came to Southern Nevada in 1908, she sought out Helen Stewart. Before the visit had concluded, Stewart was president of the Southern Nevada branch.

There had always been a place for native people on the Stewart Ranch while Helen ran it. In 1911, the federal government decided to establish an Indian reservation in or around Las Vegas, and asked for bids for the land. Whether Stewart donated the land, or was paid for it, is unclear. But it was she who provided the site for today's Las Vegas Paiute Colony on North Main Street.

Stewart became one of the state's foremost authorities on the history of Southern Nevada, and was a sought-after speaker all over the state. In 1915, she became the first woman elected to the local school board, and in 1916, the first woman to sit on a jury.

In 1914, Will Stewart's second wife, after a difficult delivery, gave birth to a daughter whom they named Helen J. Stewart. They did not realize until later that the child was mentally retarded. "The doting grandmother had a special love for this exceptional granddaughter, and took great pleasure in each small, slow step forward the child took," wrote Townley. The Helen J. Stewart School, she notes, was named for the granddaughter, not for the famous grandmother.

Helen Stewart died of cancer on March 6, 1926. The loss of a great pioneer woman was bad enough, and it was aggravated by the fact that her executors sold her treasured basket collection at auction the following year.

Her funeral was one of the largest the city had seen. Mourners from all over the state paid homage to the legendary lady who had wrung a living from a harsh land, suffered hardships modern people cannot imagine, and ultimately prevailed. She was interred in a special vault hammered out of caliche on her "Four Acres." In the 1970s, the burial plot was purchased by Bunker Brothers Mortuary, which owned the adjacent land. The remains of Archie and Helen Stewart, as well as those of their sons Hiram and Will, are now in Bunker's Eden Vale Mausoleum, a stone's throw from the site of the old home place.

"If any woman ever tackled the world by herself," wrote Townley, "that woman was Helen J. Stewart." ✍

Las Vegas Ranch, undated
(UNLV Special Collections)

Woman on Las Vegas Creek shooting ducks, one of Helen Stewart's favorite pastimes
(UNLV Special Collections)

George F. Colton (1862–?)

Visions of gold in the Lost Dutchman Mine led an independent pipe-smoking speculator to a dusty ridge, where he found enough ore to strike it rich in Searchlight. **BY K.J. EVANS**

"My dad would go downtown every weekend night and try to find the biggest miner to pick a fight with. And he said that every Friday and Saturday night he would come home with his ass whipped. Shortly after his sixteenth birthday, he beat the guy. It was his way of showing he had become a man. So I'm assuming that was an inherited trait."

—Stanton Colton
George Colton's great-grandson

George Frederick Colton went looking for the Lost Dutchman Mine, but instead found his fortune in Searchlight. How he made the discovery and how the town got its name are the stuff of legend and speculation.

Colton was born November 22, 1862, in Provo, Utah, and grew up to marry Matilda Bybee in Brigham City, Utah, in May 1883.

According to Gale Colton, his granddaughter, George Colton was on his way from Utah to Arizona in the late 1890s, bound for the Superstition Mountains, where he hoped to locate the legendary Lost Dutchman Mine. There had been extensive prospecting and mining along the lower Colorado River since the arrival of the Spanish in the 18th century. Most activity was in Eldorado Canyon, about 20 miles from current-day Searchlight. In May 1897, Colton located a promising ledge of ore on top of a hill. A few yards away, he found a second outcropping. Thus, the claim was dubbed the Duplex, and its ore yielded 72 ounces of gold per ton. The Searchlight Mining District was created the following year.

U.S. Senator Harry Reid (Democrat-Nevada), a Searchlight native and author of the only history of his hometown, observed, "The development of Searchlight came at an opportune time in the history of Nevada, since the Comstock Lode was all but exhausted by the time Colton struck gold in 1897. The shipment of ore from the Searchlight District followed a 20-year slump in Nevada mining and gave the state increased visibility nationwide."

As for George Colton, he didn't have much to say about his find. In fact, his family knows very little about him. A fiercely independent and close-mouthed man, he tended to his own business and was annoyed with people who tried to mind his.

"When Dun and Bradstreet asked for a report on the Duplex," says Gale Colton, "he said, 'My property is not for sale; I'm not promoting it and not asking for anyone to invest in it, so whatever it's worth is my business and none of yours.' He talked to nobody; he gave no interviews."

When, in 1907, the movement to divide Lincoln County began to gain momentum, George Colton opposed it. Stanton Colton, his great-grandson, thinks it was because the county seat, with its meddlesome officials, was 250 miles away in Pioche, and Colton preferred it that way.

At that time, according to Reid, Searchlight had twice as many registered voters as did Las Vegas, and therefore was likely to become the county seat. But by the time of the division in 1909, Las Vegas' population had surpassed that of Searchlight. Besides, Las Vegas was centrally located on the railroad.

George Colton's taciturn nature is the reason for a controversy that seems destined never to die—how did Searchlight get its peculiar name? He was never interviewed concerning the circumstances of his strike, except to acknowledge that he did, indeed, find gold.

The most widely circulated explanation is that the town was named for Searchlight matches, a popular brand used by Colton, who smoked a pipe. Another tale claims that it was named for a man named Lloyd Searchlight. There is no record of any man by that name, but there are records of a Lloyd-Searchlight Mining Company.

Yet another story has it that Colton and some other man had spent a particularly grueling and futile day combing the area. Returning to camp, Colton declared, "There is something here, boys, but it would take a searchlight to find it." A few days later, so the story goes, he found the Duplex

Colton in Southern Nevada

POP.*	DECADE
n/a **	pre-1900
30	1900
945	1910
2,686	1920
5,952	1930
13,937	1940
45,577	1950
123,667	1960
273,288	1970
463,087	1980
715,587	1990

■ Time spent in Southern Nev.
* - Population figures are for greater Las Vegas area (*Source: Nevada State Data Center*).
** - Colton arrived in Southern Nevada in 1897.

George Frederick Colton, founder of Searchlight
(*UNLV Special Collections*)

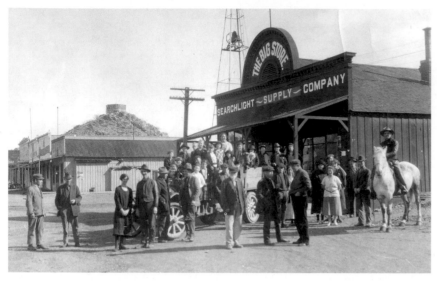

The grand opening of the Searchlight Supply Company was the occasion for this group portrait in 1919. Joining owner Ella Knolls are her sister Frances Knolls, Dick Arnold, Frank Guswell, Neal Scott, George Scott, Harvey Cashman and family, Arda Haenzel, Vance Brite (on horse), Major Allured and family, Sid Garnes, Lucy Weaver and father, Willet Barton, Roy Croft and family, and Harry Russell and wife.
(Review-Journal files)

Searchlight (bottom right) was in decline when this photo was taken in 1937.
(Review-Journal files)

Today, Searchlight is a popular way station for recreationists traveling to Lake Mohave and Laughlin, and incoming retirees are boosting the population back toward 1907 levels.

outcropping, and called his new firm the Searchlight Mining Company.

It is impossible to prove any of these theories. The most widely accepted one, according to Reid, is the story about Colton saying it would take a searchlight to find gold. However, according to family tradition, says Gale Colton, the Searchlight match theory is closest to the truth. She says her grandfather had been warned to beware of marauding Indians. Indeed, there had been Indian trouble in the area, and would be again. As Colton was approaching current-day Searchlight, he saw an Indian riding toward him and climbed a hill to hide and watch his potential attacker. At dusk, he made camp, but not a fire. He did strike a Searchlight match to light his pipe, and by its faint glow, saw he was sitting on a ledge of ore.

Colton's discovery set off a rush to Searchlight. Between 1907 and 1910, the mining camp produced almost $7 million in gold and other precious minerals, and reached a population peak of about 1,500. Colton built a large home on Hobson Street, then the town's main drag. The ruins still stand.

In his day, George F. Colton was a leading citizen—when he was in town. Unlike many pioneers who were nipped by the "Desert Bug," he does not seem to have embraced the desert aesthetic. And he never sought or held public office. "But he controlled those people who did," adds Gale Colton.

As to whether George Colton was a scuffler, Stanton Colton says he doesn't know of any particular incidents, but suspects that he could handle himself. "That is," says Stanton Colton, "if he was anything like my father. My dad would go downtown every weekend night and try to find the biggest miner to pick a fight with. And he said that

every Friday and Saturday night he would come home with his ass whipped. Shortly after his sixteenth birthday, he beat the guy. It was his way of showing he had become a man. So I'm assuming that was an inherited trait."

By 1917, Searchlight's mines were in decline, though they were periodically leased and mined with some success until about 1953. Most of the Coltons, including George Colton, had moved on to California. Some, like Gale Colton's father, remained. Stanton Colton served for many years as the Clark County registrar of voters and the state treasurer, and was a candidate for governor.

Searchlight also produced other people who went on to bigger things. Edith Head, the famous Hollywood costume designer, was a native, as was William Nellis, a heroic aviator in World War II for whom Nellis Air Force Base is named. Silent film stars Clara Bow—the "It Girl"—and her husband, cowboy star Rex Bell, had a home at the Walking Box Ranch west of town. Bell became involved in politics and was subsequently elected lieutenant governor of Nevada.

Unlike the majority of Nevada mining camps, Searchlight survived. It was on the main auto route between Las Vegas and Los Angeles, the Arrowhead Highway, and hung on by catering to desert-weary travelers. But in 1927, U.S. Highway 91 (now Interstate 15) was completed, bypassing the town. Searchlight hit rock bottom, with a population of only 50.

In the early 1930s, with Hoover Dam rising, the town enjoyed another boom, owing to the thirst of construction workers and an increase in the price of gold, which made the old diggings profitable again. In the 1940s, the town developed a reputation as one of the last outposts of quasi-legal prostitution in the region, when a pimp named Willie Martello opened the El Rey Club. The bordello avoided the anti-prostitution crusade of the late 1950s

by burning to the ground.

Unfortunately for historians, George Frederick Colton simply faded away. The family isn't sure exactly when he died. Gale Colton believes he is buried in Southern California, but isn't certain where.

Today, Searchlight is a popular way station for recreationists traveling to Lake Mohave and Laughlin, and incoming retirees are boosting the population back toward 1907 levels. George Colton's town seems to have adopted the motto that appears on the Colton coat of arms: "Never Despair." ✍

Unlike many pioneers who came to Southern Nevada and were nipped by the "Desert Bug," George Colton does not seem to have embraced the desert aesthetic.

William Andrews Clark (1839–1925)

A man full of contradictions—and remembered most for buying a Senate seat—left his name to the county that Las Vegas calls home. BY A.D. HOPKINS

In 1899, Clark simply tried to buy the legislature. More than one 19th-century senator had done so, including a couple who represented Nevada, but Clark got caught red-handed. A legislator dumped $30,000 before his fellow members and declared it had been advanced to him and three others for their votes. And the sordid episode became one of the final straws that led to a constitutional amendment mandating popular election of senators.

He left his name to Clark County and built one of the West's important railroads. He won fights with copper bosses and railroad robber barons. It took him perhaps 10 years to build Montana's largest fortune and not much longer to build one of America's largest business empires. Yet within a few years of William A. Clark's death, his empire was dismantled, and today he is remembered more often for buying a seat in the U.S. Senate than for all his accomplishments.

Clark was a gifted public speaker, but privately close-mouthed. Driven apparently by plain greed, he had such a Midas touch that gold rubbed off the corners of his operations, enriching people who didn't even know him.

He was born in Pennsylvania in 1839, the son of Scotch-Irish parents, and when he was 17, the family moved to Iowa as homesteaders. A bright student, Clark taught school and went to law school, but never practiced. Despite roots in Yankee Pennsylvania, he served the Confederate side in the Civil War. But by 1862, Clark was out of the South, sinking a mineshaft into the hard rock of Bob Tail Hill, Colorado.

Hearing of new claims in Montana, Clark and his partners headed north and made a small stake in a claim near Bannack. But Clark soon recognized that capital invested in a developing country could turn a profit as fast and as large as panning for gold, and was far more certain.

Journeying to Salt Lake City, he brought a wagonload of groceries back to Virginia City, Montana, and sold out immediately. The highest profits were made on eggs. "I bought case after case," he said later. "I knew they would be frozen, but they were suitable for making Tom and Jerrys." The cold-weather beverage was a favorite in Montana bars, and he sold the eggs for $3 a dozen—at a time when miners on Nevada's

Comstock, earning $4 a day, were called the highest-paid working men in America.

Always, Clark seized opportunities to provide support services to a mining economy. When a tobacco shortage loomed, he raced to Salt Lake City for a wagonload of plug-cut and twist, and made another killing. Gold dust was accepted as currency in Montana, but it was unhandy. So every Sunday morning, when miners were paid, Clark showed up with cash to buy dust at $18 an ounce.

By 1872, Butte was in decline. Dust and nuggets had been panned out. There was plenty of gold left, but it was locked up in quartz ore. Clark bought quartz claims cheap, then got hold of a quartz mill and made a fortune processing ore.

There were other men of vision in Montana, and one was Marcus Daly. He partnered with mining magnate George Hearst to buy a silver claim called the Anaconda. The silver prospects proved unfounded, but miners uncovered a seam of copper 50 feet wide—the biggest ever found and the basis of the great Anaconda Copper Company. But when Daly wanted to build a smelter, he discovered that Clark had secretly bought all the readily available water rights necessary to operate it. Thus Clark created an able and unforgiving enemy.

In 1888 Clark sought a territorial seat in Congress on the Democratic ticket. Daly, one of four men who controlled the Democratic Party in Mon-

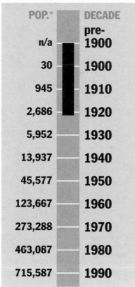

W. Clark in Southern Nevada

POP.*	DECADE
n/a	pre-1900
30	1900
945	1910
2,686	1920
5,952	1930
13,937	1940
45,577	1950
123,667	1960
273,288	1970
463,087	1980
715,587	1990

■ Time spent in Southern Nev.
* - Population figures are for greater Las Vegas area (*Source: Nevada State Data Center*).

William A. Clark controlled one of America's largest business empires and built a railroad to bring his copper mines closer to the Pacific. Incidental to this goal, he turned Las Vegas Ranch into a town where his railroads could be serviced and train crews housed. He called it Las Vegas.
(Union Pacific Railroad)

tana, supported a Republican. Clark and Daly each ran for the U.S. Senate in 1893, but neither could achieve a majority in the state Legislature, which elected senators in those days, and Montana simply did without a senator. In 1898, masked men tried to steal the ballot box in one precinct. Two election officials were shot down; one died. Who ordered the raid was never proved, but when the ballots were counted, there were 307 for Daly's candidates and only 17 for Clark's.

In 1899 Clark simply tried to buy the Legislature. More than one 19th-century senator had done so, including a couple who represented Nevada, but Clark got caught red-handed when a legislator dumped $30,000 before his fellow members and declared it had been advanced to him and three others for their votes. This sordid episode became one of the final straws that led to a constitutional amendment mandating popular election of senators.

Clark won a Senate seat, more or less legitimately, in 1901, with the help of a miners' union. He promised to legislate an eight-hour day for mines, mills, and smelters; a law that would permit a worker to sue a company for damages caused by a co-employee's negligence; and a law permitting employees to shop where they liked instead of being required to patronize overpriced company stores.

He did not keep these promises. In fact, he did surprisingly little with the position. However, Clark believed the United States should cede all federal lands to the states, and he did try to maintain the policy allowing timber to be cut from public lands without payment, ostensibly for mining development. He and many others built lumber empires this way.

Clark had more than one reason for building the San Pedro, Los Angeles, and Salt Lake railroad. It would shorten the distance between his Montana mines and a seaport by 663 miles. It also would open the mineral country of Utah. And Mary Montana Farrell, who wrote a master's thesis on Clark, believed the project appealed to "his imagination as a means of leaving behind him an imperishable monument to himself as one of the great developers of the West … another 'empire builder.'"

Much of the credit for the railroad, however, should go to the senator's younger brother, J. Ross Clark. While William Clark financed the railroad, documents donated to UNLV Special Collections in 1979 suggest that Ross saw the opportunity first.

J. Ross Clark was rail thin and 6 feet tall, towering over his senatorial brother, who was 11 years his senior. Ross Clark was an able banker and mining man in his own right. Poor health drove him to Los Angeles in 1892. His health improved, and he settled in. In 1896 the two brothers bought thousands of acres in Los Angeles County, planted sugar beets, and built a factory to process them, introducing a new industry.

Los Angeles' major ambition in those days was a railroad to Salt Lake City, but the field was littered with the slain pocketbooks of those who had tried to finance this dream. The Union Pacific had failed twice. But the Clark brothers, who owned their enterprises personally, from the president's private car to the janitor's broom, had the money to do it.

At a banquet thrown in honor of the new venture, J. Ross Clark assured guests "that this has been entered upon as an independent project. … It is not the thought, much less the intention of any of the proprietors … that it shall ever become the part of any existing railway." This was the first of many Clark denials to widespread reports that their railroad would be controlled by the same chummy interests who already overcharged for freight. Particularly feared was E.H. Harriman, who had rebuilt the bankrupt Union Pacific by rapid, ruthless expansion.

After one of the earlier attempts, the Union Pacific abandoned a section of completed grade, and Nevada's Lincoln County reclaimed it for nonpayment of taxes. Clark bought this grade in 1900 and started construction. However, Harriman tried to reclaim the grade through the Oregon Short Line, which he controlled.

A yellowed news clipping in the J. Ross Clark papers tells what happened next: "Sunday the Short Line people arrived at … the terminus of

Clark left his railroad interests to the care of others, and occasionally toured his properties in his private railroad car.

their line, with rails, ties, wagons, and men, and commenced to lay track on the old grade. Late in the afternoon C.O. Whittemore, chief attorney for the San Pedro, Los Angeles, and Salt Lake Railroad, arrived and at once proceeded to the grade in Lincoln County, and put men and teams to work with a view to holding the grade. ... When [the Short Line workers] attempted to cross the line, Whittemore and his force with uplifted shovels beat the men and teams back."

A compromise was reached in July 1902, giving each side half the stock in the San Pedro, Los Angeles, and Salt Lake Railroad, but the Clarks were to retain control. The final spike was driven home on January 30, 1905, at a point about four miles from Jean.

The Clarks tried to deal fairly when laying out their own townsite for Las Vegas proper. They advertised lots at specific prices, and accepted applications and down payments, implying sales on a first-come, first-served basis. But at the last moment, with buyers on the scene ready to build, Ross Clark received a telegram from W.H. Bancroft, who represented the Harriman interests in the partnership. Bancroft wished to exploit the unexpected demand by selling the lots at auction, instead of at the advertised prices. Ross Clark wired back that to do so would be impossible, as deposits already had been accepted on most lots. Back to Clark hummed the reply: "Auction or nothing. Bancroft." Deposits were returned, and lots were sold to the highest bidders.

The Clarks tried to diversify the economy, employing men to prospect for gypsum and other minerals, and helping to found the Home Building and Loan Association in 1905, as well as the First State Bank. But the biggest economic opportunity was in the freight and passenger business to the emerging mining region of central Nevada and the promising camps of Rhyolite, Beatty, Goldfield, and Tonopah.

Francis E. "Borax" Smith realized a spur heading that way would pass near his Death Valley borax claims, liberating him from the 20-mule teams that contributed more romance than profit.

By the time Smith had built his own railroad grade nearly to Corn Creek (near today's Lee Canyon turnoff), the Clarks had decided they wanted to control this northbound spur.

"First they started charging Smith high rates to haul road-building materials ... contrary to all railroad practice," said rail historian Art Rader. "If somebody is building a feeder line to your railroad, you give him a big discount." They also started a motor stage line to Rhyolite, which would compete for passenger business. Ultimately the Clarks forced Smith out and began building the feeder line themselves. Borax Smith built a rival railroad from Ludlow, California.

The Clarks' railroad would be called the Las Vegas and Tonopah. Despite the name, it never reached Tonopah, stopping at Goldfield. But it was a big day when the railroad arrived in Beatty. One journalist reported: "The entire population was on hand with dynamite bombs, sky rockets, and hurrahs. ... The corks popped, [and] men threw their arms round each other and shouted their joy at the final coming of the railway that linked the great little camp to the outside world."

After that, however, the Clarks' popularity declined. Forced to testify before the Interstate Commerce Commission, J. Ross Clark admitted that neither he nor Senator Clark made the decisions that really mattered. When it came to deciding which towns got spur lines, or setting freight rates, the notorious Harriman called the shots. This testimony helped break Harriman's railroad trust.

Although the Union Pacific bought out the Clarks' interests in 1921, J. Ross Clark would remain involved in Las Vegas affairs almost until his death in 1927. William Clark would not concern himself closely with Las Vegas or the railroad. In 1907, he essentially quit living in Montana.

He set up headquarters in a mansion on Fifth Avenue in New York, and tried to build the finest house in America, buying entire quarries and a bronze foundry to ensure first-class material. The exterior was concrete, shaped to resemble logs. There were more than 100 rooms, excluding ser-

vants' quarters; the main banquet room had a marble fireplace 15 feet across and was roofed with wood from Sherwood Forest; a breakfast room had 200 carved panels, none of the same design. Clark filled his mansion with original Gothic tapestries and paintings gathered in Europe. The home would remain his castle until he died there on March 2, 1925, at the age of 86.

Clark had married a childhood friend, Katherine Stauffer, in 1869. By 1878 Katherine and their children lived in Europe most of the time, and Clark commuted across the Atlantic every winter. Katherine died in 1893. Shortly after her death, Clark took a mistress, Eugenia LaChapelle, who bore him two children. Clark gave her diamonds, a luxurious apartment, and $1 million. He also left her $2.5 million in his will.

His children by Katherine inherited an estate worth $200 million in 1925 dollars. By 1935 they had sold the assets, divided the proceeds, and gone separate ways. His art collection eventually went to the Corcoran Gallery in Washington, D.C.

The magnificently ostentatious house was razed three years after Clark's death. The *New Republic* questioned the loss: "The Clark house was a scandal even more than it was a joke. ... Decent people were indignant and considered it an affront to the city and to themselves. But time has consecrated its ugliness and it is almost an act of vandalism to tear it down. ... It should be presented to the city as a permanent curiosity ... as a monument to one of the strangest of millionaires, as a crystallization of the pioneer imagination, a reminder of our recent past, a treatise on copper, and a tribute to the state of Montana." ⋈

Railroad operations on the San Pedro, Los Angeles, and Salt Lake Railroad were supervised by J. Ross Clark, the senator's younger and very capable brother. Pictured below are Ross Clark, his wife Miriam, and their grandson J. Ross Clark II.
(UNLV Special Collections)

Walter Bracken (1870–1950)

In Bracken's lifetime, more than one Las Vegan had made a fortune buying a piece of some "single-blanket, jackass prospector" who eventually struck it rich. But in 1948 Bracken told a newsman, "Through the years I spent plenty of money grubstaking but have never gotten back a dollar."

In on the ground floor, the railroad's man kept his lip buttoned during his tenure while holding other offices, such as postmaster and water agent. **BY A.D. HOPKINS**

In the 1940s, a few Las Vegans used to brag that they had seen the 1905 land auction, when downtown lots sold for an average of $452 and the best hotel was made of canvas. Having arrived on a train for the auction was the Western equivalent of having an ancestor on the Mayflower.

Walter Bracken, however, was here to meet the train. And from the town's very beginnings until Bracken's death in 1950, Las Vegas' story and Bracken's were intertwined. Agent for the railroad that decreed a town would be built, and for the land and water company that directed its growth, Bracken was seen in his time as a local Pilate to the railroad Caesars. He, in fact, toiled much of his career under micromanaging bosses, yet managed to steer Las Vegas in the directions he thought best.

Born in 1870 in Ohio, Bracken became a civil engineer. He first saw Las Vegas in 1901, from a horse-drawn buckboard, as part of a team picking a route for the San Pedro, Los Angeles, and Salt Lake Railroad. The survey party recommended buying Las Vegas Ranch, already a well-known rest stop. Its location and water meant it could be more than a "jerkwater town"; it would be a substantial community, where steam engines could be serviced and where train crews and mechanics could be housed.

Bracken took possession of the old ranch and in 1904 became the postmaster; his post office was a tent in which he lived. Bracken was involved in surveying for a new townsite, and arranged to give free lots to any denomination that would agree to establish a church. He set aside the land

on which a city library and even the Clark County Courthouse eventually were built—even though Las Vegas was then part of Lincoln County, with a county seat in Pioche.

In the spring of 1905, the railroad announced that its lots would be sold only at auction. It offered special passenger rates for those traveling to the auction ($16 from Los Angeles, $20 from Salt Lake City, to be rebated if the ticketholders actually purchased a lot). On May 15, when bidding opened, more than 1,000 people stood in the growing heat, hoping to claim a piece of the new town. When the final gavel dropped, 176 choice lots—there were 1,200 available—had been sold, and Bracken owned one.

As soon as the auction was over, he caught a train for Salt Lake City and married a schoolmarm named Anna Johnson. Anna was born in Eureka and was a graduate of the University of Nevada. She taught at Delamar, now a ghost town but then a booming mining community. Surveying work had brought Bracken to Delamar, and into Anna's heart.

The couple honeymooned in San Francisco. On returning to Las Vegas, Anna was introduced with a big party at the ranch. An account of the occasion topped a local newspaper: "Splendid Reception at Ranch Resort," read the first headline deck. A subhead elaborated, "Lavish Banquet Enjoyed by Many Guests." The dining hall was decorated with "trailing vines, ferns, and willows gathered from the banks of the creek."

The Brackens soon built a big gray stone home at 410 Fremont Street, where they lived for 37 years before selling it for business development.

In 1942 the couple moved to 417 South Seventh Street, where they would spend the rest of their lives.

Bracken served as the railroad agent in Las Vegas but was more active as agent of the Las Vegas Land and Water Company, the subsidiary set up by the railroad to develop its land holdings. To most Las Vegans, that made him "The

Walter Bracken at the home he and Anna built on Fremont Street, one of the finest in Las Vegas at the time. Note the collection of Paiute basketry.
(UNLV Special Collections)

Man," the individual who seemed to run the town. But in the first 25 years of his long career, Bracken was carrying out orders of distant superiors.

The relationship was proved in 1989, when Bob Coffin, a Nevada state senator, rare book dealer, and amateur historian, dug up a trove of documents from the railroad. "They were in the basement of this building in Los Angeles. ... Sometimes the fungus and mold was so bad I had to wear a mask," remembered Coffin. He saved more than 300,000 pages, and eventually sold the collection and index for $330,000 to his alma mater, UNLV. These documents prove that the railroad thoroughly micromanaged Las Vegas operations. "They had to account for every horseshoe nail," said Coffin.

Letters from about 1910 relate Bracken's efforts to buy an automobile for company use. J. Ross Clark, president of the company and vice president of the entire railroad, had his own chauffeur inspect the car, then told Bracken not to buy it. The subject of this painstaking attention was a used Ford.

Bracken directed the installation of the town's first water system, using pipes made of redwood staves, bound with metal hoops. Redwood pipes weren't as good as iron, but they were cheaper, and in the view of the San Pedro, Los Angeles, and Salt Lake, that settled the choice. The railroad interests also were slow to pave the streets made it harder to dig up and maintain water mains. There was no significant city park or civic center until the New Deal, said Michael Green, a historian who teaches at the Community College of Southern Nevada.

"They were also very slow to run water lines beyond the original townsite," Green added. The idea, he explained, was to ensure that growth stayed close to the railroad, where it was easy to serve. "But the real effect was that developers drilled their own wells. So eventually, you had a hundred uncapped artesian wells in the valley, pouring out water constantly. Certainly that contributed to the dropping of the water table."

Though Bracken lacked authority, he buttoned his lip and accepted blame. But when W.M. Jeffers became president of the Union Pacific in the 1930s, he decided to give Bracken the authority everybody thought he already had.

Green says some of the Union Pacific's old-fashioned policies continued even after Bracken had the power to change them: "You find restrictive covenants in deeds in the earlier years." He doubts Bracken set the policy, but he implemented it, and it confined black residents to Block 17, adjacent to Las Vegas' infamous redlight district, Block 16. In the 1940s, the city brought heavy-handed pressure on black businessmen downtown to remove themselves to West Las Vegas. "It isn't clear who is responsible, but they moved on his watch. ... Certainly none of this makes Bracken unique; he reflected his times."

During Bracken's first few years here, Las Vegas was the jumping-off place for mining booms at Rhyolite and Goldfield. More than one town dweller made a fortune buying a piece of some "single-blanket, jackass prospector" who eventually struck it rich. Bracken tried it but had no luck. "Through the years I spent plenty of money grubstaking but have never gotten back a dollar," he told a local newsman in 1948.

The Brackens enjoyed a rich social life and Bracken was active in virtually all community organizations. But while his wife traveled fashionably in Europe, nobody remembers Bracken taking a vacation during a career that spanned more than 40 years. Failing eyesight forced his retirement in 1946.

On January 2, 1950, after actively participating in the social events of Las Vegas' holiday season, Anna Bracken remarked that she felt ill. Before a doctor could arrive, she died of a heart attack. Already in failing health, Walter Bracken quickly grew worse without his mate of 45 years. He survived her by only seven months, dying on July 13, 1950. ✍

The Las Vegas Land and Water Company offices, built in 1905 at the southeast corner of Main Street and Ogden Avenue. Identities are uncertain, but the man on the left may be Walter Bracken.
(Nevada State Museum)

Walter Bracken gives a tour of one of his water projects to Las Vegas Mayor Ernie Cragin.
(Nevada State Museum)

Bracken in Southern Nevada

POP.*	DECADE
n/a	pre-1900
30	1900
945	1910
2,6686	1920
5,952	1930
13,937	1940
45,577	1950
123,667	1960
273,288	1970
463,087	1980
715,587	1990

■ Time spent in Southern Nev.
* - Population figures are for greater Las Vegas area (*Source: Nevada State Data Center*).

J.T. McWilliams (1863–1941)

A one-time railroad surveyor takes on his former employer over water service and finds a home in Southern Nevada. **BY K. J. EVANS**

His face was as red as his hair when J.T. McWilliams reached the crest of the Spring Mountain Range. He paused, wiped the sweat from his face and thick spectacles, and peered down at the heavily forested Lee Canyon.

On that day in 1894, he saw more trees than he had seen anywhere since he came West, and he saw money to make from timber sales. But as he explored the canyon, he saw a higher use for the land, and he would spend the next four decades working to open the mountain canyon to public recreational use, and to preserve its natural splendor.

McWilliams had been in the region for about a year and was working in Goodsprings as a surveyor and civil engineer. There, he met Noah Clark, who operated a sawmill in Clark Canyon, on the Pahrump side of the Spring Mountains. Clark told him of the vast, unclaimed forest on the other side, and McWilliams set out on foot to inspect it. He surveyed the land and claimed about 1,300 acres of it.

"This proved a long and expensive process because others who had money and great influence were also smitten with the ambition to secure this timber for its value as lumber," said the *Las Vegas Age* of August 20, 1937. It was not surprising, therefore, that in 1906, through the power of some Washington politicians, the McWilliams permits were canceled.

The surveyor suspected it was the work of William A. Clark, who was a U.S. senator (from Montana), as well as the proprietor of the San Pedro, Los Angeles, and Salt Lake Railroad, which had built Las Vegas and controlled most local development. Clark had made fortunes not only in copper but also by exploiting timber, and furthermore, seemed to consider McWilliams an enemy.

McWilliams retaliated by writing a long letter to President Theodore Roosevelt, no lover of the big railroads, and telegraphing it to Washington. Within four days, his claims were revalidated. This was one of many battles the feisty McWilliams would wage with the railroad between 1902 and his death in 1941—and one of the few he would win.

John Thomas McWilliams was born at Owen Sound, Ontario, Canada, on December 10, 1863, one of four brothers. His father, John McWilliams, was a building contractor who had emigrated from Ulster in what is now Northern Ireland. Young McWilliams learned surveying by working as an apprentice, but aspired to a career in engineering.

On a visit to the United States in 1879, J.T. McWilliams decided he liked America and moved to Detroit, where he worked in a wholesale grocery. In 1883, he moved to Chicago. During the day, he was a grocer; at night, he attended classes in civil engineering at the University of Chicago. By the next year, he was employed by the Northern Pacific Railroad in its engineering corps.

In 1893, he was in Southern California, where he found a wealth of work for a man with his skills. He was on a job in Needles, California, in 1897, when he met his future wife, Iona. She had been born in Grand Rapids, Minnesota, in 1876, had been educated as a schoolteacher in Philadelphia, and had moved to Needles on the advice of her doctor when she developed a lung ail-

John Thomas McWilliams, as he appeared in middle age
(Jim Day/Review-Journal)

McWilliams in Southern Nevada

POP.*	DECADE
n/a	pre-1900
30	1900
945	1910
2,686	1920
5,592	1930
13,937	1940
45,577	1950
123,667	1960
273,288	1970
463,087	1980
715,587	1990

■ Time spent in Southern Nev.
* - Population figures are for greater Las Vegas area (*Source: Nevada State Data Center*).

ment. She had fully recovered by the time she married McWilliams at Fort Mohave in 1897.

His next job took the newlyweds to Flagstaff, Arizona, where McWilliams designed the town's first water system, and the couple welcomed their second child, Nellie, in 1898. (Their first child, a boy, had died at birth.) In 1899, they moved to the Grand Canyon, where McWilliams surveyed the Bright Angel Trail into the canyon.

In 1901, the family moved to Goodsprings, determined to settle in that booming little town. A particularly interesting job came McWilliams' way in 1902, when William McDermott, who represented the newly formed San Pedro, Los Angeles, and Salt Lake Railroad, summoned him to Helen J. Stewart's Las Vegas Ranch. The railroad wanted him to survey the 1,840-acre ranch, which it was considering as a new townsite and railroad division point.

McWilliams, who probably knew the region as well as anyone of the time, and was aware of the valley's huge artesian water belt, peered through his surveyor's transit and saw opportunity. It would be the last time for a long time that he would deal with the railroad on friendly terms.

Around 1904, he purchased from Stewart 80 acres of land on the west side of the railroad right of way, and laid out an orderly townsite with broad avenues. McWilliams saw it as the ideal site, close to Las Vegas Creek and accessible to the road to Rhyolite, Goldfield, and Tonopah.

To an extent, he was right. The lots sold well through the winter of 1904-1905, and the town reached a peak of 2,000-3,000 people, many of those teamsters who plied the trails between Las Vegas and the northern mines. But the railroad was not about to allow an upstart surveyor to reap any benefits that it could retain for itself.

The company established its own subdivision, the Las Vegas Land and Water Company, which laid out Las Vegas Townsite, the core of today's downtown Las Vegas. Lots were sold during a two-day auction in May 1905. The high demand can be explained in a word: water. The railroad owned nearly all the water from Big

Springs, the source of Las Vegas Creek, and lots in the townsite came with the promise of water. McWilliamstown got water from a hodgepodge of small wells, some of which served several lots. Many people who had originally bought lots there and erected permanent structures put them on skids and dragged them across the tracks to the new townsite.

Still, optimism flourished. McWilliams built his house there, and he persuaded well-known impresario Chauncy Pulsifer to build a vaudeville theater, the Trocadero. Work began on the 800-seat theater in May 1905, and ceased a few weeks after the Las Vegas lot auction. The unfinished building languished, and finally was felled by one

of a series of fires that destroyed most of the town's few remaining wooden buildings.

Until the 1930s, the town would consist mostly of tents and shacks. By 1906, the year McWilliams was appointed state water rights surveyor for the region, snobs across the tracks were calling his development "Ragtown." McWilliams insisted that it be called "the Original Las Vegas Townsite." Both he and Senator Clark's Las Vegas Land and Water Company had, since early 1905, been advertising heavily in the Los Angeles newspapers. Clark's ads touted the easy availability of water; McWilliams', his low prices and easy terms.

There was no love lost between Walter Bracken, the railroad's lackey in Las Vegas, and the feisty surveyor. But it was the fabled icehouse incident that upgraded their mutual disdain to outright hatred. C.P. "Pop" Squires, editor of the *Las Vegas Age*, recalled in a 1933 article that the construction of an icehouse was a priority in the early years of the town, and that Senator Clark himself rode past a plot of land on the north end of town and indicated that he wanted the ice plant located there. His will was done, and workers soon had completed the foundations for a fine, large structure.

Meanwhile, McWilliams, who had been in Los Angeles when the work commenced, returned. He took one look at the site, must have laughed, and fetched his surveying instruments. His suspicions were confirmed; the ice house was on his property. (It was a small, triangular section of land located at what is now the corner of Main Street and Bonanza Road.)

It is unclear whether McWilliams deliberately waited until the work was well along before notifying the railroad of its mistake, or if he had actually been unaware of what was happening. In either case, McWilliams apprised Bracken of the error and offered to sell the lot for $1,000. Bracken, who was responsible to the company for such screw-ups, took the position that McWilliams was once again trying to take advantage of the poor railroad. There was no sale.

McWilliams responded to the cancellation of his claims by writing a long letter to President Theodore Roosevelt, no lover of the big railroads, and telegraphing it to Washington. Within four days, his claims were revalidated.

J.T. McWilliams surveying his property in Lee Canyon, about 1936
(UNLV Special Collections)

Claude Mackey (left) with J.T. McWilliams at Lee Canyon, early 1930s
(UNLV Special Collections)

The railroad simply ceased work and moved the project elsewhere. McWilliams later sold the land for several thousand dollars.

McWilliams thereby discovered a new hobby: annoying Bracken. The surveyor seemed to enjoy the role of gadfly, and it was certainly a job that needed to be done in such a solid company town. On the other hand, it may have been in McWilliams' nature. There is plenty of evidence that he possessed the Celtic cultural trait of enjoying a good row.

Sometime around 1914, McWilliams was beaten senseless by Joe May, who had taken exception to something McWilliams had said about him. McWilliams filed charges of assault and battery, and May demanded a jury trial. The defense "called several witnesses to prove that McWilliams' reputation for peace and quietude is bad," the *Las Vegas Age* reported. "Sheriff Woodard was called in rebuttal and testified that McWilliams has been on good behavior for the past six months." May was fined $50.

Though he was not among the city's original elite because of his estrangement from the railroad, McWilliams continually showed his interest in the town and the region. And as the town grew, his reputation grew along with it. He maintained his civil engineering practice, and he produced more than 3,000 maps of Clark County and all its subdivisions, a project that kept him busy the rest of his life. Not so busy, though, that he couldn't pause to give Bracken a bellyache.

In their book *Water: A History of Las Vegas,* Florence Lee Jones and John Cahlan provided a detailed account of the next battle between Bracken and McWilliams. In May 1912, McWilliams happened upon some workmen emptying the cesspool of the railroad shops directly into Las Vegas Creek. He wrote to Bracken, noting that a herd of dairy cattle, from which the city obtained all of its milk, was drinking from the creek below where the dumping was going on. He also pointed out that the creek was used by the ranch's slaughterhouse, and said, "The only supply of meat Las Vegas has is butchered in the slaughterhouse, and must be washed with sewerage water."

The railroad ceased dumping and laid a water line to the slaughterhouse. By 1916, McWilliams and the residents of what had come to be called "Old Town" were pressuring the railroad's land-and-water subsidiary to provide water to the subdivision, and the Las Vegas City Commission passed a resolution that year asking it to do so.

However, the clamor continued until 1926, when residents of Old Town petitioned the Nevada Public Service Commission for service. Long, complicated, and occasionally rancorous negotiations continued until the fall of 1927, when it was finally agreed that Old Town—and no other subdivisions—would receive city water. McWilliams was hired to lay out the system. In the end, the cost to the railroad company to deliver water to Old Town was $87.40 per month, while income from water sales amounted to $271.81 per month.

McWilliams didn't have water on the brain, though, and through all his water battles, he saved time for his pet project, the development of his land in Lee Canyon. As early as 1910, he and his wife had established a camp in the pines, and advertised it in the *Las Vegas Age,* advising customers to "bring your own grub and bedding."

By the early 1930s, McWilliams owned or controlled more than 2,000 acres of the best land in Lee Canyon. He was deluged with offers from entrepreneurs who wanted to log the property, most of which were declined. What McWilliams had in mind was a small community of rustic cabins, with campgrounds, hiking trails, and access roads throughout the area.

He got acquainted with Claude Mackey, local representative for the Works Progress Administration, one of the Roosevelt administration's New Deal programs. McWilliams offered the WPA 10 acres of his best forest land if the government would build a public playground for Southern Nevada children. Naturally, with the feds involved, the scope of the project increased dramatically. Mackey asked for an additional 40 acres, then another 10 acres. Then he asked for still another 50 acres and, finally, another 10 acres on top of that to build a ski course. During 1937, a unit of the Civilian Conservation Corps (CCC) was installed, and the boys worked wonders on the area. In addition to building the main road—under the direction of McWilliams—they built a full-blown mountain resort with cabins, a kitchen and dining hall, and hot showers.

C.P. Squires, on a visit in 1937, was impressed: "McWilliams Park is the splendid result of determination and tenacity of purpose not often experienced in these days of dollar-grabbing."

A transalpine road to Death Valley was never completed, though it might have been if McWilliams had lived through the war. In the fall of 1941, he suffered a heart attack and died a few days later. His wife continued to live in the house on Wilson Street that her husband had built in 1904, until she was put into a nursing home in 1968.

The outsider who bucked the railroad big boys had gained considerable status since his arrival, and his death was front-page news. His "crank" individualism was lauded, and he was recalled as a great pioneer. In 1927, he made a statement, in passing, that sounded suspiciously like the utterance of a visionary. "I gladly gave my time," he said, "for the future of what will be a magic city." ☙

> *"I gladly gave my time for the future of what will be a magic city."*
>
> —J.T. McWilliams

SAM GAY (1860–1932)

An honest man who knew how to break up a drunken brawl without a gun, Clark County's
second sheriff bowed out when asked to enforce laws he didn't believe in. **BY K.J. EVANS**

I t was right after Christmas in 1910. Clark County Deputy Sheriff Sam Gay was going about his duties, busting up a hobo camp. A couple of muggers were arrested, stolen goods and money were recovered, and an escaped convict from Idaho was nabbed. Meanwhile, someone stole a furnished house and carried it away. Just a tent house, with a wooden foundation, mind you, but the house was gone and was never recovered. This just wasn't the kind of case in which Sam Gay excelled. But even though he wasn't a great detective nor a slick politician, voters kept re-electing him.

Gay was big—6 foot and 260 pounds—fearless, and equipped with fists so efficient he almost never saw the need to carry a gun, let alone use it. He was also compassionate, never known to abuse his authority or mistreat prisoners. In fact, he was constantly criticized for being too lenient. But he was the most popular and beloved lawman Clark County has ever had.

In later years, he described the town he policed this way: "From 1905 to 1910, Las Vegas was a rough and tumble western town. Five men dead for breakfast one Sunday morning and 10 men wounded. The boys put on a show that would make Bill Hart ashamed of himself [in reference to William S. Hart, a cowboy star of the silent film era]."

Sam Gay was, in a sense, one of those "boys." He enjoyed whiskey and sporting fisticuffs, and thought the men who toiled in mines or drove freight wagons were entitled to get drunk, gamble, and raise hell. His job was to keep them from killing, robbing, or seriously injuring each other. This view was not shared by all of the other leading citizens of Las Vegas.

Born March 1, 1860, in Canada, Gay grew up on a Massachusetts farm. Like many of his generation, he went West. Just before the turn of the century, he was in San Diego, working as a streetcar conductor; in 1900, he moved to Nome, Alaska, lured by the gold rush, but returned to San Diego the following year. By 1902, he was in Goldfield, swinging a pick in deep mines, but was soon hired as a bouncer at Tex Rickard's Northern Club.

In the autumn of 1905, at age 45, Gay arrived in the embryonic town of Las Vegas and again was hired as a bouncer, this time by J.O. McIntosh, owner of the Arizona Club. The joint was situated in Block 16, the only part of town where booze and prostitution were allowed. Gay was adept at handling the roughest of customers without resorting to the gun. Lincoln County Sheriff Jake Johnson liked his style and, in January 1906, made Gay Las Vegas' night watchman. He was elected town constable a short time later. When Orrin K. Smith was elected sheriff of Lincoln County in 1908, he hired Big Sam as his deputy for the southern part of the vast county.

Gay's technique was to grab combatants by the scruffs of their necks and bash their heads together, repeating this as required. If the warriors persisted, they were tied together at a hitching post and hosed down until their tempers cooled.

In 1909, Clark County split off from Lincoln County. Charles C. Corkhill was elected sheriff, and he retained Big Sam as his deputy. But the two men were very different. Corkhill was "by the book"; Gay relied on his wits. Their first clash

Though slow to draw his weapon on a man, Gay enjoyed blasting the newfangled electric lights. One night, after he darkened Fremont Street, District Attorney Albert Henderson charged him with gross intoxication. In court, Gay rose and declared, "So long as I am sheriff of Clark County, I will not take a drink of intoxicating liquor. If I do, I will hand in my resignation."

Sam Gay, second sheriff of Clark County
(Nevada Historical Society)

Interior of the Arizona Club (following page), downtown Las Vegas, circa 1912. The tall man with the moustache, at center, is Sheriff Sam Gay.
(UNLV Special Collections)

Gay in Southern Nevada

POP.*	DECADE
n/a	pre-1900
30	1900
945	1910
2,686	1920
5,952	1930
13,937	1940
45,577	1950
123,667	1960
273,288	1970
463,087	1980
715,587	1990

■ Time spent in Southern Nev.
* - Population figures are for greater Las Vegas area (*Source: Nevada State Data Center*).

was not long in coming.

The town jail was a large, windowless shack built of sheet metal and railroad ties, airless and rat-infested. In the summer of 1910, Sam Gay opened the jail, chained the men together, marched them to Las Vegas Creek, and tied them loosely to the giant cottonwoods, where they were able to stay cool. Corkhill was infuriated and fired Gay, which was a mistake. The well-liked deputy challenged him at the polls and, in 1911, Gay became the second sheriff of Clark County.

His popularity saved him when he faced his next major crisis in 1915. Though slow to draw his weapon on a man, he enjoyed blasting the newfangled electric lights. One night, after Sam darkened Fremont Street, District Attorney Albert Henderson charged him with gross intoxication. In court, Gay rose and declared, "So long as I am sheriff of Clark County, I will not take a drink of intoxicating liquor. If I do, I will hand in my resignation." The charges were dropped, but it was the start of a long feud between Henderson and Gay.

Gay seemed to keep his temperance pledge. In later years, he said that Prohibition, which started in 1919, helped him stay sober. "I quit after they started making the stuff out of old shoes," he explained.

One day, a 5-year-old girl, Marjorie Schaeffer, met Gay on the street, handed him a small box marked "Sheriff Sam," and scampered away. Inside the box was a solid gold badge with the words "Sheriff, Clark County, Nevada" on its face, and the inscription "Compliments of Las Vegas friends." The big man was quite moved and vowed to keep the badge "bright and unsullied."

Technically, gambling had been outlawed in Nevada since 1910, but the law was rarely enforced. This did not perturb Gay, who enjoyed a friendly game himself. In 1916, District Attorney Henderson charged Gay's young deputy, Joe Keate, with participating in a poker game. Gay fired Keate—but only for a day.

Keate had his own feud with Justice of the Peace William Harkins, which erupted on September 19, 1917. Keate had been ordered to fetch a prisoner to the courtroom and arrived an hour late, whereupon Harkins slapped him with a $5 contempt of court charge.

Keate refused to pay, ran out of the courtroom, and returned with a borrowed gun. Harkins was still on the bench, and Keate threw the gun down in front of Harkins and "called him out." Gay heard the ruckus and went into the courtroom. There he found the enraged Keate with a hand twitching over his holstered gun, and the ashen-faced Harkins, petrified and staring at the second pistol lying in front of him. Henderson screamed for Gay to arrest his deputy, but Gay waited until Keate had calmed down a bit, then led him away.

Gay was sacked for failing to discharge his duties, but he asserted that as an elected official, he couldn't be fired. The case went all the way to the Nevada Supreme Court, which upheld the firing, but Gay was re-elected in 1918.

In the summer of 1922, a railroad strike threatened to turn violent, and Sam Gay took the side of the working men, deputizing several of them to keep the peace. They did.

Gay, at age 66, was re-elected in 1926, but didn't run in 1930. "Too many crooks coming to Las Vegas, now [that] they're building Boulder Dam," he said in announcing his retirement. "I'm used to tough hombres who shot each other up once in a while. I'm used to gunfights. But I ain't much good running down racketeers. My notions is too old-fashioned. You can't deal with these new gunmen with a single-action .45. Need a machine gun. I'm too old to learn to run one, so I quit." In truth, he was sick of enforcing anti-drinking and anti-gambling laws he thought were foolish.

In the summer of 1932, Gay was in California for a holiday when he suffered a minor heart attack, which went untreated. On his return to Las Vegas in August, the big one came and he died in the local hospital. He was buried with his solid gold badge.

"Sam Gay numbered his friends by the thousands, and was always the friend of the underdog," wrote Al Cahlan in the *Las Vegas Evening Review*. "That's why men used to ride hundreds of miles to cast their ballots for him when election time rolled around. He had a following that was loyal almost beyond belief, and that, more than any words I might say, constitutes a eulogy complete. Sam Gay was a Clark County institution." ✍

> *"Sam Gay numbered his friends by the thousands, and was always the friend of the underdog. That's why men used to ride hundreds of miles to cast their ballots for him when election time rolled around."*
> —Al Cahlan
> *Las Vegas Evening Review*

C.P. "Pop" Squires (1865–1958)

"Perhaps that bright and glorious morning after the misery of the long night gave this spot a particularly tender place in my heart."
—C.P. Squires
Upon seeing Las Vegas

A Minnesota man saw a desert way station as the land of opportunity, and used a tiny newspaper to rescue it from the doldrums. **BY K.J. EVANS**

If there is any individual who deserves the title "The Father of Las Vegas," it is Charles Pember Squires, a native of Austin, Minnesota, who spent more than 50 years here — building, boosting, and ballyhooing his city. Fellow citizens who knew him during that time in Las Vegas greeted him with the sobriquet of "Pop," and his wife, Delphine, as "Mom."

Born in 1865, Squires moved with his family to Redlands, California, where he set himself up in a real estate and title insurance business. Once established, he proposed by mail to his high-school sweetheart, Delphine Anderson, and they were married in August 1889. Their first two children, Florence and James, were born in Redlands.

The panic of 1893 caused a sharp drop in real estate transactions, and Squires later sold his business. In 1903, he became secretary and manager of the Union League Club, where he heard about the plans of Senator William A. Clark to extend his San Pedro and Los Angeles Railroad all the way to Salt Lake City. Part of the plan was to establish a new town in a desert valley that happened to contain quite a bit of water. It had long been known as Las Vegas, "The Meadows."

Squires smelled opportunity. In partnership with J. Ross Clark, Frank Waters, and Chris N. Brown, he borrowed $25,000 from banker John H. Pirtle to establish a bank, a hotel, a lumberyard, and a real-estate firm. Squires invited Brown to join him on an inspection tour of the site. Getting there, however, was a problem, as the railroad was using all of its cars to carry the equipment needed to lay out and subdivide the town. "We were free to stow away as best we could on gondola cars loaded with plows, scrapers, wagons, and other dirt-moving appliances," Squires recalled.

The only spot they could find aboard the train was in a small space at the front of a gondola car, which exposed them directly to the freezing desert night. After traveling most of the night, the train stopped near the current site of Jean, and the conductor ordered them off the train, promising to return. Several hours later he did, with the engine at the rear of the train and a caboose at its front. Squires and Brown were allowed to ride in its relative comfort.

At about 7 a.m., Squires stepped out onto the platform of the caboose and peered out across the wide valley. In the distance, he spotted several tiny white dots. "What is that?" he asked the conductor.

The conductor cleared his throat and spat vigorously. "That is Las Vegas," he replied.

Outwardly, the landscape was no different from that of a dozen desert valleys. But Squires was impressed. He didn't know why. "Perhaps," he said, "that bright and glorious morning after the misery of the long night gave this spot a particularly tender place in my heart."

The only lodging house in town was a tent owned by "Captain" James Ladd, who had a novel way of making sure that his premises were free of lice and other vermin. When a lodger arrived, Ladd made him sit by the stove for a while. If he started scratching, he got the boot. If he didn't, he was welcome to pay his $1 and share a bed with another man for eight hours.

Each of Squires' partners put up $1,250 to capitalize what became known as the First State Bank, and Los Angeles banker John S. Park was brought in to run it. Squires went back to Los Angeles, where he bought

Squires in Southern Nevada

POP.*	DECADE
n/a	pre-1900
30	1900
945	1910
2,686	1920
5,952	1930
13,937	1940
45,577	1950
123,667	1960
273,288	1970
463,087	1980
715,587	1990

■ Time spent in Southern Nev.
* - Population figures are for greater Las Vegas area (*Source: Nevada State Data Center*).

Charles Pember Squires about age 20
(*UNLV Special Collections*)

One of the first passenger trains to Las Vegas came for the townsite auction of May 15, 1905. C.P. Squires had just finished setting up his tent hotel in anticipation of its arrival.
(Review-Journal files)

Pop Squires was well-acquainted with Republican royalty. Here, he visits with failed presidential candidate Thomas Dewey.
(UNLV Special Collections)

a set of books, a desk, chairs, and a mighty iron safe, calculated to inspire confidence in depositors.

On May 15, 1905, Squires was among the bidders gathered around the platform when the town lots were being auctioned. He bought numerous parcels, including an entire block between Fourth and Fifth streets to be used for residential development. By June 1906, Squires had completed his own home at Fourth and Fremont, and had brought his family to join him.

Las Vegas was not a pleasant place. There was no sewage system, and flies brought on by human and animal waste besieged the town like a plague from the Old Testament. An ordinance was passed requiring that all privies be enclosed in metal boxes. Since the nearest law was in Pioche, Squires made it his business to see that the ordinance was enforced.

Of greater concern, however, were fires, usually started by kerosene lamps. Squires got to work on his next big project, electrifying Las Vegas. The Consolidated Power and Telephone Company was incorporated March 20, 1906, with Chris Brown as president, Robert Graham as vice president, John S. Park as treasurer, and Squires as secretary.

Job one was a distribution system—power poles and wires. Squires purchased a pair of 90-horsepower gasoline engines and a pair of 50-kilowatt Westinghouse generators, capable of producing 110-volt alternating current, along with 50 telephones, enough for everyone in town who wanted one.

But by 1908, another "panic" had hit the nation—and Las Vegas. Money was tight. Squires traveled to Minnesota and Chicago, seeking investors willing to take a chance on the promising young desert town. He had no luck: "It was a black-looking world and poor, sick Las Vegas was about the lowest in spirit that a town could get. … There were still some people here, most of them unable to get away and having no other place to land which was any better. The train crews operating the railroad were the only people who had any income, and that none too generous."

It was against this backdrop that Charles Pember Squires, now nearing age 40, almost missed the opportunity that would make his fortune.

In 1905, there had been three newspapers in Las Vegas: the *Las Vegas Times*, the *Las Vegas Advance*, and the *Las Vegas Age*. The *Advance* lasted only a couple of months. The publisher of the *Las Vegas Times* decided that Las Vegas was hopeless and moved his newspaper to Caliente. This left the *Las Vegas Age*, owned by C.W. Nicklin.

Nicklin was anxious to get out of town. He approached Squires and asked if he would like to enter the exciting world of journalism. Squires had an immediate answer. "What on earth would I do with a newspaper? I have troubles enough already," he cried.

The next day, Nicklin came again, this time offering the *Age* to Squires at a deep discount, if he would take it right away. He "firmly and very decisively" declined the offer. "But something had started a train of thought which I was unable to sidetrack," recalled Squires. "Now, just suppose I had a newspaper in Las Vegas; perhaps I could help revive the poor, sick little town."

On his third visit, Nicklin offered Squires the newspaper at the "ridiculously low price" of $2,300. Squires hesitated, then accepted. Charles Pember Squires now had what his hero, Teddy Roosevelt, would call a "Bully Pulpit"

for expounding his views, and he used it. But before he started crusading in earnest, he began to improve the little paper. Sometime between 1908 and 1909, he began his tenure as Las Vegas' official and unofficial weather observer, and installed a small weather station behind the newspaper office at 411 East Fremont Street. The *Age* now was able to report the weather, and on July 26, 1931, he logged the highest recorded temperature ever—118 degrees.

To a newspaperman of his generation, it would have been unthinkable not to become directly involved in civic matters, including politics. In 1907, Squires served on the finance committee of the Lincoln County Division Club, which advocated breaking off the southern half of the enormous county and creating a new one.

In 1909, the Nevada Legislature approved the split, but at a heavy cost. The indebtedness of Lincoln County was to be divided between Lincoln and Clark counties. This included the debt from the notorious "Million Dollar Courthouse" in Pioche. Needlessly elaborate for its time and place, the courthouse had cost $20,000 to build in 1871, and mismanagement of the debt service had swelled the debt to $640,000 by 1909. The cost was split in proportion to the assessed valuation of

each county, so the fledgling Clark County began life $430,000 in debt. Furthermore, noted Squires, the new county had "no money, no county property. Lincoln County had its courthouse. It was a bitter pill, but county division was worth it."

In late 1910, Squires and three other leading citizens drafted Las Vegas' city charter and marshaled it through the legislature. The charter was signed by Governor Tasker L. Oddie on March 17, 1911.

In 1920, Squires embarked on the project that would ultimately ensure the survival of Las Vegas, and likewise ensure his place as a major figure in the history of Nevada. A promotional organization, the League of the Southwest, consisting of representatives from Southern California and Nevada, met in Los Angeles in April 1920 to discuss the possibility of developing the Colorado River—specifically, building a dam on it.

Squires approached Nevada Governor Emmett Boyle and asked him to lend his support to the effort. Boyle declined to be personally involved, but deputized Squires. "I appoint you my personal representative and will stand behind whatever you see fit to

do," the governor declared. The first thing Squires did was select three other Las Vegans—Dr. Royce W. Martin, James Cashman, and E.W. Griffith—and Boyle confirmed all of them as delegates to the convention of the League of the Southwest.

Squires was appointed to the committee on resolutions, chaired by Governor D.W. Davis of Idaho. The first day of the convention was given over to protests from those who believed that building a dam would flood the Grand Canyon. At the end of the second day, no resolutions had emerged.

"Nobody had any ideas," Squires recalled. Davis asked Squires to write a resolution that evening. He spent most of the night drafting it, and it was accepted and adopted with only minor changes the next day. The resolution called for a high dam to be built at or near Boulder Canyon "in order to preserve the Imperial Valley from destruction and to provide water for the growing cities of the Southwest."

Another meeting of the league was held in Denver, and it was there that Squires pointed out that the U.S. Constitution allows states to form treaties or compacts among themselves. The governor of Colorado volunteered that a man in his office, Delph Carpenter, was an authority on interstate compacts. Carpenter explained that it would be virtually impossible for a private enterprise to finance and build a dam on the Colorado River. The states would have to agree upon a compact and put it before the U.S. Congress. "We knew then that our dreams for early construction of a dam on the Colorado River were hopeless," Squires said.

In January 1921, the legislatures of each of the seven states adopted a resolution asking that a commission be formed to hammer out the necessary interstate compact. Commerce Secretary Herbert Hoover represented the federal government and was chairman of the Colorado River Commission. Nevada State Engineer James Scrugham, Ed W. Clark, and Squires were appointed to represent Nevada.

The first meeting of the Colorado River Commission was held at the Bishop's Lodge in Santa Fe, New Mexico, in early 1922. After more than 20 days in session, Hoover managed to get the delegation—with the exception of Arizona—to agree on a Colorado River Compact, which allocated water to each of the states and set forth a basic plan of action. It was ratified by six of the seven state legislatures in 1923.

In early 1928, the commission again met at Santa Fe, this time determined to bring Arizona into the fold. It was finally decided that the six states that were in agreement could sign the compact, and Arizona could join when it had a change of heart. By the end of that year, the Swing-Johnson Bill, named for Representative Phil Swing and Senator Hyrum Johnson, both of California, had been passed into law.

In 1940, Squires sold the *Las Vegas Age* to Frank Garside, who then owned the *Las Vegas Review-Journal.*

In November 1944, a woman named Margaret Folsom bought a 40-acre tract of land far out on the Los Angeles highway from Squires for $7,500. He had originally paid $8.75 an acre for it. The land was then conveyed to a Los Angeleno named Billy Wilkerson, who began work on a very large hotel. When Wilkerson, a heavy gambler, ran out of funds to complete the project, a handsome gangster named Benjamin "Bugsy" Siegel took control. Long after the Fabulous Flamingo had been built and Bugsy had been whacked, Squires recalled Siegel as "a pleasant chap."

Squires had the good fortune not shared by many of the other 1905 pioneers; he lived long enough to see the fly-infested tent town grow into a booming city, which was continuing to boom when he died in 1958, at age 93.

In a page-one obituary in the *Las Vegas Sun,* reporter Bob Faiss summarized Charles P. Squires' contributions concisely and accurately: "It seems strange that Las Vegas, a modern boomtown ... established as one of the vacation centers of the world, should owe so much to the foresight of one man. But there is little we have today that wasn't given an initial shove by 'Pop' Squires." ✍

Charles and Della Squires in later years. He holds a copy of his newspaper, the Las Vegas Age.
(UNLV Special Collections)

As unofficial Las Vegas weatherman, C.P. "Pop" Squires recorded Las Vegas' highest temperature ever, 118 degrees in July 1931.
(UNLV Special Collections)

The Squires home (previous page, lower right) on Fremont Street, about 1907
(UNLV Special Collections)

PETE BUOL (1873–1939)

When he discovered he didn't have a big enough bankroll to invest in booming Goldfield, the first mayor of Las Vegas decided the way to fame and fortune was via the valley's artesian wells. **BY A.D. HOPKINS**

"Somebody got an idea the town needed a mayor, so Bill Hawkins and I decided to run against each other. Nobody else wanted to run."

—Pete Buol
In a 1933 interview

Pete Buol spent only two decades in Las Vegas, but he convinced everyone else that Las Vegas had the brightest future in the West. "He was a one-man chamber of commerce," a newspaper observed at the time of his death. Of course, Buol also predicted a bright future for the town of Johnnie, which is today merely a wide place in the road. But in the case of Las Vegas, he was right, and a lot of those who believed him got rich.

Buol was the city's first mayor and represented Clark County in Nevada's Assembly and Senate, but his main contributions were in hastening development that otherwise would have had to wait on the notoriously slow land-and-water subsidiary of the San Pedro, Los Angeles, and Salt Lake Railroad.

He outlined his philosophy of irrepressible optimism in publications during his campaign for mayor in 1911: "Ability doesn't count, knowledge is useless, experience has no worth without the driving force of optimism." Buol had the courage of his homilies.

The son of a Swiss immigrant, he was born in Chicago on October 1, 1873. Sixty years later he told a Las Vegas journalist that he made his first dollar as a newsboy, selling papers for a nickel apiece. His father, Frank Buol, had been a master chef in Switzerland and trained all five of his sons. Peter finished the eighth grade before going to work full time for his father, peeling potatoes for 50 cents a day.

He was only 19 when he won $100,000 on a lottery ticket, an absolute fortune for the times.

He spent the money on a yacht and the lifestyle that went with it, and in a remarkably short time was back peeling potatoes. Later Buol was a chef for the dining cars operated by Fred S. Harvey on the Santa Fe Railroad—diners noted for excellent food served with class. He also had a food concession at a Chicago fair, serving 5,000 people a day at 25 cents a meal. In 1901, he moved west.

Buol told an interviewer that he decided to invest in Las Vegas because his bankroll was too small to have much impact in booming Goldfield, where property values were sky-high. Looking for

a place to get in on the ground floor, he came to Las Vegas by stagecoach, before the planned railroad was built. "I really shouldn't use the name Las Vegas yet," he said, "for when I got here there was no town, only the two old ranches, the Stewart and Kiel, and a couple of tents. I immediately went into the mining, insurance, and real estate games."

By the time the railroad auctioned its lots in the official townsite—May 15, 1905—lots in Buol's adjacent subdivisions had already been on sale for two months. "I was fast in those days," he observed in 1933.

Buol soon realized that the key to making money in Las Vegas real estate was having water to develop the properties. Although the railroad had tied up water rights to Big Springs, the artesian pools that fed Las Vegas Creek and the meadows along its banks, Buol noticed that smaller artesian springs bubbled forth at other places in the valley. By November 1905, he was manager of the Vegas Artesian Water Syndicate. The syndicate and others began drilling wells here and there throughout the valley, and by 1908, a local newspaper headline was crowing, "Another Big Artesian Well … J.F. Evey Gets 100-Inch Spouter on His Ranch South of Vegas."

In 1910 Buol brought in a large artesian well near Sixth and Fremont streets, the site of his "Buck's Addition." Until this time, the railroad-owned land company had ensured its own lands were developed first by refusing to extend water lines beyond its original townsite. Now homebuyers had a different option. The area, generally bounded on the north by today's Las Ve-

Buol in Southern Nevada

POP.*	DECADE
n/a	pre-1900
30	1900
945	1910
2,686	1920
5,952	1930
13,937	1940
45,577	1950
123,667	1960
273,288	1970
463,087	1980
715,587	1990

■ Time spent in Southern Nev.
* - Population figures are for greater Las Vegas area (*Source: Nevada State Data Center*).

Mayor Pete Buol
(*UNLV Special Collections*)

gas Expressway and on the south by Fremont Street, and extending from today's Las Vegas Boulevard to Ninth Street, promptly became the fashionable residential neighborhood.

That same year, fire broke out in the Overland Hotel, and with no firefighting equipment except hose carts, volunteer firefighters never had a chance to stop it. The hotel's destruction focused attention on the many things Las Vegas needed but couldn't afford, and precipitated incorporation as a city.

"Somebody got an idea the town needed a mayor, so Bill Hawkins and I decided to run against each other. Nobody else wanted to run," Buol told an interviewer in 1933. "Some little accident happened and I beat him by about 10 votes."

His salary as mayor was $15 a month. He took office in June 1911 and served through May 1913, when Bill Hawkins, the man he defeated in the first election, succeeded him. Buol also was elected to the Nevada Assembly in 1912, and after one term was elected to the state Senate. His legislative career is best remembered for a three-county manhunt for the missing Senator Buol.

On his way to Carson City for a legislative meeting, Buol decided to inspect some mines in Lincoln and Nye counties. He didn't show up in Carson City, and all feared the worst. Men set afoot in eastern Nevada at midwinter were usually found as frozen corpses. And nobody knew exactly where Buol was supposed to be.

The Clark County sheriff headed north with six automobiles full of deputies and volunteers, but had to abandon three cars in the mud of a "dry" lake. From Ely in White Pine County, the sheriff headed south with seven deputies, two autos, and a buckboard. From Pioche in Lincoln County, the sheriff drove northwest in a car, with seven men going before, on horseback, to break trail. Forty miles northwest of Pioche, they found Buol, marooned by auto trouble. Far from despairing, he had passed the time prospecting for ore.

In 1913, Buol and his wife, the former Lorena Patterson, built a home at North Seventh Street and Ogden Avenue in the area Buol's well had opened for development. With walls 8 inches thick, adobe inside and brick without, porches on all four sides, and a peaked roof, the house was said to be the coolest in summer and warmest in winter of any in town. Its eight rooms were heated with wood fireplaces.

When Lorena Buol entertained other women, Buol dusted off his chef training and prepared gourmet dishes with folded paper garnishes. In their big yard, the Buols gave parties for their adopted daughter, Dorothy, entertaining as many as 40 children with puppet shows and elegant sweets.

Buol was as interested in mining as in real estate, and sometimes these interests overlapped. He ran ads in the Las Vegas newspapers offering lots in "The Bustling Booming Town of Johnnie," adding in finer print that the land was merely close to the "Famous Johnnie Mine" (using large type once more). The ad continued, "The Town of Johnnie has an abundant supply of pure arte-

sian water and is the only available place for a town in that entire section of country." The Johnnie Mine did ship bullion in 1908 and for years thereafter, but today, some 90 years later, Pahrump may soon absorb the few buildings left of Johnnie.

Buol developed a lime deposit that became the foundation of the small community now known as Sloan. With some partners, he located a borax claim that was sold to Francis E. "Borax" Smith for a price reported as $250,000. He also mined for the ores of mercury near Tonopah and in eastern California.

His wife and daughter, like many Las Vegans who could afford to flee the punishing summers of Southern Nevada, spent part of every year on the California Coast. In 1925 the Buols moved there permanently.

About 1929 Buol was injured in a mine cave-in at Pioche, and friends said he never completely recovered. He had a stroke in 1937 and died in 1939 in Los Angeles. Comparatively poor when he died, Buol left the impression of a man who lived a life of personal booms and busts, and merely happened to depart it on the bust stroke. ✍

Pete Buol (left) participated in the ceremonial planting of the first tree in Las Vegas' new courthouse park about March 1911. The man with the tree is District Judge E.J.L. Tober; holding the shovel is E.W. Clark, a prominent Democrat who helped split Clark County away from Lincoln County.
(UNLV Special Collections)

Pete Buol watches the gratifying flow from a new artesian well near Sixth and Fremont streets, which enabled him to begin developing property beyond limits of the original railroad townsite. At right is William Pike, an early insurance agent.
(Review-Journal files)

Ed Clark (1871-1946)

Although Clark County is named for another man, this entrepreneur was instrumental in establishing the county, its financial institutions, and its utilities. BY A.D. HOPKINS

Ed Clark never liked the spotlight, but if you looked behind the scenes, he had his hand on the switches. For 40 years, very little got done in Southern Nevada without Clark's help.

He seemed always to know what needed to be done, then did it before anybody else thought of it. When Las Vegas became the railhead serving rich mines to the north, Clark hauled the freight. When the time came to break away from Lincoln County, Clark did much of the political engineering. He ran Las Vegas' first bank, its first telephone company, and its first power company. He helped bring Hoover Dam to reality and, perhaps most important, obtained for Nevada a share of the electricity the dam would generate.

Politically, Clark County became a Democratic stronghold largely because of Ed Clark. His father, Jacob C. Clark, was a Democrat before him and was the first sheriff elected in Storey County after Nevada became a state—a surprising result, because in the election year of 1864, many equated being a Democrat with being a traitor to the Union. Sheriff Clark kept order on the Comstock Lode during two of its liveliest years, 1865 and 1866, but would die soon after the birth of his son in 1871, in San Jose, California.

His widow, Julia Clark, moved that same year to the booming silver camp of Pioche. She operated a boarding house for bachelor miners and educated her own children; Ed would boast later that he was "a graduate of *McGuffey's Third Reader.*" He grew up helping run his mother's business and was only 17 when he started his own cattle outfit in the Wilson Creek range of northern Lincoln County.

Pioche was not served by a railroad, so Clark went into the freight business, hauling supplies from the Mormon farming communities in western Utah. In the 1890s he went into partnership with C.C. Ronnow of Panaca, and from that day forward the fates of the two families would be intertwined, and both would become part of Southern Nevada history. Clark made his home with the Ronnow family and was called "Uncle Ed" by their children. Ronnow and Clark operated the Ed W. Clark Forwarding Company, which carried freight from the end of the Union Pacific Railroad, then at Milford, Utah, into the mining country of Southern Nevada.

Clark was elected treasurer of Lincoln County, but he soon found it difficult to please everybody. E.H. Harriman, who controlled the Union Pacific, wanted to extend his railroad westward, while Montana Senator William Clark wanted to build his own railroad eastward from the port of San Pedro, California, to Southern Utah. There was only one good route through Lincoln County, however, and the two interests came to an actual battle over it, with railroad workers slugging it out with shovels and pick handles on a disputed grade.

Meanwhile, a war also was waged on the political front, and Ed Clark, though no relation, became aligned with the senator of the same last name and for whom the county is named. Harriman sent Ed Clark a message: This county isn't big enough for both of us. In the early 1900s, such a message from Harriman was taken as seriously as one from the Mafia would be in the 1950s. But Ed Clark foiled Harriman, according to folklore, by finagling an appointment as postmaster of Caliente. Even Harriman didn't dare molest a federal appointee.

The truculent tycoons eventually agreed that William Clark would control the railroad in Nevada. By 1905 Clark Forwarding Company was headquartered in the new town built by the railroad, Las Vegas, and was hauling freight into mining camps such as Beatty and Rhyolite to the north and into Eldorado Canyon to the south.

The success of the relatively new communities of southern Lincoln County—Las Vegas and Searchlight—compared to the declining fortunes of Pioche, created tension. Las Vegans, and particularly Searchlighters, had to travel for days to

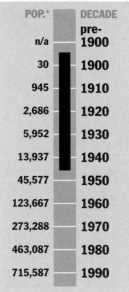

E. Clark in Southern Nevada

POP.*	DECADE
n/a	pre-1900
30	1900
945	1910
2,686	1920
5,952	1930
13,937	1940
45,577	1950
123,667	1960
273,288	1970
463,087	1980
715,587	1990

■ Time spent in Southern Nev.
* - Population figures are for greater Las Vegas area (*Source: Nevada State Data Center*).

Ed Clark, at about age 25, a few years before he moved to Las Vegas and became one of the town's founding fathers. His nickname in some quarters was "Handsome Ed."
(UNLV Special Collections)

do business at the courthouse in Pioche. During the summer the trip could be so difficult that some travelers actually died. Argument arose that the county seat should be moved to Las Vegas, but there were many counterarguments. It was just as far from Pioche to Las Vegas as the other way around, and an expensive courthouse already existed in Pioche. Residents in the north end were offended in 1905 when the upstart *Las Vegas Age* wrested the county printing contract away from the venerable *Pioche Record*. Then Ed Clark attracted controversy when the Lincoln County public funds, formerly kept in a Salt Lake City bank, found their way to the First State Bank of Las Vegas, operated by his friend John S. Park and the railroad interests.

Gradually, a new idea emerged: Let Pioche keep the county seat, and give Las Vegas and Searchlight their own county. A bipartisan organization, the Lincoln County Division Club, was formed to push the idea. Support was by no means unanimous, even in the south. Searchlighters recognized that a new county seat would end up in Las Vegas, cutting their 233-mile trip to the courthouse by three-fourths but leaving them with the hardest part—the 55-mile pull from Searchlight to the railroad at Las Vegas. They wondered if the shorter trip would be worth the additional expense. Many business interests opposed division for fear of higher taxes.

Once Treasurer Clark announced his intention to keep Lincoln County deposits in Las Vegas, he attracted the opposition of his old hometowns. In 1908 he lost the office to Henry H. Lee, a member of the pioneer family who founded Panaca.

Most candidates elected that fall, however, supported the Division Club, and in January 1909 it asked the Nevada Legislature to form the new county. As usual, the role Ed Clark played was behind the scenes. Harley E. Harmon, son of one of Clark's political allies, recalled years later, "The story is told that Clark County was bought by a case of Yellowstone Whiskey purchased with money provided by Clark."

The new county promptly elected Ed Clark

its treasurer. Not long thereafter, he also became a director of the First State Bank, where the county funds remained. He already had become associated with Park in the Consolidated Power and Telephone Company, the tiny predecessor to the giant corporations that now serve Las Vegas.

Ed Clark remained a bachelor all his life. He lived with the Ronnows next to the store at Clark and Main streets. "It was really quite odd that he wasn't related to us but lived there with my grandparents," said C.C. Ronnow's granddaughter, Mary Lee Coleman. "He was a staunch Democrat and my grandfather was a strong Republican. They would each go to the political conventions and they would have heated discussions about politics. Also, he was a Catholic and my grandfather was very active in the Mormon Church, and went on a mission to Denmark even after he was married.

"Ed's half brother, Fred McFadden, cared for their invalid sister and, after their mother's death, came to live with the Ronnows, too. It was a nice house for the times, but it must have been crowded. There was only one bathroom."

When young Gerald Crowe came to live with them, Clark shared his bedroom with the boy. Crowe was the son of Mrs. Ronnow's sister, who was divorced and died in the Spanish Flu epidemics of World War I. "There was a hint that if she had lived, he [Clark] would have married Gerald Crowe's mother," said Cecile Crowe, Gerald's widow, who married Gerald in 1932. But if Clark's bachelorhood resulted from grieving for a lost love, she couldn't say.

The forwarding company kept changing with the times. When the

Las Vegas and Tonopah Railroad built northward toward Beatty and gobbled up the freight business, Clark and Ronnow adapted by stressing the mercantile end of their business.

The store attracted the attentions of outlaws, as well as solid citizens. In November 1923, a 17-year-old Gerald Crowe accidentally surprised two burglars, who crashed through a glass door in hasty departure. The *Las Vegas Age* reported: "Ed W. Clark, eating dinner in the Ronnow home close to the store, heard the crash of the breaking glass and ran out in time to see the … robber sprinting away at a lively rate." Clark chased him but, be-

The interior of Clark Forwarding Company in its earlier years. The man at right is Ed Clark's partner, C.C. Ronnow, with whom he shared a house. Ronnow was a county commissioner and active in efforts to improve local schools, and he is remembered in the name of a grade school near Washington Avenue and Pecos Road.

(Review-Journal files)

ing already more than 50 years of age, was soon outdistanced.

"This is the 'steenth time the Clark Store has been entered in recent years and Ed Clark is able to keep in good physical condition by chasing the burglars," reported the *Age*. "With the practice he has had, he expects to make a capture in the next chase." Less than two weeks later, Clark did capture a burglar by surprising him with a double-barreled shotgun and chasing him around the corner, into the grasp of Crowe and C.C. Ronnow's son, C.L.

Like other prominent Las Vegans, Clark pushed the effort to build a dam on the Colorado River. He also served 25 years on the interstate commission that finally persuaded Congress to build it. Harley E. Harmon credited Clark with originating the idea of the commission, and with conceiving the Nevada amendments to the enabling legislation. Those amendments gave Nevada and Arizona shares of the water and power provided by the dam.

After years of work, enabling legislation for Boulder Dam was signed on December 21, 1928. In Las Vegas, the shop whistle blew, and every business closed except those that sold liquor. And when the hangovers cleared, folks realized that while Hoover Dam was going to make a lot of people rich, nobody was going to do better than Ed Clark.

Quietly, Clark had placed himself in control of at least three of the town's more important growth industries. For years he had been a minor owner in the First State Bank, which was run by cashier John S. Park. Park's major partner was J. Ross Clark, who had built and run the railroad for his brother and financial backer, William. In

After years of work, enabling legislation for Boulder Dam was signed on December 21, 1928. In Las Vegas, the shop whistle blew, and every business closed except those that sold liquor. And when the hangovers cleared, folks realized that while Hoover Dam was going to make a lot of people rich, nobody was going to do better than Ed Clark.

1926 the elderly Park and J. Ross Clark retired, and Ed Clark bought them out and became president. He would hold the position until 1937, when he sold the bank to First National Bank of Nevada. Thus, within two years of the time he bought the only bank in a one-horse town, that town was marked to become America's hottest boomtown.

Clark continued many conservative policies instituted by Park, who had earned the nickname "Ten Percent John" for the high interest rates he charged on risky loans. In Joe Midmond's *First National Bank of Nevada*, a book commissioned by the financial institution, Gerald Crowe related how handily First State weathered the dark days of 1932. On November 1 of that year, trying to save Nevada's Wingfield Banks from panic withdrawals, the governor declared a bank holiday requiring banks to close their doors. First State Bank complied—barely. "The front door was closed but I was stationed at the door and anyone who wanted his money was allowed in," said Crowe.

Once admitted by Crowe, customers encountered a shotgun-bearing guard, nervously pacing back and forth in front of a counter groaning with the weight of coins and paper money—hundreds of thousands worth. Behind the piled money stood Ed Clark, smiling reassuringly. A sign announced: "This is your money. It is safe." Harley E. Harmon, then a youngster who would grow up to run banks of his own, elaborated, "He'd give them money to pay a grocery bill or the rent or anything like that. But if they wanted it all, he wouldn't let them have it. He said, 'This bank is sound and you're not going to break it.'"

In 1924, Clark became president of Consolidated Power and Telephone Company. He reor-

ganized into different companies, which have become Sprint of Nevada and Nevada Power Company. In 1937 his company, then known as Southern Nevada Power, became the first utility to distribute electricity from the newly-created dam. This source would satisfy all local electrical needs for 16 years.

Clark's political influence helped bring a war industry to Nevada, the event that started the city of Henderson. He could have been a governor or a senator himself, but turned down nominations more than once. His original Las Vegas company evolved into Clark County Mercantile, and one of its divisions survives today as the venerable Clark County Auto Parts at 505 South Main Street.

Clark died in April 1946, of heart disease and pneumonia, at the age of 74. He left no descendants. Though his estate included much valuable real estate and utility stock, the official report showed only $85,000 cash. He left $10,000 to the Sisters of the Holy Family for their charity work in Clark County, and $10,000 to a niece, Georgia McFadden. Crowe and C.L. Ronnow, the men who helped him bag the burglar back in 1923 and had been trusted associates in later endeavors, received $5,000 each to educate their respective daughters, and J.L. Ronnow got $10,000 to educate his two sons. Clark left $5,000 and real estate to Alice Ronnow, the widow of his old partner, C.C. Ronnow.

The stock in his growing utility companies he left to his half brothers, Fred and Clarence McFadden, two nieces, and a nephew. The rest of his estate was divided among the half brothers and three former employees: C.S. Wengert, longtime cashier of the bank; S.J. Lawson, who would succeed him as president of the power company; and C.L. Ronnow, the power company's vice president. All were men he had mentored and, to Clark, all the family he required. ✍

Ed Clark as he was caricatured in 1935 by an artist covering the Nevada Legislature.
(Review-Journal files)

LEGISLATIVE LIGHTS AND SHADOWS

ED CLARK
DEMOCRATIC
NATIONAL
COMMITTEEMAN
FOR
NEVADA

QUEHO (1880?–1935?)

**An American Indian who lived by his own rules found himself
at odds with white residents of early Clark County.** BY K.J. EVANS

It is impossible to discern, through the haze of time, bigotry, and conjecture, whether the man known as Queho was a murderous scoundrel or a scapegoat. He was indeed a killer, as were many men of the 19th century. There was such a thing in those days as "justifiable homicide," a doctrine that has become largely ignored in the modern legal system. But Queho was an Indian. He killed white people in a time and place where white men made the rules.

Of his alleged crimes, much is known; of the man, virtually nothing, except what was reported by the press of the day. "Just how many people Queho killed, and under what circumstances, will probably never be known. During the course of his career, he was accused of practically every murder committed in the vicinity of Eldorado Canyon. His story has been hammered and mauled and shaped by writers across the entire spread of America, and Lord only knows where some of them got their material," said *Review-Journal* writer Ray Chesson, whose story was as questionable as any of those he criticized.

Queho's tribal affiliation is uncertain. He was supposedly born around 1880 on Cottonwood Island, the illegitimate son of a Mexican miner and a local Indian

girl. Queho was employed in odd jobs around the Eldorado Canyon mines. He also gathered driftwood along the Colorado and sold it to the miners. At some point, he broke his leg or his foot, leaving him with a characteristic limp, supposedly detectable from his footprints in the dirt.

In late 1910, he was hired by J.M. Woodworth to cut trees on Timber Mountain in the McCullough Range near Searchlight. Somehow, Woodworth angered Queho, who fatally brained his boss with a chunk of cedar.

Harry Reid, in his 1998 book, *Searchlight, The*

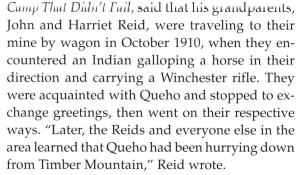

Camp That Didn't Fail, said that his grandparents, John and Harriet Reid, were traveling to their mine by wagon in October 1910, when they encountered an Indian galloping a horse in their direction and carrying a Winchester rifle. They were acquainted with Queho and stopped to exchange greetings, then went on their respective ways. "Later, the Reids and everyone else in the area learned that Queho had been hurrying down from Timber Mountain," Reid wrote.

Shortly thereafter, an elderly night watchman at the Gold Bug Mine, across the river in Arizona, was found dead of a bullet wound to the head. All of his food and his badge were missing.

From Pioche to Searchlight, the word was out: A renegade savage was on the loose. They knew who it was by his distinctive footprints. Posses were assembled and trackers hired. Every lead was pursued. Queho eluded them all. "Local lawmen, who viewed Queho as little more than an ignorant savage, thought catching him would be child's play," wrote Reid. "They couldn't have been more wrong."

In 1913, a 100-year-old blind Indian known as Canyon Charlie was found dead, a pickax wound in his head. Queho was blamed, but this crime probably wasn't committed by him, since Charlie was his friend and confidant.

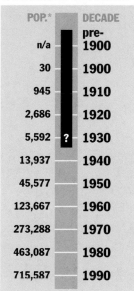

Queho in Southern Nevada

POP.*	DECADE
n/a	pre-1900
30	1900
945	1910
2,686	1920
5,592 ?	1930
13,937	1940
45,577	1950
123,667	1960
273,288	1970
463,087	1980
715,587	1990

■ Time spent in Southern Nev.
* - Population figures are for greater Las Vegas area (*Source: Nevada State Data Center*).
? - Queho was active here from 1880 until probably some time in the 1930s.

The posse that recovered Queho's remains stands at the mouth of his cave hideout. From left, Coroner A.J. Nelson, Frank Wait, Queho's remains, and Art Schroeder.
(*UNLV Special Collections*)

Within the next two months, two more miners, who were working claims at Jenny Springs on the Arizona side of the river, were found dead, shot in the back. An Indian woman also was found dead. Queho got the blame for her death, as well as that of James Patterson, who disappeared but turned up some days later unhurt.

As Queho hysteria grew, so did the rewards for his capture, eventually reaching $2,000. And the *Searchlight Bulletin* reminded its readers of the principle that guided most European/American Indian relations in the 19th century. "A good Indian is a dead Indian," it thundered.

On a cold January day in 1919, two prospectors named Hancock and Taylor set out from their camp near St. Thomas on the Muddy River, and were later found murdered and robbed of their

Queho's mummified remains were found surrounded by all his possessions.
(UNLV Special Collections)

shoes. Queho was the prime suspect.

About a week later, Maud Douglas, the wife of an Eldorado Canyon miner, woke up to investigate a noise in her kitchen. She was killed by a shotgun blast at close range. On the floor, canned goods and cornmeal were piled, evidently left behind by the fleeing killer. Reid believes Queho was the killer, but adds that there is room for doubt. A four-year-old boy living with the Douglas family at the time later stated that Arvin Douglas, Maud's husband, had killed her.

It was an atrocity that motivated Southern Nevada. Sheriff Sam Gay ordered Deputy Frank Wait to round up a posse, hire the best trackers, and once and for all kill or capture Queho. Wait led the posse from Las Vegas Wash to Callville to Muddy Mountain and on to Black Canyon. By this time the exhausted and demoralized posse had dwindled to three men, and when Wait caught influenza, they gave up and returned to Las Vegas.

Queho was not without friends. His fellow Indians certainly assisted him, while at the same time unanimously declaring that he was long dead. And, despite his fugitive status, many whites helped Queho as well. Murl Emery, who operated a ferry at Nelson's Landing in Eldorado Canyon for many years, never hid the fact that he saw Queho often, liked him, and wasn't slow in lending him a hand. "Why don't you let the poor Indian rest?" he once asked.

The hunt for Red Queho finally ended in February 1940. Charley Kenyon and brothers Art and Ed Schroeder were prospecting along the Colorado River, about 10 miles below Hoover Dam, when they discovered a shallow cave about 2,000 feet above the river. Inside the cave were the mummified remains of an American Indian male. He had been

bitten by a rattlesnake, which probably was the cause of death.

"Some of his old pursuers," said Reid, "not wanting to acknowledge that they had been outsmarted, tried to say he had been dead since 1919." Not true. Blasting caps, dynamite, and sheets of plywood, stolen from the Hoover Dam job site, confirmed that Queho had been active into the early 1930s. (He used the blasting caps to reload his own cartridges.) Also in the cave were the badge of the night watchman from the Gold Bug Mine, a .30-30 Winchester saddle rifle, a repeating shotgun, a high-quality bow and a quiver of steel-tipped arrows, and numerous pairs of shoes of various sizes. Frank Wait, then Las Vegas chief of police, went to the cave with a party of 10, including Coroner A. J. Nelson, who held an inquest on the spot. The verdict was death by natural causes.

A squabble erupted over who owned the remains. The option of simply burying them doesn't seem to have been considered. Sheriff Gene Ward put the bones and artifacts in a display case in the county courthouse. The bones and artifacts then came into the possession of the Las Vegas Elks, who produced what was then the city's biggest public celebration—Helldorado. The Elks built a replica of Queho's cave and furnished it with what was left of him and his effects. The bones and plunder were later stolen from Helldorado Village. Years later, remains thought to be Queho's were recovered and were buried at Cathedral Canyon, near Pahrump.

To some, the story of Queho is no more than a tale of a brutish killer. To others, it is the story of a man who was abused, hounded his entire life, then, in death, rendered into a cheap carnival attraction.

"Indians were granted no respect," Reid wrote. "And they were harassed and discriminated against in increasingly offensive ways. It is no wonder that Queho's fellow Indians helped him. Nor is it surprising that he became known among the few Indians of the area as someone who had stood up to the white man." ⌀

ROY MARTIN

(1874–1943)

"I think it probable that no citizen of Las Vegas during all those long, lean, and disappointing years had such supreme faith in the high destiny of Las Vegas, or sacrificed so much of himself in the effort to bring that destiny to fruition."

—C.P. "Pop" Squires
After Martin's death

For $10 he won from a foot race, a young physician bought a medical practice in Las Vegas and stayed another 38 years. BY K.J. EVANS

The young doctor stepped off the train that had deposited him in the desiccated tent town of Las Vegas. He was not impressed. It was August, and the temperature was past the century mark. Only three months before, the town had been created in the span of two days when the San Pedro, Los Angeles, and Salt Lake Railroad auctioned off townsites in what is now the core of downtown.

Dr. Royce Wood Martin, who went by "Roy," surveyed a cluster of wood-framed tents, one of which was a "hotel" where dust-covered men paid a dollar for the privilege of sleeping in a bed with a stranger. "There was only one train a day then, and it left at night," Martin recalled in later years. "I was going to take it that same night." His destination was the Bullfrog Mining District and the town of Rhyolite.

To kill time, Martin strolled the bustling streets of Las Vegas, stopping to talk to the locals, who were unanimous in their denunciation of the Bullfrog District as a "has-been" place, and in their confidence about their own fledgling community. At one point, Martin met another physician, quite disenchanted with Las Vegas, who offered to sell him his entire practice, with equipment, for $10, the cost of a railroad ticket to Los Angeles.

Martin didn't have a spare sawbuck. To raise it, he asked around until he had located the town's fastest runner, and challenged him to a foot race. The purse was $10. Martin, a sprinter in his college days, won the race, collected the money, paid off the doctor, and decided that Las Vegas might be a good place to stop for a while. He stayed 38 years.

Martin was born November 16, 1874, at Table Rock, Nebraska, the eldest of five children. He earned his M.D. in 1903 at the University Medical College in Kansas City, Missouri. Martin married his high-school sweetheart, Nellie Cotton, and for a wedding gift gave her a grand piano, which is now owned by his granddaughter, Julie Jones of Las Vegas. The couple subsequently had two daughters, Frances and Mazie. The family home, situated on the southwest corner of Fifth and Fremont streets, was a concrete block structure described by *Las Vegas Age* Editor C.P. "Pop" Squires as being "of Japanese design."

The town was crude, some of its inhabitants cruder still, but it was infused with the optimism that characterizes most boomtowns, and seemed to hold promise for an entrepreneurial young doctor. Martin hung his first shingle on an 8-foot by 10-foot framed tent at Stewart Avenue and Third Street. Four months after his arrival, he was appointed chief surgeon for the Las Vegas and Tonopah Railroad, a position he held for nearly 12 years. The railroad provided him a second hospital—another tent. But it had 10 cots and, according to his daughter, Mazie Martin Jones, a "makeshift operating room where only minor surgery was done, except in emergency cases." His counterpart was Dr. Halle Hewetson, the surgeon for the San Pedro, Los Angeles, and Salt Lake Railroad. The two doctors often assisted and relieved each other.

According to Squires, neither surgeon did much cutting in their tent hospitals, particularly in summer when oppressive heat made it too risky for the patient. The standard procedure was to stabilize patients and put them on the train to Los Angeles. If surgery was essential, the operation would be performed at 4 a.m., the coolest time of day.

Martin made house calls. He also made calls to the mining camp at Goodsprings and to more

Martin in Southern Nevada

POP.*	DECADE
n/a	pre-1900
30	1900
945	1910
2,686	1920
5,952	1930
13,937	1940
45,577	1950
123,667	1960
273,288	1970
463,087	1980
715,587	1990

■ Time spent in Southern Nev.
* - Population figures are for greater Las Vegas area (*Source: Nevada State Data Center*).

Royce Wood Martin, M.D., in the 1920s
(UNLV Special Collections)

remote workings, to the brothels of Block 16, and to the Paiute colony. "He would answer any call for help from anyone, anywhere, anytime," said Frances Donnelly, his eldest daughter. "He paid a lot of attention to the minorities in this town; at his funeral, people of all colors came to pay their respects."

Martin was a country doctor in a very large country, often as much a race car driver as a physician. In what must have been a record for the time, he drove from Las Vegas to Arden, where a U.S. Gypsum worker had been injured in a rock fall. Martin gave the man first aid, then loaded him aboard the No. 4 train to Las Vegas. The train slid along on smooth steel rails, while Martin bounded along on a dusty, rutted cowpath—and beat the train to Las Vegas. In 1927, he drove to Baker, California, a distance of more than 90 miles—on a road that was mostly sand, rocks, and misfortune—in less than two hours.

Sometimes the problem was the patient, not the terrain. Once Martin was summoned to a home where a screaming wife in labor had sent her husband into hysterics. The husband threatened Martin with violence if he did not alleviate his wife's pain. Asked in later years how he handled the situation, Martin offered a simple explanation. "I knocked him out," he said. Mother, baby, and dad all recovered nicely.

Roy Martin and Las Vegas socialite Alta Ham, photo dated 1929
(UNLV Special Collections)

To maintain the stamina needed to keep up the pace he set for himself, Martin adhered to a rigorous diet, avoiding fatty foods and eating plenty of fresh fruits and vegetables. His one vice, said Donnelly, was unfiltered Lucky Strike cigarettes. Sadly, that habit may have contributed to his eventual demise.

Aside from the inevitable mining accidents, most of Martin's business was provided by the gun, the knife, and the stork. One of his first patients was night watchman Joe Mulholland.

He and William McCarthy were drinking at Arthur Frye's saloon on First Street, when a quarrel erupted over ownership of a ring. McCarthy settled it by drawing a pistol and giving Mulholland a hot lead injection. Martin couldn't help, and the watchman died.

In June 1906, Martin moved his hospital to a suite of offices upstairs in the Thomas Building at First and Fremont streets. It was a great improvement with a dozen beds, a private room, and a pharmacy. In 1911, Martin and his colleague, Dr. H.H. Clark, remodeled the facility. It then boasted its own heating plant, electric fans and appliances, an X-ray machine, and a kitchen. In 1916, he built the first hospital in booming Goodsprings.

The following year, Martin purchased the Palace Hotel, plus two cottages on Second Street, for about $10,000. The Palace had been the first two-story building in Las Vegas. Martin modernized it, and when the work was completed, the facility had 12 beds and a second-story balcony that wrapped around the entire structure, providing patients with a place to take the cool evening breezes. His associates were Dr. Forrest Mildren and Dr. F.M. Ferguson.

In early 1931, Drs. Martin, Ferguson, and R.D. Balcum formed the Las Vegas Hospital Association, with the intention of building a first-rate facility. They agreed that Martin would build the structure and the other doctors would furnish and supply it. In April 1931, Martin bought 16 lots on Eighth Street between Ogden and Stewart avenues. He told the *Las Vegas Evening Review-Journal* that he had retained architect A.L. Warwick to design the hospital, which would be "a two-story structure, built of gypsum blocks, stuccoed outside, finished in white with a red tiled roof, in the typical Spanish style so well adapted for this country." The total cost would be about $100,000. The Las Vegas Hospital was a state-of-the art, 35-bed

facility. It had laboratories, a maternity ward, an X-ray machine, five treatment rooms, a tilting operating table, and an advanced lighting system in the operating room.

As the summer of 1931 approached, Martin sent his wife and daughters on a tour of Europe. "With his family out of the way, he could focus on planning his hospital," Frances Donnelly said in retrospect. The new facility opened in December 1931.

Martin sold his interest in the hospital in 1937, planning to retire. But, according to daughter Mazie Martin Jones, he was stuck with more than $80,000 in debts he couldn't collect. Even so, he joined his old Las Vegas Hospital on Second Street with a house he owned next door to create the El Patio Motel, which he operated until 1941.

Martin was a Republican and was elected to the Clark County Republican Committee in 1910 and 1924. He later was a delegate to the 1928 national convention that nominated Herbert Hoover for president.

In 1923, Martin was elected to the state assembly. One of his assignments was the committee on roads and highways. Having suffered the bumps, bruises, and breakdowns inflicted by the state's primitive roads, Martin was a vociferous advocate of improving them. He was especially keen on linking Las Vegas with Yerington; the only decent road sent travelers through California. The road to Los Angeles ran down through Searchlight, then to Needles and Barstow. The road advocated by Martin was more direct. Highway 91 and, later, Interstate 15 both followed his proposed route.

Late 1926 found Martin in Reno, where he purchased a new Cadillac. He convinced his friend, former Governor James Scrugham, to ride with him to Las Vegas in order to inspect the road. It was a grueling journey, climaxing when Mar-

> *"He was a busy, energetic man, and he was preoccupied with one thing or another most of the time. But on Sundays, he made time for his family."*
> —**Frances Donnelly**
> **Roy Martin's daughter**

tin lost control of the car north of Las Vegas and it overturned. Neither man was hurt, but Scrugham was so exhausted that Martin checked him into the hospital for a week.

It wasn't Martin's first motoring mishap. The worst incident involved his family. "He was a busy, energetic man," recalls Donnelly, "and he was preoccupied with one thing or another most of the time. But on Sundays, he made time for his family." Usually this came in the form of a family outing.

In July 1918, Martin, his family, and the daughter of a fellow Las Vegas physician set out in an open Franklin motorcar to visit friends in Pioche. The party arrived at Hiko, stayed the night at a ranch, and asked for directions to Pioche. They were directed to a shortcut across the mountains to Caliente. Martin drove the rocky, rutted roads for 84 miles before conceding that he was lost, and turned back toward Hiko. The gasoline gave out 75 miles from there. Provisions consisted of a quart of water, a can of beans, and a few graham crackers.

"We opened the can of beans with a nail file," said Donnelly. A small cloudburst appeared, and the women hurried to rig funnels to collect the rain, finally resorting to licking the moisture off

the car. Meanwhile, Martin began the hike to Hiko. It was a nightmarish ordeal. He hallucinated springs of fresh water gushing across the road. At one point, he turned himself around, following his own tracks and marveling that some fool had been hiking in this barren wilderness. He drank water from cow tracks and, after 28 hours, he reached John Wright's ranch at Hiko. They immediately cranked up Wright's Model T and raced to aid the doctor's stranded family, nearly dead from thirst.

"My first memory was someone shoving ginger snaps down my throat with milk," said Donnelly. "It was a long time before I could eat ginger snaps again." At the insistence of the girls, the Martins continued on their trip to Pioche. "He had promised us," said Donnelly, "and when he made a promise, he kept it."

Even after the near calamity, Martin remained an inveterate desert explorer and became something of an expert on extracting vehicles from the inevitable sand traps. His skill came in handy in 1935, when President Franklin D. Roosevelt, in Nevada to dedicate Hoover Dam, decided to visit the Civilian Conservation Corps Camp at Harris Springs, adjacent to Martin's property. The road was narrow, the presidential entourage was long,

and FDR found himself stranded in his car on a steep road with no place to turn around. "The newspaper stories of the time tell about the president being delayed," said Donnelly. "But they don't say that it was Dr. Martin who got them out of the situation and back on the road."

But Martin is perhaps best remembered by old-timers for his contribution to the rescue of the Prettyman party in 1937. In December of that year, Lee Prettyman, his wife, their cook, two friends, two cats, and a dog set out in a new Packard sedan to inspect the Groom Mine, owned by Prettyman. It was a hard winter, and the group was soon stranded in deep snow near the mine. Lee Prettyman walked to civilization and organized a rescue. The *Las Vegas Evening Review-Journal* followed each development of the ensuing drama as it unfolded over a week. An airplane rescue was impossible, and several attempts to reach the party by tractor were thwarted by new snowstorms.

By midweek, it was learned that one of the men had attempted to walk out and had died of exposure on the shore of Groom Lake. Concern soon shifted to the 20-member rescue party, which included Martin. It was making slow progress toward the stranded group, which was living off of canned corned beef and snow. Ultimately the rescue succeeded, with Martin providing first aid to survivors who were more dead than alive. So dramatic was the misadventure that the following year, the National Broadcasting Company (NBC) produced a radio drama about it.

Martin came out of retirement in 1942, at the onset of World War II, because of the shortage of civilian doctors. He practiced at Basic Hospital in Henderson until December 27, 1943, when he died after suffering two heart attacks in close succession.

Of Martin, Squires wrote: "I think it probable that no citizen of Las Vegas during all those long, lean, and disappointing years had such supreme faith in the high destiny of Las Vegas, or sacrificed so much of himself in the effort to bring that destiny to fruition." ⌀

The Las Vegas Hospital built by Dr. Roy Martin at Eighth Street and Ogden Avenue. The photo was taken shortly after the hospital's completion in December 1931.
(UNLV Special Collections)

Ed Von Tobel

(1873–1967)

Las Vegans did not try to insulate children from real life. On Sunday afternoons, when the Von Tobels had guests, 9-year-old Jake was sent to buy a bucket of beer. He bought it in the closest place that had a bar, which happened to be a brothel.

A cold winter in St. Louis pushed a young man to head west, where his family trade became a Las Vegas institution. BY A.D. HOPKINS

Coming to Las Vegas was a lark for Ed Von Tobel Sr., but staying sure wasn't. The Von Tobel family hung on by its fingernails when less tenacious folk drifted away. And during more than 90 years here, they've made business history.

The son of a Swiss immigrant, Ed was born in 1873 in Fairbury, Illinois. He dropped out of high school but continued his education informally, working in his father's lumberyard, traveling in Europe, and reading newspapers voraciously. He was 20 years old in November 1903, when he sat in a St. Louis cafe with his boyhood buddy, Jake Beckley, drinking beer and reading a paper.

"It reported that the temperature in Los Angeles was 72 degrees, and it was zero in St. Louis," Von Tobel related in a 1964 interview. "There also was an advertisement for the Santa Fe Railroad, offering a 'settler's rate,' one-way to California for $30."

Von Tobel hated cold weather, and the two chums borrowed money for tickets. Ed found work in a Los Angeles lumberyard, and Jake worked as a barber. But less than two years later, another newspaper ad caught their eyes, this one suggesting that readers could "get in on the ground floor" when lots were auctioned in a brand-new town, on the new railroad linking Los Angeles and Salt Lake City. Round-trip tickets cost only $22. However, with less than $100 between them after buying their tickets, Von Tobel and Beckley didn't expect to "get in on the ground floor"—or even a walk-up.

The young men stepped down from the car at a town consisting of one passenger railroad car, parked on a siding, equipped with a sign saying "Las Vegas." Beneath a big mesquite tree, on what is now North Main Street, stood a rude lumber platform, where an auctioneer and railroad officials could sit in the shade as the auction progressed. Bidders stood in the full sun as the temperature climbed to 110—a scorcher, even for May in Las Vegas. Men shucked coats and vests, but still sweat poured as the auctioneer's gavel rapped out the future of Las Vegas.

The only reason nobody left, Von Tobel would recall later, was the fear of missing the bargain of a lifetime. With more than 2,000 people present, choice business lots sold for $750, but who knew how long it would be till the well-heeled bidders were satisfied and lots might go for a few dollars? And that's what happened. As bidders and their enthusiasm wilted, the railroad freshened them up by announcing that the round-trip fare some had paid could be deducted from a down payment, which was a fourth of the cost of a lot. Beckley and Von Tobel bought adjoining $100 lots for a

Von Tobel in Southern Nevada

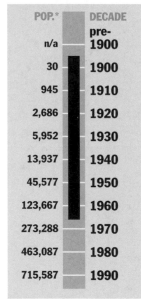

POP.*	DECADE
n/a	pre-1900
30	1900
945	1910
2,686	1920
5,952	1930
13,937	1940
45,577	1950
123,667	1960
273,288	1970
463,087	1980
715,587	1990

■ Time spent in Southern Nev.
* - Population figures are for greater Las Vegas area (*Source: Nevada State Data Center*).

Ed Von Tobel, an American bachelor in Europe in 1900, reads a newspaper in the home of his Swiss cousins.
(UNLV Special Collections)

cash outlay of $3 each and a ticket stub.

The feeling of good fortune must have sustained Von Tobel until he returned to his Los Angeles job, only to find he no longer had one. His employer had seen him at the land auction and had hired a replacement. Until then, Von Tobel hadn't made up his mind to move to Las Vegas. But with no other immediate prospects, he borrowed money from his father to buy lumber, nails, hardware, a delivery wagon, and a team to pull it. Beckley became his partner. Surely a lumberyard would make money fast in a town being built from the ground up. But when the partners alighted in the new settlement, seven other lumberyards were already in business. To add the final insult, one of them was operated by Von Tobel's former employer.

Life was like that for the next several years, relates Von Tobel's son, Ed Jr., interviewed at the age of 85 in the office he still maintains on South Maryland Parkway. His dad got some breaks, but each good fortune was followed by some blow. "Once the town was built, there wasn't enough business" to keep all those lumberyards going, said Ed Jr. "My dad bought out two. It got to the point there wasn't enough business to even keep two families, so he bought out Jake, and Jake went to work for his brother Will, who had a men's clothing store."

At a dance, Ed met a pretty girl from Bavaria and they married in 1908. Mary Von Tobel's first son, Jake, was born in late 1909, followed by a daughter, Elizabeth, in 1911, Ed Jr. in 1913, and George Jr. in 1918.

Las Vegans did not try to insulate children from real life. On Sunday afternoons, when the Von Tobels had guests, 9-year-old Jake was sent to buy a bucket of beer. He bought it in the closest place that had a bar, which happened to be a brothel.

Each of the boys, as he reached the age of 9 or 10, had the job of repackaging turpentine and linseed oil, which came in 50-gallon drums but was sold by the pint. "We would buy empty beer and whiskey bottles from transients for maybe a penny. We filled those, put a cork in it, and a label. We got maybe 25 cents or 50 cents a day for this, which was enough to keep you in candy." Elizabeth was still in high school when she broke in as bookkeeper. All four children would take part in the business as adults, and for Jake and Ed Jr., it would be the main endeavor of their lives.

Ed Sr. lived to be 94 and went to work every day until he was almost 90. He was a hands-on manager most of that time: "He used to keep his desk right behind the front counter because he wanted to see every customer who came in. He wanted to say hello."

Hoover Dam created a housing boom in the 1930s, followed by a bust. World War II brought another boom, but the Von Tobels didn't reap the profits because lumber shortages virtually shut them down. Short supply and a downtown location less convenient for contractors' large trucks forced the Von Tobels to cater to the do-it-yourself trade. Few realized how big this trade would

become as droves of ex-GIs married and moved into tract houses. Young men who had lately whipped the Axis were confident enough to build their own picnic tables.

The Von Tobels invented new ways to serve such customers. "We experimented back in the 1950s with letting people come into the hardware store and use shopping baskets and check out through a check stand, and that was the forerunner of all the Home Depot style operations you have today," said Ed Jr.

Jake also experimented with the then-radical concept of letting customers walk into a building and carry out their lumber, instead of driving into a yard to load it. "He proved they would do it," said Ed. That meant the Von Tobels could keep lumber in a climate-controlled building. Shopping became more comfortable, leveling out summer slumps in the business, which had been so pronounced in earlier years that Ed Sr. endured the occasional day without a single customer.

About 1966, Pay and Save Corporation bought out the Von Tobel stores, and since then the family has concentrated on real estate interests, developing a shopping center and other commercial properties. Ed Jr., like his father, was still going to the office at the age of 85.

His father worked hard to make Las Vegas succeed, said Ed Jr. But he didn't enjoy any special insight into the future in those early years, when family after family left Las Vegas for an easier life. "I asked my dad why they didn't pull out too, and he said, 'I had your mother and you kids here and a house here. I just had to tough it out.'" ⬠

Freight wagons like this one carried lumber and other building materials in the Von Tobels' early years in business.
(Courtesy Von Tobel family)

On February 27, 1944, Lt. George Von Tobel of the U.S. Army Corps of Engineers was home on leave and joined the other Von Tobel men on the porch of the family home at 214 S. Second Street. From left were Ed Von Tobel Sr., known to his boys as "Boss"; Jake Von Tobel, who succeeded him as president of Von Tobel Lumber Company; Ed Von Tobel Jr.; and Lt. Von Tobel. Ed and George would both become vice presidents.
(UNLV Special Collections)

BILL TOMIYASU (1882–1969)

A Japanese immigrant popularized many of the trees and
plants found today in Las Vegas Valley yards. **BY JOAN WHITELY**

He wasn't an engineer or a construction worker, but Yonema "Bill" Tomiyasu just as surely helped build Hoover Dam. He was a local farmer who fed the dam's workers with the literal fruits, and vegetables, of his labor: fresh tomatoes, asparagus, luscious watermelons, and canteloupe. All were items of produce that, prior to Tomiyasu's innovative farming techniques, mostly had to be shipped to Las Vegas from elsewhere, at added expense.

A Japanese-born immigrant who planted roots in Southern Nevada in 1914, Tomiyasu was one of the first Asian Americans to settle here. He arrived with the specific intention of owning and operating a ranch—which people of Japanese origin were not permitted to do, at the time, in neighboring California, where Tomiyasu had been living.

He went on to help his adopted country fight his land of birth during World War II, delivering produce and poultry to the mess hall of the airplane gunnery school near Las Vegas, which today is Nellis Air Force Base. Then the Las Vegas Valley began to urbanize. The Indian labor that Tomiyasu used to hire for ranch hands became scarce, and gradually he switched from agriculture to raising landscape plants.

Bill Tomiyasu's son, Nanyu, 80, today is completing the final contracts for the family's horticulture business as he readies for retirement. His own grown sons have declined to follow him in the back-breaking occupation. So the Tomiyasu business dynasty is ending. But signs of a Tomiyasu legacy remain.

A street, Tomiyasu Lane, still runs where the family ranch used to lie, though the land itself—in southeast Las Vegas, near the intersection of Pecos and Sunset roads—is broken up into many private upper-crust estates, just south of Wayne Newton's property. A public building also bears the family name: the Bill Y. Tomiyasu Elementary School at 5445 Annie Oakley Drive. And throughout the valley, trees continue to prosper that were germinated and raised to saplings by Bill Tomiyasu.

Nanyu Tomiyasu recounts the story his dad personally told of the exodus from Japan to California, and then of his eventual move to Las Vegas.

Yonema was born near Nagasaki, Japan, the son of a sugar cane farmer who also raised chickens. There he learned the skills that would carry him through life. But times were hard for the Japanese peasant class. Nanyu recalls that his father's family could hardly ever afford to eat any of the eggs their hens laid. So, Yonema vowed to become affluent one day. "He said, 'One thing's a must for me. I'm going to have six eggs a day.' And he did," Nanyu says.

In 1898, at age 16, Yonema left Japan for the United States to "have a look-see," as Nanyu puts it. He landed in British Columbia, Canada, then made his way to California, near San Jose, where a sister was already living. He made ends meet by picking fruit. But "he gradually drifted on down toward Fresno, Santa Barbara," taking jobs in gardening and plant nursery work, Nanyu says. By 1910, Yonema—still single—was living in San Bernardino. He had hired on at an Elks Club as a groundskeeper, but eventually transferred to the kitchen and became head cook.

"An Elks member who was a real estate agent … came up to Las Vegas to sell lots," Nanyu continues. On his return, the agent, M.M. Riley, "walked in the kitchen and told my dad, 'You'd better go to Las Vegas. There's lots of water, lots of land up there. It's hot, and gets fairly cold [in winter]. But if you can stand the weather conditions, you can make a living up there.'"

Nanyu took the advice. Soon, on April 25, 1914, the *Las Vegas Age* newspaper reported, "B.Y. Tomiyasu, secretary of the Japanese Association of San Bernardino, California, has been in Vegas the past week making arrangements to begin work on the 40 acres on Winterwood Boulevard recently purchased by him."

In 1916, Yonema permanently moved to Las Vegas. In 1917, he married. "It was an arranged marriage, what they call a 'picture' marriage," says Nanyu, referring to the practice of agreeing to wed on the basis of a matchmaker's recommendation and an

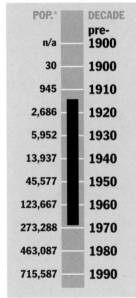

Tomiyasu in Southern Nevada

POP.*	DECADE
n/a	pre-1900
30	1900
945	1910
2,686	1920
5,952	1930
13,937	1940
45,577	1950
123,667	1960
273,288	1970
463,087	1980
715,587	1990

■ Time spent in Southern Nev.
* - Population figures are for greater Las Vegas area (*Source: Nevada State Data Center*).

Yonema "Bill" Tomiyasu in Sunday best in 1935
(Courtesy Tomiyasu family)

exchange of letters between prospective spouses, which usually included photo portraits.

Yonema's bride, Toyono, came from urban Sendai, Japan, to desolate Southern Nevada. Data from the 1920 census measured the entire Las Vegas population at 2,304. That year, the county recorded 62 residents of Japanese extraction. "She told me, when I was 6 or 7, her first couple years were really scary. She'd never heard a coyote howl," recalls Nanyu, their oldest son, born in 1918.

But farming in Southern Nevada wasn't as simple as reproducing the methods Yonema had used in Japan or California. In his early years of experimentation with food crops, Tomiyasu depended on alfalfa as his money crop. "He got seed catalogs from Los Angeles and got all their planting guides. And they were absolutely worthless here," says Nanyu. "He said, 'OK, I'm going to plant all these crops every two or three weeks, and find the best schedule.'"

After five or six years, he had succeeded in developing planting timetables for a cornucopia of produce: onions, green onions, carrots, radishes, beets, cabbage, cauliflower, Brussels sprouts, endive, bell peppers, melons.

In his "From Where I Sit" column in the June 28, 1930, *Las Vegas Evening Review-Journal*, co-owner Al Cahlan mentioned Tomiyasu's efforts to cultivate the Colorado River bottomlands: "It seems like about the time you get disgusted trying to find a good melon in the shipments from other climes, the home-grown melons land in town, and the search is over. … Bill Tomiyasu and Fred Haganuma (also of Japanese descent) are pioneering the game down on the river bank, near Searchlight, building each year, and bring new raw acreage into production. They are demonstrating just what can be done under the influ-

ence of this remarkable Clark County climate, with water on the desert lands."

During Nanyu's childhood years, the family—which had grown to include three more siblings—spent most of its time working the fields. "We supplied restaurants" in Beatty, Jean, Goodsprings, and Sloan, Nanyu recalls. The children and their mother helped Tomiyasu harvest, clean, and bundle the produce. Regularly, Nanyu went with his father on his delivery rounds, bouncing along dirt roads in a heavily laden family truck.

In the 1930s Tomiyasu struck a great coup for the family business, landing a long-term contract with the Six Companies—a consortium of companies building Hoover Dam—to supply food to their construction camp mess halls.

Before World War II, Japanese truck farmers in the West had already distinguished themselves as hard-working. "Issei (Japanese-born) men and women farmed side by side, often paid higher rents, and sustained their families on smaller profit margins," Andrew B. Russell wrote in his 1996 master's thesis for UNLV, which is titled *Friends, Neighbors, Foes, and Invaders: Conflicting Images and Experiences of Japanese Americans in Wartime Nevada.*

In California, the Japanese knack for agriculture aroused ethnic-based resentment on the part of what Russell calls "whites attempting to break into the farming 'aristocracy.' … California growers at first recruited large numbers of Japanese as farm laborers but turned suspicious of the Issei when they put their outstanding talent for horticulture to their own uses."

Anti-Japanese bias in California, Oregon, and Washington culminated in the forced relocation of Japanese to internment camps during World War II. Such bias wasn't so evident in prewar

Southern Nevada.

In the decades before the war, Nanyu and his siblings attended a one-room elementary school in the Paradise Valley School District. "It was one of the most integrated schools I've ever been to," says Nanyu. In addition to the four Tomiyasu children, its enrollment included a Japanese-American cousin, the six children of a white Mormon family, and the child of a black rancher. Later, the Tomiyasus were assigned to a downtown Las Vegas grammar school when several districts consolidated. In Las Vegas at large, Nanyu says, "Socially, we weren't integrated. But as far as gaining respect of the community for what he did, my father got that."

Russell theorizes in his thesis that the earliest Japanese in Clark County—who arrived soon after the first Las Vegas lots were sold in 1905— were able to keep a low profile. They did not earn unwanted prejudicial attention because most had a language barrier, worked solely for the railroad, and lived together in a compound. As World War II loomed, though, anti-Japanese sentiment kept on building in California, with

"Socially, we weren't integrated. But as far as gaining respect of the community for what he did, my father got that."
—Nanyu Tomiyasu
Bill Tomiyasu's son

Yonema Tomiyasu's four children attended a one-room schoolhouse in Paradise Valley.
(Courtesy Tomiyasu family)

Ranch hand Shigemura stands with the boss, Yonema Tomiyasu, and the Tomiyasu family, in about 1920. Toyono Tomiyasu holds 1-year-old Nanyu on her lap.
(Courtesy Tomiyasu family)

Yonema Tomiyasu works in a Paradise Valley lettuce field with sons Kiyo (at left) and Nanyu.
(Courtesy Tomiyasu family)

Gathered around the truck (bottom right) that figured in the Tomiyasu truck farming business in 1924 are (from left) Kyo Tomiyasu, Yoshiko Nagamatsu, Nanyu, Uwamie, and Maymi Tomiyasu.
(Courtesy Tomiyasu family)

To celebrate the first birthday of their youngest child in December 1924, the Tomiyasus posed for this family portrait. The adults (from left) are Yonema and Toyono Tomiyasu and Toyono's sister, Shimayo Nagamatsu. The children (from left) are Maymi, birthday girl Uwamie, Kiyo, and Nanyu Tomiyasu, and their cousin, Yoshiko Nagamatsu.
(Courtesy Tomiyasu family)

some spillover to Nevada.

"Nevada's preoccupation with these immigrants was a reaction to California's more successful efforts at restricting the Japanese. These, it was feared, might cause a great influx of Japanese into Nevada," writes Russell in another article, about the Japanese in Nevada from 1905 to 1945, which was published in the spring 1988 *Nevada Historical Society Quarterly.*

But the forecast never materialized for Southern Nevada. The census for 1940 showed 49 residents of Japanese race in Clark County, compared to a total Las Vegas population of 8,422 residents. Anti-Japanese events did occur sporadically during that four-decade span in certain Nevada communities—such as Reno and Fallon—but none occurred in the southern part of the state, perhaps because of the low percentage of Japanese in the overall population.

Yet the federal war agenda did affect Nevadans. No internment camps were located in Nevada. Nor were Nevadans of Japanese descent interned into camps, except for a few suspected of unionizing activity in the mining and rail towns of Ruth and McGill in White Pine County. But hundreds of workers there did petition to have Japanese employees fired, and by mid-1942 most Japanese-Americans had moved away from those two towns.

Even upstanding Japanese Nevadans were kept under surveillance to a certain extent. Throughout the state, Japanese followed federal policy by turn-

ing in short-wave parts from their radios, cameras, and even flashlights. Several of the Tomiyasu children, who were in college in California, stopped their studies and returned home. Nanyu Tomiyasu was instructed by the government—as were many sons of white farmers—to stay and help his father on the ranch, to maximize its output during the war years.

In Clark County, Sheriff Gene Ward—whom Nanyu remembers as a family friend—"staunchly defended the Japanese farm families of the area," reports Russell. "One Las Vegas Issei was interned. ... But that action came only after this individual had publicly aired his sympathy for Japan through letters to the local newspaper," Russell writes in *Friends, Neighbors, Foes, and Invaders.*

At one point in the war, Nanyu says he and his brother, Kiyo, received special dispensation from the FBI to drive across Hoover Dam, classified as a military target from which Japanese were to be restricted. The two then followed a route, also prescribed by the FBI, to pick up a Japanese-American family friend who was being released from an internment camp in Poston, Arizona. The friend, Seiji Iyemura, had been Tomiyasu's helper at the Elks Club in San Bernardino, and spent the rest of the war working at the Tomiyasu ranch. "He was able to track when he came to the United States, where he worked, where they worked together. My father vouched for him," Nanyu says.

The elder Tomiyasu was not

embittered by the U.S. wartime treatment of Japanese, not even the internment, according to Nanyu. His father's attitude was, "That's fate. There's nothing you can do about it."

After the war Tomiyasu prospered, until the 1960s, when he obtained a loan to expand his nursery operations. The way Nanyu remembers it, a member of their church invited them to take the loan. In an ensuing lawsuit, the Tomiyasus claimed that someone fraudulently obscured the repayment terms in such a way that the Tomiyasu family ended up delinquent.

In a controversial foreclosure that made Las Vegas headlines and went to the Nevada Supreme Court, Tomiyasu lost the entire 100-acre ranch—valued then at $240,000 and today some of the most valuable land in Paradise Valley—over an $18,000, second-trust deed. The supreme court ruled 2-1 for the purchasers of the foreclosed property. The family was evicted, but resumed nursery operations at another location.

Yonema Tomiyasu died in 1969 at the age of 87. But his legacy lives on, in several ways. Nanyu jokes that allergy sufferers can thank his father for the abundance of fruitless mulberry trees that dot the Las Vegas landscape—and dust it every spring with their pollens. ⌂

James Scrugham (1880–1945)

Scrugham was the first Nevada governor to propose setting aside public lands for recreational purposes. In his message to the Legislature in 1923, he said, "It appears entirely practicable to segregate areas within the forest reserves as state recreation grounds or game refuges."

An engineer by trade and a politician by chance, he was the first governor to treat Southern Nevada as part of the state. BY K.J. EVANS

One-term politicians are rarely celebrated by history, unless they were comically inept or criminally inclined. Colonel James Scrugham, elected in 1923, was neither. But his insistence on being the first Nevada governor ever to pay any serious attention to Southern Nevada may have cost him his re-election.

To say that Nevada was a much different place in 1920 would be an extreme understatement. Mining and agriculture were the dominant industries, political power was based solidly in the north, and Clark County was viewed by most Nevadans as an overheated appendage on the state's bottom. It was absurd, said Scrugham's detractors, that a governor should become personally involved in something as frivolous as the Lost City archeological project, or in that pie-in-the-sky Boulder Canyon Project. But before he died, he would see the pre-history of his state documented and his beloved dam constructed.

James Graves Scrugham was born January 19, 1880, in Lexington, Kentucky, and attended the State University of Kentucky, where he earned bachelor's and master's degrees in engineering. He worked for engineering firms in Cincinnati, Chicago, and San Francisco before coming to Nevada.

In 1903, he was hired as an assistant professor of mechanical engineering at the University

of Nevada. The following year, he felt sufficiently prosperous to go back to Kentucky and marry a Lexington girl, Julia McCann. The couple had two children, James Jr. and Martha. By 1914, Scrugham was dean of the college of engineering, which today bears his name.

In 1917, Governor Emmet Boyle, a fellow Democrat, appointed him state engineer. It was an important post, since the state engineer arbi-

trated disputes over water rights. Scrugham never again returned to academia. He enlisted in the Army in World War I, served only one year on active duty, but rose to the rank of lieutenant colonel in the Army Reserve. He was thereafter known as "Colonel Scrugham." In 1919, he was one of the founding members of the American Legion.

Upon his return to the office of state engineer, he embarked on what would become his life's work—constructing a high dam on the Colorado River. His quest was to make sure that the dam was built on a river stretch bordering Nevada, and that the state reaped its benefits.

As early as 1920, the U.S. Reclamation Service had been studying the feasibility of such a dam. The agency had estimated the cost to be around $200 million, and Director Arthur Powell Davis in 1921 voiced doubts about federal participation in such a costly venture. That same year, the Southern California Edison Company was approached, but dismissed the idea.

In late 1922, representatives of seven Western states and the federal government met at the Bishop's Lodge in Santa Fe, New Mexico. The assembly comprised the original Colorado River Commission. Secretary of Commerce Herbert Hoover, himself an engineer, chaired the commission, and Scrugham headed the Nevada delegation. The commission's task was to hammer out a pact among the states bordering the river.

Scrugham in Southern Nevada

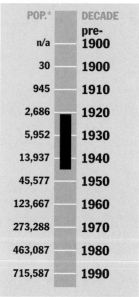

POP.*	DECADE
n/a	pre-1900
30	1900
945	1910
2,686	1920
5,952	1930
13,937	1940
45,577	1950
123,667	1960
273,288	1970
463,087	1980
715,587	1990

■ Time spent in Southern Nev.
* - Population figures are for greater Las Vegas area (*Source: Nevada State Data Center*).

Governor James Graves Scrugham, from his official portrait that hangs in the state capitol

(*Nevada State Archives*)

Among the issues were flood control, water storage, and electrical generation. The greatest issue of all was who got how much water and electric power. The commission agreed on general principles, but those greater issues would remain unresolved for years to come. The state of Nevada also formed a Colorado River Commission, chaired by Scrugham.

By mid-1923, Scrugham had abandoned the idea that the dam might be built by private enterprise. "It is my firm belief," he told the *Los Angeles Times*, "that the government is the only agency that should build the dam. Afterward, state, municipal, or private agencies can operate it. What we want is the dam built and built quickly."

He might have gotten that last wish were it not for Governor George Hunt of Arizona, who had been elected on a "no dam" platform. Six of the seven states involved had immediately signed the Colorado River Compact. Arizona was the holdout, and the matter could not be put before Congress until that state had also signed the compact.

Governor Boyle completed his second term in 1923, and he urged Scrugham to run for the office. He was elected by 2,222 votes, and quickly became known as "The Governor on Wheels" and "Gasoline Jimmy." The Colonel liked to get around the state, and he usually drove.

The problem was, Nevada roads of the time were primitive or nonexistent. There were no gasoline stations or repair shops between Reno and Las Vegas. If it rained, the road washed out; if it snowed, drivers were stranded. In fact, a 120-mile stretch of north-south road, between Beatty and Las Vegas, was the abandoned bed of the Las Vegas and Tonopah

Railroad. At Scrugham's urging, the 1923 Legislature imposed a 2-cent-per-gallon fuel tax to be used for road improvements. In 1924, Scrugham reported to the Legislature the completion of 769 miles of improved roads, 510 miles of which were gravel.

Scrugham was the first Nevada governor to propose setting aside public lands for recreational purposes. In his message to the Legislature in 1923, he said, "It appears entirely practicable to segregate areas within the forest reserves as state recreation grounds or game refuges." In response, the Legislature enacted a bill allowing the governor to designate 25 such areas, to be administered by the State Fish and Game Commission. This was the beginning of the modern Nevada Division of State Parks. Although Scrugham wanted the Valley of Fire to become a national park, it would become a Nevada State Park.

"He had a statewide view of Nevada and its resources," says Dr. James Hulse, professor emeritus of history at the University of Nevada-Reno. "He was probably the most active governor in developing the state's resources up to that time. And he recognized the importance of Southern Nevada far sooner than did most politicians."

The political complexion of the Legislature changed abruptly in 1924, when Republicans gained control, and Scrugham did not enhance his chances of re-election by becoming directly involved in an archaeological project in a remote part of the state.

Sometime in 1924, Scrugham received a package from Fay Perkins, a member of a pioneer Mormon clan of the Moapa Valley. In the package were Indian artifacts Perkins had found along the Muddy River. Scrugham was fascinated and contacted Mark R. Harrington, who was then excavating the Lovelock Cave, 90 miles east of Reno. Harrington agreed to take a closer look, and Perkins led the archaeologist to where he had found the relics. Harrington became very excited, talking about a lost city beneath the riverside dunes.

Scrugham walked up in time to catch the last

of the conversation. "A buried city, hey?" he said. "How old do you think it might be?"

"It's hard to tell right off the bat," Harrington replied. "But this black on white pottery is pretty old stuff. A thousand years maybe, or even two thousand."

"This will jolt some of those smart Easterners," said the governor, chuckling, "the fellows who say Nevada is so raw and new. They think we have no past, no background of antiquity."

Harrington was in Nevada under the auspices of the Museum of the American Indian, headed by George Gustav Heye. Scrugham asked Heye to put Harrington in charge of the excavation, which he did. The governor also obtained funding from the Smithsonian and Carnegie institutions. And he dispatched state trucks, equipment, and workers to aid the effort.

In 1926, Scrugham stood for re-election, but was defeated by GOP challenger Fred Balzar. The *Reno Evening Gazette* characterized Scrugham as a spendthrift and added, "No Nevada governor has shown less ability as an executive."

The *Gazette* editors also took a rather condescending tone regarding his interest in the Lost City excavation: "It is impossible to discern the grounds upon which Governor Scrugham can base any serious claims to a second term. He takes much interest in archaeology, lectures on ancient civilizations, has conducted a considerable amount of research in old Indian graveyards, and for fours years has actively canvassed the state for re-election. But these qualifications and matters have nothing to do with the administration of government. He seems more interested in tourist roads than in highways that will serve the farms, the stockmen, and the mining industry."

Hulse, however, believes that Scrugham's defeat had more to do with the national and statewide trend toward Republicanism, than with any north-south rivalry.

Scrugham's knowledge of the issues surrounding the Boulder Canyon Project earned him a post of special adviser to U.S. Secretary of the Interior Hubert Work in 1927. That same year,

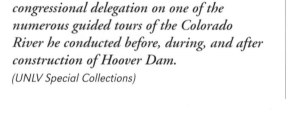

James Scrugham (first from left) with a congressional delegation on one of the numerous guided tours of the Colorado River he conducted before, during, and after construction of Hoover Dam.
(UNLV Special Collections)

Scrugham also purchased the *Nevada State Journal* in Reno for just over $100,000. He followed the example of the previous governor, Boyle, who bought the newspaper after he left office in 1922. The acquisition did not really represent a new career for Scrugham, since Nevada newspapers of the day usually aligned themselves with one political party or the other, bellowed the party line, and rarely made any pretense of objectivity. The *Las Vegas Age* acknowledged this, saying, "The purchase by Governor Scrugham is taken to mean that he will continue actively in state politics."

With the onset of the Great Depression, the Democrats were again in ascendancy, and Scrugham ran for Nevada's lone congressional seat in 1932. He beat Republican Sam Arentz by a large margin, riding comfortably on the coattails of Franklin D. Roosevelt, along with the legendary Patrick A. McCarran, who was elected to the Senate.

> "*He didn't know what it meant to relax. He regarded an hour lost when he wasn't doing something for Nevada. No man could last forever at that pace, even though he possessed the qualities of a human dynamo. Jim Scrugham gave his life to the people of Nevada.*"
> —Al Cahlan
> Editor of the
> *Review-Journal* in 1945

Although it is today a pejorative term, "pork barrel" politics, in earlier times, was viewed differently by the American public. Senators and congressmen were expected to use their clout to obtain federal works projects and funds for their home state. It is an especially proud tradition in Nevada. Scrugham proved a prodigious pork procurer, and FDR set a bountiful barrel in front of the solons.

In April of 1933, Scrugham sliced off his first slab, asking Roosevelt to increase, from 200 to 1,000, the number of youths assigned to Nevada as part of the proposed "Reforestation Army." (This became the Civilian Conservation Corps, part of the Works Progress Administration.) "The reason for asking for the extra allotment," Scrugham wrote, "is the distressing condition of thousands of able-bodied men drawn to Las Vegas through hopes of obtaining employment on the Boulder Canyon Project. They cannot be allowed to starve."

By 1934, Southern Nevada had two CCC camps, one at Boulder City and the other at Mount Charleston. Scrugham also obtained $5,900 and the manpower needed to finally build a museum at Overton to house the artifacts unearthed at the Lost City excavation. A camp also was established at Panaca in Lincoln County, and the CCC boys did extensive work developing Cathedral Gorge, Kershaw-Ryan, and Beaver Dam state parks.

With the completion of Hoover Dam in 1935,

Scrugham went to work to develop "Boulder Lake" into a first-rate recreational center. He obtained an appropriation of $60,000 to build the first fish hatchery, and badgered federal fish and wildlife authorities to install it posthaste.

The question of how the huge lake would be administered had not yet been resolved in 1935. In late fall, Scrugham conducted one of his many excursions on the lake and the river, taking with him several federal officials. The idea of incorporating the lake and dam into Grand Canyon National Park had been advanced, but Scrugham opposed it. He was concerned that park status would do harm to adjacent mining and ranching operations, and limit public recreational access. He favored an entirely new concept, a national recreation area, and Lake Mead became the first such unit in the federal system.

In 1942, Scrugham won the senate seat vacated by the death of veteran Democrat Key Pittman. Though Scrugham had been instrumental in establishing Basic Magnesium in 1941, it was as U.S. senator that he tried to ensure the plant would continue to operate after the war. (The plant today is owned by Basic Investments Inc. and houses four industrial firms.)

Scrugham did not live to see the magnitude of Southern Nevada's postwar prosperity, although he did see the birth of the resort row that would become the Strip. Shortly after his election, his health began to fail, and he spent the last two years of his life in and out of hospitals. On June 6, 1945, he died at the Naval Hospital in San Diego.

Al Cahlan of the *Las Vegas Review-Journal* had first met Scrugham when he went to the University of Nevada to study engineering. He was amazed at the pace Scrugham set for himself then, and later in public office. "He didn't know what it meant to relax," eulogized Cahlan. "He regarded an hour lost when he wasn't doing something for Nevada. No man could last forever at that pace, even though he possessed the qualities of a human dynamo. Jim Scrugham gave his life to the people of Nevada." ✍

> "*The reason for asking for the extra allotment is the distressing condition of thousands of able-bodied men drawn to Las Vegas through hopes of obtaining employment on the Boulder Canyon Project. They cannot be allowed to starve.*"
> —James Scrugham
> Asking for more men to be
> assigned to the "Reforestation Army"

This photo was probably taken near the Black Canyon damsite in the 1920s, when James Scrugham was governor, or in the 1930s, when the dam was under construction.
(UNLV Special Collections)

MARK HARRINGTON

(1882–1971)

"To follow the trail of a forgotten people, to play detective upon the doings of a man who has been dead 10,000 years or so is a thrilling pastime to an explorer under any circumstances. But when the trail leads into a rich virgin field never disturbed by the spade of the relic hunter, then your sunburned desert rat of an archaeologist thinks he has discovered a real paradise."

—Mark Harrington

An archaeologist found paradise amid the ruins of the Lost City, and proved that Nevada was inhabited long before modern times. **BY K.J. EVANS**

Mark Harrington knew within minutes that he was standing on something of monumental scientific importance. It was a fall day in 1924, and the famed archaeologist was on the bank of the Muddy River in the Moapa Valley. With him were James Scrugham, the governor of Nevada, and two brothers, John and Fay Perkins, members of a local pioneer Mormon family. Fay Perkins had found odd Indian artifacts along the river and had sent them to Scrugham, who sent for Harrington. "We had not been there two minutes," Harrington recalled, "when my eyes rested upon a scrap of painted pottery lying on the sand beside a prickly mesquite bush. It was our first clue!"

Harrington examined the piece. It was a neat pattern in black on white, which his trained eye quickly identified as an early example of Pueblo craft, made at a time when that people were just beginning to develop their characteristic pottery. In New Mexico and Arizona, such a find might possibly be expected. But not west of the Colorado River in Nevada. "Look at this pottery; it's early Pueblo," he said excitedly, and handed the shard to Fay Perkins, who tossed it back casually.

"I wouldn't get all worked up and excited over just one piece," Perkins advised. "You'll find that kind of stuff scattered all along the river here for five or six miles."

"If that's true," said Harrington, "and you really saw all those old foundations you've been telling about, I'll bet we've found a regular buried city."

Harrington left the Moapa Valley the next day. He would return, and what he would find would exceed his wildest expectations. "Even then," he wrote, "with all our enthusiasm over the new find, we did not realize just how old it was; that we had struck the trail of some of the very first Pueblos."

Many of Harrington's conclusions came into question in later years and many were disproved. Dr. Margaret Lyneis, professor of anthropology at UNLV, says Harrington's initial findings were "fundamentally right" and his chronology, with a few exceptions, was good. "While many of his results got changed in later studies, he drew attention to the importance of the sites he excavated, and that resulted in further studies. All three of his excavations—the Lost City, Gypsum Cave, and Tule Springs—were pioneering pieces of work."

Harrington knew Indian ways. During his career, he lived with or visited 43 Indian tribes and bands in North America and was adopted into several. He wrote fanciful adventure stories, published under his pen name, Ramon de la Cuevas (Raymond of the Caves). In later years, he would even try peyote, a powerful hallucinogenic drug used by some tribes to attain spiritual enlightenment. It is hard to determine from his cryptic account whether he was enlightened, but he was definitely impressed.

Mark Raymond Harrington was born on the campus of the University of Michigan in Ann Arbor on July 6, 1882. From his earliest years, Raymond, as he preferred to be called, was fascinated by Native American culture, and local Indian friends helped him learn some of their language.

When his family moved to Mount Vernon, New York, there were no Indians, but there was

Harrington in Southern Nevada

POP.*	DECADE
n/a	pre-1900
30	1900
945	1910
2.686	1920
5,952	1930
13,937	1940
45,577	1950
123,667	1960
273,288	1970
463,087	1980
715,587	1990

■ Time spent in Southern Nev.
* - Population figures are for greater Las Vegas area (*Source: Nevada State Data Center*).

Mark Harrington practices flint-knapping, about 1928.

(Southwest Museum)

plenty of physical evidence that there once had been. Harrington dug up pot shards and arrowheads, which he eventually took to F.W. Putnam, head of the anthropology department at the American Museum in New York City. When his father's illness forced Harrington to quit high school, Putnam hired him as a trainee field archaeologist and would become his mentor and lifelong friend.

Harrington earned a master's degree in anthropology from Columbia University in 1908, and soon thereafter, George Gustav Heye, a rich banker who was fascinated with Indian lore, hired Harrington to collect materials that would make up the inventory of the Museum of the American Indian in New York City.

The chain of events that resulted in Harrington coming to Nevada began in 1911. That year, James Hart and Samuel Pugh discovered a shallow cave in the West Humboldt Range, near Lovelock. Inside the cave was a fortune in bat guano, prized as fertilizer. Hart and Pugh filed a mining claim on the cave and began to excavate. To their chagrin, the poop wasn't pure. It was contaminated with all manner of bows, arrows, baskets, pottery, and clothing. So thick were the relics, they abandoned the claim.

The men kept the showiest goodies and donated some to the Nevada Historical Society, which contacted the University of California at Berkeley. Between April and August of 1912, Dr. Llewellyn Loud took 10,000 specimens from the cave. George Heye obtained a rabbit net and some other artifacts from the cave and showed them to Harrington in 1924. Heye sent Harrington to see if there was anything worth saving from the ravaged site, and Harrington invited Loud to join him.

The cave was a jumbled mass of bat guano, artifacts, and dirt. In those days before carbon dating, the way an archaeologist usually determined the age of a site was by studying the layers of dirt and relics. Loud had simply cataloged the artifacts in "lots." Harrington found one tiny area of the cave floor undisturbed and reckoned that the earliest inhabitants had moved in around 2,000 B.C.; the last, about 900 A.D. Modern studies have shown that the cave was occupied or used between 2,600 B.C. and 1850 A.D.

Among Harrington's findings was a bundle of very well preserved duck decoys. These had been fashioned from bundles of reeds, then decorated with the feathers of the birds being hunted. Harrington's find proved that people had hunted and fished on the shores of ancient Lake Lahontan. When the lake dried up, the people departed.

While at work in the Lovelock Cave, Harrington was contacted by Governor Scrugham concerning the mysterious relics and ruins along the Muddy River. By 1925, Harrington was eager to tackle the excavation of the place Scrugham had named "El Pueblo Grande de Nevada."

When Harrington arrived, he was met by newspaper and magazine reporters, film crews, and an astonishing number of private citizens. To raise money for the project—and to get favorable publicity for his state—Scrugham threw a pageant, depicting the valley's prehistory and history. It was held May 23, 1925, at the end of the digging season. A replica of a pueblo was constructed for a stage, and the show drew some 6,000 people.

Harrington's right-hand men—and close friends—were George and Willis Evans, members of the Pitt River Tribe. A group of Zunis from New Mexico showed up and went to work, along with Indians of several other tribes. "It is only right that they should have a hand in uncovering the ancient history of their ancestors," said Harrington.

During his initial expedition, 1925–26, Harrington's party excavated 46 prehistoric structures, the largest of which had nearly 100 rooms. He determined almost immediately that more than one culture had occupied the site. First came the Basketmakers. He dated their time at around 1500 B.C., but modern studies place the period at about 300–500 B.C. The Basketmakers found at the site were characterized by long, rather than round, skulls. They practiced agriculture and wove fine baskets and cloth, but they made no pottery. They did not use the bow and arrow, relying on the atlatl, a special stick used to hurl light spears called "darts."

Excavation of the first site in the Lost City, or "Pueblo Grande de Nevada," November 22, 1924. From left, George Evans, excavator; Mark R. Harrington, archaeologist in charge, and his son; Governor James G. Scrugham; Mr. Wright, a newsman; Dr. C.W. West of Reno; State Senator Levi Syphus of Clark County; and State Police Sergeant MacSherry.
(UNLV Special Collections)

"Fortunately for archaeologists," wrote Harrington, "these people had the custom of burying their dead and storing their belongings in caves so dry that specimens of practically everything they owned, even highly perishable articles made of fur and feathers, have come down to us in a remarkable state of preservation."

But to Harrington, the most exciting finds were those of the Pueblos. These were the people who built houses of stone and adobe. They were entirely dependent upon agriculture and grew cotton, which they wove into fine cloth. They seem to have mastered irrigation, since early settlers recorded finding many ditches running from the Muddy River. Harrington overestimated the antiquity of this culture, and later archaeologists set it at about 700–1150 A.D.

In 1928, Harrington became curator of the Southwest Museum in Los Angeles, and represented the museum when he returned to Southern Nevada in 1929. His mission was a complete survey of the Moapa Valley. Harrington's survey recorded 77 ruins on a 16-mile stretch of the Muddy River. Meanwhile, a colleague, Irwin Hayden, began digging Mesa House, a large pueblo arranged in a courtyard fashion. He unearthed 84 rooms and single-family dwellings, most of them from the last period of the Pueblo occupation. Harrington believed that these single-story adobe structures were the precursors to the gigantic multistory pueblos that these people built in New Mexico and Arizona, after they left the valley sometime after 1100 A.D.

Mark Harrington (left) and his assistant, S.M. Wheeler, unpack artifacts from an archaeological expedition, 1930s.
(Southwest Museum)

In 1930, Harrington began work in Gypsum Cave, which John Perkins had told him about in 1924. The cave is in a limestone spur of the Frenchman Mountain Range east of Las Vegas. Harrington and his crew dug 8 feet into the floor of the cave. They found atlatl darts, indicating the presence of Basketmaker people, and they found huge deposits of dung, which Harrington surmised had come from a large animal. Further digging turned up the bones and a skull from a species of extinct ground sloth (Nothrotheriops shastensis). Then, at a deeper level, beneath the dung of the ice-age creature, were more atlatl points, the remains of cooking fires, and evidence of vegetation that does not exist in the area today.

This raised an important question. Did these people live at the same time as the ice-age sloth? Harrington produced bones that he believed had been split for their marrow, since they bore the marks of what seemed to be a stone knife. He concluded that the Basketmakers had indeed met the sloths, and he placed the time at 8,500 B.C. This was a revolutionary and controversial finding. And it was wrong. Recent radiometric tests have shown that the sloth leavings dated to 9,700–6,500 B.C., and the human artifacts went back to 900–400 B.C. This by no means settled the controversy among archaeologists, which continues today.

Equally controversial was Harrington's dating of bones and weapon points at Tule Springs. Amateurs had been turning up bones and artifacts there since the turn of the century. The site had first been excavated by scholars in 1932, when Fernley Hunter and Dr. Albert Silberling, under the auspices of the American Museum of Natural History, unearthed the bones of two ground sloths, a camelops—the largest of the American camels—and a partial skeleton of a mammoth. Among the bones, in an ancient campfire pit, they found an obsidian weapon point. So astonishing was this find that they unearthed the fire pit intact and shipped it to Dr. George G. Simpson at the American Museum of Natural History. Simpson was excited by the find, but hesitant to go against the prevailing wisdom that ice-age beasts and man had never met. In 1933, he published a paper with the cautious title "A Nevada Fauna of Pleistocene Type and Its Probable Association with Man," which stopped short of stating that the ancient bones and human relics were from the same time period.

A few months later, Hunter turned the site over to the Southwest Museum, and Harrington, along with Fay Perkins, went to Tule Springs. Harrington was overcome when he saw bones of the long-extinct animals strewn among the black charcoal of the fireplaces. "I think if I had been wearing a hat, I would have taken it off," he wrote. In his opinion, the Tule Springs site was a camel hunter's camp and was "considerably more than 10,000 years old, more like 25,000 years old." He published his conclusions in an unequivocal piece titled "Man's Oldest Date in America."

Unfortunately, his dates have not stood up to the scrutiny of more recent examinations. It is now generally agreed that the shortage of human artifacts at Tule Springs does not yet allow scientists to make a solid connection between prehistoric man and animals.

In 1933, Harrington was summoned by the National Park Service to direct the Civilian Conservation Corps in salvaging what could be found before the entire Lost City site disappeared under the new lake formed by Hoover Dam. The CCC excavated 17 more pueblos, laboring until water literally lapped at their feet. At the same time, Harrington directed construction of the Lost City Museum near Overton and restoration of ruins above the high-water line.

His work for the government ended in 1935, and except for sporadic work in Southern Nevada, he spent the rest of his career exploring the antiquities of Southern California. He died on June 30, 1971, well established as a legend in his profession.

In a 1927 magazine article, Mark Raymond Harrington explained why he chose such a dusty, difficult, and often frustrating career. He wrote: "To follow the trail of a forgotten people, to play detective upon the doings of a man who has been dead 10,000 years or so is a thrilling pastime to an explorer under any circumstances. But when the trail leads into a rich virgin field never disturbed by the spade of the relic hunter, then your sunburned desert rat of an archaeologist thinks he has discovered a real paradise." ✍

DAVID G. LORENZI

(1874–1962)

"There isn't an old-timer in Las Vegas who hasn't sweet memories of picnicking and dancing cheek-to-cheek and swimming in one of the West's largest outdoor pools in the days when Twin Lakes was a country retreat from the heat."

—Bill Vincent
Magazine editor

A Frenchman's dream of not one but two lakes in the desert with recreational facilities for all became a magnet for heat-stricken Las Vegans and tourists alike. **BY K.J. EVANS**

Bill Vincent, the mild-mannered editor of the *Review-Journal's* Sunday magazine, *Nevadan,* was incensed when he sat down at his typewriter that June day in 1966. The city of Las Vegas had acquired the old Twin Lakes resort and was converting it to a public park. Vincent titled his piece "How to Ruin a City Park" and went on to deplore the cutting of the many trees and foliage, the destruction of the old 1920s dance pavilion, and the desecration of David G. Lorenzi's unique dream of a recreational oasis in the desert.

"There isn't an old-timer in Las Vegas who hasn't sweet memories of picnicking and dancing cheek-to-cheek and swimming in one of the West's largest outdoor pools in the days when Twin Lakes was a country retreat from the heat," Vincent wrote. Moreover, the place was a reflection of the man, whose statue in Lorenzi Park now looks out over the body of water he created.

David Gerald Lorenzi was born December 29, 1874, in Montougne, France, a minor aristocrat and second cousin to the King of Monaco. He came to the United States first at age 15, then returned when he was 20 and spent time in New York, Texas, and San Diego. During his travels, he heard of the new town of Las Vegas, which was supposed to have unlimited artesian well water suitable for farming. He arrived in Las Vegas in the fall of 1911 and purchased an 80-acre site two miles from the railroad tracks.

His first task was to find more water, and after several weeks of drilling, he hit the fluid lode, one of the most prodigious water wells in the valley at the time. Lorenzi thinned the thick mesquite and built arbors to encourage the growth of the native grapevines, later grafting

domestic grapes onto the rootstock. His daughter, Louise Lorenzi Fountain, recalled in a 1980 interview that her father foresaw a giant desert vineyard producing European-quality wines. The grapes did well and the wine was adequate, but the public demand was low. Las Vegas was a beer and whiskey town.

Lorenzi had sufficient irrigation water, and plenty to spare. All that was needed to make the place a bonafide oasis was a shimmering body of water. Using a team of mules and a drag line, Lorenzi undertook the Herculean task of excavating two lakes. One would be higher than the other, and their outflow would irrigate the fields at the lowest point on the property.

In early 1913, Lorenzi married Julia Traverse Moore, and they opened a downtown confectionery store they called "The Palms," which offered homemade candies, ice cream, and fresh fruits and melons.

By 1921, the first lake was complete; it encompassed three acres and was 10 feet deep. Each lake had an island. One was connected to the mainland with a wooden bridge, which had a locked iron gate on its landward end. On the island was a small building where leading Las Vegas citizens gathered to socialize, play cards, and ignore Prohibition. The building had a trap door in the floor, covered by a rug. If a lawman showed up, the trap door was opened, the illegal hootch was stashed, and the cop was invited in for a friendly game.

Lorenzi in Southern Nevada

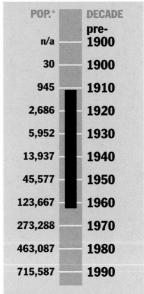

POP.*	DECADE
n/a	pre-1900
30	1900
945	1910
2,686	1920
5,952	1930
13,937	1940
45,577	1950
123,667	1960
273,288	1970
463,087	1980
715,587	1990

■ Time spent in Southern Nev.
* - Population figures are for greater Las Vegas area (*Source: Nevada State Data Center*).

David G. Lorenzi in later life
(Review-Journal files)

The musicians union band prepares for a performance in the band-shell-on-the-island at Twin Lakes Resort, 1956.
(UNLV Special Collections)

Aerial view of Twin Lakes Lodge as it appeared before city acquisition. Notice the two lakes and two islands. The large building at center is the dance pavilion; the small body of water at right center is the trout pond; the riding stables are at far left.
(UNLV Special Collections)

On the other island was a band shell, which also had a movie screen. Rowboaters would lazily circle the island, listening to the band as lights in the trees reflected in the placid waters. Or they enjoyed the world's first row-in theater.

The lakes were stocked with bluegill, crappie, black bass, and gigantic bullfrogs. Critics said the fish would not survive in the lakes, but they thrived. When Lake Mead began to rise behind Hoover Dam, it was initially stocked with thousands of fingerling fish from Lorenzi's pond.

Just in time for the 1926 sweating season, Lorenzi completed a 90-foot by 100-foot swimming pool with a large fountain at its center. It was the largest swimming pool in Nevada at the time, and its waters were remarkably refreshing, since Lorenzi's "flow-through" water system negated the need for chemicals. Corrals and riding stables were built nearby, along with a dance pavilion capable of handling 2,000 people. It extended over the lake on pylons.

The resort opened to the public in May 1926, but the July 4 celebration was a major hit with Las Vegans. Newspaper reports told of a queue of 1,000 cars lining the road into town. The festivities that day included fireworks, bathing beauties, and a 4,000-foot parachute drop.

Admission to Lorenzi's Resort was one thin dime, which entitled the visitor to use any or all of its facilities. As might be expected in those pre-air-conditioned days, the park became the city's favorite summer retreat, and Lorenzi accommodated guests with as many diversions as his fertile imagination could conjure. There were beauty pageants, dance contests, prizefights, and horse races.

Few old-timers who witnessed his 1931 Independence Day fireworks pageant will forget the spectacle. The theme was the Spanish-American War, and Lorenzi built a replica of the Battleship U.S.S. Maine, which had been blown up in Ha-

vana in 1898. The event drew the largest crowd ever, about 4,400 people.

Two summers before, when it was announced that the president had signed the Boulder Canyon Project Act of June 1929, authorizing the construction of Boulder (later Hoover) Dam, the town poured out to the park for a frenzied soiree that lasted three days and three nights. "We knew that it meant the beginning of Las Vegas as a city," said daughter Louise in a 1964 interview.

On the resort grounds, Lorenzi built an ice manufacturing plant, which served as the backdrop for his first and only brush with the law. In May 1931, lawmen discovered a steam brewery at the icehouse, along with 2,500 gallons of beer. Lorenzi protested that he knew nothing of the operation, since he had recently leased the icehouse to a man who had changed the locks. Even so, he was arrested. Exactly two months later, the charges were dropped for lack of evidence.

The resort was Lorenzi's pride and joy, but it wasn't profitable. He wanted his property to become a public park, and in 1936 offered it to the city for $70,000. The city fathers pleaded poverty and declined. (The city paid $750,000 for it in 1965.) In 1937, Thomas Sharp, a San Diego businessman, purchased it for $59,000 but did nothing more than fence it off and allow its lakes to degenerate into swamps. The venerable oasis was

saved 10 years later when Sharp leased it to Lloyd St. John, who drained the lakes, then dredged and refilled them. He renamed the resort Twin Lakes Lodge and built a 48-unit motel. Under St. John, the resort became as popular as it had been during the 1920s and '30s. It was a playground for celebrities and a staging ground for political rallies and conventions.

Lorenzi was a singularly talented stonemason and built several church shrines and colorful stone structures. One of the most visible of those is the historical marker for the old Las Vegas Fort, built in 1939 and still standing at Washington Avenue and Las Vegas Boulevard North. What isn't generally known, says Fountain, is that the monument is a time capsule, containing relics and artifacts telling the history of the Lorenzi family.

Lorenzi died in January 1962 at age 86. Commenting some years before on his heroic labors in creating the verdant resort, *Las Vegas Evening Review-Journal* Editor John Cahlan said, "It took Lorenzi 11 years of hard work to bring about the development of which he had dreamed. Las Vegans, then as now, were a little reticent to accept the dream which Lorenzi had, because they were certain he would not succeed and leave the place half-completed. They reckoned, however, without taking a good peek at the man himself." ✍

BOB HAUSLER (?–?)

Las Vegas showed up on aviators' maps largely through the efforts of one man, who made Anderson Field planeworthy. BY K.J. EVANS

Not counting annual visits by Santa Claus, the first aircraft to land in Las Vegas touched down on the afternoon of May 7, 1920. Matter of fact, that flight had a lot in common with those of the jolly old man. Jake Beckley was the surrogate Santa in this tale; his sled, an old Curtiss "Jenny" biplane. The part of his reindeer was played by Randall Henderson of Blythe, California, a newspaper editor and pilot in the Army Reserve.

Dropping to 500 feet, Henderson made a wide banking turn over the tiny town of Las Vegas, then came in low and slow over the home of Jake's brother, Will, at 120 S. Fourth Street. Jake peered over the side of the open cockpit, spotted the green square of lawn, and dropped a doll for his niece, Virginia. The Beckley brothers were pioneer retailers and owned stores in Las Vegas and Blythe. Henderson then pointed the machine south and looked for the plot of naked dirt that was Anderson Field, named for property owner Harry Anderson and located near what is now the corner of Paradise Road and Sahara Avenue.

The arrival did not go unnoticed by the local citizenry. Their reaction was akin to what might happen today if the space shuttle were to make an unannounced landing on the Strip. Businessmen locked their shops, housewives shed their aprons and donned their newest hats, and bare-foot kids bolted, followed by a riot of barking dogs. All were off to see the wondrous flying machine. So enthralled was the crowd that Henderson spent that day, and then three more, taking passengers aloft in the wood-and-canvas craft.

"Las Vegas has at last experienced the joy of flying, at least some of Las Vegas has," wrote C.P. Squires in the *Las Vegas Age*. "All the rest of us are taking treatment for dislocated necks and sunburned tonsils."

No one was experiencing the joy of flying that day more than Bob Hausler, a young mechanic who had worked in the railroad shops since the previous year. Like an aspiring actor who grudgingly waits tables, he was biding his time until he

Hausler in Southern Nevada

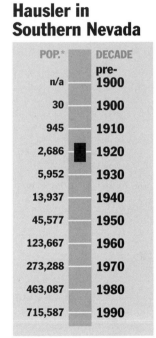

POP.*	DECADE
n/a	pre-1900
30	1900
945	1910
2,686	1920
5,952	1930
13,937	1940
45,577	1950
123,667	1960
273,288	1970
463,087	1980
715,587	1990

■ Time spent in Southern Nev.
* - Population figures are for greater Las Vegas area (*Source: Nevada State Data Center*).

Legendary daredevil aviator Clarence O. Prest brought his plane, "Poison: Dose, One Drop," to Las Vegas for Bob Hausler's air show on Thanksgiving Day, 1920. The dwarf biplane's name proved to be prophetic. When a mechanic mixed the fuel improperly and the engine got a dose, the plane dropped. Prest survived.
(Jim Day/Review-Journal)

could find a way to make a living in the aviation business.

As an Army aviator, Hausler had in 1918 piloted one of five planes that had flown from Los Angeles to Salt Lake City—passing near Las Vegas—then on to Reno and Sacramento, California. The mission of the squadron had been to scout potential airmail routes. Hausler believed that the Los Angeles to Salt Lake City route was superior to the one from Salt Lake to Sacramento. The latter required fliers to cross the Sierra Nevada range west of Reno, and to negotiate the perilous 7,329-foot Donner Pass. The southern route over the Mojave was much lower, with mountain passes only half as high, and much less prone to blizzards.

Hausler had scraped out a very rough landing field in 1919. He wanted to create a field that was up to the standards of the Aero Clubs and the military. If Las Vegas could establish itself as a modern facility, he reasoned, it might stand a chance of being included on the new airmail routes. He also wanted to establish a flying school and aircraft service station. Unfortunately, the airmail route across Nevada bypassed Las Vegas in 1920, following instead the northern route through Reno and over the Sierra.

But Hausler remained optimistic and continued to make improvements to Anderson Field. By November of 1920, he had cleared, leveled, and smoothed the field, constructed a small building, and completed an L-shaped runway, which would allow pilots to land without regard for the direction of the wind. The field was now up to standard and could be included in the aviation guidebooks published by the Aero Clubs. Thanks to Hausler, Las Vegas was on the aviation map.

Hausler proposed a full-blown air show on Thanksgiving Day to celebrate the completion of Anderson Field. "The matter of an aviation meet in this city Thanksgiving Day was not undertaken with the expectation of any immediate profit," wrote Squires. "Mr. Robert Hausler, who is promoting the enterprise, is giving his own time and

On the afternoon of Turkey Day, three biplanes, one piloted by Hausler, set down at Anderson Field and were surrounded by most of the population of Las Vegas. But the real star of that air show was a peculiar dwarf biplane emblazoned with a skull and crossbones, and bearing the legend "Poison: Dose, One Drop."

some of his money for the work. His object is to place Las Vegas on the air map, with a view to future business. … Another plan which Mr. Hausler hopes to realize is the establishment of a flying school here."

On the afternoon of Turkey Day, three biplanes, one piloted by Hausler, set down at Anderson Field and were immediately surrounded by most of the population of Las Vegas, hurrahing and waving flags. But the real star of that air show was a peculiar dwarf biplane, emblazoned with a skull and crossbones, and bearing the legend "Poison: Dose, One Drop."

It was an experimental craft—as most planes of that time were—and was designed and owned by C.O. Prest, who had built it at Crawford Airplane Company in Venice, California. Prest was a veteran airplane builder, having designed his first craft in 1909. Poison had a wingspan of 18 feet, was 14.5 feet long, and weighed 500 pounds. Designed for short takeoffs, it could get airborne on only 100 feet of runway and climbed at a rate of 1,400 feet per minute. The aircraft had been shipped to Las Vegas via rail because Prest was unsure of the plane's ceiling, and of whether it could clear the mountains between Los Angeles and Las Vegas.

"Poison is some kid," opined Squires. "He is about the size of a good fat jitney [a small bus] but has a sassy look, all sleeked out in a new coat of red paint. Mr. Prest claims that Poison is a nice little thing to travel with, although inclined to be a little flighty and noisy."

Poison was powered by a 7-cylinder, two-stroke, 50-horsepower rotary engine. Practically all modern vehicles are powered by four-stroke engines, allowing their parts to be lubricated by a reservoir of oil, while two-stroke engines require oil to be mixed with the gasoline. But in Poison's time, two-stroke engines were used in nearly all aircraft because they were capable of a higher number of revolutions per minute than were four-stroke engines of the same size, and could therefore spin a propeller faster. All of which is related here to explain what next hap-

pened to Poison.

The crowd stood in breathless silence as Prest taxied the little plane into a headwind, then gave her full throttle. Poison roared, Prest pulled back on the stick, and the plane shot into the sky. At about 75 feet, however, the engine abruptly quit and the plane nosed down into the dirt. Amid screams and shouts, the crowd rushed toward the crash, expecting the worst.

But the drop of Poison didn't kill Prest. In fact, other than a case of the shakes, he was unharmed. As it turned out, the castor oil that had been mixed with the plane's fuel either was contaminated or had not been mixed properly. The biplane wasn't seriously damaged, but Prest decided to dismantle it and use the parts to build a monoplane.

The airshow served the very important purpose of making the Las Vegas public aware of aviation and its potential as an economic development tool. As for Hausler, he had found his aviation career. In an era when no such occupation existed, he had become an "airport expert." He went on to design airports in Victorville and Caliente, creating a chain of state-of-the-art fields between Los Angeles and Salt Lake City, certainly a factor in the later decision to establish an airmail route between those two cities.

However, try as he would, Hausler could not make a financial success of his flight school and airplane repair enterprises at Anderson Field. In 1923, an advertisement in the *Las Vegas Age* identified him as the distributing agent for Perfection Pressure Cookers. By 1924, he had left Las Vegas for good.

Hausler later was named field secretary for the Western Aero League, a position that entailed traveling around the West, exhorting various cities and towns to develop their own airports. In 1925 the *Winslow Mail* (an Arizona newspaper) published a special edition to honor him for his work in developing western aviation. The editor's introduction lauded Hausler's persistence and energy, and stated that the edition was "dedicated to Bob Hausler, who should be called Bob Hustler." ✍

Robert Griffith (1899-1978)

By the late 1930s, Griffith all but stood alone as the community's aviation expert. He spent his own money and used his political pull with U.S. Senator Pat McCarran to get an Army Air Force base here. … Griffith's plan was the launching pad for today's Clark County airport system.

While he had dreams of helping to build a city brick by brick, a civil engineer soon became a civil servant whose eye on the sky brought air service to Southern Nevada. BY ROBERT STOLDAL

Robert "Bob" Griffith was fond of saying, "I was lucky. As a boy I came to Las Vegas when the town was new; it raised me and I tried to raise it." Most think he raised it well. He gave the city airmail service, airports, and even an Air Force base.

Griffith first saw Las Vegas on May 14, 1905, when he was 6 years old. His father, E.W. Griffith, had brought his son to Southern Nevada to witness the now-famous Clark Townsite auction. It was at this auction, on May 15 and 16, that the land on which modern Las Vegas now stands was sold. E.W. Griffith purchased two of the lots.

A month later, father and son moved to Las Vegas. The boy's mother had died when he was 3. Griffith helped his father hammer tent stakes into the ground for their first Las Vegas home on the southwest corner of Second and Fremont. In 1923 he graduated with a degree in civil engineering from the University of Nevada in Reno, and that same year he married Ruth Atcheson. With a degree in one hand, and a new wife on his arm, Griffith returned to Southern Nevada.

A year after his return, a new opportunity would appear. Late in 1924, C.P. Squires, publisher of the *Las Vegas Age* newspaper, said he planned to retire as the community's postmaster. Griffith went after the job. Passing the postmaster test, he received his appointment on January 1, 1925. The Griffiths' only child, a daughter, had just been born, and the $225-a-month postmaster's salary was "big money," Ruth Griffith later recalled.

As the Griffiths celebrated the birth of their daughter and their newfound wealth, local residents were celebrating the town's 20th birthday. Las Vegas was still small, with fewer than 4,000 full-time residents. As a desert oasis, it was isolated. Neither radio nor long-distance telephone service was yet a local reality. Travel by auto was still for the adventuresome.

So it was left to the railroad to connect Southern Nevada to the outside world. But in the summer of 1925, the federal government announced plans to link Los Angeles to the national airmail route, via Salt Lake City. A new airline, Western Air Express, won the right to fly mail between

Los Angeles and Salt Lake City, with one stop— Las Vegas.

On November 10, Griffith reported to the Las Vegas Chamber of Commerce that he had received a letter from Western asking if the community could make ready an airfield. The chamber appointed Griffith to look into the matter. His first stop was Anderson Field. While several flat spots on the Southern Nevada desert were called "landing strips," Anderson Field (situated on the current site of a Sahara Hotel parking lot) was listed on most maps as the official landing field. However, by 1925 it was overgrown with brush.

When it became public that Las Vegas was in the running to become an airmail stop, ownership of Anderson Field quietly changed hands. On December 21, 1925, the Rockwell Brothers, Leon and Earl, acquired the land. The Rockwells offered to lease the land to the chamber of commerce without charge. But the chamber would have to absorb the cost of bringing the field up to Western's specifications, and pay to bring telephone, power, and water to the site. One other thing: The name of the airstrip would have to be changed from Anderson to Rockwell Field.

Griffith "borrowed" a piece of railroad track, and with the help of James Cashman and his tractor, leveled the desert landing strip. Boy Scouts cleaned up broken bottles from an old saloon that used to occupy the south end of the property.

At 10:05 on Saturday morning, April 17, 1926, Las Vegas was connected to the outside world by airmail. The flight from Los Angeles took two hours and 30 minutes. The honor of being the first to land in Las Vegas goes to pilot Maury Graham.

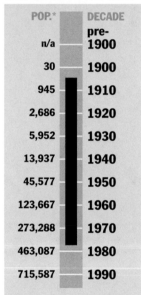

Griffith in Southern Nevada

POP.*	DECADE
n/a	pre-1900
30	1900
945	1910
2,686	1920
5,952	1930
13,937	1940
45,577	1950
123,667	1960
273,288	1970
463,087	1980
715,587	1990

■ Time spent in Southern Nev.
* - Population figures are for greater Las Vegas area (*Source: Nevada State Data Center*).

Robert B. Griffith in middle age
(UNLV Special Collections)

With a .45-caliber pistol strapped to his belt, Graham pulled back his goggles, stood up, and waved to "more than two hundred automobiles loaded with spectators." The crowd cheered, dogs barked, and Griffith loaded his first shipment of airmail letters heading east.

Once the big day had come and gone, Griffith went back to work to get the lease with the Rockwells wrapped up. It was clear to Griffith that once improvements to the land were made, the Rockwells intended to sell it. Quietly, Griffith began looking for a new landing field.

The Las Vegas Post Office Building on Fremont Street, early 1930s
(Review-Journal files)

The entire town of Las Vegas turned out on April 17, 1926, to greet the first Western Air Express. This photo was taken at Rockwell Field, near what is now the corner of Sahara Avenue and Paradise Road.
(UNLV Special Collections)

At this point a new aerial entrepreneur, Roscoe Turner, showed up with plans to establish a route between Los Angeles, Las Vegas, and Reno. Turner, an internationally known pilot, worked out a deal with local gas-station operator P.A. "Pop" Simon. Simon would provide the land and would get the rights to sell gasoline at the airport; Turner would get his field and provide the first regular air traffic. The site they selected was eight miles from the city, a spot regarded by many Las Vegans as the middle of nowhere. It is now Nellis Air Force Base. When Turner's company failed a few months later, Griffith, the chamber, and Western Air Express moved in, and a 20-year lease was negotiated.

Griffith resigned as postmaster on March 31, 1930, and focused his attention on taking care of his father, who had become seriously ill. The elder Griffith died in October 1932. By the late 1930s Bob Griffith all but stood alone as the community's aviation expert. He spent his own money and used his political pull with U.S. Senator Pat McCarran to get an Army Air Force base here.

John Cahlan, a longtime Las Vegas newspaperman and a friend of the Griffiths, remembered it this way: "It was in 1940 that Bob saw an airman in the Apache Hotel [in downtown Las Vegas]. Uniforms were not very numerous in the community at that time, and he got to talking to the sergeant, who said, 'Well, my major and I are surveying the western area for a gunnery range.' That's the first that we heard of it." Cahlan said Griffith immediately began lobbying the government to build the base in Southern Nevada.

Las Vegas was soon selected as the spot for the gunnery school. To make the plan work, the city obtained funds from the federal government to buy what was then called Western Air Express Field. In turn, the city leased the field to both the Army and Western. In March of 1941, the public

> *"I was lucky. As a boy I came to Las Vegas when the town was new; it raised me and I tried to raise it."*
> —**Robert Griffith**

side of the field was renamed McCarran Field, honoring the senator who funneled federal funds to the city.

With the Army air base in place, Griffith, now 42, headed up the chamber of commerce. In this role, he once again lobbied with McCarran for federal funds to build a municipal airport. It was clear that the Army would take over the field and that the community would soon need its own. This time, Griffith suggested that the community build an airport south of the city, where McCarran International Airport is now located.

But his vision was broader still. In June 1945, he proposed that local governments begin "acquiring land preparing for the future to develop a countywide system of airports for the use of postwar travelers." Griffith's plan was the launching pad for today's Clark County airport system.

At this point in his community career, Griffith turned his efforts to securing water for Southern Nevada's future. During World War II, Griffith and several other community leaders convinced the government to build a water pipeline from Lake Mead to the Las Vegas Valley. This pipeline would be large enough to serve both the defense contractors in Henderson and the citizens of the valley, and enabled Las Vegas to grow after the war. Griffith was appointed to the Colorado River Commission in 1957 and elected chairman in 1966. While he headed the commission, it drew up the "first plans for utilization of Nevada's share of the Lake Mead water."

Up until his death at the age of 79, Griffith continued to believe and share in the future of Las Vegas. When he died on March 23, 1978, Cahlan said, "If ever there was a man who deserved to be called 'Mr. Las Vegas,' it was Bob Griffith. He was active in every major project. Bob Griffith was a dreamer, but fortunately for the present citizens of Las Vegas, he made his dreams come true." ✍

DEATH OF A HERO BY K.J. EVANS

It had been snowing sporadically for two days when Western Air Express pilot Maury Graham set down at Las Vegas, en route to Salt Lake City, on January 11, 1930. Graham was a decorated World War I aviator and later brought the first airmail plane into Las Vegas. He was generally known as a cautious man. On the other hand, he also had a reputation among his peers as the guy who was always on time. Today, snow or no snow, he would continue his run to Salt Lake City.

Shortly after his Boeing 95 plane disappeared into the clouds, mechanics at the field heard an airplane engine overhead and thought it was Graham attempting to return to the airport. When he didn't, they concluded that he couldn't see the runway lights. As all had feared, he failed to show up in Salt Lake City, and his friends and fellow pilots began a search that would last six months.

"One of the reasons for the prolonged search," said aviation historian Gary Kissel, "was that the people who knew him well, and especially his wife, would not believe that Graham had crashed and was killed. Instead, they believed that he set his plane down safely and was either waiting out the weather so he could take off again, or that he was injured in the landing and was waiting for help."

It was a harrowing search, given the rugged terrain and deep snow. The air route followed the Union Pacific Railroad in most places, but Graham's plane wasn't found along its tracks. As the search intensified, 24 Army and Navy airplanes joined the effort, but they were all grounded by another snowstorm January 18. By the end of the month, the military planes had pulled out, and the search wound down.

But Graham's comrades, Fred Kelly and Jimmy James, refused to give up, and Western allowed them to continue their search as long as they continued their scheduled runs. The airline offered rewards ranging from $3,000 to $10,000 for Graham's recovery.

Kelly, exhausted after more than 150 hours in the cockpit, was hedge-hopping in the canyons near St. George when he scraped a wingtip on the ground and crashed. He walked away from the wreck to a highway, holding his head in his hands to support a broken neck. He was taken to a hospital by a passing motorist.

On June 24, two sheepherders finally discovered Graham's red and silver biplane in the Kanarra Mountains, 22 miles south of Cedar City, Utah. But Maury Graham wasn't with it. The plane had evidently landed, but had damaged a wingtip and the landing gear. It appeared that Graham had attempted to walk out through the 8-foot snowdrifts.

Further examination determined that the plane had five gallons of fuel in its tank, meaning that Graham had probably landed deliberately. He had removed the plane's tool kit and had attempted to remove a section of the fuselage, possibly to use as a sled, but probably realized it was too heavy. Melting snow had obliterated any track Graham may have left, so the searchers fanned out over a wide area. Three weeks after the plane's discovery, Graham's body was found about six miles from his plane, at the bottom of a sheer cliff overlooking Zion National Park.

Investigators believed Graham had sustained a head injury in the crash and had simply stumbled over the precipice. In his right hand, he had a revolver, with several empty casings, indicating he had attempted to signal for help. On his chest was his pocket knife; nearby, a half-opened can of food. Graham's body was flown from Utah to Los Angeles in a Western Air Express Fokker Tri-Motor, and he was buried in Glendale, California. ✍

THE STOWAWAY BY K.J. EVANS

Major Corliss C. Moseley, vice president in charge of operations for Western Air Express, was becoming impatient with his mechanic. Just as the major was trying to get his heavily laden DeHavilland biplane off the ground, his mechanic, seated behind him, started pounding on the back of his head. The plane had begun to pull strongly to the right, and Moseley turned around to ask the mechanic if he could diagnose the problem—and perhaps stop beating on his skull.

Finally, he turned around to face the mechanic, who gestured to the right lower wing. As Moseley watched, he saw a hand groping for a hold on the wing's outer leading edge. The hand got a grip and hauled the rest of the body onto the wing.

At the time, August 1925, Western Air Express was not yet in the passenger carrying business. But on that day, Moseley had been in town on an inspection tour, meeting with Las Vegas Postmaster Robert Griffith and making plans for the airmail service that would begin the following year.

Griffith witnessed the bizarre incident and later recalled that one of two "hobos who had been admiring the plane" had sprinted after it as it started to take off. The hobo then grasped the under wing guard, a loop of metal on the underside of the wing that prevented the plane from touching a wingtip to the ground, much as a motorcycle crash bar protects more important bike parts.

Meanwhile, up in the sky, Moseley had coaxed the stowaway, a 16-year-old boy, off the wing and up against the fuselage. But the lad was paralyzed with fear and could not be persuaded into the cockpit. Moseley slowed the plane as much as he safely could, but 90-mph winds blasted the boy, who crouched and tried to shield himself. The wind, however, prevailed, and by the time Moseley reached Los Angeles, the boy had been stripped of every stitch of his clothing except his cuffs and collar.

The next day, the *Las Vegas Evening Review*, always looking for superlatives that could be applied to Las Vegas, crowed: "This little ol' burg can honestly announce to the whole world that it has the honor of having entertained the most modern and up-to-date hobo on the face of the universe."

As for the stowaway, he was never named, but was reportedly given a train ticket back to Las Vegas. And, for the record, Western's first "official" passenger was A.B. DeNault, vice president of the Piggly Wiggly grocery store chain. ✍

MAUDE FRAZIER

(1881–1963)

"I was cast in the wrong mold to fit comfortably as a teacher of that period. I was not able to understand why a teacher should not enjoy a ball game, skate on the pond in the winter, and swim there in the summer. Why couldn't she have beaux just as the other girls did, wear dresses of gypsy red if they looked well on her, and dress her hair in the prevailing pompadour style?"

—Maude Frazier

A woman who was unimpressed with what others thought she should and should not do made a life teaching Southern Nevada's children to think for themselves. BY A.D. HOPKINS

Maude Frazier was a lady to her toenails, but she wouldn't run from a fight, and she had no problem calling a spade a doggone shovel. She spent a long life making liars of those who said some job or another was no calling for a woman.

Arriving in 1921 in the whistle-stop town of Las Vegas, she stayed to build a good school system and even a university. She served repeatedly in the Nevada Assembly and was the first woman to serve as lieutenant governor. "I was well aware that when a woman takes over work done by a man, she has to do it better, has more of it to do, and usually for less pay," Frazier once wrote. She was not happy about any of those conditions, but accepted them as realities. And if today's rules are more fair, Frazier gets some of the credit.

People say that in her prime she was nearly 6 feet tall and straight as a teacher's ruler. She dressed in lace collars and wire-rimmed glasses, pursed her lips, and sucked her teeth. But the schoolmarmish appearance belied the spirited personality within.

Frazier was born in 1881 and reared on a farm in Sauk County, Wisconsin. Her family pressed her to become a teacher, as others in the family had done. But she questioned the choice in her unpublished memoirs. "It is quite possible that it was never intended by the good Lord that I should

be a schoolteacher," she wrote. "At least not so soon after the turn of the Twentieth Century. ... Early in the 1900s, women teachers suffered most of the restrictions of nuns, with none of the advantages they enjoyed. The members of the school board not only hired a teacher to teach, they made the rules for her private life and worked overtime enforcing them."

She added, "I was cast in the wrong mold to fit comfortably as a teacher of that period. I was not able to understand why a teacher should not enjoy a ball game, skate on the pond in the winter, and swim there in the summer. Why couldn't she have beaux just as the other girls did, wear dresses of gypsy red if they looked well on her, and dress her hair in the prevailing pompadour style?"

Even though her parents wanted her to teach, they did not believe in educating women beyond high school. It was still possible to get a teaching credential by passing an examination, so Frazier did, starting her career in the mining and timber camps of the region.

"Memories of my early mistakes because of lack of training haunt me to this day," she wrote, "but these errors which torment me yet were not the errors so evident to the school board. The board criticized me because I wore a dress with too many ruffles. They called them flounces. I rode a bicycle too, something which no nice girl would think of doing. Their objection to such a means of

getting about always appeared incongruous to me, since the board members expect this same dignified teacher to perform all the undignified tasks of janitor work."

Frazier decided that if she was going to be a teacher, she was going to be a good one. On a salary of $22 a month, she saved what she could and augmented it by working in the summer as a

Maude Frazier
(UNLV Special Collections)

Frazier in Southern Nevada

POP.*	DECADE
n/a	pre-1900
30	1900
945	1910
2,686	1920
5,952	1930
13,937	1940
45,577	1950
123,667	1960
273,288	1970
463,087	1980
715,587	1990

■ Time spent in Southern Nev.
* - Population figures are for greater Las Vegas area (*Source: Nevada State Data Center*).

storekeeper and seamstress, until she had enough money to start two years at a teachers college. She worked her way through, on finances so thin that she owned but one winter skirt. "There were plenty of girls better dressed at graduation, but all the diplomas were the same size," she wrote later.

But her diploma won no added respect from the region's school boards. The next time she and her associates were asked to sign contracts, they found that something new had been added: "We must promise not to dance. Neither were we to play cards. This was to apply, not only in the town where we were teaching, but everywhere else. Of course as a group, we were scarcely what could be considered riotous livers, but as soon as we read these restrictions, our comments could have burned holes in asbestos."

Frazier refused to sign. Having met mining engineers who were enthusiastic about the emerging West, in 1906 she took a job as a teaching principal in Genoa, Nevada. The pride she must have felt in being hired was soon taken down a peg, when the superintendent explained that the vacancy she had filled was created after a big fight on the school board. "Most of the board members blamed the principal, who was from a nearby town. … One member had moved that they elect their next principal from as far away as possible. So that was it," she wrote. "Distance rather than qualifications had gotten me this position. I might have been the best teacher in the world, or the worst."

But out here, a teacher's life was her own. The energetic Frazier thrived on hard work and freedom. In Nevada, she learned to ride with cowboys and sometimes rode 12 miles to dance Virginia reels. Over the next 15 years, her résumé would read like the itinerary of a politician running for governor. She taught at Lovelock, even then a stable agricultural community. Seven

> *"A good school is a thing of the mind and spirit, and not a thing of gadgets."*
> —Maude Frazier

Troughs, a new mining camp, hired her to start a new school in a tent, and moved a brothel to make way for a schoolhouse. There were jobs in Beatty, Goldfield, and Sparks.

Conditions varied wildly. Goldfield, prosperous in those days, could afford a fine modern school and a piano for every classroom. At Genoa, not even books were furnished, so students brought what they could find. At Seven Troughs, coal had to be hauled so far that it cost $36 a ton, more than twice the price that was charged in cities served by railroads, so students and teachers wore multiple coats and fur-lined boots, and on windy days, they wrapped themselves in blankets. So roughly constructed was the new building that every pencil dropped on the floor rolled through the cracks. When the supply ran low, a boy would crawl under the tent and retrieve them.

Yet the school was blessed with miners' children, who knew what it was to be uneducated, and feared it: "There was never a complaint about too much homework. There was no playing hooky." The shack schoolhouse had what Frazier called "the two essentials important to any good school—pupils who wanted to learn, and a teacher who wanted to teach." She wrote in her memoirs, "A good school is a thing of the mind and spirit, and not a thing of gadgets."

In 1921 she applied for a position as deputy superintendent in the State Department of Education. The job involved supervising all public schools in Clark, Lincoln, Esmeralda, and Nye counties. "Four men had given up on that particular territory, saying nobody on earth could get over that desert country," she wrote. No roads. Wild coyotes. Long stretches without water. She was warned of hostile denizens who would refuse her food or a place to sleep.

Frazier bought a used Dodge roadster she named Teddy "because he was such a rough rider," she wrote. "Teddy and I became a team as we covered the trail. Garage men were our friends. They drew crude maps on any scrap of material available … made lists of supplies I must carry. I would need a shovel, an ax, tow ropes, two jacks, good tire pump, canteens of water, gas, and oil. Neither must I ever be without an abundance of canned goods, which in turn necessitated a can opener." She also carried two flashlights, plenty of magazines, and a deck of cards.

Her headquarters were in Las Vegas, then a town of 2,500, and the *Las Vegas Age* hailed Frazier as the first person to drive the 180 miles to Goldfield in a single day. At the time, the best route to Goldfield and Tonopah was along the abandoned bed of the Las Vegas and Tonopah Railroad, which the federal government had forced to close dur-

Maude Frazier encouraged and attended ceremonies such as this flag raising at Vegas Heights Elementary School in 1946. The flag was donated in honor of a World War II casualty. The boy at center is Dale J. Douglas, soloist singing "The Star Spangled Banner." The widow of the serviceman, not further identified, stands at right in the dark dress, next to Frazier in the checkered dress.
(UNLV Special Collections)

Las Vegas High School faculty, 1931–32. Maude Frazier, the principal, is the woman wearing glasses in the row next to the back.
(UNLV Special Collections)

ing World War I as a superfluous route. "The rails had been removed because Uncle Sam wanted the steel," Frazier wrote. "Most of the ties had been taken out and used by desert dwellers in building their houses." This made for a bumpy road indeed, and at some points autos had to drive in the ditch alongside the roadbed. "This ditch was filled with fine silt, which, at times, caused visibility to be zero. Often I had to stop and let the dust settle before I could see ahead of me at all."

In 1927 Frazier took a job as superintendent of the Las Vegas Union School District, consisting of two local elementary schools and the high school. (She was also principal of the high school.) This put her in charge during the population boom brought about by the construction of Hoover Dam.

She found the local high school so old and unsuitably built that she feared it would explode in flames, burning students alive. Fire did destroy the building, but not during school hours, so nobody was seriously hurt. Frazier and others worked all night salvaging desks and other equipment, and convened school the next day in temporary classrooms all over town. Fortunately, Frazier had already persuaded the public to pass a $350,000 bond issue to build Las Vegas High School (now Las Vegas Academy), a school so architecturally memorable that it is now listed on the National Register of Historic Places. She was criticized for building "rooms which will never be used."

Many wondered if the busy and stern Frazier ever had time for romance. Eva Adams, a Las Vegas teacher who eventually became director of the U.S. Mint, recalled in an oral history that Frazier indeed did. "There was a man who had a ranch outside of Beatty, and poor Miss Frazier had great struggles about whether or not to marry this farmer," said Adams. "And when she found out that he, and I'm quoting, 'hadn't the gumption to run a pipe from the well into the house,' she decided that she wasn't going to marry him."

Frazier retired from the school district in 1946, but couldn't bring herself to take it easy. She ran for the Nevada Assembly in 1948, lost, then won in 1950. She served in the Legislature for 12 years, and Harley E. Harmon, who began his long career in public life about the same time, remembers her as an effective legislator. Legislation can be passed in Nevada by horsetrading, gladhanding, and a variety of other methods. "Her method was to do her homework," said Harmon. "She knew to the penny how much money was available, knew by heart how many students would be affected by a bill."

Her most popular issue was getting a college of some sort in Southern Nevada. "Getting the college was hard, because Washoe County outnumbered us in the Legislature," said Harmon. Washoe, home of the University of Nevada, foresaw that a college in Southern Nevada would compete for funds, students, prestige, and the loyalty of Nevadans.

In 1955 Frazier persuaded legislators to appropriate $200,000 for a Southern Nevada campus, but they attached a big, fat string. The money would be forthcoming only if Las Vegas raised $100,000 from private sources. R. Guild Gray, the superintendent of schools at that time, chaired the fund-raising effort, with the help of Frazier and Archie Grant. They kicked off the campaign on May 24, 1955, with a one-hour telecast featuring Strip entertainers, as well as civic leaders and educators. They exceeded the goal by $35,000, and in April 1956, Frazier dug out the first spadeful of soil for what would become a junior college and, eventually, UNLV.

During her last term in the Legislature, Frazier fell and broke her hip while touring Hyde Park Junior High School. The accident wouldn't stop Maude Frazier. That same year, when Lieutenant Governor Rex Bell died suddenly in office, Governor Grant Sawyer appointed Frazier as Bell's replacement. She was the first woman to hold the office.

Brent Adams, a Washoe County district judge who grew up in Las Vegas, knew her in those days. "She was up in the Legislature, coming back to testify on an education bill, and Floyd Lamb opposed it," Adams recalled. "She was hobbling out on crutches and Floyd spoke to her. He said, 'Sometimes you have to act like a politician.' She just whirled around on those crutches, glared at him, and snapped, 'I didn't expect you to act like a politician; I expected you to act like a senator!'"

Later, Frazier was confined for a time to a wheelchair, and Adams visited her home. "She was frying chicken in her kitchen," he said. "She had this bowl of flour set on the floor. She would drop each piece of chicken into the flour, pick it out, and then would throw it all the way across the room and see if she could hit the frying pan."

Interviewed by a local newspaper in April 1963, she asked the photographer to let her pose without crutches and asked the reporter not to mention them. "They're not typical of me, and I don't intend to wear them forever," she said.

Six weeks later, she died in her sleep. She never liked long speeches, and the Reverend Walter Hanne, presiding over her funeral at First Presbyterian Church, kept the service to 15 minutes. Every newspaper in Nevada wrote a tribute, but if Maude Frazier can be summed up in words, let them be her own:

"Our schools tend too much to uniformity. We turn out people who know the same things, do the same things, think the same way. Yet it has been the nonconformists, the people who dared to be different … who have contributed most to the world—the Edisons, the Wrights, the Marconis. Instead of trying to make people to fit into a certain mold, we should encourage them to furnish their own mold." ✑

HARLEY A. HARMON

(1882–1947)

As district attorney for a county just coming into its own, a self-taught lawyer set a high standard for law enforcement amid an influx of lawlessness BY A.D. HOPKINS

It was a matter of money, not honor, said Harley A. Harmon. And a man who took a life for that reason should breathe the cyanide gas in Nevada's state prison. No life sentences, no long years at hard labor, no breaks.

Men and women oozed sweat in the undercooled Clark County Courthouse of September 1931, while Harmon and attorney Louis Cohen battled for the life of John Hall. Hall and his wife, Eva, and the victim, Jack O'Brien, were all newcomers. They were part of the flood of boomers and outlaws who washed over Las Vegas as construction began on Hoover Dam. O'Brien stole money from Hall; Hall claimed he also tried to assault Eva sexually. He confronted O'Brien as he tried to drive away, saying, "I want to talk to you about that money." O'Brien turned and tried to strike Hall, and Hall shot him.

"People we used to call friends are submerged beneath the new arrivals flocking into our fold," Harmon told the jury. "We welcome these people into our arms and our hearts, and will work with them and mingle with them. But let them leave their guns behind; we want no murderers here!"

The jurors deliberated late, slept on it, reconvened at 8 a.m., and a short time later announced a verdict. Foreman Frank Williams handed the verdict to Judge William Orr, who handed it to the clerk. She stood and her voice trembled as she

read, "We the jury … find the defendant John Hall guilty of murder in the first degree and sentence him to death."

The dapper district attorney had set the market price for murder. Rackets were a growth industry in 1931, and guns were tools of the trade, but Las Vegas would honor no trade discounts on human lives. Harmon and his assistant dis-

trict attorney, Roger Foley, tried five murder cases that year. Four killers were sentenced to the gas chamber, and the fifth survived with a life sentence.

Summing up Harmon's life years later, the *Review-Journal* wrote that he was "credited with stemming the rising tide of lawlessness which swept the area with the start of Boulder Dam construction." Harmon was a self-taught country lawyer and first ran for office by stumping the county in a buckboard; his son, as a county commissioner, would build an airport for jet airliners.

Born in Kansas in 1882, Harmon himself was the son of a self-taught lawyer but ambled far from those footsteps. He worked as an assistant circulation manager for a Los Angeles newspaper, then as a railroad fireman, then as an engineer. He came to Las Vegas in 1905 as a crewman on the new San Pedro, Los Angeles, and Salt Lake Railroad, and was stationed here in 1908. In 1909, the *Las Vegas Age* carried a story under the headline "Frightful Explosion."

"On Sunday morning last, at 5:15, a train of 31 cars of oranges, with two engines ahead and one pushing, was coming up the hill from Kelso to Cima, engine No. 3670 in the lead. Without an instant's warning, the crown sheet of No. 3670 dropped—a roar and it was all over. [The crown sheet is part of the firebox under a steam boiler, a fact that didn't require explaining to the readers of 1908.] Harley Harmon, engineer of the wrecked

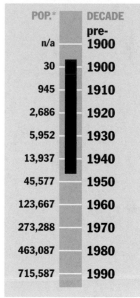

Harmon in Southern Nevada

POP.*	DECADE
n/a	pre-1900
30	1900
945	1910
2,686	1920
5,952	1930
13,937	1940
45,577	1950
123,667	1960
273,288	1970
463,087	1980
715,587	1990

■ Time spent in Southern Nev.
* - Population figures are for greater Las Vegas area (*Source: Nevada State Data Center*).

Harley A. Harmon in the early 1920s with his two sons, Harley E. Harmon (left) and Charles E. Harmon
(UNLV Special Collections)

engine, and G.W. Hogue, fireman, had their first knowledge of the explosion when they regained consciousness about 40 feet from the track, where they had been hurled from the cab. They were uninjured except for some slight burns from the escaping steam."

Harmon found a telephone and notified his superiors. He related the damage but assured the brass that he and all hands had miraculously escaped alive. The exact words of the boss have been lost to history, but can be paraphrased: "You're fired, Harmon!"

"The hell I am," responded Harmon. "I quit 15 minutes ago."

Though he was an engineer without an engine, Harmon had political talents. When a convention deadlocked over whether to split Lincoln County and create a new county, it was Harmon who realized that the wheels of government sometimes needed the proper lubricants. He asked his wealthy friend, Ed Clark, to procure a case of Yellowstone whiskey, which Harmon applied at the sticking spots. The rest was history and hangovers.

An early County Commission meeting. From left are Clerk Harley A. Harmon, C.C. Ronnow, George Fayle, an unidentified man, Joseph Ira Earl, and A.S. Henderson.
(UNLV Special Collections)

Thus did Harmon land on his feet in July 1909 as clerk of newly created Clark County. When Las Vegas incorporated in 1911, Harmon got the city clerk's job as well, at a salary of $25 a month. That September he married a city commissioner's daughter, Leona McGovern. He was nearly 30 by then but looked much younger, and people started calling him, affectionately, "The County Kid." Leona, shy but poised and beautiful, was nearly as popular as her husband. They had two sons: Charles, born in 1913, and Harley Emmett Harmon, born in 1918. Charles died of a ruptured appendix while still in his teens. The younger son would become well-known as Harley E. Harmon, legislator, insurance agent, banker, and pivotal player on the Clark County Commission.

Interviewed in September 1998, Harley E. Harmon explained that his father's duties as county clerk drew him into law. "He used to love to go into the courtroom and watch the attorneys," said Harley E. Meanwhile, he added, a former Stanford law professor, forced by tuberculosis to seek a desert climate, "took a liking to my dad and thought he should study the law." Studying in his spare time, Harley A. was admitted to the bar in 1919. Only two years later, he ran for district attorney and won the post.

Whatever happiness victory might have brought, however, was smothered in sorrow. Leona caught strep throat. Antibiotics hadn't been discovered yet, and she battled the illness a month before dying in October 1921 at the age of 29. Her boys would be left to the care of their widowed father and their grandparents, until the elder Harmon remarried in 1924, to Veronica Wengert. The second Mrs. Harmon lived to the age of 96.

One of Harley E.'s earliest memories is of seeing a burned-out Ku Klux Klan cross on Fremont Street, near his grandmother's house. He was not yet 4 years old in 1922, when his father launched an investigation of the local klavern. A membership list of the local organization turned up. ... District Attorney Harmon got the list and, apparently, let the locals know he had it. Craig F. Swallow, who gathered a history of Nevada's Klans as a master's thesis at UNLV, wrote, "Though the membership roster was not publicly disclosed, the loss of anonymity was a deterrent to Ku Klux Klan activity. The Las Vegas Klavern suspended activity and soon ceased to exist."

One of Harley E.'s earliest memories is of seeing a burned-out Ku Klux Klan cross on Fremont Street. He was not yet 4 years old in 1922, when his father launched an investigation of the local klavern. A membership list of the local organization had turned up when Los Angeles police raided the Klan's Pacific Domain headquarters. District Attorney Harmon got the list and, apparently, let the locals know he had it. Craig F. Swallow, who gathered a history of Nevada's Klans as a master's thesis at UNLV, wrote, "Though the membership roster was not publicly disclosed, the loss of anonymity was a deterrent to Ku Klux Klan activity. The Las Vegas Klavern suspended activity and soon ceased to exist."

Harmon's duties didn't require him to enforce Prohibition, as it was a federal law rather than a state one. He didn't follow it, either. Once he was traveling in the northern end of the state with C.P. "Pop" Squires, the prissy-looking publisher of the *Las Vegas Age,* and the two men went into a hotel bar. "They had green rivers, sarsaparilla, and like that to drink," related Harley E. "My father gave the password so they could go in back and have a real drink." When the bartender ignored him, the D.A. asked why. "The bartender says, 'That guy looks like a minister, and we're not going to let you in as long as you got that minister with you.' My father said, 'He's not a minister. He's a son-of-a-bitching Republican!'"

Harley A. Harmon was a yellow-dog Democrat and proud of it. He ran twice for governor, but was unable to overcome favorite-son candidates from Northern Nevada, which then had most of the voters. He served four years on the Public Service Commission, became interested in the rapidly changing field of transportation law, and served as attorney, lobbyist, and organizer for the Nevada Trucking Association.

In 1947, the old warrior was called to speak at a gathering of the Young Democrats in Reno. The *Review-Journal* reported: "As he warmed up to his subject, urging his listeners to carry forward the party banner in 1948, many seemed to sense here was an outstanding oratorical appeal. Old-timers nudged each other and whispered it was the best speech of a long career. ... As he reached the climax of his address, the speaker declared dramatically, 'I'd give my last breath for the Democratic Party!'" Harley A. Harmon sat down—and slumped to the floor with a fatal heart attack.

Meanwhile, Harley E. had learned the political ropes. When he decided to go to law school in Washington, D.C., Senator Berkeley Bunker got him a job operating the elevator in the Senate Office Building. At the time, Harley E. disliked Nevada's senior senator, Patrick McCarran. His father had helped McCarran get elected and had expected to be named U.S. attorney for Nevada, but McCarran appointed somebody else.

Harley E. took the only revenge he could. "Any time I opened the door and saw McCarran, I would close it and go either down or up," he said. "One Saturday morning ... he put his foot in the door and said, 'Senate's not in session today. Drive this thing up to the top floor and shut it off, because you and I are going to have a talk.'" McCarran did most of the talking, explaining that the elder Harmon's letter requesting appointment had been intentionally sidetracked by a secretary who was friendly to another attorney who

wanted, and got, the federal appointment. Eventually, McCarran become a mentor for the younger Harmon.

In World War II, Harley E. Harmon served in the U.S. Navy gun crews of merchant ships running military supplies through hostile waters. He lost interest in law school, returned to Las Vegas in 1946, and married Cleo Katsaros in 1947. Their sons, Harley L. and Jeff, would eventually take over the Harmon business interests.

In 1947, Harley E. Harmon served his first and only term in the Legislature. He started an insurance agency in Clark County, got elected to the Clark County Commission in 1950, and discovered that he who won a commission seat quickly became a successful insurance agent. "I make no bones about it," he said. "Business came to you. For instance, I wrote the Dunes Hotel exclusively. I wrote the original Stardust. I'm not kidding myself. I was a county commissioner!"

But not having to worry about making money, in those tolerant times, gave commissioners leisure to address the pressing problems of their offices. "We revamped the road department and started building roads, like Nellis Boulevard," said Harmon. "At the time, all those enlisted men and officers from Nellis Air Force Base, in order to get into town, had to come through North Las Vegas and Las Vegas, and North Las Vegas was ticketing them." A Nellis brass hat ran into Harmon at a Lions' Club meeting in Henderson and asked him to build a road connecting Henderson, where many Air Force personnel lived, to the base. The road became an important artery, but its original purpose was to bypass a speed trap.

Harmon was instrumental in getting sewer service into Paradise Valley, which was a larger

> *"[Harmon was] credited with stemming the rising tide of lawlessness which swept the area with the start of Boulder Dam construction."*
> —Review-Journal
> **Years later**

accomplishment than it sounds in retrospect, with long-term consequences. "We had water in Paradise Valley but were at the beck and call of the city of Las Vegas as far as sewerage was concerned," he said. "C.D. Baker was mayor and wanted to annex. I said I had no objection to annexation, 'but how long's it gonna take you to get sewerage out to those hotels?'

"He said, 'Well, we might get around to it in three or four, five years.' I said, 'Well, that's not right. You're going to increase our taxes; you ought to be able to do better than that.' One day I was sitting in my office and [a] guy walked in and introduced himself. Said, 'I hear that you wanta build an outhouse.'" Actually, Harmon said, the guy put it less delicately, but Harmon cleaned up the quote. The caller was Walt Gibbs. "All I want is, I'll sell the bonds and take my profit from the sale," said Gibbs.

The county providing urban services removed any incentive Strip powers might have had to consent to city annexation. That froze the city limit at Sahara Avenue, where it remains to this day.

Harmon served 12 years on the commission and helped build the airport that brings most tourists to Las Vegas. Like his father before him, Harley E. was offered more than one chance to run for governor; unlike his father, he never ran. He elected instead to concentrate on business as one of the founders of Frontier Fidelity. Later he put together a group of local investors to buy Nevada State Bank, and talked Parry Thomas of Bank of Las Vegas into financing the deal.

Under Harmon's leadership, the bank grew from assets of $7 million in the early '60s to some $105 million by the time he sold out in 1976. Its strength lay in being locally owned and therefore understanding local issues and opportunities. ∅

Harley E. Harmon, Harley A.'s son, in 1998 at age 79. He led the County Commission in the 1950s and '60s.
(Steve Andrascik/Review-Journal)

A.E. "AL" CAHLAN (1899–1968)

The valley's political and civic future was shaped in part by two brothers, one of whom built the *Review-Journal* into the state's largest newspaper. BY A.D. HOPKINS

Although A.E. "Al" Cahlan came to Las Vegas as a schoolteacher, he metamorphosed into a newspaper editor, and within a few years dominated news media in Southern Nevada. Between 1926 and 1960, he transformed a 300-circulation weekly into a daily boasting 27,000 subscribers, the largest in the state. The newspaper he built, now known as the *Las Vegas Review-Journal,* retained first position, and by 1999 had a daily circulation of 151,162 and 213,619 on Sunday.

Cahlan became a political kingmaker and a civic progressive, using his newspaper and his influence to develop the community. And the editor-reporter team he hired—his brother, John F. Cahlan, and John's eventual wife, Florence Lee Jones Cahlan—were the most important scribes of their time in recording and preserving Southern Nevada's history.

Al Cahlan was born in 1899 and John in 1902 in Reno. Both attended the University of Nevada, where Al was one of three students who revived the school's sputtering student newspaper, *Sagebrush.* Both studied electrical engineering, but neither worked in the field. Maude Frazier, principal of Las Vegas High School, captured Al as a math and science teacher. But he worked summers with the Nevada Highway Department, which took him to Elko. There, the publisher of the *Elko Free Press* found out that he had worked on a college newspaper and hired him on the spot.

John Cahlan also stumbled into journalism, in 1919, as a play-by-play announcer at football games: "I'd run or walk up and down the side-lines. Through a megaphone I would tell the audience who carried the ball and how much yardage he made. When somebody was knocked out, I'd tell them who that was. Through that beginning came the regular announcing systems that they've got in the big stadiums now. I've never been able to find anybody else who would go back that far as an announcer."

Before home radios became common, many newspapers would "announce" the latest news bulletins received by telegraph, concerning events such as title fights and elections, to crowds gathered on the streets in front of their offices. Because John had developed a good announcing voice working a crowd with a megaphone, Reno's *Nevada State Journal* hired him to announce the World Series, then kept him on as sports editor.

In 1926 Frank Garside, a publisher who had operated newspapers in Tonopah and other boom towns, saw a similar opportunity in news that a huge dam would be built near Las Vegas. He bought the *Clark County Review,* a struggling Las Vegas weekly, and brought in Al Cahlan to run it. Al Cahlan became his partner.

John Cahlan, who went to work for his brother and Garside in 1929, recalled, "We had the smallest office of a newspaper that I've ever seen. We had very few tools to work with. They gave me a four-legged table that had no drawers in it, no storage space or anything. They did put a typewriter on the desk … but we had no direct connection with any news service."

John talked Al into subscribing to a syndicate for editorial cartoons and some features; about the time the paper went daily in 1929, a teletype wire service was added. "I was a very avid sports man, and I tried to make the sports stuff as good as that they could find anywhere," John recalled. "Al would write the editorials, and he was the business manager, and he would sell ads." In January 1930, Al started writing "From Where I Sit," a column that appeared for nearly 40 years.

One of the frustrations of living in Nevada was several days of uncertainty as to who had really won elections. Returns were so slow from some Southern Nevada precincts that, John Cahlan wrote, "There were times when a United States senatorial candidate had to wait for nearly a week before he could be certain that he could pack his bags and start the long journey back to Washing-

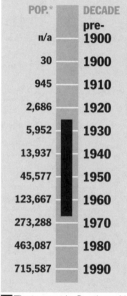

Cahlan in Southern Nevada

POP.*		DECADE
n/a		pre-1900
30		1900
945		1910
2,686		1920
5,952		1930
13,937		1940
45,577		1950
123,667		1960
273,288		1970
463,087		1980
715,587		1990

■ Time spent in Southern Nev.
* - Population figures are for greater Las Vegas area (*Source: Nevada State Data Center*).

A.E. Cahlan built his 300-circulation weekly into the state's largest daily. He also turned himself into a political kingmaker.
(Review-Journal files)

ton, D.C." Rural precincts didn't always bother to count votes the same day they were cast.

Al Cahlan thought this was no way to run a state. About 1928 he convinced the county commissioners to establish a policy that election officials were to stay at their posts on election eve until all votes were counted. "The commissioners were not happy to accept this program because the county coffers were not overflowing," wrote John Cahlan. "Hiring the extra personnel this required might mean that the road to Logandale would not be fixed." But the commissioners complied, grudgingly.

Al Cahlan then recruited a citizen in every precinct and got him to swear a blood oath that he would get the results to the newspaper that very night. Runners got to the nearest phone by bicycles, autos, pedestrian enterprise, even horseback. Precinct returns were tallied in the newsroom by the entire staff of four or five, including advertising staff. Sometimes politicians themselves helped. Every hour a partial count would be posted on a blackboard outside the building, where political junkies gathered. Meanwhile, inside, John Cahlan would use the results to put out an extra edition.

In their low-budget way, the Cahlan team succeeded with surprising speed. Within five months of taking over the *Review* on May 1, 1926, they added another edition each week. In 1927 the paper became a tri-weekly, and then became a daily in 1928. The *Las Vegas Age,* run by C.P. "Pop" Squires and the most important paper until that time, was quickly surpassed. In 1929 Cahlan and Garside bought out the *Las Vegas Journal,* published by former Governor James G. Scrugham.

Michael Green, a history teacher at the Community College of Southern Nevada, says the Cahlan-Garside team overwhelmed Scrugham and Squires with competence. In a 1988 article for the *Nevada Historical Society Journal,* Green also asserted, "The *Las Vegas Evening Review-Journal* prospered because it was staunchly Democratic in a predominately Democratic city." And in the 1930s, when both the Nevada congressional delegation and the national administration became overwhelmingly Democratic, the paper's owners were wired "into the national administration better." Being reared in Reno, when it was still the seat of power in Nevada, gave the Cahlans contacts in state government. And Garside knew rural Nevada like his back yard.

"Pop Squires knew the ruling elite of Las Vegas just as well as they did," explained Green. "But his competitors were better connected to the world beyond Las Vegas." Squires slanted his news coverage to favor Republicans and discredit Democrats. The Cahlans were better at keeping opinions and facts separate, and in any case, Al was soon part of the power elite.

John Cahlan explained: "The power structure of Las Vegas in the '30s was headed by Ed W. Clark. Ed Clark was to Las Vegas what George Wingfield was to Reno. He controlled most of the economy of the community through his banking facilities. … Ed usually chose who he wanted as members of the city commission and county commission and those powerful bodies. … When Al came down here to run the newspaper, he became very close to Ed Clark; Al was his lieutenant, I would say. Al controlled the American Legion because he was state commander and quite active in the post here. Between the two of them, they pretty well controlled the politics of the community."

Clark was Democratic national committeeman

Ed Clark was Democratic national committeeman for Nevada. "At the time of Ed's death, Al became national committeeman and followed more or less Ed's ideas. I think you can say that Ed Clark and Al Cahlan were the two most powerful people in the 1930s and early '40s," said John Cahlan.

for Nevada. "At the time of Ed's death, Al became national committeeman and followed more or less Ed's ideas," said John Cahlan. "I think you can say that Ed Clark and Al Cahlan were the two most powerful people in the 1930s and early '40s."

Al Cahlan at various times represented Clark County in the Nevada Assembly, served on the Las Vegas Planning Commission and chaired it, served on the Colorado River Commission, and helped engineer the deal by which the war industries in Henderson would be bought from the federal government and kept open in private hands.

The Cahlans were community boosters and proud of it. They would point out community shortcomings, but their main job, they believed, was to point out the silver opportunity lining every civic cloud, and to back any idea that would turn that opportunity into gold.

John Cahlan (kneeling) helped organize the first Helldorado in 1935 and shared a light moment with the costumed gentry.
(Review-Journal files)

The late Ed Oncken, himself a longtime Las Vegas journalist, wrote about one such instance: "In 1929 Las Vegas experienced its first boom in history, when Congress passed the Boulder Dam bill. The immediate influx of population and new business had neglected to find out that money to carry out the great project had not yet been appropriated. For six months the *Review* kept the town alive by propaganda, seizing any type of optimistic news to cheer up hard-pressed merchants, who were doing no business."

Later, as the dam neared completion, the Depression seemed determined to go on forever. The Cahlans got behind the Helldorado celebration, which was started in 1935 to develop Las Vegas tourism and replace the business that left with the construction crews.

As World War II loomed on the horizon, the Army established an airfield here to train aerial machine gunners. But because not all of Congress believed war was inevitable, the effort was badly underfunded. The base didn't even have enough money to buy guns. Training for each gunner, explained John Cahlan, "started with BB guns, then .22s, then shotguns, and finally .50-caliber machine guns." Because the first three types of weapons were commonly owned by civilians, the *Review-Journal* started a successful drive to get locals to donate them.

About that same time, Al Cahlan suffered a devastating blow to his political aspirations. Key Pittman, who represented Nevada in the Senate, died in office a few days after his re-election in 1940. It fell to Governor E.P. "Ted" Carville to appoint a successor. Al Cahlan had helped Carville get elected governor in 1938, and many say that Carville promised to appoint Cahlan as Pittman's successor. Instead,

In 1987, the year he died, John Cahlan visited an exhibit of pioneer printing equipment at the Clark County Heritage Museum, and found much that was still in use during his newspaper career, which stretched from the late 1920s to the 1960s.
(Review-Journal files)

Carville appointed Berkeley Bunker, who had managed his campaign in Southern Nevada.

It cost Al Cahlan political power in a curious way. He walked away from it. Technically, he held the same leadership roles he had held before; he would even achieve higher ones. But John Cahlan said, "He became disinterested, let's say. He wasn't as avid a Democrat as he was prior to that time. I can see why, because the Democratic party kicked him in the pants, and that was it."

Al considered himself a newsman first, though. Don Digilio, who came to work at the *Review-Journal* in 1960 and eventually became editor, said, "Al actually wore a green eyeshade around the office. He wore suspenders, and garters around his shirtsleeves. This was in 1960, and I never knew anybody else in the news business who was still doing that."

Meanwhile, Al Cahlan and Garside had developed diverging views about the future of Las Vegas and its newspaper. "Al needed a new press," explained John Cahlan. "An eight-page press meant that we had to insert every time they had anything over eight pages, and that was costly. But Garside thought the town would blow away because Hoover Dam was already built. ... He had been in so many communities where it was a boom and bust, and he thought Las Vegas was the same thing." He absolutely refused to invest the money for a new press.

According to Al Cahlan's son, Forest Cahlan, an attorney who lives in Pahrump, there was also a difference of opinion on how to deal with unions at the *Review-Journal*. "Garside said we keep the unions; Dad said that if we keep the unions, and give them what they want, we go under. The paper was making money, but not nearly enough to give the unions all the luxuries they expected."

Garside wouldn't sell his interest to Al Cahlan, but did agree to sell to a third party if

> *"I don't expect to be the* New York Times. *I want to be what Al Cahlan was."*
> —Bob Brown
> Publisher of the *Valley Times*, a short-lived third Las Vegas daily

Cahlan found one. Cahlan found Don Reynolds, a self-made newspaper tycoon, who bought Garside's controlling interest in 1949 and hired Cahlan to run the paper as general manager. However, Cahlan agreed to sell his stock to Reynolds at any time Reynolds chose. The arrangement worked for more than a decade, during which the *Review-Journal* prospered. But in December 1960, with the circulation at approximately 27,000, Cahlan resigned and Reynolds bought out his stock.

Al Cahlan turned his considerable energies to civic life and politics, ran unsuccessfully for the county commission, and was associated with a printing company. He resumed writing his column, which was published by the *Review-Journal's* rival, the *Las Vegas Sun*. In 1968 he suffered a stroke and died three weeks later, at age 69, in Southern Nevada Memorial Hospital.

John Cahlan stayed at the *Review-Journal* briefly as editor, long enough for Reynolds to find his replacement in Robert L. Brown, a former wire-service reporter. John Cahlan built another career as an executive of the Southern Nevada Industrial Foundation and a lobbyist for the Las Vegas Chamber of Commerce. He collaborated on a book, *Water: A History of Las Vegas*, with his wife and former star reporter, Florence Lee Jones Cahlan. John Cahlan died in 1987 at the age of 85.

Nearly 13 years after replacing John Cahlan as editor, Brown would make his own play for the big time, buying a moribund North Las Vegas tri-weekly, the *Valley Times*, and turning it for a while into a third Las Vegas daily. Brown paid Al Cahlan a high compliment when he described his editorial strategy: "I don't expect to be the *New York Times*. I want to be what Al Cahlan was." ⌀

FLORENCE LEE JONES

(1910–1985)

"I was always treated with the highest respect because I behaved like a lady. The communications field should inspire people to be better and to reach higher. I take pride that I have been at the beginning of many wonderful things."

—Florence Lee Jones
In a 1983 interview

Chronicling the events—whether they were tea parties or murder trials—that made Las Vegas a city was this journalist's first love; her second love was the city itself. **BY A.D. HOPKINS**

Florence Lee Jones had a chance to be Las Vegas' most sensational journalist, jerking tears with tales of women wronged and justice miscarried. Instead, she became a meticulous scribe, documenting the people who built a city. She was the first important female journalist in Southern Nevada. Only after proving herself as a hard news reporter did she concentrate on society news; she then dominated that field locally for 20 years.

"I have been in the business of building Las Vegas since I wrote my first story," she told a younger journalist in 1984, a year before her death. "I think I helped make the town happen."

Born in Missouri in 1910, Jones spent some of her teen years in Sumatra, where her father was teaching Shell Oil crews how to use new rotary drills. Living in small camps newly carved from the jungle, the Jones kids were taught to smell the outside air the moment they opened a door. A heavy, musky odor meant a tiger might be lurking under the house, waiting for an American breakfast.

Her family returned to Missouri so Florence could attend college there, but in 1931, her father and mother were scheduled to go back to Sumatra. "Dad and Mother … were on their way to Long Beach, the port from which they were to embark," said Florence's brother, Herb Jones. "They were in Kingman, and somebody told them

about this little town across the river where they were starting to build a big dam. They took a ferry across, Dad looked around, and [he] said, 'I'm not going back to the jungle.'"

The elder Jones built a service station on the road to Boulder Dam, near Pittman, and later went into real estate. His sons, Herb and Cliff, would work their way through college with jobs on the dam and would became prominent Las Vegas attorneys. Cliff also would serve as lieutenant governor and hold interests in casinos throughout the world.

Florence Jones graduated from the University of Missouri with a bachelor's degree in journalism in 1933, but that was a poor year to be in the job market. "Only three in our class of 100 went into journalism," she recalled 50 years later. "Men were store clerks and gas station attendants. Those were the only jobs they could find."

Jones joined her family in Las Vegas and lucked into a temporary job at the *Evening Review-Journal*. "I was hired to cover a special story," she wrote later. "My assignment was the famous Kraus trial, which related to claims of a truck driver in the tunnels of Boulder Dam that he had lost his sexual powers because of exposure to the carbon monoxide fumes in the tunnels. The defendants were the Six Companies Inc., the contractors on the dam construction."

The defendants hired undercover agents, who befriended Kraus and introduced him to ladies of the evening. No journalism course had prepared Jones for the explicit testimony extracted from the prostitutes. Kraus' lawsuit didn't succeed, but Jones' trial by fiery language did. The *Review-Journal* hired her full time.

John F. Cahlan, the wire and sports editor, also wrote some stories, but Jones was the only full-time reporter. She was immediately assigned to cover the biggest story Las Vegas offered—the construction of Hoover Dam. "I made a trip on

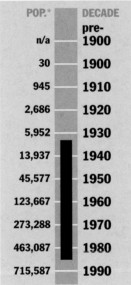

Jones in Southern Nevada

POP.*	DECADE
n/a	pre-1900
30	1900
945	1910
2,686	1920
5,952	1930
13,937	1940
45,577	1950
123,667	1960
273,288	1970
463,087	1980
715,587	1990

■ Time spent in Southern Nev.
* - Population figures are for greater Las Vegas area (*Source: Nevada State Data Center*).

Florence Lee Jones, Review-Journal writer and editor, not only covered Las Vegas but also helped found some of its most enduring community organizations, then wrote and edited some of the area's most reliable history texts.

(Review-Journal files)

Florence Lee Jones and advertising salesman Bill Bailey were proud of all the work they did for the Review-Journal's *1955 special edition commemorating the 50th anniversary of the city. Historians say this special edition is the only surviving source for some of the region's early history.*
(Nevada State Museum)

It fell to young Florence Jones (left) to cover celebrity weddings. Actress Margarita Bolado (center), known to the public as "Margo," married Francis Lederer on October 18, 1937. They supposedly wed impulsively after a romantic moonlight ride in the Nevada desert.
(Nevada State Museum)

Lake Mead with the National Park Service during which we named various scenic points, of which Iceberg Canyon still retains the name," Jones wrote in a column marking her retirement in 1983.

She was especially skillful at covering court news. Her editor and mentor, John Cahlan, recalled being caught up in a dramatic crime story. The perpetrator was a sympathetic figure, cultured and articulate, all but deserted by her husband. A policeman gave her a tiny pistol to protect herself, and she put a tiny bullet through the husband's heart. Cahlan grew flushed with excitement as he described the opportunity. Why, Florence could become a modern version of Nellie Bly, the *Denver Post* reporter who won fame by sensational coverage of important trials. It was a fine idea, except Cahlan had overlooked one important element, Jones told her boss. "The woman is *guilty*," she emphasized.

Jones wrote the story straight, and she kept writing the same way for 50 years. In 1940 she married Cahlan, and an oral history he recorded in the 1980s implies that this aspect of her personality was one of the foundations of their relationship. She was a clear-thinking person who never lost sight of the moral shoreline. While she admired most of his brainstorms, she shot down the ones that had no business in the air.

World War II brought the hardest years Jones would see as a journalist. She felt obliged to report the movements of Las Vegans in service, and the only way to do it was to correspond with them. Meanwhile, she was working 12- and 14-hour days covering everything from coroners' inquests to ladies' club meetings. After peace came, the women who had worked as volunteers—for the American Red Cross, the USO, Travelers' Aid, rationing boards, and war bond drives—wondered whether their demonstrated abilities could

be tapped to address postwar problems. "Seven young matrons formed the nucleus of the organization now known as the Service League," Jones wrote.

In the league's early years, members helped the health department run clinics, rounded up clothes for needy children and sometimes made them by hand, lobbied the Legislature for child welfare laws, and assisted in fund drives for charities. Jones served as president of the Service League for the first two years, and the organization eventually evolved into the Junior League, probably the most active and influential working charity for women in Las Vegas.

By 1951, Jones was the *Review-Journal's* full-time women's editor, and Maisie Gibson Ronnow was her assistant. Ronnow says that Jones' volunteer work was hard to separate from her journalism: "It almost seemed that she gave 100 percent of her time to each of them."

Jones kept thousands of 3-by-5 index cards filled with personal information about people. The card for Mrs. J.D. Smith starts with the following information: "Nurse in World War I. Sister, Mrs. Pauline Gibson of Toronto, Canada. Visited in summer, 1942. Has son, Eugene, of Toronto. Daughter Mary (Mrs. Sidney C. Wooten, Was. D.C.). Wed summer, 1942, after LV divorce."

At some later time, with a different typewriter, Jones added the names of the foster parents who had raised Mrs. Smith, the date of the foster parents' golden wedding anniversary, the maiden and married names of Mrs. Smith's niece, the fact that the niece had a baby, and a reminder that the niece had visited Las Vegas in 1944. Nothing derogatory—just the sort of details that make stories sparkle.

Jones retired in 1953 because of a serious illness and spent the next decade doing free-lance projects. In 1955 she wrote a vo-

luminous special section for the *Review-Journal*, marking the town's 50th anniversary. She interviewed old-timers who were still alive and the aging offspring of others. "You find things in that edition that aren't found anywhere else," said David Millman of the Nevada State Museum.

She resumed writing a social column for the *Review-Journal* in 1963, but found time to serve on the Governor's Commission on Nevada History in 1967 and also chaired the commission that ran the Lost City Museum at Overton. In 1972 she became the first woman selected to the board of trustees of the Nevada State Museum. With Cahlan, she wrote *Water: A History of Las Vegas*, which explains how the development of the city was determined by the availability of water. The book was published in 1975.

Jones retired for good in 1983, and died of cancer in 1985. In her last important interview, in 1983, she told the *Review-Journal's* Ed Vogel that she never found any trouble melding her respected position in the community with work in the sometimes gritty field of journalism. "I was always treated with the highest respect because I behaved like a lady," she said. "The communications field should inspire people to be better and to reach higher. I take pride that I have been at the beginning of many wonderful things." ✍

FRANK CROWE

(1882–1946)

"He'd get you a job, like he got me a job here, but if I'd have got fired or laid off the next couple of days, it would have been too bad. And that's the type he was. He'd give you a boost, but you'd better look out for yourself."

—Marion Allen
Worker on both the Hoover and Shasta dams

A civil engineer went from public to private employment just for the chance to build Hoover Dam, putting Boulder City on the map. **BY DENNIS MCBRIDE**

When Frank Crowe died in 1946, the American Society of Civil Engineers published a memorial essay outlining his life and achievements. Crowe still loomed large in the public mind a decade after he completed his career's crowning project: Hoover Dam. The society wrote: "His projects will stand forever as monuments to his great ability as a constructor, but he will be best remembered by his many friends and close associates for his ever-present human understanding, his extreme fair-mindedness, his wonderful sense of humor, and his absolute integrity—once his word was given it was carried out, no matter what his personal sacrifices might be."

Crowe was a far more complicated man than his eulogy implies, and his behavior in some situations was far from laudable. But Crowe's work as a dam builder forever changed the face of the American West, and his successful completion of Hoover Dam in 1935 made possible the Southern Nevada we know today.

Crowe was born in 1882 in Quebec, where his father owned a woolen mill. The family moved to the United States in 1888, settling in Massachusetts. In 1901, Crowe entered the University of Maine, where he studied civil engineering.

In January 1904, Crowe attended a series of lectures by Frank Weymouth, an engineer for the Bureau of Reclamation, known then as the Recla-

mation Service, which had been founded just two years before. Crowe listened in awe as Weymouth described the government's plans to "reclaim" huge areas of the West with dams and irrigation projects. Crowe asked Weymouth for a job. Weymouth obliged, and Crowe spent the summer of 1904 working for the Reclamation Service on a survey crew along the Lower Yellowstone

River. For a young man who'd grown up in the cramped landscapes of New England, the unlimited vistas of the West promised equally unlimited professional opportunities.

Crowe also seemed a man made to thrive in the West; he was more than 6 feet tall and had an open, driven, and forward-looking personality. True to the nickname he earned in later years, "Hurry-Up Crowe" didn't even wait for his 1905 commencement exercises and diploma before joining the Reclamation Service and heading West.

For the next 20 years, Crowe roamed the West working for both the Reclamation Service and private construction firms. He was involved in the construction of Arrowrock Dam in Idaho, the Jackson Lake Dam in Wyoming, and Washington's Tieton Dam. He soon proved his mechanical genius by designing construction methods for delivering concrete and moving equipment through the use of cable ways. His systems, which initially propelled dam construction out of the era of mules and scrapers, reached their technological epitome on the Boulder Canyon Project.

Throughout his early professional life, Crowe looked for the one project that would be not only the pivotal event of his own career, but also an undertaking of monumental importance in itself. Marion Allen, who helped build Hoover Dam, said Crowe told his father in 1921, a decade before construction would start, "I'm going to build Boulder Dam!" (The name of the dam has changed

Crowe in Southern Nevada

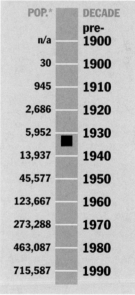

POP.*	DECADE
n/a	pre-1900
30	1900
945	1910
2,686	1920
5,952	1930
13,937	1940
45,577	1950
123,667	1960
273,288	1970
463,087	1980
715,587	1990

■ Time spent in Southern Nev.
* - Population figures are for greater Las Vegas area (*Source: Nevada State Data Center*).

Frank Crowe, nicknamed "Hurry-Up" for his driven insistence on completing projects on schedule or earlier, was construction superintendent on Hoover Dam. When a construction speed-up was ordered, the man and his moment had met.

(Courtesy Dennis McBride)

An inspection party accompanying Secretary of the Interior Ray L. Wilbur was photographed in front of the outlet from one of the diversion tunnels built to bypass the damsite temporarily and give the builders a dry spot to pour concrete. From left are William E. Stringfellow of the reservation police; Sims Ely, city manager; Walker R. Young, construction engineer; H.J. Kaiser, a director of Six Companies; Wilbur; W.A. Bechtel, president of Six Companies; W.L. Honnald, chairman of the engineering committee for the Los Angeles Metropolitan Water District; S.D. Bechtel, a director of Six Companies; W.P. Whitsett, president of the water district; and Frank Crowe, construction superintendent.

(Courtesy Dennis McBride)

more than once; it was referred to as "Boulder Dam" at the time.)

Crowe admitted his passion for Hoover Dam in a 1943 interview in *Fortune* magazine: "I was wild to build this dam. I had spent my life in the river bottoms and [Hoover Dam] meant a wonderful climax—the biggest dam ever built by anyone anywhere."

Crowe spent 20 years developing contacts who afforded him an inside track on getting to build it. He had worked with Walker Young, who would be construction engineer on the Boulder Canyon Project. In 1919 Crowe and Reclamation Commissioner Arthur Powell Davis produced a rough cost estimate for a dam on the lower Colorado River, and in 1924 Crowe helped with the dam's preliminary design.

But in 1925 the Reclamation Service changed the way it approached construction projects. Rather than building its own dams, the service began contracting the work out to private firms,

so Frank Crowe faced a dilemma: Stay on with the service and become a pencil-pusher, or leave government for private industry. He went to work for the Morrison-Knudsen Construction Company. When the government announced that construction would proceed, Crowe persuaded Harry Morrison, president of Morrison-Knudsen, to organize the Six Companies and make a construction bid, using figures Crowe himself had worked up. The Six Companies agreed to make Crowe their construction superintendent on Hoover Dam, and on March 4, 1931, they won the contract with a bid of $48,890,955. The winning bid was only about $24,000 higher than the cost calculated by Bureau of Reclamation engineers.

Crowe arrived in Las Vegas on March 11, 1931, to start work. The first problem he faced was the government's plans for Boulder City. The government had expected to have Boulder City built for workers before dam construction began, but by the time Crowe arrived, Boulder City consisted of a rail yard and a government survey camp, surrounded by a makeshift camp called McKeeversville.

Urban planner Saco DeBoer had designed an elaborate town with a greenbelt forest and an 18-hole golf course. Crowe took Walker Young out to the townsite with a roll of drawing paper. They sketched a simpler plan, based loosely on DeBoer's, and crews broke ground within a week. That design—which, incidentally, still serves today as the basis for Boulder City's master planning—included a large, sumptuously furnished hacienda on a granite knoll at the north end of town, overlooking monotonous rows of slapdash wooden cottages. Completed in January 1932, this mansion was

home for Crowe, his wife Linnie, and their two daughters, Patricia and Elizabeth "Bettee" Jean.

The first real test Crowe faced on the dam project was the labor strike of August 1931. That summer, men had died of heat prostration in temperatures exceeding 130 degrees; workers complained of poor food, bad drinking water, and the Six Companies' lack of safety precautions, which killed and injured a number of laborers. "Muckers" did perhaps the hardest and hottest work on the dam—shoveling up dynamite-loosened rock to be hauled away—yet got the lowest pay. When Six Companies announced a wage cut for muckers, it was the final straw, and a strike was called.

In his book, *Hoover Dam: An American Adventure,* Joseph Stevens notes, "Crowe had the reputation of being tough but fair in labor disputes and because he knew so many of the men and valued their skills and experience so highly, they thought he might intercede on their behalf with the Six Companies' directors."

But that didn't happen. Crowe told a reporter from the *Las Vegas Age* that the strike was largely a result of agitators and that Six Companies "would be glad to get rid of such." Indeed, Six Companies' chief of security, Glen E. "Bud" Bodell, together with Boulder City Manager Sims Ely, had been conducting covert surveillance to weed out, blacklist, and otherwise harass men perceived to be union agitators. Between October 1931 and October 1932, more than a thousand were rounded up and thrown out of town, many of them only to be arrested and jailed in Las Vegas.

Despite Bureau of Reclamation records that listed 15 deaths on the project in July 1931, Crowe claimed that his own records showed no job-related fatalities. Technically he was right: Men had died of heat prostration, disease, auto crashes, and drowning. Crowe proved himself to be the company's man. He shut down the job, fired everyone, and began hiring new crews. Labor strife was never again a serious concern for Crowe on the Boulder Canyon Project.

Another situation in which Crowe's behavior was questionable was in drilling the diversion tunnels that shunted the Colorado River around the construction site. In direct violation of state law, he allowed the use of ordinary motor trucks inside these tunnels without adequate ventilation to remove the carbon monoxide spewed by their exhaust. "Driving trucks through those tunnels, there was a gas problem there, real bad at times," recalled Curley Francis. "We usually could tell by looking at the lights in the tunnel. If they had a blue ring around them, we would know the gas was getting pretty rough in there."

River man Murl Emery, who carried men to work in his boats, had a hand in rescuing workers. "They were hauling men out of those tunnels like cord wood," he remembered. "They had been gassed. I laid them on the bottom of the boat, along the seats and what not. ... They were real sick from being gassed working in that tunnel along with the running trucks ... so they hauled them out of there. And that diehard Frank Crowe in the courthouse swore that to the best of his knowledge, there never had been men gassed underground working."

When the state of Nevada sued Six Companies to stop the practice, a panel of federal judges found in favor of the company. Lawsuits brought by injured workers, however, went on for several years. Six Companies resorted to pimping, intimidating witnesses, and jury tampering. In January 1936 the company settled out of court and sent checks to all the plaintiffs.

Then there was the Frank Crowe who improved construction methods to the benefit of both the Hoover Dam project and its workers. "Everybody who worked down here knew who Frank Crowe was," said Bob Parker. "Very tall and erect, kind of [a] stately looking person, a very likable fellow. He was all over the job. His workmen, he knew them by their first name, nearly every one of them. ...

"He came to work every morning wearing a brand spanking newly ironed white shirt. His daughters told me ... that's one part that their mother played in the building of Hoover Dam. She never let him go out of the house ... without a clean white shirt on and that was his trademark, that and a large Stetson hat. ... He never forgot you if you crossed him. Men that had worked for him 15, 20 years before this dam started, if they ever did anything wrong, he knew it. He remembered it."

"On the other hand," remembered Marion Allen, "he'd get you a job, like he got me a job here, but if I'd have got fired or laid off the next couple of days, it would have been too bad. And that's the type he was. He'd give you a boost, but you'd better look out for yourself."

Saul "Red" Wixson had followed Crowe from job to job for years. "[Crowe] had an awesome job, and if he wasn't in his office, he was down at the dam," Wixson noted. "It'd never surprise me to see him down there at 2 o'clock in the morning looking around. ... If something went wrong he was there ... to explain what was wrong, fix it. He was there to help you, not to fire you."

There was a generous side to Frank Crowe, too. After Hoover Dam was finished, Crowe and many of his workers helped build Shasta Dam in California. Marion Allen and his family were among them. "I remember when my brother died on Shasta Dam," Allen said. "[Frank Crowe] came down to see my dad and he said, 'Val, you might be short a little money. I better give you a couple hundred. ... Pay me back whenever you get to it.'"

One of Crowe's great talents was his ability to deal with different people on different levels, which went a long way toward keeping the dam project moving smoothly. "One thing he knew was men," said Wixson. "Everyone has a different temperament and he knew how to treat you. For instance, he never bawled me out, 'cause he knew I was the wrong kind of guy to bawl out. I'd eat my heart out. And there was other guys he could nibble at a little bit. One time he said to me, 'I got to nibble on Jack, 'cause he's got to be pushed along a little bit.'"

Crowe designed and built for Hoover Dam the most sophisticated and extensive cable system ever built. It was used to deliver concrete and workers throughout the canyon. Frank Crowe finished Hoover Dam two years ahead of schedule, and on February 29, 1936, he handed the finished project over to the Bureau of Reclamation.

Just two days later, Al Cahlan of the *Las Vegas Evening Review-Journal* interviewed Crowe for the last time. "I feel like hell," Crowe admitted. "I'm looking for a job and want to go right on building dams as long as I live. Somehow I can't imagine myself in a big city skyscraper acting as a consulting engineer. ... I'm going to keep my feet in the dirt some way—that's where I'm happiest. ... I've got to find a dam to build somewhere."

Crowe did find other projects after Hoover: Parker Dam, 155 miles downstream from Hoover; Copper Basin and Gene Wash dams on the Colorado Aqueduct system; and Shasta Dam in Northern California. All were important, but none approached the mythic scale or mystique of Hoover Dam. He retired in 1944 to his 20,000-acre cattle ranch near Redding, California, where he died of a heart attack on February 26, 1946.

Crowe's obituaries recognized that if he hadn't completed Hoover Dam, Boulder City would not exist, Las Vegas would still be a wide spot on the road, and the power required to run the World War II industries in Southern California would not have been available. Hoover Dam was the pivotal project Crowe had looked for all his life, and it is the one thing for which he is most remembered. ⌀

A piece of penstock pipe is lowered into place.
(Review-Journal files)

SIMS ELY (1862–1954)

The rigid influence of the man who controlled the lives of the workers who built Hoover Dam, and the town where they lived, is still felt in that town's legacy of no gambling. BY DENNIS MCBRIDE

On June 2, 1935, Boulder City Manager Sims Ely delivered a speech over NBC radio. Referring to Boulder City and the nearly completed Hoover Dam, Ely said, "There have been manifested here in a very actual way some of the principles that have distinguished the Bureau of Reclamation … human sympathy, courage, and common sense. … The thousands of workers who soon will be leaving here will always remember Boulder City as a town of fine artistic planning and beautiful landscaping; a town of happy living conditions … where the highest American ideas were fostered."

The idyllic life Ely describes was almost entirely his own creation, since he controlled every aspect of the city's economy and morality.

He was "an honest, upright, and thoughtful man," wrote Ray Lyman Wilbur Jr. in his 1935 master's thesis about Boulder City.

"He was a little Hitler," remembered former dam worker Tex Nunley.

Ely was born January 7, 1862, in Overton County, Tennessee, and was educated at the College of Commerce in Bloomington, Illinois. He edited a newspaper in Hutchinson, Kansas, and later was editor and publisher of the *Arizona Republic* in Phoenix.

Ely's first link with the Boulder Canyon Project was his membership in the League of the Southwest, a private organization that promoted Western development. During a meeting in Los Angeles in April 1920, the league urged the federal government to build a dam on the Colorado River in Boulder Canyon. Delph Carpenter of Colorado and Ely of Arizona suggested a water-rights pact among the seven Colorado River states, leading to the Colorado River Compact, which made Hoover Dam possible.

In his book, *Hoover Dam: An American Adventure,* Joseph Stevens writes that Secretary of the Interior Ray Lyman Wilbur decided Boulder City and the Boulder Canyon Project Federal Reservation would be run by an appointed city manager. Wilbur wanted "a highly skilled administrator, an executive who was supremely self-confident but not openly arrogant, a leader combining the attributes of firmness, impartiality, and incorruptibility, an authority figure who could command total respect without being hated or feared."

The man he chose was Ely, then 69 years old and approaching the age of mandatory retirement. As Wilbur noted in his memoirs, Ely "would have full control and would keep off the reservation those who socially misbehaved in any way. In a state as free and easy as Nevada, this was important, but not always popular."

Sims Ely moved to his office in Boulder City's new Municipal Building on February 29, 1932. His power was near absolute. The police force took its orders directly from him. Ely could approve or refuse commercial and residential lease applications, and through this power control competition and prices. He could have men fired and thrown off the reservation.

For all the effort to create a "model American community," Boulder City was a dictatorship. The Bureau of Rec-

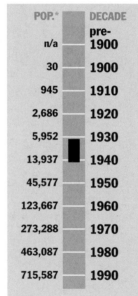

Ely in Southern Nevada

POP.*	DECADE
n/a	pre-1900
30	1900
945	1910
2,686	1920
5,952	1930
13,937	1940
45,577	1950
123,667	1960
273,288	1970
463,087	1980
715,587	1990

■ Time spent in Southern Nev.
* - Population figures are for greater Las Vegas area (*Source: Nevada State Data Center*).

Sims Ely, Boulder City manager, in October 1931
(U.S. Bureau of Reclamation)

lamation did establish a three-member advisory committee, but its members were picked by project construction engineer Walker Young and served at his pleasure. This commission advised Ely, who reported to Young. The commission had no authority to override decisions by Ely or Young, its meetings were private, and it stopped keeping minutes after the first few.

As Wilbur Jr., son of the secretary of Interior, wrote, "It is true that by his actions Mr. Ely gradually became a very powerful influence in the community and could make rules as he pleased, but he was always subject to his superiors. However, the construction engineer [Walker Young], the commissioner [of Reclamation, Dr. Elwood Mead], and the secretary [of the Interior, Ray Lyman Wilbur Sr.] backed him up in all his major decisions and activities."

A case could be made for such iron-fisted control. "A lot of your construction stiffs, they lived by their own rules," said Floyd Jenne, who worked for Ely as a Boulder City ranger. "If they disagreed, they went out and hashed it out. And if they disagreed with you, why, they either beat hell out of you or you beat hell out of them. That was just the way it worked. In a construction town [with families], you couldn't have that kind of a set-up."

Mary Ann Merrill remembered that Ely "was fair in a lot of ways, but he had his own ideas and he put them into practice. And you had to go by his rules. He thought of it as his town. I've heard that said so many times: 'This is Sims' town.'"

Boulder City was built in part so the government could keep liquor, gambling, and prostitution away from its workers. Cars were stopped at the reservation gate near Railroad Pass and searched for liquor. If any was found, the car was impounded and the guilty individuals banned from the reservation. There were no exceptions, even after Prohibition was repealed in 1933.

On December 28, 1932, Ely issued this broad-side: "In the interest of the workers here, it should be understood by everybody that to be drunk on the Boulder Canyon Project Federal Reservation means expulsion from the reservation with consequent loss of job. It is unfortunate that some of the men working here have very short memories concerning the terrible conditions of unemployment which prevail elsewhere. Within a short time after getting their jobs, they forget all about the privations, hardships, and despair they underwent before they secured employment, and they proceed to 'blow' their money with bootleggers and toss away the jobs for which they have waited so long. If the workers on this reservation cannot refrain from getting drunk, they must step aside for the sober men who are anxious for employment on this work. It is a matter of choosing between drink and the job."

The sale of alcoholic beverages was not legal in Boulder City until 1969. The enthusiasm with which Ely enforced anti-liquor and anti-gaming laws contributed to Las Vegas' growth. Construction workers with money burning holes in their pockets found their way to the bars and brothels of downtown Las Vegas and to those that lined the road to Boulder City.

Another way Ely made sure that vice didn't find its way into Boulder City was through his minute investigation of applications for business permits. Ely granted leases and permits "on the basis of personal, financial, and service fitness, and on training and experience."

One applicant for a taxi-dance hall assured Ely that his dancers would be "respectable girls on salary." Unconvinced these respectable girls wouldn't really be hookers, Ely refused the application. He also revoked a permit for a cab service when he discovered that owner Frank Gotwalls had arranged to deliver customers from Boulder City to the Railroad Pass Casino on the road to Las Vegas, with the casino paying the fare.

> *"[Ely is] an honest, upright, and thoughtful man."*
> Ray Lyman Wilbur Jr.
> Scholar and son of Ely's boss

To this day, gambling and prostitution remain illegal in Boulder City through deed restrictions.

Ely's control of the business permit system also kept Boulder City from becoming a typical boom-and-bust Western town. Ely often refused to grant a business permit if, in his opinion, there was no chance of the venture's success.

Despite flying in the face of traditional American free enterprise, the system worked. As Ely reported in August 1932, "[T]here has been no business failure ... and all establishments are doing fairly well. They, of course, are not doing so well as they would like, but all are probably doing better than they would do anywhere else just now."

Ely was appointed superintendent of the Boulder City grammar schools, and in that capacity he selected the teachers and supervised administration until Clark County took responsibility in 1933. He also enforced school rules and punished "antisocial" behavior among pupils. A form letter Ely composed to send home to parents of truant youngsters read, "Certain pupils enrolled in the Boulder City schools are creating an intolerable evil in school control by absenting themselves without leave. ... The bad example thus set has a demoralizing influence on pupils of studious habits and better impulses."

And it was Sims Ely and Boulder City businesswoman Ida Browder who established the town's municipal library. They prevailed upon the Library of Congress to donate 3,000 discarded volumes. Ely's involvement didn't end there. Carl Merrill had several overdue library books he'd been unable to return when his shift was changed at the dam. "I got a call from Sims Ely about these books," Merrill said, "and I had to go up and see him and pay the fine to him."

Sims Ely's power over Boulder City residents depended upon the reality that those he chose to evict from Boulder City would return to the grim Hoovervilles whence they had come. Even if evicted workers managed to hold on to their jobs, little other housing was available. This camp was near Boulder City; the men in the truck are believed to be relief workers delivering food.
(UNLV Special Collections)

Ely was particularly concerned with family matters and didn't hesitate to punish a worker who mistreated his family. "If a man beat up his wife," said Mary Eaton, "he'd lose his job. Sims Ely would say, 'You just get off the reservation and don't ever come back.'"

In another incident, Ely actually took a child away from her family for her own safety. "There was a girl who lived down the street from us," remembered Lida Buck. "Her stepfather drank and she was afraid of him. ... Her mother drank, too—neither of them was worth a hoot. One night [the girl] came up to our house in her nightie and didn't want to go home. I let her stay the night and called Sims the next day." Ely told Buck to keep the girl and she would get paid to care for her. The girl's parents were run out of town and the Bucks raised the girl for several years. Despite Ely's promise, Buck added, "I never got a cent for it."

Boulder City was more at the mercy of Sims Ely than in his care. He believed no one employed on the reservation had the right to keep his job just because he was a good worker. He had to abide by Ely's unwritten rules. Nadean Voss' first husband, Dave Laughery, nearly lost his ranger job because he wanted to invest in real estate. "When we wanted to buy one of the fourplex apartments over on Avenue B," Voss recalled, "Sims didn't want us to, and he threatened to fire my husband if he did." Macie Felts remembers that Ely threatened to have her husband fired from his job as an electrician on the dam if he went ahead with his plans to build a house in Boulder out of native rock.

The only plausible expla- nation for Ely to discourage buying or building houses in Boulder City is that most of Boulder City was supposed to be demolished when the dam was finished. But that didn't happen, and many people missed out on property ownership because of Sims Ely's dictums.

Ely often ordered landlords to lower their rent. Since the landlords were subleasing property they had leased from the government, Ely could control them. "Nobody in the world could live up to the terms of those leases," Jenne said. "You could find any number of little things you could cancel a lease for. So Sims would say, 'Forty dollars a month's the most you can charge for this house.'"

There were times when Ely seemed to exercise his power merely for the sake of letting everyone know he was the law. He lived in a house on Utah Street across from the government park where there was a tennis court, and just beyond lay Smith's Root Beer Stand, both of which were popular with Boulder City's teenagers. Ely liked to go to bed early and often called out the rangers to send everyone in the park or at the root beer stand home so he could sleep. Sometimes Ely would stalk out of his house and cross the street to send the kids home himself. "He had this cap on and his gown—he looked just like the Ku Klux Klan," recalled Eileen Conners, who was a teenager then.

There was also an element of racism in some of Ely's threats. Bob Parker related that at Boulder City's popular Green Hut restaurant, "Clarence Newlin [hired] ... a black cook by the name of McKinley Sayles. Somebody went to Sims Ely and told him that Clarence Newlin had a black cook ... and that there oughtn't to be any blacks in Boulder City. Sims Ely took it upon himself to tell [Newlin] he had to get rid of his black cook." Newlin refused and Ely's appeal to Washington went nowhere.

It was one of the rare instances in which Ely failed to impose his will. There was an appeal process for those who felt Sims Ely had been unfair. But Wilbur Jr. wrote, "Young had uniformly sustained Mr. Ely so that practice of appealing [was] seldom attempted."

Appeals and complaints were seldom attempted for another reason. "Letters criticizing Ely were intercepted by someone in the government," said Erma Godbey. "Ely would find out who wrote the letters, then make their life miserable and nothing was ever done about it."

Ely retained his position and his power for nearly 10 years after the Hoover administration that appointed him disappeared into history. He finally retired on April 16, 1941, when he was 79. The Bureau of Reclamation's director of power retained control of Boulder City until 1960, but abolished the position of city manager and ran the community through a city administrative officer, who had nowhere near the sweeping authority Sims Ely had wielded. Today, Boulder City's government is headed by a city manager, but one with conventional powers.

Ely went on to write a book about the Lost Dutchman Mine. He died in a Rockville, Maryland, sanitarium in 1954 at age 92.

When Ely retired, Bureau of Reclamation Commissioner John Page paid tribute to him in a speech at the Boulder Dam Hotel. "The conscientious attention to detail exercised by Mr. Ely in his position of city manager of Boulder City will be greatly missed," Page said. "It was this quality, plus Mr. Ely's firmness of purpose in carrying out his difficult duties, that no doubt gave Boulder City the reputation of being a model government town."

Don Belding expressed an opinion more typical of a Boulder City resident. He remembered being in a local tavern one evening after Ely retired. A prominent Boulder businessman was lamenting Ely's absence. "He'd had things almost his own way when his friend Ely controlled the permit system and Boulder City," Belding said. "And now he wasn't getting his way and he was upset. I wanted to knock him in the head." ⌀

> *"He was a little Hitler."*
> —Tex Nunley
> **Former dam worker**

Life in Boulder City was organized but not luxurious; common buildings lacked air conditioning and even lacked exterior walls. A barber cut hair outside, where the light was better.
(UNLV Special Collections)

MAYME STOCKER

(1875–1972)

"They're trying to lay all this crime we have today on the hookers and the pimps. Well, if that's the problem, why the hell don't they legalize it [prostitution] so they can regulate it, as they basically did on Block 16? Regulating it is all you can hope to do, because they have never succeeded in eliminating it in a thousand years of trying."

—Harold Stocker
Mayme's son

To keep her railroad-working husband and sons respectable, a woman who had no background in gaming held Las Vegas' first casino license. BY A.D. HOPKINS

Not all the pioneers of the Las Vegas casino business were mobsters. In fact, Las Vegas' first lawful casino license was held by Mayme Stocker, a wife and mother so respectable that her birthday parties were covered in the Las Vegas newspaper society pages.

Born in 1875 in Reading, Pennsylvania, Mayme was the daughter of a railroad man and married one at the age of 16. She and her husband, Oscar, had three sons: Clarence, Harold, and Lester.

Railroads in those days hired, fired, and transferred their employees at will. By the time Oscar got a job as an engine foreman in the Las Vegas railroad yards, the family was tired of moving every couple of years. They vowed to stay in their new home as long as they could, even if it turned out to be on the doorstep of hell. Which it seemed to be.

"Anybody who lives here is out of his mind," Mayme remarked on her arrival in 1911. She remembered the comment 37 years later for a *Review-Journal* reporter. "There were no streets or sidewalks, and there were no flowers, lawns, or trees," she recalled in the 1948 interview. In the hot summers, she said, "A familiar scene was the family groups hiking to the 'Old Ranch' for picnics and a few hours of relaxation in the shade of the large trees there. The older children in the family were usually seen pulling the younger tots in small wagons along the dust-covered trail made by horse-drawn vehicles."

She could recall only three forms of public entertainment: "Ben Emrick and his four-piece German band, which played on the street corners on Saturday night, Ladd's swimming pool on East Fremont Street, and the Princess Theater, where a

5-cent movie could be viewed."

Family duty rescued her temporarily from the boredom that was Las Vegas; she learned that one of her two sisters in Butte, Montana, had not much longer to live. Mayme Stocker went to care for her and took along her son, Harold, then 11. It was a fateful trip, for it provided little Harold an introduction to the whiskey business.

"Both my aunts were married to saloon owners on opposite sides of the street," Harold Stocker recalled in 1981. "One made a lot of money in Prohibition; he bought three carloads of liquor for 50 cents a quart, just before Prohibition went in. The people sold it cheap because Prohibition was coming, and my uncle bought it because he didn't believe they would ratify Prohibition. When they did, he was stuck with it. Three years later he sold it anyway, and he got $25 a quart."

In the meantime, Harold had moved back to Las Vegas. Then the local school burned down. Since the family worked for the railroad and could commute free, Mayme took Harold to Los Angeles and enrolled him in school there.

"I went to work as a dealer one summer, met somebody who got me a job in a casino in Tijuana," Harold told the *Review-Journal* in 1981. "I was only 17, but it wasn't illegal; there was no regulation there at all. I started out stacking chips at a roulette wheel. That was the game that had the most play in those days. That and '21,' which we dealt with gold coins and big pesos.

Stocker in Southern Nevada

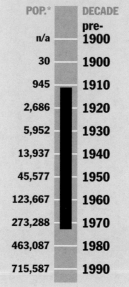

POP.*	DECADE
n/a	pre-1900
30	1900
945	1910
2,686	1920
5,952	1930
13,937	1940
45,577	1950
123,667	1960
273,288	1970
463,087	1980
715,587	1990

■ Time spent in Southern Nev.
* - Population figures are for greater Las Vegas area (*Source: Nevada State Data Center*).

Old-fashioned girls Geraldine Stocker (left), one of Harold's several ex-wives, and his mother, Mayme Stocker, in front of Las Vegas' first licensed casino, the Northern Club. They are dressed for the first Helldorado celebration in 1935. The lad is a young relative.
(*UNLV Special Collections*)

California Supreme Court, during the litigation he continued to reap profits of more than $200,000 a month.

By 1939 the struggle between Cornero and the protectors of public morality had reached a climax. California Attorney General Earl Warren launched a full-scale attack on both the *Rex* and the water taxis. Warren announced, "We're prepared to besiege them until they give up." Cornero replied that he would go down with his ship. Nine days later he surrendered, claiming he changed his mind because, he said, "I have to get a haircut and the only thing I haven't got aboard ship is a barber."

The federal government then decided that gambling ships would hamper preparations for a possible conflict in the Pacific. When the Coast Guard seized the *Rex* in November 1939, Admiral Cornero announced that he would operate a legitimate shipping company. He did so through 1944.

In spite of the earlier failure of the Meadows, Cornero remained convinced that Las Vegas could be a gambling mecca. He contacted Pietro Orlando Silvagni, builder of the Apache Hotel, leased its casino, and changed its name to S.S. Rex.

City commissioners publicly told Silvagni that his association with Tony Cornero was the reason for a 3-2 vote denying a gaming license. Commissioner Al Coradetti explained: "I would like to see P.O. Silvagni clean house. It is our business to see that we know who is going to run this place for Silvagni. I don't want Bugsy Siegel and people of his stripe in here, and until I know who is going to run Silvagni's place, I'll vote against the license."

Two weeks later, on December 22, 1944, Coradetti, apparently persuaded that Cornero would not actually control the casino, joined two other city commissioners in voting to give Silvagni his license. Cornero continued to be associated with the S.S. Rex for six months,

until Silvagni, facing another licensing battle, severed his connections with him.

Cornero was not discouraged. Rather, he returned to Southern California and bought a new ship, the *Lux*, which he anchored off the Long Beach coast. Thousands of citizens took the short trip to the *Lux* while local and state officials fumed. The guardians of public morality then seized the water taxis, surrounded the *Lux*, and exchanged insults with the admiral and his crew. Eventually Cornero surrendered, went to trial and was found innocent, and immediately reopened the *Lux*.

Once again, though, the feds were the admiral's nemesis. The Coast Guard seized the ship because it was not fulfilling the purpose of its license. Instead of engaging in coastal trade, the *Lux* was anchored offshore, functioning as a floating casino. Cornero realized that his days as an admiral were over as congressional support grew for a bill to outlaw gambling in the U.S. coastal waters. When Congress passed the bill in 1948, he was already planning to invest his capital and gambling expertise in Mexico's Baja California.

But again he faced adversity. Answering the door at his Beverly Hills home, he was shot by an unidentified gunman. The bullet entered Cornero's stomach and tore out part of his intestine. He was in serious condition for several weeks. The victim was treated unsympathetically by the police. One law enforcement officer reported that "Cornero was evasive as a typical gangster." Another said, "Whenever I tried to pin him down, he acted like he was in pain."

Cornero began sharing his dream of building the biggest, plushest hotel along the Strip. He settled on the name Stardust and shared his vision with potential investors. Of course, Cornero didn't worry about the finer points of federal or state law as he raised capital. Like so many Strip entrepreneurs in the 1950s, he kept records of investments in his head or on paper he often carried with him. Perhaps $10,000 would bring to

the investor 5 percent of the profits of the showroom, or 2 percent of the profits of the hotel. Cornero pushed forward with his grand plan to build a 1,000-room hotel on the Strip, and by July 1955, he had spent more than $3 million and had personally overseen construction of about 70 percent of the Stardust.

Cornero's Beverly Hills brush with death did not change his outlook on life. He worked hard and played hard, and he loved to gamble. He spent many hours at the gaming tables of the nearby Desert Inn. On the morning of July 31, 1955, he made his last roll of the dice, clutched his chest, and collapsed. The next day, Las Vegas newspapers carried front-page stories about his life and death. *Review-Journal* reporter Bob Holdorf wrote:

"Tony died the way he had lived. He died at a gambling table. Probably, the diminutive gambler was happy as hell when he felt the surging heat whip across his chest and blot out the world. What other way was there for him to go? In a bed? Never! In a gun battle? They tried that! In an ambush? They tried that, too! Tony went the way any tough gambling hombre wants to get it. ... He had crapped out."

Desert Inn owner Moe Dalitz and his Cleveland associates oversaw the completion of a slightly less lavish Stardust than Cornero had envisioned. ✍

Tony Cornero conceived the Stardust hotel and had it about 70 percent built by the time of his death in 1955. It looked like this a couple of years later.
(Las Vegas News Bureau)

Employees watch the Meadows' hotel wing burn on Labor Day, 1931. Dorothy Baker, a dancer, has her back to the camera.
(UNLV Special Collections)

Tom Williams (1880-1939)

A church-goer who was never a hypocrite, the man who founded North Las Vegas believed in the motto live and let live — without government interference. **BY K.J. EVANS**

The early history of North Las Vegas unfolded pretty much as its founder intended that it should. Except, perhaps, for the illegal booze.

Tom Williams was a libertarian, though he probably wouldn't have recognized the term. He simply thought government was a bad idea. His utopia would be free of building codes, land-use regulations, laws concerning livestock, nosy cops—and people of color. The founding father of North Las Vegas also was a racist.

Las Vegas had been formed overnight in May 1905, when the San Pedro, Los Angeles, and Salt Lake City Railroad auctioned townsites to an enthusiastic horde of bidders. By 1911, Las Vegas was an incorporated city replete with politicians and bureaucrats feverishly compiling an ever-lengthening list of dos and don'ts for the populace. Still, it was a fairly crude and rough-edged place when Williams arrived for a visit in 1917.

Whether Williams disliked Las Vegas because of its rowdiness—he was a pious, churchgoing man—or was put off by its attempts at municipal regimentation, he decided that Las Vegas was not for him. What he did like was the valley, with its seemingly inexhaustible supply of artesian water and potential for agricultural development. In 1919, he moved his wife Lola and his sons Don, Bert, and Tom Jr. from Eureka, Utah, to a barren 160-acre tract about a mile down the hill from Las Vegas. He paid $8 an acre for the property.

He wasn't the first man to attempt to establish a community in what would become North Las Vegas. In the 1860s, Conrad Kiel had a ranch near what is now the corner of Carey Street and Losee Road; Kiel's ranch had come into the hands of Las Vegas banker John S. Park by the time of Williams' arrival. Peter Buol, the first mayor of Las Vegas, had drilled wells in what became the Craig Ranch and formed the Las Vegas Land and Investment Company to interest settlers in land north of town.

But it was Williams who started an actual town. In 1919, he built his family a house, then subdivided 100 of his 160 acres, sunk a well, graded roads, extended power lines a mile down the hill from Las Vegas, and installed a system of irrigation ditches. The nucleus of Tom Williams' town is near the current site of Jerry's Nugget on Las Vegas Boulevard North.

The lots were offered at $10 down, which included water and power. Williams was especially eager to attract churches. Free sites were offered to any church willing to locate in the townsite. His view was that churches and church people, not civil authorities, should govern the town and keep the peace. The first was the Emanuel Church, which became the town's social center.

Williams' ideology proved to be a boon for development in the face of a federal experiment in social engineering—the Volstead Act, which went into effect in 1919, prohibiting the manufacture, sale, possession, or consumption of alcoholic beverages. The result was that Las Vegas bootleggers, though only nominally persecuted in Las Vegas, moved their operations to the new community, which had somehow picked up the nickname of "Old Town." There were no local laws against hooch, and no one to enforce them even if there had been.

One of the enduring legends of North Las Vegas is that of the first 80 lots sold in Williams' subdivision, 31 were purchased by moonshiners. The founder seems to have been unaware of this, though he surely became aware of it in a hurry. But even though he was a teetotaler, he was not a hypocrite. As far as Tom Williams was concerned, if a man wished to make his living manufacturing liver lubricants, it was his own business.

The new cottage industry required enormous amounts of fresh grain mash. The standard cover story was that it was for livestock. If this had actually been true, the town would have had a bovine population second only to the Fort Worth stockyards. Williams stuck with legal farming, but in 1920 he seems to have unknowingly provided the moonshiners with the makings for an unusual batch of brew. His first big crop of watermelons came in that year, but at market time

Williams in Southern Nevada

POP.*	DECADE
n/a	pre-1900
30	1900
945	1910
2,686	1920
5,952	1930
13,937	1940
45,577	1950
123,667	1960
273,288	1970
463,087	1980
715,587	1990

■ Time spent in Southern Nev.
* - Population figures are for greater Las Vegas area (*Source: Nevada State Data Center*).

"North Las Vegas was a maze of tunnels. But I'm not saying where they are or who built them. It was sure one wet town, though."

—**Don Borax**
Former Las Vegas police chief

be blocked. He called for raising the speed limit to a realistic 20 mph, then enforcing it. He wanted parking banned from 1 a.m. to 6 a.m., so streets could be swept, and parking in alleys banned altogether, for fire safety.

In mid-1932 Cragin fired the police chief, Clay H. Williams, for running a department that wrote too many traffic tickets for petty offenses and left too many visitors determined not to come back.

Paradoxically, the dam boom that brought prosperity to local businesses brought poverty to city government. The population needed civic services and facilities faster than revenues were found to pay for them. Work on a badly needed expansion to the city sewer system began in early 1932, but in 1933 Cragin was forced to cut city salaries, including his own. Some employees were

Ernie Cragin shows Walter Bracken of Las Vegas Land and Water Company the new artesian well drilled on the Mayor's homesite. The photo is thought to date from 1946.
(Nevada State Museum)

laid off.

However, the election of Franklin D. Roosevelt and his New Deal policies changed this picture. Federal money became available for civic improvements. "With Senators [Key] Pittman and [Pat] McCarran casting vital swing votes for many New Deal programs, the Roosevelt Administration was particularly responsive to the needs of Las Vegas, Reno, and other Nevada communities," wrote Eugene P. Moehring in *Resort City in the Sunbelt*, his history of Las Vegas from 1930 to 1970.

Cragin, as part of the Democratic machine that supported the two powerful U.S. senators, was well-positioned to tap the pork barrel. New Deal money put sewers into the suburbs, paved streets, finished a city park, and helped the American Legion Post 8 build its War Memorial Building on the present site of City Hall. (Public funds were available because the building would also serve as a civic auditorium; it became the city's first convention center as well.)

Most things accomplished under the New Deal had been part of Cragin's platform even before Roosevelt was elected. Yet despite an enviable track record of promises kept, Cragin was turned out of office partly for fighting still another New Deal project. Councilman Leonard Arnett decided that Southern Nevada Power Company's rates were too high, and began seeking New Deal funds for a municipal power plant and to bring power to Las Vegas from Hoover Dam. He also began seeking the mayor's seat occupied by Cragin.

Arnett was able to convince voters that Cragin represented the power company's interests and not the public's. In the municipal election of 1935, Arnett beat Cragin 1,472 to 1,093. But after all Arnett's trouble, the municipal power project never came to pass, and he would resign in disgust in 1938.

Cragin threw himself into the Elks' Helldorado celebration, a community-wide festival launched in 1935 to attract tourism by saluting Las Vegas' Western heritage. Strangely, in a

town whose actual history was studded with gunfighters and renegade Indians, where aged "single-blanket jackass prospectors" still told stories for drinks and companionship, the Elks rented costumes from Hollywood and dressed up everybody to fit movie stereotypes. Cragin, who normally wore tailor-made business suits, showed up in publicity photos as a tall "cowboy" lifting a "dance hall gal," who was, in mundane fact, his respectable wife.

Meanwhile, Las Vegas' city administration dissolved into bickering and fiscal crisis. When Cragin offered to take up the reins again in 1943, nobody else filed for the office, and he became mayor by default.

Cragin's administration launched an ambitious program of publicly funded civic improvements, such as a new police station, street pavements, and public swimming pools. But his best bet to pay for the needed improvements went awry in 1946 when he tried to annex the Strip. He argued that the few Strip resorts really fed off the fame of Fremont Street, which was the older and then bigger casino district. But opponents needed only 50 percent of the affected residents to block the annexation; they got more than 90 percent to oppose it.

In 1950, Gus Greenbaum, the mobster who ran the Flamingo after Bugsy Siegel was assassinated, led a successful campaign to make Paradise Valley, which included the Strip, an unincorporated town. This meant the area could not be annexed without the approval of county commissioners, an event expected to happen the same day suckers get an even break.

For Las Vegas, failing to annex meant that tax revenues remained limited and expenditures had to be carefully prioritized. And it was in prioritizing that Cragin's reputation has suffered the most. By the accounts of black Las Vegans, he didn't prioritize fairly.

Whatever problems West Las Vegas retains today, the neighborhood offers gracious living compared to the shantytown that emerged there in the '30s and '40s. It wasn't entirely Cragin's fault,

but Cragin may have been the only person who could have kept the area from becoming a ghetto and a slum—and he didn't.

Las Vegas has had a black population almost from its beginning. It has been estimated that 50 blacks lived here as early as 1925, with adults employed largely as railroad porters, track crewmen, janitors, or maids. In a research paper called "The Mississippi of the West," historian Perry Kaufman found that blacks in those days could go where they liked, except within movie theaters. In Cragin's El Portal, recalled Harley E. Harmon, blacks and the noticeably Hispanic were steered to the left; whites could sit on the right or in the middle. Another theater confined blacks to the balcony.

In the 1930s, according to Kaufman, blacks mostly lived interspersed with whites in an eight-block area between First and Fifth streets and from Stewart to Ogden. Beginning in the 1930s, however, this formerly residential area was increasingly devoted to bars, brothels, and restaurants. Both blacks and whites began moving away, but blacks, because of limited employment opportunities and consequent lack of money, gravitated to inexpensive properties in West Las Vegas. Restrictive deed covenants, prohibiting sales or rentals to blacks, also limited their choices.

The black population exploded during World War II, when many were hired to build and work in the war industry at Henderson. Most came from the Deep South and were surprised to encounter living conditions worse than any they had previously known. Most were unable to find housing anywhere other than in the segregated facilities built in connection with the war plants, or in West Las Vegas. Because few construction materials were available to the private market during wartime, much housing was in tents and makeshift shanties.

In the South, restaurants, bars, and stores often required blacks to use the back door and take all orders "to go," but in Las Vegas, downtown businesses, particularly the emerging casinos and nightclubs, increasingly refused to serve blacks at all. In the 1940s, the city of Las Vegas refused to renew business licenses for black-owned businesses in downtown Las Vegas, unless owners agreed to move to West Las Vegas.

After Cragin's election in 1943, Las Vegas police actively enforced segregation. Officers closed the Star Bar in West Las Vegas; the *Review-Journal* reported that this was because the bar had been "playing to a mixed trade, with Negroes and whites encouraged to congregate in the establishment promiscuously."

Many soldiers stationed or trained in the Southwest, including the entire military police regiment assigned to protect Boulder Dam from saboteurs, were black, and often visited Las Vegas. Those who had been reared in the North were particularly offended at being denied access to Las Vegas' already famous nightlife. They clashed with police in West Las Vegas in August 1943, and one man on each side was wounded by gunfire. In 1944 rioting and gunfire broke out again; one soldier was killed, three were wounded, and one policeman was also slightly wounded. Army and city officials responded by restricting blacks further. One base declared Las Vegas off limits to its black troops.

Partly because of these tensions, the American Federation of Labor constructed a communal facility with showers and laundry tubs for West Las Vegas, and a USO was set up there for black soldiers. But West Las Vegas remained mostly a shantytown without adequate sewers, fire plugs, street lights, or pavement on most roads. Appeals to Cragin went unanswered; at least twice he told community leaders that property values there did not justify extending services.

In 1944 city bulldozers leveled 75 shacks that didn't meet fire or building codes. In 1945 they cleared another 300. But as Eugene Moehring has pointed out, "While the move pleased health reformers, it only promoted more overcrowding in the Westside, because black residents … had nowhere else to live."

Cragin's administration did build a swimming pool in West Las Vegas. It opened in 1947, just a few weeks before one opened on the white side of the railroad tracks.

Lubertha Johnson, who told of her civil-rights work in Las Vegas in an oral history published by the University of Nevada-Reno, said Cragin's anti-black attitude was extreme even for the times: "He talked down to us as if we were really stupid for thinking we should be treated like anybody else. … Most people … like to avoid showing that they are really prejudiced. [But Cragin] conducted himself as if it was really the right thing to do."

Cragin held on to the mayor's post until 1951, when he was defeated in a re-election bid by C.D. Baker. His political career over, Cragin worked every day in the insurance office in the El Portal building. In 1959 he dropped dead at his desk of a heart attack. He was 64. ✍

Mr. and Mrs. E.W. Cragin on their wedding day, October 3, 1917, in Bill Pike's car
(UNLV Special Collections)

The El Portal Theatre featured top stars Temple, Cooper, and Lombard, but the newfangled refrigeration air conditioning got even bigger billing as "manufactured weather."
(UNLV Special Collections)

JIM CASHMAN (1884–1962)

A man of firsts — first automobile dealership, first community celebration, first highway to Las Vegas — found humor in almost every situation. BY A.D. HOPKINS

Big towns run on money, but small ones run on heart. For 40 years, much of the pulse of little Las Vegas emanated from the pudgy chest of Big Jim Cashman. Whether it was starting a baseball team, building a new road, or attracting some new business, Big Jim had a big hand in it. Often, it was two hands and both feet.

His nickname sounds like that of an old-time political boss, bullying people till he got his way. In fact, Big Jim was the opposite. He didn't drive people, but led them. His tool kit was full of charm, humor, and a logic-defying insistence that everything was *fun.* You could prove it by numbers: The more blisters and empty bottles, the more fun you'd had.

The first time he hit town, Cashman didn't make a dent. It was 1904, Las Vegas was nothing but a tent town on an unfinished railroad, and Cashman was a 19-year-old farm boy from Missouri looking for work and, according to family tradition, carrying exactly 10 cents. He found work washing dishes and waiting tables in the chow tent of a railroad grading camp. He grew friendly with the cook, Charlie Rowe, and shortly the two quit the railroad to operate a lunch counter in a tent saloon.

"We got along fine and were doing quite a business, but we spent all the money every night that we'd made during the day," Cashman told interviewer Ed Reid in 1960. "Finally we decided we weren't getting ahead, so instead of going out every night, we would go to bed early and save

our money. Whoever happened to count the cash when we closed up put it in his pocket, and it happened that the first night we agreed to stay home, Charlie had the money in his pocket. I went to bed, but Charlie didn't." The following morning, Cashman discovered he was back to his original stake of 10 cents. That ended the partnership.

Over the next few years, Cashman took whatever jobs he could. One was repairing the neglected telephone system that served the mines around Searchlight, then a bigger town than Las Vegas. "The lines were in such bad shape that whenever the wind blew, the wires would all get crossed up and the poles and lines would fall to the ground," he told Reid. "I got a team and a wagon with some water barrels, and I started out over the line, resetting the poles that had fallen down and pulling up the slack wire. After sending back three helpers in a week's time because they couldn't keep up, I had earned the reputation of being able to work."

The owners ended up leasing the company to Cashman. On the strength of that concrete accomplishment, he borrowed $500 from his brother and started a sort of rural taxi service. Later, Cashman got a contract hauling ore from local mines, enabling him to borrow money to buy a 5-ton, solid-tire White truck. To get ore to the railroad at Kingman, he set up his own ferries to cross the Colorado River. They were essentially barges attached to cables and drawn back

and forth by gasoline engines mounted on the shore.

"Because he did have those trucks and the auto was just getting started," explained his son, James Jr., in a 1998 interview, "he had the only

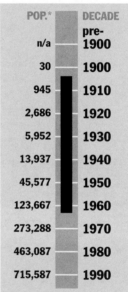

Cashman in Southern Nevada

POP.*		DECADE
n/a		pre-1900
30		1900
945		1910
2,686		1920
5,952		1930
13,937		1940
45,577		1950
123,667		1960
273,288		1970
463,087		1980
715,587		1990

■ Time spent in Southern Nev.
* - Population figures are for greater Las Vegas area (*Source: Nevada State Data Center*).

Big Jim Cashman with the fancy saddle he used in Helldorado parades
(Courtesy James Cashman Jr.)

repair facility anywhere between Southern California and St. George." Cashman's Searchlight Garage, opened in 1910, became a lifesaving landmark for travelers. He also became an auto dealer; he had no distribution franchise, but could buy from dealers in bigger cities and deliver to local customers.

Searchlight was situated on what passed for a main road in those days, and Las Vegas was served by a railroad, so the auto caught on faster in Searchlight. "When I came into Las Vegas, I would have the only car in town," Cashman told Reid. Sighting an auto would bring media comment such as this item in the *Las Vegas Age* in June 1912: "James Cashman drove over from Searchlight in his Oldsmobile bringing T.S. Wilson, T.A. Brown, and C.E. Burdick." By 1917, Cashman was selling enough autos that the newspaper referred to him as "the Searchlight automobile magnate."

Then came Tri-State. As James Jr. explains it, "Some real-estate speculators from California talked his friends into trying to develop Tri-State," a new town near the intersection of California, Nevada, and Arizona. In September 1921, Cashman and his friends organized a townsite auction on the order of the one that so successfully launched Las Vegas.

"We built a dance platform, hired an Indian band from Needles, and put on a barbecue," related Big Jim 40 years later. It was a glorious party lasting two days. There were fist fights, and one drunk decided that a blackjack dealer deserved whipping with "the cat." The drunk tried to do it with a live feline, which didn't cooperate, so both the dealer and the black cat escaped unharmed.

But only $2,700 worth of lots were auctioned, and Cashman said later that the bidders never paid for even those. The venture, begun on borrowed capital, was $20,000 in the hole. "That broke him," said his son. "He was the only one of the partners who had any money and was willing to stand up." One partner left the country, but Big Jim stayed and paid back the loan in three years.

Searchlight's boom cooled off about that time. Cashman set up a garage next to the Overland Hotel in Las Vegas and gradually came to consider Las Vegas his home. His line of autos expanded to include Buicks, LaSalles, Pontiacs, Oldsmobiles, and GMC trucks.

Leah Barker, born and reared in Reno, was the first home economics major to graduate from the University of Nevada, then she became an agent for the university's extension service. She traveled the back roads teaching cooking and housekeeping to farm women. She needed a car for her travels and bought it from Jim Cashman.

"On her first trip, she had to go to Caliente, in Lincoln County," James Jr. related. "Dad said, 'I'm going with you to make sure you don't get in trouble.' About halfway to Caliente, she got a flat tire. He got out of the car, got underneath a bush in the shade, and watched her change the tire. She didn't know how. And she was so mad at him because he wouldn't help her. He told her what to do, but he made her do it. Said that was the only way she'd learn to do it. 'I can't go with

you on every trip,' he told her."

It made her mad, but Leah married Jim in 1923, and their romance lasted until her death nearly 40 years later. They had a daughter, Tona, born in 1924, and James Jr. was born in 1926.

Elected a county commissioner in 1920, Cashman made good roads a primary concern. The main road across Southern Nevada went through Searchlight and bypassed Las Vegas. "With the Clark County equipment, and the backing of San Bernardino County's money, they punched a road from Las Vegas up over Mountain Pass into Baker, California," explained James Jr. The new road opened in 1927 and is today's Interstate 15.

Cashman also was a delegate to the League of the Southwest, which was responsible for getting Congress to fund Hoover Dam. In 1929 he had a 25-passenger boat built to run tours of the lake. The business lasted 10 years, though it wasn't a roaring success. Other ventures, however, were more successful. Frank Crowe, construction superintendent of Hoover Dam, mentioned to Cashman that the dam would require many Caterpillar tractors. Big Jim got the Caterpillar franchise.

Hoover Dam was a cash cow for every sort of business, but when the dam neared completion in 1935, and the free-spending construction crews began moving on, business got slow fast. That year a showman named Clyde Zerby, with previous experience in organizing festivals to bring tourism to small towns, pitched the idea here. The Las Vegas Elks lodge sponsored the festival, named it Helldorado, and got the whole town behind it. Western movie costumes were rented from Hollywood, most local business people wore them and posed for publicity photos, and Helldorado touched off a party that has drawn visitors and money annually ever since.

The original celebration was held in a tent village near Sixth and Fremont streets. But Helldorado outgrew that after two years, so the Elks decided to build a more permanent facility near Las Vegas Boulevard and Bonanza Road.

The first Helldorado was publicized with shots like this one, in which a "prospector" (in a costume rented from a Hollywood studio) "deposited" gold at a local bank. Big Jim is the dude in the stovepipe hat.
(Courtesy James Cashman Jr.)

Leah Cashman contemplates the display set up at the Cashman auto dealership when her husband and son were fighting a heavy-handed union attempt to organize the business. The display implied that Uncle Sam was literally on Cashman's side of the picket line.
(Courtesy James Cashman Jr.)

They spent weekends cutting timber for Helldorado Village, a sort of carnival midway reminiscent of movie-set Western towns, on property that Big Jim owned in Lee Canyon.

In 1948 Helldorado needed still more facilities, and again there was little money to build. And again, Big Jim scrounged up the materials and dragooned the labor. Ed Von Tobel Jr. remembers one Saturday when Big Jim called his father, operator of a local hardware store and lumberyard, and within a minute or two, talked Von Tobel into donating an entire railroad carload of cement. "It was hard to say no to Big Jim," said Ed Jr.

What emerged was Las Vegas' first stadium, consisting mostly of concrete bleachers built into a hillside but big and versatile enough to accommodate not only a rodeo, but also a minor-league baseball team and the city's first exhibition big-league game. Cashman ended up getting most of the credit. The Elks named that stadium Cashman Field, and the Las Vegas Convention Authority retained the name when it built today's modern stadium on the same site. But Big Jim was always quick to point out that it was a community effort, not his alone.

On his travels to Los Angeles in the 1930s, Big Jim usually stayed at the Hollywood Roosevelt, where he got to know the operator, Tommy Hull. Hull began visiting Las Vegas and, early one morning in 1940, he sat with Big Jim at a sidewalk table in front of the Apache Hotel on Fremont Street, having a few drinks. In those wee hours, even Fremont Street was dead, and Big Jim suggested that Hull liven things up by building another hotel here. A drink or two later, Hull decided to do it, and El Rancho Vegas became the first big-time resort on what would soon be known as the Las Vegas Strip.

Cashman's business interests suffered while he threw himself into community projects, but he had a plan to resolve that: Tona and James Jr. His parents expected Tona to be the socially graceful and housewifely "Miss Perfect," said James Jr. But they also encouraged her to learn the family busi-

ness, even when it was unfashionable for women to work, and she became vice president and co-owner. Tona Cashman Siefert died in 1996.

James Jr. worked in every department of the automotive business, starting at age 14. And when he came home from World War II, Big Jim told him to forget about college, because he was about to have the whole magilla—car dealership and heavy equipment sales, real-estate holdings, and even the chairmanship of the Helldorado parade—dumped into his youthful lap. So James Jr. dutifully went to work: "He wanted me to run the business so he could do what he wanted."

In the early '50s, local unions tried to organize the auto dealership. The effort was led by Ralph Alsup, Thomas Hanley, and Bill Carter. All three were tough; Alsup had served time for wounding a man in a union-hall shooting, and to call Hanley a labor racketeer would be letting him off lightly.

The Cashmans fought back with humor. When pickets appeared in front of their house, they tied a mule outside bearing a sign saying, "I'm a picket, too, but I have an excuse. I was born a jackass." They also had a live monkey on exhibit, and when union bosses showed up across the street, the Cashmans turned on loudspeakers with a recording of Spike Jones giving the horse-laugh. Before it was over, said James Jr., he was receiving death threats, made to his face.

Finally, the union men gave up. The Cashmans opened a new auto showroom and invited the whole town. Two days later, the business burned down. Somehow, in the middle of the night, a 55-gallon drum of paint thinner had overturned and ignited. "Later that day I got a call from Tom Hanley," James Jr. recalled. "He said, 'You won the battle, but I won the war.'"

But the war wasn't over. The Cashmans not only rebuilt, but also helped pass a right-to-work law in Nevada. Alsup was shotgunned to death in 1966 outside his home in Paradise Valley. Hanley and two other men were charged with the murder, but the key witness also was murdered—by firebombing—and Hanley went free. More

than a decade later, he kidnapped and murdered Al Bramlet, head of the Las Vegas local of the Culinary Workers Union. Hanley died in 1979, a federal prisoner and one of the most despised men in Nevada history.

Big Jim Cashman died at home in 1962, one of the most beloved. He was 77.

It would be his son and daughter, and grandsons, the late James Cashman III and Tim Cashman, who would turn his small-town businesses into the large operations they are today. In addition, each has continued Big Jim's tradition of volunteerism.

Big Jim was so busy that his son never got to spend as much time with his father as he would have liked. "But it didn't bother me," said James Jr. "I was pretty busy doing all the things I was supposed to do. ... It taught me that when I got to be his age, I had to contribute myself. And I taught my two sons that. The town has been good to us, the state has, and we've got a debt to pay back. I loved my dad, and my mother, and if I had my choice, I wouldn't have changed a thing." ⌀

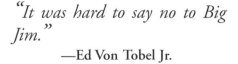

"It was hard to say no to Big Jim."

—Ed Von Tobel Jr.

Jim Cashman (left) and his family on a desert outing in the late 1920s. Leah, seated on the running board, is wearing the light-colored dress; the child at her left knee is Tona and the one at her right is James Jr. Other folks are unidentified.
(Courtesy James Cashman Jr.)

THE FIRST 100

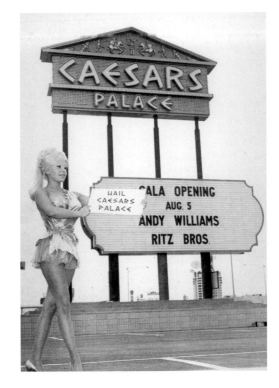

PART II:

Resort Rising

THOMAS HULL (1893–1964)

A visionary, whose El Rancho gave one of the more famous streets in the world its start, began a trend in hotel-casinos in Las Vegas. **BY A.D. HOPKINS**

Even Fremont Street was deserted in the wee morning hours in 1940, when Tommy Hull and Jim Cashman were having a few drinks on the sidewalk in front of the Apache Hotel. They fell to discussing opportunities that might be found along this street, which at the time was one of the few in America where gambling was actually legal.

Big Jim said, "What we really need here is a real resort," or words to that effect. The next day, he claimed later, the two men were looking at sites big enough to build the kind of operation Hull wanted. Cashman, who was a one-man chamber of commerce, suggested a tract at what is today Maryland Parkway and Sahara (San Francisco) Avenue.

"I don't want to build there," Hull said. "I want to build on the road going into town." He pointed at the corner of San Francisco and the Los Angeles Highway. There's a popular story that Hull selected that site because he once had a flat tire there and idly counted the cars that came by while he was waiting for a tow truck. He saw that the traffic would support a roadside resort. Another story claims that the

main reason he bought the site was that it was owned by a single individual with no partners, so the deal could be closed quickly.

Whatever his reasons, his decision put Las Vegas in the resort business. The Las Vegas Strip started with Hull both chronologically and geographically, for the Strip corridor took shape from his resort south.

Tommy Hull was not afraid to take chances. He was an adventurer and a plunger, who had

risked both life and fortune when occasion demanded. Born in Colorado Springs on October 3, 1893, he graduated from the Colorado Agricultural and Mining College in 1913. Hull then tried to ply his mining trade in Mexico, but ran into trouble in those revolutionary times and walked 600 miles back to safety.

He ran a movie theater in New Mexico but was unsuccessful. During World War I he became an officer and a flight instructor for the Army. Following the war, he tried running movie theaters in Austin, Texas. Hull sold his operations to a larger corporation at a profit, then joined his father in the hotel business in San Francisco. He eventually acquired the Bellevue in San Francisco, and traded on his own background as a pilot to make it a gathering spot for America's first generation of aviation heroes, such as Charles Lindbergh, Eddie Rickenbacker, Wiley Post, and Clyde Pangborn.

In September 1932, he took over Los Angeles' Mayfair Hotel, soon adding Hollywood's Roosevelt and the Hotel Senator in Sacramento. By the time he started the venture in Las Vegas, eight other hotels were under his man-

Hull in Southern Nevada

POP.[1]	DECADE
n/a	pre-1900
30	1900
945	1910
2,686	1920
5,952	1930
13,937	1940 ■
45,577	1950
123,667	1960
273,288	1970
463,087	1980
715,587	1990
1,360,000[2]	2000

■ Time spent in Southern Nev.
1 - Population figures are for greater Las Vegas area (*Source: Nevada State Data Center*).
2 - Estimate

Tommy Hull and his wife, former entertainer Lynn Starr Hull, were still celebrities when they visited Las Vegas 20 years after he started the Strip.

(Review-Journal files)

agement.

One of Hull's innovations was extending the services and ambience of first-class hotels into motels and auto courts, places where luxury had been previously unseen. He dubbed each of his new auto hotels "El Rancho," and the one in Las Vegas, opened April 3, 1941, was his third. Hull figured a main function of the Las Vegas version would be offering refreshment and rest to travelers on the hot journey from Los Angeles to Salt Lake City. He built a tempting swimming pool only a few feet from the highway.

His original plan didn't even call for a casino, according to the late John Cahlan, who was managing editor of the *Review-Journal* when Hull arrived. In an oral history done for the University of Nevada-Reno, Cahlan said, "When he started his motel, several of his friends that he had made here in Las Vegas … said, 'Why don't you build a casino building?'"

The casino and a small dining room, surrounded by 65 guest cottages, constituted El Rancho Vegas. "The dining room was built sort of in the form of a corral, with the dance floor being the center of the corral," remembered Cahlan. Walls were brick, and the ceiling had open wood beams and chandeliers made out of wagon wheels. There was a wishing well against one wall. Each table was lit by a hurricane lamp with a leather lampshade; chairs were also of stitched leather.

Entertainment Director Maxine Lewis "set the tempo … for the acts that were in use up until 1960," recalled Cahlan. "She would have a singer, a standing comedian, and then the star of the show with dance girls." One of the first bands to play El Rancho was Garwood Van's. The leader settled in and spent the rest of his life here, founding a local music company.

Las Vegans booked the dining room for wedding parties and banquets. "They'd been waiting for a resort hotel for 40 years, and they thought that this was the best offer that they'd had, and they greeted it very well," said Cahlan. "But they were skeptical, because it was clear out of town."

There was so much business, however, that even celebrities couldn't always get a table. Garwood Van told Las Vegas writer George Stamos about an evening when movie star Wallace Beery and his family were denied a table. "I don't want to see no goddamned show; I just want to have dinner!" roared Beery. Van, who by that time had acquired some authority beyond his role as a bandleader, had a table set up for the family at poolside, converting an unavoidable snub into a memorable evening for the Beery family.

Tommy Hull was the man who decided that Las Vegas wouldn't be a black-tie-only resort. On opening night many Las Vegans wore formal evening wear. Hull showed up in jeans, boots, and a cowboy shirt. By now an urbane sophisticate, he reverted to his native Western drawl and, according to newspaper reports, repeatedly uttered the words that became a motto: "Come as you are."

Hull hadn't been open long when another Western-style casino would try to rustle some of the patrons from El Rancho. R.E. Griffith, who had built and run a chain of movie theaters in the South, and his nephew and architect William J. Moore, were thinking of expanding into the hotel business. Chancing to visit Las Vegas, they decided to do it here.

In a coincidence that seems to defy mathematical odds, Griffith and Moore also had planned to name their new hotel El Rancho. Finding Hull was already using that name, they settled on the Last Frontier. And like Hull, they chose to operate south of town on the Los Angeles Highway.

In 1982 Moore was in-

terviewed for the Pioneer Tapes, an oral history project sponsored jointly by UNLV, the Nevada Humanities Committee, and the *Las Vegas Review-Journal.* Moore pointed out to a UNLV interviewer that arriving in December 1941 meant building during World War II, when construction was supposed to be limited to projects for the war effort.

"They exempted anybody that had started construction … providing they could prove that they had the material before the institution of the War Production Board," he told the UNLV interviewer. Moore's group proved it, but then ran into a catch: The board also had authority to seize construction materials for the war effort. Proving they had the materials handed the government a list of what was available to commandeer. "So they came in on our construction job at the hotel and essentially grabbed all of the material we had having to do with anything electrical and took the material in trucks to the Army air base."

Moore solved that problem by buying a couple of mines and stripping the wire and conduit out of them. To avoid wasting material, he incorporated an existing roadhouse and casino— formerly the Pair-O-Dice but then known as the

The Last Frontier grounds played upon America's fascination with the rural West. Many of the buildings and vehicles were not reproductions, but actual specimens moved from Nevada's ghost towns.
(Las Vegas News Bureau/LVCVA)

91 Club—into the Last Frontier. He bought a bar and the barroom entrance out of the historic Arizona Club in Las Vegas' old Block 16 red-light district, and used them in the new hotel. In the end, Moore and Griffith managed to build a 100-room resort, slightly smaller than their original intention.

They opened their hotel on December 10, 1942, but their home-front war wasn't over. Rationing made it hard to get food for the hotel dining room, so the Last Frontier bought ranches and raised its own cattle for meat and milk. Las Vegas war babies were raised partly on the surplus, sold to the public.

Griffith and Moore were experienced promoters who had helped build the theater business to the dominance it enjoyed in the 1940s, when many Americans attended movies three or four times a week. They used their connections to bring in stars to entertain their resort's visitors. Tommy Hull had no such connections, so he raided their stable of performers to supply his own showroom, sometimes offering stars twice the salary they were making at the Last Frontier. "We were creating jobs, yes. But we were also in the position of furnishing our own competition," said Moore. "We had no alternative."

Griffith died less than a year after the hotel opened. It was Moore who carried out the dream, often attributed to Griffith, of establishing the Frontier Village, celebrating Nevada's colorful past. This was no hokey heap of used sets from forgotten B-movies, but consisted largely of the actual buildings and relics of Nevada's yesteryears.

Most of it came from the collection of Robert "Dobie Doc" Caudill, Moore said. "Dobie Doc" was an abbreviation of the name under which Caudill had once run a construction-repair business: the Adobe Doctor. Caudill was a gambler who would later hold a small interest in Benny Binion's Horseshoe Casino. He was also a compulsive collector of Western memorabilia—so compulsive, in fact, that many called him a kleptomaniac.

It is uncertain whether Frontier management understood the doubtfulness of title by which Doc held many of his collectibles. But those it bought from him and displayed included Elko's joss house—a small temple built for Chinese railroad workers in the 1860s and said to be the oldest surviving in the United States. There was the wooden jail that served Tuscarora in the 1870s. Its interior walls were still equipped with leg irons and charred from an escape-by-fire plot, which went awry and burned to death the man trying to escape. There were real prairie schooners, real horse-drawn fire engines.

Under Moore, the Last Frontier ran some of the first junkets, booking the planes through an obscure airline operator named Kirk Kerkorian.

Well-established before Benjamin "Bugsy" Siegel began building the Flamingo in 1946, Moore stood up to the reputed killer when he tried to throw his weight around Las Vegas. About 1980 Moore related to *Review-Journal* gaming reporter Clyde Weiss how Siegel had become enraged at some imagined offense by the Frontier against his new Flamingo. Siegel sent his goons with bottles of acid, which they dripped onto the carpet up and down the Frontier hallways.

A summit meeting was called and Siegel showed, guarded by some cronies wearing size-19 collars and size-6 hats. But Moore brought some of his own dealers, and Siegel quickly perceived that while Moore was a college boy, some of his employees had been instructors in the school of hard knocks. Siegel paid for the carpet, Moore claimed, and made no more trouble in Las Vegas. Siegel died soon thereafter of a .30-caliber bullet through the brain precipitated by his mismanagement of the Flamingo for his silent partners.

"It became obvious to those of us who had been in business here in town that if somebody didn't get control of this business, sooner or later there was going to be no business," Moore said. In some Nevada counties, he added, the way to get a gaming license was to bribe the sheriff, and human nature dictated this would sooner or later become the case in Las Vegas. Even the mob front guys who succeeded Siegel, said Moore, saw that this trend would wreck the gravy train. So they supported Moore's idea of getting the Nevada Tax Commission to take over gaming licensing. The Tax Commission agreed on condition that Moore accept an appointment to the commission.

By this time, Tommy Hull was long gone from the Strip he started. The conventional wisdom said his unexpected sale of the El Rancho in June 1943 was precipitated by fear of competing with the competent Bill Moore. But John Cahlan discounted that story. "I think he kind of welcomed the competition," said Cahlan. And Hull would be back, for a while, as a partner in the Flamingo. He died in 1964, at the age of 70, of a heart attack at his home in Beverly Hills. The El Rancho burned in 1960.

Moore left the Frontier in 1951, when major stockholders decided to sell the hotel. He would rejuvenate downtown's El Cortez hotel and build the Showboat on Boulder Highway before drifting out of the resort business into real-estate development, oil drilling, and—improbably—pioneering the potato agribusiness in northwestern Nevada. He died in 1982 at the age of 68, still a Las Vegas resident.

Both Hull and Moore went on to make many another mark, but during the war years, the two entrepreneurs were inventing the Las Vegas Strip. ✍

> *"They'd been waiting for a resort hotel for 40 years, and they thought that this was the best offer that they'd had, and they greeted it very well. But they were skeptical, because it was clear out of town."*
>
> — **John Cahlan**
> Former *Review-Journal* managing editor speaking about Tommy Hull's brainchild

William Moore, an experienced promoter from the movie business and also an architect, upstaged El Rancho with the Last Frontier, an early themed resort that featured authentic artifacts of Nevada's past.
(UNLV Special Collections)

HOWARD EELLS
(1893–1978)

Despite facing numerous obstacles, he built the world's biggest magnesium plant during World War II. **BY A.D. HOPKINS**

"It detracts nothing from the splendor of the Boulder [Dam] accomplishment to point out that the big job at Basic is of even more gigantic proportions. At the peak of employment the dam project had 5,250 at work. Last week the employment count on the Basic job was 13,618. The weekly payroll at this project is greater than the monthly payroll at the dam. Anderson's [the company that contracted to feed workers] had a mess hall at the dam that seated 1,300. Anderson's here can serve 2,500 at a sitting."

—"The Big Job"
BMI newsletter, July 30, 1942

The city he started was named for somebody else, and others ended up running the industry he brought to Nevada. Far from spreading the welcome mat, one of Nevada's U.S. senators demanded that Congress investigate him. But Howard Eells endured it all, and Henderson exists because he did. Now the third largest city in Nevada, Henderson is also one of the youngest. Most people born the same year as Henderson, 1941, aren't even retired yet.

Eells, of Cleveland, inherited his father's manufacturing business in 1919. In the 1930s he made firebrick, used to line furnaces and fireplaces. And in 1939 he sent geologists into the mountains of Nye County looking for heat-resistant materials. They found or acquired deposits of magnesite and brucite containing more than 70 million tons of good ore—the largest deposit ever found.

Hitler's invasion of Poland reminded Eells that his ore had other uses. German dive bombers could turn on a dime because of lightweight magnesium components. German paratroopers had a huge advantage over other infantry, for they were able to carry their own artillery—lightweight 25mm cannon made of magnesium.

Magnesium was the key component of bright-burning tracer bullets, essential to accurate machine-gun fire. It was the key component of incendiary bombs and of the flares used to light battlefields or signal rescue craft. Yet the United States had been caught napping; little magnesium was made in this country. And through patents, Dow Chemical Company and Alcoa monopolized even this.

Eells tracked down Major John P. Ball, who had bought production patents from a German operation shortly after World War I and founded a company to produce magnesium in England. Ball would provide know-how to make the light metal in America. But getting plans for a magnesium factory proved difficult. Dispatched to America in six large crates accompanied by two of Ball's employees, the first set of plans went down when the ship was torpedoed. Both escorts were rescued. A second set of plans was microfilmed and sent by airplane, while the waterlogged escorts boarded a different plane as a decoy. Both airplanes got through.

Meanwhile, Eells searched the country for financing and friends. He found the friends in Nevada Senators Key Pittman and Patrick McCarran. It helped that Charles P. Henderson, a former U.S. senator from Nevada, was chairman of the Reconstruction Finance Corporation, a federal agency that financed businesses, including defense plants. They considered locating the factory near the magnesite deposits at Gabbs, but the site lacked both water and electrical power. Making magnesium requires plenty of both. They eventually settled on a site about halfway between the generating facilities of Hoover Dam and the railroads at Las Vegas.

However, some contend it wasn't logical to build a new factory at all, and especially not in Nevada. In his book *Resort City in the Sunbelt*, UNLV history professor Eugene P. Moehring explained why it happened anyway. Both men (Ball and Eells) needed a factory, and Nevada's congressional delegation had the clout to build it, wrote Moehring. Efficiency would have dictated that the ore be hauled to existing plants in Cali-

Howard Eells, founder of Henderson
(Courtesy Maryellen Sadovich)

Eells in Southern Nevada

POP.[1]	DECADE
n/a	pre-1900
30	1900
945	1910
2,686	1920
5,952	1930
13,937	1940
45,577	1950
123,667	1960
273,288	1970
463,087	1980
715,587	1990
1,360,000[2]	2000

■ Time spent in Southern Nev.
1 - Population figures are for greater Las Vegas area (*Source: Nevada State Data Center*).
2 - Estimate

fornia, but then Nevada would have lost the factory. Efficiency also might have demanded that the magnesium deposits in nearby Overton (only 50 miles from Las Vegas) be used, but then Eells owned the deposits at Gabbs, 350 miles away. So, at first, the federal government paid an exorbitant price to transport Gabbs magnesite 1,100 miles by rail via Salt Lake City to Las Vegas. Eventually, Washington built road connections (including a new Las Vegas thoroughfare, Rancho Drive, to prevent the heavy trucks from tearing up existing city roads).

There are some counter arguments. C.F. DeArmond, an engineer and member of the Colorado River Commission, said in 1941 that nearby ores were more expensive to process, so using Gabbs ore was cheaper even when transportation costs were calculated.

Southern Nevada folk wisdom holds that the

Workmen in May 1942 remove a node assembly from a lead mold to install in the plant that produced dangerous chlorine for use in the plant's own process and to sell to other defense industries.
(Courtesy Maryellen Sadovich)

site was chosen to disperse war industry and make it harder to hit should carrier-based Japanese aircraft attack the mainland. The neighboring mountains would require bombers to fly high and make their bombing less accurate. Eells took the trouble to deny that in 1953. "The selection had nothing whatever to do with 'decentralization against enemy attacks,'" he wrote in a letter to *Business Week*, clarifying mistakes in a story.

On July 5, 1941, the U.S. Defense Plant Corporation signed an agreement with Eells' newly formed Basic Magnesium Inc. to build the plant. With war looming, the federal government was to own all buildings, land, equipment, and magnesium produced. It controlled sales and production quotas, and it paid the workers. But BMI ran the operation and recruited, hired, and fired.

A few days after the contract was signed, the government asked Eells to build a plant 10 times the size originally contemplated. It would be a mile and three-quarters long and three-quarters of a mile wide, the largest magnesium plant in the world. The scale of the construction staggers the imagination, even today.

The BMI newsletter, appropriately named "The Big Job," commented on July 30, 1942: "It detracts nothing from the splendor of the Boulder [Dam] accomplishment to point out that the big job at Basic is of even more gigantic proportions. At the peak of employment the dam project had 5,250 at work. Last week the employment count on the Basic job was 13,618. The weekly payroll at this project is greater than the monthly payroll at the dam. Anderson's [the company that contracted to feed workers] had a mess hall at the dam that seated 1,300. Anderson's here can serve 2,500 at a sitting."

The 13,000-plus workers constituted 10 percent of Nevada's population, and that didn't even include the number building a second plant at Gabbs to partially refine the ore, reducing the weight by half before shipping it.

Workers still trying to rebuild their bankrolls from the waning Depression hastened to Las Vegas, and their numbers quickly overwhelmed lo-

cal accommodations. Ragtag campsites, which would have been called "Hoovervilles" only a few years before, grew up along Boulder Highway. There were tents, trailers, makeshift shacks—even some hogans built by Indians working on the plant. Eells wanted to house workers in Boulder City, a town originally built for dam workers. But when the Bureau of Reclamation, which still ran Boulder City, said it couldn't handle so many workers, Eells started talking about building housing near the plant.

Las Vegas business interests promptly declared the honeymoon over. They had missed out on many economic benefits from Hoover Dam, because the federal government built Boulder City as a complete town with its own stores, entertainment, and restaurants. Now Las Vegans saw the same thing about to happen again.

Their champion became Berkeley Bunker, the Las Vegan appointed to the Senate after Pittman's unexpected death in 1940. Bunker wrote the president of the Defense Finance Corporation, urging that Las Vegas be designated the official homesite for the plant and charging that Eells wanted to build a new townsite based on "visions of personal financial profit."

Eells didn't even want a company town, just worker housing. But growth-hungry Las Vegas had never developed water, sewer, and street facilities to accommodate such a windfall of new population. In the end, federal authorities forced Eells to do what neither he nor Las Vegas wanted. DFC refused to finance housing unless it met U.S. Public Health Service standards requiring on-site stores, streets, and recreational facilities. A company town was born.

Construction began on February 17, 1942. As a concession to Las Vegas interests, the houses were built on wood foundations so they could easily be moved after the war. Some were moved, but many remain today, their temporary foundations long since replaced with concrete.

McNeil Construction Company of Los Angeles got the contract to build both the plant and the townsite. President Bruce McNeil became a

Nevada hero when the BMI administration office, containing all the plans for the plant, caught fire. McNeil drove a bulldozer through flames to push out the filing cabinets containing the critical plans.

Bunker publicly suggested that the fire had been intentionally set to cover the facts about the "company town." This led to a fact-finding mission by Senator Harry Truman, chairman of the Senate Investigation Committee. He held hearings in Las Vegas, and though he never bothered to visit the plant site, Truman issued a report calling the new plant "one of the most flagrant attempts at war profiteering."

Bunker faced re-election in 1942. If he was trying to make hay with his anti-BMI crusade, he was badly out of touch with constituents. Democrats voted to nominate not Bunker, but former Governor James Scrugham, a pro-BMI candidate, who subsequently won the general election.

Meanwhile, Eells sold BMI and its management contract to Anaconda Copper Mining Company in 1942. It would remain for Anaconda to complete the townsite and bring the plant to full production. The town was named for Charles P. Henderson, at the urging of the Colorado River Commission, in gratitude for the former senator's role in getting the plant financed and built.

Despite work that was brutally hot and hard, and created serious turnover problems, BMI under Anaconda management broke both production and safety records. So hard did the war workers toil that by July 1943, the plant was producing magnesium at 10 percent greater than its rated capacity. So much did it make that in November 1944, with fighting still raging in Europe and the Pacific, the federal government decided it needed no more magnesium, and Basic Magnesium was ordered to suspend production. Within a few days, the production lines closed down and workers were dismissed.

Finding a new job in the war-hot economy was no great hardship, but the jobs were somewhere else, so more than half the houses soon stood empty. Henderson nearly became one more Nevada ghost town. But Charles Henderson, Pat

McCarran, Vail Pittman, and many other Southern Nevada leaders were determined to have another outcome. The War Assets Administration sought to sell the whole operation—factory, tools, hospital, and Henderson itself—to private industry. Some assets were sold, but the WAA retained the real estate for several years, largely because title was clouded. In the housing shortage brought on by Las Vegas' postwar boom, all the single-family dwellings built for the townsite, and most of the apartments, were once more occupied.

In 1948, through negotiations involving the Colorado River Commission, the state purchased the entire complex for $24 million—with $1 down. The announcement in the March 17 *Review-Journal* noted, "As a tribute to Senator McCarran, WAA rushed through all legal entanglements so transfer would be formally recorded on St. Patrick's Day."

New manufacturing firms were found to use portions of the plant, giving Southern Nevada the industrial base that had been a civic goal for more than 40 years. In 1951 the tenants organized a company called Basic Management Inc. The new BMI bought the property from the state in 1952. Another legacy of the plant was the federally financed water line from Lake Mead, which became a basis for the Las Vegas Valley Water District.

Industrialization had brought great changes to the social order. Women had worked outside the home, in large numbers, for the first time. Many of them never went back to traditional roles. The plants offered jobs to blacks from poverty-stricken Southern regions and changed the racial demographics of Clark County. Organized labor became important. Henderson became a city.

Meanwhile, the man who started it was forgotten. Then, in the 1960s, Maryellen Sadovich, a writer who had come to Henderson in 1954 when her

miner husband was transferred to one of the new plants, began wondering who was originally responsible for the war industry. Nobody knew.

Someone had heard it was a guy from Cleveland. "Then some photographer told me he thought the guy's name was Eells," said Sadovich in 1998, then age 73. "I looked his name up in the Cleveland phone book and wrote him a letter. … I ended up going to Cleveland and interviewing him in his office."

Eells gave her dozens of boxes of correspondence, photographs, documents, and souvenirs relating to the nativity of Henderson's war industry. Sadovich based her master's thesis on those materials and gave most of them to the UNLV archives, to ensure that her city's founder would never again be forgotten.

Eells died in 1978, at the age of 85. ⌀

Aerial view of the Basic Magnesium Inc. complex on November 10, 1941, emerging from the empty desert that would become Henderson.

(Courtesy Maryellen Sadovich)

"Magnesium Maggie" (1942–1945)

Female workers flourished during the war years in positions formerly considered too difficult for women. BY A.D. HOPKINS

Call her "Magnesium Maggie." She was Nevada's version of Rosie the Riveter, and she spent the war years making magnesium ingots, then stacking and shipping them to factories where they would be turned into tracer bullets and aerial flares and incendiary bombs.

Maggie never got the attention Rosie did, but Irene Rostine, herself a former war worker, vows that Maggie won't be forgotten. Rostine is gathering stories of the women war workers as her master's thesis at UNLV and hopes to publish the collection in a book. "I wanted to find out about them [the women] and put them in the public eye," said Rostine. "There are movies about Rosie the Riveter and about the women who built ships in Seattle, and we had women who did something just as important."

Rostine dubbed these women "Magnesium Maggies" because the largest group of them worked at the Basic Magnesium plant in what is now Henderson. But with the manpower shortages of war, women took jobs throughout the local economy that formerly had been associated with men. "At BMI they [women] drove forklifts," Rostine said. "They drove taxis, which were used to get around the plant because it was so big. They handled and wrapped ingots for shipping." Some made asbestos gloves to handle the ingots; some repaired gas masks.

The late Thelma Lindquist was called "Chlorine Kate" because she operated a cell that made chlorine gas, hydrogen, and caustic soda, which were used in the magnesium manufacturing process and also were sold as byproducts. "Workers who ran these cells had to wear rubber shoes to prevent electrocution from the electrodes that were operating in the tanks of brine, and they had to carry a gas mask at all times," said Rostine. "It was easily 130 degrees in that section in the summer, and in the winter it was so cold she [Lindquist] would crawl up on top of the cells to get warm, even though it was dangerous and forbidden." The job was so rough that most people who tried it lasted one day, but Lindquist stuck with it through war and peace, until her retirement in 1955.

Magnesium production shut down in 1944, but portions of the huge plant were converted to other purposes. Rheem Manufacturing Company rented the machine shop in May 1945 to make artillery shells and tracer ammunition. At the time

Maxine Buckles worked in a Boulder City bank. "I learned I could make as much money in a week at Rheem as I made in a month at the bank, so I applied," she said. She learned to operate a lathe, machining shells down to exact size. "It wasn't difficult work, but the shift was from 5 p.m. to 5 a.m. I got so I couldn't sleep at night, I was so used to working."

When the shell delivered to her for milling was too big, it would break the lathe. The worker who came to fix it, Benjamin Buckles, was an Army man employed there while on convalescent leave after being injured in the Pacific. He married Maxine before going back to finish the war.

Though many women married or at least dated men they met on the job, sexual harassment was rare. Women interviewed for this story, and all those interviewed by Rostine, said neither they nor any of their friends had such problems. Rostine thinks that may have been partly because Henderson was a company town, which did not blend into

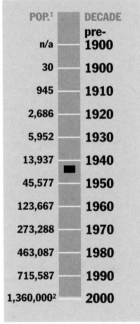

'Maggies' in Southern Nevada

POP.[1]	DECADE
n/a	pre-1900
30	1900
945	1910
2,686	1920
5,952	1930
13,937	1940
45,577	1950
123,667	1960
273,288	1970
463,087	1980
715,587	1990
1,360,000[2]	2000

■ Time spent in Southern Nev.
1 - Population figures are for greater Las Vegas area (*Source: Nevada State Data Center*).
2 - Estimate

Winnie Cooper Prince saved her identification badge from her job at the Rheem Manufacturing Company ammunition plant.

(Courtesy Winnie Cooper Prince)

some larger society: "The town was built because of the plant, so everybody knew everybody. That would discourage it." Most people were married, and a would-be Lothario might run into a suspicious spouse at his own job or in the local bar.

Women's previous life experiences adapted them to the work, suggested Rostine: "The metalworkers section at Basic was very dangerous, working over molten metal. But one woman said, 'It's nothing more than working over a hot cookstove.'" The women's safety record was better than the men's, but the women tended to get hurt in different ways. "They dropped things on their feet, or were hit by an object, or tripped," said Rostine. "The kind of thing that happens to you when you are not used to a factory setting and find yourself in one."

Economic opportunity was an important reason women worked in war industries, but so was patriotism. Rostine's mother-in-law, Della Mae Rostine, was a machinist, though so tiny at 90 pounds that she could not always pull the safety cover down over her machine. Sometimes the cover sprang back and lifted her off her feet. "She complained to the foreman, and he gave her a clipboard and made her keep track of downtime on the machines," said Rostine. "But that was boring so she asked for a different job. The foreman said, 'I don't have a different one; if you want to help the war effort, you gotta do this.' So she kept doing it, even though she hated it."

Although Buckles worked in another war plant in Utah after the Henderson ammo factory closed, she was glad when the manpower shortage was over and she felt she could honorably quit. "I don't want to do what men do," she said. "I did it as a patriotic effort, but if they wanted me to do a man's job now, I wouldn't want to do it."

Winnie Prince, who also worked at Rheems, said, "I didn't have any intention of staying [in the labor force]. … We had a goal. We wanted to earn enough money to take our family to Salt Lake for the Centennial in 1947." It was a goal she and her husband realized.

Most Magnesium Maggies enjoyed their first taste of equal pay for equal work—generally 90 cents an hour for Henderson production workers. Federal rules requiring equal pay, said Rostine, "were riddled with loopholes, but BMI apparently didn't take advantage of them. All the women I found said they were paid the same as men."

Even those who went back to the family cookstove, said Rostine, "cut a path for other women. They did jobs that were men's jobs before."

> *"I consider myself a local historian, trying to fill in the missing pieces in a puzzle. I feel that these women, who got up and went to work every day at a difficult job, helped make the community what it is. So without knowing about them, our understanding of the community is incomplete."*
> —**Irene Rostine**
> **Former war worker**

By the time the war emergency was over, she added, there were women in most classes of jobs. While breakthroughs into management remained in the future, the door to industrial employment would never again be as tightly closed as it had been in prewar days.

Although the Henderson plants were the most conspicuous examples, said Rostine, much of Southern Nevada's economy was marshaled into support of the war, and wherever they could, women went to bat for their country. Rostine herself made tail cones for B-17 bombers in New York before her family moved here in 1941.

"I went to work for the telephone company," she said, "and that was considered war work because communications were so important. … Operators had to pledge not to disclose anything. You were under constant supervision, so it would have been hard to eavesdrop, but you might have overheard something." She parlayed her phone company experience into good postwar jobs setting up phone systems and supervising operators at resort hotels. Later she owned Shamrock Realty.

Rostine was born in 1924 and graduated from high school in 1941, when a job in an aircraft factory seemed infinitely more important than a college education. She was past retirement age when she found time to enter UNLV, and was taking a class in social history when she decided to research women war workers.

She's been at the task ever since: "I consider myself a local historian, trying to fill in the missing pieces in a puzzle. I feel that these women, who got up and went to work every day at a difficult job, helped make the community what it is. So without knowing about them, our understanding of the community is incomplete." ✍

Women workers on October 1, 1943, wrapping ingots of magnesium for shipping to factories where they would be made into tracer bullets, bombs, and lightweight equipment.
(Courtesy Maryellen Sadovich)

Young women learned to master bicep-building tasks like driving a forklift to load the tall stacks of ingots for shipping.
(UNLV Special Collections)

BERKELEY BUNKER
(1906–1999)

"The fact of the matter is, I managed [Carville's] Southern Nevada campaign when he ran for governor. ... When I was speaker, we worked closely on legislation, and we were very close friends. But why he chose me, I'll never know. I didn't campaign for it; I didn't lift a finger. I was the most surprised man in the state when it came."

—Berkeley Bunker

A member of a pioneer Mormon family, who found himself thrust into a national office after a key official died, returned to the city he loved and made himself and his family proud. BY K.J. EVANS

O f all the bizarre tales of Nevada politics—and there are plenty of them—none is stranger than the one in which a dead U.S. senator, on the eve of his re-election in 1940, was preserved on ice in a hotel bathtub by his campaign aides until the vote was final. That senator was Democrat Key Pittman, first elected in 1912. Having hit the end of the campaign trail, the rarely sober senator began hitting the bottle, and subsequently suffered a heart attack in his room at the Riverside Hotel in Reno.

The politician-on-ice story is almost certainly bogus; researchers have concluded that Pittman was rushed to the hospital, where he died after the election. Pittman's death did, however, set into motion an equally strange series of events in the career of a serious-minded young man named Berkeley Bunker. He would be celebrated as the first Southern Nevadan—and the first Nevada Mormon—to hold national office.

The Bunkers are a pioneer Morman family of the Moapa Valley. Martin and Euphamie Bunker moved there from St. George, Utah, in 1877 and established the family ranch at St. Thomas. Berkeley was born there in August 1906, one of five boys and two girls. The family moved to Las Vegas when Berkeley was 17. Impressed with the modern conveniences of electricity and indoor plumbing, young Berkeley promptly became a city boy. "I said, 'This is for me,' and I fell in love with town—and I've loved it ever since," he said in a 1988 interview.

He was one of 26 graduates of the Clark County High School class of 1926, and then was called on a church mission to the Deep South. On his return in 1933, he married Lucile Whitehead, a fellow Moapan.

The fall of 1935 was the season of petroleum and politics, as Bunker was elected vice president of the Nevada Young Democrats Club and leased a Mobil service station at the corner of Las Vegas Boulevard and Carson Street. Shortly after that, he opened a Texaco station at Fifth and Fremont streets.

Bunker's first foray into politics was in the summer of 1936, when he entered the race for the state Assembly. During his first term in 1937, he astonished everyone by garnering an appointment to the Assembly Ways and Means Committee. He easily won a second term in the 1939 Legislature, and surprised everyone again when he challenged William Kennett of Tonopah for the position of Assembly speaker—and won. Bunker had not planned to seek a third term, but at the urging of party leaders he filed for re-election in 1940 and won again.

Then Key Pittman died. Responsibility for naming Pittman's successor fell on Governor E.P. "Ted" Carville, who was instantly set upon by a horde of eager applicants, including Key Pittman's brother, Vail Pittman.

On November 26, 1940, Carville announced his choice—Berkeley Bunker. "Bunker's appointment can perhaps be seen as a slap at anti-Mormonism," said Michael Green, history professor at the Community College of Southern Nevada. "It was also an acknowledgment that the Mormon Church, and its adherents in Southern Nevada, were gaining political power."

Offering his own explanation for the appointment, Bunker said: "The fact of the matter is, I managed [Carville's] Southern Nevada campaign when he ran for governor. ... When I was speaker,

Bunker in Southern Nevada

POP.[1]	DECADE
n/a	pre-1900
30	1900
945	1910
2,686	1920
5,952	1930
13,937	1940
45,577	1950
123,667	1960
273,288	1970
463,087	1980
715,587	1990
1,360,000[2]	2000

■ Time spent in Southern Nev.
1 - Population figures are for greater Las Vegas area (*Source: Nevada State Data Center*).
2 - Estimate

The annual equestrian appearance in the Helldorado Days parade was standard practice for local dignitaries, and Berkeley Bunker was no exception.

(Courtesy Della Lee Bunker)

we worked closely on legislation, and we were very close friends. But why he chose me, I'll never know. I didn't campaign for it; I didn't lift a finger. I was the most surprised man in the state when it came."

With little knowledge of international affairs, and a war already going in Europe, Bunker's public utterances concerning foreign policy were cautious. "I shall be a strong advocate for a strong national defense program, but I am not in favor of sending our men to Europe," he said. "I think the British can win the war with the assistance the United States can render under the lend-lease bill."

But isolationists became extinct on Sunday, December 7, 1941, when the Japanese attacked Pearl Harbor. With war under way, Bunker cast himself in the role of gadfly, harshly criticizing plans by Basic Magnesium and the Defense Plant Corporation to build a company town—which would become Henderson. The senator insisted that housing also was needed in Las Vegas proper and, as a result, several hundred new houses were built in the Huntridge district, near East Charleston and Maryland Parkway.

Bunker continued the pressure, accusing BMI and the DPC of drawing up a contract that would result in an annual profit to BMI of more than 4,000 percent. "If the agreement between the Defense Plant Corporation and Basic Magnesium

represents a cross section of conduct on the part of the DPC," he said, "I can come to only one conclusion: We are tolerating the existence of an agency of the government that is so corrupt that it would make profiteering in the last war look like petty larceny by comparison."

Bunker later explained that he tackled the BMI issue because he was concerned the plant would not survive into the competitive postwar marketplace unless it were put on sound financial and managerial footing from the outset. The BMI complex has survived to this day.

The freshman senator was obliged by law to stand for election in 1942 and, to his chagrin, his opponent in the primary was former Governor James Scrugham, then one of the top Democrats in the state. Bunker's 1,100-vote loss to Scrugham was his first political setback, and left him feeling "kind of empty."

But he bounced back in 1944, announcing his candidacy for Nevada's lone congressional seat, challenging and beating incumbent Democrat Maurice Sullivan in the primary. "Bunker surprised the wiseacres by beating Sullivan in his home county of Washoe," crowed the *Las Vegas Review-Journal*. The general election, in which he faced silent film star Rex Bell, was a 14,000-vote landslide for Bunker.

The next year, 1945, Scrugham died, vacating the very seat Bunker had once warmed. Governor Carville again had to name a replacement, and Bunker was a top contender. But Carville had a better idea. He made a deal with Lieutenant Governor Vail Pittman: Carville would resign, Pittman would become governor, and he would appoint Carville to the Senate. The only catch was that Carville would have to stand for election in 1946.

It was more than Bunker could tolerate. He announced that he would challenge his former benefactor in the 1946 Democratic primary, a move that he would later admit was "the biggest mistake" of his political career. Bunker eas-

ily defeated Carville and was expected to trounce Republican George "Molly" Malone in the general elections. But so fragmented was the Democratic vote that Malone rode to an easy victory—though it should be noted that 1946 was a very good year for the GOP nationwide.

Back home again, Bunker was hired by P.O. Silvagni to manage the Apache Hotel. (The property would later be leased by Benny Binion and renamed the Horseshoe Club.) Bunker stayed for less than a year, resigning because his duties required him to work every Sunday, a day that Mormons set aside exclusively for worship and church activities.

As an LDS bishop, Bunker was much in demand among his brethren as a funeral preacher. And his years in politics had enhanced his oratorical skills. For a deeply religious man, the job of "preaching people into heaven" was quite satisfying. "I never knew the real heartbeat of the people until I became a bishop of the LDS church," he said. "When you hold a funeral, clasp the hand of the dying, and prepare for the last rites … you feel the true pulse of the people." So Berkeley joined his elder brother Bryan in the mortuary business.

Berkeley Bunker made one last bid for elected office in 1962 when he got his party's nomination for lieutenant governor. He lost to relative newcomer Paul Laxalt.

In 1988, Lucile Bunker died, and the following year, Berkeley married Della Lee, a native of Panaca. She would care for him as his health deteriorated, until his death on January 21, 1999, at age 92.

Among the members of his church, Bunker will certainly be best remembered as chairman of the fund-raising committee that finally gathered the money needed to construct the long-anticipated Las Vegas Temple, the gleaming spired structure at the base of Frenchman's Mountain. ✍

Berkeley Bunker was a member of the Las Vegas High School basketball team of 1926. Front row (left to right): Coach Carver, Jack Sandy, Fred Whiteneck, Fermin Goodwin, Clair Wadsworth, Ebbie Davis, and Bunker. Back row (left to right): Lawrence Whiteneck, Jimmie Down, John McDonald, and George Bremner.
(UNLV Special Collections)

Berkeley Bunker held the title of patriarch in the Mormon Church and was a patriarch in the secular sense as well. Here, he leads a Bible study session with some younger family members.
(Review-Journal files)

PAT McCARRAN (1876–1954)

The Silver State's champion, who served as a Nevada Supreme Court justice, found himself on the losing side of many an election until he was able to win a seat in the U.S. Senate. BY A.D. HOPKINS

For 20 years, Pat McCarran's political machine ran Nevada. It replaced the machine of George Wingfield, which had existed mostly to enrich Wingfield and his cronies. McCarran believed his machine served the interests of all Nevadans.

He helped bring heavy industry to Southern Nevada and keep it here. He was one of those responsible for Nellis Air Force Base and civil aviation. He helped keep Nevada silver in every American's pocket change, and he helped keep Franklin Roosevelt from packing the U.S. Supreme Court with New Deal Democrats.

McCarran was a second-generation Irish-American. During the Potato Famine of the 1840s, "his father came over at the age of 14, his family having starved, and his mother came over in steerage," wrote McCarran's daughter, the nun Sister Margaret P. McCarran.

Patrick McCarran, born in 1876, grew up on his father's sheep ranch on the Truckee River, about 15 miles east of Reno. He had no childhood playmates, and as an adult never developed a social life. The few mandatory Masses of his Catholic faith gave him an opportunity to converse and roughhouse with others his age. He remembered those occasions with special fondness in a letter to his daughter: "We would together kneel and examine the conscience and read the prayers before Confession, then to the dear little

Confessional where the freckled-faced boy told all the terrible sins which a freckled-faced boy with only a dog for a playmate might be guilty of committing."

He didn't start grade school until he was 10. Being more mature than his classmates had its payoffs; graduating from Reno High School at nearly 21 years of age, he was valedictorian and

had broken school records for both the 50- and the 100-yard dash. At the University of Nevada he excelled in debate and wrote for the school newspaper. However, he dropped out when his father's ill health required him to take over the family ranch.

In 1902, Silver Democrats recruited him to run for the Nevada Legislature. Though silver was primarily a national issue, the silver crowd needed to control the Legislature because it would select a new U.S. senator. McCarran's platform also included eight-hour-day, pro-labor, and anti-trust planks. He won the election, and soon was recognized as an able and particularly hard-working legislator, largely because he got himself appointed correspondent for a Reno newspaper and wasn't shy about mentioning himself in his stories.

McCarran married in 1903, then ran for the Nevada Senate in 1904 and lost decisively. He educated himself in law by private reading and passed the bar exam in 1905. He moved to Tonopah the same year.

Tonopah had sprung up in 1900 around an important silver strike, and another strike in 1902 spawned nearby Goldfield. One of McCarran's biographers, Jerome Edwards, thinks McCarran realized that "the political center of Nevada had gravitated to the mining-boom towns. Tonopah was new; there was no established element jealously guarding its political and financial prerogatives. Everyone was in on the ground floor; ev-

McCarran in Southern Nevada

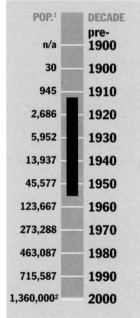

POP.[1]	DECADE
n/a	pre-1900
30	1900
945	1910
2,686	1920
5,952	1930
13,937	1940
45,577	1950
123,667	1960
273,288	1970
463,087	1980
715,587	1990
1,360,000[2]	2000

■ Time spent in Southern Nev.
1 - Population figures are for greater Las Vegas area (*Source: Nevada State Data Center*).
2 - Estimate

Pat McCarran as he looked in the 1950s; he died in 1954 at age 78.
(Nevada State Museum and Historical Society)

eryone was a carpetbagger."

McCarran proved himself a brilliant defense lawyer, good enough to get elected district attorney. But he was not as successful at prosecution. "His heart was with the sinner," explains Edwards.

It was during his Tonopah years that he ran afoul of George Wingfield, sometimes called the "owner and operator of Nevada." McCarran represented Wingfield's wife in a divorce suit, but Wingfield won annulment instead of divorce. During labor troubles that began in 1907, McCarran again alienated Wingfield and his mine-owner allies by criticizing the Nevada governor for calling in troops and, later, forming a Nevada State Police Force.

"The plan of Governor Sparks to equip a body of Texas Rangers and vest these horsemen with power to use their shooting irons at will in the settlement of labor controversies would be more than a state disgrace," McCarran said. Edwards says such statements got McCarran a reputation as a dangerous radical. When he ran for Congress in 1908, Democratic Party bosses shunned him like a leper.

In 1912 McCarran was elected to the Nevada

P. A. McCARRAN

Supreme Court and was good at the job, writing decisions admired and cited these 80-plus years later. But in 1916, before completing his term, he sought the nomination for a seat in the U.S. Senate against Democratic incumbent Key Pittman. Democrats chose Pittman, and two years later refused to work for McCarran's re-election. Thus he managed to become one of the few incumbent justices who failed to win a Supreme Court race. For the next 14 years, he was a perennial loser.

In 1932 McCarran challenged U.S. Senator Tasker Oddie. The Republican Oddie was popular and had lots of money. McCarran ran on a shoestring, but the Democratic Party allowed him to coast through the primary without an opponent: Nobody else would risk getting slaughtered by Oddie in the general. Most folks thought it would take a miracle to beat Oddie, but a bank failure sufficed. Wingfield's bank chain failed a few days before the election, and most of Nevada's state funds were in these banks. Oddie, closely associated with Wingfield, got some of the blame.

McCarran also profited from a landslide turnout in the presidential election of his fellow Democrat, Franklin Roosevelt. In addition, Southern Nevada's population had boomed with the construction of Hoover Dam. Nearly all newcomers were working folk, disproportionately from the South, and Democrats for both reasons.

McCarran went into the Senate by 21,398 votes to 19,706. He was already 56, yet would serve more than 20 years. He had learned a great deal about political machines in 30 years of being trampled by one and promptly began building his own. McCarran's machine eventually replaced Wingfield's and enlisted some of Wingfield's veterans. Even Wingfield eventually became friendly.

Despite recent Democratic backing, McCarran couldn't count on continued support because the party was led by his sometime enemy, Senator Pittman. So

McCarran devised a machine that would be only secondarily loyal to the Democratic cause but primarily loyal to him.

He wrested control of many federal appointments in Nevada from the senior senator who normally would have made them. He did this by threatening to oppose Pittman's important appointments on the Senate floor, unless he was allowed to appoint underlings in the same office. McCarran also controlled many state and even city appointments. Each McCarran appointee knew part of the deal was working for McCarran in federal elections. This was illegal, but the Hatch Act was ignored in Nevada.

Around 1937 McCarran made an alliance of convenience with gubernatorial candidate E.P. "Ted" Carville. Though Pittman remained the theoretical head of Nevada's Democratic Party, he was falling into complete alcoholism and was more interested in national and international issues. McCarran became the real power and soon fell out with Carville.

Pittman died in 1940 and Carville, by then governor, appointed Las Vegan Berkeley Bunker to replace him in the Senate. Bunker served out the term, but lost the next Democratic primary to a McCarran-backed man. In 1945, when Bunker's successor died in office, Carville essentially named himself to the Senate. McCarran got Bunker to run against Carville, and Bunker beat him in the Democratic primary but lost to a Republican dark horse, George "Molly" Malone, in the general.

If McCarran was deeply disturbed about losing a Democratic seat in the U.S. Senate, he never showed it convincingly. Carville, too independent for McCarran's taste, was out of his hair. In 1950, McCarran backed Republican Charles Russell for the governor's seat against Vail Pittman, brother to the late senator and the candidate of McCarran's party. Russell won.

McCarran, however, knew Jesse James' secret: You can kill a few people as long as you're nice to

"*Normally the door was always open between my office and the senator's. This man closed the door. All of a sudden that door flew open; the senator had him by the back of the neck and the seat of the pants propelling him out of the office. And it was tragic, because he was trying to give the senator $2,000 to get his son this job, which the senator had already gotten for him. But oh, he was insulted!*"

—Eva Adams
McCarran's office manager

The future senator, Pat McCarran, as drawn by newspaper cartoonist Arthur Buel for a book published around 1910. The tiny jackass in the left corner was a trademark that appeared in most of Buel's newspaper cartoons; it was not an editorial comment.
(Nevada State Museum and Historical Society)

everyone you don't yet need to kill. Most Nevadans were in the latter category, and therefore loved the nice man in Washington.

Young Harley E. Harmon wanted a job in civilian aviation and went to McCarran's office to ask for a contact. Harmon described the meeting in an interview, nearly 60 years later, with the *Las Vegas Review-Journal:* "He got on the phone and said, 'Get me the chairman of the board of Pan American Airlines.' Somebody told him, 'He's in a meeting.' He said, 'I don't give a damn where he is. I want to talk to him.'"

A half-hour later, the chairman of the board of Pan American Airlines was on the phone, offering an unknown young Nevadan a meeting with the airline's personnel director himself. All Harmon had to do was get to New York. "No, no," said McCarran. "You have him come down here and we'll interview him in my office." The personnel director did come to Washington, and Harmon was hired.

The senator juggled his staff to require more part-time than full-time workers, so more Nevada kids could work there while attending Washington-area law schools. Some of these men, such as Grant Sawyer, Jon Collins, and Harvey Dickerson, became the next generation of leaders for Nevada.

McCarran believed that nearly anything could be accomplished through politics. Joe McDonald Jr., son of a Reno newspaper publisher, was captured by the Japanese when Wake Island fell during World War II. McCarran tried to get the young man released by declaring him a working journalist, which was at least arguably true. He contacted the Vatican. Some say he even asked his friend Francisco Franco, the fascist but neutral dictator of Spain, to pull strings in Japan. McCarran never gave up until nuclear weapons ended the war and brought freedom for surviving POWs, including McDonald.

Senator McCarran worried about money and had a bad reputation for not paying even ordinary expenses, such as gasoline bills and mortgages. Yet while some of his appointees used their offices for personal gain, most believe McCarran never did.

Eva Adams, his office manager and later director of the U.S. Mint, remembered an incident in which McCarran asked her to find somebody a job on Capitol Hill. In an oral history collected by the University of Nevada-Reno, she explained that she had found a job and all was fine until the candidate's father showed up.

"Normally the door was always open between my office and the senator's," Adams said. "This man closed the door. All of a sudden that door flew open; the senator had him by the back of the neck and the seat of the pants propelling him out of the office. And it was tragic, because he was trying to give the senator $2,000 to get his son this job, which the senator had already gotten for him. But oh, he was insulted!"

The senator was involved in bringing war industries to the site that eventually became Henderson, and after the war helped make sure they were converted to private production instead of being dismantled.

After the Kefauver Committee hearings in 1951 gave gambling a new black eye, a bill was introduced in Congress to place a 10-percent tax on all gaming transactions. Not the profits, but individual bets. That would have killed casino gaming. McCarran fired his ammo and then threw the pistol, trading votes on important national issues for those that would save casinos, which he did.

McCarran also fought obsessively for the remonetization of silver, which endeared him in the Silver State but appeared small-minded elsewhere. Ironically, Eva Adams, his protégé, would be director of the U.S. Mint a decade after his death, when the final blow was struck and the government quit using silver in coins.

McCarran International Airport is named for him, not merely because he was a senator from Nevada, but because he did much for aviation.

McCarran wrote the Civil Aeronautics Act of 1938, the Federal Airport Act, and the National Aircraft Theft Act. He also was the first to introduce a bill for a separate air force, in 1933.

McCarran, who considered himself a conservative Democrat, opposed many of Franklin Roosevelt's New Deal programs. McCarran got out of a sickbed in 1937 to speak against Roosevelt's transparent plan to expand the nine-justice Supreme Court to as many as 15 seats. Of course, the expansion would have allowed Roosevelt to appoint a decisive and lasting liberal majority.

His anti-Communist fears led McCarran into an ill-advised red-hunting alliance with Senator Joseph McCarthy. McCarthy is remembered today only as a lip-shooting bully, and association with him tarred McCarran's reputation as well.

McCarran also came out second-best in his feud with *Las Vegas Sun* publisher Herman "Hank" Greenspun. In March 1952, most of the important casinos simultaneously withdrew advertising from the *Sun.* Greenspun sued, then located a key witness to support the proposition that McCarran had ordered the boycott. That forced an out-of-court settlement in early 1953. All the settlement money came from casino owners, but it cost the senator politically. Greenspun had challenged McCarran's power and had won.

In September 1954, McCarran spoke at a Democratic rally in Hawthorne. He hammered his favorite themes of fighting Communism and the necessity of maintaining a Democratic Senate so he could retain chairmanship of the Judiciary Committee.

A few moments later, he dropped dead, clutching a tiny gold box of nitroglycerine pills. The nameless International News Service correspondent who covered the speech noted that some of McCarran's last words "urged united support of the Democratic ticket, something he seldom did in the 15 years he ruled the Nevada branch of the party."

That speech was too much for his 78-year-old heart. ✄

The senator and some fellow Democratic bigwigs ride in a Fremont Street parade on Nevada Day, 1944.
(UNLV Special Collections)

EVA ADAMS

1910–1991

Worth her weight in silver, the woman who ran Senator Patrick McCarran's office
was so highly organized that President Kennedy asked her to manage the U.S. Mint. BY A.D. HOPKINS

Eva Adams was from a town that doesn't even exist today, yet she became one of the most powerful women in Washington. Though only a pint-sized 5-foot-1 with her hair up, she had brains enough for two, and they served her well as a teacher at Las Vegas High School and the University of Nevada, as the director of Senator Pat McCarran's Washington office, and as a director of the U.S. Mint.

Because she was pretty and never married, she was rumored to be McCarran's mistress. But she denied it to a journalist in 1989, when she was 79 years old: "They said that I visited Senator McCarran ... and that the place was full of cigarettes with lipstick on them. Now, that alone should have exonerated me, because I didn't know how to smoke."

Adams was born in 1910 in Wonder, a mining camp in Churchill County, east of Fallon. Her father worked for the mining magnate George Wingfield. "When Mr. Wingfield started a camp, he would send my father to set up the hotel and the commissary, the bar, and such things as that," Adams explained to Mary Ellen Glass, an oral historian for the University of Nevada-Reno.

The one-room schoolhouses of mining camps enabled her to advance at her own pace, so when she entered high school in Reno, she was ahead of her peers. "I had an inferiority complex, of course, because of being fat. But ... I was too busy

to brood. ... I was in every sport ... and I've often wondered because I couldn't run fast, but I think it was my enthusiasm." She graduated from high school at 14.

Adams won a scholarship to Vassar, but that campus was too far away and too expensive. So she stayed in Reno to attend the University of Nevada, and by the age of 19 she was teaching at Las Vegas High School. "Many of the students worked on the railroad, and sometimes they would drop out," she told Glass. "They would work for two or three years—before they went to high school, mind you. ... So I encountered probably as tough and difficult a group of young people as you ever saw. ... One young fellow ... stood in the study hall and he wouldn't behave, and he had a basketball and he just threw it at me. And I picked that thing up and I threw it back at him and hit him right in the nose. ... Never had trouble with him after that."

It was in Las Vegas, through her landlady, that Adams began socializing with people like politi-

Eva Adams, who managed Senator Patrick McCarran's office so well that she trained the staffs of other senators, was formerly a librarian at Las Vegas High School and a faculty member at the University of Nevada-Reno.
(UNLV Special Collections)

Adams in Southern Nevada

POP.[1]	DECADE
n/a	pre-1900
30	1900
945	1910
2,686	1920
5,952	1930
13,937	1940
45,577	1950
123,667	1960
273,288	1970
463,087	1980
715,587	1990
1,360,000[2]	2000

■ Time spent in Southern Nev.
1 - Population figures are for greater Las Vegas area (*Source: Nevada State Data Center*).
2 - Estimate

cal kingmaker Al Cahlan and his wife Ruth, and with Ed Clark, who ran the Clark County Democratic Party. She met Pat McCarran on a holiday journey home, when a snowstorm stranded about 40 motorists at the Goldfield Hotel: "He came in and he bought drinks for everybody, and he wasn't running, and I thought what a nice man."

Adams attended graduate school at Columbia University and was teaching in the English department at the University of Nevada in 1940, when McCarran hired her to work in his Washington office. She shortly found herself in charge and had the good fortune to learn, very soon, how far she could go.

"The secretary of the Senate had an open bar," Adams recalled, "which created problems, frequently, and this night it was a great problem, because Senator McCarran had been at this open bar. He came stomping into the office." McCarran then dictated a number of exceedingly rude telegrams to some of the most important people in the aviation industry, ordering them to be in his office at 10 a.m. the following morning. Adams stared at the telegrams, decided not to send them, and cleaned out her desk for her pending discharge from McCarran's employment.

McCarran didn't even show up till 10:30, a half-hour late for his meeting with the bigwigs. Later in the day, he seemed to recall having ordered something, and she showed him the telegrams. "My God! Did you send those?" gasped the senator.

"No, and I'm resigning," said Adams.

McCarran laughed. "You don't have to resign, and thank you for not sending them," he said.

> *"Dress like a queen. Act like a lady. Think like a man. Work like a dog."*
> —**Eva Adams**

> *After McCarran's death in 1954, Adams managed the office for his successors, Ernest Brown and Alan Bible, until 1961, when the new president, Jack Kennedy, invited her to have lunch in the Senate cafeteria and, by the way, to run the U.S. Mint.*

Thus they established their relationship: Adams and her staff would quietly protect McCarran from his worst character traits and let his best shine.

McCarran's office was recognized as the most efficient in the Senate. The Department of Agriculture, which for some reason gave classes on running a senator's office, asked Adams to teach. "To my utter astonishment, several senators came with their staffs," she recalled. "Margaret Chase Smith never missed a meeting."

After McCarran's death in 1954, Adams managed the office for his successors, Ernest Brown and Alan Bible, until 1961, when the new president, Jack Kennedy, invited her to have lunch in the Senate cafeteria and, by the way, to run the U.S. Mint.

Bible had suggested that Kennedy hire her for more than one reason. It would help to have a mint director who understood something about precious metals and the states that produced them. In addition, Bible and Adams did not get along well. Yet Bible couldn't fire somebody so famously competent; the best thing was to find a new use for her organizational abilities.

Adams soon found she would need them all: The mint was a disorganized mess. It was full of over-the-hill oddballs who did their jobs as they liked. Nobody had bothered to order new presses to deal with a looming coin shortage created by coin-operated machines and an economy surging back from the Eisenhower recession.

One can't just run out to the nearest hardware store and buy a coin press, however: "We're the only ones who use them, so nobody makes them to sell to anybody who comes along, thank goodness." Coin presses are built to order, which takes months. So under Adams' encouragement, mint workers modified existing machines to produce more coins with the same number of blows; they raided government arsenals for machines, originally designed for making jackets for rifle bullets, and turned those into coin presses. They even took the presses from the old Carson City Mint, still maintained in Nevada for their historical interest, and pressed them back into service.

Congress complicated the issue by ordering, almost simultaneously, that silver be taken out of coins. This was necessary, said Adams, because the market price of silver tended to stay higher than the face value of coins containing it. There was supposed to be almost an ounce of silver in a dollar's worth of coins, but the market price was $1.29 an ounce. Adams saw no way to continue minting coins that were mostly silver, but thought the government should have found a way to back money with precious metal. She was overruled.

The mint began issuing "sandwich money" made of common metals. Once that happened, the older silver coins were hoarded by collectors, survivalists, and speculators who melted the coins for their bullion value. Silver coins disappeared from common circulation, compounding the coin shortage.

Eva Adams resigned from the U.S. Mint in 1969, pressed out by Richard Nixon, who wanted the director's job for a Republican. She worked in the Washington offices of Mutual of Omaha before retiring to Reno, where she died in 1991 at the age of 80.

How much she had remained a Nevadan is evident in a story set during the furor over the sandwich money. Repeatedly assured that the new coins would work fine in any coin-operated machine, Adams checked herself. On a visit to Nevada, she smuggled along a quantity of the blanks from which the new coins would be made, and arranged to personally test them in slot machines.

Pat McCarran probably smiled his approval. ✍

MAXWELL KELCH (1911–1977)

A radio man with a gift for promotion, KENO's first owner proved to the rest of Las Vegas that publicity is everything. BY K.J. EVANS

One morning in 1940, Maxwell Kelch answered his phone. The caller, an official with the Federal Communications Commission in Washington, D.C., apologized in advance for delivering the bad news: The radio call letters that Kelch had requested for his new station had already been assigned to a ship at sea. Kelch would have to settle for his second choice—KENO.

The FCC guy probably wondered why Kelch sounded so happy when he hung up. It was because he'd gotten the call letters he really wanted. "We leaped up and down, and I cried," recalled his wife, Laura Belle Kelch. "That was *the* name to have for Las Vegas. But we knew our illustrious Federal Communications Commission would never grant a gambling-game name to a radio station."

Laura Belle explained that the application form for a radio station license contained spaces for three choices of call letters. Certain KENO would be denied, the Kelches listed as their first choice KLVN. For their second, they picked KENO. Just for the hell of it.

Laura Belle Kelch also recalled seeing a mountain bluebird land outside her window just after they had received the news, and she took it as an omen of good luck. But it was vision and energy, not luck, that advanced the fortunes of Maxwell Kelch and his family.

Vision brought Kelch to Las Vegas to found the valley's first radio station. Energy and business acumen placed him at the forefront of the postwar push to make Las Vegas one of the world's best-known destinations. "If we trace the ancestry of efforts to publicize Las Vegas as a tour-

ist attraction," says Michael Green, a professor of history at the Community College of Southern Nevada, "then Max Kelch is the founding father."

The son of a Los Angeles lawyer, Kelch was born there on July 17, 1911. He grew up on Hollywood Boulevard at a time when that star-studded street still had lima bean farms. By the time he was in high school, he was already licensed as a ham radio operator, spending his evenings chatting with other hams all over the world.

In 1933, Kelch earned a bachelor's degree in physics from UCLA and set his sights on becoming a college professor. His amateur radio license helped finance his education, landing him engineering jobs at several Los Angeles radio stations. In 1936, he received a master's degree in physics from the California Institute of Technology. But by then, Kelch was having second thoughts about a career in academia. The pay was lousy, and the job market was tight. "By golly, I couldn't get a job," he later recalled, "because teachers weren't dropping out."

On the other hand, opportunities for qualified technicians in radio, film, and recording were abundant. Between 1936 and 1939, Kelch was an engineer at radio station KFWB in Los Angeles. It was associated with the National Broadcasting Network, Warner Brothers Pictures, and Decca Records. Kelch worked as a design engineer for Warner Brothers and was technical supervisor for network programs such as "Amos and Andy." For

Kelch in Southern Nevada

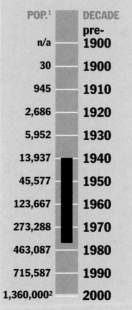

POP.[1]	DECADE
n/a	pre-1900
30	1900
945	1910
2,686	1920
5,952	1930
13,937	1940
45,577	1950
123,667	1960
273,288	1970
463,087	1980
715,587	1990
1,360,000[2]	2000

■ Time spent in Southern Nev.
1 - Population figures are for greater Las Vegas area (*Source: Nevada State Data Center*).
2 - Estimate

Maxwell Kelch, January 1, 1944
(Review-Journal files)

Max Kelch finishes planting his Chamber of Commerce sign, late 1940s, in front of the newly completed KENO studio, then located on the Strip, slightly north of current-day Circus Circus Drive.
(Courtesy Kelch family)

Max and Laura Belle Kelch in 1977
(UNLV Special Collections)

Max Kelch as "Maxine" (center) at a Branding Iron Club dinner spoof of Las Vegas production shows at the El Rancho Vegas, early 1950s
(Courtesy Kelch family)

Decca, he served as a recording engineer for artists like Bing Crosby and Francis Langford.

Laura Belle Gang was a native of Cincinnati who had lived in New York before coming to Los Angeles. In the late 1930s, she met Kelch at KFWB. "I was doing dramatic parts for an acting group," she recalled.

In 1939, when Kelch took the job of chief engineer at station KGDM in the Sacramento Valley city of Stockton, Laura Belle went with him. That same year, they crossed the Sierra to Carson City and got married. They had already decided they wanted their own radio station by the time they were married. Kelch just needed to find the most promising spot to locate.

"We did a survey of the Southwest, because that's where we wanted to live," said Laura Belle. Their research revealed that Las Vegas once had a radio station, KGIX, but it had gone off the air. No competition. Further inquiries revealed that the local business community would support a new station.

"I thought it [Las Vegas] was wonderful," said Laura Belle, who was able to ride her horse downtown on errands. "I had never been in, or lived in, a small town before." Of course, Las Vegas lacked the cultural amenities of larger cities, and she soon found herself up to her elbows in civic and service activities. She was active in improving the Las Vegas Library and, as an accomplished watercolorist, was a founding member of the Las Vegas Art League.

KENO went on the air in the fall of 1940, an ABC affiliate serving a population of only 8,700. "Included in the entertainment," reported the Evening Review-Journal, "will be … 'Our Scenic Southwest,' devoted to promoting tourist interest in Southern Nevada and adjacent areas."

KENO's first broadcast facility was the old Meadows Club, which Laura Belle dubbed "the extinct nightclub." It had been built in 1931 by gambler Tony "The Admiral" Cornero on the Boulder Highway at the site now occupied by Montgomery Ward. The building itself was without heat in winter or cooling in summer, and was literally falling down.

Shortly after he opened El Rancho Vegas in 1941, casino man Tommy Hull made Kelch an offer he couldn't refuse. "Max, if I moved your radio station, your tower, everything, to my property, would you move over there?" Hull asked. Kelch agreed instantly. It was free studio space in a high-visibility location. Hull got a good deal, too. Every 20 minutes or so, the announcer would identify the radio station and note that it was "broadcasting from the grounds of the fabulous El Rancho Vegas." Later, Kelch built a new studio on the Strip, just north of where Circus Circus would one day stand.

When the war started, Kelch reacted in the same way as most American men. "He wanted to join the service and build radio stations abroad wherever they needed them, but they refused him," says Laura Belle. "They told him he was more important here." And they meant it. An edict came from the feds requiring civilian radio station operators to carry sidearms while on duty.

"The essential radio service to everyone in the area was KENO," recalls the Kelches' son Rob. "It was where you tuned if there was an invasion on the West Coast. This was a tremendous scare; people really believed it was going to happen. They were afraid that if they had to evacuate the West Coast in an invasion, Las Vegas would be one of the staging points on the inland move where it

would be very critical to have good radio communications."

And Southern Nevada itself was a prime target. A successful attack on Hoover Dam could have cut power to Southern California war industries. Basic Magnesium was another potential target, as was the Las Vegas Air Corps Gunnery School.

KENO was also the community's voice. Laura Belle Kelch, under the name "Peggy Maxwell," hosted a program called "Listen Ladies," which provided tips on the domestic arts and how to get the most out of ration books. Charles "Pop" Squires took the mike occasionally to recall some slice of local history, or to hold forth on his own brand of rock-ribbed Republicanism. Kelch even offered the Las Vegas Evening Review-Journal a slot to pass along the day's headlines.

And, of course, Kelch joined the Las Vegas Chamber of Commerce. By 1944, he was elected president. Rob Kelch attended many chamber meetings with his father. Typically, said Rob, while everyone else in the room was voicing opinions, his father would sit quietly taking notes. If numbers were bandied about, he would whip out his slide rule and check them.

"When everybody else had their say, he would come in and draw it all together, bring clarity to the situation, bring it to a point," said Rob. "And more often than not, everybody would say, 'Sounds good to me.' He could summarize very well, and part of that was his mathematics background."

Green notes that Kelch's combination of intellect and market savvy was rare. "The image of the scientist is of a guy tucked away in a lab with test animals, chemicals, and a slide rule," says the historian. "Max Kelch stood that image on its head. Most people of an academic bent are not going to be as good at salesmanship as he was."

The first idea Kelch sold to his chamber colleagues was that if Las Vegas was serious about wanting to build strong postwar tourism, it had to start planning before the war was over. "Everybody is going to have to do their share to help bring the tourists and continued prosperity to Las Vegas after the war," he told a gathering of merchants in the summer of 1944. "In short, we are going to have to stop paying more money to have our garbage collected than we have been paying to bring business to Las Vegas."

Kelch conceived of Las Vegas as a product, like a box of soap or a car. And the way to sell a product was to advertise it. "This was a quantum leap that really was Dad's," said Rob Kelch. "It was the first time the concept had been applied to Las Vegas."

Kelch and the chamber budgeted $75,000 for publicity in 1945 and, in February of that year, launched one of the most ambitious fundraising campaigns in Nevada history, the "Live Wire" fund. The "Live Wires" were chamber members who agreed to contribute from 1 percent to 5 percent of their annual gross receipts for promotion. The large resorts pledged to match whatever amount was raised, up to $50,000.

UNLV history professor Eugene Moehring, in *Resort City in the Sunbelt,* said that Kelch and the chamber recognized "the crucial role played by propaganda in cementing support for the war." They responded to the fundraising campaign accordingly.

"From its inception," Moehring wrote, "the Live Wire campaign was a roaring success: $84,000 was raised that first year alone, with greater amounts thereafter." The money allowed the agency to hire one of the nation's largest advertising firms, J. Walter Thompson, and later the legendary publicity agency Steve Hannagan and Associates, which had engineered very effective campaigns for Miami Beach and Sun Valley, Idaho.

By 1950, the chamber could no longer afford Hannagan, but his techniques would remain. They would even be copied by other cities, said Don Payne, former manager of the Las Vegas News Bureau. Payne credits Kelch with appreciating Hannagan's genius and "borrowing" his modus operandi. "That's why we named the Las Vegas News Bureau building in [Kelch's] honor and placed a memorial plaque at the front door," says Payne.

In fact, Kelch's ethical standards made him something of an oddity in the Las Vegas of the 1940s and 1950s. He never ran for public office, nor invested in a casino. The reason he resisted both temptations, explains his son, is that both were infested with people who could best be described as ethically elastic.

"There's two businesses you don't get involved in," Max Kelch told his son. "One's liquor; the other's gaming."

"It wasn't that he had moral objections to it," explains Rob Kelch. "He just thought that there were so many other opportunities, why get involved with businesses that tend to have a rather rough clientele?"

After selling KENO in 1955, Kelch got the local franchise for Muzak. He also designed and installed the public-address system for the Pioneer Club that provided Vegas Vic, the club's marquee mascot, with his two-word vocabulary: "Howdy Podner." Rob Kelch was pretty sure his dad's voice became the cowboy's drawl that resonated down Fremont Street for decades.

A private pilot and a skilled boatman, Max spent part of every summer plying the Pacific Coast with Laura Belle in one of the three yachts they christened *Keno.* Kelch also wrote a book on celestial navigation and taught that subject at the community college in the 1970s.

Both of Max and Laura Belle's children remain in Las Vegas. Rob and his sister, Marilyn Gubler, operate a property management business and a gym.

Maxwell Kelch's death in 1977 at age 66 was certainly a loss for Las Vegas, but his son also laments that his techno-crazed dad never had a chance to see the technology of later times. "He would have loved computers," says Rob Kelch. "He would be designing them by now." ✍

Before coming to Las Vegas, a young Max Kelch tried his hand at gold panning in the Calaveras River in the Sierra Nevada, 1930s.
(Courtesy Kelch family)

BENJAMIN SIEGEL (1905–1947)

"When he [Siegel] got killed, you wouldn't believe how many employees broke down in tears. He was very generous with the help and very well-liked. He was good to people. He was good to me and my wife."

—Lou Wiener Jr.
Siegel's Vegas attorney

The mobster with the movie-star looks and the certifiable paranoia brought Las Vegas much more attention after his death than he did during his short life. **BY JOHN L. SMITH**

For an incurable paranoid who had only a few moments left to live, Benjamin "Bugsy" Siegel was probably feeling pretty content. It was June 20, 1947. Siegel had escaped the stifling Las Vegas heat for the cool shadows of the Moorish-style house at 810 Linden Drive in Beverly Hills. He'd just returned there from Ocean Park after a late dinner at Jack's-at-the-Beach. Settling onto the chintz sofa in the living room, a copy of the *Los Angeles Times* before him and his trusted pal, Al Smiley, a few feet away, the dapper Siegel was the picture of confidence.

He was probably as self-satisfied as a sociopath with a blood-soaked portfolio could be. After his Flamingo's disastrous grand opening on December 26, 1946—the strains of Jimmy Durante's one-liners and Xavier Cugat's band fading amid the word that the casino had lost a fortune—the shiny new Las Vegas resort was reopened March 27 and was finally turning a profit. That fact was almost certain to quiet the whispered rumors from New York and Miami Beach that his days as a Las Vegas casino mogul were numbered. Even his hell-raising girlfriend, the fiery Virginia Hill, was in Europe and out of shouting distance.

At age 41, Ben Siegel had carved out a notorious name for himself in the annals of organized crime and in Las Vegas history as well. Somehow, he had managed to walk between the raindrops and avoid conviction on a plethora of crimes ranging from bootlegging to murder. If he had not become a silver-screen gangster, which his closest friends believed he secretly wanted to be, he had accomplished the next best thing: He had become a genuine gangster with movie-star looks and had surrounded himself with the Hollywood glitterati.

In a few seconds, his name would become permanently etched in the American psyche. When people thought of Las Vegas, they would always think of Benny Siegel. Not because he had turned the Fabulous Flamingo into the snazziest carpet joint in Sin City, but because, at that moment, an assassin wielding an Army-issue carbine aimed at the back of Siegel's carefully coifed head and blew his brains and one of his pretty blue eyes all over the living room. Smiley was untouched. The shooter was never identified.

Siegel's .30-caliber sendoff not only made headlines from L.A. to London, but also linked the handsome psychopath forever with the fortunes of Las Vegas. In a town with more than its share of wiseguy misfortune, what makes Siegel's demise so special? For that matter, what makes the infamous Bugsy worthy of a place in the pantheon of local historical figures? Several things, really.

In an odd way, Siegel was better for business in death than in life. Had Siegel lived a long time, he might have ended up respectable or in the penitentiary. Had he died of a heart attack or the gout,

This undated photo of Benjamin Siegel was probably taken after his acquittal at a murder trial.

(Los Angeles Public Library)

Siegel in Southern Nevada

POP.[1]	DECADE
n/a	pre-1900
30	1900
945	1910
2,686	1920
5,952	1930
13,937	1940
45,577	1950
123,667	1960
273,288	1970
463,087	1980
715,587	1990
1,360,000[2]	2000

■ Time spent in Southern Nev.
1 - Population figures are for greater Las Vegas area (*Source: Nevada State Data Center*).
2 - Estimate

he might have become a footnote in time. Instead, he died violently and, in a sense, got to live forever.

Through the years, Siegel has been credited for everything from putting the glow in neon to inventing Las Vegas. The fact that the Flamingo wasn't even his idea tells you something about how myths are made.

The Flamingo was the creation of Billy Wilkerson, a Hollywood nightclub owner and one of the founders of the *Hollywood Reporter*. Wilkerson had plenty of big ideas and no shortage of friends in the underworld. The Flamingo was to be his crowning glory. By the mid-1940s, it was an unfinished dream deferred.

Enter Siegel. Bugsy was not only a wealthy man in his own right and a big-time earner for his mob friends, but he also had access to all the money the New York, Chicago, and Miami Beach underworld could generate. Numerous published accounts of Siegel's status rank him as one of the most respected and feared names in the syndicate. He carried the sort of clout that was capable of persuading tightwads like Charlie "Lucky" Luciano and Meyer Lansky to invest in his desert dream. And they did.

Siegel and the boys bankrolled construction of the Flamingo with $1.5 million, but in the months following the end of World War II, materials were scarce. The job immediately ran over budget.

It didn't help that the four-floor Flamingo was built like a fortress, a testament to Siegel's paranoia. The thick concrete walls were reinforced with steel acquired from Naval shipyards. Siegel's top-floor suite was riddled with trap doors and escape hatches, one leading to a getaway car in his private garage. There were gun portals and hallways leading nowhere. The Flamingo was a physical manifestation of Bugsy Siegel's troubled brain.

But it also was filled with the sort of posh amenities never before seen in Las Vegas. Siegel poured big money into carpets and fixtures, and spared no expense on a pool, tennis courts, and riding stables. Siegel's idea, his first Las Vegas attorney, the late Lou Wiener Jr., once said, was to create a real resort capable not only of attracting the Hollywood set, but also of giving gamblers a variety of diversions from their inevitable losses at the tables. Siegel envisioned adding a championship golf course to the Flamingo, but his plans were interrupted.

Theft at the Flamingo construction site was legendary, a big part of the reason the hotel ultimately cost $6 million, an incredible figure for the times. "A lot of characters, I think, duped him," Wiener said. "They'd go through the front gates with materials and drive out the back."

But at least one author suggests Siegel's own sticky fingers were responsible. Says Richard Hammer in his well-researched *Playboy's Illustrated History of Organized Crime:* "Siegel was not only a flop as an impresario, but, Lansky said, he was a thief as well. Lansky had learned that Miss Hill was making frequent trips to Europe, depositing several hundred thousand dollars in cash in a numbered account in Switzerland; the cash had come from the Flamingo's building fund.

"Nobody, not even an old trusted comrade like Siegel, steals from his underworld friends and gets away with it. Siegel's execution was ordered, but first he would be given time to prove that his Nevada dream might actually come true."

It is possible, too, that Siegel's Hollywood profile became so high that he became an embarrassment to his associates. He was a silver-screen sycophant and groomed the acquaintance of major players such as Jack Warner, Cary Grant, Barbara Hutton, Jean Harlow, and every hoodlum's favorite actor, George Raft. American gangsters learned how to walk by watching George Raft on the screen. They learned how to talk by listening to his snappy, wiseguy patter.

"He [Siegel] was a frustrated actor and secretly wanted a movie career, but he never quite had nerve enough to ask for a part in one of my pictures," Raft once said of his pal.

Las Vegas history buffs know Siegel as the man who developed the Flamingo, but few appreciate just how big a hoodlum he really was. Born in the Williamsburg section of Brooklyn in 1905, as a boy Siegel befriended Meyer Lansky. Together with a gang of teen-age toughs known as the Bug and Meyer Mob, they provided protection and efficiently performed a string of contract killings on behalf of the city's bootlegging fraternity. By the time World War II broke out, Siegel and Lansky had made the post-Prohibition transition from illegal whiskey running to illegal bookmaking, numbers running, and gambling. Siegel lived at the Waldorf Astoria and traveled in a bullet-proof limousine with the requisite pair of torpedoes posing as bodyguards.

After coming West to oversee the Capone mob's successful takeover of the race wire business, Siegel's infatuation with Hollywood began to show—and his profile began to rise dangerously high. At the same time that he was mus-

The Flamingo under construction, circa 1946
(Courtesy Flamingo Hilton)

cling in on illegal gambling throughout Southern California, buying percentages of small Las Vegas casinos, clipping Tony Cornero's *Rex* gambling ship, and strong-arming his way into the Agua Caliente racetrack in Tijuana, as well as into a California dog track, Siegel was busy being seen in the company of Harlow and Raft and many other stars. Continental race wire sales to Las Vegas sports books alone generated $25,000 a month, according to *The Green Felt Jungle,* and Siegel bought into the Golden Nugget and the Last Frontier at a time when his pal Lansky was picking up a piece of the El Cortez.

Siegel was one of the schemers behind opening a pipeline of narcotics trafficking from Mexico to the United States, and he raked a percentage of the profits from the largest prostitution ring in the West. If it moved in the netherworld of illegality, Benny Siegel got his pinch.

Siegel's temper was legendary. No one dared call him "Bugsy" to his face, and anyone with a smart-aleck comment about his height or thinning hair was likely to get his teeth knocked down his throat. To some local observers, Siegel's maniacal chest-puffing set the pattern for several generations of big-shot casino moguls.

Las Vegan Herb McDonald, then a young assistant general manager at El Rancho Vegas, met Siegel through Billy Wilkerson. For a short time, McDonald knew Siegel only as a casino man. "We played gin rummy, and I won 28 bucks," McDonald said in an article in *Nevada* magazine. "When I saw Ben Siegel again, he asked me when I was going to give him a chance to win some of his money back. I said, 'Any time you think you're good enough.'"

A short while later, McDonald learned Siegel's true background as a member of the board of Murder Inc. "My knees buckled," McDonald said. "Had I known that, I would have lost it [the gin game]."

But Wiener knew Bugsy as an intense character who was not without a charitable streak. Siegel was a soft touch for the Damon Runyon Cancer Fund. "When he got killed, you wouldn't believe how many employees broke down in tears," Wiener recalled. "He was very generous with the help and very well-liked. He was good to people. He was good to me and my wife."

But others knew Siegel as a textbook paranoid. "He used to go down to Los Angeles about every two weeks," said the Flamingo's first engineer, Don Garvin. "He'd have me change the lock on the door of his room almost every week. He and Virginia would sit out in the hall while I worked. He was a little leery. It got to where I would pretend to change it [the lock] and hand him the same key."

But in 1947, no amount of caution could prevent the boys from disciplining one of their own. Wallace Turner put it bluntly in his breakthrough 1965 book, *Gamblers' Money:* "Siegel was murdered reportedly to effect a change in management. There are those who firmly believe that this killing of the hoodlum Siegel irrevocably set the pattern for Las Vegas' development as a gambling center. The Mob was in, these observers hold, and the Mob has stayed.

"In a sense he [Siegel] was the Christopher Columbus for the Mob; he went exploring and found the New World in the desert. But Siegel failed to adapt. It is possible that he became confused between the two ways of doing business and thought that because his name was on so many pieces of paper, he really owned the Flamingo Hotel. He was wrong."

Today, the Flamingo Hilton is one of the largest casino resorts in the world. It has long since shed its association with Siegel's kind, but management saw fit to honor the Flamingo's founder with a bronze plaque and a small rose garden not far from the original site of the Flamingo's first pool.

What is Siegel's legacy? "I think what it shows more than anything else is the public's fascination with gangster-type characters," Flamingo Publicity Director Terry Lindberg said. "[His death] turned a man who was basically not a historical figure into somebody who was a lot larger than life."

Others give Siegel more credit. UNLV Public Administration Department Chairman William Thompson said: "It's folklore, it's mythology. … His death let the world know we had casinos. … It was important that we turned the corner and quit being just a cowboy town and became a resort town. He was responsible for that."

It is a sentiment echoed by UNLV history professor Hal Rothman, author of *Devil's Bargain: Tourism in the Twentieth-Century American West.* "The most important thing about Siegel is he raised the ante here," said Rothman. "He had an idea, however bizarre, of what class was. As we become a resort destination, we actually owe him more and more."

Las Vegas historian Frank Wright notes: "His [Siegel's] death was a great advertisement for the city of Las Vegas, in a sense. It certainly brought attention to Las Vegas and created a sort of sense of illicit excitement about Las Vegas."

Ever a defender of the image of his old friend, Wiener credited Siegel with setting a standard others are still trying to match. "He was one of the most progressive businessmen I've ever met," Wiener once said. "Had he been alive today, he probably would have had the first 3,000-room hotel in Las Vegas."

But Ben Siegel was not meant for such a tame fate. By spilling his blood, the Mob ensured that Bugsy would live forever in Las Vegas history. ⌀

> *"The most important thing about Siegel is he raised the ante here. He had an idea, however bizarre, of what class was. As we become a resort destination, we actually owe him more and more."*
> —Hal Rothman
> UNLV history professor

After Bugsy Siegel's death, the Flamingo came into the hands of a new crop of wiseguys. Poolside at the Flamingo (left to right) are Israel "Icepick Willie" Alderman, Joe Rosenberg, and Gus Greenbaum. Greenbaum presumably ran afoul of mob mavens; he was murdered, along with his wife, in Phoenix.
(Las Vegas News Bureau/LVCVA)

THOMAS YOUNG
(1895–1971)

"We had something they needed, and we were the only ones who could produce it. And they paid their bills. They were people of honor as far as we knew."
—Tom Young Jr.
Speaking about the gaming industry

A father of six with a flair for lettering found his niche in the neon-bathed streets of a fledgling gambling town called Las Vegas. **BY DAVE BERNS**

It was 1931, and the guy figured the new dam would be good for business. After all, the turbines of Boulder Dam would generate more than enough electricity to light the fledgling gambling city of Las Vegas.

So, on returning from one of his road trips between his Salt Lake City home and the customers of Los Angeles, Tom Young Sr. cruised through the isolated town before going home to his family. "They've just legalized gambling in Las Vegas, and we've got to build casino signs," the sign maker told his wife, Elmina. "Mama, we've got to do that."

For the British-born son of Mormons, it was logical, though he had qualms about profiting from the proceeds of games of chance. "But Dad was dealing with these decent, honest people," Tom Young Jr. remembered. "Sure they were in the gambling industry, but if they weren't cheating, weren't loading their dice, they were honest."

Young Sr.'s decision soon transformed his Young Electric Sign Company (Yesco) into the dominant sign maker for the emerging casino industry. If Bugsy Siegel's Flamingo was Hollywood's playground, if the Rat Pack established the Sands as party central for Camelot-era chic, Yesco's signs were the exclamation mark over it all.

Young came to the United States in 1910 with his entire family, who settled in Ogden, Utah. A creative youngster with an entrepreneurial bent, he grew up sketching people and animals before becoming an apprentice sign maker. After receiving a pair of art degrees from correspondence schools, he went to work for a sign construction company before opening Yesco in 1920 with $300. With a flair for lettering, the 25-year-old Young would take a camel-hair brush and produce sign boards that merchants would purchase for $2 down and a dollar a week.

Decades later, Mark Laymon offers the lament of a Vegas old-timer: "It's not the town it used to be." As the 38-year-old Yesco foreman cruises along the Las Vegas Strip, he eyes the computerized sign boards that have popped up in recent years. The MGM Grand, Monte Carlo, Bellagio—they all have them. They're a new generation of computer chip towers that can be rapidly reprogrammed to flash messages designed to separate casino-goers from their cash. To the out-of-towner, the multimillion dollar boards are the logical extension of the dot-com generation, where the high-tech world meets the high-risk town. Yet, Laymon remembers the very recent past.

"It used to be about neon," he says. "It was a town known for its neon." True neon lighting, which relies on passing electric current through glass tubing filled with exotic gasses, is no longer common. Expert glassblowers could bend these tubes and combine them into almost any picture imaginable, and some classics of the art have been preserved in a sort of museum exhibit at the Fremont Street Experience.

Neon established Yesco's reputation. When Young took to the road to meet with customers, he would sketch sign ideas on a hunk of wood, a paper napkin, or linen. The original sign for the

Young in Southern Nevada

POP.[1]	DECADE
n/a	pre-1900
30	1900
945	1910
2,686	1920
5,952	1930
13,937	1940
45,577	1950
123,667	1960
273,288	1970
463,087	1980
715,587	1990
1,360,000[2]	2000

■ Time spent in Southern Nev.
1 - Population figures are for greater Las Vegas area (*Source: Nevada State Data Center*).
2 - Estimate

Tom Young Sr. founded Young Electric Sign Company in 1920 with $300 and a flair for lettering.
(Courtesy Yesco)

To eye pictures of Yesco's oldest offerings is akin to scanning the pages of a scrapbook. Yesco's neon creations, like the one for the Mint, became the trademark for Las Vegas, and their glare could be spotted by astronauts orbiting Earth. Throughout Las Vegas' history, Yesco's signs have often provided the backdrop for the city's showgirl-dominated entertainment scene.

(Courtesy Yesco)

Young would take a camel-hair brush and produce sign boards for merchants.

(Courtesy Yesco)

1930s-era Boulder Club was sketched on a piece of butcher paper. "It was the first spectacular in Las Vegas," Tom Young Jr. remembers.

Rather than selling his signs, the elder Young developed a program for leasing them, making them more affordable for new business owners while Yesco retained ownership of the equipment. The arrangement saw Yesco signs pop up throughout the West for banks, restaurants, and hardware stores.

By the end of World War II, larger casinos had begun to open. Owners of El Rancho Vegas, the Pioneer Club, and the Las Vegas Club competed for the dollars of returning troops. The Golden Nugget joined the game in 1946; all worked with Yesco to create the biggest magnets. A deal with Northern Nevada sign maker Dewey Laughlin helped. The pair sliced the state in half, giving Laughlin and his QRS Neon the profitable Reno market, while Young took the emerging Las Vegas territory. The deal lasted until 1964.

Throughout the early years, the Youngs dealt with the boys from the East, mobsters who financed the postwar Las Vegas boom with money earned from bootlegging, illegal bookmaking, and prostitution. "People would say, 'You're really in a hotbed down there,' but I can honestly say that was never apparent in our dealings," Young Jr. said. "We had something they needed, and we were the only ones who could produce it. And they paid their bills. They were people of honor as far as we knew."

Don Lesson has been working at Yesco since the mid-1960s. An assistant manager at the company's Las Vegas production plant, Lesson's job description requires him to oversee service, maintenance, and sign changes. As he speaks of the evolution of gaming signage, he flips through a photo album of some of his favorite work. To flip through those pages is to wander through a graphic history. There were the combos: "Tony Orlando + Dawn." The ever present: "Wayne Newton." The one-name icons: "Dean" and "Sinatra."

"All of these were custom made," Lesson says. "They are like art by themselves." Sammy Davis Jr. loved his signs, and they had to be just right. If not, he'd threaten to cancel his show until the sign was fixed to his liking. Latina bombshell Charo said hers, which included an artist's image of her face, made her nose look like a pig's snout. Rodney Dangerfield loved his sign so much—it included a cartoonist's version of his memorable visage—that one day he visited the company's Las Vegas warehouse to ensure that it was in stock. After finding his beloved sign, he stuck around long enough to shoot some hoops with the afternoon crew.

The ultimate Las Vegas sign may be the Fremont Street Experience, the $75 million canopy of two million bulbs that was opened in 1995 to lure tourists and locals to the troubled downtown casino market. Ron Ischer has been overseeing the maintenance of the Fremont Street Experience since its opening. "Our job is monotonous because we take care of that structure every night, over and over and over," Ischer reflects. "But it's like show business for us. The less flaws you see, the better for us."

The 36-year-old high-school dropout did some crazy things during his younger days as a journeyman light repairman. He's hung over the top of buildings without a protective harness, 300 feet above the roadway, to replace one last burnt-out sign bulb. There was the time that Ischer climbed inside the old Vegas World sign in a wind storm. Perched more than 200 feet above Las Vegas Boulevard, the sign swayed four feet back and forth, as he repaired a light in Bob Stupak's neon signature.

With 1,050 employees at 25 offices, Yesco bills itself as the largest sign company in the country. An estimated 37 percent of its 1998 revenue came from its casino operations, a market that has expanded with the use of interior signage to lure gamblers to slot banks. Tom Young Sr., who died in 1971 at the age of 76, may have unwittingly stumbled onto the formula: Use your highly visible casino signs as marketing tools for your noncasino business. Overall, the privately held company generated 1998 revenues that were in the "high eight figures," Young Jr. says. The company anticipates a 10 percent revenue jump for 1999.

The son is the first to admit that he's different from his father. "He was tougher-fisted and tougher-minded than I am," Young Jr. says. "Verbally, businesswise, I wouldn't say he was feisty, but if you got into a business deal with him, you didn't push Tom Young around. By the time I came around, I could hire people to do that for me." ✍

EDMUND CONVERSE (1906–1981)

"His grandfather had an endowment at Stanford University, which I guess goes back a long, long time. He told me that this gift that his grandfather made to the law school haunted him while he went to Stanford. When he went to his first class, his instructor said, 'I hope you don't think you're going to get by in my class just because your grandfather gave all this money.' It was an embarrassment to him, and it hurt him, and I felt sorry for him."

—Florence Murphy
Nevada's first female commercial pilot

A wealthy man who wanted to make his own way in the world brought Southern Nevada into the commuter aviation age by developing its own scheduled airline. **BY K. J. EVANS**

Bonanza Airlines pilot Dick Hall had just left Reno on a bright June day in 1947 and had climbed to an altitude where he could see the azure waters of Lake Tahoe out the starboard window. A call came from the Reno tower instructing him to return to the field. Annoyed, Hall demanded to know why. He was told that the Washoe County sheriff's office had ordered the plane back because it carried two criminal suspects. Hall paused, then pressed the transmit button on the microphone. "Negative," he said, explaining that Las Vegas was expecting bad weather and he wanted to arrive there ahead of it. He signed off.

The flight landed on schedule at Las Vegas, beneath cloudless, sunny skies, and local deputies took the men into custody. Later that day, Edmund Converse, the founder and president of the tiny company, confronted Hall and asked him why he had ignored the Reno tower. "What?" exclaimed Hall. "And have those two guys demand their fare back? This way, we flew them to Las Vegas and kept the fare." Converse must have laughed. He tried to hire people who were aviation savvy and loaded with chutzpah.

"He was scared to death of airplanes; I don't think he ever became comfortable in one," says Florence Murphy, the first female commercial pilot in Nevada history. She served as Bonanza's vice president and corporate secretary from 1946

until 1958, and was the person Converse relied upon to recruit the highest quality people.

The story of Edmund Converse is not a Horatio Alger story. His family was extremely wealthy, having made most of its fortune in the stock market and in banking. "He told me that he was the first man in his family in three generations to have worked," says Murphy. "He said he

Edmund Converse
(Review-Journal files)

wanted to do something with himself by himself." He succeeded. Bonanza Airlines was the state's first successful commuter airline, the first to offer jet passenger service to Las Vegas, and a major factor in the city's postwar tourism boom.

Converse was born in New York in 1906. When little Eddie was 2, his family bought a cattle ranch in California, where he grew up and went to public schools. He attended Stanford University, graduating in 1928 with a bachelor's degree in economics. "His first job was at Banker's Trust Company in New York, which his family owned," says Murphy. "He made $75 a week and went to work in a chauffer-driven limousine."

After two years, Converse decided to attend law school. "His grandfather had an endowment at Stanford University, which I guess goes back a long, long time," Murphy said. "He told me that this gift that his grandfather made to the law school haunted him while he went to Stanford. When he went to his first class, his instructor said, 'I hope you don't think you're going to get by in my class just because your grandfather gave all this money.' It was an embarrassment to him, and it hurt him, and I felt sorry for him."

He earned his law degree in 1934 and practiced law until 1937, when he was hired onto the staff of a Republican senator from New Hampshire. In World War II, Converse was assigned to Naval Intelligence. During the war, he visited Las Vegas and found it to be teeming with optimistic,

Converse in Southern Nevada

POP.[1]	DECADE
n/a	pre-1900
30	1900
945	1910
2,686	1920
5,952	1930
13,937	1940
45,577	1950
123,667	1960
273,288	1970
463,087	1980
715,587	1990
1,360,000[2]	2000

■ Time spent in Southern Nev.
1 - Population figures are for greater Las Vegas area (*Source: Nevada State Data Center*).
2 - Estimate

self-made people, precisely the environment he sought. He bought a house and made plans to start a law practice in Las Vegas.

At the time, Las Vegas was served by two commercial airlines: Western Airlines provided service from Los Angeles, and TWA had one stop in each direction on its Newark-San Francisco route. The best way to get to Reno was to drive the two-lane blacktop or charter a plane. There was no scheduled service between Nevada's two largest cities.

Converse had made some friends soon after his arrival. They included Charlie Keene, a pilot who had flown charters in California, and June Simon, daughter of "Pop" Simon, the man who built the airfield that would become Nellis Air Force Base. June was an officer in the Las Vegas Chamber of Commerce and believed that the future of the town was in making it easily accessible to tourists. A Las Vegas-based airline would accomplish this, the trio decided, and Converse had the deep pockets to create one.

Deep, but not bottomless. The firm was incorporated December 31, 1945, but its assets consisted only of some furniture, a ticket counter in the lobby of El Rancho Vegas, and a leased single-engine, three-seat Cessna Skymaster. The airline was strictly a charter business, and it operated from the primitive Sky Haven landing field built by John and Florence Murphy in 1941. The field had no weather station, no communications gear, no landing lights. Converse and Simon would take turns running out and lighting flare pots along the runway when Charlie Keene was due in from a charter.

The following year, Bonanza moved from Sky Haven to Alamo Airport, now McCarran International, then a few months later to McCarran Field, now Nellis Air Force Base. The Bonanza fleet had expanded to include two Piper Cubs, a Stearman biplane, and a twin-engine, five-seat Cessna.

In 1946, the Federal War Assets Admin-

istration noticed that it had a huge surplus of twin-engine C-47s, the paratroop-dropping, supply-hauling workhorses of the war. They were sold as-is and where-is, cheap. It also was possible to lease a C-47 from the government, which Converse decided to do. Keene and two other pilots went to Oak Ridge, Tennessee, to pick up what they called "the bucket of bolts" and bring it back to Las Vegas, where they would transform it into its civilian counterpart, a Douglas DC-3 airliner.

Coincidentally, the day they departed Tennes-

see, the national railroad union called a general strike. There were only two ways to move freight, by truck or plane, and Bonanza's phones began to ring steadily. Farmers in the Moapa Valley were frantic. They had to move their vegetable crops to market or lose them. The redecoration of the "bucket" was put on hold while basic mechanical repairs were made. By early spring 1946, Bonanza was in the produce-shipping business. Everyone from Converse on down pitched in to load crate after crate of celery and tomato bedding plants, which went to gardeners as far east as

A Bonanza Airlines Fokker-Fairchild F27A approaches McCarran Airport in the 1960s.
(Review-Journal files)

Rochester, New York.

With the railroad union strike settled, the old war veteran was made over into an elegant lady of the skies, and made its inaugural Reno-Las Vegas flight on August 6, 1946. Initially, there were three round-trip flights a week, about all that a single plane could manage. Weekends were reserved for charters, the most profitable part of Bonanza operations.

One day, after the plane had been loaded with passengers, one of them looked out the window and saw a tanker truck pull up to the plane and begin fueling it. "Well," he commented, "I guess they had to sell us the tickets first so they'd have dough enough to buy gasoline to make the flight." The man was joking, but he also was partly correct. Bonanza had no income other than passenger fares and charters. No mail contract like Western, no federal subsidy.

"He was scared to death of airplanes; I don't think he ever became comfortable in one."
—Florence Murphy

Converse huddled with one of his stockholders, former Nevada Governor Morley Griswold, and they hit upon a simple, yet effective, way to boost passenger counts. Delegations from Bonanza and the Las Vegas Chamber of Commerce traveled to Reno and convinced that city's chamber of commerce that it would be to their mutual advantage to advertise their attractions in each other's cities. In one of the rare times in Nevada history when Reno and Las Vegas have cooperated in anything, advertising for Reno began to appear in the *Las Vegas Review-Journal* and *Age*. Ads for Las Vegas began to appear in the *Reno Evening Gazette* and the *Nevada State Journal*.

It worked. Converse reported a small profit for April 1947, the first ever for Bonanza, and stops were added in Tonopah and Hawthorne. More of the sturdy DC-3s were purchased, eventually totaling 10. By 1949, Bonanza had been certified as an interstate carrier and was flying from Las Vegas to Phoenix with several intermediate stops.

Converse was fighting for new routes, mail contracts, and subsidies. It was a long and grueling process. He and his dedicated staff became adept hoop-jumpers and were assisted through interminable hearings by Las Vegas civic leaders. By 1958, Bonanza was serving 20 cities in four states.

Though reliable and easy to service, the old airplanes were simply obsolete. They weren't pressurized, meaning they had a limited ceiling and had to fly through, rather than over, rough weather. They also were slow, taking two hours from Las Vegas to Reno.

In mid-1958, Bonanza Airlines, already a public company, got approval from the Securities and Exchange Commission to issue $1,175,000 in stocks. At the same time, the Civil Aeronautics Board approved a $4,324,500 loan. All that money was needed for Bonanza's next great leap forward—into the jet age.

Converse spent time in Europe looking for just the right aircraft. American aircraft makers were more interested in chasing military contracts and long-range, high-capacity passenger jets than in producing mid-size passenger jets. He found the prop jet Fokker-Fairchild F27A. It carried 40 passengers, twice that of a DC-3, and had a cruising speed of 300 mph. Converse ordered six of the planes at $820,000 each, and spent more than $150,000 on a modern corporate headquarters at McCarran Field.

The new Bonanza paint scheme, tangerine and black, plus the number of flights arriving and departing daily, made the airline a familiar part of the Las Vegas skyscape. Bonanza was Nevada's airline. There were many swelled chests locally when Converse announced in June 1964 that Bonanza had ordered three state-of-the-art Douglas DC-9 fanjets, capable of carrying 64 passengers at 560 mph.

Converse was justifiably proud of Bonanza's safety record. It was perfect. But 1964 was a bad year for aviation in Nevada. In March an airliner had gone down near Lake Tahoe, killing 85 people. In May an F-105 fighter jet crashed into a North Las Vegas residential neighborhood, killing five. Then, in November, Bonanza Airlines had its one and only air disaster.

Shortly after 8 p.m. on Sunday, November 15, Hank Fitzpatrick was at the controls of his Fokker-Fairchild F27A, Flight 114 from Phoenix, about 12 miles southwest of McCarran Airport over the Spring Mountains. A freak snowstorm, the worst to hit the area in 15 years, had reduced visibility to zero. Two other planes ahead of Flight 114 had attempted to make the approach and were diverted to California. Fitzpatrick was on a ground-control approach, meaning that McCarran tower was guiding him in.

Fitzpatrick radioed the tower at 8:23, "Ah, roger, one-fourteen is out of seven," meaning that he had dropped below 7,000 feet. About a minute later, he radioed, "Bonanza Flight one-fourteen is ..." and the Fokker-Fairchild F27A disappeared from radar.

The plane clipped the summit of a 5,000-foot peak and disintegrated, killing all 29 people aboard. "Another 10 feet and the pilot would have cleared the peak," said Sheriff Ralph Lamb, whose men would have the arduous and unhappy duty of fighting their way through giant snowdrifts to recover the victims.

The next year, a disagreement erupted between Bonanza Airlines and Clark County over the taxes to be levied on the new DC-9 jets, which were to go into service in 1966. Offered a better tax deal by Phoenix, Converse announced that Bonanza would pull out of Las Vegas and make its new headquarters in the Valley of the Sun. Ultimately, Bonanza merged with Pacific Airlines and West Coast Airlines to form Air West, which was shortly thereafter purchased by Howard Hughes.

Converse died in the Phoenix suburb of Scottsdale in 1981. "Eddie was a good man," says Florence Murphy. "He could be proud of what he accomplished, and that he accomplished it himself." ⌀

FLORENCE MURPHY (1912–   )

When soaring through the clouds was a man's domain, this female flier helped put Las Vegas on the aviation map and bring commercial air travel to the valley. **BY K.J. EVANS**

"When we got airborne, the pilot, who was sitting in the rear, tapped me on the shoulder and said, 'Take a hold of the stick; it's all yours,' and he threw his hands in the air. So I tried to level her off, and I had a pretty hard time doing it. But as I went along, it became easier, and finally I was able to look out and the wings weren't flapping up and down. I was up there about a half-hour and I just loved it."

—Florence Murphy

There was a buzz in the air that day in 1936. It emanated from a two-seat Piper Cub circling Las Vegas. John and Florence Murphy knew it was an itinerant pilot offering rides, and that he would continue buzzing Vegas until a respectable crowd gathered out at Rockwell Field, near the current-day corner of Paradise and Sahara.

"We went out there because we were both interested in airplanes," says Florence Murphy. "My husband took a ride, came back and asked me if I wanted to go, and I said, 'Of course.' When we got airborne, the pilot, who was sitting in the rear, tapped me on the shoulder and said, 'Take a hold of the stick; it's all yours,' and he threw his hands in the air. So I tried to level her off, and I had a pretty hard time doing it. But as I went along, it became easier, and finally I was able to look out and the wings weren't flapping up and down. I was up there about a half-hour and I just loved it."

Murphy had aviation fuel in her blood, and a head for business. With her husband, she built the facility that is now the North Las Vegas Airport. Later, her business acumen would help make a success of the first Las Vegas-based commercial airline.

Florence Jones was born in 1912 in Fernley, one of seven children—five of them boys. "I was a tomboy," Murphy says, laughing. "And what-ever my brothers could do, I could do too." Except fly an airplane. "It was an impossible dream then," she says.

Murphy attended the University of Nevada for two years before marrying John Murphy, an engineer for the State Highway Department, in 1930. In 1936, John was made a division engineer and transferred to Las Vegas. Florence went to work as a legal secretary. Both took flying lessons and, by 1938, both had private pilot's licenses. At the time, the only public airfield was old McCarran Field, now the site of Nellis Air Force Base. In early 1941, the U.S. Army took over the facility. This left private pilots with no place to land in the valley, and it opened up an opportunity for the person who would provide one.

The Murphys bought 200 acres of flat ground just off the old Tonopah Highway, and scraped off three runways. A hangar was hauled from the Las Vegas Air Base. With a few finishing touches, Sky Haven airfield was ready. With plans to operate a charter service and a flight school, Florence received her instructor's license in 1941, and her commercial pilot's license in 1944—the first woman in Nevada to earn that credential. A grand opening was scheduled for Sunday, December 7, 1941.

"Tommy Hull [builder of the El Rancho Vegas Hotel] was our master of ceremonies," Murphy recalls. "The town was small, so everyone was out there … and we had also gotten in touch with all of our flying friends from California, Utah, wherever we knew there were flying clubs." The celebration attracted at least 150 airplanes. "We had a great day. We were having spot-landing contests, bomb-dropping contests, and aerobatics—just having a great time."

Late in the afternoon, Murphy saw a low-wing monoplane coming from the direction of the

Florence Murphy with a Bonanza Airlines DC-3 in 1956
(Courtesy Florence Murphy)

Murphy in Southern Nevada

POP.[1]	DECADE
n/a	pre-1900
30	1900
945	1910
2,686	1920
5,952	1930
13,937	1940
45,577	1950
123,667	1960
273,288	1970
463,087	1980
715,587	1990
1,360,000[2]	2000

■ Time spent in Southern Nev.
1 - Population figures are for greater Las Vegas area (*Source: Nevada State Data Center*).
2 - Estimate

Army field. "He was hedge-hopping, flying very low," she says. "We thought he was just showing off and was coming over to join us, and we all went out to greet him. He said, 'You're grounded, all of you!' and then he told us that Pearl Harbor had been bombed by the Japanese. We were awestruck. People had flown in and couldn't fly back. We had to get special permission, but not before we were fingerprinted and relicensed." For those who were from out of town, the Army speeded up the process—they were able to fly home in a couple of weeks. "I didn't get my license back for two months," says Murphy.

John Murphy immediately volunteered for service and was made a civilian flight instructor; Florence decided to join the Women's Army Special Services (WASPS). But her four-year-old daughter, Margaret Lynne, cried and begged her mother not to go. In the end, maternalism won out over patriotism, and Murphy spent the war running her airfield.

A friend, Lawrence McNeil, introduced John and Florence to a just-discharged Navy veteran, Edmund Converse, who planned to set up a law practice in Las Vegas. In 1945, Converse and two associates, June Simon and Charlie Keene, convinced that Southern Nevada was ready for real commercial air service, formed the partnership of Bonanza Air. The fleet was a rented single-engine, three-seat Cessna Skymaster, and its first home base was Murphy's Sky Haven Airport.

In early 1946, Bonanza moved briefly to George and Peggy Crockett's Alamo Airport, a

small facility now part of McCarran International Airport. That fall, Bonanza moved into an old wooden hangar at the old Army Air Field, where Western and TWA airlines made their infrequent Las Vegas stops.

That was the year Florence Murphy cast her lot with the fledgling company, at the urging of her friend June Simon. Murphy's duties were "management of the maintenance department, ordering supplies, licensing planes, setting up traffic schedules, and helping with any problems in the new air service." The company had a couple of twin-engine Cessna five-seaters for the charter trade. "We started out with one flight a week to Reno," she says. Demand was high, and the two-hour flights were soon departing daily.

In 1946, the U.S. military began selling off C-47 airplanes, the military version of the Douglas DC-3. The gutted planes received an interior makeover, with passenger comfort in mind. Bonanza eventually bought nine of them. Meanwhile, Murphy had risen to the position of vice president and secretary of the company—the only female airline vice president in the country. She also was Bonanza's director of personnel and handled labor relations.

But Florence Murphy, for all her administrative ability, was a flier. She was licensed to make those scheduled runs to Reno, and she did. "I was afraid people would jump out if they saw me flying," she says, laughing. "It was a man's world; women were *not* in aviation. I had to prove myself. But I finally gained their respect."

Bonanza's in-state operations were rarely profitable, and only by obtaining an interstate route and an airmail franchise, could the company receive government subsidies. The more airmail routes a line attained, the larger the subsidy.

"We bought TWA's route from here to Phoenix, and that made us interstate and we could carry mail," Murphy explains. "Our first subsidy was $25,000 for one year. So we started going after more mail routes and getting more subsidies

all the time. And that was why I broke with Bonanza in 1958. You see, when you're receiving subsidies from the government, your earnings are also limited. I just don't believe in the government trap anyway; I wasn't brought up that way."

Murphy says she tried to get Converse out of the subsidy game: "I told him, 'We can do it on our own, without subsidy, if we provide the service.' That was our main disagreement, and the main reason I left." She has been in the real-estate business ever since.

One of Murphy's most poignant memories is a hand-drawn picture, rendered by her daughter when she was 9. It shows an airplane, all the people at Bonanza Airlines, and their positions. With the clarity of a child, Ed Converse is labeled "the man with the money." Beside her mother's picture is the legend "the lady with the brains." ⌀

Florence Murphy at the controls of a DC-3 en route to Reno in 1953. She had to be discreet entering the cabin. Passengers weren't yet ready to accept female pilots.
(Courtesy Florence Murphy)

VIP flights were important in building public support during Bonanza's early years. This 1948 flight is just concluding. From left: Gloria Mapes, Alta Ham, Florence Murphy, Nita Gueswelle, Delphine "Mom" Squires, Phil Cherry, Ruth Ferron, Mal Morledge, Lola Woodbury, Leah Cashman, unidentified, Clara Breeze, Jean Boggs, and Anna Fayle.
(Courtesy Florence Murphy)

STEVE HANNAGAN (1899–1953)

"We would go to all the hotels—there were about four of them at the time—and look for attractive couples. The idea was to take a photo of people vacationing and send it back to the subject's local newspaper. It would run the picture of this couple sitting by the pool, and a neighbor would see someone he knew and say, 'Well, if the Joneses can afford to go to Las Vegas, then we can, too.' And we did a saturation job with those pictures."

— Don English
Former Hannagan photographer

Without ever living in Las Vegas, a publicist left his mark on the town. BY K.J. EVANS

Steve Hannagan, publicist extraordinaire, never made Las Vegas his home and rarely set foot in the town. His agency, Steve Hannagan and Associates, represented Las Vegas for less than two years during 1948 and 1949. But the "Hannagan Method" was adopted by the Las Vegas News Bureau, and it became one of the most effective publicity machines in the world. Like many good ideas, one of Hannagan's best was also one of his simplest.

"Every morning, we would have a 'home-town run,'" recalls veteran photographer Don English, a former Hannagan employee who came to Las Vegas in 1949 and stayed until retirement. "We would go to all the hotels—there were about four of them at the time—and look for attractive couples. The idea was to photograph people vacationing and send it back to the subject's local newspaper. It would run the picture of this couple sitting by the pool, and a neighbor would see someone he knew and say, 'Well, if the Joneses can afford to go to Las Vegas, then we can, too.' And we did a saturation job with those pictures." Editors also were saturated with Las Vegas cheesecake—featuring an abundance of swimming pools and showgirls.

Hannagan was a native of Indiana, born in Lafayette in 1899, who began his career as a correspondent for United Press. His first public-relations job was promoting the Indianapolis 500. His success earned him a position as a publicist

for Miami Beach—and the money to open his own agency in New York City.

In the mid-1930s, Hannagan came to the attention of W. Averell Harriman, chairman of the Union Pacific Railroad. Harriman, according to his biographer, Rudy Abramson, wanted to develop a ski resort like those he had seen in Europe. It was a totally new concept in the United States, and one that Harriman hoped would build ridership on his trains. He purchased some property in the mountain cow town of Ketchum, Idaho, and hired Hannagan to develop a publicity strategy.

"Hannagan had earned a reputation as a promotional genius by mesmerizing snowbound New Yorkers with images of sun, golden sand, and tropical luxury at Miami Beach," Abramson wrote. "He had all the machinery and contacts that Harriman needed to sell the novel idea of a winter vacation in Idaho." The resort, dubbed "Sun Valley," opened in December 1936, by which time Hannagan had become a legend.

Meanwhile, the little railroad town of Las Vegas was slowly becoming aware of an entirely new industry. Since 1931, people had been coming through Las Vegas, en route to Boulder Dam, then under construction. After the dam was finished in 1935, people continued to come.

By 1944, Maxwell Kelch, founder of radio station KENO, had been elected cham-

ber president, and was exhorting his fellow business people to get behind a regional advertising and publicity campaign that would make Southern Nevada a well-known postwar travel destination. The means to that end was dubbed the

Hannagan in Southern Nevada

POP.[1]	DECADE
n/a	pre-1900
30	1900
945	1910
2,686	1920
5,952	1930
13,937	1940
45,577	1950
123,667	1960
273,288	1970
463,087	1980
715,587	1990
1,360,000[2]	2000

■ Time spent in Southern Nev.
1 - Population figures are for greater Las Vegas area (*Source: Nevada State Data Center*).
2 - Estimate

Steve Hannagan mugs for the camera. The gag is that News Bureau photographers had to be reminded to let the receptionist, Annie, know where they were going. Coincidentally, Hannagan's girlfriend was film star Ann Sheridan.

(Courtesy Harvey Diederich)

"Live Wire Fund." Kelch persuaded nearly every business in the chamber to contribute from 1 percent to 5 percent of its annual gross receipts. The final tally was $84,000.

The prestigious New York-based J. Walter Thompson agency was hired, but its performance was unremarkable. West-Marquis Advertising was hired next, and gets credit for inventing "Vegas Vic," the rangy, cigarette-smoking cowboy who became the city's mascot. The agency handled only advertising. Publicity was handled directly by the chamber. By definition, publicity involves persuading newspapers, magazines, and broadcasters that your product—or city—is worthy of a story.

In 1948, George Ashby, a resident of Las Vegas and president of the Union Pacific Railroad, offered Hannagan's services to the chamber, paying half of his $50,000 annual fee. That summer, Hannagan's publicity machine, headed by Neil T. Regan, popped its clutch and roared off to "Operation Las Vegas," establishing the "Desert Sea News Bureau." (The name refers to Lake Mead, and later would be changed to the Las Vegas News Bureau.)

"Hannagan made it clear that he would ignore the obvious glamour of gaming, divorce, and marriage chapels, and would instead publicize Las Vegas as the hub of a surrounding scenic wonderland," wrote Perry Kaufman in *City Boosters, Las Vegas Style*. "He felt that the coverage by outside writers on the land of Sodom and Gomorrah made Las Vegas known as a gambling resort, and wanted to diversify the other images in order to entice wives and families to come."

For 1950, Hannagan submitted a bid of $87,000 to continue his services. The chamber turned it down. Union Pacific was under fire from other towns on its line who wanted a sweetheart deal; instead, the railroad ended the subsidy.

"The chamber announced that it will set up its own publicity bureau modeled and staffed as closely as possible along the lines of the current Hannagan operation," wrote the *Review-Journal* in October 1949. Hired to head the new Las Vegas Bureau was Ken Frogley, one of several Hannaganites who stayed aboard. Hannagan died February 3, 1953, and was buried in his hometown of Lafayette.

It is unknown what Hannagan would have made of the advent of above-ground nuclear testing in 1951. But it's probably safe to assume that he would have approved of the way the Las Vegas News Bureau handled atomic testing as another tourist attraction.

Bomb tests were difficult to cover, and especially difficult to photograph. A photographer might spend several days on the road, and there was always a good chance the shot would be postponed. The other option was to rely on the photographers of the Las Vegas News Bureau. They were reliable and provided a lot of unsolicited material involving celebrities and pretty women at poolside. "It was an opportunity for the Las Vegas News Bureau to service the L.A. papers and wire services and to get a rapport with those people," says English. "And it worked. It was very successful."

Jerry Abbott, who was the bureau's head photographer for several years, recalled in a 1988 interview that his guys were always looking for a new way of presenting the atomic "shot" photos. One lensman, Joe Buck, decided that he could illustrate the "false dawn" created by the early morning blasts. His idea was to pose a rooster on an antenna, backlit by the blast. He obtained a suitable bird and froze it. On the appointed day, he perched the bird and waited. The test was canceled and the rooster returned to cold storage. Another date was set, and Buck and his rooster were there. No go. With each partial thawing, the rooster's feathers were becoming increasingly disheveled. "After about the third time, the bomb finally went, and this rooster looks like it's really getting blasted off the antenna," Abbott said, laughing. Even so, the picture went out and was widely used.

In the late 1960s, the News Bureau's function began to change. Las Vegas was by then a household word, and the News Bureau increasingly functioned as a liaison between travel writers and hotel publicists. But in mid-1992, the Chamber of Commerce, headed by Bob Maxey, decided the Las Vegas News Bureau had completed its mission. The board voted not to provide its $650,000 annual budget. The bureau's huge archive of historic photographs, along with its equipment, was handed over to the Las Vegas Convention and Visitors Authority, which reopened a much smaller bureau later that year. ✍

The News Bureau provided photo coverage of all atomic bomb tests during the 1950s and '60s for United Press International, and its work was featured in virtually every newspaper and magazine in the world.
(Las Vegas News Bureau/LVCVA)

The photographers of the Las Vegas News Bureau, 1959. They took their work seriously, but not themselves. Left to right are Joe Buck, Jerry Abbott, and Milt Palmer; the fall guy at center is Don English.
(Las Vegas News Bureau/LVCVA)

HARVEY DIEDERICH (1920–)

"I think we were very instrumental in developing Las Vegas into an international destination during the 1950s and into the 1960s. I think through the efforts of all of us, we were able to call international attention to Las Vegas, basically through the appearances here of Hollywood personalities, and a lot of creative publicity. And there was creative use of showgirls."
—Harvey Diederich

Publicity played a big part in Las Vegas' formative years as a resort destination, and one publicist used every cornball stunt he could think of to get hotels' showgirls global exposure. BY K.J. EVANS

There were a lot of moving parts in the great postwar Las Vegas publicity engine, but it would certainly have stalled if not for the efforts of the Las Vegas News Bureau and resort publicists like Harvey Diederich, who touted his town from 1952 until his retirement in 1988.

"I think we were very instrumental in developing Las Vegas into an international destination during the 1950s and into the 1960s," he says. "I think through the efforts of all of us, we were able to call international attention to Las Vegas, basically through the appearances here of Hollywood personalities, and a lot of creative publicity." He pauses and a sly grin appears. "And there was creative use of showgirls."

One Valentine's Day, Diederich had a life-size playing card, a queen of hearts, made. The center was cut out, and a girl in a bathing suit was posed stepping through the hole. Like practically every publicity photo of the period, it was at poolside. "But it got play," says Diederich.

Born February 8, 1920, in Chicago, Harvey Diederich served as an Army medic in the Pacific during World War II. After the war, he earned a bachelor's degree in journalism from the University of Southern California in 1950. That summer, he heard of a publicist's job in the ski resort town of Sun Valley, Idaho. The sleepy mountain town was a gathering place for the rich and famous

largely because of the legendary Steve Hannagan, who invented the concept of promoting entire resort cities, and who hired Diederich. It was a plum job, Diederich recalls, but by 1952 he was ready for a change. Las Vegas publicity man Herb McDonald tipped him to a job at The Last Frontier, and Diederich landed it.

Hannagan had come to Las Vegas and gone, leaving a formidable publicity machine, the Las

Harvey Diederich, as a young publicist at the Tropicana, in the early 1960s
(Courtesy Harvey Diederich)

Vegas News Bureau. Don English, who came to Las Vegas in 1949 as a photographer for Hannagan, struck up a lifelong friendship with Diederich. "The News Bureau was the photographic arm and the writing aide to all the Las Vegas press agents in those days," English says. "We fed off each other. An idea would pop up, and we would discuss it and develop it together. It might originate with the News Bureau or an individual hotel, and the creativity blended both."

From 1954 to 1956, Diederich worked for Hannagan in the Bahamas and then did a short stint with a publicity firm in New York before coming back to Las Vegas, where he had friends, good memories, and a solid reputation. "I came back to town without a job, driving a station wagon with a trailer with all our household goods, four children, a parakeet, and a dog with a litter of pups," he recalled.

He immediately landed a job at the Hacienda, then moved to the Tropicana in 1957. "The Tropicana was pure class in those days," he said. "We adopted the motto, 'The Tiffany of the Strip.' That phrase actually came from a magazine writer, but we borrowed it."

Diederich even wrung publicity from the 1956 presidential election. He and photographer English posed a showgirl poolside in a bathing suit. In her right hand, she held a cardboard campaign poster for Republican Dwight D. Eisenhower; in her left, a poster for Democrat Adlai Stevenson.

Diederich in Southern Nevada

POP.[1]	DECADE
n/a	pre-1900
30	1900
945	1910
2,686	1920
5,952	1930
13,937	1940
45,577	1950
123,667	1960
273,288	1970
463,087	1980
715,587	1990
1,360,000[2]	2000

■ Time spent in Southern Nev.
1 - Population figures are for greater Las Vegas area (*Source: Nevada State Data Center*).
2 - Estimate

"I suggested we name her Miss Bea Sure N. Vote," says English. To his and Diederich's surprise, the photo got a lot of play.

Cornball sold, and so did screwball. Diederich recalls that one of his most successful pictures was taken in 1956 when he was working for the Hacienda, which at the time had a golf course. After dark, a showgirl in a very short nightie was posed at the first hole swinging at a golf ball. The caption was "Night-Tee-Time," and the photo was used by lecherous newspaper editors across the nation.

Holidays were prime time for themed cheesecake photos. One Thanksgiving, English recalls, Diederich ordered the Tropicana Hotel chef to carve an enormous ice sculpture of a turkey. A showgirl straddled its back in an equestrian pose. "Cold Turkey" was the photo's caption. "There were a lot of groans," says English with a laugh,

"but again, it worked."

Aside from cheesecake, the other staple of the Las Vegas publicity mill was celebrities. Most celebrities were amenable to posing for the publicist's camera, especially those under contract with a Hollywood studio. "In those days, the studios really owned the performer," said Diederich. "And when they wanted to go to Las Vegas, the studios probably welcomed the trip, but not unless they were completely cooperative with us."

When Ronald Reagan made his one and only Las Vegas appearance at The Last Frontier in 1954, Diederich and photographers marched him and Nancy around The Last Frontier Village, posing them on old cars and wagons, then sent them out to Lake Mead for a cruise on The Last Frontier's yacht, where they were photographed sunbathing, eating lunch, and pretending to fish. Diederich recalls that the resulting pictures were a great hit with fan magazine editors.

The dawn of the television age offered new opportunities for free publicity, says Diederich. Early TV programming managers were eager for "filler" material. The 1950s were a time when practically every celebrity in Hollywood was putting together a Las Vegas lounge act. Even Reagan, Marlene Dietrich, and Mae West appeared. Despite the rather dubious news value, the Los Angeles stations would readily air film showing an aging West on stage surrounded by men in swimsuits.

Of course, not all of the publicity stunts were hatched by Diederich, who drops the names of his peers of the period, such as Gene Murphy at the Desert Inn and Bert Perry at the Flamingo. Old-time Las Vegas publicists speak in reverential tones about Al Freeman, the legendary publicist for the Sands, whom Diederich describes as "a remarkable talent."

It was Freeman who engineered what is perhaps the most famous Las Vegas publicity shot in history—the "floating" crap game. That picture, taken July 1, 1953, depicts a group of gamblers in swimsuits standing waist deep in the hotel pool around a crap table. It wasn't a prop, but a real crap table that Freeman had removed from the casino.

English recalls Freeman as the kind of publicist who saw opportunities everywhere. One evening in the early 1960s, comedian Red Skelton was well into his act on the Sands' Copa Room stage, when a lightning storm knocked out all power on the Strip. Skelton was unperturbed, says English: "He asked everybody to bring the candles from their tables forward and put them around the edge of the stage, like footlights, and he kept the show going." English was summoned to record the scene on celluloid. "The next morning," he says, "it was on the front page of the Los Angeles Mirror, two or three columns, with the caption 'The Show Must Go On.' They were mighty pleased."

Diederich worked at the Sahara between 1957 and 1961, then returned to the Tropicana, where he remained until 1972. In 1973, he was hired to open the new MGM Grand (now Bally's), and ended his career as a Las Vegas publicity man at the Union Plaza, where he served from 1980 to 1988.

He was disappointed when the Chamber of Commerce turned over the operation of the News Bureau to the Las Vegas Convention and Visitors Authority, which spends far more on advertising than it does on publicity, and cut back the staff of the News Bureau drastically. "Publicity far, far exceeds the value of advertising," Diederich says. "Basically, it's more believable." ✍

Harvey Diederich (at rear) hobnobs with (from left) Danny Kaye, George Burns, and Sahara Hotel owner Milton Prell, 1961.
(Las Vegas News Bureau /LVCVA)

Diederich, with an unidentified model, directs a "cheesecake" photo shoot. This one seems to be in celebration of Funny Hats Week.
(Courtesy Harvey Diederich)

MORRIS B. "MOE" DALITZ (1899–1989)

If local police detectives and FBI men suspected Dalitz of wrongdoing during his latter years, they dared not whisper such criticism without ample evidence. By the time Dalitz reached his prime, his financial empire and formidable string of businesses were legitimate. It didn't start out that way.

Shady dealings did little to dull the luster that this private man brought to the city of glitz — both on and off the Strip. BY JOHN L. SMITH

If you want to understand Las Vegas history, you must get to know Moe Dalitz. Consider that no mean feat, as Dalitz died in 1989 and in life was a private man. He gave few in-depth interviews, but much was written about him. Las Vegas history is filled with characters who lived double lives. The life of Moe Dalitz is perhaps the best example of a gambling man existing in sunshine and in shadow. His story might have been penned by Horatio Alger had he written scripts for "The Untouchables."

Early in his life, Dalitz was a bootlegger and racketeer mentioned in the same breath as Meyer Lansky and Benjamin "Bugsy" Siegel. In Cleveland, one longtime member of law enforcement would tell the Kefauver Commission, "Ruthless beatings, unsolved murders and shakedowns, threats and bribery came to this community as a result of gangsters' rise to power." Dalitz was considered part of that rise.

Given the nation's fascination with organized crime, fueled in no small part by Hollywood and blood-soaked banner headlines during Prohibition's many whiskey wars, Dalitz reached something akin to a celebrity status early in his life as a runner of rum and operator of roadhouse gambling parlors from Cleveland to Newport, Kentucky. If Dalitz never achieved Lansky's moniker of "financial genius of organized crime," it was not because he was less successful.

Unlike Lansky, whose inability to shake off early-won infamy forced him into the shadows throughout his life, Dalitz made the improbable transition from underworld figure to legitimate citizen. If local police detectives and FBI men suspected Dalitz of wrongdoing during his latter years, they dared not whisper such criticism without ample evidence. By the time Dalitz reached his prime, his financial empire and formidable string of businesses were legitimate. It didn't start out that way.

Morris Barney Dalitz was born December 24, 1899, in Boston. The son of a laundry operator, Barney, Moe grew up at his father's side. The family moved to Michigan when Moe was still a child, and his father opened Varsity Laundry in Ann Arbor, which served University of Michigan students. Although he would become known first as an illegal liquor and gambling racketeer, Moe was a successful laundry operator throughout most of his life. It was a labor action associated with his laundry business that introduced Moe Dalitz to Jimmy Hoffa, future president of the Teamsters union, the labor organization that one day would be responsible for lending Nevada gamblers the millions it would take to build the first wave of casino resorts in Las Vegas. Dalitz was attempting to keep his laundries from organizing and, according to

author James Neff, at one point hired Mafia thugs to make his point.

Once he became associated with mob muscle, a door opened and Dalitz gravitated toward the lucrative and dangerous Prohibition-era liquor

Morris B. "Moe" Dalitz in 1982, at age 83
(Review-Journal files)

Dalitz in Southern Nevada

POP.[1]	DECADE
n/a	pre-1900
30	1900
945	1910
2,686	1920
5,952	1930
13,937	1940
45,577	1950
123,667	1960
273,288	1970
463,087	1980
715,587	1990
1,360,000[2]	2000

■ Time spent in Southern Nev.
1 - Population figures are for greater Las Vegas area (*Source: Nevada State Data Center*).
2 - Estimate

trade. All the while he took profits and invested them in legitimate businesses in Detroit and later in Cleveland, where law enforcement noted that he had become associated with the Mayfield Road Gang.

In fact, by the 1930s his list of legitimate businesses was impressive. Dalitz held an interest in the Michigan Industrial Laundry Company in Detroit and the Pioneer Linen Supply Company in Cleveland and percentages in the Reliance Steel Company and the Detroit Steel Company. And there were Milco Sales, Dalitz Realty, Berdene Realty, and the Liberty Ice Cream Company. He even owned a piece of the Chicago and Rock Island Railroad.

Unlike common rumrunners, who wound up either dead or incarcerated, Dalitz was not a simple man. His operation ran Canadian whiskey in trucks floated on barges across the Great Lakes. During Cleveland's liquor wars, when local mob factions battled for market share, Dalitz came away unscathed. By the time the Volstead Act was repealed, he had opened a series of illegal casinos with names like the Mound Club, the Pettibone Club, the Jungle Inn, the Beverly Hills Club, and the Lookout House.

"How was I to know those gambling joints were illegal?" Dalitz once quipped to a friend. "There were so many judges and politicians in them, I figured they had to be all right."

In the 1940s Dalitz served his country more than cards, dice, and clean shirts. He also served in the Army, rising to the rank of second lieutenant. But when the war ended, he found himself reluctantly returning to an increasingly complex business life at home. Stated bluntly, the heat was on across America as law enforcement and high-ranking politicians vilified illegal gamblers and their ilk as a societal scourge.

So Moe Dalitz did what any gifted businessman in his racket might have done. He migrated to Las Vegas, where casino games were legal and gamblers were men to be respected. At the time, Las Vegas and Havana vied for dominance as legal gambling centers. Dalitz dabbled in Cuban casinos, where his friend and bootlegging ally Meyer Lansky had invested many millions, but was more impressed with what was happening in the Silver State.

Dalitz led a group of Cleveland investors, including Sam Tucker, Thomas McGinty, and Morris Kleinman, in the purchase of the then-incomplete Desert Inn, which opened in 1950. Dalitz not only was an experienced casino man, but also understood that gamblers wanted more than green felt. He gave them greens as well, developing the Desert Inn Country Club and creating the Tournament of Champions golf competition, which focused a positive national spotlight on Las Vegas.

A year after the Desert Inn opened, Senator Estes Kefauver focused another kind of spotlight on gambling. The Kefauver hearings concerned themselves with the phenomenon of gambling and organized crime in America, as well as with promoting the political careers of senators who portrayed themselves as mob-busting puritans. Dalitz appeared before the Kefauver committee and more than held his own.

Kefauver: "As a matter of fact, you had been making a great deal of money in recent years, so I suppose from your profits from one investment, you would then go ahead and make another investment. Now, to get your investments started off, you did get yourself a pretty good little nest egg out of rumrunning, didn't you?"

Dalitz: "Well, I didn't inherit any money, Senator. ... If you people wouldn't have drunk it, I wouldn't have bootlegged it."

The critics came and went, but Dalitz kept on building his financial empire and paying his taxes. (In a lifetime of nefarious-activity allegations, Dalitz was indicted twice: once in 1930 in Buffalo, New York, for bootlegging; once in 1965 in Los Angeles for tax evasion. Both charges were dismissed.)

In 1958, Dalitz and his associates used millions in Teamsters loans and dollars borrowed from Louis Jacobs' Emprise Corporation to take over the Stardust from a group led by Jake "The Barber" Factor. The new crew of efficient casino men turned the Stardust into a winner by expanding the number of rooms and the gaming area, and by adding a Parisian-style floorshow.

Dalitz shied away from interviews, which sooner or later usually led to hard questions about his notorious days in the rackets. But he was not without a sense of humor and his own sense of image-making. "When I left home, it was during Prohibition in Ann Arbor, Michigan, and I went into the liquor business while it was illegal," Dalitz once told a local reporter. "Then when the

Moe Dalitz and his Cleveland buddies rescued the underfinanced and incomplete Desert Inn, which celebrated one of its early anniversaries with the "cutting" of a giant birthday cake.
(UNLV Special Collections)

"How was I to know those gambling joints were illegal? There were so many judges and politicians in them, I figured they had to be all right."
—**Moe Dalitz**

rules: You had to have a license, and you had to run a square game.

Born in Ogden, Utah, in 1905, Cahill spent his childhood in the Nevada railroad town of Sparks, where his father was stationed as a conductor and his mother ran a rooming house for railroad men. He attended the University of Nevada in Reno and was a popular fraternity man, he confessed in his old age, largely because of his friendships with Sparks bootleggers.

Cahill was doing well in the corporate world until the Depression blew it apart. He drifted back to Sparks and to a job as a grease monkey. "It was not easy to go back to your hometown as a college graduate … to work in a job that I could've worked at when I left the eighth grade," he said

in an oral history recorded by the University of Nevada-Reno in the 1970s. He saved enough money to open his own garage on a shoestring.

Sparks was a small town that enrolled all the willing, and some who weren't, for public service. Cahill was drawn into politics as a member of the school board, and then was elected to the Legislature and happened to chair the Ways and Means Committee. In the late '30s the state was very solvent, so it reduced the tax rate and began to brag about it. A sign at the state line announced: "Nevada, One Sound State, Cyclone Cellar of the Tax Oppressed, No Sales Tax, No Income Tax, No Inheritance Tax."

Cahill took a job in the state controller's office and discovered that the state's lax and

patched-together insurance laws permitted promoters to sell insurance policies backed by no assets. He got the code rewritten into a consistent whole.

In 1945 Cahill was appointed secretary to the Nevada Tax Commission, which administered gaming licenses because gaming was seen primarily as a source of license fees. Commissioners were part-timers who met only once in a while, so Cahill did much of their official work.

He had the bad timing to come aboard just as Benjamin "Bugsy" Siegel became prominent in Southern Nevada, and Siegel was one of the people who didn't pay his gaming tax. Cahill sent an employee, Dewey Ebert, to collect the overdue $5,000. Ebert called Cahill in Carson City, from Siegel's office at the Flamingo, and said that Siegel refused to pay. Finally Siegel himself picked up the phone. "What'll you do if I don't pay?" he asked.

"Well, we'll revoke your license immediately," said Cahill.

"You wouldn't dare do it," said Siegel.

And Cahill responded, "Well, maybe you'd better try us."

Siegel still refused to turn over a check, but agreed to write one and mail it while Ebert watched. When Cahill hung up, his secretary congratulated him for bravery toward a killer. "Who's afraid of Bugsy Siegel over the telephone 500 miles away?" Cahill thought. Then he remembered that Ebert had been face to face with a killer who was not called Bugsy for being even-tempered. But Ebert was a brave ex-policeman, and a good bluffer, too.

Bluffing was all he and Cahill were doing, Cahill recalled in an interview with the *Review-Journal* in 1990. In the early days, the Tax Commission didn't yet have the authority to revoke a license. In fact, said Cahill in his oral his-

In 1977 Harold J. Erickson (left), director of UNLV's Dickinson Library, and Robbins Cahill look over the library's copy of Cahill's oral history. The six-volume work was then the longest ever collected by the University of Nevada-Reno, and has become a standard source for researchers into Nevada's political history.
(UNLV Special Collections)

tory, it was Siegel's murder in 1947 that nudged the control of gambling out of county hands, where it had resided since legalization in 1931. Las Vegans no longer winked at Siegel's reputation as a member of Murder Inc. His slaying put the town into an uproar, and P.O. Silvagni, the operator of downtown's Apache Hotel, spoke the fears of all: "Blood is gonna run into the streets!" Suddenly, boosters *did* care who brought money and where they got it. Because many counties didn't have the resources to do background checks, they wanted the state to handle it.

Later that year, Cahill got an opinion from Attorney General Alan Bible, saying that the commission had implied authority to investigate backgrounds and deny a license to unsuitable individuals, and in 1949 the Legislature spelled it out in statutes. It also permitted the commission to require fingerprinting of gaming employees, which drove many an outlaw from the trade and reduced the probability of cheating.

One of the bigger challenges to the state's licensing authority was the Thunderbird incident, precipitated by a Byzantine sting in which an undercover agent, posing as a criminal seeking to bribe his way into a liquor license for a move into Las Vegas, recorded compromising conversations with public officials.

One of the tapes implied that crime lord Meyer Lansky held a hidden interest in the Thunderbird resort on the Strip. Cahill's own follow-up investigation showed a loan from Meyer's brother, Jake, through an intermediary, to Thunderbird licensee Marion Hicks. In 1955, the Tax Commission moved to revoke the gaming licenses of Hicks and his partner, Lieutenant Governor Cliff Jones. "We didn't have to prove that it was Meyer Lansky's money," pointed out Cahill

> *"When we brought the point of question, were they Mafia people, were they hoodlums, we were told no. These people are seen in their clubs … they tolerate them. But no, they weren't Mafia. … They don't operate in this manner."*
> —Robbins Cahill

in a 1987 interview with the *Review-Journal*. A hidden interest was prohibited no matter who held it.

Both sides eventually won in a sense, said Cahill. Courts confirmed that the state had authority over the issue. They also ruled that a loan did not constitute a hidden interest, so Jones and Hicks got to keep their licenses, although they soon sold the Thunderbird. Hicks died not long after, but Jones went on to hold interests in casinos throughout the world.

Even though Cahill fought to keep the Lanskys out of Nevada, he was criticized all his life for issuing licenses to gamblers with alleged connections to criminal organizations. Much of the controversy centered on Morris "Moe" Dalitz, the most prominent member of the group that took control of the Desert Inn from its financially strapped founder, Wilbur Clark.

Yet Dalitz also was the example Cahill chose to defend his practice. Everywhere his personnel went, in investigating Dalitz' background, they were told that Dalitz had been involved in selling bootleg whiskey and smuggling it from Canada. But they also were told: "They run a good tight business; they run an ethical business. Yes, maybe they have to pay off people to keep an illegal operation."

Cahill recalled, "When we brought the point of question, were they Mafia people, were they hoodlums, we were told no. These people are seen in their clubs … they tolerate them. But no, they weren't Mafia. … They don't operate in this manner."

Time proved him right, Cahill claimed. The Desert Inn became one of the more stable and most reputable Las Vegas casinos. Cahill often said that people who had gained gambling experience in illegal operations were the best casino operators. In fact, he believed the casino failures

of the '50s and '60s were brought on by ventures of "the butcher, the baker, and the candlestick maker" into a business they didn't understand. And that's why he preferred operators who had run a joint before, albeit an illegal one. However, he tried to avoid licensing any more of the Siegel type who practiced murder and extortion.

In 1959, at the urging of Governor Grant Sawyer, the Legislature split the gaming regulatory apparatus away from the Nevada Tax Commission and created the Nevada Gaming Commission. Cahill thought the changes were in order, but chose to remain with the Tax Commission. After four more years, he left state government to become Clark County manager.

Harley E. Harmon, who also served on the County Commission in those days, said Cahill professionalized county administration. "He was probably the most informed man in the state," said Harmon. "He could give you an answer right now."

Cahill returned to the gaming business as executive director of the Nevada Resort Association, which represented major resorts in lobbying and labor negotiations, then served three years as executive director of the Gaming Association of Northern Nevada before retiring in 1980.

Cahill was married twice. Elsie Compston Cahill died about 1956 after separating from Cahill; he married Margaret Moffatt Newton, a longtime Las Vegan, in 1957. Margaret died in 1998. The couple had two sons: Robert Cahill became a high-school teacher in Reno; William Newton, a landscape architect in San Francisco.

Robert remembered that his father was easy to get along with, but was so wrapped up in work that he didn't get to spend as much time with his family as everyone would have liked: "He was like most men who had influential positions at the time."

But in retirement, he made time. In 1994 when Margaret fell ill and had to be moved to an assisted living facility, Cahill refused to be separated from her and moved there with her. Thought to be in good health for a man of 89, he fell ill that December and died in a few days. ✍

DEL E. WEBB

(1899–1974)

"The guy I worked for was kinda on a shoestring. We would need material, and he'd show up with a board or two and then disappear. … One Friday I drew my paycheck from this guy and walked to the bank. I figured I'd check out and maybe go to the Grand Canyon, where I had heard there was some work. The bank refused to cash the check, saying it wasn't any good. … The next day [the client who needed a building faster than he was getting it] came to me and said, 'You seem to know what you're doing. Why don't you go ahead and finish this building?' From then on, I was in the contracting business."

—Del E. Webb

A developer, who did much more than just build houses, will continue to have an impact on Las Vegas well into the next millennium. BY A.D. HOPKINS

Del Webb had friends in high places and low, and was not yet sure where he should count Ben Siegel, his new client. Webb, a Phoenix construction man with a can-do reputation, had taken on an unfinished Nevada hotel as a favor to a banker friend with serious money at stake. But before he knew it, Webb found himself bound by contract to a man of doubtful repute.

And before very long, Siegel would remove all doubts. Siegel bragged that he had personally killed 12 people. Now another mob figure was getting under his skin. "I'm going to kill that SOB, too," he said. Webb's face must have reflected his shock, for Siegel then reassured him: "Del, don't worry. We only kill each other."

Webb walked a thin and dangerous line with Siegel, but it was all in a life's work. Construction contracting was inherently risky. Somebody in his company once observed that it was a business where things *do not* even out. Bid too low, you lose money; bid too high, you don't get the job. But even by construction standards, Webb was daring. He took jobs nobody else had tried, finished them fast, and did them well. He helped shape not only Nevada but also its gaming industry, the entire American Southwest, and even major-league baseball.

Born to a wealthy Fresno, California, family in 1899, Webb saw his father go broke about 1914.

His father lost his shirt in construction. Webb originally had learned carpentry as a hobby, but then turned to it as a livelihood, dropping out of high school.

But his main job, as he saw it, was playing baseball. Webb played for minor-league teams in Oakland, Alameda, Modesto, and other places, sometimes under an assumed name. A pitcher, he might have made it to the big leagues had it not been for an exhibition game at San Quentin prison in 1927. He caught typhoid fever from an inmate,

nearly died of it, and for a year was unable to play baseball.

More than 6 feet tall, he normally weighed 200 pounds; his weight dropped to 99 pounds. Webb and his young wife, Hazel, moved to Phoenix in hopes that he would recover his health. He did. He even played baseball again.

Margaret Finnerty, who wrote a biography of Del Webb, encountered at least three versions of how he got into the contracting business; two of those were from reputable journalists quoting Webb himself. All versions, however, involved a construction job gone bad.

"The guy I worked for was kinda on a shoestring," Webb said in one case. "We would need material, and he'd show up with a board or two and then disappear. … One Friday I drew my paycheck from this guy and walked to the bank. I figured I'd check out and maybe go to the Grand Canyon, where I had heard there was some work. The bank refused to cash the check, saying it wasn't any good. … The next day [the client who needed a building faster than he was getting it] came to me and said, 'You seem to know what you're doing. Why don't you go ahead and finish this building?' From then on, I was in the contracting business."

Webb's total beginning assets in 1928 are now legendary: "a concrete mixer, 10 wheelbarrows, 20 shovels, and 10 picks." The *Los Angeles Times* reported, years later, that the company was a $3

Del Webb was on the cover of Time magazine in 1964.
(Courtesy Del Webb Corporation)

Del Webb, in an undated photo probably taken in the late 1940s
(Courtesy Del Webb Corporation)

million operation by 1933, the height of the Depression. In 1935 Webb opened a branch office in Los Angeles. In 1938 he built an addition on the Arizona State Capitol.

Webb had great personal will power. In the 1940s he came down with what was presumed to be the flu. A doctor began asking him routine questions for medical background. "When I told him I drank 10 to 20 bourbons a day, he damn near dropped his teeth," Webb related later. "He said I ought to cut down, but I told him I damn well would quit. And I did. Not another drop of whiskey has passed my lips since that day. All that time I spent drinking I could now spend working."

Herb McDonald, now director of special events at the Showboat Hotel and Casino and formerly a vice president of Del Webb Hotels, remembers that Webb ordered the same meal every time they dined together: "New York steak, green beans, no bread, maybe a baked potato, and one scoop of vanilla ice cream."

Most construction companies banged together job-site shacks of unfinished framing lumber, but Webb used portable offices—identical in color, furniture, and what went on inside. A manual outlined procedures, down to where a given report would hang on the office wall. That organizational mania paid off richly in the frantic opening days of World War II, when new military facilities and war plants had to be built yesterday. World War II made Webb rich.

Having seen his father lose everything in construction, Webb put some eggs in other baskets. It was in this mood that he struck what he would call "the best deal I ever made." With a partner, Al Topping, Webb acquired the New York Yankees in January 1945. The acquisition included not only the famous club but also its farm teams, for a total of 450 players. And it included stadiums in New York, Newark, and Kansas City.

The partners paid $2.8 million for the Yankees and promptly sold some unneeded land for $2 million. They would sell the club itself at the end of the 1964 season for $14 million. In the inter-

vening years, the Yankees won 15 pennants and 10 World Series. Yankees tickets clinched deals for corporate construction contracts and made Webb a friend to senators with pork-barrel projects to build.

Webb claimed he didn't quite understand who Benjamin "Bugsy" Siegel was when he agreed to finish Siegel's new Las Vegas hotel. Robert Johnson, a longtime employee Webb assigned to work on the Flamingo and who later became president of Del Webb Corporation, remembered that the job was plagued by elegant, but ill-conceived, design: "We never had a complete set of plans. We would build what he [Siegel] wanted, and then the architect would draw what we had built." Webb went on to build dozens of important structures in Las Vegas, including its present City Hall and both Clark and Valley high schools.

But it was not Webb himself who put the corporation into the casino business. It was L.C. Jacobson, an ex-carpenter whom Webb hired as a timekeeper in 1938 and who eventually served as the company's president from 1962 to 1966. In 1965 Jacobson told *Fortune* magazine that his original interest in gambling was shooting the dice: "I was never what you'd call a high roller, but I've taken my share of lickings up there—up to $9,000 or $10,000 on a few nights. … I thought it was high time I got some of it back."

Through playing craps, Jacobson made the acquaintance of Alfred Winter, who ran gambling operations illegally in Portland, Oregon, and later legally in Las Vegas. In 1951, Winter wanted to build a bigger joint but didn't know how to raise money. He asked Jacobson for help and got it; Jacobson, then executive vice president for Del Webb Corporation, also landed the construction job for his company. And in return for his help, Jacobson was allowed to personally buy 20 percent

of the stock in the new hotel, which was called the Sahara and became, for some time, the most prestigious temporary address a visitor or a top performer could have in Las Vegas.

In 1961, Jacobson brokered a deal turning over the interests of the Winter group, including himself, in exchange for 1.5 million shares of Del Webb Corporation stock. William Bennett, who joined the corporation not long afterward and rose to operate two of its hotels, explained: "All these hotels originally belonged to owners who owned a percent here, a percent there, which is a bum deal, because those guys think they have a license to steal. And they don't. Jacobson and Winter got tired of having 15 guys in the count room taking a little for their bosses. So they made a deal to sell the thing to Del Webb for stock, and that enabled us to clean it up."

Del Webb Corporation had gone public in 1960, and the purchase marked the first entry of a respected public stock corporation into Las Vegas gaming. In those days Wall Street was afraid of gaming, and Nevada gaming authorities were afraid of Wall Street. After a series of scandals involving mob investments in casinos, Nevada had passed a law requiring licensing and background investigations for new casino owners. That rule

Webb in Southern Nevada

POP.[1]	DECADE
n/a	pre-1900
30	1900
945	1910
2,686	1920
5,952	1930
13,937	1940
45,577	1950
123,667	1960
273,288	1970
463,087	1980
715,587	1990
1,360,000[2]	2000

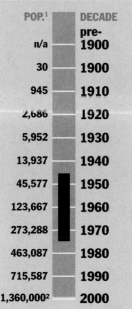

■ Time spent in Southern Nev.
1 - Population figures are for greater Las Vegas area (*Source: Nevada State Data Center*).
2 - Estimate

Henrietta Webb and her boys take a spin on the family cow. From left are Henrietta, Marvin, Halmar, and Del. Halmar became one of Webb's managers, and Marvin became an electrician.
(Courtesy Del Webb Corporation)

Del Webb, as Yankees owner, practices batting with star Joe DiMaggio.
(Courtesy Del Webb Corporation)

Del Webb Corporation entered Nevada gaming after building, then buying, the Sahara Hotel, marking the first time that a publicly held corporation had a major role in running casinos.
(Courtesy Del Webb Corporation)

seemed to eliminate public corporations, whose stock is traded every day. Del Webb Corporation, however, devised a system of operating companies that "leased" casinos. Bennett said the arrangement was a polite fiction: "You just ignored it and ran the whole place."

Del Webb Corporation quickly expanded, buying the Thunderbird Hotel and the Lucky Club downtown. The corporation also expanded the Mint and built a new casino at Lake Tahoe. In 1978 the company was the largest gaming employer in Nevada, with some 7,000 workers.

It isn't clear whether Webb's entry into Nevada gaming inspired Howard Hughes' entry. They shared interests in flying and played golf together in the 1940s. After Hughes lapsed into eccentricity and reclusiveness, Webb was one of the few people Hughes would meet with face to face.

Robert Johnson told Webb's biographer how those meetings were arranged: "He [Hughes] would call Mr. Webb, give him directions, like 'Go 10 miles to a dirt road, then go five miles to the top of a sand dune, then blink your lights twice.' They'd get together and talk until maybe 4 in the morning. But whatever Hughes wanted, the company did it." Webb did more than $1 billion worth of business with Hughes.

Unlike the group of hotels that Hughes would assemble, Webb operations were innovative. It was the Sahara that sponsored the Beatles appearance in Las Vegas in 1964. Booking an act that at the time appealed mostly to teens, who couldn't gamble, was daring.

Webb did not simply acquire classy hotels and wait for rich people to go on vacation; his hotels targeted wealthy subcultures. The Sahara Invitational was a highlight of the PGA tour. The Webb hotels also sponsored trap shoots, realizing that men and women who could afford to burn 100 shotgun shells every outing also might throw dollars at a hardway eight. In the 1970s, the Mint 400 off-road race exploited interest in trendy vehicles.

The Nevada resort operations did the main thing they were supposed to do for Del Webb Cor-

poration—insulate the company against misfortune in other endeavors. Webb's planned communities, aimed specifically at the retirement market, are considered landmark innovations in both American sociology and American business, and they have been very profitable in the long run. But they weren't profitable every month.

Del Webb Corporation officials acknowledge that they weren't the first to think of a retirement community, but nobody had done it on the scale Webb did. No one knew if a sizable market really existed, and some thought the elderly would grow depressed and die early if separated from extended families.

Market research, however, disclosed that putting substantial distance between themselves and their extended families was a major benefit many Americans hoped to get out of retirement, and, yes, they would move to Arizona to get it. Del Webb Corporation struck a deal to gradually take over and develop a former cotton ranch as the first Sun City.

The opening of model homes on New Year's Day, 1960, showed that the market for retirement communities was larger than expected. Del Webb Corporation had hoped to get 10,000 people over the three-day grand opening; it got 100,000 and sold 237 homes during the first weekend.

The company continued its diversification program until early 1974, when Webb fell ill. He had taken care of his health religiously since the 1940s and had a checkup at the Mayo Clinic every year. He was famous for the "No Smoking" sign on his desk at a time when most adult males smoked. Yet it was lung cancer that felled Webb. He died on July 4, 1974.

Webb's marriage to his childhood sweetheart, Hazel, broke up in 1952. Nine years

later he married Toni Ince, a millinery buyer for a Phoenix department store. Toni Webb now lives in Beverly Hills. Neither marriage produced children, and much of Webb's fortune went into the Del E. Webb Foundation, which funds medical projects in Arizona, California, and Nevada.

In 1988, the same year it sold its last Las Vegas resort, Del Webb Corporation brought the Sun City concept to Las Vegas with the construction of Sun City Summerlin for 14,000 seniors. The company followed up with Sun City McDonald Ranch in Henderson, which will accommodate about 9,500 homes.

And in October 1998 Del Webb Corporation opened models for Anthem, a master-planned community in southwest Henderson that will include not only a section for the retirement market, but also a gated country-club community and a section of traditional homes. Some 12,000 homes will accommodate a population projected at 30,000.

Webb's final contribution to Las Vegas may be a sea change in desert demographics. He found Las Vegas a fast, young city full of young men and women on the make. And his upscale retirement communities will leave it a gracefully paced home for those who have it made. ✍

C.D. BAKER (1901–1972)

With his no-nonsense approach, former Las Vegas Mayor C.D. Baker helped bring the city's dilapidated infrastructure out of the Depression and into the modern era.   BY K.J. EVANS

The second world war was over by 1951, another had started in Korea, and the battle of Las Vegas was under way. The growth the city had encouraged and nurtured for so many years was threatening to strangle it.

There was a shortage of housing and electricity. A large percentage of the city's streets were unpaved. The demand for phone service increased daily, and the wait for hookups often ran into months. Nellis Air Force Base had been reactivated, and the Nevada Test Site had just opened. People were pouring into town.

Worst of all, the town was running out of water—fast. Since modern air conditioning was then an expensive indulgence, residents relied on swamp coolers. Problem was, on some days, the water pressure wasn't strong enough to push water up onto the roof and over the cooler pads. Lawns and gardens died. Deodorant sales soared.

Enter Charles Duncan Baker, combat engineer and mayor of Las Vegas from 1951 to 1959. He would redesign what was essentially a Depression-era city infrastructure and guide Las Vegas through the frantic '50s and into the modern era.

Baker was an old-style politician, meaning that he probably couldn't get elected in the TV age. When he thought an idea was stupid, he didn't call it "ill-advised"; he called it "stupid." As a military man, he was used to giving orders, and he was equipped with fine vocal cords, which emitted a sandpapered growl or an arresting bark. The cigar clamped between his teeth rounded out the picture.

Tumultuous city commission meetings were often called to order by the mayor without the use of a gavel. "Sit down and shut up," he would roar.

The crusty colonel was born in 1901 in Terre Haute, Indiana, graduated from Rose Polytechnical Institute, and by 1922 was in Las Vegas teaching high-school mathematics and coaching the basketball team. Soon after his arrival, he married Florence Goldfield Knox.

In 1924, Baker started an engineering firm that dovetailed nicely with his other business, real-estate speculation. In an advertisement in the *Las Vegas Age* newspaper in the early 1930s, he asked, "You wouldn't go to a blacksmith to buy a hat; why not consult a civil engineer when you buy land?"

It was during the Depression that Baker's administrative skills first came to public light. In May of 1933, he led 10 young men into Kyle Canyon below Mount Charleston. Baker, representing the U.S. Forest Service, was charged with building a camp to house the "Reforestation Army." This was one of President Franklin D. Roosevelt's New Deal programs, which would eventually be renamed the Civilian Conservation Corps (CCC). Less than two months later, Baker's boys numbered 212. They had completed the camp; had started work on trails, recreation areas, and water systems; and had strung the first telephone

C.D. Baker, the surveyor, late 1940s

Baker in Southern Nevada

POP.[1]	DECADE
n/a	pre-1900
30	1900
945	1910
2,686	1920
5,952	1930
13,937	1940
45,577	1950
123,667	1960
273,288	1970
463,087	1980
715,587	1990
1,360,000[2]	2000

■ Time spent in Southern Nev.
1 - Population figures are for greater Las Vegas area (*Source: Nevada State Data Center*).
2 - Estimate

line into the canyon.

In 1933 Baker was named engineer-examiner for the Nevada and California Works Progress Administration (WPA), at the lordly salary of $3,300 per year. This made him the local liaison with the feds in mapping out and administering public-works programs.

From 1935 to 1938, Baker was Las Vegas' city engineer. He also was active in the Clark County Democratic Central Committee, which generally dominated local politics, but his first run for the Las Vegas mayor's chair, in 1939, failed. Further political plans were delayed by a call in April 1941 to active duty in the U.S. Army Corps of Engineers.

Captain Baker spent the remainder of that year designing and building airstrips in the South Pacific. In November 1941, he was completing an airstrip on Canton Island, a barren coral atoll. His outfit, the 1399th Engineer Construction Battalion, was made up mostly of Hawaiians descended from Japanese. After U.S. forces recovered from

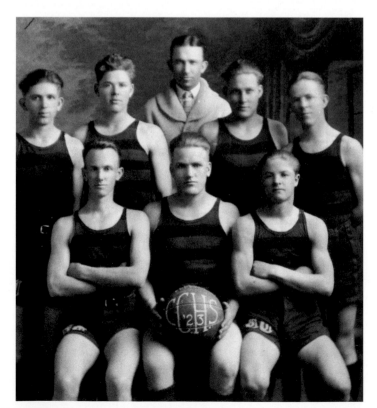

C.D. Baker coached the Clark County High School basketball team of 1923. Front row (left to right): Leonard Noblitt, Lester Leavitt, and Floyd Knickerbocker. Back row (left to right): Donald Schuyler, Jack Sandy, Coach Baker, Julian Anderson, and Gerald Crowe.
(UNLV Special Collections)

the surprise attack of December 7, Baker followed Allied troops in their island-hopping campaign across the South Pacific toward Japan. He built airfields, bases, and hospitals on Kwajalein, Guam, and Okinawa, as well as in the Marshall Islands. He attained the rank of lieutenant colonel, plus was awarded several commendations and decorations. At war's end, in 1946, Baker ran successfully for the state Senate, serving in the 1947 and 1949 legislative sessions.

With the economic survival of the county at stake, the Clark County delegation of 1947 focused on passing two vital pieces of legislation. The first created the Las Vegas Valley Water District, empowered to buy the dilapidated city water system from the Union Pacific Railroad, gaining control of the valley's primary underground water source. The other bill authorized the state to negotiate with the federal government for the purchase of Basic Magnesium Inc. in Henderson, which would give the water district access to the only water pipeline from Lake Mead.

Florence Lee Jones and John Cahlan, in *Water, A History of Las Vegas*, pointed out that passing these bills was no small task, since Clark County had only five of the 41 Assembly seats. Like all 17 counties at the time, it had one senator—Baker.

To convince their colleagues of the importance of the legislation, the southerners flew the entire Legislature to Las Vegas for a tour. "For many of the Northern Nevada legislators," said Jones, "it was their first trip into the southern part of the state." The legislation passed, and Vegas Valley voters approved formation of the water district by a vote of 4,171 to 538.

In 1947, wearing his Elk's Club antlers, Exalted Ruler C.D. Baker announced that the club would build "one of the finest all-purpose stadiums of any smaller community in the Southwest." The Elks produced the city's annual Helldorado

Days, and members had planned since before the war to construct a facility, but material shortages had caused it to be postponed.

The club bought a piece of railroad land near the old Las Vegas Ranch, and an impressive group of Elks set itself to work. The exalted ruler was an engineer, and the construction committee included James Cashman, who sold heavy equipment, and J.M. Murphy, a state road engineer.

There was no need to erect a costly grandstand; Baker carved an amphitheater out of a bluff on the property. Elks Stadium and Cashman Field, as the complex was named, had baseball and football fields, and rodeo grounds.

For its time, the stadium was enormous, capable of accommodating 20,000 people. In the 1950s and 1960s, Helldorado was the year's most important event for locals, as well as a strong tourist draw, and the new facility gave the annual lollapalooza a home.

Baker ensured the survival of the community of Henderson in 1949, when he pushed through a bill allowing Henderson residents to purchase the company houses where they lived. Most had been war workers at Basic Magnesium, and their homes were rented from the company. Baker's bill also allowed industrial buildings at the BMI complex to be leased or sold to private industries. This legislation transformed Henderson from a temporary company town to a community in its own right.

In June 1950 Baker announced that he wouldn't seek a third term in the Senate. He had done all he could for Southern Nevada at the state level, and it was time to head home. (Coincidentally, that same year, he went to Washington, D.C., to attend the command school and general staff college, and was promoted from lieutenant colonel to full colonel in the reserves.)

Baker and local attorney George Franklin Jr. both challenged incumbent Ernie Cragin in the 1951 mayoral race. Baker made a campaign issue of the city's poor water, power, and phone services, and chided Cragin for failing to call those shortcomings to the attention of the Nevada Public Service Commission.

Baker prevailed. Upon election, he promised a progressive administration, and it was so. His top priority, he said, would be to establish assessment districts to pay for much-needed improvements in the city's water, sewer, electrical, and phone systems. The streets in mostly black West Las Vegas were still unpaved when Baker took office, and he astonished many when he kept his campaign promise and spent $10,000 to pave B, C, and E streets. By 1955, property values in the area had risen enough to justify paving the remaining streets.

Following up locally on legislation he had pushed as a state senator, Baker headed the drive for an $8.7 million bond issue, which passed by 82 percent in the fall of 1953. The money was used to buy the railroad's water system and improve it, and to construct pumping stations and pipelines to carry Lake Mead water into the valley.

That same year, 1953, according to UNLV History Professor Eugene Moehring in *Resort City in the Sunbelt: Las Vegas 1930–1970,* Baker "inspired the public with a bold agenda." In addition to supporting the proposed convention center, he called for more than $1 million in new bond issues to pay for a city fire-alarm-box system, for a railroad underpass at Owens Avenue, and for expansion of the city's overtaxed sewage treatment plant. Voters did not feel overtaxed, though. They approved the bond issues and returned Baker to the mayor's chair.

"Within four years of taking office," Florence Lee Jones wrote, "Baker and the board that served with him had doubled the miles of paving and sewer lines in the city, tripled the number of streetlights and miles of sidewalk, and more than doubled park acreage in the city."

But since progress often resembles chaos, Baker's projects were a mixed blessing. Locals often found streets dug up and suffered the occasional water, power, or phone outage. Baker responded to complainers in late 1954, calling them "snipers" and stating simply, "These things have to be done."

Despite his no-nonsense demeanor, Baker was increasingly tourism-conscious and willing to step out of character in the interests of boosterism. In 1953, his honor was a guest, along with Tennessee Ernie Ford, on the "Edgar Bergen and Charlie McCarthy Show" on NBC Radio. Ford and McCarthy, the latter a dummy manipulated by ventriloquist Bergen, enacted a melodrama in which they were Pony Express riders, carrying an important and mysterious package to Las Vegas. As they delivered the package to Baker, he revealed that it contained "cherries for our slot machines."

Less amusing was the time Baker almost fell into the ocean from a great height. He was aboard a TWA Constellation in 1956, en route back to Las Vegas from a political conference in San Francisco. As the plane circled the Bay, an emergency door flew open and slammed into the seat occupied by Baker. The mayor and his aide, Robert Notti, struggled to get the door closed, and eventually succeeded when the captain left the cockpit to lend a hand. Notti and Baker then exchanged seats.

Baker's break with his former ally, Senator Pat McCarran, came in 1952. The senator had been repeatedly blasted by *Las Vegas Sun* publisher Herman "Hank" Greenspun for supporting his Commie-baiting colleague, Joseph McCarthy. In retaliation, McCarran contacted owners of certain Strip casinos and urged them to pull advertising from the newspaper. The boycott quickly spread to downtown. When he learned of McCarran's move, Greenspun filed a $225,000 lawsuit against McCarran and some 40 hotel executives, claiming a criminal conspiracy.

According to Greenspun's autobiography, Baker called together the downtown casino bosses, and he didn't mince words: "No man from Washington, or ex-con man out on the Strip is going to run this city, or ruin a legitimate business. It should be straightened out immediately; but if they want war, they shall have it." The boycott ended, and Greenspun won an $80,500 settlement.

McCarran faced re-election in 1956, and in 1954 Baker announced that he would run for the Senate seat McCarran held. But McCarran died that same year, and so did Baker's plan. Levelheaded Alan Bible was appointed to fill McCarran's unexpired term, and Baker backed him for re-election.

Baker retired from the mayor's office in 1959 and devoted himself to his business interests, the state party organization, and free-lance boosterism. In late March 1963, he appeared in the Legislature as president of the Nevada State Association of Realtors to speak in favor of a bill "allowing apartment house tenants to own their individual rooms." Baker explained that the new class of housing was fairly common in the East, where tenant-owned apartments were called "condominiums." The bill passed.

In March 1966, Baker publicly announced his retirement from politics, business, and everything else. "I'll be turning 65 soon," he growled. "I guess I'll have to apply for my Social Security." He would live until 1972.

But his old bluntness surfaced when, after retirement, he was asked by a reporter to predict the future of Southern Nevada. Baker replied that he was confident that better elements of Southern Nevada society would ultimately head off "interlopers and the infiltration of hoodlums." He was less optimistic about the future of Nevada politics: "I deplore the lack of interest of people in preventing low-caliber persons from getting into public places."

Thus spoke the colonel. Dismissed. ✍

> *"Within four years of taking office, Baker and the board that served with him had doubled the miles of paving and sewer lines in the city, tripled the number of street lights and miles of sidewalk, and more than doubled park acreage in the city."*
> —Florence Lee Jones
> In *Water, A History of Las Vegas*

ALFRED O'DONNELL (1922-)

"Coming from the Pacific and having seen the tremendous megaton bombs, destroying whole fleets of battleships with one bomb, these out here were like little firecrackers."
—Alfred O'Donnell

Proving himself up to the task on the Nevada Proving Grounds—now the Nevada Test Site—gave a young Bostonian the chance to see a new era emerge from the desert. **BY K.J. EVANS**

The U.S.S.R. had just exploded an atomic bomb. Mao Tse-tung's communists had seized power in China. North Korea had invaded South Korea. Faced with this tumult in December 1950, President Harry S. Truman authorized a permanent nuclear bomb testing facility in the continental United States. Southern Nevada was approved for the site on January 11, 1951.

In the vanguard of the resulting migration to Las Vegas of well-educated professionals was a young technician named Alfred O'Donnell. "We brought in the first high-level type of professional people," says O'Donnell, now retired. "Physicists, engineers, doctors. Every type of person you couldn't find in this valley before 1950."

O'Donnell was then a young Bostonian who possessed the rare skill of knowing how to design and build a very complex little gadget that could arm an atomic bomb, start an automated countdown, set the bomb off, and collect data on how it behaved. His employers were Drs. Harold Edgerton, Kenneth Germeshausen, and Herbert Grier, three scientists who had combined their talents—and initials—to create the firm of EG&G. It was a new company in the new field of energy measurement. Specifically, the energy created when a nuclear weapon exploded.

Following a tour of duty with the U.S. Navy in the South Pacific, and while World War II was still under way, O'Donnell, then 23, returned to Boston and was hired by the Raytheon Manufacturing Company. He was assigned various tasks, but he really didn't understand the purpose of his new job: "I knew what I was doing, but I didn't know who I was doing it for or what the end game was going to be." And he wouldn't, until he received a high-level security clearance. O'Donnell had unknowingly gone to work for the super top-secret Manhattan Project, developing the first atomic bomb.

He was still in the dark when Raytheon transferred him to the Massachusetts Institute of Technology, where he met Edgerton, Germeshausen, and Grier. Later, says O'Donnell, he was conscripted by an electrical engineer named Mike Warchol, who was on loan to EG&G from General Electric. Warchol was an expert in the bomb's timing, arming, and firing devices, and he shared all he knew with O'Donnell. "Mike and I put everything together—the prints, the design, the whole thing," says O'Donnell.

In 1947, when MIT phased out its defense activities, EG&G Corporation was born—in a converted Boston garage. "We had 15 employees, including the security guard," O'Donnell recalls. But business was booming, literally and figuratively. The Truman administration had authorized "Operation Crossroads," a series of tests in the South Pacific on the coral atolls of Bikini and Eniwetok. In all, the Atomic Energy Commission conducted five tests in the Pacific Ocean between 1946 and 1948, and EG&G was charged with designing the equipment to explode the bombs, record their yield, and photograph the results.

In 1952, Grier asked O'Donnell and two colleagues, Bill Ward and Bob Morris, if they would go to Las Vegas, Nevada, and open an office and laboratory there. The three men would form the vanguard of a force of scientists and technicians who would assist the Atomic Energy Commission in its work at the Nevada Proving Grounds, as

O'Donnell in Southern Nevada

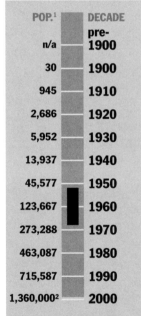

POP.[1]	DECADE
n/a	pre-1900
30	1900
945	1910
2,686	1920
5,952	1930
13,937	1940
45,577	1950
123,667	1960
273,288	1970
463,087	1980
715,587	1990
1,360,000[2]	2000

■ Time spent in Southern Nev.
1 - Population figures are for greater Las Vegas area (*Source: Nevada State Data Center*).
2 - Estimate

Alfred O'Donnell in 1955
(Courtesy Alfred O'Donnell)

the Nevada Test Site was then called.

Grier chose him, O'Donnell says, because he had become the company's expert on arming, timing, and firing devices, and was best able to recruit people who could be trained in the new technology. By the end of 1952, EG&G had recruited nearly 50 people. By the time O'Donnell retired, in 1968, more than 8,000 people were on the company payroll.

The first EG&G office in Las Vegas was another old garage, this one at 1622 S. A Street, now Commerce Street. The firm later built a facility on Sunset Road, which was demolished for airport expansion.

Las Vegas required some attitude adjustments, and the town's loose moral code sometimes interfered with EG&G's recruiting efforts. Single people, especially men, were usually eager to sign on and move to Las Vegas. Families were less so.

"It was a problem at first," says O'Donnell. On the other hand, he says, the sterling reputation enjoyed by Edgerton, Germeshausen, and Grier among scientists, plus the fact that all the research was into largely unexplored areas, was a powerful inducement.

The economic impact of the Nevada Test Site on Las Vegas was substantial, according to Eugene Moehring, UNLV history professor and author of *Resort City in the Sunbelt*. In 1951, the first year of testing, the payroll for construction alone at the test site was more than $4 million. The next year, Truman declared the Las Vegas Valley a "critical defense area." The designation made the valley eligible for more Federal Housing Administration loans, as well as funding for schools, utility improvements, and roads.

"In the long run," wrote Moehring, "the valley's designation ... as a critical defense area helped unify local governments behind a public

works agenda of systematized improvements which only promoted more growth in the metropolis." He cites figures showing that during the 1950s alone, the population of the city grew from 3,875 to 18,422.

O'Donnell notes that EG&G's move to Las Vegas created a sort of snowball effect among other high-tech firms, which also wanted to involve themselves in the new field of atomic energy. Among those were Holmes and Narver, Raytheon, and Bechtel.

While locals arose before dawn to see the awesome blasts, and newspeople from around the world trained their lenses and attention on the mushroom clouds, O'Donnell wasn't that impressed with the spectacle he helped to stage. "Coming from the Pacific and having seen the tremendous megaton bombs, destroying whole fleets of battleships with one bomb, these out here were like little firecrackers," he said.

Like most NTS veterans, O'Donnell is scornful of those who express doubts about the government's commitment to safety. Not that they didn't make occasional mistakes. Once, says O'Donnell, he sent a new technician into the field to check on the bundle of 56 color-coded wires strung between the control room and the bomb tower several miles away. It was only when the technician received radio instructions to test a wire of a certain color that the new hire confessed he was color blind.

Boredom was an occupational hazard, and it certainly was to blame for the Great Doom Town Caper. In 1951, the AEC scheduled a special shot called "Annie," which was aimed at determining how a typical American town would withstand a direct hit by a nuclear bomb. Numerous federal dignitaries were invited to tour the site and witness the demise of "Doom Town."

Homes were constructed of various materials, complete in every detail, with a car in every garage. New furniture was purchased, current magazines were laid on coffee tables, and larders were stocked with fresh foods flown in from San Francisco. The inhabitants were mannequins of the type found in department stores.

O'Donnell and two other men, Bernard Murphy and Ed Tucker, had finished their jobs, were bored, and decided to have a look at the finished town. "Because of the type of clearance we had, we could go anywhere on the test site; we could go up in the tower and sit on the bomb and eat our lunch if we wanted to," says O'Donnell. As they walked through the houses, it struck them that the mannequins were not as lifelike as they could be. It was, after all, evening—time to retire. "So," says O'Donnell, "we took Pa out of his rocking chair and took Ma from the kitchen sink, and we took them upstairs to the bedrooms."

When the Washington bigwigs arrived to see how tax dollars were being used, they discovered houses full of dummies engaged, as O'Donnell politely puts it, "in compromising positions."

"The repercussions from that were terrible," he says, laughing. "Nobody knew who did it, of course, and I'll deny it ever happened." ⌀

The nucleus of EG&G pose in the company's Boston headquarters in 1947. They are (clockwise, left to right) Bill McKinley, George Hansen, Alfred O'Donnell, Bill Bjork, and Don McClellan.
(Courtesy Alfred O'Donnell)

A nonserious credential earned by Alfred O'Donnell when he participated in the 1953 "Grable" test. The shot was controlled entirely by the military, which wanted to see if an atomic bomb could be fired through a 280-millimeter cannon. It could.
(Courtesy Alfred O'Donnell)

ERNEST BECKER

(1920–   )

"Home building is exciting. There's no place a person spends more time in his life than in his home. When you have a nice house and you drive down the street and turn into your driveway, you feel excited. You raise your kids there. You live your life there. That feeling doesn't happen with a car or a boat. I can't imagine doing anything else."

—Ernest A. Becker III
In a 1988 interview

Taking his cue from Howard Hughes, a Southern Californian found the land on the west side of Las Vegas to be a bountiful construction spot for thousands of houses. **BY K.J. EVANS**

Howard Hughes was not famous for providing inside tips to fellow entrepreneurs. But he did it at least once, though it wasn't intentional. In the late 1940s, Hughes' personal secretary told her husband, Jay Sims, that the eccentric billionaire was quietly planning to move Hughes Aircraft from Southern California to the west side of the Las Vegas Valley. Sims, in turn, passed the tip to his business partner, a young Southern California home builder named Ernie Becker, and urged him to buy all the land he could in the area of West Charleston.

"He took the advice," says Barry, the second of Becker's four sons. "So they came up and bought the original 250 acres that is Charleston Heights." In so doing, Ernest A. Becker III initiated and expedited development of the western half of the Las Vegas Valley, which continues to this day.

Hughes had traded 73,000 acres of land he owned in five Northern Nevada counties for 25,000 acres of Bureau of Land Management property near the base of the Spring Mountains. He told the BLM he wanted to develop "guided-missile devices." Becker moved to Las Vegas, but Hughes didn't, mainly because his top scientists, technicians, and executives let him know they had no intention of being shipped out into the wastes of Nevada. But Hughes kept the land.

With or without Hughes, Becker sized up Las Vegas as a winning proposition. The Nevada Test Site was being established, and an entire new work force was moving to town. The Korean War was under way, the Air Force base had been reopened, and GIs were moving into the area. Las Vegas was short of everything, especially houses.

"At the time, Charleston Boulevard was paved as far as Highland Avenue," eldest son Ernest IV recalls. Charleston also was the only one of Las Vegas' main thoroughfares that reached all the way to the Spring Mountains and Red Rock. Becker's first tract was at the corner of Alta Drive and Falcon Way, just west of Decatur Boulevard.

He called his community "Charleston Heights."

In the fall of 1952, Becker announced plans to build what was, up until that time, the largest residential development in the region—1,400 homes. The first problem was water: No city lines reached that far west. "He had to drill his own wells and he had to form his own water company, which he called the Charleston Heights Water Company," says Ernest IV.

A few years later, Becker was fighting the newly created Las Vegas Valley Water District, which claimed that small private wells were drawing down the valley's water supply. The give-and-take continued until August 1965, when Becker sold his wells and distribution system to the district for $438,000.

Ernest August Becker III was the grandson of a successful land speculator. Ernest I dealt in undeveloped land parcels, and the family created the Los Angeles suburb of Eagle Rock. Ernest II was the family's first real builder, constructing homes and other real estate all over Southern California. Ernest III built his first housing tract by the time he was a junior at the University of Southern California, which he attended from 1938 to 1940, distinguishing himself on the Trojan football team.

In 1941, the Beckers became part of one of Southern California's most famous pioneer families when Ernest III married Betty Weddington. Grandfather Weddington had been the first sheriff in the San

Ernest A. Becker III
(Courtesy Becker family)

Fernando Valley, and his family founded the L.A. suburb that became North Hollywood.

Discharged from the U.S. Coast Guard in 1945, Ernie III resumed residential construction. But young Becker found the postwar Southern California bureaucracy to be a pain.

Nowhere was the housing market hotter than in Las Vegas. Becker's homes sold even while they were just artists' sketches on paper. The first homes sold for under $10,000. "He really couldn't keep up with the demand," says Ernest IV, "so he would go into joint ventures or subdivide lots to keep up with it.

"There are about 63 subdivisions under the Charleston Heights name that he developed, but we were at our height in the 1960s, turning out developed lots, about 3,000 of them a year, for Sproul Homes." The combined house output of Becker homes, including the various partnerships, is probably in excess of 10,000, and at one time in the 1960s, Sproul Homes alone was turning out 27 houses a week.

Ernest IV explains that his dad learned from experience that the most profitable and least troublesome way of building new neighborhoods is to develop lots, sell them to other home builders, then erect and run the shopping centers needed by the new residents. The nucleus of the commercial district established by Becker in the early 1960s was the Charleston Heights Shopping Center at Decatur and Alta. It boasted a Safeway Supermarket, Walgreen's Drugs, Grant's Department Store, and numerous smaller shops, including a tavern with slot machines. In 1963, just south of the shopping center, Becker built the one business essential to any respectable middle-class 1960s neighborhood—a bowling alley. It had 36 lanes. And slot machines.

The family sometimes sold the commercial buildings and sometimes leased them. But in all cases, if there were slot machines on the premises,

they were owned by the family. In 1974, says Ernest IV, the family established a slot-route company called Sunset Coin to service its own machines and began to enjoy the fruits of an entirely new enterprise—gaming. As the number of Becker-built shopping centers increased, so did the size of Sunset Coin.

Becker's sons—Ernest, Barry, Randall, and Bruce—would join him at Las Vegas job sites while they were still in high school, spending their summers framing houses, digging ditches, and busting up caliche with picks. "It was part of the indoctrination into the business," says Barry. "We used to work from sunup to sundown, and we did virtually everything. We had a significant amount of experience before we went to work full time. If you can call us executives, we're working executives."

One day at a family meeting, Ernest IV recalls, Bruce announced that he would like to build a hotel-casino onto the bowling alley. "Since the casinos are adding bowling alleys to their casinos, I want to add a casino to my bowling alley," Bruce joked to reporters when the project was announced.

A proud family, the Beckers wanted to name the place in honor of one of their forebears. Presumably, "Ernie's" or "Becker's" lacked the needed pizzazz. They settled on a colorful but distant relative, "Arizona" Charlie Meadows. According to family lore, Meadows had been a sharpshooter in Buffalo Bill's Wild West Show.

It was to be a "neighborhood" hotel-casino. Most of these were a few blocks off the Strip or Fremont Street, and some lined the Boulder Highway as they had since the time of Hoover Dam's construction. Predictably, when plans for the resort were announced in early 1987, a howl of protest arose from nearby residents. Too much traffic, too many drunks, they complained. The hotel would overload the sewer system, some posited. Others predicted that property values would

tumble, though local real-estate agents predicted the exact opposite.

The $18 million resort, Arizona Charlie's, opened in April 1988. In 1994, it underwent a $40 million expansion, and the bowling alley went into the gutter to make way for a larger casino. A failed attempt to expand into the Missouri riverboat gaming market in the early 1990s pushed the otherwise successful Arizona Charlie's into bankruptcy. The venture was backed by some $40 million in bonds, and when Missouri regulators refused Bruce Becker's licensing application, more than half the bonds were purchased at fire-sale prices by corporate raider Carl Icahn, who presently still supervises operations of the company.

An outgoing and personable man, Ernest Becker III was active in the state and local Republican party, and in the National Association of Homebuilders. But his favorite cause probably was college athletics. For most of his life, he has sported the flat-top crew cut he wore on the USC gridiron. He donated 40 acres of land each to USC and UNLV, and served on the UNLV Academic Foundation. He also served on the committees that brought football coach Ron Meyer, as well as basketball coach Jerry Tarkanian, to UNLV.

When schools had to be built in a new Becker neighborhood, the land was donated by the Beckers. When a church needed some land, the congregation asked Ernie. Parks are also part of a complete neighborhood, and Ernie Becker donated the land. In addition, he gave land to youth groups.

A wealthy man for a very long time, Ernest Becker III could have embarked upon any business venture that struck his fancy. But building homes was always his first love. "Home building is exciting," he said in a 1988 interview. "There's no place a person spends more time in his life than in his home. When you have a nice house and you drive down the street and turn into your driveway, you feel excited. You raise your kids there. You live your life there. That feeling doesn't happen with a car or a boat. I can't imagine doing anything else." ⌘

"We have not had a boom yet. It's going to occur around 1992."
—Ernest August Becker III, 1988

Ernest Becker as a young Coast Guardsman during World War II
(Courtesy Becker family)

An enthusiastic UNLV sports booster, Ernie Becker presented Vice President Gerald Ford with a souvenir football in 1973.
(Courtesy Becker family)

GEORGE "BUD" ALBRIGHT (1909–1996)

In January 1957, Albright announced that construction would commence on the $4.5 million convention center. Albright worked out the financing formula himself. The answer was a room tax, collected each time an out-of-towner checked into a local hotel or motel. Kenny Albright remembers that his father hunkered over his adding machine, trying to figure out how much revenue a room tax would produce at various rates. The numbers he generated were enormous.

Not willing to bet his town's future on a roll of the dice, a county commissioner pushed and received backing for an unconventional idea amid all this gaming—a convention center. BY K.J. EVANS

Nobody has to tell you when Comdex or the Consumer Electronics Show is in town. The traffic on and around the Strip is gridlocked. The sidewalks are packed with business suits, and nary a fanny pack is in sight. It's a mess.

Blame it on Bud. He was George "Bud" Albright, the man who virtually built the Las Vegas Convention Center and conceived the self-perpetuating funding mechanism by which to expand and promote it. But if you blame Bud for the commotion and disruption caused by more than 40 million visitors who attended 35,348 conventions at the facility since it opened in 1959, then credit him for the $35 billion they left in Las Vegas.

Albright was born in Pittsburgh on December 6, 1909, to George and Bertha Mae Albright. By the time he was 10, his father had contracted tuberculosis, and the family moved to Albuquerque, New Mexico. His father died when Bud was 17, leaving the breadwinning duties to him and his elder brother Jack. Bud had to leave high school in his early teens. At 18, he married Marjorie Hageman and they had one son, George LaVerne. The couple divorced after three years. George LaVerne, who goes by "Vern," is now a Las Vegas attorney.

In 1931, Bud Albright struck out for Las Vegas, where he joined his brother Jack in the type-writer and office machine business. Their staple client was the Six Companies building Hoover Dam, and business was brisk. The dust from the construction project took a heavy toll on office machines, and they had to be constantly cleaned and repaired. In fact, says Vern, after the Albright brothers had trucked a load of machines from Las Vegas out the unpaved Boulder Highway, they were usually so clogged with dust that they had to be taken apart at the site and thoroughly cleaned.

In Las Vegas, Bud married Ellen Finnerty, and they had two sons: Karl Thomas, a retired 20-year veteran of the Clark County Sheriff's Department who now owns a carpet and floor-covering business, and Kenneth Edward, a business management consultant.

The three sons gathered around a table to discuss their father are reverential. That is, until they start telling Dad stories. "He once told us, 'My boys, there is nothing your Pappy can't do,'" says Karl. And it wasn't an idle boast. Bud

Albright could stitch up a badly injured dog one day and supervise construction of a great public building the next. He could rebuild a carburetor or perform a valve job on a 1951 Chevy, then fly off to Carson City and shepherd a pet bill through the Legislature.

He learned by doing and by reading. In his final years, recalls Vern, his mortality worried him less than his failing eyesight: "He was terrified that he would go blind and wouldn't be able to read."

Or build things. Bud was a hyperactive tinkerer who often would walk into the house after a full day's work and head directly for his shop. The boys remember the toys best. There were the 9-foot kites that they could pull behind a pickup; there was the roller coaster on skate wheels that went from the second-story balcony to the street.

They also remember their father as an incorrigible prankster. Sometimes, he would pluck a sleeping son from bed and lay him on the grass

County Commissioner George "Bud" Albright, early 1950s
(Courtesy Albright Family)

Albright in Southern Nevada

POP.[1]	DECADE
n/a	pre-1900
30	1900
945	1910
2,686	1920
5,952	1930
13,937	1940
45,577	1950
123,667	1960
273,288	1970
463,087	1980
715,587	1990
1,360,000[2]	2000

■ Time spent in Southern Nev.
1 - Population figures are for greater Las Vegas area (*Source: Nevada State Data Center*).
2 - Estimate

in the back yard. He would be watching through a window at sunrise, giggling, when the victim awoke. An avid hunter, he liked to lead large parties and serve as camp cook. Someone would invariably cut into a pancake with a tin can lid buried inside.

In 1933, Jack Albright was commissioned by the Las Vegas Chamber of Commerce to build a model of the as-yet unfinished Hoover Dam. It would be displayed at the Los Angeles County Fair. Bud and younger brother Kenny were enlisted in the project, which took 57 days to complete. The model was not precisely to scale and not accurate in details, but it wowed the fairgoers.

With the completion of Hoover Dam in 1935, Jack and Bud set out to build what Albright later would describe as "a romance in concrete and steel, a symphony in physical material." The second model of the dam took two years to complete, cost $25,000 to build, and cost Jack and Bud the life of 17-year-old Kenny. It was hard for Bud Albright to talk about the tragedy, so none of his sons is certain exactly what happened that day.

It is known that a fire erupted in a bucket of gasoline in the shop. One version of the story has it that someone grabbed the flaming bucket, kicked the door open, and flung the contents all over Kenny, who was just coming through the door. Another has it that Kenny spilled the burning liquid on himself as he tried to get the bucket outside. Consumed by flames, Kenny ran across the lot pursued by Jack and Bud, who tried to get him to the ground and roll out the flames. But he had been fatally burned.

As for the model, it was completed in time for the 1939 World's Fair in San Francisco. The model has sidewalks, flagpoles, and cars. It is rendered at 1 inch per 25 feet, and depicts 1 square mile; it is 18 feet long, 8 feet wide, 8 feet high, and weighs 8,000 pounds. It uses 1,000 gallons of water to demonstrate the workings of the dam, tunnels, tubes, and spillways. The topography of Black Canyon also is rendered in perfect scale. Today, the model is in storage at the Las Vegas Convention Center.

In 1941, Albright joined the electrical firm of Luce and Goodfellow, where—learning on the job—he became a master electrician and wired the first Strip resort, El Rancho Vegas. In 1950, he formed Albright's Courtesy Electric, an appliance and contracting firm.

By that time, he had been appointed to the Clark County Juvenile Advisory Board and had been serving as chairman since 1946. The only juvenile detention facility was on Bonanza Road, a dirt-floored tin shack, with open holes for windows. It was totally unfit for human habitation. Albright launched a crusade to construct a decent juvenile home on Shadow Lane, near today's Clark County Health Department.

Its first inmates were sons Karl and Kenny Albright. They had been playing "war" in an alley and lit some garbage cans on fire to create the proper ambiance. Dad caught them in the act, marched them to the new juvie, and booked 'em.

In 1952, Albright was elected to the first of three terms on the Clark County Commission, and he almost immediately saw the need for a convention center. He wasn't especially concerned about increasing casino profits, since he regarded gambling as a foolish pastime, a sentiment he shared with one of his sons who had seen a slot machine and wanted to know what it was. "Well," explained Albright, "with this machine, you put $500 into it, and it gives you back $200."

Albright's interest in the convention center was based on the belief that relying solely on leisure travelers to support Las Vegas' lifeblood industry made the city more vulnerable to economic downturns and the perennial slow seasons. Moreover, Albright understood that simply increasing the volume of visitors would result in a "multiplier" effect on nongaming businesses.

In 1955 the city and county formed a joint convention-hall subcommittee, comprised of Horseshoe Club executive Joe W. Brown, Last Frontier founder William J. Moore, and Bonanza Airlines President Edmund Converse. They

Bud Albright takes center stage to announce construction of the Las Vegas Convention Center, 1957.
(Courtesy Albright Family)

eventually chose a piece of Brown's land bordering Paradise Road.

In January 1957, Albright announced that construction would commence on the $4.5 million convention center. Albright worked out the financing formula himself. The answer was a room tax, collected each time an out-of-towner checked into a local hotel or motel. Kenny Albright remembers his father hunkered over his adding machine, trying to figure out how much revenue a room tax would produce at various rates. The numbers he generated were enormous.

"He thought he had put the decimal in the wrong place," says Kenny. "He called Mom in and said, 'Do this with me; I must be doing something

George "Bud" Albright and the carriage dog "Sport" in Albuquerque, New Mexico, 1925
(Courtesy Albright Family)

wrong.'" He wasn't.

Still, the attitude of the hotels was that collecting room taxes would be a nuisance. They had plenty of business—most of it weekend and summer leisure travelers, not conventioneers. "And that was the selling point," says Karl Albright. "He [Bud Albright] said, 'We'll bring conventions here, not just in the summer, but also in the winter.'"

Bud was chairman of the Clark County Fair and Recreation Board and, as such, the project was his baby. In his characteristic hands-on approach, he spent as much time at the construction site as many of the workers. He drove contractors crazy, carefully scrutinizing the placement of practically every beam, poking batches of concrete to make sure they were mixed properly, and always offering suggestions about how something could be done better or faster.

The Las Vegas Convention Center was completed in early 1959, and the city's first big convention—The World Congress of Flight—was booked for April. Congress organizers were worried because, as the date drew closer, there still was no one in charge of running the center. So Albright was drafted. He sold his business, resigned his seat on the county commission, and was named executive director at a then-generous salary of $25,000 per year.

Those who had supported the convention center expected that the grand new building would soon be bursting at the seams with conventioneers every single day. That would happen eventually, but in those early days, Albright took a lot of heat for the lulls between conventions. Herman "Hank" Greenspun, publisher of the *Las Vegas Sun*, was particularly vocal in his denunciations of Albright's management.

"He said one time that he thought he and Greenspun had buried the hatchet," recalls Kenny Albright. "Until he opened the paper the next morning and found out where he [Greenspun] had buried it." However, in the late 1960s, Albright was named "Convention Man of the Year" by the local chapter of the National Hotel Convention Sales Managers' Association.

In July 1967, he was fired in a secret meeting held by the five-member Convention and Visitors Authority, chaired by Mayor Oran Gragson. Gragson told reporters that Albright's actions "contributed to the community's lack of confidence in the operation of the convention authority in the past few years." Albright's sons agree that the main reason for the firing was Greenspun's interminable broadsides against their dad, but Karl allows that his father's plainspoken manner may have chafed some of the powers that were. "Dad was not famous for being tactful," Karl says.

Actually, the reason may have been money. In 1967, Albright was being paid $29,500 per year. Gragson made a point of informing reporters that the salary of Albright's replacement, Radford Cox, "will not exceed $17,500."

Less than a year later, Albright was hired by Clark County with the title of director of special projects. The room tax he had created helped him fund parks, swimming pools, and recreational facilities. He was also placed in charge of acquiring land for the ongoing expansion of McCarran International Airport.

In 1973, Ellen Albright died, and the following year, Albright took his third wife, Flora Grant. In 1979, at age 69, he retired but stayed active in the Masonic Lodge and the Kiwanis Club, where he was a 50-year member, as well as in the Clark County Sheriff's Mounted Posse. "We had lunch with him once a week for 35 years, except when one of us was out of town," says Vern.

By the time Bud Albright died in 1996, he was generally acknowledged as "The Father of the Convention Center." ✍

Monsignor Thomas Collins (1906–1983)

> *"Bishop Gorman needed an energetic man to get a Catholic Welfare agency organized, and he found him in Thomas Collins."*
> —Reverend Caesar Caviglia
> Former pastor of St. Peter's Catholic
> Church in Henderson, now retired

With a lilting Irish brogue and a head for business, a not-so-wealthy young man found his calling in a vast wasteland. **BY K.J. EVANS**

S can the pages of old issues of the *Las Vegas Age* and the *Las Vegas Evening Review*, and you may come across the word "floater," as in "the sheriff gave him a floater out of town." It meant that the person was obliged to remove himself forthwith, by whatever means possible, from the town. It was a popular and cost-effective means of dispensing with moonshiners, bootleggers, opium den operators, card cheats, suspected thieves, and—most of all—vagrants or "vags," as the newspapers called them.

In 1930, yet another not-so-wealthy young man was wandering through America, seeking his place in a new country, and stopped to have a look at Houston. He stayed only a short while, presumably to raise some traveling funds, before making his way to San Francisco. His name was Thomas F. Collins, and he was a native of Tralee, County Kerry, Ireland, one of 12 children born to John and Nora Barrett Collins. The family owned a small farm. Young Tom graduated from the public schools of Tralee and received his secondary education in Wexford. In 1932, Collins was called to the priesthood and entered St. Patrick's Seminary in Menlo Park, California.

A year earlier, in 1931, Pope Pius XI had detached Nevada from the administration of the Dioceses of Sacramento and Salt Lake, and had created the Diocese of Reno, encompassing all of Nevada. This had happened by chance when Chicago's Cardinal Mundelein was traveling by train to San Francisco. Awed by the vast spaces outside his window, the cardinal asked where he was. When informed that the train was in Nevada, he asked who served as bishop of this huge area and was amazed to learn that of all 48 states, Ne-

> *"My study of sociology led me into a different kind of world altogether, and that's the world of being concerned and being compassionate and caring about those less fortunate than ourselves."*
> —Thomas Collins
> In a 1977 interview

vada was the only one with no bishop and no diocese of its own.

Thomas K. Gorman was named the first bishop of the new diocese, and when Collins graduated from seminary in May 1936, he became the first priest ordained in the Diocese of Reno. His first assignment was as secretary to Gorman and vice-chancellor of the diocese.

The bishop soon realized that the diminutive priest with the lilting brogue was an extraordinarily competent and hard-working administrator. "Bishop Gorman needed an energetic man to get a Catholic Welfare agency organized, and he found him in Thomas Collins," says retired Reverend Caesar Caviglia, formerly the pastor of St. Peter's Catholic Church in Henderson.

Collins was sent to the Catholic University of America in New York, where he graduated in 1940 with a master's degree cum laude in social sciences. "My study of sociology led me into a different kind of world altogether," he recalled in a 1977 interview, "and that's the world of being concerned and being compassionate and caring about those less fortunate than ourselves."

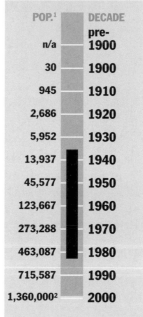

Collins in Southern Nevada

POP.[1]	DECADE
n/a	pre-1900
30	1900
945	1910
2,686	1920
5,952	1930
13,937	1940
45,577	1950
123,667	1960
273,288	1970
463,087	1980
715,587	1990
1,360,000[2]	2000

■ Time spent in Southern Nev.
1 - Population figures are for greater Las Vegas area (*Source: Nevada State Data Center*).
2 - Estimate

Monsignor Thomas F. Collins, about 1954
(Review-Journal files)

He was immediately named diocesan director of Catholic Welfare and, in 1940, established the Catholic Welfare Program, opening offices in Las Vegas and Reno. Soup kitchens were the first step, and the program also offered shelter for homeless families on an emergency basis.

During the war years, Collins served as auxiliary chaplain at the now-closed Stead Air Force Base in Reno, and turned most of his attention to the needs of the thousands of military men who poured into Nevada. He opened three USO Clubs in Las Vegas and later built another USO Club in Boulder City, two in Reno, and one in Hawthorne. Because of this work, Collins was named a national director of the USO and was honored with a special citation from the War Department.

"He moved around in secular circles very easily," Caviglia recalls. "He identified with Nevada—the regular people, the poor people, and the political people."

One of the latter, Governor E.P. Carville, appointed Collins to the State Welfare Board in 1943, and he served until 1949. He was an outspoken advocate for improving the living conditions of children who had become wards of the state and for tightening up Nevada's lax adoption laws. He also was instrumental in establishing the first

Nevada laws providing aid to dependent children. As an adviser to the Nevada State Mental Hospital, Collins pushed for, and got, recreational and occupational therapy programs instituted.

"He was the leader in the state of Nevada in all social welfare areas, and especially in establishing the State Children's Home in Carson City," says the Reverend John McVeigh, pastor emeritus of St. Anne's Catholic Church.

Collins was not hesitant about importing specialized talent when he was faced with a difficult task. While trying to work out the logistics of redesigning the Nevada orphanage, he consulted with Father Edward Flanagan, the priest who founded Boy's Town. Flannigan gave Collins some advice that he often repeated throughout his career. "Always remember you have a product to sell," said Flannigan, "and always remember we have the best product to sell—Christian charity to our fellow man."

Word of Collins' accomplishments eventually reached the top of the church hierarchy and, in 1947, he was elevated by Pope Pius XII to the rank of domestic prelate with the title of Monsignor. For a priest of 41, this was an unheard-of honor, usually reserved for much older priests. Shortly afterward, he was named pastor of the Little Flower Church, then became pastor of St. Thomas Aquinas Cathedral, both in Reno.

In 1953, Collins was named pastor of St. Joan of Arc Church and Dean of Southern Nevada, representing the bishop. His tenure lasted only two years, but in that time he remodeled Las Vegas' first Catholic Church, installing carpet and Italian statuary. He then returned to the Little Flower Church in Reno to establish a Catholic School. In 1962, his mission accomplished, he returned to St. Joan of Arc Parish,

where he spent the rest of his career.

McVeigh, who was required to tend the monsignor's flock while he was away, recalls that sometimes it was hard to get him back to work. "He would travel to Ireland ostensibly for a three-weekend visit," says McVeigh. Shortly before Collins was due back, McVeigh would pick up the phone and hear the monsignor's familiar brogue. "Now, Johnny," he would say, "would you give me just another weekend?"

Caviglia remembers Collins as the man to whom recently arrived and culture-shocked Irish priests would turn for advice. "He was familiar with American culture and very sharp in business dealings," says Caviglia, who notes that Collins acquired many choice sites for new parishes at bargain prices. He also used his business acumen to devise a sort of retirement plan for his fellow priests. In those days, Caviglia explains, there was no church pension plan for priests. Collins would acquaint them with the workings of the booming Las Vegas real-estate market, and they would purchase a piece of land to be sold off later for their retirement money.

At the end of June 1977, after 14 years in Las Vegas and 41 years in the priesthood, Collins retired. He reflected upon his career and upon American society: "It's frightening the type of society we have developed. We cannot change society at all for the better through money or by hiring extra police. … We must start with the children. … If we don't get love, we grow up frustrated, because you can never give to others what you don't have. If you want to change society, you have to go to the source of the troubles … but nobody wants to do that because you step on too many people's toes.

"We have lost the consciousness of sin. Today, anything you do is not wrong. As long as you get away or are not caught, it's all right. We've lost our sense of guilt, and that's the frightening thing."

In 1982, Collins returned to his native Ireland, where he died the following year. ✍

Monsignor Collins receives the Distinguished Nevadan Award from UNLV President Donald Baepler during commencement exercises in 1976.
(Review-Journal files)

JAMES B. McMILLAN

(1917–1999)

"I think the mobsters decided it was better to negotiate than to have cars burning on the Strip. We would have had to do something like that, you see. If not, they would just have sat on the sidewalk and laughed at us."

—James B. McMillan

A dentist whose mother was horsewhipped by the Ku Klux Klan found that the Mississippi of the West had its own share of prejudice—something he fought his entire life. BY A.D. HOPKINS

James B. McMillan was 5 years old when he saw the Ku Klux Klan horsewhip his mother. It was supposed to deter any other blacks who might be tempted to stand up for themselves. But McMillan was not deterred. He got angry and stayed that way long enough to overturn the Jim Crow policies that once earned Las Vegas the name "The Mississippi of the West."

McMillan, a Las Vegas dentist and former president of the local NAACP, was born in 1917 in the actual Mississippi, where the whipping occurred. McMillan explained that his ex-slave grandmother had three children by a white veterinarian. Interracial marriage was prohibited in Mississippi, but because a veterinarian was important in a rural community, his mixed-blood family was never mistreated. That changed suddenly after the veterinarian grew old, blind, and less important.

The vet also had a daughter by marriage to a white woman. This daughter resembled McMillan's light-skinned mother, Rosalie McMillan, and the half-sisters were friendly with one another. One day Rosalie was in the downtown five-and-dime where her half-sister worked. The white woman's boyfriend walked in, mistook Rosalie for his girl, covered her eyes from behind, and yelled, "Guess who?"

"She turned and slapped him," related McMillan in an interview in January 1999. "He got mad, but apologized. Her half-sister got mad and yelled, 'That's my nigger sister!' And my mother raised so much hell that the Klan came."

The Klan butted into a private misunderstanding to "discipline" Rosalie for raising her hand and voice to whites. Masked men went to her home a day or two later and hauled Rosalie downtown. There, they tore off her blouse and lashed her bare back 15 times with a buggy whip. "From the front porch of our house on the hill, I could look down and see this," remembered McMillan in his 1997 autobiography. "But there was nothing I could do and I just cried."

Not long after, Rosalie and her family were driving across a wooden bridge and found a black man dangling in a noose. "My mother put the whip to the buggy, and we went on home," said McMillan. "My recollection is we left Mississippi the next week."

McMillan's autobiography was written with the help of Gary E. Elliott, a history teacher at the Community College of Southern Nevada, and R.T. King, director of the oral history program at the University of Nevada-Reno. They titled the book *Fighting Back*, because it is primarily concerned with McMillan's lifelong struggle against racism.

McMillan grew up in New York City, Philadelphia, Pontiac, and Detroit. His father died in the Spanish flu epidemic when McMillan was an infant. His mother eventually married a man with the knack of making money—in concrete, until the Depression crushed construction, and thereafter in operating an illegal numbers game.

McMillan said ghetto schools didn't teach him much science or literature, but he did learn to deal with bullies: "One guy pushed me around a whole semester. He'd run up when I wasn't looking and jump on me and knock me down. So something said to me, I have to fight him. The day I made up my mind to fight him, I saw him out of the corner of my eye, [and] he started running at me. I flipped him over my back

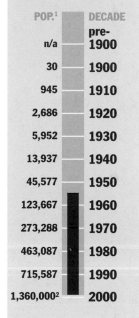

McMillan in Southern Nevada

POP.[1]	DECADE
n/a	pre-1900
30	1900
945	1910
2,686	1920
5,952	1930
13,937	1940
45,577	1950
123,667	1960
273,288	1970
463,087	1980
715,587	1990
1,360,000[2]	2000

■ Time spent in Southern Nev.
1 - Population figures are for greater Las Vegas area (*Source: Nevada State Data Center*).
2 - Estimate

Dr. James B. McMillan
(Courtesy James B. McMillan)

onto the ground and kicked him in the head. He started crying. … And he and I were friends after that, all the way through high school."

McMillan was the only black player on the University of Detroit football team. Teammates accepted him, but in his junior year the school administration kicked him off the team and revoked his athletic scholarship for dating a white girl. He paid for the rest of his education by working in an auto factory.

James McMillan at his profession, 1979. When he first opened a Las Vegas office, he had to stay open at night to get patients.
(Review-Journal files)

He entered dental school in 1941. When World War II broke out, McMillan and many other dental students were deferred from active duty. After graduation in 1944, he practiced dentistry in the U.S. Army and rose to the rank of captain. He once was arrested for refusing to move to the back of an Army bus and getting into a fight with the driver, who tried to throw him off the bus. But his one night in the stockade resulted in victory. The base commander brought the whole camp to attention and announced: "As long as I am in command here, this type of thing will not happen. There will be no difference in races." McMillan served again during the Korean War, after the armed forces were integrated.

He set up private practice in Detroit and became friends with Dr. Charles West, a black medical doctor in the same neighborhood. West married a showgirl and began commuting to the West Coast, where his new wife was working, and once happened to take an alternate route through Las Vegas. "He liked the weather, the nightlife, and the gambling," said McMillan. West soon settled in Las Vegas.

Not long after, McMillan went to his office on a winter morning. "We had those window units, combination of heaters and air conditioners, and they weren't working, and it was just miserable. … I called Dr. West and asked him what the temperature was in Las Vegas, and he said 75 degrees. I said, 'I'll be out this week.'"

On arriving in Las Vegas, McMillan asked the cab driver to take him to Dr. West's office at 524 Wyatt Avenue. The driver was unfamiliar with the address and radioed his dispatcher for directions. "That's over where them niggers live," squawked the radio. The driver apologized and delivered McMillan to West's office.

So when McMillan moved here in 1955, he was not surprised at the cool reception he received. Even after he passed his Nevada dental examination with high grades, it took months for the board of dental examiners to license him. Dr. Quannah McCall, a board member who was an American Indian, cut the red tape. Approval of a license required a unanimous vote, and some board members were dead set against approving a black dentist, McCall later related to McMillan. "I told them that if they didn't pass you, nobody else would pass as long as I was on the board," McCall said, so McMillan got his license.

There was a dental association, which didn't welcome its new member; the dental wives' club disbanded rather than welcome his spouse. "You couldn't live in the best places," McMillan said. "There was disrespect everywhere."

But there were already people working to end it: "David Hoggard, Woodrow Wilson, Lubertha Johnson, and a couple of preachers were here before I got here and were working tremendously hard. Hoggard was on the police force, and he was a truant officer and had good contacts with most politicians. He would try that way to get things done.

"Mrs. Johnson had a grocery store, and she would hire blacks, and built up the economy.

Woodrow Wilson was an outspoken guy, worked out at Basic Magnesium, and would try to get political action going through the union. They did not yet have enough muster to do a picket, and maybe the community wasn't ready, but this movement could not have started without the efforts of those people."

Hoggard and Wilson drew McMillan into the local chapter of the National Association for the Advancement of Colored People. One night, out of the blue, somebody nominated him to be its next president. "I didn't seek the office, but once I had it, I decided there were things I should do," McMillan said.

Members noticed that Highland Dairy and Anderson Dairy both delivered milk to the black community of West Las Vegas, yet wouldn't hire blacks as delivery men. First McMillan wrote the companies asking that they hire blacks. When there was no response, the NAACP decided to target the businesses, one at a time. They picketed Highland Dairy, without results. So blacks quit buying milk from Highland Dairy, and it went out of business. Anderson Dairy began hiring blacks.

Around 1957 Hoggard, McMillan, and a third man started a newspaper called the *Missile*. It was published from the NAACP office, and members donated money to support it. Until that time, explained McMillan, it was difficult for the NAACP to get coverage: "If we decided to boycott the Sands, for instance, we couldn't get that in the paper and particularly not in the *Review-Journal.* Hank Greenspun would print some of our news in the *Sun,* but only what he agreed with. Not everything."

After three years, the founders decided they couldn't continue pouring time and money into the *Missile,* so they sold it to Dr. West. He changed the newspaper's name to the *Voice,* somehow turned a profit, and later sold it to a retired Air Force colonel, the late Ed Brown. Some 40 years later, the newspaper survives as the *Las Vegas Sentinel Voice.*

In 1960, four black college students sat down

at the whites-only Woolworth lunch counter in Greensboro, North Carolina, and refused to leave. This first "sit-in" inspired similar ones. The NAACP sent letters to all its branches asking them to press forward while the mood of the country seemed receptive.

The most glaring offenders in Las Vegas were casinos and restaurants, where black would-be patrons were denied admission. "So," said McMillan, "I sent a letter to the mayor … and gave him 30 days." If the mayor failed to respond with a plan to eliminate discrimination, blacks would march on the casino districts.

Mayor Oran Gragson and City Commissioner Reed Whipple made a counteroffer: If the demonstration was called off, there would be more city jobs for blacks, and Whipple, an officer of First National Bank, would see that blacks started getting loans to build houses and start businesses. But they didn't promise to force resorts to admit blacks, claiming they lacked jurisdiction.

To his dying day, McMillan wondered whether he made the right decision when he rejected the deal. Had he accepted the proposition, West Las Vegas might not have remained as undeveloped and jobless as it did. "But … I felt that by eliminating the prejudice, the development would come anyway," he said.

McMillan was bluffing. He had not actually organized a protest and didn't know whether he could. He had only 10 days to do it. The NAACP held meetings in West Las Vegas churches, trying to get citizens to commit to marching, perhaps facing fire hoses and clubbing and jail.

Meanwhile, McMillan was getting death threats from the Ku Klux Klan. Sergeant Wilbur Jackson and the rest of Las Vegas' handful of black police officers invented endless reasons as to why

their duties required them to drive by McMillan's house several times a night. Entertainer William "Bob" Bailey organized volunteers to defend McMillan and his family.

Then McMillan got a phone call from Oscar Crozier, who owned a small gambling club in West Las Vegas. Crozier had been chosen to deliver a message from some of the hidden, mob-connected owners of Strip hotels: "Cut it out or we'll drop you in Lake Mead."

McMillan sent a message back through Crozier, saying, as he recalled it, "All I'm trying to do is make this a cosmopolitan city, and that will make more money for them. You tell them that and let me know what they say."

"I was almost ready to throw in the towel," McMillan admitted in his autobiography. "If he had come back to me and said, 'Man, they said no. You better cut this crap out,' I would have peeked at my hole card."

Instead, Crozier came back and said, "Mac, it's OK. They're going to make their people let blacks stay in the hotels. … Black people can go

into restaurants and stay at hotels and gamble and eat and everything else."

Recalling the incident, James McMillan said: "I think the mobsters decided it was better to negotiate than to have cars burning on the Strip. We would have had to do something like that, you see. If not, they would just have sat on the sidewalk and laughed at us."

The decision was announced at the Moulin Rouge and has become known as "The Moulin Rouge Agreement." McMillan resigned his position as head of the NAACP in 1961. He would serve two more two-year terms, but his reputation will forever stand on the 1960 confrontation when the mob blinked before he did.

He ran for the U.S. Senate against Howard Cannon and Harry Claiborne, and ran for the County Commission against Bob Baskin and Harley Harmon. McMillan lost each time. He did defeat an incumbent school board member, John Rhodes, and served one term before he was defeated in 1996 by a professional educator, Shirley Barber.

McMillan died of cancer on March 20, 1999. Only two months before that, he was still outspoken about his disappointment in public education, and advising that the public not take it lying down. "I don't think teachers are doing a good job," he said. "It seemed impossible that we are taking kids all the way through sixth grade and they are not yet able to read, write, or spell. Yet they are promoting a lot of kids instead of holding them back."

Schools remain poor because parents accept it, McMillan added. "We need people to raise hell," he said. "And if they can't get the school district to function through their school board representatives, they need to picket, march, and do whatever they can until it changes." ⌀

A March 1960 meeting at the Moulin Rouge announced an agreement to end segregation on the Las Vegas Strip. James McMillan is at the head of the table, with Las Vegas Sun *publisher Hank Greenspun on McMillan's right. On McMillan's left are Mayor Oran Gragson, Dr. Charles West, and Las Vegas Police Chief Ray Schaeffer.*
(Review-Journal files)

ORAN K. GRAGSON (1911–)

"One of the newspapers said I had about as much of a chance of being the first man to land on the moon as I did to be elected mayor of Las Vegas. I didn't get hardly any votes from the Westside. About 19 votes, I think. Also, I was from the South, and I think a lot of voters over there assumed I was a bigot. The second time I ran [1963], I got 89 percent of the vote there."

—Oran K. Gragson

A businessman, who got into politics to stop a few crooked police officers from robbing him blind, became one of the city's more well-regarded leaders. BY K.J. EVANS

I f those crooked cops hadn't insisted on repeatedly letting themselves into his appliance store at night and carrying away his television sets, Oran Gragson probably wouldn't have run for mayor in 1959. But those cops. Someone had to do something. So Gragson ran, won the election, and held the post for 16 years, becoming one of the most popular mayors the city has ever known.

Gragson was born in 1911, and the Great Depression found him riding the rails, seeking work. In the fall of 1932, he was headed for the site of what would be Hoover Dam. "I caught a freight train out of Oklahoma," he recalls. "Six days later, I arrived in Las Vegas, Nevada, at 11 o'clock at night." His personal fortune totaled $2.70, more than enough for the 25-cent blue-plate special at the Busy Bee Cafe—a full-pound hamburger steak, potatoes and gravy, and coffee.

Gragson landed a job at the dam, worked for two weeks, but failed the first company physical—he had a hernia—and was dismissed. It wasn't such a blow. He was earning 40 cents per hour on the dam job. Three days later, he went to work at $1 an hour driving a truck for J.C. Compton, a road construction outfit.

He continued to correspond with Bonnie Henley, his childhood sweetheart back in Mansfield, Arkansas. In December 1934, they married. Bonnie was not impressed with the little railroad town. "Fact is, she told me that I could

stay here if I wanted to, but she was going back," Gragson says, laughing.

Gragson called upon the diplomatic skills that would serve him so well in later years. "I walked her out on the street, showed her the bank, the other buildings," he said. "Then I told her, 'One of these days I'm going to be mayor of this town.'" He was only kidding, he now admits, but Bonnie stayed.

For a short time, they left for the heartland to run a dairy. But, he said, "I got tired of the day and night work, 16 to 18 hours a day, so we bundled everything up and came back to Las Vegas." The couple then briefly went to work for Pete Peccole, who operated a bar and cafe at Railroad Pass.

Back then everyone was an entrepreneur. Gragson's first enterprise was the Little Secondhand Store, opened December 18, 1937. It was in the 100 block of South First Street, and Gragson was a partner. He says he kept the place stocked by scouting the town for cast-offs.

In 1944, Gragson was drafted. For the same reasons that precluded employment at Hoover Dam, he was excused from military service. However, in his brief absence, his partners closed the secondhand store. So he went to work for a while at Basic Magnesium, then went into partnership in a furniture store with George Skylstead at 1100 E. Charleston Avenue. Gragson later sold his interest to Skylstead and opened his own store at 808 N. Main Street, a piece of land he still owns.

He began to sell television sets before there was actually a television station in town. But one was being planned, and Gragson owned an 18 percent interest in it. It would become KLAS-TV, Channel 8.

"Later I sold my interest to Hank Greenspun, and I made a mistake by doing that," says Gragson. "But I needed the money to expand my

Mayor Oran K. Gragson in his last term
(Review-Journal files)

Gragson in Southern Nevada

POP.[1]	DECADE
n/a	pre-1900
30	1900
945	1910
2,686	1920
5,952	1930
13,937	1940
45,577	1950
123,667	1960
273,288	1970
463,087	1980
715,587	1990
1,360,000[2]	2000

■ Time spent in Southern Nev.
1 - Population figures are for greater Las Vegas area (*Source: Nevada State Data Center*).
2 - Estimate

furniture business." Specifically, he wanted to buy more television sets. "I got into the TV business because I knew it was coming. My TVs were Admirals, and they had a radio, a TV, and a record player. My theory was that people would buy them, use the radio and record player now, and watch the TV when it came on the air."

In those early days, local police officers often carried keys to businesses, supposedly to allow the cops access in case of a burglary or fire. After a few strange incidents, Gragson began to get the picture. "I locked the door myself; I knew it was locked," he recalls. "At about 11 that night, I'd get a call from the police telling me that they'd found my door open and a television stolen." This happened three or four times, Bonnie adds. "If they hadn't have done that, I would never have run for mayor," Gragson declares.

Not long after Gragson's election as mayor in 1959, an investigation uncovered a full-blown burglary ring within the Las Vegas Police Depart-

ment, which ultimately led to the indictment by a Clark County grand jury of the police chief and the city manager. The charges later were dropped, but both men resigned.

Having satisfactorily resolved the mystery of the shanghaied Admirals, Gragson immersed himself in planning the Fremont West Expressway, also called the Oran Gragson Expressway and now part of U.S. Highway 95. One proposed interchange was at Rainbow Boulevard. Twenty acres of land at the interchange was owned, coincidentally, by a group of speculators, the L&L Land Development Company, which had purchased the land in 1961 for some $50,000. The group included several city executives.

The acquisition, by the standards of the day, was not seen as improper. Two of the city-employed principals spoke freely of their investment with reporters. But to Gragson, the deal reeked. "Before anyone else knew anything about it," he recalls, "they were buying up choice pieces of property at the intersections. I didn't think that was proper." The mayor voted to fire the two, but was overruled. Gragson went on to devise and implement a code of ethics for all city employees.

In the election of 1959, Oran Gragson was not the favorite. He lacked political or governmental experience. "One of the newspapers said I had about as much of a chance of being the first man to land on the moon as I did to be elected mayor of Las Vegas," he says. "I didn't get hardly any votes from the West side. About 19 votes, I think. Also, I was from the South, and I think a lot of voters over there assumed I was a bigot. The second time I ran [1963], I got 89 percent of the vote there."

The reason for the surge in popularity was Gragson's introduction of equal representation. He discovered there was a city fund earmarked for depressed areas, and West Las Vegas, with its mostly unpaved, mostly unlit streets, certainly fit the definition. "And the majority of that money went for improvements on the West side," he says.

Three days before the 30th anniversary of his furniture store in 1967, Gragson closed it to de-

vote his full attention to his mayoral duties. "I could not have done both as well as I did one," he says simply.

And there was a big project on the horizon. The city had long outgrown its old City Hall. "I proposed to build us a City Hall a couple of years before we did," says Gragson. "The commission didn't approve it. Later we did build it. So what would have cost us $5 million then, wound up costing us $8 million when we did it." Even so, he regards it as his single greatest accomplishment.

He proposed Cashman Field Center while mayor. And it was on Gragson's watch that the city embarked on an ambitious park-building program, acquiring Lorenzi Park and Tule Springs, along with its artesian water well.

On July 4, 1962, Lieutenant Governor Rex Bell, campaigning as a Republican candidate for governor, suddenly collapsed and died of heart failure. "When he died, a group of us [Republicans] came together, knowing full well that it was almost impossible to beat Grant Sawyer," says Gragson. "But we did want the Republican Party represented." Gragson ran and won the primary but, as expected, lost to Sawyer in the general election.

Gragson was elected to his third mayoral term with no opposition, and it was during this term that the new City Hall was completed. He was challenged in the 1971 election by Bill Briare. Like nearly every campaign in which Gragson has been involved, it was a very civil contest.

"He was running for a fourth term," said Briare, "and I thought a fourth term back then should never occur." Briare lost, but he was elected mayor in 1975—with Gragson's endorsement—and served for 12 years.

"I never thought I had all the answers," Gragson says. "So I weighed every decision pretty thoroughly before I made it. And I hope I didn't make too damn many bad ones." ⌀

Oran Gragson in 1985, beside the portion of U.S. Highway 95 that bears his name
(Review-Journal files)

Oran Gragson with Reverend Martin Luther King Jr., April 1964
(Review-Journal files)

public lands in Nevada away from the federal government.

Sawyer was a civil rights advocate at a time when he had nothing to gain from it, note historians. The minority vote had no viable options except supporting him, but there were plenty of white Southern Democrats he risked alienating.

"He just believed in it," said local attorney Bob Faiss, a former Las Vegas editor who became Grant Sawyer's executive assistant. Sawyer, added Faiss, was the first governor to demand that minorities be considered for state jobs: "Up until then, you would go into any state office and see nothing but white faces."

Sawyer drove through a law requiring color-blind hiring in state offices, but couldn't get the state civil rights law he wanted. He did get a weak civil rights commission, which was able to bring about some changes simply by publicizing injustices. In 1963, when frustrated blacks threatened to march on the Strip against Jim Crow hiring practices, Sawyer and others worked out a compromise by which casinos opened up nonmenial jobs.

From such efforts, Sawyer acquired moral authority. In 1965, riots broke out in Watts, and Las Vegas police notified Sawyer of a report that black militants were heading for Las Vegas to start another. "It was almost as if a riot would be forced on the city by the mobilization to prevent one," recalled Faiss in the eulogy at Sawyer's funeral. "Grant Sawyer felt he had to do something, so he drove into the black neighborhoods … to talk with residents throughout the night. The next morning, he publicly an-

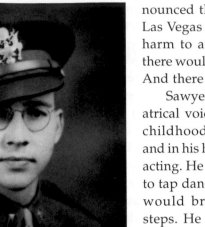

nounced that no citizen of Las Vegas was threatening harm to anyone else, and there would be no violence. And there wasn't."

Sawyer had a deep, theatrical voice, developed in childhood voice training and in his hobby of amateur acting. He also had learned to tap dance as a child and would break into dance steps. He usually insisted on driving the governor's official car himself. "He was a terrible driver; he got tickets," Faiss recalled.

Sawyer had the courage to take on even the dangerous J. Edgar Hoover, director of the FBI. Hoover was a hero to most Americans, but savvy politicians knew he assembled ruinous dossiers about public figures, much of the information of dubious authenticity, and would leak those dossiers to the media if angered.

In 1963, Carl Cohen, a 10 percent owner of the Sands, found microphones in his office. Other wiretaps began to turn up. Sawyer wrote Bobby Kennedy, who was ostensibly Hoover's boss, but received no satisfactory answers. So Sawyer publicly criticized Hoover for the wiretaps, which he believed were illegally planted without court orders.

Hoover retaliated, inserting himself into Sawyer's 1966 campaign for a third term. The FBI director wrote a letter, which was published on the front page of the *Las Vegas Sun*, urging Nevadans not to vote for Sawyer. It implied a Sawyer link to organized crime.

Elliott said, "I think his utter disdain for J. Edgar Hoover, his dislike of Bobby Kennedy, may have created a false impression that he stood for the status quo. I don't think he did. Remember, he had taken big heat over the Black Book. He

simply felt Hoover, in his zeal to put people in jail, ran all over people's civil rights. … He found the government violating people's rights more frightening than any gangster." Even so, Sawyer's position enabled his opponent, Lieutenant Governor Paul Laxalt, to portray himself as somebody who could outdo Sawyer in legitimizing the casino industry.

Other factors also worked against his re-election. Sawyer violated tradition by seeking a third term. "He didn't want to run, but there was nobody else to do it," explained Bette Sawyer in a 1998 TV interview. Polls indicated that Sawyer was the only Democrat who might beat the popular Laxalt, who was lieutenant governor during Sawyer's second term, so party leaders talked him into running. But Sawyer was wounded in the primary by one of his own appointees. Attorney General Charles Springer ran against him and made dubious, but damaging, accusations about Sawyer's ethics. Laxalt defeated Sawyer 71,807 to 65,870.

Sawyer was less than 50 years old when he finished serving in the last elective office he would ever hold. He formed a partnership with Las Vegas lawyer Sam Lionel, and Justice Jon Collins later resigned from the Nevada Supreme Court to join the firm that became Lionel, Sawyer, and Collins.

The new governor changed gaming laws to permit corporate ownership of casinos—something Sawyer had always opposed because he thought it would be impossible to do background checks on individual stockholders. The change created enormous amounts of legal work, as corporations acquired casinos or casinos became corporations. And Lionel, Sawyer, and Collins did a lot of the work. Elliott remembered that in later years, Sawyer commented, "Irony of ironies, Paul Laxalt made me rich."

Grant Sawyer suffered a stroke in 1993, and the complications of that stroke killed him in three years. And on February 24, 1996, it seemed as if all Nevada came to Las Vegas' Palm Mortuary to bury him, and to praise his accomplishments. ⌀

BOB BAILEY (1927–)

A singer who worked with Count Basie and at the Moulin Rouge would not be silenced in his fight against segregation. **BY A.D. HOPKINS**

"It is a proud thing to look at television and see somebody that looks like you. It gave a certain pride to the African-American community to see a black man interview celebrities, to be taken seriously."

—Bob Bailey

Bob Bailey had been a star singer with the Count Basie Orchestra, but when he got a job in broadcasting, he had to use the service entrance to reach the TV studios in the Fremont Hotel.

"Flora Dungan was the accountant for Channel 13," remembered Bailey. "She was so outraged when she learned they wouldn't let me in the front door that she invited me for lunch. They kept us waiting and waiting, and finally they called her away from the table. Of course, that was to tell her they wouldn't serve her as long as she was with me."

Bailey met with Eddie Levinson, operator of the Fremont, asking for access to his work and maybe to a lunch counter once in a while. Levinson said he'd think about it. But, recalled Bailey, "I got impatient and went on the air and said if I was late getting onto the show some day, it would be because I had to come in the back way."

Levinson called Bailey's boss and raised hell, but eventually he relented, and for a while Bailey was the only black who could dine at the Fremont. Nobody seemed to resent the exclusivity of his arrangement, said Bailey: "All the hired help was very proud that somebody had broken the color line. ... There's a saying, 'If you let one in, they'll all come.' Well, there's truth in that. Somebody has to start it."

William H. "Bob" Bailey has spent the rest of his life starting it. He was born on February 14, 1927, in Detroit. When his father lost his job during the Depression, the family moved to Cleveland.

The Bailey family has a strong musical tradi-

tion; vocal star Pearl Bailey was Bob's second cousin. "I had a quartet called the Four Notes, and we won every amateur show in Cleveland," recalled Bailey. "We sang a little scat and a little do-wop. We fashioned ourselves pretty much after the Ink Spots."

Bailey's ambition was to be a lawyer. But it was music, combined with his good grades, that won him a voice scholarship to Morehouse College in Atlanta, and paid his bills. He was performing in a local nightclub when two white guys asked if he would be interested in singing with

Count Basie.

"I thought they were queer or something," Bailey said, laughing. It seemed impossible such an offer could be legitimate, but it was.

On Christmas break Bailey auditioned with Basie himself and became one of the band's two featured singers. "We played two kinds of theaters," he said. "One was called the Chitlin' Circuit, in the black communities of big cities, but we also played a lot of RKO theaters, which were patronized by the general public. I got a lot of exposure there because I sang stuff like 'Danny Boy,' the kind of things Sinatra and Perry Como did." Bailey had three hit records: "Danny Boy," "The Worst Blues I Ever Had," and "Blue and Sentimental."

The job vanished in 1950 when Basie broke up his big band. By then Bailey had become enchanted with television, and he attended the School of Radio and Television in New York City. But nobody was hiring black talent. After it became clear that he wasn't going to get hired for on-air work, he tried for technical jobs, also without luck. He couldn't even get hired as a gofer.

Then somebody thought up the Moulin Rouge. In a Las Vegas that was still highly segregated, the Moulin Rouge casino and hotel would be open to all comers. Clarence Robinson created a show with black entertainers, and in 1955 he brought Bailey to Las Vegas as co-producer and master of ceremonies.

The Moulin Rouge show was a hit, drawing a hip, interracial crowd, particularly after midnight. And that's one reason the Moulin Rouge closed in six months, Bailey believes. "Entertain-

Bailey in Southern Nevada

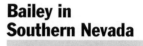

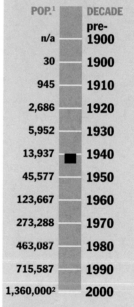

POP.[1]	DECADE
n/a	pre-1900
30	1900
945	1910
2,686	1920
5,952	1930
13,937	1940
45,577	1950
123,667	1960
273,288	1970
463,087	1980
715,587	1990
1,360,000[2]	2000

■ Time spent in Southern Nev.
1 - Population figures are for greater Las Vegas area (*Source: Nevada State Data Center*).
2 - Estimate

Bob Bailey, the dapper ex-singer, became Nevada's first black television personality and used his prominence to encourage social change for the better.
(Courtesy Bob Bailey)

Bailey came to Las Vegas as co-producer and master of ceremonies in the Moulin Rouge's **Tropicana Revue.** *Bailey and cast members are reading a performance contract.*
(Courtesy Bob Bailey)

Bailey had a role in the movie **Let's Do It Again.** *From left are Bill Cosby, Bailey, George Foreman, and Sidney Poitier.*
(Courtesy Bob Bailey)

ers congregate according to talent, not color," he said. "So they [the showgirls] all wanted to see our show, and would come over and watch. And as the showgirls go, so go the players." Strip hotels retaliated by putting up notices in dressing rooms that cast members who went to the Moulin Rouge would be fired.

The short gig with the Moulin Rouge, however, brought Bailey a long-sought break—a role in TV. He had a 13-week contract to host a show sponsored by the Moulin Rouge: "I was in week seven when it [the Moulin Rouge] closed. The show had attracted its own audience by then. Hank Greenspun owned KLAS television in those days, and he said he liked that show and wanted it continued. That meant his ad people had to find sponsors, and in a short time they did.

The original program was a variety show, featuring interviews with entertainers who happened to be appearing in town. Later Bailey did a Sunday show recapping and commenting on the weeks' news.

"I had been to school for this, yet could not get any kind of job in TV, anywhere in the country, then it falls into my hands in Las Vegas, the Mississippi of the West. And I'm not only in the door, but I'm doing my own show." Bailey clung to his foothold, and spent most of the next 16 years as a newsman and host at various Las Vegas TV stations.

The importance of breaking into television, said Bailey, was not that he did it, but that some black did it. "It is a proud thing to look at television and see somebody that looks like you," he said. "It gave a certain pride to the African-American community to see a black man interview celebrities, to be taken seriously."

Bailey was a Republican, and is again, but he changed parties to work for gubernatorial candidate Grant Sawyer in 1958. "He indicated that if he were elected governor, certain changes would be made," Bailey said. "He struck me as a man you could believe."

The Legislature of 1961 established a commission to find out whether discrimination existed. It was the best tool for social change that Sawyer could get, and he appointed Bailey its chairman.

"We did not have any money, but they did give us the power of subpoena, and that was enough to get to the information we needed," said Bailey. "I probably signed more subpoenas than the Kefauver Commission. We showed what was going on and used that as the basis of getting the Equal Rights Law that we have today. ... We were able to open a public dialogue about why there were no black bellmen, no desk clerks, no waiters. ... And their position was nobody is qualified, and it made them look ridiculous. We could say, 'Blacks have been waiting on white people and carrying their baggage a hundred years, and we're not qualified?'"

Progress thereafter didn't come easy, but it came. In 1971 Bailey was chosen to direct a Manpower Services program, which trained minorities for jobs formerly reserved for whites—especially casino dealing. He developed a nightclub—the famous Sugar Hill—and the Pan-Afro Auditorium. Later he established the Nevada Economic Development Corporation, which for 19 years helped minority businesses get funds for startups and expansion.

Bailey's success led to his appoinment by President George Bush as a deputy director of the Minority Business Development Agency, overseeing a $66 million national budget. Today, Bailey is back in Las Vegas running New Ventures Inc., which certifies small businesses to participate in a new Small Business Administration program.

Bailey was invited to stay in Washington, he said. But by that time, Nevada no longer seemed like the Mississippi of the West. It just seemed like home. ✍

CHARLES KELLAR (1909–)

"I started suing police for violating people's civil rights. At that time they had the idea that you could not sue the state, that the police were part of the state and you therefore couldn't sue them. But after my pressing for a couple of lawsuits, they learned you could. These were over excessive use of force. They would beat the hell out of you and say it was essential to subdue you."

—Charles Kellar

A tenacious lawyer with a knack for investments financed his own courthouse crusade for civil rights. BY A.D. HOPKINS

Charles Kellar was already a lawyer when he moved to Nevada, yet it took him five years and a Nevada Supreme Court decision to get admitted to practice. Once he did, the first move he made was to file a lawsuit that ultimately desegregated Clark County schools. One by one, he targeted practices and institutions that denied full citizenship to Southern Nevada's blacks.

He will be 90 this year and wonders aloud who is going to finish the fight. Kellar mentions young black lawyers reared in Las Vegas who got good educations partly because of battles fought in the 1960s by activists like him. "Did you ever hear of those young people taking on anything for blacks?" he asks rhetorically.

Kellar was born on June 11, 1909, in Barbados. "My mother, when she became 12 years of age, was hired out to the home of a plantation owner, and during the course of her engagement with the family, she was seduced and produced me six days after she became 16 years of age," said Kellar.

His father's refusal to acknowledge him was not a product of racial prejudice, but of class. "My father was said to be the richest black man in Barbados," said Kellar. Whether black or white, he explained, "It was the practice of rich folks to take advantage of pretty young girls."

After the birth of a second child a year later, Kellar said, his grandmother hauled her daughter off to Bridgetown, the largest city in Barbados, where she met a man who brought the family to Brooklyn, New York, when Charles was 11. "The man who became my stepfather was a very industrious person who was an itinerant caretaker for the houses of wealthy persons," Kellar said.

Within three or four years, the family had become middle class.

Kellar attended City College of New York and worked as a probation officer, but seven years later he decided to become a lawyer. "I saw such discrimination in the courts," he explained. "I saw that blacks could not find persons to represent them, so I decided to do it."

He eventually headed a law firm with five other attorneys working for him. "I started suing police for violating people's civil rights," he said. "These were over excessive use of force. They would beat the hell out of you and say it was essential to subdue you."

Kellar made money elsewhere to subsidize civil rights cases. "In those days," he said, "we had the problem that whites moved out of areas where blacks were invading, so they left all those beautiful old houses unoccupied and you could buy them very cheaply. I, at one time, had 50 of those with my own staff to sublet and take care of them. I had an income of more than $1 million a year."

At that time, the head of the NAACP legal division was Thurgood Marshall, who encouraged black lawyers to relocate in states where there weren't any. So, said Kellar, "I sold my houses and went to Nevada."

In those days, one had to live in Nevada a year before taking the bar examination, and Kellar spent the time studying for his real-estate license.

Kellar in Southern Nevada

POP.[1]	DECADE
n/a	pre-1900
30	1900
945	1910
2,686	1920
5,952	1930
13,937	1940
45,577	1950
123,667	1960
273,288	1970
463,087	1980
715,587	1990
1,360,000[2]	2000

■ Time spent in Southern Nev.
1 - Population figures are for greater Las Vegas area (*Source: Nevada State Data Center*).
2 - Estimate

Kellar relaxes as much as is possible in front of his picture window, which somebody filled with bullet holes, 1967. Despite the reward Kellar posted, the perpetrators were never caught.

(Review-Journal files)

Donald M. Clark and Charles Kellar before a meeting with Nevada Governor Grant Sawyer concerning jobs in the gaming industry, 1961.
(Review-Journal files)

Charles Kellar in 1970, when he led the Las Vegas chapter of the NAACP
(Review-Journal files)

When he went to Reno to take the bar exam, he said, the hotel where he had made reservations took one look at him and refused admission. He had no time to find another room and slept two nights in the airport.

"When the results were published, they didn't publish any results for me," Kellar said. He was told that his score was so high that it was assumed he had somehow cheated.

His response was to go on the radio, saying Nevada refused to admit blacks to the bar.

The accusation sent bar members scurrying to Howard University, where it was made known that blacks could take the Nevada bar exam. Kellar believes two good students were handpicked because they were almost certain to pass: "One of them was Earl White, who later became a judge. I don't remember if they both passed, but Earl did for sure." Kellar's admission was still delayed, so he sued, and the Nevada Supreme Court finally ordered him admitted in 1965.

"The first case I filed was a lawsuit to provide equal opportunity in the schools," said Kellar. Clark County schools had no written segregation policy, but they did have ironclad school zoning. Combined with widespread discriminatory housing practices, zoning confined nearly all black elementary students to schools in West Las Vegas. "I wanted it so you could live anywhere and go to any school," he said.

Kellar won a partial victory. The Clark County School District converted West Las Vegas schools into sixth-grade centers, which would be fully integrated. White sixth-graders would be bused to the centers, and black sixth-graders would walk. In the other 11 grades, black students would be bused out of West Las Vegas.

Kellar sued over employment of blacks, housing, and public accommodations. He overturned death penalties. He pursued many cases to the Nevada Supreme Court and claims he never lost one.

His courtroom demeanor would get Kellar in trouble more than once. On one occasion, Judge Tom Foley fined him for punching another lawyer in Clark County District Court. "He was taking advantage of me," said Kellar. "He told me, 'Oh, you sit down,' and I said, 'We'll see you sit down,' and hit him with my fist."

Kellar served as president of the Brooklyn and Las Vegas chapters of the National Association for the Advancement of Colored People, and served for many years as the Las Vegas group's legal counsel and spokesman. In April 1967 he announced that the NAACP executive board would consider "a march in front of Strip hotels to protest unequal employment of Negroes."

By June, somebody was shooting rifle bullets through his windows. He offered a $5,000 reward for information leading to arrest and conviction, but nobody collected. In July, an explosive blew an 8-inch hole in the rear door of his office. Police made no arrests. "I don't think they ever investigated," he said recently. "It was said on the street that the police were doing it."

It certainly didn't tone him down. Later that month at a public gathering, Kellar urged blacks to apply for their share of some 1,900 new jobs at the recently opened Frontier Hotel and the soon-to-open Landmark resort.

"White folks are coming to realize that they have to talk with us or fight with us," he said. "There are 25 million Negroes, and that's a lot of folks to have to kill."

But Kellar eventually took that fight to the courts, not the streets. It was one of the few he did not carry through to settlement, taking a back seat when the Justice Department stepped into the case. The suit was settled when Las Vegas resorts and various unions signed consent decrees opening jobs to blacks and other minorities.

Nobody ever bothered his family. "As a matter of fact, my wife was very popular," Kellar said. "She was a high-class secretary and insurance broker." The late Cornelia Street Kellar was the mother of Michael Charles Kellar, who now practices law in Marina Valley, California. Kellar has another son, Charles Jr., from a previous marriage. He lives in Las Vegas and is retired from a career in the culinary arts.

In 1970, Kellar stepped down from office with the Las Vegas NAACP to take a regional job with the same organization. After his wife's death, he got into a dispute with another NAACP official, Bettye Clark Black.

So he asked her to marry him. "They all told me not to marry him—you'll never get him to shut up," Bettye said laughing. "I never did get him to, and I don't guess I want to." ⌀

RALPH DENTON (1925–)

A lawyer who fought for civil rights when it was not popular to do so was his own man, regardless of whom his influential friends might be. **BY K.J. EVANS**

"The lawyers and judges used to come up from Las Vegas about once a month. And they were dressed in fine suits, and everybody I knew was dressed in bib overalls or Levis. And it struck me that being a lawyer was a hell of a lot better than shining shoes."

— Ralph Denton

If you have never heard Nevada called "the Mississippi of the West," it is in large part because of people like Ralph Denton. They fought racism at a time when it was totally acceptable and helped elect reform Governor Grant Sawyer, who bashed Jim Crow in the beak. Denton is a lawyer, a liberal, and a politician—the latter, sporadically. He also is an activist, whether as an attorney, a political operative, or an office holder.

Ralph Lloyd Denton was born in Caliente on September 8, 1925, the youngest of four children of Floyd and Hazel Denton. Floyd Denton was undersheriff of Lincoln County, and Hazel, after 35 years as a teacher and school board member, was elected to the Legislature in 1953 and 1955, where she backed the failed attempt to pass a state civil rights act. Tolerance was taught in the Denton household.

As a boy, Ralph Denton shined shoes at the barber shop in Caliente. "The lawyers and judges used to come up from Las Vegas about once a month," he said. "And they were dressed in fine suits, and everybody I knew was dressed in bib overalls or Levis. And it struck me that being a lawyer was a hell of a lot better than shining shoes."

In the 1930s, with Floyd out of work, the family took in boarders. One day, Bill Roberson, a U.S. Soil and Conservation Service engineer, came to the door and asked if he could take his meals at

Hazel Denton's table. He arrived that evening for dinner and, when he left, a couple of boarders took Hazel Denton aside. "They told her they didn't want to have dinner with a nigger," says Denton. Hazel thought Mr. Roberson seemed like a nice man and refused to turn him away. The bigoted boarders grumbled, but didn't move out.

In later years, Roberson was a guest at Denton's Las Vegas home and took Denton's children, Mark and Sally, to the nearby White Cross Drug Store for ice cream. The lunch counter refused service to Roberson. He stood on the sidewalk eating an ice cream cone while the kids sat inside, perplexed.

Denton attended the University of Utah before enlisting in the U.S. Army in 1943. He earned a second lieutenant's commission in the field artillery, but saw no combat.

It was in the winter of 1946-47 that Denton first met Grant Sawyer. Both were among the 50 or so "McCarran Boys" attending law school on patronage jobs provided by powerful U.S. Senator Patrick McCarran.

Denton graduated from law school in 1951. Driving back to Reno, he stopped overnight in Elko, where Sawyer had been elected district attorney. "We made a few sacrifices on the altar of friendship, and laughed and joked and had a good time, at which time he offered me the job of deputy district attorney if I passed the bar," says Denton, who served from 1951 to 1953.

Denton moved to Las Vegas in 1955 and started a private practice. In 1958, Sawyer ran for governor, and Denton, whom Sawyer called "my closest friend," became his Southern Nevada campaign chairman.

"Ralph and I had both been quite active in

Ralph Lloyd Denton, October 1978
(Review-Journal files)

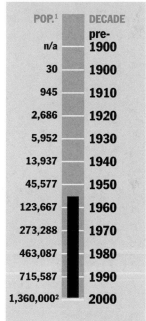

Denton in Southern Nevada

POP.[1]	DECADE
n/a	pre-1900
30	1900
945	1910
2,686	1920
5,952	1930
13,937	1940
45,577	1950
123,667	1960
273,288	1970
463,087	1980
715,587	1990
1,360,000[2]	2000

■ Time spent in Southern Nev.
1 - Population figures are for greater Las Vegas area (*Source: Nevada State Data Center*).
2 - Estimate

the party," said Sawyer. "And were always in the same conspiracies when it came to Democratic conventions. He was liberal and he was gutsy, and we were pretty much soul mates on political issues."

In the 1958 Democratic primary, Sawyer beat Attorney General Harvey Dickerson and George Franklin, taking about one-third of the Clark County Democratic vote. "And all of a sudden, all these so-called big shots are beating down the door," Denton says, laughing. Now in the mainstream, and with a good following in the northern counties, Sawyer beat popular incumbent Charles Russell by more than 16,000 votes.

Even though they were best friends, Denton says that he was careful not to make presumptions about his relationship to Sawyer, and offered advice only when asked. "We had an understanding," says Denton. "He recognized, as did I, from reading the newspapers, that I was supposedly the fix man, the bagman, the hatchet man. So we had this arrangement. If I ever wrote him a letter recommending anything, he was not to pay any attention to it. If it was something I really considered important, I would call him. So I could write letters for people, recommending them for this or that, and give them copies, and if he wanted to make the appointment, that was fine, but it wasn't my suggestion."

"He isn't a Sawyer man," confirmed Sawyer. "He's his own man."

While Sawyer tried to get a state civil rights act through the Legislature, Denton tried to coax color-blind justice from judges and juries. He also raised eyebrows when he hired the town's first black legal secretary, Micki McMillan.

"We did ACLU cases," says Denton. "In those days, to say anything good about the ACLU was to brand you as a communist. So there were two or three lawyers here, George Rudiak, Dean Breeze, and I, who would handle ACLU cases, but we didn't want anybody to know they were ACLU cases."

But one of his most significant civil rights cases was home-grown. "I take some pride in the fact that I represented a black guy in what I think was the first suit against a police department for police brutality," Denton said. The man was skycap Cliff Burns. The time was the early 1960s. Burns was driving a lady friend home when a quarrel erupted. He kicked her out of the car and went home. The next day the North Las Vegas police knocked on Burns' door. The woman had accused him of stealing her purse. The cops marched him out to his car and, sure enough, the purse was on the seat. The cops beat Burns well enough that he required hospitalization. At the hospital, it was discovered that he was blind in one eye, the result of trauma.

Denton, confident of victory, asked the jury for $300,000. But the defense did some deep research on Burns and discovered that he had lost the eye at least 20 years before. Burns had not shared this fact with Denton, who then had to make his closing argument to the jury.

"I guess I asked for too much money in this case," Denton told the jurors. "I was under the impression that he was blinded by the trauma inflicted by the policemen. Apparently, I was wrong. But I wasn't wrong that they beat him up without cause; he was hospitalized and he's entitled to substantial damages. I leave it to you as to what damages to give him." The all-white jury awarded Burns $10,000.

Though he tried and nearly succeeded in 1966, Denton was never able to unseat fellow Democrat Walter S. Baring, who relied on his conservative power base to keep him in congress for 10 terms.

In April of 1963, Sawyer named Denton to the Clark County Commission, where he upset Dunes hotel operator Major Riddle by voting against changing the name of Flamingo Road to Dunes Road, and fought the acquisition by the county of the Winterwood Golf Course.

Developers offered to sell the golf course to the county at their cost, but the Winterwood development was in a flood channel and too close to the sewage treatment plant. Denton consulted several real-estate brokers and all agreed that the place, well, stunk. County Manager Robbins Cahill and the county recreation director recommended against the aquisition, but Denton was the only commissioner to vote against it.

"I was really shocked that my four colleagues just rolled over and played dead," he said. ◢

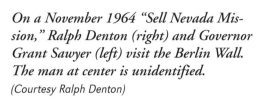

On a November 1964 "Sell Nevada Mission," Ralph Denton (right) and Governor Grant Sawyer (left) visit the Berlin Wall. The man at center is unidentified.
(Courtesy Ralph Denton)

The candidate poses with his campaign van at the University of Nevada-Reno in 1964.
(Courtesy Ralph Denton)

E. PARRY THOMAS (1921–)

A banker who was not afraid to loan money to casinos rode the wave of
development within the gaming industry. **BY JOHN G. EDWARDS**

I t was no coincidence that billionaire Howard Hughes asked E. Parry Thomas, chief executive officer of Bank of Las Vegas, to acquire a Las Vegas home for Hughes' actress wife, Jean Peters, in the late 1960s.

Bob Maheu, a former FBI agent who was Hughes' top aide, can't recall any major piece of valley real estate—including six casinos—that Hughes acquired without consulting Thomas. The banker bought properties as nominee for Hughes so the seller wouldn't know that the richest man in the world was bidding for the property.

Thomas, probably more than any other single person, fostered the development of Las Vegas' casino industry, and with it Las Vegas. For 20 years, he and his late partner, Jerry Mack, ran the only bank willing to make loans to local casinos. Before Thomas' arrival, Las Vegas casinos were forced to rely on their own cash for projects, says Jack Binion, former president of Binion's Horseshoe and now chairman of Horseshoe Gaming. "If Vegas had to be built for cash all these years, figure how it would be stunted for growth," Binion said.

Parry Thomas was born on June 29, 1921, in Ogden, Utah. His father was a successful plumbing contractor, so successful that he found himself the biggest depositor in a bank that failed during the Depression. He took over the bank, and Parry helped his father collect loan payments.

When World War II started, Parry was trained as a paratrooper-skier and worked for an intelligence unit in Europe.

After the war, he joined Continental Bank and Trust Company of Salt Lake City. Walter Cosgriff,

who headed the bank, also owned a stake in the Bank of Las Vegas, which opened in 1954. The Bank of Las Vegas was struggling, so Cosgriff sent Thomas to find out whether the bank should be closed. Thomas was enthusiastic about the bank's potential and ultimately was assigned to work in Las Vegas full time.

Thomas was smart, hard-working, handsome, likable, a good judge of character, a risk taker, and an opportunist. He viewed Las Vegas' gaming industry in terms of basic economics. First came the pioneering phase. Then, if that proved successful, expansion followed. And finally, the industry entered into a consolidation.

The Utah banker arrived during the pioneering phase. "We had a road map in front of us," he explained. "All we had to do was to follow it."

In 1955, the Bank of Las Vegas made its first casino loan to Milton Prell for the Sahara. The $750,000 enabled Prell to build the Congo Room and 120 hotel rooms, and to make other improvements.

Nate Mack was the chairman of Bank of Las Vegas, and his only son, Jerry, was involved in real estate. At the suggestion of Nate Mack, Jerry and Parry became business partners. "Jerry was closer to my dad than his own brothers and sisters," said Peter Thomas, Parry's son. When Cosgriff died in 1961, Parry Thomas was promoted to bank president.

By the 1960s, the owners of the casinos were

Thomas in Southern Nevada

POP.[1]	DECADE
n/a	pre-1900
30	1900
945	1910
2,686	1920
5,952	1930
13,937	1940
45,577	1950
123,667	1960
273,288	1970
463,087	1980
715,587	1990
1,360,000[2]	2000

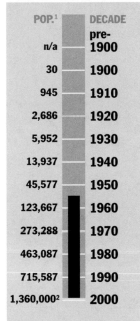

■ Time spent in Southern Nev.
1 - Population figures are for greater Las Vegas area (*Source: Nevada State Data Center*).
2 - Estimate

E. Parry Thomas

getting old. Many were ready to sell, but Nevada law required that all owners be licensed, which resulted in casinos selling at a discount. The law prevented publicly held companies from acquiring casinos, because it was impractical for every stockholder to obtain a license.

Some thought corporate control would open the industry to hidden ownership. "Just the opposite was true," Parry Thomas said. He proposed changing the law about 1965. Northern Nevada controlled the Legislature, and Bill Harrah of Harrah's casinos figured he didn't need investors on Wall Street.

Thomas urged Harrah and his attorney, Mead Dixon, to join him in supporting the bill. Otherwise, asked Thomas, "What was [Harrah's company] going to do when he died?" Dixon "understood immediately," Thomas said. "He convinced Bill Harrah it was the proper thing to do." The bill became law in 1967 and was refined with a 1969 amendment. Since then, small investors have

> *"The gaming industry protected the bank against problems. They didn't want their only bank to have a problem."*
> — Peter Thomas
> Parry Thomas' son

Beginning in 1976, Parry Thomas suggested that corporations make a commitment to the visual arts in Nevada. The Valley Bank collection, including the statue in this 1988 photo, grew to more than 500 pieces.
(Review-Journal files)

been allowed to buy shares of casino corporations without obtaining a gaming license. Only those investors holding 10 percent or more of the stock are required to be licensed.

In 1968, Bank of Las Vegas merged with Valley Bank of Reno, which had the same major stockholders. Thomas and Mack named the combined institution Valley Bank. The proud people of Reno wouldn't do business with an institution called the Bank of Las Vegas, which referred to a place they considered a disreputable, dusty desert town.

By 1975, Thomas and Mack could view the city from the 17th floor of the $15 million Valley Bank Plaza in downtown Las Vegas. Thomas "wanted to build Valley Bank into a Southwest banking powerhouse," explained Irwin Molasky, who developed the bank building. "He knew that the way to do that was through appearances. Parry wanted the biggest building in downtown Las Vegas."

Thomas and Mack started scouting real estate near the University of Nevada-Las Vegas for a computer center. They discovered that UNLV itself owned only 55 acres. The bankers knew that land prices around the university would skyrocket if UNLV waited to purchase land until the state appropriated funds. The university would be forced to erect high-rise buildings or to use a split campus. So the two bankers formed the Nevada Southern University Land Foundation, then personally guaranteed loans to it. The foundation used that money to acquire 300 acres and resell it to the university at cost whenever the college had money to buy.

Thomas, Mack, and others thought the Community Chest, a local charity fund, was controlled by a few charities. They established

the United Way to distribute funds based on merit, rather than on personal ties.

At a Boy Scout testimonial recently, Irwin Molasky asked the audience to visualize how different Las Vegas would be without Parry Thomas. "It is still 1998, but the Strip looks different. There is no Mirage, Treasure Island, Bellagio, no MGM or New York-New York," the developer said. "Caesars Palace, the Desert Inn, and the Flamingo are all small, 300- to 500-room hotels. No Sunrise Hospital; over two million patients would never have been cured. Boulevard Mall, not there. Instead, maybe a post office and grocery store."

Parry Thomas also helped casinos tap Teamster pension funds in the 1960s. Casinos paid higher interest rates than other businesses, and lending to casinos "helped put their members to work" in Las Vegas, Peter Thomas said.

Thomas became a mentor to several casino entrepreneurs. "He's like a son to me; he's like a fifth son," Thomas said of casino executive Steve Wynn. "I like him personally. I like his attitude. He's brilliant. He's bright."

Parry Thomas helped Wynn get a liquor distributing company and was impressed with Wynn's success. Then Thomas saw an opportunity for a coup at the Golden Nugget in downtown Las Vegas. "The Golden Nugget, of all the properties downtown, was by far and away the most attractive to me personally," he said. The Nugget's managers, "a small clique of old-timers," didn't own much stock in the casino.

"The management really wasn't doing anything, and it was going to languish if somebody didn't give it a swift kick," Thomas said. Stock in the Golden Nugget didn't reflect the enormous value of the real estate the company owned. So Wynn and a group of investors bought controlling interest and turned the company around.

Bank of Las Vegas started in 1954 with $250,000 in equity or net worth. By the time Bank of America took over in 1992, the Valley Bank's stockholders had $400 million in equity. ⌀

BILL MILLER (1904–)

An agent extraordinaire, who began his career as a hoofer with chutzpah, virtually invented the lounge show and brought everyone from Mae West to Elvis to Las Vegas. BY K.J. EVANS

Seductive 1930s screen actress Mae West still looked pretty good by the mid-1950s, enough so that she still was able to pack the guys in just by showing up. They came to see flashy costumes wrapped tightly around her generous hourglass figure. And, of course, to hear her famed witticisms. She would slither up to a front-row customer, give him the up-and-down scan, and issue her trademark invitation: "Why don't you come up and see me some time? Make it Tuesday; that's amateur night." But she was a screen star, not a nightclub performer.

"I brought in people nobody believed could do a nightclub act," says Bill Miller, the man who virtually invented the Las Vegas lounge show. "For instance, do you think you could ever get Mae West to play in a nightclub? I did."

Adds his former colleague, Bill Layne, "He was an innovator; he brought in stars nobody else could get to play Las Vegas, and by doing that, he permanently raised the standard for Las Vegas entertainment."

Miller, a relatively robust 94, allowed that time was on his side when he booked West at the Sahara in 1954. Her last major screen appearance was 11 years behind her, she was 61 years old, and she was traveling with a marginally successful stage revue. Miller hired a group of spectacularly buffed-out male bodybuilders. Clad only in bathing trunks, they posed, flexed, and strutted.

West leered; inspected lats, delts, and pects; and fluttered her eyelashes in excitement.

"I wrote her a song for the very finish," says Miller. "It went, 'I've got something for the girls: boys, boys, boys.'" Not only were Mae West and her muscular minions a crowd-pleaser in Las Vegas, they subsequently played to sellout crowds in New York and Atlantic City.

Miller admits to booking only one real flop—Zsa Zsa Gabor. "People came to see her, but she didn't really have an act," he says with a shrug.

William Miller was born in 1904 in Pinsk, Russia, the son of David and Lena, Jews who wanted to get to America. "I was 1 year old when they brought me over," he says.

Miller doesn't know his original family name. He suspects it was lost at Ellis Island when an official asked David his name, and he instead told him his occupation. Somehow, the immigration official heard "Miller" and that became the family's American name. "And that's as far as we know about it," says Miller. "And I never did find out."

The family settled first in Brooklyn, then moved to Jersey City. David Miller was an accomplished building tradesman and was soon making a good living. "We

went through the Depression," Bill says. "But I never remember ever being hungry at home."

By the end of his second year in high school, Miller had already decided on a show business career, and he dropped out of school to pursue it.

Miller in Southern Nevada

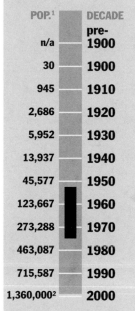

POP.[1]	DECADE
n/a	pre-1900
30	1900
945	1910
2,686	1920
5,952	1930
13,937	1940
45,577	1950
123,667	1960
273,288	1970
463,087	1980
715,587	1990
1,360,000[2]	2000

■ Time spent in Southern Nev.
1 - Population figures are for greater Las Vegas area (*Source: Nevada State Data Center*).
2 - Estimate

Alex Shoofy (left) general manager of the under-construction International Hotel (now the Las Vegas Hilton) signs a contract with Elvis Presley and Bill Miller.
(Courtesy Bill Miller)

His father obligingly provided him with 50 cents a week to take violin lessons. He took a few, but he usually spent the half-buck to see a vaudeville show. "I loved the theater," he recalled, "and in those days it was all live shows, no movies or anything. I fell in love with the dancers. I'd follow their steps, then go home and practice. I finally had enough steps for a good routine."

At an amateur show in the early 1920s, Miller performed his dance, then watched in amazement as another young man did virtually the same act. Miller surmised that the lad had learned his steps the same way Miller had.

According to Miller, the producer said, "You two fellows dance so much alike, we can't use both of you doing the same routine. Why don't you get together?" Thus was born the dancing duo of Miller and Peterson. They decided they needed an agent and struck out for New York's Palace Theatre, where several talent agents kept offices.

Sharing a laugh with Peter Marshall (left) and legendary composer Sammy Cahn is Bill Miller (center) 1974.
(Courtesy Bill Miller)

On the way over, they noticed signs plastered all over town advertising the spectacular "Miller and Lyle Revue." Miller hatched a scheme. Arriving at the Palace, he whispered to Peterson, "You just sit. I'll do the talking." Brimming with chutzpah, Miller strode to the receptionist and asked to speak to an agent: "Tell him Bill Miller, the son of Miller and Lyle, would like to see him."

The agent was concluding a phone call as Miller was escorted into his office. He hung up, looked around, then called the receptionist. "So where's this Miller kid?" he asked.

"He's there in your office," she said.

The agent turned to young Bill: "You're Bill Miller, the son of Miller and Lyle?"

"Yes, I am."

"You know, I'm your Dad's closest friend. I even keep a pic-ture of him here. Would you like to see it?"

"I'd love to."

The agent held up a portrait of the famous Mr. Miller, who was obviously of African ancestry. More amused than annoyed, the agent steered the pair to the Palace Theatre Ballroom, where auditions were being held for a new revue. They were signed at the astronomical salary of $75 per week—each. It was their first paying gig, and it was at the venerable Palace.

"The ambition of every performer, and I mean every performer, was to play the Palace in New York," Miller said. "We played there for four weeks."

He eventually put together his own successful musical comedy revue, with singers, comics, and an orchestra dressed in the uniforms of West Point cadets. But, he said, "After 10 or 12 years, I had enough; dancing was too tough." Approaching his 30th birthday, he was ready for a change.

At one of his last engagements, in 1929, the audience was sparse. Up the street, though, people were lining up for blocks to see the new "talking picture," starring Al Jolson in the title role of *The Jazz Singer*.

"I decided that my part of the business was over, so I'll become an agent," Miller said. "And that's what I did for several years."

One of the nightclubs where Miller booked many of his clients was the Riviera in Fort Lee, New Jersey. It was a swank joint with an illegal casino upstairs. When World War II commenced, it was closed. Miller bought the club in 1945, renamed it "Bill Miller's Riviera," and reopened. It was touch-and-go for the first year, partly because Miller insisted on doing without gambling. "Re-gardless of what I did, everyone wanted to know when I was going to open the room upstairs," he says.

"We finally got [Elvis] on one condition. [Colonel Tom] Parker didn't want him to open in that big 2,000-seat theater. He said that we would have to put someone else in to open, and Elvis would follow. So I went to work on Barbra Streisand. She was leaving, on her way to Europe, when I got her to sign the contract. And she opened the International."
—Bill Miller

Miller was the agent for crooner Tony Martin, who was at the zenith of his career and was booked at the Copacabana. Miller offered to double Martin's salary to $10,000 per week if he would open the Riviera. He accepted. "He was the biggest smash you ever saw," says Miller. The lineup of acts that followed reads like a who's who of mid-century popular entertainment.

"Every one of the Rat Pack came from the Riviera," says Miller. "Sinatra played there; so did Dean Martin and Jerry Lewis when nobody knew who they were. I brought in the Will Mastin Trio, starring Sammy Davis Jr., and also Joey Bishop."

When the Copacabana Club closed in New York, one of its employees, Jack Entratter, was sent to Las Vegas to handle entertainment at the new Sands Hotel. "I was still open, and all the acts that I had, he brought to Vegas," says Miller. "A year later, I found out my place was going to be closed because they were building a highway through it."

Milton Prell, who had opened the Sahara Hotel in 1952, heard about the closing of Bill Miller's Riviera and called Miller. "We'd love for you to come out and take a piece of this place, and be part of our group," said Prell. Miller bought a 10 percent interest in the property and was named entertainment director in 1953.

"But all my acts were already taken [by Entratter], so I had to start from scratch," Miller says. "Ray Bolger was the first act I booked at the Sahara." Bolger, best known as the scarecrow in *The Wizard of Oz*, was also a popular dancer.

"The trouble with Ray Bolger was that nobody knew how to use him in a nightclub act," says Miller. "He was a dancer. How many numbers can you do?"

Miller created an act for Bolger, casting him in the role of master of ceremonies of a variety show. Bolger would do a dance bit before introducing each act. Bolger was a hit, as was Miller's next booking, Donald O'Conner, another hoofer with strong credentials in film and dance revues. And there was Marlene Dietrich, who brought crowds who just wanted to see a legend in the flesh.

But Miller wanted to create a new entertainment venue, one unique to Las Vegas. He thought lounges could produce profits on their own.

"Truthfully, the lounges were a joke," says Miller. "Oh, they had a violin player or a guitar player or something. I said, 'This is ridiculous.

I've made all my money in show business selling whiskey. I can make more money selling whiskey than you can gambling.'"

As a talent agent, he had formerly represented trumpeter and gravel-voiced vocalist Louis Prima, a Sicilian-American who had earned some success with energetic arrangements combining swing, Dixieland jazz, Italian folk songs, and comedy. In 1954, Prima called Miller looking for work.

"How would you like to have a seven-year deal?" Miller asked. He offered $3,500 per week for Prima, $3,500 for his partner and wife, Keely Smith, and $3,500 to be split among the backup band, Sam Butera and the Witnesses. He also informed Prima that he would be working in the Sahara's Casbah Lounge.

"Lounge?" exclaimed Prima.

"You're going into the lounge, Louie," said Miller firmly. "You're going to be there seven years. You're going to live in the town and you're going to make more money than you ever did."

"And there was no one, ever, in the history of show business, that did the business that this man did from midnight until 6 in the morning," says Miller. "You could not get into that club. That was really one of the biggest things that happened in Vegas. It created people like Shecky Green. All the lounge acts started with Louis Prima."

In 1955, Miller left the Sahara and bought an interest in the new Dunes Hotel and signed on as entertainment director. The show budget was tight, but Miller solved it by booking, for $9,500 per week, what would today be called a "production show." It was called *Smart Affairs*.

"That started all the big production shows you have in Vegas today," says Miller. "From there, they brought in the *Lido de Paris* and the *Folies Bergere*." Miller's former producer in New Jersey, Donn Arden, came to Las Vegas in the vanguard of the feather-show phenomenon, and he would become one of the city's leading show pro-

ducers.

While at the Dunes in 1956, Miller decided to catch a show at the New Frontier. It featured a 21-year-old kid who had made his TV debut on the "Ed Sullivan Show" only a few weeks before.

Miller claims he recognized Elvis Presley's potential the first time he saw him on stage. "I said, 'Boy, some day I'm going to fire up this guy's career.'" In 1967 Miller, then the owner and operator of a hotel in the Dutch West Indies, was lured back to Las Vegas to become the Flamingo entertainment director.

Miller sought unusual acts. One was the husband-and-wife vocal team of Sonny and Cher. "They needed the job, and I thought she was great," says Miller. It was on the Flamingo stage that the couple invented the bickering banter that later segued into a hit network television show.

When Flamingo owner Kirk Kerkorian opened the International Hotel in 1969, Miller had a chance to "fire up" Elvis Presley's career. Of course, Miller had to arm-wrestle "Colonel" Tom Parker.

"We finally got [Elvis] on one condition," says Miller. "Parker didn't want him to open in that big 2,000-seat theater. He said that we would have to put someone else in to open, and Elvis would follow. "So I went to work on Barbra Streisand. She was leaving, on her way to Europe, when I got her to sign the contract. And she opened the International."

Miller retired to Palm Springs in the mid-1970s.

Longtime Las Vegas showman Ralph Young, half of the act of Tony Sandler and Ralph Young, sums up Miller's career: "He's the last of the most knowledgable entertainment directors. He had his finger on the pulse of what was happening at the time." ⚑

Las Vegas perennial Tom Jones got his start here when Bill Miller booked him in the lounge of the Flamingo in the late 1960s.
(Las Vegas News Bureau/LVCVA)

Bill Miller (left) with co-hoofer Nat Peterson, 1925. The pair made their New York debut at the venerable Palace Theatre.
(Courtesy Bill Miller)

FRANK SINATRA (1915–1998)

The Chairman found his way back to the top of the heap by bringing sophistication
to a stretch of road that he traveled with his Rat Pack friends. **BY MIKE WEATHERFORD**

He made the city swing. And that is neither to undersell nor overstate Frank Sinatra's contribution to Las Vegas. Sinatra was a pop music legend, not a civic leader or entrepreneur. But he was a one-man chamber of commerce who gave Las Vegas something equally important: an image. And he did so in the mid-1950s, before demographics and visitor volume were buzzwords.

It was a simpler day in a smaller town, and Sinatra's magic was more easily described: gambling, womanizing, drinking till dawn—and all of it with style.

"He brought unmatched excitement to the Strip and defined the word 'swinger' for all times," said actor Gregory Peck at the Las Vegas golf tournament that bears Sinatra's name. "With his little gang of merry men, he established forever a sense of free-floating fun and frolic that captured the imagination of the world," Peck told celebrities two weeks after Sinatra's death in May 1998.

Sinatra was a Las Vegas fixture for 43 years, from his first gig in September 1951 until May 1994. He first worked the glorified motel that was the Desert Inn and last performed at the 5,000-room MGM Grand. Even before his death, his life was legend. "That Sinatra aura brought international royalty and made us a global destination," says Lieutenant Governor Lorraine Hunt, a former entertainer and Clark County commissioner.

Aspects of the saga surely bend the corners of reality as all legends do. However embellished, the Rat Pack image of all-night ring-a-ding-dinging still holds a grasp on the "Cocktail Nation" of young swing-dance enthusiasts in the waning days of the century.

But trying to extract Sinatra's legend from real Las Vegas history is tough. To play a game of "What if there had been no Sinatra?" is nearly impossible, because the rise of the singer and the Strip were inseparable.

"Prior to Sinatra, we were more of a Western-feeling town," asserted Hunt. "He brought a sophistication to the Strip." Hunt was a teen-aged friend of Carol Entratter, daughter of Sands impresario Jack Entratter. His legacy also is inseparable from Sinatra's.

When publicity agent Monte Prosser bought New York's Copacabana club in 1946, he named Jack Entratter as its general manager. A year later, Entratter owned stock in the club and by 1949 had a controlling interest. But in 1952, the 38-year-old Entratter cashed out to become general manager of a new carpet joint called the Sands. He relied on the loyalty of Lena Horne, Danny Thomas, and other Copacabana stars to book the hotel's Copa Room.

"That was an era when the hotel owners were all walking around in cowboy hats, and all these guys came in with the mohair tuxes with the black satin shoes. That look was so cool," Hunt recalls. "I remember, being a teen-ager, I was so attracted to those shiny shoes."

The Sands came along at a perfect time for Sinatra. His first visit to Las Vegas had been less than auspicious, coming in the midst of a nation-

Sinatra in Southern Nevada

POP.[1]	DECADE
n/a	pre-1900
30	1900
945	1910
2,686	1920
5,952	1930
13,937	1940
45,577	1950
123,667	1960
273,288	1970
463,087	1980
715,587	1990
1,360,000[2]	2000

■ Time spent in Southern Nev.
1 - Population figures are for greater Las Vegas area (*Source: Nevada State Data Center*).
2 - Estimate

Frank Sinatra onstage in the Sands' Copa Room, 1953
(Las Vegas News Bureau/LVCVA)

wide scandal over leaving his wife Nancy for actress Ava Gardner.

Though only 35, Sinatra was virtually a has-been. The young sensation from Hoboken, New Jersey, had risen to the top since his first jobs singing for the Harry James and Tommy Dorsey bands in 1939. His distinctive voice, boyish charm, and lanky, nonthreatening build made him a favorite of the female "bobby-soxers" who crowded New York's Paramount theater during World War II.

Sinatra's career seemed to stabilize after the war and he looked like a permanent presence. But by the end of the decade, it had all gone sour. His records for Columbia weren't selling, his movies weren't popular, and the bobby-soxers had moved on to postwar nesting.

Sinatra first played Wilbur Clark's Desert Inn on September 4, 1951, just a few days after a reported suicide attempt in Lake Tahoe that was quickly discounted by both the singer and local authorities. He called it a sleeping-pill miscalculation; others called it Ava-baiting. By the time he debuted at the Sands on October 7, 1953, he had divorced, remarried, and was almost divorced again. The next March, he picked up a Best Supporting Actor Oscar for *From Here to Eternity*.

Sinatra's renewed momentum had carried over to his recording career. Leaving Columbia for Capitol, he entered a second, more mature phase. Working with arranger Nelson Riddle, he emerged from the winter of 1953 with "Songs for Young Lovers," one of the first conceptual long-play record albums. Vegas suddenly had a new soundtrack, albeit in old standards such as "My Funny Valentine" and "I Get a Kick Out of You."

"Sinatra perpetuated this music of Gershwin and Porter," singer Paul Anka notes. "Pop music was at its infancy stage and just growing. … It was just a bunch of us kids," says Anka, who first played the Sahara in 1959 when he was only 18. "So consequently [the casinos] went to these older established acts" from the nightclub circuit.

Television also was coming of age. It was a revolution that helped Las Vegas, and not just because it was right in the pathway to the West Coast TV mecca. Stay-at-home viewing habits suddenly put the crunch on supper clubs in other cities—giving Las Vegas casinos a clean sweep at the acts.

But nightclub veterans such as Jimmy Durante and Joe E. Lewis were really holdovers from a pre-war era. Suddenly, with the Rat Pack, it all jelled. "Now you've got the greatest, cool, hippest entertainers around," Anka says of the expanding circle of hepcats.

By the end of the decade, that circle included Dean Martin—who split with partner Jerry Lewis and began working the nightclubs as a solo act in 1957—and Sammy Davis Jr., the young breakout sensation of the Will Mastin Trio. Joey Bishop, who had been working steadily as an opening act, was welcomed into the fold as a warm-up and uncredited gag writer for much of the "improvised" mayhem onstage. There was even room onstage for the less-heralded journeyman comedian, Buddy Lester.

The nascent Strip wasn't full of theme architecture and daytime diversions as it is today. "The stars were the draw. They weren't the cherry on the cake like they are today. They were the cake," Anka says.

And the stars came to see Sinatra. "He was actually the king of Las Vegas, because the minute he stepped in town, money was here," says veteran Las Vegas lounge singer Sonny King, a longtime friend of Sinatra. "He drew all the big money people. Every celebrity in Hollywood would come to Las Vegas to see him, one night or another."

And the Sands became his playground. Part of it was loyalty, part of it business. "Sinatra's allegiance to Jack Entratter was because [at the Copacabana club] Jack stood by him through all his troubles," says veteran lounge singer Freddie Bell.

Entratter also was, King notes, "the first guy to give them points in the hotel. If you messed up and didn't show up, you would lose money." Within weeks of Sinatra's first engagement, Nevada gaming authorities approved his application to buy 2 percent of the Sands for $54,000. By 1961, Sinatra owned a reported 9 percent share of the hotel, valued at $380,000.

As the Rat Pack charmed Eisenhower-era America separately and together through every available forum—radio, television, movies, and nightclubs—the Strip continued its expansion. By the end of the '50s, the Tropicana, Dunes, Stardust, and Riviera had joined the horizon, while older hotels expanded.

The shining pop culture moment for both Sinatra and the city came with the "Summit at the Sands," held from January 26 through February 16, 1960, playing on a summit meeting in Paris between President Eisenhower, Russian leader Nikita Khrushchev, and French President Charles De Gaulle.

For the Rat Pack, the legendary showroom nights—performing all together or in various combinations—anchored the filming of *Ocean's Eleven*. The caper comedy was produced by Sinatra's own Dorchester Productions as a vehicle for the entire Rat Pack. The gang now included Peter Lawford, convenient in an election year when Sinatra was enamored of Lawford's famous in-law, Senator John F. Kennedy.

The routine became famous: Two freewheeling, seltzer-spraying shows each night in the Copa Room, followed by a 2 a.m. sojourn in a carefully guarded Sands lounge, where the boys would in-

> *"He brought unmatched excitement to the Strip and defined the word 'swinger' for all times. With his little gang of merry men he established forever a sense of free-floating fun and frolic that captured the imagination of the world."*
> —**Gregory Peck**
> **Actor**

variably end up onstage again. Then sleep—depending upon when the filming schedule required a couple of hours on the set from one or more of the stars. Around 5 p.m. everyone convened in the steam room.

"Nothing has ever, or will ever, compare to that evening," Governor Bob Miller recalls of the Rat Pack show he saw as a teen-ager. "That was clearly the best show in the history of this community." The magic was fueled by the Camelot spirit of the election year, capped by a visit from JFK himself on February 8. But Kennedy's November 1963 assassination began to close the door on the era. Vietnam, civil unrest, and the Beatles would change the face of pop culture.

Sinatra and Dean Martin ham it up at the Jerry Lewis Labor Day Telethon, Sahara Hotel, 1976.

(Las Vegas News Bureau/LVCVA)

Two months earlier, on September 11, 1963, the Nevada Gaming Control Board had recommended that Sinatra's gambling license be revoked for allowing Chicago crime boss Sam Giancana to visit the Cal-Neva Lodge at Lake Tahoe. Nevada had published a "List of Excluded Persons," who were not allowed in casinos even as customers, and Giancana was infamously on that list.

Sinatra "never could understand" the stigma of friendship with Giancana, said Phyllis McGuire, who was Giancana's girlfriend during the controversy. "He'd been friends with the boys for years, ever since he needed to get out of his contract with Tommy Dorsey." Sinatra surrendered his casino license at the Cal-Neva and agreed to sell his interest in the Cal-Neva casino and in the Sands.

The whole country seemed to fly offtrack in the '60s, and the desire to run with the new youth culture may help explain why a 50-year-old Sinatra married a 21-year-old Mia Farrow at the Sands on July 19, 1966. The marriage would last two years.

The biggest change for Sinatra came when Howard Hughes bought the Sands in 1967. The new management failed to continue the liberal accounting policies used to justify Sinatra's casino debt, and the singer flew off the handle one night in September after his credit was cut off.

"He got up on that table and started yelling and screaming right in the middle of the casino," says Anka, who claims to have witnessed the debacle. Hotel Vice President Carl Cohen was summoned, and when Sinatra threw a chair his way, the burly casino boss punched him in the mouth. The blow knocked the caps off Sinatra's two front teeth, according to newspaper reports at the time.

Sinatra jumped ship to Caesars Palace in November 1968. But there was trouble again in 1970, when casino executive Sanford Waterman pulled a gun on Sinatra after another argument over casino credit. Sheriff Ralph Lamb threatened to throw the singer in jail: "I'm tired of the way he has been acting around here anyway."

"The love affair slowly started to unravel," Anka says of the crooner and Las Vegas. Sinatra said he had "suffered enough indignities. … If the public officials who seek newspaper exposure by harassing me and other entertainers don't get off my back, it is of little moment to me if I ever play Las Vegas again."

That was a precursor to a show business "retirement" that lasted from 1971 until a ballyhooed return to Caesars Palace on January 25, 1974. "He omitted 'My Way' (because the end is no longer near?) and did a graceful exit with 'I've Got the World on a String,'" *Review-Journal* columnist Forrest Duke wrote of the comeback.

The mellowed singer performed at least six annual concerts that raised more than $5 million for the UNLV athletic program. (The university presented him with an honorary doctorate in 1976.) And the singer's name was instrumental in launching the "Nite of Stars" benefit for St. Jude's Ranch for Children in 1966.

As Sinatra and Barbara—his wife from 1976 until his death—began to spend more of their time and charity at home in Palm Springs, California, Nevada gaming controllers gradually put to rest the rift that stemmed back to 1963. In 1981, Sinatra listed President Reagan as a character reference and called Peck to testify on his behalf when applying for a license as an entertainment consultant at Caesars Palace. The Gaming Commission voted 4-1 for approval.

The late 1970s and early '80s were perhaps the nadir of Sinatra's tuxedo-clad hipness, but the "has-been" never missed a year of packing showrooms in Las Vegas. Buoyed by his last hit, 1980's "Theme from 'New York, New York,'" he continued to play Caesars, then young casino executive Steve Wynn's revitalized Golden Nugget downtown from 1984 through 1987. From October 1987 through 1990, he joined old friends Martin and Davis in the rotation at Bally's.

"As much as people have said Las Vegas was the burial ground [for entertainers], I totally disagree," says Richard Sturm, the MGM Grand's vice president of entertainment and marketing, who booked the Bally's showroom in those days. "There was certainly a new audience watching Sinatra. You could see tons of younger people really standing up and getting into it."

The Desert Inn celebrated Sinatra's 77th birthday with a gala in December 1992, and the singer struggled to remember lyrics. Paul Anka said a year later, "If I know this man, he must work. To tell him he can't work—it ain't gonna fly."

Sinatra cast his long shadow on one more hotel, the new MGM Grand, during the grand-opening New Year's holiday of 1993-'94.

The lights dimmed on the Strip the night after Sinatra's fatal heart attack at his Palm Springs home on May 14, 1998. But the Chairman would never have wanted the action to slow for long. ✍

BENNY BINION (1904–1989)

A Texan who knew horse trading and gambling camped on Fremont Street and changed the face of Western hospitality. **BY A.D. HOPKINS**

Men and cities can be judged by their heroes, and it tells you something of Las Vegas that there are only two historic equestrian statues in the city. There's Rafael Rivera, said to be the first white man to find the Las Vegas Valley, and there's Benny Binion, said to be the first to give gamblers a fair shot at winning big.

The Binion statue suggests that Las Vegans value the Western traditions of individuality, fairness, and a good gamble.

In some 40 years of operating Las Vegas casinos, Binion injected courage into an industry too timid to take a high bet. He forced gambling houses to change from sawdust joints to classy, carpeted casinos. He and his sons changed poker from a kitchen-table pastime into an important casino game. He was one of the boosters who made Las Vegas the home of the National Finals Rodeo.

Binion did not merely create tourist attractions, but was so famously colorful that he personally became one. Born in 1904 in Grayson County, Texas, about 60 miles north of Dallas, Binion was often seriously ill as a child. His parents decided to let him accompany his father on journeys as a horse trader, hoping the outdoor life would restore his health. It did, but Benny never got around to attending school.

He became skilled at horse trading and skilled at gambling in the campgrounds where traders gathered awaiting market days. "Everybody had his little way of doing something to the cards," he told an oral historian from the University of Nevada in the 1970s. "I wasn't too long on wisin' up to that. Some of 'em had different ways of markin' 'em, crimpin' 'em. … There was fellows … that had what they call 'daub' they put on dice.

And you could roll the dice on a layout, and this daub caused the dice to hesitate, slow down, and turn up on their number. … I never did learn how to do any of these tricks like cheat people, which I'm kind of proud of now. But I was always pretty capable about keeping from gettin' cheated."

First the boy ran errands for gamblers. Then the young man steered customers to clandestine gambling joints. Meanwhile, he made money in the bootlegging business. Around 1928 he opened an illegal "policy" game, or lottery.

In 1936 Dallas unofficially adopted a policy of tolerance toward minor vices, the better to host the Texas Centennial celebration. Police wouldn't put gamblers out of business, but would raid and fine them from time to time. Binion had crap tables built specially in crates labeled as containing hotel beds. "If we had half an hour's notice we were going to be raided, we could clear it out," Binion told a reporter in the '70s.

Even in the Depression, Dallas was flush with oil money. During World War II, entire divisions of GIs learned to shoot craps in barracks and motor pools, and many headed for Dallas to buck the bigger banks and honest dice Binion was known to provide.

This river of money also attracted pirates. In those days Binion carried three pistols—two .45 automatics and a small .38 revolver. In 1931, he suspected that fellow bootlegger Frank Bolding had stolen some liquor and argued with him in a

Binion in Southern Nevada

POP.[1]	DECADE
n/a	pre-1900
30	1900
945	1910
2,686	1920
5,952	1930
13,937	1940
45,577	1950
123,667	1960
273,288	1970
463,087	1980
715,587	1990
1,360,000[2]	2000

■ Time spent in Southern Nev.
1 - Population figures are for greater Las Vegas area (*Source: Nevada State Data Center*).
2 - Estimate

Benny Binion in the 1970s, on a cold day on his Montana ranch. His buffalo coat became a trademark after this photo was published in 1975.

(Courtesy Binion's Horseshoe)

One of Binion's gimmicks was giving visitors the opportunity to see $1 million in one place and to have their photos taken in front of the display. Risk of theft was low, not only because the money was guarded, but also because $10,000 bills are no longer circulated and would be impossible to spend.

(Review-Journal files)

Teddy Jane Binion, Benny's wife, ran the casino cage. That's $4 million stacked in front of her, stakes on deposit for the 1985 World Series of Poker.

(Review-Journal files)

back yard. "This guy was a real bad man, had a reputation for killing people by stabbing them," related Binion's son, the late Lonnie "Ted" Binion, after Benny's death. "He stood up real quick, and Dad felt like he was going to stab him and rolled back off the log, pulled his gun, and shot upward from the ground. Hit him through the neck and killed him."

This athletic marksmanship was the genesis of Binion's nickname "the Cowboy," but also earned him a murder conviction. Bolding did have a knife on him, but hadn't pulled it. Yet Binion got only a two-year suspended sentence, said Ted, because the deceased's reputation was so bad.

Five years later, Binion shot and killed a rival numbers operator, Ben Frieden. Wounded, Binion was cleared on grounds of self-defense. No other killings were ever officially attributed to Binion, though a number of his rivals—and a number of his allies—died in a gang war that broke out in 1938.

Herbert Noble was called "the Cat," for he was thought to have nine lives. In 1946 he was shot in the back; in 1948 his car was riddled with bullets; in 1949 he found dynamite wired to the starter of his car and later got shot in another high-speed chase. But when somebody blew up his car, killing his wife instead of him, he blamed Binion and spent the rest of his life trying to even the score.

Noble was a pilot, and in 1951 a police officer caught Noble rigging an airplane with two large bombs, one high explosive and one incendiary. He had a map with Benny Binion's Las Vegas home—the structure that still stands on Bonanza Road—clearly marked. Noble escaped or survived 11 known attempts to kill him—involving bombs and automatic rifle and machine-gun fire—before a bomb planted in front of his mailbox got him in 1951.

Binion denied responsibility for the eventfulness of Noble's final years, and particularly for the death of Noble's wife. By then a reform administration had encouraged Binion to leave Dallas, and he settled in Las Vegas. "When I realized how good it could be up here, I said, 'Let 'em have Texas.'"

Binion opened a club on Fremont Street in partnership with J.K. Houssels, but soon split with him, though they remained lifelong friends. The split was over Binion's desire to increase the limit on the size of bets the house would accept. When he opened his own place in 1951, naming it Binion's Horseshoe, he set the craps limit at $500—10 times the maximum at other casinos.

Most gamblers use some sort of system. Commonly, if a gambler wins a $10 bet, he will then bet the original $10, plus the $10 won. All gamblers dream of riding a streak of luck and a system into real money, but casino owners have nightmares about the same event.

The house limit made it harder to do. A person betting $10 and doubling it each time he won would be blocked on the fourth bet by the $50 limit. Under Binion's $500 limit, he could keep doubling until the seventh bet. If the doubler won all seven bets, he could win $1,130 at Binion's compared to $270 anywhere else. The new limits made Binion's famous immediately, and other casinos were forced to raise their own limits accordingly.

Some in the industry didn't go along willingly. "He was going to raise the keno limit to $500," related Ted Binion, a few years before the younger Binion's death in 1998. "Dave Berman said if he raised it, he'd kill him." It was one of the few times on record that Benny backed down. He had no doubt that Berman would try to make good his threat, and Binion did not want another gang war. The difference was worked out in some fashion unknown to him, said Ted, and the limit was raised a few months later without incident.

> *"Everybody was comping big players, but Benny comped little players. He said, 'If you wanta get rich, make little people feel like big people.'"*
> —Leo Lewis
> **Binion's comptroller**

Over 40 years, the Binions pushed the limits ever upward to $10,000. Gamblers who felt like going higher could do so, as long as they did it on the first bet. Back in 1980, a player named William Lee Bergstrom asked if he could really bet $1 million. He didn't have the money at the time, but the Binions told him he could.

A few months later he showed up with $777,000, apologizing that he couldn't raise a whole million. They never bothered to convert the money to chips, but laid the whole suitcase of cash on the "don't pass" line, and the woman holding the dice sevened out in three rolls. Binion's counted out another $777,000 to Bergstrom, and Ted Binion escorted him to his car.

Bergstrom came back over the next few years. He bet $590,000 and won. Bet $190,000 and won. Bet $90,000 and won. Then, in November 1984, he brought in a whole million. He deposited it in the casino cage, and Ted told him he could bet it on any game. Ted recalled, "He run a few feet ahead, up to a crap table, put his finger on the table, and said, '$1 million on the don't pass.' It was the come-out roll, so the shooter wanted a seven, and they come ace-six. It was all over in one roll. I felt like electricity run through me. And

Bergstrom pulled his finger off that table like it was on fire!"

Three months later Bergstrom committed suicide. "But you know, he was still $400,000 winner," pointed out Ted. He knew Bergstrom by then, and believed he died not for money, but for love.

Jack Binion, who became president of the casino, remembered that his father was first to put a carpet in a downtown casino, first to have limousines to pick up customers at the airport, and first to offer free drinks to slot machine players.

"Everybody was comping big players, but Benny comped little players," noted Leo Lewis, who was comptroller at Binion's and later ran Strip resorts. "He said, 'If you wanta get rich, make little people feel like big people.'"

In the 1950s Benny served a hitch in prison for tax evasion, stemming not from the casino profits but from his Texas operations. He had to sell majority interest in the casino to finance his legal fights. The family regained control in 1964, with Jack becoming president, Ted becoming casino manager, and their mother, Teddy Jane, managing the casino cage almost until her death in 1994. Three Binion daughters—Barbara, Brenda, and Becky—owned percentages but were not active in operations until 1998, when Jack, after a bitter legal fight among the siblings, surrendered the presidency to Becky and sold her his interest. Jack Binion became active in gambling in other states.

Benny himself never held a gambling license after going to prison, but until his death in 1989 was on the payroll as a "consultant." In the 1970s he bragged that the Binion brothers, then in their 30s and veteran casino executives, "mind me like a couple of 6-year-olds."

Insiders, however, understood that the boys had good ideas of their own, which Benny was smart enough to rubberstamp. The most famous was the World Series of Poker. Tom Morehead of the Riverside Casino in Reno actually started it, but got out of the gambling business and allowed Jack and Ted to take over the tournament in 1970, when it was still in its infancy.

At that time, the Binions didn't even offer poker in their famous but small casino; floor space was too precious to waste on a game in which players vied for each other's money, and in which the casino could collect fees for running the game but had no chance to win big. (Much later, when they acquired an adjacent high-rise hotel, the Binions added a poker room.)

Many other casinos also did not offer poker because the game was not entirely respectable. The game is hard to police, and was associated with cheating long after other Nevada casino games were universally honest. A few casinos offered it as a customer service, but intentionally kept it inconspicuous.

The Binions, by contrast, promoted poker. Their original World Series games were winner-take-all challenges (today the prize money is split among numerous finalists) and were not invitational but open to anybody with $10,000 to buy in. The open aspect was the secret of success; it lured rich suckers and unknown poker prodigies, but it also lured legendary pros such as "Amarillo Slim" Preston and Johnny Moss, who hoped to pluck the newcomers. They usually did, but sometimes the new guys won and themselves became legends, and that hope kept them coming back year after year.

The Binions devised special rules to force the game to a resolution before everyone got bored with it, making it an event that could be, and still is, nationally televised. Within a few years tournament poker was played everywhere poker was legal. And the positive national attention brushed off the lingering grains of disrepute, so that nearly every casino added the game to the attractions.

One of Binion's final gifts to the city was the hand he played in attracting the National Finals Rodeo to Las Vegas every December.

While the second generation of Binions evolved into modern businessmen and businesswomen, Benny remained a Texas tough guy with eclectic tastes. He wore gold coins for buttons on his cowboy shirts, but was never seen in neckties. He didn't shave every day. Despite felony convictions that normally prohibit ownership of firearms, he carried at least one pistol all his life and kept a sawed-off shotgun handy.

In the 1970s, if the police needed lots of money on short notice to execute a drug sting operation, they could get it from Binion's casino cage. Yet he didn't ask the police for such ordinary services as arresting a slot cheater or pickpocket caught on the premises. Those duties were handled by burly, surly security guards, and the perpetrators rarely sinned again until their casts were removed.

Binion ran what was thought to be the most profitable casino in Las Vegas (privately held, it never had to report earnings publicly), but he didn't keep an office; he did business from a booth in the downstairs restaurant. Nobody needed an appointment to talk to him; they asked him personally for his ear, and usually got it. When he invited someone to sit down and have a bowl of the Horseshoe's famous chili, the guest was often a senator or federal judge. And just as often, it was some old Texan from a one-windmill spread, trading stories of rodeos and crap games.

"He was a guy you could shake hands with and feel you had met a real American character," said Howard Schwartz, who has documented the development of Las Vegas as an editor at Gambler's Book Club. "That was what made the place. It wasn't the classiest joint in town, but it was an authentic and unique experience. When you met Benny Binion, you felt you'd been part of history." ✍

Another famous son of Texas, Willie Nelson, shared the mike with Benny at his 83rd birthday party in 1987.
(Review-Journal files)

The statue of Benny Binion at the corner of Second Street and Ogden Avenue was donated by his family.
(Review-Journal files)

WALTER BARING

(1911–1975)

A Democrat who didn't like JFK, minorities, foreign aid, or the federal government defied his detractors by being re-elected to Congress 10 times. **BY K.J. EVANS**

"With all these demonstrations, the NAACP is violating more laws than the states are. The big thing this country has overlooked is J. Edgar Hoover's statement that the civil rights movement is communistically inspired, and J. Edgar Hoover knows what he's talking about. It's been shown that Martin Luther King [Jr.] is connected with several subversive groups, and yet he calls himself a reverend."

—Walter S. Baring
Nevada congressman

He has been called by his detractors the least effective congressman in Nevada history and a demagogue who would say anything to get re-elected. But Walter S. Baring's constituents returned him to office 10 times. His motto was: "Nobody likes Walter Baring but the voters."

He was a 250-pound bear who liked both his rhetoric and his cigarettes unfiltered. To him, liberalism and socialism were synonymous, intellectuals were eggheads, and the most noble virtue a person could possess was unqualified patriotism. "I don't think he believed most of the things he said himself," says former Senator Howard Cannon, who served in Congress at the same time Baring did.

The congressman called himself a "Jeffersonian States' Rights Democrat." He was born in 1911 in Goldfield, where his father was chairman of the Esmeralda County Commission. The family later moved to Reno, where Baring graduated from the University of Nevada in 1934 with two bachelor's degrees. He then managed his father's store for a while—one of the few times in his life he would work in the private sector—before getting his first government job as a collector for the Internal Revenue Service.

In 1936, he was elected to the state Assembly. Jerome Edwards, in his biography of Senator Patrick McCarran, said Baring was suspended from his IRS job at McCarran's behest, because he criticized President Franklin Roosevelt's attempt to pack the U.S. Supreme Court. His job was saved by Senator Key Pittman.

Baring was re-elected to the assembly in 1942, but shortly thereafter resigned and joined the U.S. Navy. Before shipping out, he married Geraldine Buchanan. The couple eventually had four sons.

After the war, he was elected to the Reno City Council, and in 1948 defeated incumbent Republican congressman Charles Russell. Re-elected in 1950, Baring was a mainstream liberal Democrat.

But 1952 was Eisenhower's year, and that year Baring lost his seat to Republican Cliff Young by 771 votes. Baring tried again in 1954, but was rebuffed by 7,000 votes. In 1956, Young ran for the Senate, leaving the congressional race open. Baring first defeated Las Vegas City Attorney Howard Cannon in the Democratic primary, then Republican Robert C. Horton in the general election.

Baring was a different man this time. He aligned himself with the clique of Southern congressmen known as "Dixiecrats" and tended to vote their way—conservatively.

Baring didn't like John F. Kennedy or his politics, and made it clear in a speech before the Reno Chamber of Commerce in mid-1962. "I am seriously concerned over the foreign aid giveaway programs and the constant spirit of defeatism which has existed over the last 10 years," he said. Baring instantly became his party's pariah.

In later years, he would take credit for helping push through the vital Southern Nevada Water Project, which delivered Nevada's full allotment of Colorado River water to Las Vegas. But in reality, the measure passed in spite of Baring: His antagonism toward President Lyndon Johnson almost scuttled it. But the project was a pet of Senators Bible and Cannon, both strong

Congressman Walter S. Baring

Baring in Southern Nevada

POP.[1]	DECADE
n/a	pre-1900
30	1900
945	1910
2,686	1920
5,952	1930
13,937	1940
45,577	1950
123,667	1960
273,288	1970
463,087	1980
715,587	1990
1,360,000[2]	2000

■ Time spent in Southern Nev.
1 - Population figures are for greater Las Vegas area (*Source: Nevada State Data Center*).
2 - Estimate

Johnson men, so the president couldn't realistically veto it just to spite Baring. LBJ was content to sit on it for a while to make him sweat. Johnson's antipathy toward Baring went back to 1964, when Baring led the charge in the house to defeat the Civil Rights Act. (Cannon was instrumental in saving it.)

In an interview at a Lovelock casino with William Trombley of the *Los Angeles Times*, Baring spoke his mind on several issues, among them the United Nations. "The communists have dominated that organization since its inception, when Alger Hiss, a convicted communist, helped to found it." Baring also bashed college professors, "those awful ultra-left professors who are putting that pornography and other stuff into the minds of our youth."

Baring was a man who could get things undone. An example was his success in denying his home state its only national park. In 1958 Senator Bible first proposed a national park in the Snake Mountains of eastern Nevada, one of the most spectacular ranges in the state. The area, what is now Great Basin National Park, included Lehman Caves National Monument, created in 1922.

In 1959, Bible introduced a bill to create a 147,000-acre Great Basin National Park. Baring evidently hadn't yet heard from his ranching and mining constituents, because he introduced a companion bill in the House of Representatives. During hearings before the Senate Subcommittee on Public Lands, he heard from the constituents—loudly. Bible modified the bill to allow grazing in the park for 25 years. The mining industry protested that the park would "lock up" mineral resources in the Snake Range, though there had been little mining there. Bible conceded 24,000 acres in the northeast, which some thought contained beryllium deposits.

The bill passed the Senate easily and went to the House, where Baring, as a member of the House Subcommittee on Public Lands, was expected to lead the push for passage of the 123,000-acre park. Instead, he drafted his own bill, paring down the park to 53,000 acres and allowing mining and grazing in perpetuity. Interior Secretary Stewart Udall flatly rejected Baring's idea, since it contained no provision to protect the ancient bristlecone pines, the nation's southernmost glacier, or any of the region's unique natural resources.

Governor Grant Sawyer went to Washington to try and break the impasse between Baring and Udall. Bible also made a public plea to Baring to work out a compromise. "If we cannot reach an agreement within the delegation on the scope of the proposed park," Bible wrote in a letter to Baring, "then we should at least agree on a course to bring action on a park bill in both houses. Short of this, the Great Basin National Park is dead in the 89th Congress and probably forever. If this occurs, you should be prepared to accept full responsibility for its death."

But Baring would not budge. By 1966, the Great Basin National Park idea was all but abandoned. The park was finally established in October 1986.

Though savage in his defense of antiquated mining laws, and generally a foe of any public lands use policy that raised an eyebrow among ranchers, Baring backed a few causes that seem inconsistent with those positions. One of the causes was protecting wild horses and burros. In the early 1960s he pushed a bill through Congress forbidding the use of aircraft to round up wild horses. Eleven years later, he was chief sponsor of the wild horse and burro protection law that exists today.

He also pushed for passage of the 1971 Clean Water Restoration Act and for $1.25 billion to fund it. And he co-sponsored a bill to prohibit capturing or killing ocean mammals.

Baring worked to get a Veterans Affairs Hospital built in Southern Nevada, but succeeded only in getting an outpatient clinic.

Walter Baring's time had run out by 1972. Seven candidates filed for his congressional seat. In his own party, attorney James Bilbray emerged as his main primary challenger. Only a few months into the election season, Baring was hospitalized in Reno for what his aides described as "a virus." However, it is more likely that Baring was suffering from emphysema and a weak heart, and the rumors of his ill health did not help his campaign. Bilbray won the Democratic nomination, carrying both Clark and Washoe counties.

In July 1975, Baring entered Hollywood Presbyterian Hospital for surgery on his hip, which had troubled him for several years. The strain of the procedure was too great, and he died of heart and lung failure at age 63. ⌀

Walter Baring (second from right) with a group of veterans, 1972
(Review-Journal files)

THE FIRST 100

PART III:

A City in Full

KIRK KERKORIAN (1917–)

The father of the megaresort, this daredevil pilot turned his high-flying ways into high-roller profits by building the world's biggest hotels, both on and off the Strip. BY K. J. EVANS

"When you're a self-made man, you start very early in life. In my case it was at 9 years old when I started bringing income into the family. You get a drive that's a little different, maybe a little stronger, than somebody who inherited."

—Kirk Kerkorian

Kirk Kerkorian, father of the Las Vegas megaresort, dropped out of school in the eighth grade to become a professional boxer, flew suicide missions for the Royal Air Force, made a small fortune in surplus military airplanes, and parlayed that fortune into an even bigger one in the airline business. In Las Vegas, he built three hotels that were the largest in the world in their time and proved that, contrary to the wisdom of the day, courting the convention and family travel markets could be profitable. Today, Kerkorian is the 41st richest man in the country, worth about $5.7 billion.

Kerkorian rarely attends board meetings and never gives speeches. He is shy, but a tough negotiator. Those who know him describe him not as a Hughesian hermit, but as a gentle, gracious, normal guy.

"I'm far from being reclusive," declares Kerkorian. "I have 30- or 40-year friendships that I prefer to meeting new people. I go to an occasional party, but just because I don't go to a lot of events and I'm not out in public all the time doesn't mean I'm anti-social or a recluse. I'm at a restaurant three or four nights a week, here or in Las Vegas."

His dark, motionless eyes are set below thick salt-and-pepper eyebrows. The tanned, deeply lined poker face reveals nothing. He may be amused, bored, or about to knock his interviewer through the second-story window of his office in Beverly Hills, California. He still looks capable of demonstrating why he was called "Rifle Right Kerkorian" in the boxing ring.

Kirk Kerkorian was born in Fresno, California, on June 6, 1917, the youngest of Ahron and Lily Kerkorian's four children. When the recession of 1921-1922 wiped out the family, the Kerkorians moved to Los Angeles. Kirk sold newspapers and hustled odd jobs.

"When you're a self-made man, you start very early in life," he says. "In my case it was at 9 years old when I started bringing income into the family. You get a drive that's a little different, maybe a little stronger, than somebody who inherited."

The Kerkorians moved often, and Kirk was always the new kid in school, obliged to prove himself. Big brother Nish, a pro boxer, coached him. Kerkorian became the Pacific amateur welterweight champion and wanted to box professionally. He might have slugged himself into addled obscurity. Instead, in the autumn of 1939, he met Ted O'Flaherty.

Both were earning 45 cents an hour installing wall furnaces. Kerkorian sometimes joined O'Flaherty on his lunchtime trips to Alhambra Airport and watched him train for his pilot's license in a Piper Cub. Originally disinterested, Kerkorian consented one day to go aloft with O'Flaherty. As the plane rose and the Southern California landscape became visible from the mountains to the ocean, Kerkorian experienced a defining moment.

"He was sold on it right then," O'Flaherty later recalled. "The very next day, he was back out at the field to take his first flying lesson."

With war clouds darkening Europe, Kerkorian worried that he would be drafted into the infantry before he became a licensed pilot. So one day in 1940, he showed up at the Happy Bottom Ranch in the Mojave Desert adjacent to Muroc Field, now Edwards Air Force Base. Owned by Florence "Pancho" Barnes, a pioneer female aviator, the ranch was a combination flight school and dairy farm.

"I haven't got any money," Kerkorian told Barnes. "I haven't got any education. I want to learn to fly. I don't know how I can do it. Can you help me?" No college was needed, just the willingness

Kerkorian in Southern Nevada

POP.[1]	DECADE
n/a	pre-1900
30	1900
945	1910
2,686	1920
5,952	1930
13,937	1940
45,577	1950
123,667	1960
273,288	1970
463,087	1980
715,587	1990
1,360,000[2]	2000

■ Time spent in Southern Nev.
1 - Population figures are for greater Las Vegas area (*Source: Nevada State Data Center*).
2 - Estimate

Kirk Kerkorian with hard hat and blueprints as the International Hotel rises in the background, October 21, 1968.
(Las Vegas News Bureau/LVCVA)

to pull teats and shovel bovine backwash. Within six months, Kerkorian had a commercial pilot's license and a job as a flight instructor. But teaching bored him.

"I heard about the Royal Air Force flying out of Montreal, Canada, and I went up there and got hired right away," he recalls. "They were paying money I couldn't believe—$1,000 a trip."

The mission of the RAF Air Transport Command was to fly Canadian-built Mosquito bombers from Labrador to Scotland. Only one in four made it. The Mosquito's fuel tanks carried it 1,400 miles; it was 2,200 miles to Scotland. Pilots had only two possible routes, both equally dangerous.

The roundabout route was Montreal-Labrador-Greenland-Iceland-Scotland, but the plane's high-performance wings could be distorted by a paper-thin coating of ice, causing it to fall out of the sky. Or one could fly straight across the Atlantic, riding a west-to-east airflow called the "Iceland Wave." It blew at jet speeds, but it wasn't constant. If it waned in midflight, plane and pilot were lost.

Kerkorian and his wing commander, J.D. Woolridge, rode the wave in May 1944 and broke the old crossing record. Woolridge got to Scotland in six hours, 46 minutes; Kerkorian, in seven hours, nine minutes. The following month Kerkorian tried again, but the Iceland Wave died halfway across. The sun set. In a cloud bank, with the reserve tank empty, he prepared to ditch. His navigator begged him to drop low just once. As they broke through the cloud, the lights of Prestwick, Scotland, twinkled ahead. Kerkorian made a perfect landing.

In two and a half years with the RAF, Kerkorian delivered 33 planes, logged thousands of hours, traveled to four continents, and flew his first four-engine plane. He also saved most of his generous salary.

Kerkorian clearly recalls his first visit to Las Vegas in July 1945. His RAF service completed, he paid $5,000 for a single-engine Cessna in which to train pilots. "I used that same plane to fly charters," he says. "That's what got me into the trans-portation end of the business." Jerry Williams, a Los Angeles scrap iron dealer, hired Kerkorian's plane two or three times a week to fly to Las Vegas. "I was just overwhelmed at the level of excitement in this little town," Kerkorian remembers. "The best times of my life were in Las Vegas."

One morning, he and Williams emerged into the dawn after a fruitless night at the tables. They had $5 between them, and Williams suggested they save it for breakfast. "What good's five dollars going to do?" asked Kerkorian, and headed back to the craps table, where he won $700. Kerkorian became well-known as a high roller in Las Vegas during the 1940s and 1950s. He was always unruffled when he won, or lost, $50,000 to $80,000 per night, but eventually he quit gambling entirely.

Married twice, Kerkorian met his second wife in Las Vegas. She was Jean Maree Hardy, a former dancer at the Thunderbird. The marriage produced Kerkorian's two daughters, Tracy and Linda; he named his personal holding company Tracinda Corporation.

In 1947, Kerkorian purchased a tiny charter line, Los Angeles Air Service. He later changed the name to Trans International Airlines and offered the first jet service on a nonscheduled airline. In 1965, he took TIA public. Armenian-Americans knew of Kerkorian and bought the TIA stock. It rose from a low of $9.75 per share to a high of $32.

"It brought the stock up to begin with, and then our earnings were great, too, and it kept going up until we sold to TransAmerica," says Kerkorian. In that 1968 deal, he received about $85 million worth of stock in the TransAmerica conglomerate, making him its biggest shareholder.

In 1962, Kerkorian pulled off what *Fortune* magazine called "one of the most successful land speculations in Las Vegas' history." He bought 80 acres across the Strip from the Flamingo for $960,000. The price was low even then, and for good reason: A narrow band of property cut the 80 acres off from the Strip.

"It was landlocked," says Kerkorian. "We traded the owners four or five acres for all of this thin strip that they could never build on. Then I got a call from Jay Sarno, and that's how Caesars Palace got started." Kerkorian collected $4 million in rent before selling the land to Caesars for another $5 million in 1968.

With the cash from the Caesars sale and his TransAmerica stock, Kerkorian was ready to build his first Las Vegas megaresort. In early 1967, he had bought 82 acres on Paradise Road for $5 million and hired Fred Benninger. "All I knew about Las Vegas came from the other side of the table—the contributing end," Benninger recalled years later.

"I'm not a firm believer that you have to have 30 years of experience, if you've got good, common sense," says Kerkorian. "I knew he could cut the mustard and he did. He helped, no, he built the International. He built the old MGM and he built this MGM. It was all Fred Benninger. I can't take much credit except for seeing the big picture—the amount of rooms, what kind of showrooms, I'm into that part of it. But when you get to the nitty-gritty, I don't have the education to really get in there and dissect it."

Given the size of the International, the two men decided to buy an existing hotel and use it to train staff. The Flamingo Hotel fit the bill. Benninger installed Sahara Hotel Vice President Alex Shoofey as the Flamingo's president, and Shoofey stole 33 of the Sahara's top executives.

In February 1969, Kerkorian's International Leisure was given the go-ahead by the U.S. Securities and Exchange Commission to offer the public about 17 percent of the

> *"I'm not a firm believer that you have to have 30 years of experience, if you've got good, common sense."*
>
> —**Kirk Kerkorian**

An early artist's rendition of the International Hotel. The large tower at center went up first.
(Las Vegas News Bureau/LVCVA)

Kerkorian with friend Cary Grant, at the opening of the International Hotel, 1969
(Review-Journal files)

Kerkorian and singer Steve Lawrence backstage at the Desert Inn, 1994
(Las Vegas News Bureau/LVCVA)

company's stock at $5 per share. This was not a routine approval, though. The Justice Department was investigating the Flamingo's previous owners and had identified Meyer Lansky, Bugsy Siegel's old partner in Murder Inc., as a hidden partner in the Flamingo. Skimming was suspected, and Kerkorian more or less proved it.

"The reason I think they allowed us to go public," says Kerkorian, "was that I don't think the Flamingo ever showed anything more than $300,000 or $400,000 in profits. In our first year, 1968, we showed about $3 million."

The International Hotel, at 30 stories and 1,512 rooms, was the largest hotel in the world when it opened July 1, 1969. The International had a "Youth Hostel," where kids could play and swim while their parents were doing grown-up stuff. The hostel organized field trips for the kids to Lake Mead, Mount Charleston, and other local attractions.

"We opened that hotel with Barbra Streisand in the main showroom," says Kerkorian. "The rock musical *Hair* was in the other showroom, and the opening lounge act was Ike and Tina Turner. Elvis followed Barbra in the main showroom. I don't know of any hotel that went that big on entertainment."

One month before the hotel made its debut, International Leisure common stock, which had opened at $5 per share, was selling over the counter for $50. But Kerkorian had some expensive European loans to pay off. He was confident he could retire them with a second offering of International Leisure stock.

The SEC refused to allow the sale on the grounds that Kerkorian had failed to disclose financial information about the Flamingo's previous owners. Kerkorian's people believe this information was not important to the SEC, but to the Justice Department's investigation. "They employed a form of economic blackmail to try and get information out of us," said a Kerkorian lawyer. By the time the SEC relented, Kerkorian's company was all but destroyed. To pay off his debts, he was forced to sell half of his shares in

International Leisure to Hilton Hotels. He got $16.5 million for stock worth $180 million only six months earlier.

At the same time that he was making his splash in Las Vegas, Kerkorian was acquiring a controlling interest in ailing MGM studios. In 1971, less than a year after the sale of the International, MGM announced it would "embark on a significant and far-reaching diversification into the leisure field by building … the world's largest resort hotel in Las Vegas." Now Bally's, it was originally the MGM Grand, named for the 1932 MGM film *Grand Hotel*. (Today's MGM Grand is a different property.) At 26 stories, the $107 million megaresort had 2,084 rooms, a 1,200-seat showroom, and amenities like a shopping arcade, movie theater, and jai alai fronton.

When it opened December 5, 1973, it was the largest hotel in the world—just as the International had been. The MGM Grand also was the site of the city's biggest disaster: In November 1980, a fire started by electrical problems raged through the casino and the upper floors of the MGM, killing 87 and injuring hundreds.

The great poker face softens and the brown eyes lower when the catastrophe is mentioned. "It's something I rarely ever talk about, because how do you talk about it?" Kerkorian says quietly. "I was in New York in a meeting with people from Columbia Studios, and I had an emergency call telling me that the hotel was on television, on fire, and in less than two hours I was at the airport and on my way to Las Vegas. The two people I really felt for at the time were Fred Benninger and Al Benedict, because they were on the front lines through everything that happened."

"I figured there was no way we could come out of this," said

Benedict, who was hotel president at the time. "I think the idea of walking away and forgetting about rebuilding the property was in the back of everybody's mind. That's what most people would have done."

Not Kerkorian. Eight months later, the MGM Grand reopened. "How could I walk away while that whole team was out there, taking the brunt from everybody?" he said. "I had to be a part of it. I couldn't walk away; I just couldn't." In 1986, Kerkorian sold the Las Vegas and Reno MGMs to Bally Manufacturing Corporation for $594 million.

The current MGM Grand Hotel, opened in 1993, has 5,000 rooms, eight restaurants, a health club, a monorail, the 15,000-seat MGM Grand Garden, and a theme park as big as Disneyland when it opened in 1955.

As for the health of the Las Vegas resort industry, Kerkorian remains as bullish as he was in 1945. "Personally, I wouldn't say it's headed for a fall," commented Kerkorian, "except that there will be a leveling-out time, and the best hotels and the best operators are going to suffer less than the others." ◢

WALTER LIBERACE

(1919–1987)

"I'd like to think that the most enduring quality about me will be the music, because everything I'm doing … is to promote the music of future talent. My foundation is based on promoting new talent, and I feel that my longevity will survive through other people in this business because I'm going to provide a lasting support and a foundation for artists."

—Liberace

A renowned pianist with a flair for the outlandish, Liberace gave his audiences impeccable performances while clad in sequined capes. **BY K.J. EVANS**

As he strolled down Fremont Street, the cherub-faced young man with the dark, wavy hair offered passersby a broad grin, his hand, and a handbill that introduced him. "Have You Heard Liberace?" it asked. If they hadn't, Walter Liberace would first correct their pronunciation of his name—"It's Liber-AH-chee"—then ask them to come to his show at the Last Frontier resort.

It was November 1944, and the young pianist was making his Las Vegas debut. The city would become the entertainer's home—one of many around the country—but more important, it would become the place where he would develop his spectacular stage persona. Liberace would pack Las Vegas showrooms for the rest of his life, and after his death his collection of antiques, custom cars, and elaborate costumes would fill a museum that is, in itself, one of the city's more popular tourist attractions. The museum is the financial wellspring that funds scholarships for aspiring musicians and artists.

Asked in a 1985 interview how he wished to be remembered, Liberace replied: "I'd like to think that the most enduring quality about me will be the music, because everything I'm doing … is to promote the music of future talent. My foundation is based on promoting new talent, and I feel that my longevity will survive through other people in this business because I'm going to provide a lasting support and a foundation for artists."

It was, after all, a scholarship that provided musical training for the boy who would become "Mr. Showmanship."

Wladziu Valentino Liberace was born in 1919. His father, an Italian immigrant who played French horn in orchestras providing background music for silent movies, required his children to learn music. Walter was capable of picking out

tunes at age 4. By his pre-teen years, he was playing piano for dance classes.

"Except for music, there wasn't much beauty in my childhood," he later recalled. "We lived in one of those featureless bungalows in a featureless neighborhood. I hated shabbiness. I'd walk 27 blocks and pay 15 cents to sit in a new, clean movie house when I could have walked five blocks and paid 5 cents to sit in an old, dirty one."

He excelled academically at West Milwaukee High School and was active in extracurricular activities, excluding sports. (He couldn't stand to get dirty.) One of the school's traditions was "Character Day." Every student was supposed to dress up as a famous character from history, and Walter nearly always won. He appeared one year as Emperor Haille Selassie of Ethiopia and another time as Yankee Doodle Dandy. One year he came in full drag as Greta Garbo.

Liberace's big break came in 1939 with an audition for Dr. Frederick Stock of the Chicago Symphony. His audition was flawless, and he was invited to play at the Pabst Theatre in Milwaukee.

Sometime in 1942, perhaps emulating his idol, the great Polish pianist Paderewski, Walter Liberace dropped his first name altogether. His friends would thereafter simply call him "Lee." The idea of his trademark candelabrum was borrowed from the film *A Song to Remember*, in which Polish composer Frederic Chopin was shown

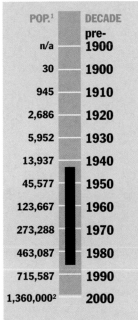

Liberace in Southern Nevada

POP.[1]	DECADE
n/a	pre-1900
30	1900
945	1910
2,686	1920
5,952	1930
13,937	1940
45,577	1950
123,667	1960
273,288	1970
463,087	1980
715,587	1990
1,360,000[2]	2000

■ Time spent in Southern Nev.
1 - Population figures are for greater Las Vegas area (*Source: Nevada State Data Center*).
2 - Estimate

To his mother, Liberace was always "Walter."
(Liberace Museum)

At their first meeting backstage at the Riviera Hotel in 1956, Liberace and a young Elvis Presley swapped jackets and instruments to ham it up for the camera.
(Las Vegas News Bureau)

with a single candelabrum on his piano.

In 1944, while performing at the Mount Royal Hotel in Montreal, Liberace received a phone call from Maxine Lewis, entertainment director at the Last Frontier. She asked him if he would be interested in playing Las Vegas. He was. She asked how much he was currently making. "Seven hundred and fifty a week," he lied. His salary was $350, but Lewis agreed to $750 per week.

Liberace sized up his first-night audience and decided to delete several of the classical pieces, concentrating on boogie-woogie and popular tunes. The audience went wild, and Maxine Lewis called him to her office, where she tore up the $750-per-week contract and gave him a new one for $1,500 per week. Later he would sign a 10-year contract with the hotel at an even higher salary.

In 1947, Liberace made a return engagement at the Last Frontier and, as usual, the audience loved him. After the show, he milled in the casino with the crowd, chatting and signing autographs. As Liberace biographer Bob Thomas tells the story, Liberace felt a hand grip his arm and a gruff voice say, "Hey, kid, I want to talk to you." Liberace protested and moved away. The man followed. Liberace asked a security guard, "Who is that creep over there, the one who looks like a gangster?"

"He is a gangster," said the guard. "That's Bugsy Siegel."

Terrified that he had offended a known killer, Liberace went to prepare for his second show. After the performance, he received word that Siegel wanted to see him in the lobby. The Bug wasn't angry; he was just trying to steal the Last Frontier's headliner for his new Flamingo Hotel. He offered to double Liberace's $2,000-per-week salary.

"A classy act like you should be playing the Flamingo, not this cheesy dump," said Siegel, who then left Liberace to fret over whether to accept the offer and insult his current benefactor, or to refuse and risk an abrupt end to his career. The problem solved itself a few months later when

Siegel was shot dead in his girlfriend's home in Beverly Hills, California.

Liberace's public persona, that of an effeminate mama's boy, often brought caustic comments. At a concert in San Francisco, he responded to his detractors with characteristic wit: "I don't mind the bad reviews, but [my brother] George cries all the way to the bank."

The question of Liberace's sexual orientation can still start an argument. But it is fairly certain that he was, indeed, gay. "In fact," wrote Thomas, "Liberace was confused about his sexual identity." Thomas explains that Liberace's first sexual encounter, with a female blues singer who practically raped him in a car, had "obliterated any boyish notions he had about romance."

Aside from the occasional one-night stand, Liberace seems not to have had a regular gay partner, at least in his early days. Publicly, he steadfastly maintained that he was just waiting for the right woman to come along, and even had some high-profile courtships to quell the rumors. His most devoted fans, middle-aged and elderly females, were, in his mind, the group most likely to desert him if he stepped out of the closet.

In the fall of 1956, Liberace toured Great Britain. Adoring crowds of women swarmed him at every stop, and groups of male homophobes screamed things such as "Queer go home" and "Send the fairy back to the States."

A scribe for the tabloid *Daily Mirror*, William Connor, writing under the name "Cassandra," wrote perhaps one of the nastiest reviews ever suffered by Liberace, called him "the biggest sentimental vomit of all time," and went on to describe him as "this deadly, winking, sniggering, snuggling, chromium-plated, scent-impregnated, luminous, quivering, giggling, fruit-flavored, mincing, ice-covered heap of mother love."

It was that crack about "fruit-flavored" that prompted Liberace to sue the paper for libel, and caused him to bluster: "If ... my appearances didn't depend on my hands, I would knock Cassandra's teeth down his throat. And I ain't kidding." The British High Court ruled in

Liberace's favor, and a jury later awarded him $22,400 in damages.

But by the late 1950s, Liberace was letting his guard down more, inviting young men to his homes in Malibu, Palm Springs, and Las Vegas. While few of his business associates ever recalled seeing him in the company of a male paramour, George Liberace knew all too well of Lee's secret dalliances. One day, he confronted his younger brother. "Goddamm it, Lee," he said. "How can you keep saying in public and in courtrooms that you're not a homosexual and then hang out in the Springs with a bunch of faggots? You're gonna get nailed someday."

Furious, Liberace fired him, then rehired him under pressure from their mother, who boycotted Lee's concerts until the brothers reconciled. However, according to Thomas, it would be many years before they were friends again.

In the early 1980s Liberace hired an 18-year-old named Scott Thorsen as his private, live-in chauffeur, bodyguard, and secretary. In 1982, Liberace had Thorsen bodily ejected from the house, ostensibly because of drug use and because he had made a death threat against the entertainer.

Thorsen filed suit for palimony, asking for $380 million and claiming that part of his initial agreement with Liberace had been that sex would be part of his job description. Thorsen asserted that since he had been Liberace's de facto spouse, he was entitled to half of his assets. After some lurid testimony, a few spicy tabloid articles, and some unnerving interviews by the media, a California judge ruled in Liberace's favor, dismissing the palimony claims as being void because they were essentially a contract to perform an illegal act—prostitution. Later, the entertainer would find a more suitable companion in 19-year-old Cary James, who was content to remain quiet.

Liberace was perhaps the most ardent collector of art, antiques, and curios since William Randolph Hearst. Everywhere Liberace went, he frequented antique stores, junk shops, and garage sales. He sought out and bought rare pianos—one owned by Frederic Chopin, another by

George Gershwin. Soon, like Hearst, he had filled warehouses to their ceilings with objects he called "Happy Happys."

However, unlike Hearst, Liberace wanted to display his goodies—all of them. So he bought houses and incorporated his collections into their startlingly elaborate interior schemes. As his fortune grew, so did the number of customized houses he owned. He explained that while his profession required him to travel, he preferred to own homes in the cities where he worked most. In his life, he owned homes in Sherman Oaks, Hollywood Hills, Palm Springs, Malibu, Los Angeles, Lake Tahoe, Lake Arrowhead, and New York as well as several in Las Vegas. When he was forced to stay in a hotel room, he often redecorated it.

Always a fop, Liberace had, in his early years, appeared clad in the concert pianist's uniform—black tux and tails. When he appeared at the Hollywood Bowl in the early 1950s, he had been concerned about being visible against the black-suited orchestra and had gone onstage in a white tux. At the conclusion of the show, someone asked him what he would wear at his next appearance, in Las Vegas. Standing next to him was a woman in a gold lamé dress.

"I'll be wearing a gold lamé dinner jacket," he answered. He did. For Liberace, the fact that the audience responded to gay apparel was all he needed to know. Next came the diamond shirt studs, the multicolored tuxes, the capes and furs and boas and rhinestones and sequins, and the dashes backstage with the parting quip, "Pardon me while I slip into something more spectacular."

"I hate to admit it, but I just keep piling things on and on," he later said of his act. Las Vegas, he found, was the perfect venue for his increasingly elaborate productions.

Liberace opened at the Las Vegas Hilton in 1972 at a salary of $300,000 per week. Las Vegas became his legal residence, and he played the city about 16 weeks a year, plus four weeks in Reno and Lake Tahoe.

He purchased an unremarkable tract home, then the adjacent house, and linked them together into one mansion. He then set about giving them the Liberace touch. A reproduction of Michelangelo's ceiling painting in the Sistine Chapel loomed over his bed; an indoor lagoon had a miniature version of the "dancing waters" show that was part of his act.

He also decided that his collection of "Happy Happys," which had grown to include several rare autos, works of art, and a desk once used by Czar Nicholas II, constituted the raw material for a museum. He found a moderately-priced shopping center on East Tropicana Avenue in Las Vegas and opened his museum on Easter Sunday in 1979. Today it draws more than 100,000 visitors a year.

In August of 1986, Liberace returned to Caesars Palace for a two-week engagement. It was his final Las Vegas show. His friends, the staff, and the Caesars stagehands noticed that the normally ebullient and gregarious Liberace was quiet and spent most of his offstage time in his dressing room. His obviously deteriorating health prompted many inquiries from the media. Liberace laughed them off, explaining that he had gone on a "watermelon diet" that had made him ill.

He remained secluded in his Palm Springs home until he died February 4, 1987, at age 67. The rumors that he was dying of AIDS began even before his passing, but were all dismissed by his staff and family. His Las Vegas physician, Dr. Elias Ghanem, would not comment.

His Palm Springs physician, Dr. Ronald Daniels, filed a death certificate stating that Liberace had died of heart failure, brought on by a brain inflammation. However, before the pianist could be put to rest, his body was seized by Riverside County Coroner Raymond Carrillo and autopsied. The coroner announced that Liberace had indeed been carrying the HIV virus.

Liberace was buried in a 6-foot-tall tomb at Forest Lawn Memorial Park in the Hollywood Hills. The tomb stands between a pair of flowering pear trees trimmed to resemble candelabra. ♫

One of the most widely distributed publicity photos ever to come out of Las Vegas was of Liberace in his red, white, and blue "hot pants" ensemble. Caesars Palace, May 1971.
(Las Vegas News Bureau)

A snappy dresser even in high school, Liberace (far right) posed for this photo with his band, "The Mixers," in the late 1930s.
(Liberace Museum)

H.M. "Hank" Greenspun (1909–1989)

"Every time they tried to close a door, he kicked it down. If somebody hadn't done that—and people capable of doing it were rare—we would not have had the second generation of builders, the Steve Wynns and the Kerkorians, who came here confident they would be allowed to fulfill their dreams. They would have gone somewhere else."

—Brian Greenspun
Talking about his father

A seasoned newspaperman with a strong sense of community, Hank Greenspun gave the good-old-boy system a run for its money. BY A.D. HOPKINS

Nobody who knew him was neutral about Hank Greenspun. He was hated or loved, feared or trusted, respected as a crusader or dismissed as a journalistic loose cannon, admired as an entrepreneur or advanced as an example of how not to run a business.

Greenspun was born August 27, 1909, in Brooklyn, New York. His father was a Talmudic scholar too kind and idealistic to succeed at business; his mother was a practical merchant. In his 1966 autobiography *Where I Stand*, Greenspun described what happened when a customer on his paper route refused to pay and added anti-Semitic insult to financial injury.

Mrs. Greenspun scolded her 8-year-old son: "You let him insult you? And you didn't even insult him back? What's the matter with you?" She marched Hank back to confront the customer, who hurled hot water on mother and son. But Mrs. Greenspun charged in, slapping and clawing, while the boy kicked the offender's shins. They collected the bill and an apology.

Greenspun became a lawyer but disliked it, and drifted into business before being drafted into the Army. He spent most of World War II as a captain in the ordnance corps, responsible for maintaining weapons, ammunition, and related equipment. In Northern Ireland he met Barbara Ritchie and married her in 1943.

Greenspun visited Las Vegas in 1946, ran into a college buddy, Ralph Pearl, and became his partner in *Las Vegas Life,* a weekly entertainment magazine. They lost money, so Hank took a job as publicity agent for the new Flamingo Hotel, operated by Ben "Bugsy" Siegel. When Siegel was murdered, Greenspun quit the Flamingo and became a partner in a new radio station, KRAM. Later he founded Las Vegas' CBS affiliate station, KLAS-TV, Channel 8, which he sold to Howard

Hughes in the late 1960s.

In late 1947, Greenspun was recruited by Haganah, the Jewish self-defense organization. The nation of Israel was to be re-established in 1948 as a homeland for Jews. War with the Arabs was certain.

His autobiography describes clandestine expeditions to buy artillery and rifles in Latin America, and airplane engines and machine guns from a surplus yard in Hawaii. Greenspun got caught and in 1950 pleaded guilty to violating the Neutrality Act. He was fined $10,000 but the judge, attributing the crime to noble motives, refused to sentence him to prison.

Meanwhile, the International Typographical Union, during a labor dispute with the daily *Las Vegas Review-Journal,* had launched its own competing tri-weekly newspaper. Greenspun bought it in 1950 for $1,000 down on a total purchase price of $104,000, renamed it the *Las Vegas Sun,* and turned it into a daily.

"If he hadn't done that, Las Vegas would have remained a community completely in the grip of people who … were focused on their own interests, instead of those of the community," said Brian, Greenspun's son and now editor of the *Sun.* "The good old boys didn't want competition. Every time they tried to close a door, he kicked it down. If somebody hadn't done that—and people capable of doing it were rare—we would not have had the second generation of builders, the Steve

Greenspun in Southern Nevada

POP.[1]	DECADE
n/a	pre-1900
30	1900
945	1910
2,686	1920
5,952	1930
13,937	1940
45,577	1950
123,667	1960
273,288	1970
463,087	1980
715,587	1990
1,360,000[2]	2000

■ Time spent in Southern Nev.
1 - Population figures are for greater Las Vegas area (*Source: Nevada State Data Center*).
2 - Estimate

H.M. "Hank" Greenspun chose this photo for the cover of his autobiography, **Where I Stand,** *published in 1966. The gesture and pose were typical of Greenspun who used them in making a point with a reporter or responding to threats of libel litigation.*
(Courtesy Barbara Greenspun)

Wynns and the Kerkorians, who came here confident they would be allowed to fulfill their dreams. They would have gone somewhere else."

The most famous vested interest he tackled was Nevada's U.S. Senator Pat McCarran and the political machine he used to control Nevada. Greenspun's anti-McCarran campaign escalated to include McCarran's ill-chosen ally, the red-baiting Senator Joe McCarthy of Wisconsin. When a Greenspun column predicted that McCarthy would be slain by some unfortunate McCarthy had ruined, Greenspun was indicted for publishing and mailing matter "tending to incite murder or assassination." He was acquitted.

Greenspun's newspaper influenced political campaigns with devastating exposés. In 1954, Greenspun accused Clark County Sheriff Glen Jones of having a financial interest in a brothel. Jones sued, so Greenspun hired an undercover agent to gather defense evidence by posing as a mobster trying to buy the brothel and the protection of Nevada politicians. Secretly recorded conversations touched on names more important than the sheriff's. Greenspun published the most damaging implications. The sheriff withdrew his libel suit, and Lieutenant Governor Cliff Jones resigned as Democratic national committeeman for Nevada and never again held an important public office.

The *Las Vegas Sun* lost much of its youthful energy when fire destroyed the *Sun's* offices and production plant in November 1963. Investigators blamed spontaneous combustion, but Greenspun suspected arson by labor racketeer Tom Hanley, who at the time was embroiled in a fight with the newspaper. Hanley died a convict after murdering a union boss.

By the mid-1970s hiring and salary freezes limited the *Sun's* reporting staff. There weren't enough typewriters for even those few, and stories missed deadline each day because reporters had to wait for a typewriter. Used office typewriters in perfect condition sold for $25 at the time. Greenspun's widow, Barbara, who succeeded her late husband as publisher, said earlier this year, "We didn't have the $25. In those days nobody was paying their advertising bills. I used to go down … to collect $5 at a time." In the same era, however, visitors in Greenspun's office could admire the unusual paperweights on his desk: fist-sized bars of silver bullion.

Greenspun, or his immediate family, was active in dozens of charities ranging from People for the Ethical Treatment of Animals to the Sun Summer Camp Fund, which solicits money from the public to provide camp for children who couldn't otherwise afford it. This year, said Barbara, the Greenspuns expect to send 1,000 children to camp at a total cost of $185,000, and to make up the difference out of the family pocket if they fail to raise enough money.

In the final months of his life, in 1989, Greenspun helped negotiate a joint operating agreement by which the rival *Las Vegas Review-Journal* sells the advertising for the *Sun,* prints the newspaper, and distributes it. The *Sun* retains independent editorial control and demonstrates it regularly with bitter attacks on the *Review-Journal*. In mid-1999, the *Sun* had 33,466 daily circulation to the *Review-Journal's* 156,382.

The newspaper was neglected because Greenspun had other fish to fry. For years, said Barbara, every spare dime the family had went into land investments. But much of the Greenspun fortune was based on a single, controversial land deal. The city of Henderson was surrounded by federal land and had no room to grow. Congress released thousands of acres to the city, and Greenspun asked Henderson to sell him a large share of the land. Council members who opposed the deal were hammered mercilessly by the *Henderson Home News,* which was owned by Greenspun ally Morry Zenoff.

In 1971 the council sold the most desirable land—4,720 acres lying near the upscale Paradise Valley suburb of Las Vegas—to Greenspun for $1.3 million, or about $280 an acre. The council did so largely because he promised to include the land in his proposed Green Valley development, increasing the city's tax base and establishing nearby residential areas and amenities, which would attract further development in the stagnating small town.

Instead, Greenspun sold much of that land right away, at $3,000 to $5,000 an acre, and started Green Valley in 1973 on land that he already had owned. Although Henderson had annexed this land as part of its deal with Greenspun, this meant that Green Valley became a suburb of Las Vegas, rather than of Henderson. However, Henderson did get its increased tax base and became one of the fastest-growing cities in the United States.

The Greenspuns won franchises to provide cable television to most of the Las Vegas Valley. Their company, which became known as Prime Cable, began serving Las Vegas households in 1980. The company had more than 300,000 subscribers in 1998, when Cox Communications, an Atlanta-based media group, bought an 80 percent interest for $1.3 billion.

Greenspun died of cancer in July 1989. His estate became a major benefactor of UNLV, where two institutions bear his name: The Greenspun College of Urban Affairs and the Hank Greenspun School of Communications, fitting memorials for a man who changed his city and built a fortune on the power of words. ✍

Greenspun about 1973, being interviewed by UPI Correspondent Myram Borders (far right) and a pack of TV journalists
(Las Vegas News Bureau/LVCVA)

Aftermath of the fire that destroyed the Las Vegas Sun *in 1963. Brian Greenspun said the paper continued to publish but was unable to deliver papers in a timely fashion, and as a result fell too far behind in circulation to catch up with the competing* Review-Journal.
(Las Vegas News Bureau/LVCVA)

John C. Mowbray (1918–1997)

"Don't ever be afraid to do the right thing. I always tried to do that, and no matter how many cases I decided, I've always been able to go to sleep at night."

—John C. Mowbray
As told by his son John

A man who loved to sing and was born to lead spent 25 years on the Nevada Supreme Court in an effort to make sure the state kept its promises to the people. BY A.D. HOPKINS

John Code Mowbray once found himself the military governor of a province of Korea, recently liberated from the Japanese. In the first growing season, he forced peasant farmers to withhold from market enough rice to keep themselves until the next harvest. The farmers gave the rice up reluctantly, for any rice "stored" by the Japanese had never been returned. That winter, another province, where nobody had mandated food storage, was running out of rice. One of Major Mowbray's superiors, a colonel, ordered rice to be seized from Mowbray's province and redistributed to the other.

"I can't do that," Mowbray protested. "I got this rice at the point of a bayonet with my solemn promise that it would be returned to them. My people will starve."

The colonel was unmoved. Mowbray prepared a contingency plan to defy orders and hide the rice. But he also went over the colonel's head to a general, arguing that the military government ought to keep its promise. Mowbray prevailed, but the experience left a bitter memory. He saw the farmers at the mercy of a military with god-like powers. The farmers never got to present their own arguments and could not have appealed had they lost.

Mowbray spent the rest of his life, 25 years of it on the Nevada Supreme Court, seeing that any citizen of Nevada could have his day in court.

Along the way, he helped build Southern Nevada's social safety net of privately funded charities and it's best-known parochial school.

Mowbray was born September 20, 1918, in Bradford, Illinois. He graduated from high school in mid-Depression and worked his way through college, earning a teaching credential, by waiting tables and doing odd jobs. When World War II intervened, he became an Army Air Corps pilot but was tapped to run a photo reconnaissance school in the United States and never saw combat.

After post-war service in Korea, Mowbray went to Notre Dame law school. Students there weren't permitted automobiles, and he was hitchhiking the day Kathlyn "Kax" Hammes gave him a ride. They later married and moved to Las Vegas in 1949.

Kax' father, Romy Hammes of Kankakee, Illinois, was an American success story so spectacular that *Life* magazine did articles on him in 1938 and 1946. Hammes started his career as an auto mechanic but didn't like it, and in 1917—at age 17—he became a part-time Ford salesman. By 1926 he was named the best Ford salesman in the United States; in 1929 he bought the first of five dealerships.

Hammes' other ventures included real estate development. One of Mowbray's first Las Vegas roles was helping Hammes develop the Marycrest neighborhood, which generally surrounds Bishop

Gorman High School and St. Anne's Elementary School off Maryland Parkway. Both schools were part of the neighborhood plan. Gorman became the preferred high school not only for Las Vegas' Catholic youth but also for the elite of other faiths.

Mowbray also helped found the Home of the

Three generations: The aging justice (right), his son John H., and his grandson John Tyler
(Courtesy John H. Mowbray)

Mowbray in Southern Nevada

POP.[1]	DECADE
n/a	pre-1900
30	1900
945	1910
2,686	1920
5,952	1930
13,937	1940
45,577	1950
123,667	1960
273,288	1970
463,087	1980
715,587	1990
1,360,000[2]	2000

■ Time spent in Southern Nev.
1 - Population figures are for greater Las Vegas area (*Source: Nevada State Data Center*).
2 - Estimate

Good Shepherd, a charity that served as a sort of halfway house for girls with discipline problems. Meanwhile, he had begun his legal career as a Clark County deputy district attorney.

Decades later, he still carried haunting memories of children harmed by adults. A Searchlight child's schoolteacher "told us the child came in with his face green from being beaten," Mowbray recalled. The boy was forced to do adult chores and was severely punished when they proved beyond his ability. Mowbray said he warned the judge that if the boy were left in that environment, he would not survive. "Sure enough, in about six months, this boy was trying to start a fire with kerosene and was burned all over his body." The boy died. Mowbray lobbied the Nevada Legislature and won the state's child abuse law.

In 1959, Governor Grant Sawyer appointed Mowbray to the bench of Clark County District Court. At the time, there was such a backlog that the court actually refused to accept new civil cases. Mowbray cleared the logjam by devising a "master calendar system," which his son describes as "similar to having airplanes stacked up in a holding pattern over an airport."

Mowbray was also dissatisfied with the system used to provide lawyers for indigent defendants. William Morse, who began practicing law in Las Vegas in 1950, remembers that each judge had a calendar call on Fridays: "If they needed an appointment for an indigent, the judge would look out over the courtroom and pick somebody and say, 'You're it.' You did this basically for free. I remember that George Dickerson spent literally years defending one guy, and I think he got $500."

Mowbray applied to the Ford Foundation for a grant to set up a public defender system, and he appointed young Richard Bryan, who would eventually become a U.S. Senator, as the first public defender.

The judge spent many weekends with Boy Scout Troop 108, sponsored by St. Anne's Catholic Church. "We would camp at Willow Beach, Red Rock, Mount Charleston," said John. "Sometimes we would be gathered on Friday night, and a bailiff would show up and say, 'He's still on the bench but he's still coming.'"

Once, as a patrol leader, the judge's son chewed out a patrol member in front of the others. "My dad came over and said, 'You better never do that again! You have something to say to a guy, you tell him in private.' And he said that about four times," just to let John the Younger know how it felt.

John H. and two of his three brothers became Eagle Scouts, and the judge received the Silver Beaver Award. Mowbray also served as president of City of Hope and the National Conference of Christians and Jews, and as a board member of the local YMCA.

In 1967 the Nevada Supreme Court was expanded from three to five members, and Governor Paul Laxalt appointed not only a fellow Republican, Cameron Batjer, but also Mowbray, a Democrat. At the time, Laxalt said he chose men with conservative legal philosophies.

Justice Cliff Young, who served many years with Mowbray, said he rarely let a technicality overturn a just verdict. Once, Young related, an attorney wanted to argue such a point. Mowbray responded: "Counselor, you know what that man did? He raped that little 2-year-old! Why, he oughta be taken out and shot! But let's give him a fair hearing first."

In 1991, Mowbray was one of the majority who ruled that even though Nevada companies might fire employees "at will," whatever disciplinary procedures they announced in employee handbooks were binding on employers as well.

About 1989, Mowbray had eye surgery for glaucoma, and by 1991 he no longer felt competent to drive his own car. His vision deteriorated to almost complete blindness. Even so, he accepted the post of chief justice for 1991 and 1992, but delegated liaison with the Legislature, one of the job's important duties, to Young. When Mowbray was assigned to write a legal opinion, assistants who were also attorneys looked up citations and wrote the draft under his supervision and oral editing.

Other justices began to question whether he was still carrying his load. Their concern evolved into a bitter fight, and the pressure to resign made Mowbray determined to seek re-election. His sons, however, wanted him to begin a peaceful retirement. He had planned to file for re-election on the last possible day; his son Jerry spent the day driving around with his father, purposely dawdling until he missed the deadline.

When his term expired at the end of 1992, Mowbray retired to Las Vegas, where he died on March 5, 1997. Not long before his death, his son John got him to speak, however obliquely, about the fights he had weathered on the Supreme Court.

"As we came to the end of it," recalled John, "he said, 'Don't ever be afraid to do the right thing. I always tried to do that, and no matter how many cases I decided, I've always been able to go to sleep at night.'" ✍

John C. Mowbray and Kax in a St. Patrick's Day parade
(Courtesy John H. Mowbray)

First at Notre Dame and later as an army officer, Mowbray polished his singing voice. All his life he sang at weddings, St. Patrick's Day celebrations, and anywhere else he could. His signature song was "Danny Boy."
(Courtesy John H. Mowbray)

DONN ARDEN

(1917–1994)

Splashy production numbers were nothing to the don of destruction, who pitted beauty against special-effects beasts to become Las Vegas' premier producer. **BY MICHAEL PASKEVICH**

Donn Arden didn't invent topless showgirls parading sensually wearing heavy feathered headdresses, glittering costumes, and omnipresent smiles. He was not the first in showbiz to employ quirky novelty acts, handsome lead singers, and winsome chorus dancers, then surround them with massive stage sets and mind-boggling special effects.

But the late producer was certainly the first to fuse these elements into creative, over-the-top presentations that would become known worldwide as Las Vegas showroom spectaculars. His flair for blending beauty and good old song-and-dance with amazing restagings of disasters such as the sinking of the Titanic and the 1906 San Francisco earthquake earned Arden the titles of king of the modern production show and the "Master of Disaster."

His impact is still felt today, nearly five years after his death and almost 50 years since Arden's showgirls and boys performed with headlining ventriloquist Edgar Bergen and singer Vivian Blaine at the 1950 opening of Wilbur Clark's Desert Inn. Some Donn Arden show has been running ever since.

Bally's *Jubilee!*, a bare-flesh-laden spectacle that's sunk the Titanic more than 15,000 times since it opened in 1981, is the last living testament to Arden's genius. It will no doubt be the last show of its kind in this in-creasingly high-tech era.

Arden shook up the entertainment world, not to mention American morals, when he imported an "English edition" of *Lido de Paris* to the Stardust Hotel in 1958. Bare breasts had barely been seen in America. (*Minsky's Folies* at the Dunes Hotel was the first to display such natural wonders on a Vegas stage.)

Arden changed all of that when the first topless showgirl paced across the Stardust stage displaying her breasts, as well as the sensual "showgirl walk" that Arden patented and demanded of his females. "There's a certain way a girl can walk, particularly when you're going across the stage," Arden said in a 1989 interview. "By simply twisting the foot, it swings the pelvis forward, which is suggestive and sensual. If you twist right and swing that torso, you get a revolve going in there that's just right. It isn't the way a woman should walk, necessarily, unless she's a hooker. You're selling the pelvis; that's the Arden Walk."

Arden was notorious for requiring the right kind of bodies in his spectaculars such as *Hello America, Hello, Hollywood, Hello!*, and *Hallelujah Hollywood*. "We specify no girls under 5-foot-8," Arden said. He also demanded "small and firm" breasts for his women, "tight and firm" butts on his male dancers.

Fluff LeCoque, longtime company manager of *Jubilee!* and a former covered dancer for Arden, said the producer wanted to stimulate audiences without degrading the women on display. "The nudity still carries a shock value, even today, and you can't say it's not for sexual attraction," she said. "But it's not meant to be pornographic like a strip club. What he wanted to do was beautify them, like it was a painting that had come to life."

That meant looking, dancing, or sounding just right. Arden could be brutal to would-be cast members during open auditions. "He would rant and rave all the time," recalls producer Breck Wall, "but he really knew what he was doing. He had an eye for talent, and everybody else was just wasting his time."

"I think I can be very nice, and I think I

Arden in Southern Nevada

POP.[1]	DECADE
n/a	pre-1900
30	1900
945	1910
2,686	1920
5,952	1930
13,937	1940
45,577	1950
123,667	1960
273,288	1970
463,087	1980
715,587	1990
1,360,000[2]	2000

■ Time spent in Southern Nev.
1 - Population figures are for greater Las Vegas area (*Source: Nevada State Data Center*).
2 - Estimate

In 1981, Donn Arden looked on as Fluff LeCoque, longtime company manager of Jubilee!, *cut a cake for the cast of the then-new show.*
(Las Vegas News Bureau/LVCVA)

racketeers Moe Dalitz, Morris Kleinman, and Sam Tucker when his construction funds ran low.

"I felt obliged to go," Arden would say years later. "They were 'the boys' and they paid well." The mobsters had plenty of cash to spare, allowing Arden the luxury of buying the best costumes he could come up with.

Mob carte blanche also allowed Arden to design all manner of moving, gargantuan set pieces. "He dared to do things that had never been tried on a stage before," remembered LeCoque. "Some of the things he came up with didn't seem possible." Like having a DC-9 rev its engines as it seemingly prepared for takeoff, right through the audience. Like collapsing Delilah's temple in a heap of columns.

Amazons. Waterfalls. Spaceships. Celestial goddesses. Can-can girls. Argentine gauchos. Magicians. Fred Astaire and Ginger Rogers clones. Smoke and fire. Spangles. Stand-up comics. Crooners. The show itself was the star and completely nonreliant on financially risky headliners.

Bosses wanted to give Arden a lump sum for his efforts but he always declined. "With my drinking and gambling, I never believed in that," he once said. "I'd rather have the security of a weekly paycheck."

He pushed the limits in his re-creations of famous disasters, such as the burning of the Hindenburg—with "stuntmen falling from the fly loft in flames." But if anyone complained about turning human misery into a glitzy Vegas crowd-pleaser, Arden could have cited his own experi-

ence in a disaster—the November 21, 1980, fire that raced through the MGM Grand Hotel (now Bally's), killing 87 people and injuring another 700 in the worst disaster in Las Vegas history.

Arden was nearly ready to unveil *Jubilee!*, his follow-up to the recently closed *Hallelujah Hollywood*, when the fire started. "Around 7 a.m. all hell broke loose," he recalled. "I looked out in the hall and all I saw was smoke."

He rounded up friends and attempted to escape down a stairwell, only to be turned back by a crowd coming up the other way. The entire group dashed back to Arden's suite, where he began directing them like a cast, slapping some of those turning hysterical and taking control of the group's survival effort. Rescue ladders reached only to the ninth floor, but a well-positioned ramp on one side of the burning building allowed some of the party to be lowered to safety. The rest, covering their mouths with towels soaked in vodka, eventually were led to safety by a firefighter.

The fire claimed all of Arden's scenery and costumes for *Jubilee!* It took nine months of retooling before the show finally made its debut.

Although surrounded by beautiful women his entire life, Arden never married, saying he'd been engaged maybe six times early in his dance career and now couldn't be bothered.

Arden's health began to fail in the early 1990s, and he became a less frequent visitor to Las Vegas. Years of chain-smoking and the showbiz life began to take a toll on his body. When he died November 2, 1994, at his Los Angeles home, the lights on the Strip were dimmed in memory of the 78-year-old producer. ✍

The survivors in a lifeboat pass the audience while the Titanic sinks in this re-enactment, part of the Arden-originated Jubilee! *show at Bally's, photographed in March 1998.*
(Review-Journal files)

Arden was outspoken and demanding, demonstrating to cast members exactly the moves he wanted, as in this 1965 rehearsal.
(Las Vegas News Bureau/LVCVA)

can be very mean," Arden said. "But you know within the first eight bars whether they can sing or not. Sometimes you can tell in two. And the same thing applies to dancers."

A dancer himself, Arden was earning money by the age of 9, dancing for dollars in his hometown of St. Louis, Missouri, where he was born Arlyle Arden Peterson in 1917. "I'd pick up $5 on weekends doing shows at movie theaters while I was in grammar school," he said.

The son of a railway executive and a housewife, Arden tap-danced his way through his teens and, by the age of 20, was running small dance troupes. He changed his name for showbiz effect, later adding the second "n" in Donn on counsel of a numerologist who said a nine-letter name would ensure his success.

In 1950, "the boys" who ran the clubs in Cleveland told Arden about the new property they had invested in: the Desert Inn in Las Vegas, where owner Wilbur Clark brought in former

> *"He dared to do things that had never been tried on a stage before. Some of the things he came up with didn't seem possible."*
> —Fluff LeCoque
> *Jubilee!* company manager

Irwin Molasky

(1927–)

"I built my first apartment building when I was nineteen. I was too young to get a loan; it was either forge the papers or get my father to sign for me, and he signed. I didn't know what I was doing, but it was a big success."

—Irwin Molasky

From high-rise bank buildings and hospitals to horse racing and motion pictures, the projects of this construction king continue to flourish in Las Vegas and the West. BY A.D. HOPKINS

Irwin Molasky works in a cylindrical building full of ferns, open staircases, and photos of race horses and sports stars. "It's the kind of building that ought to be in the middle of a landscaped office park," he quips. "But it's in the middle of a parking lot so our tenants can find us.

"You see plans everywhere you look," he pointed out to the visitor entering a spacious but cluttered office. "This is a construction office. A place to work."

Molasky opens a conversation by establishing immediately the central theme of his life. He builds. He works. He's been doing it since boyhood and is still going strong at 72.

Since 1951, he has done it mostly in Las Vegas. Outside those who built the most innovative Strip hotels, he has probably been Las Vegas' most significant developer. He built Las Vegas' first enclosed shopping center, the Boulevard Mall; its first modern private hospital, Sunrise Hospital and Medical Center; and its best-known office building, the Bank of America Plaza. With Las Vegas partners he built the La Costa resort near San Diego and started a successful television and motion-picture production company.

His father was an Ohio businessman who had a newspaper distribution agency and managed apartment buildings. One of the most significant facts of Molasky's childhood was attending a military high school, away from home.

"It made me independent," he explained. "So I wanted to earn my own money from then on. I spent my summers working." Because his brother-in-law was in construction, he entered the business as a teenage gofer.

Molasky attended Ohio State for a year, but decided to transfer to UCLA and moved to Southern California. "But I started construction jobs to support myself and I just never did matriculate," he said. "I did everything. Waterboy, hauled lum-

Irwin Molasky, 72 and still dreaming of new projects, shows off his latest—a high-rise luxury condominium a couple of minutes off the Strip near Flamingo Road.
(Gary Thompson/Review-Journal)

Molasky in Southern Nevada

POP.[1]	DECADE
n/a	pre-1900
30	1900
945	1910
2,686	1920
5,952	1930
13,937	1940
45,577	1950
123,667	1960
273,288	1970
463,087	1980
715,587	1990
1,360,000[2]	2000

■ Time spent in Southern Nev.
1 - Population figures are for greater Las Vegas area (*Source: Nevada State Data Center*).
2 - Estimate

ber, estimating, then I took the plunge and started design and construction.

"I built my first apartment building when I was nineteen. I was too young to get a loan; it was either forge the papers or get my father to sign for me, and he signed. I didn't know what I was doing, but it was a big success." The five-unit building still stands.

Molasky was drafted in the late 1940s, but was discharged before the Korean War. He moved to Las Vegas in 1951 to take advantage of the construction opportunities. Initially, he did small jobs, such as garage conversions and home additions. A few years later he met Merv Adelson. The son of a Beverly Hills grocer, Adelson moved to Las Vegas to start Market Town, a 24-hour market at Oakey and Las Vegas Boulevard South. They founded Paradise Development Company, which remains active today.

One of their first projects was Paradise Palms, the neighborhood bounded by Desert Inn and Flamingo roads and by Maryland Parkway and Eastern Avenue. From 1957 through 1959, said Molasky, it sold a house every day for $30,000 to $40,000.

Around 1956, said Molasky, the partners started thinking about constructing a medical building, but when they approached doctors to determine interest, "every one of them said, 'We really need a hospital.'"

The main hospital in town, explained Molasky, was run by the county and was a political football. "The doctors wanted out of the politics and also they wanted to practice with modern facilities."

The hospital was originally financed by a local savings and loan business, said Molasky, "But we ran out of money and had to take in some investors." The investors included Allard Roen and Moe Dalitz, both associated with the Desert Inn.

Sunrise opened its doors in December 1958 with 58 rooms; it now has 688 and is the largest private hospital west of Chicago, said Molasky. "We started the first heart-transplant unit, the first children's surgical unit; it has 28 surgical suites

and 1,200 doctors on the staff."

Molasky's wife, Susan, sits on the hospital board. Molasky admits a "patriarchal pride," as well as gratitude toward the hospital. "One of my granddaughters had a problem at birth and that neonatal unit saved her life."

After not doing well financially with professional hospital administrators, the hospital hired Nathan Adelson, Merv's father, who had been in the grocery business. "The doctors loved him," Molasky said. "He brought ethical business practices with him. They kept him to run it long after we sold it."

Molasky continued, "Nate Adelson died of cancer, a very inhumane death. We thought there must be a better way. We heard of a program in England, at a place called St. Christopher's, where they taught people who are dying how to live their last years in dignity. So the university gave us a lease for a dollar a year to build this kind of facility here." Nathan Adelson Hospice was born. It takes all comers, said Molasky, regardless of ability to pay.

It was also through the hospital that Molasky came into contact with the Teamsters Central States, Southeast, and Southwest Pension Fund, which provided financing for some of his future projects. "The local Teamsters, as well as the Culinary Union, wanted us to take all their members for a certain amount a month," said Molasky. "It was an early form of managed care. We needed more bed space to do this." So local Teamsters loaned $1 million to expand the hospital from 58 to 120 beds.

The Teamsters also financed the famous and notorious Rancho La Costa development near San Diego. The development loans, more than $100 million, had been made in an era when the pension fund was mob-influenced. After an investigation, Molasky said the federal authorities found nothing wrong with those loans.

Although Dalitz had conducted himself respectably since moving to Las Vegas in the 1950s, he was a former bootlegger and illegal gambler who had been publicly grilled in the U.S. Senate.

His associate Roen had pleaded guilty to securities violations in a major stock fraud case in 1962.

Dalitz and Roen were partners in developing La Costa, but inactive. Neither Merv Adelson nor Molasky, the active partners, had ever been charged with a crime. Nevertheless, *Penthouse* magazine published an article asserting that the resort had been built and frequented by gangsters. "*Penthouse* made allegations that weren't true," said Molasky.

The four partners sued for libel. After years of litigation, they won no money, but *Penthouse* issued a letter saying it did not mean to imply that Adelson and Molasky "are or were members of organized crime or criminals." The statement did not include Dalitz or Roen.

Molasky was involved in the development of most of Maryland Parkway from Sahara Avenue to Flamingo Road, including the Boulevard Mall. Opened in 1968, it was the first enclosed mall in the valley. He also developed Best on the Boulevard, a smaller shopping center just south of the Boulevard Mall, concentrating on what he calls "big box" retailers such as Best Buy and Copeland Sports. He used the same concept in 1996 at the Best In the West center at Lake Mead and Rainbow boulevards.

Around 1966, related Molasky, he and Adelson met Lee Rich, who produced TV shows for ad agencies and dreamed of producing TV specials and scheduled shows. Lorimar was born.

One of their first efforts was based on the work of a then-obscure Virginia author named Earl Hamner. "He came to us with this wonderful story about a family going through Christmas after the Depression," recalled Molasky. The story became known to millions as "The Homecoming," and spun off the enormously successful series "The Waltons."

Lorimar also produced "Eight is Enough" and the less wholesome

Artist's rendering of Molasky's planned high-rise luxury condominiums, to be built in Hughes Center on Flamingo Road near the Las Vegas Strip.
(Courtesy Irwin Molasky)

"Dallas," "Knots Landing," and "Falcon Crest." Lorimar's feature films included *Sybil, Being There,* and *An Officer and a Gentleman.*

Molasky is no longer involved with Lorimar. Adelson, who reportedly had wanted to be in the entertainment industry since his Beverly Hills childhood, became more and more associated with Hollywood; he even married Barbara Walters. Lorimar eventually merged with Time-Warner and Adelson became one of its board members. But he continued to be active in Paradise Development until this year, when Molasky bought him out. Molasky says they are still friends.

Bank America Plaza was conceived when Parry Thomas, who then headed Valley Bank,

Irwin Molasky, seen here leading the horse, has been associated with racing Thoroughbreds since his boyhood.

(Courtesy Irwin Molasky)

contacted Molasky. "He said, 'I want an image and a name to be seen for many miles around.' He wanted prestige and he wanted a modern branch downtown," remembered Molasky.

"I said, 'The only way you can get that is a high-rise.'" Parry and Molasky purposely built it as the tallest downtown building, to dominate the skyline.

"It was a giant leap of faith. It was built in 1975, and it took years to fill it up," said Molasky. "But I think it really helped economic development in downtown; I believe a lot of law firms would have migrated out without it."

Molasky and Adelson were also key figures in the development of UNLV. "Parry Thomas came to me and said if we are to have an urban university, we have to have land." The partners donated 45 acres off Flamingo Road and Maryland Parkway for the campus. "Again, he came to me and said every great university needs a foundation to help guide, to help subsidize a president and a good faculty, and I can't think of anybody better than you to start it." So Molasky started the UNLV Foundation, modeling it on foundations at other institutions.

He is still a member of the foundation, though he stepped down from the board years ago, during the administration of UNLV President Robert Maxson. "I did not like Maxson's tactics," said Molasky. He blames Maxson for escalating the conflict between athletics and academics, culminating in the resignation of coach Jerry Tarkanian.

The Molaskys became mentors to several of Tarkanian's basketball players. On a place of honor on his wall hangs a picture of Sidney Green, a former University of Nevada-Las Vegas standout and NBA player, now a coach in Florida.

Molasky's interests in sports have been more than casual. He was named as a member of the "Computer Group," a ring of sports betters investigated and unsuccessfully prosecuted by the Las Vegas Organized Crime Strike Force. Molasky was given immunity, but testified in the 1992 trial

that he bet small fortunes. In 1982, he testified, he lost $30,000 betting baseball and won $350,000 betting football.

Molasky said the prosecution resulted from the government's mistaking sophisticated bettors for bookmakers: "The government indicted ten or twelve people, mostly people I didn't even know, and they were all found innocent."

Does he still gamble?

"The biggest gamble you can get in this country is building a high-rise," he said, chuckling. "I still do that."

He has another interest that he suggests is not so much gambling, as a very expensive hobby. He owns race horses. "Racing is kind of a dying sport, but I get a thrill out of having a good horse," he said. "They're like athletes." He owns the horses in partnership with the well-known trainer, Bruce Headley. One of the horses is Kona Gold, known as the nation's fastest sprinter.

Formerly an avid golfer and tennis player, Molasky quit both sports because of back trouble. He has been married twice, first to Pepi Bookbinder, a make-up artist he met in Southern California; they were divorced in 1969. In 1973 he married Susan Frey.

With 48 years invested in Las Vegas, Molasky is still plowing his energy and resources back into the town, and does not think the phenomenon has run its course. "We have such infrastructure in this community now, billion-dollar hotels, white tigers and volcanoes, so I don't see how any other community can compete with us just because of the spread of gambling," he commented. "I don't think it will continue a 5,000-a-month growth rate forever, but I don't think it will crash. I see the city going to two million in the near future.

"The only thing that could blight that future would be slow-growth or no-growth policies some are trying to put in," Molasky continued. "Managed growth, with good architectural controls—certainly we should have that, but not slow growth or no growth. Because who's to say when the right time is to cut it off?" ✍

Ralph Lamb (1927-)

Clark County's longest-serving sheriff was the top man when the city and county
law enforcement agencies merged into the Las Vegas Metropolitan Police Department. **BY A.D. HOPKINS**

Ralph Lamb walked into the old airport on Las Vegas Boulevard, and a man he had never before seen tried to kill him.

"Shot at me three or four times, and I wasn't as far as from here to that door," said the retired lawman, gesturing at a doorway perhaps 12 feet away. "And he didn't hit me once. I hit the concrete and shot at him a couple of times, and I didn't hit *him* once. Then he was running away and I would have had to shoot him in the back, so I ran him down, tackled him. He turned out to be just a wanted guy. He must have seen me coming in, maybe saw me fix my coat to cover my gun or my badge, and assumed I was coming for him."

Lamb never actually shot anybody in a lifetime of law enforcement, he said. People called him the cowboy sheriff, but gunplay wasn't his style. Fisticuffs were. Calf roping was. And politics were.

Lamb was sheriff for 10 years, longer than any Clark County sheriff. He forged a rural department into an effective urban one, and was largely responsible for merging the sheriff's office and the Las Vegas Police Department into the single police agency dubbed Metro.

"When I went to work, there was hoods here, on the Strip, and the legitimate people mostly came later," said Lamb in a recent interview at his Las Vegas home. "Everybody wants me to write a book, but I never have said I would. The first guy to come to me on something like that was Sam Peckinpah. He said we could make a great movie and he'd get Clint Eastwood to make it. We were on our way, had it kind of in outline, when he died."

The opening scenes could have been in the Mormon farming community of Alamo, where most of the Lamb family worked on ranches. The sheriff's grandfather was killed working cattle, when a horse bucked him off. Later, Lamb's father met a similar fate. On July 4, 1938, his father was helping to put on a rodeo at Tonopah. "He

was trying to catch a runaway race horse," said Lamb. "There was a young boy on the horse. My dad rode up alongside and reached for the halter, and the runaway ran into his horse, hit right behind the saddle, and knocked it off balance. His own horse rolled right over him."

The deceased Lamb left 11 children, one so young that the father died with a telegram in his pocket announcing the boy's birth. The future sheriff was only 11. "My oldest brother, Floyd, had a ranch by then," said Lamb. "He took in me and my sister Wanda."

Floyd Lamb would become a powerful state senator and the ranch would become the substantial Buckhorn, but both were still small in those Depression years. "There were mighty few jobs around, so a couple of my brothers and I cleaned the schoolhouse, dust-mopped, what have you," said Ralph. "And my mother would preserve fruit, vegetables, beef, anything we could grow and put in a bottle. And that's how we got along."

Lamb served during World War II in the Pacific with Army intelligence. He aspired to become an FBI agent, but the family's immediate need for income put college out of the question, even with the GI Bill. So he hired on as a Clark County deputy sheriff and soon became chief of detectives.

"It was pretty exciting work," he said. "You were out there on the Strip all the time,

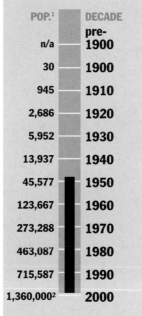

Lamb in Southern Nevada

POP.[1]	DECADE
n/a	pre-1900
30	1900
945	1910
2,686	1920
5,952	1930
13,937	1940
45,577	1950
123,667	1960
273,288	1970
463,087	1980
715,587	1990
1,360,000[2]	2000

■ Time spent in Southern Nev.
1 - Population figures are for greater Las Vegas area (*Source: Nevada State Data Center*).
2 - Estimate

In 1978 Sheriff Ralph Lamb still had his good looks, but they weren't enough to overcome a challenge by John McCarthy, who defeated him by a landslide but served only one term.

(Review-Journal files)

and mostly you dealt with guys coming here on the run. They had pulled a bank robbery, for instance, and they would come here, thinking it was an exciting place to spend their money, to kind of launder it. So we'd catch a lot of those guys.

"We knew people in all the hotels, the parking boys for instance, that we could ask, 'Is there a stranger here?' We were constantly trying to show the government we were in control of gaming," Lamb added. "That was the purpose of the work-card law." This law requires people employed in liquor and gaming operations to be fingerprinted and photographed, and to notify the sheriff's department if they move to another job.

Lamb departed the force in 1954 to form a detective agency with another ex-policeman. Their best-known client was Howard Hughes. "He was just a regular guy then," Lamb recalled. "People made him a recluse because they wouldn't leave him alone. He was getting to be so famous. But he had everybody watching each other. Once I called him from a phone booth and he said, 'Is there a guy in the phone booth next to you?' And there was. He had that guy watching me, and he was using me to check up and make sure that guy was doing it!"

Lamb ran for sheriff in 1958 against one-term incumbent Butch Leypoldt, and lost. But in 1961, when Leypoldt was named to the Nevada Gaming Control Board, the Clark County Commission appointed Lamb to the unexpired term. He won election to a full term in 1962.

Lamb modernized the department. "At first, all anybody knew was that Bugsy Siegel built the Flamingo," Lamb said. "Nobody knew who the young Turks were. So we started building an 86 file, working closely with the FBI. They would alert us that some hood was coming here, and usually we would surveil this guy awhile to see who he contacted before we ever talked to him. So that way we built up intelligence information."

When the conversation finally took place, the hood would be informed that ex-felons had to register with the sheriff. The hood was also told about the work-card law and that while the Ma-

fia and Cleveland Syndicate operated casinos, they operated at the sufferance of Lamb and other elected officials and had better confine their activities to legal ones.

Lamb became friends with a police reporter, Don Digilio, who was later promoted to managing editor of the *Review-Journal*. Lamb was a country boy who had grown up on horses; Digilio was a polished urbanite who had barely seen one. But Lamb found it hard to talk to the media, so he would try out his announcements on Digilio before making them public.

In a recent interview, Digilio remembered a 1966 discussion with Lamb about Chicago mobster Johnny Rosselli, who became posthumously famous for helping the CIA in an unsuccessful assassination plot against Cuban Premier Fidel Castro. But in December 1966 Rosselli, who had formerly visited Las Vegas without causing trouble, began making a regular circuit of Strip gambling clubs for no apparent legitimate purpose. It looked to Lamb as if Rosselli were setting up a shakedown racket. Digilio recalled, "We said, there's always a shadow hanging over the place that nobody was going to touch any of these mob guys; maybe you ought to flex your muscles."

Digilio was a body builder and former amateur wrestler who admired Lamb's willingness to get physical when necessary. But even Digilio wasn't prepared for the enthusiasm with which Lamb did so on this occasion.

Rosselli and Nicholas "Peanuts" Danolfo were sitting in a booth at the Desert Inn with Moe Dalitz, the proprietor, when Lamb sent in a rookie cop to tell Rosselli to come downtown and have that mandatory conversation with Lamb. Rosselli was 61 by then, but he had worked for Al Capone and had once beaten a narcotics rap when the arresting officer disappeared, permanently. Rosselli told the young cop to get lost, just as Lamb had expected. The sheriff had instructed the officer to be no hero that day, so the rookie retired to the parking lot, started his engine, and waited.

Now Lamb went into the resort and pointed out to Rosselli the discourtesy he had shown an

officer. Then he grabbed Rosselli by his expensive necktie, dragged him across the table, and slapped him around a while. Danolfo started to jump in but Dalitz, spotting another officer coming up behind Danolfo to sucker-punch him, grabbed *his* necktie and bade Danolfo to resume his seat, observe, and learn. Lamb threw Rosselli into the back-seat cage of the rookie's waiting cruiser and sent him to jail, ordering the extra touch of delousing. Rosselli made bail and left town. Ten years later, his corpse was found floating in a 55-gallon oil drum off Miami.

One example was worth a thousand words, and Lamb had little further annoyance with mob misbehavior. It was even claimed, never in print but quite often, that if outlaws became too troublesome, Lamb's men would simply kill them. To that assertion Lamb said recently, "I know of no policeman, in any department anywhere, who has ever participated in a murder such as you are describing."

Well, did it help to have the reputation?

"Yes," he replied.

Lamb's administration brought in a modern crime lab, a mobile crime lab, and the city's first SWAT team, which was kept secret until one of its snipers killed a bank robber who was threatening to shoot a hostage.

Lamb grabbed Rosselli by his expensive necktie, dragged him across the table, and slapped him around a while … Lamb threw him into the back-seat cage of the rookie's waiting cruiser and sent him to jail, ordering the extra touch of delousing.

Escaping from a hardscrabble childhood on working ranches, Ralph Lamb re-created his early life's more enjoyable aspects at his suburban Las Vegas home, which is equipped with stables and a ring for calf roping. This photo was taken in the late 1980s.
(Review-Journal files)

But Lamb's most important contribution was helping to form the Metropolitan Police Department. In the early 1970s, both the Las Vegas Police Department and the Clark County Sheriff's Department struggled with jurisdictional problems. People called the wrong agency to report crimes in progress, delaying police response. Both agencies were strapped for manpower, yet used a lot of it duplicating record keeping and administrative functions.

Unlike most efforts at consolidation, the Metro legislation slid through the Nevada Legislature with ease, and Lamb ended up in charge of the joint agency. Most people attributed that to Lamb's political muscle. By then his brother Floyd was an important senator, and Ralph Lamb could count on support from at least one county commissioner, his younger brother Darwin. But Lamb gives much of the credit to the late John Moran, who was then Las Vegas chief of police and would become his undersheriff.

"It wasn't hard because Moran and I were friends," said Lamb. And even policemen on the Las Vegas Police Department could see that it would be better if the agency were run by the sheriff, Lamb added. "The Las Vegas department had several good chiefs who couldn't keep the job," said Lamb. "They'd make somebody mad and they'd get replaced. So an elected head was better."

One of Lamb's efforts at efficiency, however, helped cost him the post that seemed made for him. His innovation was called the Task Force and was an elite unit of experienced officers, hand-picked by Lamb himself. If burglars became particularly aggressive, the Task Force set up sting operations, buying stolen goods and then busting the sellers. Then the Task Force moved on to

"Everybody wants me to write a book, but I never have said I would. The first guy to come to me on something like that was Sam Peckinpah. He said we could make a great movie and he'd get Clint Eastwood to make it. We were on our way, had it kind of in outline, when he died."

—Ralph Lamb

attack some other kind of crime. It made life miserable for pimps, and when a hotel building boom brought in a new crop of hoods trying to gain a foothold in casinos, Task Force officers identified and kept track of them.

Lamb still thinks it worked like a charm. But many of his officers hated it. They regarded the Task Force as an arrogant outfit, hogging the glory and leaving the real work to everybody else.

Then there was Joe Blasko. A controversial Las Vegas officer known for beating up suspects—one died—Blasko ended up in Metro's organized crime unit after the merger. In 1978 he was accused of leaking information to mob boss Tony Spilotro, and Lamb fired him. But that sort of black eye does not quickly fade.

The longtime sheriff was also weakened by his indictment in 1977 for income tax evasion. The IRS attempted to prove that Lamb spent more money than he earned as sheriff in such activities as building a home, complete with guest house and horsemanship facilities; proving the charges would mean that Lamb had concealed income and evaded the taxes on it. And the IRS attempted to prove that certain loans, including one for $30,000 from tough casino owner Benny Binion, were never meant to be repaid and were, therefore, taxable income.

However, U.S. District Judge Roger D. Foley acquitted Lamb of all charges. Foley said the IRS had failed to prove that anybody paid for the building materials, so they probably were gifts, not subject to taxation. "Many fringe benefits come to a public official which may be accepted along with the honest discharge of duty," said Foley. Similarly, said Foley, it was up to the government to prove that Binion's loan was never re-

paid, and it failed to do so. Lamb said recently he did pay Binion back.

But Lamb was politically wounded and didn't recover. The following year he lost a bid for re-election, by a landslide, to his former vice squad commander, John McCarthy. "I wasn't paying attention to the campaign, because I was worrying about the trial," Lamb said. And he admits that his past popularity may have made him overconfident.

"I guess the public didn't think my department was too bad," he commented. "Just one term later they elected my right-hand man, John Moran, to replace the guy who replaced me." Lamb ran again in 1994, losing to Jerry Keller. "A lot of guys it devastates to lose," he said. "I never let it get to that stage with me. When I lost an election, I just went on and got a job, did something else."

Now more than 70 years old, Lamb rides every day, reads Louis L'Amour westerns, and remains too busy to wish he'd done anything different. ✍

Lamb receives guests in a tach room—equipped with plumbing, air conditioning, and a refrigerator. This is where he shows off the photos of a life that made him not merely a policeman but a celebrity.
(Review-Journal files)

THE ORGANIZER

Al Bramlet (1917–1977)

"Bramlet turned off as many people as he impressed. He was embarrassing for me when I ran for governor. He essentially put out orders that people had to vote how he told them. Well, of course people resented that and I even resented him telling them that, because I knew it would hurt me more than it helped."
—Ralph Denton

The Culinary union's powerful leader in the 1970s was found dead in the desert near Mount Potosi after refusing to pay for two car bombs he ordered that failed to blow. BY A.D. HOPKINS

In February 1977 Al Bramlet, the most powerful labor leader in Nevada, arrived at McCarran Airport after a business trip to Reno. He telephoned his daughter from the airport, telling her he had just arrived and would be home shortly. Soon afterward, Sid Wyman, an executive at the Dunes Hotel, received a telephone call from Bramlet, asking him to send $10,000 to Benny Binion, operator of the Horseshoe. The cash would be used for a personal matter, Bramlet said.

Bramlet's car was still parked at the airport when police began looking for the boss of Culinary Workers Local 226. Three weeks later, a couple hiking in the desert west of Mount Potosi found his body.

Bramlet was a manifestation of a Nevada fact of life: Labor unions and those who control them can be remarkably important in an economy dominated by a single industry.

Restaurant and hotel workers were first organized in the 1890s, but the union did not become powerful until President Franklin Roosevelt sponsored laws that increased the bargaining power of relatively unskilled workers, allowing them to join forces with craftspeople like chefs. The National Labor Relations Act, also called the Wagner Act, guaranteed the right to strike.

Born on an Arkansas farm about 1917, Bramlet went to work as a dishwasher in Joliet, Illinois, at the age of 14. He later worked as a bar-

tender and then became a business agent for a Los Angeles bartenders local union. In 1946 Bramlet was sent to Las Vegas to help Culinary Workers Local 226, and in 1954 he became the local's secretary-treasurer.

By 1963, Bramlet had brought more than 8,000 workers into the local. *Review-Journal* columnist Jude Wanniski estimated that the city was "98 percent organized" despite a state right-to-work law, and noted that Bramlet had been able to negotiate a steady increase in wage scale and benefits.

In Las Vegas, working couples from the culi-

nary trades entered the middle class, owning homes and sending children to college. But union members were beginning to complain because Bramlet hogged the power. Political consultant Don Williams, who still holds an inactive Culinary union membership, said, "People just weren't being treated fairly. There weren't a thousand captain's jobs, only so many good cocktail jobs where they could make great tips, and only certain people could get those jobs." But efforts to replace Bramlet failed.

Bramlet was proud of getting contracts without many work stoppages. But in 1967, 12 downtown hotels were closed for six days before reaching a contract agreement. In 1970, Local 226 and Bartenders Local 165 struck the International (now the Las Vegas Hilton), the Desert Inn, and Caesars Palace. Management then locked out the unions at 13 other hotels.

"It was a showdown situation," Bramlet said later. "It had come to the point that management would no longer bargain because they didn't think we would go out." The four-day strike bought wage and benefit increases amounting to 31.5 percent over three years for 13,000 to 14,000 workers.

In 1976 the Culinary joined Musicians Local 369 and Stagehands Local 720 in striking 15 resorts for 15 days. The key issue was a management demand for a no-strike, no-lockout clause. It was replaced with a clause that required mem-

Bramlet in Southern Nevada

POP.[1]	DECADE
n/a	pre-1900
30	1900
945	1910
2,686	1920
5,952	1930
13,937	1940
45,577	1950
123,667	1960
273,288	1970
463,087	1980
715,587	1990
1,360,000[2]	2000

■ Time spent in Southern Nev.
1 - Population figures are for greater Las Vegas area (*Source: Nevada State Data Center*).
2 - Estimate

Al Bramlet went to work as a dishwasher at age 14 and rose to control the union that represents most of Las Vegas' resort workers.
(*Review-Journal files*)

bers to ignore picket lines of other unions in certain situations, such as jurisdictional disputes and organizational drives. Management had feared that Bramlet would use his Culinary union to organize casino dealers.

Newspapers editorialized that labor, and particularly the Culinary union, ran state government. However, Ralph Denton, who was active in the Democratic Party and ran for the congressional nomination in 1966, said Bramlet was not a political kingmaker. "Bramlet turned off as many people as he impressed," said Denton. "He was embarrassing for me when I ran for governor. He essentially put out orders that people had to vote how he told them. Well, of course people resented that and I even resented him telling them that, because I knew it would hurt me more than it helped."

But Bramlet was part of the power elite. "He knew them all; he was part of that group," said Irwin Molasky, a co-founder of Sunrise Hospital. "He was a guy who loved a joke, mixed well. I'd see him at charity events." In 1973, when City of Hope chose Bramlet to be honored at its annual banquet, the sponsoring committee consisted almost entirely of hotel executives.

Bramlet owned or had interests in private businesses that served the same industry that employed his members. One company cleaned casinos; another sold shelves and furniture to shops

in Strip resorts. Such cozy arrangements weren't illegal if disclosed to the National Labor Relations Board, and they resembled the practices of many Southern Nevada public officials of the time. An editorial in the *Valley Times* said Bramlet had become a millionaire this way. But after his death, his estate was officially estimated at $300,000.

Bramlet, however, could play rough. Hershel Leverton, owner of the Alpine Village Restaurant, claimed Bramlet showed up at his bar about 15 minutes before opening time one day in 1958: "Bramlet came in out of the blue and said we had 15 minutes to join or he'd put me out of business. 'Take your best shot,' I told him, and 15 minutes later 20 pickets started marching." The pickets would be there for the rest of Bramlet's life, nearly 20 years.

In the mid-1980s, the President's Commission on Organized Crime found that infiltration of Chicago-area locals had begun in the era of, and by the organization of, Al Capone. The commission received testimony that Tony Accardo personally picked Ed Hanley as the international union's president.

Bramlet was cherished by the parent union for his successes, but he was also resented for his independence. One of Hanley's major goals was bringing local health and welfare funds under the control of internationals. Such mergers had often led to abuses in various unions, and Bramlet was determined to keep Local 226 funds in Las Vegas.

After his death, one of the men convicted of murdering him testified that in 1976, one of mob enforcer Tony Spilotro's thugs told Bramlet he would be killed if necessary. To make the point, "They knocked his ass off the barstool and stomped him," said Gramby Hanley. Gramby Hanley and his father, Thomas Hanley, were unrelated to Ed Hanley.

The Las Vegas Hanleys were contract bomb planters and arsonists, and according to Gramby, Bramlet became their best customer. On the morning of January 12, 1976, a bomb blew up David's Place, a nonunion gourmet restaurant on West Charleston Boulevard near Rancho Drive. A year

later, sophisticated booby-trap bombs were discovered on the same night in autos outside the Village Pub on Koval Lane and the Starboard Tack restaurant on Atlantic Avenue. Each failed to ignite. These restaurants were also involved in labor disputes.

But according to later testimony, Bramlet balked at paying for bombs that didn't go off. So on February 24, 1977, the Hanleys and Eugene Vaughan waited for Bramlet in the parking lot of McCarran Airport. Bramlet had a permit to carry a .357-caliber revolver, but federal laws and the airport metal detectors meant that he would be unarmed upon arrival after a business trip to Reno. As Bramlet walked toward his car, Vaughan later testified, Gramby pointed a pistol at him and ordered, "Get in the van or I'll kill you right here." Bramlet was handcuffed and gagged with duct tape.

"You've got to come up with some money or we're all going to prison," Tom Hanley told Bramlet. So the group drove to a pay telephone and Bramlet called Wyman, asking for the loan of $10,000. Then they drove back into the desert. Tom Hanley said, "Hey, Al." Bramlet turned and Hanley shot him, Vaughan said. Bramlet was shot six times in all, including once in each ear.

Vaughan spilled the story to a woman, and eventually police learned it. Gramby and Tom Hanley pleaded guilty and got life sentences without parole, while Vaughan was sentenced to less time in return for his cooperation. Gramby Hanley later disappeared into the Federal Witness Protection Program, emerging briefly in 1982 to testify before a U.S. Senate panel investigating illegal union activities.

In 1995 the international union signed a consent decree allowing a court-appointed monitor, the former chief of the Justice Department's organized crime and racketeering unit, to oversee union activities. Four key International officers resigned about the same time, and in 1998 Ed Hanley stepped down. ✍

The 1984 contract talks, after Bramlet's death, resulted in a valleywide strike against major resorts. Here strikers and police tangle in front of the Flamingo Hilton.
(Review-Journal file)

At the height of his power, Al Bramlet drove a Lincoln past a shoulder-to-shoulder picket line in front of Caesars Palace.
(Review-Journal files)

OTTO RAVENHOLT (1927–)

Clark County's unassuming chief health officer focused only on the public's needs, not the political infighting, in his quest to improve the quality of life on all levels. **BY K. J. EVANS**

"I remember one bell captain, in his uniform and all. He'd been sitting in a chair, looking out the open window with his feet up on the sill. The chair had tipped back onto the floor, and he's sitting in this chair with his toes sticking up, dead. And that was the case with 10 to 20 people. They had died completely unsuspecting in those rooms."

—Otto Ravenholt
Recalling the MGM fire

One afternoon in 1982, Otto Ravenholt, chief health officer for the Clark County Health District, was talking to a reporter about contagious diseases and what the doctor had done about them in his 19 years in office. Ravenholt explained that the infant mortality rate had dropped dramatically. Tuberculosis, once common, was now rare, and venereal disease was dropping.

"I asked why the numbers were getting smaller," said Mike Green, the reporter and now a professor of history at the Community College of Southern Nevada. "He gave me detailed medical reasons for the decline of infant mortality and tuberculosis."

"What about venereal disease?" asked Green.

"The economy," answered Ravenholt.

"The economy?" asked Green, scribbling frantically.

"Yes," said Ravenholt. "You see, when the economy is bad, people don't have the money to do the things that give them VD."

Green was impressed with Ravenholt's insight and frankness, and with his longevity in the contentious world of local politics. During his 36-year tenure, Otto Ravenholt created the Clark County Health District. He also reformed the state's 19th-century mental health laws and reduced infant mortality by providing more and better prenatal and infant care for the poor. Per-

haps his greatest achievement, however, was setting very high standards for restaurant sanitation.

Otto Hakon Ravenholt was born May 17, 1927, on a farm in rural Wisconsin, one of the nine children of Ensgar and Kristine Peterson Ravenholt. After graduating from high school in 1946, Ravenholt enrolled in the University of Minnesota, working full time to pay his way.

In 1947, he enlisted in the U.S. Army, was sent to its language training school, and mastered Japanese. After his discharge in 1952, he returned to college to pursue a medical degree. In 1958, Ravenholt earned his M.D. and served his internship at the U.S. Public Health Service Hospital in Seattle.

"I reasoned that getting a medical degree and going into public health would be the kind of community thing that interested me," said Ravenholt. "All of my brothers and sisters more or less followed the public service track." Among his siblings are two nurses, two physicians, and a distinguished journalist.

In 1960, young Dr. Ravenholt was hired to head the Shawnee County Health Department in Topeka, Kansas. During his three-year tenure, he supervised the completion of the new county health department and traveled the state lecturing on health issues.

In January 1963, he met with members of the newly created Clark County Health Board for lunch under pink chandeliers at the Fremont Hotel. He wasn't in Kansas anymore—and he liked it. He was hired at a salary of $22,000 and was scheduled to start on September 1. Instead, he showed up in July to help persuade voters to approve a $1.2 million bond issue for construction of a new health center. The bond issue passed, and *Review-Journal* political columnist Jude Wanniski wrote, "Our new, exuberant County

Ravenholt in Southern Nevada

POP.[1]	DECADE
n/a	pre-1900
30	1900
945	1910
2,686	1920
5,952	1930
13,937	1940
45,577	1950
123,667	1960
273,288	1970
463,087	1980
715,587	1990
1,360,000[2]	2000

■ Time spent in Southern Nev.
1 - Population figures are for greater Las Vegas area (*Source: Nevada State Data Center*).
2 - Estimate

Dr. Otto Ravenholt, 1990
(Review-Journal files)

and kidneys, and is spread by dog urine. Ravenholt announced the outbreak and calmly reassured the worried public. However, he used the occasion to point out the need for a coordinated animal control program, which was not long in coming.

One of the biggest health issues in the Las Vegas Valley during the 1960s was air pollution. The building boom resulted in hundreds of square miles of land being denuded, and the attendant dust storms that periodically cloaked the valley were fierce and truly dangerous—dust-bowl magnitude. The solution was ridiculously simple, and Ravenholt implemented it. That is why today, whenever one sees graders leveling a new building site, there also will be a water truck or two following along, wetting the loose dirt to keep it in place.

By the early 1960s, Las Vegas' resort owners were beginning to realize that a tourism-dependant town could ill afford to give its guests food poisoning. Bad for repeat business. Ravenholt had a radical idea. What if the department employed only credentialed sanitarians and paid them a livable wage?

"There was a need for stronger sanitation control in the food facilities in the hotels," said Ravenholt. By the 1960s, he said, Las Vegas had become a dumping ground for worn-out restaurant equipment from Los Angeles. Refrigerators that didn't get cold, freezers that didn't freeze, lukewarm steam tables. Since the key to avoiding outbreaks of food poisoning is to keep foods sufficiently hot or cold, faulty equipment could make people sick. "We locked the door against used equipment being shipped into Las Vegas," said Ravenholt.

Of course, to some Strip bosses, Ravenholt

seemed a zealot, meddling in their business. In 1964, the Flamingo decided to test his resolve. An inspection of the hotel kitchen had shown it to be in deplorable condition, and Ravenholt politely asked to meet with the food and beverage manager to recite a long list of repairs and renovations that would have to be made at once. At the appointed time and place, Ravenholt and an aide were waiting when a cook and a dishwasher showed up. Neither knew why he had been sent.

The gauntlet was down, and Ravenholt didn't hesitate. It was Friday afternoon, and he sent a message to the food and beverage manager, informing him that at noon on Monday, the restaurant would be closed unless substantial progress had been made to remedy the problems. "They brought in quite a crew from Los Angeles, and they worked 24 hours a day to finish the job," said Ravenholt. "That was a milestone in terms of credibility. They knew we could literally close their operation."

In 1965, under a new state law, Ravenholt donned the hat of Clark County coroner and wore it 26 years through about 2,000 homicides. "Prior to that, there hadn't been any office of the coroner," said Ravenholt. "The justice of the peace was coroner by statute." He added, "I'm sure the most challenging test in the coroner thing came with the policy I initiated of holding inquests."

According to Ravenholt, the catalyst was the fatal shooting in 1969 of a 17-year-old black teen, Aaron Butler Jr., by North Las Vegas Police. District Attorney George Franklin instantly ruled the shooting justifiable. Ravenholt was suspicious and was further spurred to action by expressions of outrage in the press and from black leaders such

Otto Ravenholt (right), age 12, with his brother Reimert at the family home in Luck, Wisconsin, winter of 1939-40
(Courtesy Otto Ravenholt)

Ravenholt, as a young intelligence officer, meets with police chiefs in occupied Japan, 1948.
(Courtesy Otto Ravenholt)

Health Officer ... was just about the most gleeful fellow in town, kicking up his heels with great delight."

Ravenholt then went to work. "Our infant mortality rate in Clark County is 50 percent higher than it is nationally," he reported in October 1963. "Instead of 24 deaths per 1,000, we have 36 deaths per 1,000—through bad prenatal care and poor care in the first months of a child's life. There were 50 babies who died last year that could be living today if this department had been properly staffed." In the black community, the infant mortality rate was 45 per 1,000.

The city also had an alarming amount of venereal disease, but no real program for education or treatment.

Animal control was spotty, and there was no countywide licensing or inoculation system for pets. The area at the foot of Frenchman's Mountain, around the old county landfill and along Vegas Wash, was patrolled by packs of wild dogs, mostly litters of puppies dumped there and gone feral. In early 1964, a North Las Vegas veterinarian destroyed some 15 dogs owned by people living in the eastern valley. All the dogs had leptospirosis, a virulent disease that attacks the liver

Ravenholt and Clark County Commissioner Thalia Dondero celebrate the 20th birthday of the Clark County Health District, July 22, 1982.

(Review-Journal files)

Otto and Barbara Ravenholt, 1993

(Courtesy Otto Ravenholt)

as Charles Kellar, who called the shooting murder.

The police maintained that Butler reached under his jacket for what they believed was a weapon. An eyewitness claimed Butler had his hands in the air when he was shot. The weapon was a flashlight. Two days of testimony from 19 witnesses concluded that the shooting was justified.

In early January 1967, Governor-elect Paul Laxalt offered to make Ravenholt executive director of the Nevada Department of Health and Welfare. "I was flattered by the overture. But it turned out that this was a much more persistent thing than just an invitation," said Ravenholt. "For some reason, he was determined that I should be director." Laxalt persisted for several weeks, but Ravenholt had a personal reason behind his reluctance to accept the position.

In the mid-1930s, the Ravenholt family homestead had been foreclosed, and the family was evicted. The children were dispersed to various farms, homes, old hotels, and barns. Eventually, they were reunited on a rented farm. But father Ensgar Ravenholt had a long history of emotional problems, which became worse after the loss of his farm. He eventually was confined to the state mental hospital, and his young son got a firsthand look at the barbarity of the mental health system.

"Unpopular family members or those who were an embarrassment got committed in those days," said Ravenholt. "Once in, getting out was tough, because civil rights had been suspended. There was no voluntary exit."

So Ensgar Ravenholt escaped. A manhunt was organized, and the radio blared warnings about the dangerous escaped lunatic. One evening, 400 miles away, he walked across a field and greeted his sons, who persuaded him to return to the hos-

pital. With the help of his close-knit family and therapy, he recovered and spent the last 10 years of his life tending the Rose Garden in Los Angeles' Griffith Park.

Ravenholt told Laxalt he would take the job for six months. He kept his old one, and commuted between Carson City and Las Vegas. In wooing Ravenholt, Laxalt had promised to support any measure the doctor proposed.

"Nevada had no out-patient facilities for the mentally ill," Ravenholt recalled recently. "I wanted to modify the rules at the Sparks Mental Hospital and move mental illness treatment from in-patient to out-patient. We changed it to more of mental treatment than confinement."

Ravenholt was both the coroner and the head of Clark County Emergency Medical Services in November 1980, when the worst hotel fire in the city's history roared through the MGM Grand, now Bally's. He was in charge of recovering the bodies of the people who had died of burns and smoke inhalation, and of transporting about 700 who required hospitalization.

Ravenholt knew that a procession of body bags on stretchers coming out of the hotel would attract TV cameras and photographers, and he wanted to avoid that. Oddly, the problem took care of itself: "By 11 or 12 o'clock, there'd been an overload on the media, they had more than they could handle, and they were off to file stories and have something to eat." The grueling job of hand carrying the victims down from the upper stories began just after noon.

Ravenholt was amazed at what he found on the upper stories. Flames had not reached some floors, but poisonous gases from below had risen up the elevator shafts and leaked under doors. Many people were found sitting in their rooms, where they had been waiting calmly for the ruckus to pass, when they died.

"I remember one bell captain, in his uniform and all. He'd been sitting

in a chair, looking out the open window with his feet up on the sill. The chair had tipped back onto the floor, and he's sitting in this chair with his toes sticking up, dead. And that was the case with 10 to 20 people. They had died completely unsuspecting in those rooms."

As he speaks of the MGM Fire, Ravenholt sounds oddly detached. A bit of emotional detachment helps in politics, too.

"Frankly, in over 35 years in Las Vegas, politics were never a problem for me," said Ravenholt. "With all the winds that blow one way or another, the personalities that rise and fall, I never had any serious distress about the politics of Clark County and Las Vegas. I had a pretty good talent for friendships and comradeships when they elected someone, and at the same time for not getting too close to them. That's what gets you in trouble; you get tied up with one faction or another, and you become one of the strong boy's people. And you get to where you're keyed to what he wants, and the others get angry with you because you're in his pocket."

Then Ravenholt smiles, thrusts out his FDResque chin, and peers over his trifocals. "Of course," he says, "one of the best advantages you can have politically is if people underestimate your ability to play the game." ✍

Reed Whipple (1905–1986)

A public servant who was on the City Commission for two decades found his true reward in serving both mankind and the Mormon Church. **BY K.J. EVANS**

One afternoon in the spring of 1986, Reed Whipple lay down on the carpet in his den to take a nap. At age 81, it had become part of his daily routine. But after three hours, his wife Birdie went to check on him. He had died in his sleep. Quietly. At peace with himself and his God.

Meanwhile, out on the end of East Bonanza Road, the initial earthwork was under way for the foundation of what would be the Las Vegas Temple of the Church of Jesus Christ of Latter-day Saints. It was as though the Mormon leader's work on earth had concluded, and he had simply gone home to rest.

Whipple was first and foremost a religious leader. But he was also a secular leader, serving on the Las Vegas City Commission during two decades of phenomenal growth and keeping the civic ship on a straight fiscal course during a time when that wasn't an easy task.

"He was a straight, no-nonsense person, and I don't think he had any interests other than serving the people and city of Las Vegas," says former Mayor Oran Gragson. "When I was first elected [in 1959], I relied on his counsel in many matters."

Reed Whipple was born the same year as the city he would serve, 1905, in Pine Valley, in the mountains 30 miles from St. George, Utah. He was the second youngest of the 11 children of Edgar and Althea Whipple, both faithful Mormons who raised their children in the church. The alpine valley provided the family with most of its needs. Produce came from the earth, fish from the nearby creek, and wild venison from the woods. Edgar Whipple operated a sawmill, which provided a small cash income, and made the red bricks from which he fashioned the sturdy, two-story house where Reed was born.

By 1917, most of the older Whipple children had married and moved away, many to the country along the Virgin and Muddy Rivers of Southern Nevada. Father Whipple decided to do the same, and in September of that year the family set off with a wagon piled high with household goods. Driving a herd of cattle ahead, they spent seven days covering the 140 miles to Logandale, where Edgar Whipple purchased a 40-acre farm for $8,000 and planted a cash crop of cantaloupes to pay off the mortgage on the new place.

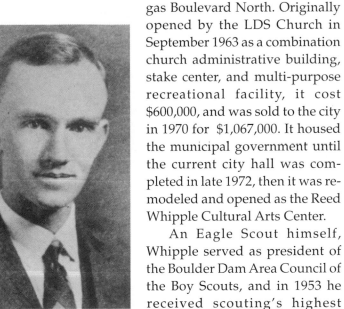

At age 17, Reed Whipple moved to Las Vegas, where he graduated from the old Clark County High School. Following a stint with the Union Pacific Railroad, the 21-year-old went to work in 1926 for First State Bank as a bookeeper at a salary of $145 per month. He would remain with the bank, after its acquisition by First National Bank, until his retirement in 1970. He reached the post of vice-president.

In 1947, Whipple was elected to his first term on the Las Vegas City Commission. Former Mayor Gragson recalls that it was Whipple who conceived the idea of municipal parking garages downtown, to keep the increasingly congested area accessible. It was also Whipple who negotiated the deal whereby the Foley Federal Building was located on Las Vegas Boulevard and Bridger Street.

The only public building bearing Whipple's name is the Reed Whipple Center at 821 Las Vegas Boulevard North. Originally opened by the LDS Church in September 1963 as a combination church administrative building, stake center, and multi-purpose recreational facility, it cost $600,000, and was sold to the city in 1970 for $1,067,000. It housed the municipal government until the current city hall was completed in late 1972, then it was remodeled and opened as the Reed Whipple Cultural Arts Center.

An Eagle Scout himself, Whipple served as president of the Boulder Dam Area Council of the Boy Scouts, and in 1953 he received scouting's highest award for adult volunteers, the Silver Beaver.

In 1955, Whipple was appointed as the city's delegate to the Clark County Fair and Recreation Board, which was finalizing plans for the Las Vegas Convention Center. Following its completion in 1959, Whipple served on the board, which

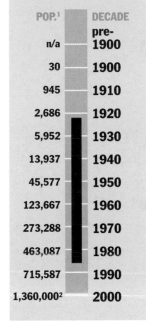

Whipple in Southern Nevada

POP.[1]	DECADE
n/a	pre-1900
30	1900
945	1910
2,686	1920
5,952	1930
13,937	1940
45,577	1950
123,667	1960
273,288	1970
463,087	1980
715,587	1990
1,360,000[2]	2000

■ Time spent in Southern Nev.
1 - Population figures are for greater Las Vegas area (*Source: Nevada State Data Center*).
2 - Estimate

Reed Whipple as a young teller at First State Bank, 1926
(*UNLV Special Collections*)

evolved into the Las Vegas Convention and Visitors Authority, until 1967.

Then, in the 1967 city commission race, Whipple was unseated by tavern owner Jim Corey. "If there was any single cause for Reed's defeat," says Gragson, "it was the widening of Maryland Parkway and Eastern Avenue." The former mayor explained that in the late 1960s, portions of those thoroughfares were narrow residential streets. Turning them into the arterials they are today upset those who owned homes along them, and it became a campaign issue. "But it had to be done," he says.

Whipple was ready to turn his full attention to church work, anyway. When Whipple arrived in 1926, Las Vegas had only one Mormon Church: the Las Vegas First Ward. It was part of the Moapa Stake. (A stake is a district of 6-10 wards and corresponds roughly to a diocese in the Roman Catholic Church.) In 1944, he was named Bishop of the First Ward. In 1946, he was chosen President of the new Las Vegas Stake and held that office until 1970, longer than any other Las Vegas Stake president before or since. During his tenure, he conducted an ambitious but necessary building program at a time when local congregations were expected to raise most, if not all, of the money for those buildings. Today, the church headquarters in Salt Lake City typically funds 100 percent of new facilities.

"The church experienced tremendous growth … during this time," Whipple wrote in 1979. "It has grown from two wards to 46." (There are currently some 120.)

In 1970, he retired from his banking job and was named president of the St. George, Utah, Temple. "Of all my church positions and service, being president of the St. George Temple was the most rewarding," said Whipple.

To the LDS faithful, the temple is the most sacred of places and is open only to members in good standing who have been recommended by their ward bishop.

Mormon doctrine holds that their church is the restored church that was originally founded by Jesus Christ. The Roman Catholic Church, and all the Protestant denominations that grew out of it, lack divine authority. This authority, they believe, was given back to church founder Joseph Smith when he founded the LDS Church in 1830. With that restoration, many sacred rites that had been lost by the other Christian churches were once again put into practice.

The most sacred rites are performed only in temples. Among those rites is the ceremony of "sealing," in which spouses and other family members pledge to follow church teachings in exchange for a promise of being reunited in the hereafter. Deceased non-Mormon family members, as well as ancestors who died before the church was founded, are baptized by proxy and can join their descendants in the highest level of Heaven.

Released from his Temple duties in 1979, Whipple returned to Las Vegas with the title of stake patriarch, a position in which, according to LDS belief, he was authorized to bestow divine blessings or guidance on people.

That same year, the *Washington County News* in St. George reported that Whipple had been named to chair a committee charged with "attracting philanthropic support for LDS programs." In fact, the primary purpose of the committee was to raise funds for the Las Vegas Temple. At the time of his death, the building fund contained some $5 million, enough to commence work.

Today, though his name is not as well known to the general public, in the Mormon culture he is legendary. "I know of no one individual," eulogized church official G. Dwayne Ence, "that can match his record of unselfishness." ♨

"He was a straight, no-nonsense person, and I don't think he had any interests other than serving the people and city of Las Vegas. When I was first elected [in 1959], I relied on his counsel in many matters."
—**Oran Gragson**
Former Las Vegas mayor

Whipple in front of the First Ward of the Church of Jesus Christ of Latter Day Saints. When he served as Bishop, beginning in 1944, there were only two Las Vegas Wards. Today, there are more than 100.

(Review-Journal files)

HOWARD HUGHES (1905–1976)

"He cleaned up the image of Las Vegas. I have had the heads of large corporate entities tell me they would never have thought of coming here before Hughes came."
—Robert A. Maheu
Hughes' right-hand man

The obsessive recluse was seen by some Nevada politicians as a cure for Las Vegas' mob-related woes in the gaming industry, but his unusual behavior was almost as embarrassing as the shadow cast by the mob. BY K.J. EVANS

The year 1966 brought Las Vegas bad news, and good news. The bad news was that mobsters were skimming Las Vegas casinos. The good news came when billionaire Howard Hughes arrived quietly and began buying casinos and real estate.

The eccentric billionaire, it was speculated, was on a mission. He would de-mob Las Vegas, make the city safe for legitimate business. In fact, mob activity did decline during Hughes' four years in Las Vegas, partly because he bought out many of the old-timers, but more because the federal government was turning up the heat.

Just by showing up, Hughes changed Las Vegas forever. If one of the richest men in the world, one of the nation's largest defense contractors, was willing to invest in Las Vegas, it must not be such a sordid, evil place after all.

"He cleaned up the image of Las Vegas," said Robert A. Maheu, who spent 13 years working for Hughes. "I have had the heads of large corporate entities tell me they would never have thought of coming here before Hughes came."

The Hughes fortune is based on a drill bit patented in 1909 by Howard Hughes Sr. and Walter Sharp. The first bit that could easily penetrate solid rock, it revolutionized oil drilling and made Hughes and Sharp rich. In 1922, Hughes' mother died; two years later, his father died. His uncle, Rupert Hughes, and the rest of his extensive fam-

ily expected the orphaned 18-year-old to finish Rice University. Instead, he dropped out of college and announced his plans to take over his father's tool company. Not content to be the majority stockholder in a family business, he bought his relatives' stock, and alienated his entire family in the process.

In Los Angeles, Hughes met an accountant and former race-car driver named Noah Dietrich

and hired him as his personal accountant in 1925. Most historians agree that it was Dietrich who transformed Hughes from a wealthy man to a billionaire. "There is no doubt about it," affirms Maheu. "He [Dietrich] was delivering Howard profits of $50 [million] to $55 million a year. Big bucks in those days."

In June 1925, Hughes married Houston socialite Ella Rice and they moved to Hollywood. He kept her isolated at home for weeks, and she returned to Houston and divorced him in 1929. His second wife, actress Jean Peters, married Hughes in Tonopah in 1957 and divorced him in 1970. Except for a brief period in 1961, they lived apart.

Meanwhile, Hughes cultivated his image as the playboy filmmaker who discovered Jean Harlow and Jane Russell and as the daredevil aviator who broke speed records in airplanes he designed. After his round-the-world flight of 1938, he had become a national hero on par with Charles Lindburgh.

In 1946, while test-piloting the XF-11 photo reconnaissance plane, Hughes crashed the plane in Beverly Hills, California. He wasn't expected to live. The crash broke nearly every bone in his body, and doctors dosed him liberally with morphine to ease his intense pain, beginning a lifelong addiction to opiates.

He had been a regular visitor to Las Vegas during the 1940s and '50s, and was seen occasion-

Hughes in Southern Nevada

POP.[1]	DECADE
n/a	pre-1900
30	1900
945	1910
2,686	1920
5,952	1930
13,937	1940
45,577	1950
123,667	1960
273,288	1970
463,087	1980
715,587	1990
1,360,000[2]	2000

■ Time spent in Southern Nev.
1 - Population figures are for greater Las Vegas area (*Source: Nevada State Data Center*)
2 - Estimate

Hughes as a young man, 1920s
(Review-Journal files)

Howard Hughes as he pictured himself. The "heroic aviator" poses in front of a Northrup Gamma, 1936.
(Review-Journal files)

ally at the tables but more often escorting a gorgeous young woman into a restaurant or showroom. In 1950, he announced that Hughes Aircraft would move from Culver City, California, to a 25,000-acre tract west of Las Vegas. He had felt oppressed since California levied an income tax in 1935. However, his key executives and technicians at Hughes Aircraft had flatly refused to be exiled to the desert, and the "Husite" property remained vacant.

By 1957, Hughes was seriously drug-addicted and in total isolation. Maheu, a former FBI special agent, was regularly taking assignments, thwarting blackmailers, spying on Hughes' girlfriends, and increasingly acting as personal emissary.

"He decided that he wanted me to become his alter ego so he would never have to make a public appearance," Maheu said. But they never met face-to-face; communications were always by phone or memo. By 1961, Maheu had moved from Washington to Los Angeles to become Hughes' surrogate. The pickings were lush. In addition to a $520,000 yearly salary, Maheu had an unlimited expense account, access to Hughes' jet, and the social status of a Saxon lord. But his king was unhappy and still wanted to move to Nevada. "I'm sick and tired of being a small fish in the big pond of Southern California," Hughes complained. "I'll be a big fish in a small pond. I want people to pay attention when I talk."

In 1966, the Desert Inn rented Hughes its entire top floor of high-roller suites, as well as the floor below, for 10 days only. Check-out time came and went, and Hughes didn't move. Moe Dalitz

and Ruby Kolod, co-owners of the Desert Inn, were furious. New Year's was looming, and the suites had been promised to high rollers. The squeeze was on Maheu. "Get the hell out of here or we'll throw your butt out," growled Kolod.

"It's your problem," Hughes told Maheu. "You work it out."

Maheu called in a favor from Teamsters Union President Jimmy Hoffa, who phoned the DI boys and asked them to leave "my friends" alone. The reprieve lasted into the new year of 1967, when Maheu told the boss he had played out his options with the DI guys. "If you want a place to sleep, you'd damned well better buy the hotel," he told Hughes.

After months of arduous log-rolling, Hughes and Dalitz agreed on a price of $13.25 million. Hughes had just received more than $546 million from the sale of all his TWA stock. The IRS taxed that money as "passive" income, at a higher rate than "active" or "working" income. After the DI purchase, Hughes discovered that the gross receipts of a casino are considered active income. Ecstatic, he called Maheu. "How many more of these toys are available?" he demanded of Maheu. "Let's buy 'em all."

"I knew that we'd never make it in the gaming business," said Maheu. "For the simple reason that he had a standing rule that we could not make a capital investment of $10,000 or more without his approval—and he never gave his approval."

Johnny Rosselli, known as the mob's "ambassador" to Las Vegas and Hollywood, approached Maheu and started naming people to executive jobs at the hotel. Maheu says he told Rosselli to go to hell. Not only was he not in bed with the mob, Maheu claimed, but he was actually working quietly to ease them out of town.

To be licensed as the operator of the Desert Inn, Hughes would have to undergo an extensive background check. He also would have to appear before the state Gaming Commission, which he had no intention of doing. Well-con-

nected Las Vegas attorney Thomas Bell was hired to handle the licensing, and he would stay on as Hughes' lobbyist in Carson City. The new governor, Paul Laxalt, persuaded the commission to allow Maheu to appear as Hughes' surrogate. "Laxalt saw Hughes as a better option than the mob," said Maheu. "He was an excellent businessman and he was totally legitimate—the kind of sugar daddy Las Vegas needed."

The next purchase was the Sands, then a Strip showplace. Dalitz was consulted and allowed that it "would be a good acquisition." Hughes paid $14.6 million for the Sands, which included 183 acres of prime real estate that would become the Howard Hughes Center. That was followed by the purchase of three more hotel casinos: The Castaways, the Silver Slipper, and the Frontier. All three properties had one thing in common: They came with enormous parcels of empty land.

He made a deal to buy the Stardust for $30.5 million, but was prevented from closing by the U.S. Securities and Exchange Commission, which was worried about Hughes holding a monopoly on Las Vegas lodging. "If we had been allowed to buy the Stardust, you wouldn't have had … all the terrible publicity from that movie *Casino*," said Maheu.

"Once he was in both [the gaming and hotel businesses], he didn't want anyone bigger than him," said Maheu. "That's why he tried to stop Kirk [Kerkorian] from building the big place. But he was not willing to do it at the expense of himself continuing to build or expanding the ground that he had. It doesn't make sense, but it happens to be the truth."

As Kerkorian's International Hotel began to rise in early 1968, so did Hughes' anxiety. He announced plans for a $100 million "Super Sands," hoping Kerkorian would flee into the desert at the news. He didn't.

Hughes saw the solution to "the Kerkorian problem" in the Landmark. The tower, a fat concrete cylinder topped with an oversized saucer, rose in the early 1960s but sat dark most of the decade. Its problem was design. It had too few rooms, too little casino space. But at 31 stories, it was slightly taller than the International. For that reason, Hughes wanted it. Maheu was ordered to pay top dollar, $17.3 million, for it. Hughes said he would personally direct planning for the grand opening. "I knew from that point on that I was in trouble," said Maheu. "He was completely incapable of making decisions."

The International was scheduled to open July 2, 1969. Maheu suggested that the Landmark open on July 1, but Hughes wanted the opening date left flexible. The International's opening act would be Barbra Streisand. Hughes' ideas bordered on fantasy. He suggested a Bob Hope-Bing Crosby reunion, or getting the Rat Pack together for a "Summit at the Landmark." He obsessed endlessly over the guest list, which made dozens of trips from Hughes' suite to Maheu's office but was never approved. "I had to go ahead and make the arrangements," said Maheu. "Otherwise we would have looked stupid."

Although one of the country's most generous campaign donors, Hughes was apolitical. He backed whichever candidate would do him the most good, but always spread plenty of cash among incumbents and challengers alike. "All the money came from the cage at the Silver Slipper," notes Maheu.

Howard Hughes didn't expect much for his largesse. He just wanted to control every aspect of Nevada public policy. He gave his attorney Thomas Bell a legislative shopping list. Hughes wanted to prevent dog racing from becoming legal; repeal the sales tax, as well as gasoline and cigarette taxes; stop the integration of Clark County schools; prevent communist-bloc entertainers from appearing on Nevada stages; pass a special law exempting him, Howard Hughes, from being forced to appear before any court or board, and a bill to outlaw rock festivals in Clark County. He also wanted to prohibit governmental agencies from realigning any streets without first consulting him. The list went on, but Hughes was especially wary of civil rights legislation. He was Afrophobic.

Maheu, a tennis devotee, had brought the Davis Cup championship to the Desert Inn. The event promised to fill the hotel with well-heeled guests, but on the night before the tournament, Hughes discovered that one of the contenders was tennis superstar Arthur Ashe, a black man. Hughes wanted the match canceled, fearing the Desert Inn would be invaded by "hordes of Negroes." Maheu quelled his fears, and the match went on.

But no one could quell his fear of disease and germs, perhaps his mother's most profound phobia. If young Howard sniffled or coughed, he was rushed to a doctor and lavished with attention and sympathy. Allene Gano Hughes saw every playmate as a disease carrier and discouraged her only son from socializing.

Paradoxically, Hughes wallowed in his own filth in his DI penthouse, which was never cleaned during his entire tenancy. He stored his bodily waste in jars in the closet, never sterilized his hypodermic needles, and rarely bathed, except when he "purified" himself with rubbing alcohol.

The Southern Nevada Water Project was the culmination of some 30 years of work by state leaders, and literally made it possible for Las Vegas to grow to its current dimensions by bringing water over the mountains from Lake Mead. Hughes wanted it stopped. His objection was that while Las Vegas drew water from the lake, it also discharged treated waste water back into it.

"Nevada must not offer its tourists water from a polluted, actually stinking lake," Hughes wrote. "This water is, in truth, nothing more or less than sewage, with the turds removed by a strainer so it can be pumped through a pipe." On one occasion Governor Laxalt listened politely on the telephone to a Hughes harangue and promptly dismissed the whole nutty notion.

During all his years as a recluse, there was only a handful of people who saw him personally each day. This was the so-called "Mormon Mafia," which took orders from Bill Gay, chief of Hughes' Los Angeles office. Its mission consisted of feeding Hughes occasionally and drugging him regularly.

On November 5, 1970, Hughes was carried from the Desert Inn and put on a jet for the Bahamas. It was, according to Maheu, a coup. "The reason I know is that that they tried to get me to join on two occasions," said Maheu.

In April 1976, at age 70, Hughes died ostensibly of kidney failure while aboard a plane en route to Houston. However, his dehydration, malnutrition, and the shards of broken hypodermic needles buried in his thin arms suggested other factors. "If sheer neglect qualifies as a weapon," said Maheu, "they killed him." Because no Hughes will was ruled legitimate, his empire was divided among his many cousins.

The company, now renamed Summa Corporation, finally began to show a profit. In 1996, the old Husite property was renamed for Hughes' grandmother, Jean Amelia Summerlin. ✍

Robert A. Maheu, Hughes "alter ego," in November 1968
(Review-Journal files)

Hughes answers questions before a U.S. Senate Investigating Committee looking into Hughes Aircraft's military contracts, late 1940s. The tycoon had been summoned to explain why he had failed to deliver aircraft on time and within budget. The honest answer was that he meddled with his aircraft company so much that it was dysfunctional. Only later, when he started a second aircraft company and vowed a hands-off management policy, did he become a successful defense contractor.
(Review-Journal files)

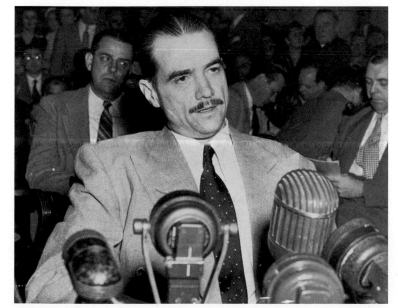

Fred Smith (1934–)

"It [Mister] was all I ever called him. It wasn't anything he demanded. It was just a respect thing. Don Reynolds was an awesome person. He came up from nothing. He had built a very strong base and because of timing I happened to be there when the growth took place."

—Fred Smith
Speaking of Don Reynolds

As a young newspaper advertising executive, he took a gamble on a place called Las Vegas and a man named Don Reynolds, and helped that man build a media empire. BY ED VOGEL

As a 27-year-old newspaper advertising executive in Fort Smith, Arkansas, Fred W. Smith was not sure what to do when he received a call asking him to become general manager of the *Las Vegas Review-Journal*.

Las Vegas in that year of 1961 was not the most glittering place in the world. It was Sin City in the eyes of many people from America's Bible Belt. What Smith really wanted was the managership of the much bigger *Southwest Times-Record* in his hometown of Fort Smith. And he was thinking about tying the knot with a local girl. Las Vegas was a longshot, but Smith took the gamble.

"It certainly was different than Arkansas," says Smith about his journey into the netherworld of Las Vegas. "I don't know if I looked at it as Sin City. But I knew if I didn't take the job, I wouldn't get another opportunity."

Now 65, Smith figures he made the right decision. Largely because of Smith's business acumen, the Donrey Media Group became a billion-dollar enterprise with 52 daily newspapers and five cable companies at its peak in the late 1980s, along with television and radio stations and outdoor advertising companies.

By 1966, he'd become vice president of Donrey's western operations. Then in 1973, he became executive vice president and chief oper-

ating officer. In 1987 he was appointed president of the company and in 1990 he became chairman.

The *Review-Journal* remains the largest newspaper in the Donrey chain. Smith's work made his boss, Donald W. Reynolds, the richest man in Nevada. And to the day Reynolds died in 1993, Smith called him "Mister," rather than by his first name.

"It was all I ever called him," Smith said. "It wasn't anything he demanded. It was just a respect thing. Don Reynolds was an awesome person. He came up from nothing. He had built a very strong base and because of timing I happened to be there when the growth took place."

That Reynolds found a Nevada niche also was a matter of luck. Oklahoma-reared, Reynolds owned a couple of newspapers in his home state and Arkansas when he made a trip to Pasadena, California, and the Rose Bowl game on New Year's Day 1949. While on his football excursion, he intended to look for a paper or two in California. Reynolds secured a complimentary ticket to the game from the Associated Press and happened to take a seat next to Al Cahlan, editor of the *Review-Journal*. Cahlan also was an AP guest at the game.

"They got to talking," Smith said. "Al Cahlan said, 'Have you considered Ne-

vada?'"

Within a few months, Reynolds bought controlling interest in the *Review-Journal*, circulation 7,000, from the Frank Garside family. He bought out the remaining partner, Cahlan, in 1960. That was the start of Reynolds' Silver State empire, which eventually consisted of four newspapers, two television stations, two outdoor advertising companies, and several radio stations.

Today Smith and his wife, Mary, look out at the clear blue skies over Lake Tahoe from their summer home along Incline Village's exclusive Lakeshore Boulevard. Their primary home re-

Fred Smith looks back at his years with the Donrey Media Group and his future with the Donrey Foundation at his home in Incline Village.

(Cathleen Allison/Review-Journal)

Smith in Southern Nevada

POP.[1]	DECADE
n/a	pre-1900
30	1900
945	1910
2,686	1920
5,952	1930
13,937	1940
45,577	1950
123,667	1960
273,288	1970
463,087	1980
715,587	1990
1,360,000[2]	2000

■ Time spent in Southern Nev.
1 - Population figures are for greater Las Vegas area (*Source: Nevada State Data Center*).
2 - Estimate

mains in Las Vegas, where two of their three children live. The other child is their Incline Village neighbor.

He retired from Donrey completely three years ago. Arkansas businessman Jackson Stephens, a Smith friend, bought Donrey after Reynolds' death.

And $804 million of the purchase price went into the Donald W. Reynolds Foundation. The foundation is fully separate and not in any part related to the Donrey Media Group and the *Review-Journal*. Smith chairs the foundation board. He has the pleasant job of spending the money Reynolds accumulated. The worthy causes include the likes of Shade Tree, a shelter for homeless women and children in Las Vegas, and the Children's Center, a facility for brain-damaged children in Bethany, Oklahoma.

"I went back there for the dedication," he said. "You come away feeling you did something good."

With a twinkle in his eye, he points out the foundation has a tough task in future years. The foundation has $1.3 billion in assets. Based on current fund growth rates, Smith expects the directors will have to give away $100 million a year for the next forty-five years before the foundation is drained.

In the last four years, the foundation has doled out $193 million in grants, much of it in Nevada. Its money built the journalism school at the University of Nevada-Reno and is building facilities at Great Basin College in Elko. A $10.4 million grant to Catholic Charities of Southern Nevada will construct a center for homeless programs in downtown Las Vegas.

"I spent forty-five years of my life making money, and now I'm giving it away," he said. "I hope I can direct giving it away intelligently. Frankly, it is easier making money than giving it away intelligently."

In all his years of building a media empire, Smith insists he never wanted the limelight. "I had no interest in it," he said. "In Las Vegas, we wanted the *Review-Journal* to be the entity. Unlike at the *Sun* where Hank Greenspun was the entity. I don't mean to criticize him, but he was bigger than the *Sun*. It wasn't my job to promote myself."

Despite the often humorous battles between the *Sun* and the *Review-Journal*, Smith contends he had a somewhat friendly relationship with Greenspun. "I knew how well we were doing and I had a pretty good idea of how badly he was doing," he said. "We talked. People weren't aware of our relationship."

Consequently in 1989, Smith and current *Sun* editor Brian Greenspun hammered out the joint operating agreement between the newspapers. Advertising, circulation, and printing functions of the two newspapers since then have been joint operations, while editorial functions remain separate.

"Hank was aware the deal was made before he died," Smith said. "Of course, it saved the *Sun*. We called him. He had been wanting to do it for twenty-five years."

Despite their control of much of the Nevada media, Smith insists he and Reynolds exerted no editorial control over their newspapers. The exception was 1964 when Reynolds decreed his chain endorse Lyndon B. Johnson, a personal friend, for president.

In the case of the powerful *Las Vegas Review-Journal,* however, Smith was one of the locals who controlled its political stances and endorsements: "Because of my association with the *Review-Journal* and the fact I lived in Las Vegas, I had more input than Bill Wright or Sherman Frederick [former publisher and current publisher of the *Review-Journal*] wished I would have, but I simply had no control. They didn't always accept my views."

Rather than influencing the politics of the state, Smith said he always campaigned for growth.

"Growth has been positive," he said. "It has allowed people like you and me to work. It is good for the community. It is good for our business." ✍

Fred Smith gets in a little putting practice on the green in the back yard of his Incline Village home.
(Cathleen Allison/Review-Journal)

Fred Smith, center, and media king Don Reynolds, at right in a pressman's paper hat, tour the Review-Journal's *new pressroom about 1985 with John Pellegren, left, an architect involved with the building's construction.*
(Review-Journal files)

Jay Sarno (1922–1984)

The man who brought fantasy and families to the Strip in the form of Caesars Palace and Circus Circus was never able to fulfill his one huge dream—building the Grandissimo. **BY A.D. HOPKINS**

You can get an argument over who started the Las Vegas Strip, but there's no question that it was Jay Sarno who changed it forever. The fast-living genius behind Caesars Palace and Circus Circus invented the fantasy resort and the modern family resort, twin ideas that have guided the past three decades of Las Vegas' growth.

He lived so large that it is difficult to exaggerate his appetites. Or, for that matter, his creativity and generosity. Unlike most casino moguls, Sarno was himself a gambler. "I would say in one evening, at craps, he could swing a quarter of a million one way or the other," said his former wife, Joyce Sarno Keys, who divorced him in 1974.

His cabinetmaker father and homemaker mother, who lived in Missouri, pinched pennies to make sure all seven of their children attended college. At the University of Missouri, Sarno set up on-campus businesses delivering laundry and selling corsages. His classmate Stanley Mallin, who would become his lifelong business partner, said Sarno was already a plunger even in those days. "He would pawn his clothes for gambling money," remembered Mallin in a 1999 interview.

Both partners served in World War II in the South Pacific. They returned to finish college, then teamed up as tile contractors in booming Miami. "If the season was good, you got paid and if it wasn't, you didn't," said Mallin. They tried their luck in Atlanta, building government-subsidized housing. The partners saw opportunity in motor hotels, but banks wouldn't loan them money.

Then, said Mallin, the partners met Teamsters boss Jimmy Hoffa and the union's money man-

ager, Allen Dorfman. The first loan Dorfman ever arranged from the Central States Pension Fund was to build the Atlanta Cabana motor hotel in 1958.

"Jimmy and Jay just hit it off," said Mallin. "They were different in some ways; Jay lived high while Jimmy lived in the same house he bought for $7,000. But they were both hard-driving guys, impulsive, almost compulsive."

It was then that Sarno met Jo Harris, an interior designer who had just finished architecture school at Georgia Tech. She asked for a job decorating the Atlanta Cabana. "Jay said, 'I like your work but if anybody is going to work for me, I expect her to be my girl,'" Harris remembered. "I said, 'I've been to Miami and I know that if I wanted to be a prostitute, I could earn six times what you're offering me.' I wanted to be hired for my ability, plus I was married. Two weeks later he called and said I wouldn't have to be his girl. He offered me $100 a day, which was all the money in the world." Harris would design for Sarno as long as he lived.

They filled the Atlanta Cabana with fountains and statues and mirrors. The operation was immediately successful, so Sarno and Mallin built Cabanas in Palo Alto, California, and in Dallas. But

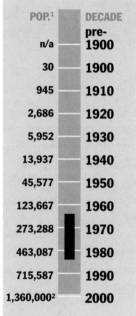
The family Sarno at a birthday party at Caesars Palace in the late 1960s. From left are Jay, September, Freddie, Jay Jr., Heidi, and Joyce. Later divorced, Joyce and Jay remained friendly and observed family occasions together as long as Jay lived.
(Courtesy Heidi Sarno Straus)

a side trip to Las Vegas changed their direction. Joyce said, "He could see the kind of money that was being exchanged, mostly going in favor of the hotels, and decided that just one big hotel with a casino would make more money than a Hilton without one."

"He was a man who loathed plain vanilla," said Sarno's daughter September. "Las Vegas hotels at that time just oozed mediocrity." They attempted to distinguish themselves by adopting names that sounded vaguely French, or vaguely Moroccan, or Western American, but the theme was skin-deep.

No one would ever say that about the hotel Sarno, Mallin, and Harris dreamed up. Caesars Palace was a fantasy world where every guest was a Caesar or a Cleopatra. "Jay insisted that people be in uniform from head to toe," said Harris. "We sketched our ideas, then brought in a wardrobe mistress, as if we were costuming a show, to execute them." Waitresses wore sexy, short, bare-shouldered togas; desk clerks wore tunics suggesting Roman military fashions. "We caught lightning in a bottle with Caesars," recalled Mallin happily. "It took right off. It was the nicest thing in Las Vegas and maybe in the country."

Caesars cost $24 million and sold in 1969 for $60 million. From the time it opened in 1966, the most successful new gambling resorts would be those that, like Caesars, carried out some escapist theme.

Meanwhile, Sarno and Mallin planned a resort embodying everyone's childhood fantasy of running away to join the circus. Circus Circus was built in the shape of a tent, and trapeze artists performed overhead. A live pink elephant "flew" around the casino on a sort of overhead tram. Sarno himself would dress up as a ringmaster and walk through the casino. By adding a midway to the casino, Sarno had

> *"He was a man who loathed plain vanilla. Las Vegas hotels at that time just oozed mediocrity."*
> —**September Sarno**
> **Daughter**

begun catering not only to families with children, but to children themselves.

None of it worked well enough to turn a profit. Mallin says the mistake was opening without hotel rooms to provide a captive casino clientele.

"About that time there was a gasoline crunch, and you could shoot a cannon down the Strip and not hit anybody," Mallin said. "We didn't weather that. We lost five or six million, so we leased it to Bill Bennett and Bill Pennington." Bennett had casino-hotel experience as an executive with Del Webb Corporation, and Pennington was his partner in a slot machine business.

"They struggled the first year, then conditions turned around, and to tell the truth, they were probably better operators than we were," said Mallin. "They exercised their option to buy after a few years, and Circus just went terrific."

Sarno was sometimes called a "front" for mob interests associated with the Teamsters. In a 1979 trial involving skimming at other casinos, gaming executive Carl Thomas testified that he had skimmed Circus Circus profits. Mallin, however, denies the Teamsters played any role except lender.

Mallin became a full-time investor. Sarno spent the rest of his life trying to raise money for a giant hotel to be called the Grandissimo. He envisioned 6,000 rooms.

The Sarnos had four children. Jay Jr. runs his own engineering firm. September is a stockbroker and senior vice president at Prudential Securities in Beverly Hills. Freddie is a stockbroker. Only Heidi Sarno Strauss remained in Las Vegas; she divides her time between her own business— a flower shop—and a family.

In the 1970s, Jay Jr. remembered, his parents brought him along to a charity auction because the items being auctioned included a number of

authentic mementos from America's space program, with which he was fascinated.

"One item was a patch from the uniform of Jack Swigert, the commander of Apollo 13, and my dad started bidding on it," said Jay Jr. "The bidding reached $10,000 and the other bidder dropped out and he got it. I thought he was just trying to show off. I asked, 'Why did you buy that?' And he said, 'To give to you.'"

With that, Sarno handed over the patch as nonchalantly as another man would present a lollipop. Jay Jr. has kept the historic patch clean and safe for nearly 30 years.

After Sarno cashed out of Circus Circus, he was simultaneously flush and frustrated at his inability to get enough financing to build the Grandissimo. His boredom led him deeper into gambling, usually at the crap tables at Caesars, where he had once ruled the empire and was still treated as royalty. Not one but two of his own brothers, the hotelman Sam and the doctor Herman, had dropped dead at these tables in the excitement of a crap game. Jay had his own fatal heart attack in a suite at the same hotel, in 1984.

Jay Sarno's influence will always be evident in Las Vegas, especially at Caesars Palace. Even today, when September comes home for a weekend in the town where she grew up, she is never an overnight guest with relatives or friends. She stays, by choice, at Caesars: "I walk through the same casino I did as a kid, and I see some of the same people." Now and then she assaults the crap tables. "It's where I grew up," she said. "I feel happy here. I feel close to my dad." ✍

Jay Sarno and his wife, Joyce, take a ride on one of Circus Circus' elephants.
(Courtesy Heidi Sarno Straus)

General R.G. "Zack" Taylor (1918–1997)

A fighter pilot turned wing commander at Nellis Air Force Base had a huge impact on the base's future as an elite training facility. **BY DICK BENOIT**

There are no streets or buildings on Nellis Air Force Base named after Major General R.G. "Zack" Taylor, whose tenure as a wing commander ran from the summer of 1966 through December 1969. Not that he would have coveted such recognition. More often than not that honor signifies a flying career cut short. Such was the fate of base namesake William Harrell Nellis, Las Vegas High School Class of 1936. Nellis met his fate two days after Christmas 1944, when he was hit by ground fire while strafing a German convoy near Bastogne, Belgium. Nellis' plane burst into flame and plunged to the ground.

Taylor also fought in Europe, and shot down six Luftwaffe aircraft to become an "ace." He fought again in Korea and trained young pilots for Vietnam. It was his understanding of military history, coupled with leadership and political savvy, that resulted in Nellis' nearly constant growth over 30 years, even as the rest of the Air Force was downsizing.

Of course, several men before and after Taylor helped shape Nellis history. Dr. Cate Willman, Air Warfare Center historian, points out figures such as Army Major David M. Schlatter, who in 1940 flew around the Southwest looking for airfields at which to establish aerial gunnery schools. He landed in Las Vegas in October.

"The Army could clearly see that war was on the horizon," said Willman. "Europe was already engulfed in World War II and we were clearly going to enter it soon.

"They needed these schools because military doctrine, then, was predicated on the ability of the bomber to defend itself against attack, which meant that it would go to a target, drop its bombs, and come home, all without any fighter escort. You needed gunners to do it," Willman said.

After Schlatter's visit, the Army leased 160 acres in Las Vegas. Lieutenant Colonel Martinus Stenseth became the first commander and set up his headquarters in the basement of the Las Vegas Post Office.

Major Richard "Moody" Suter gets credit for solving the riddle of why so many Air Force pilots were being shot down over Vietnam. In Korea, the U.S. Air Force kill-ratio over the enemy's was at least 10 to one. In Vietnam it was only half that, and pilots were also being shot out of the sky by anti-aircraft fire and surface-to-air missiles.

Suter proposed a solution—realism. That realism would become the "Red Flag" training exercises. During Red Flag, portions of the 3.1 million-acre Nellis bombing and gunnery range, become enemy territory. "Aggressor" pilots, flying specially equipped F-16C fighters, used the tactics and maneuvers of potential enemies. On the ground, missile sites seek, track, and try to electronically "shoot down" the good guys in the most realistic air-combat training ever devised.

Visionaries like Suter conceived Red Flag, and technical experts like Lieutenant Colonel Donald

Taylor in Southern Nevada

POP.[1]	DECADE
n/a	pre-1900
30	1900
945	1910
2,686	1920
5,952	1930
13,937	1940
45,577	1950
123,667	1960
273,288	1970
463,087	1980
715,587	1990
1,360,000[2]	2000

■ Time spent in Southern Nev.
1 - Population figures are for greater Las Vegas area (*Source: Nevada State Data Center*).
2 - Estimate

Captain R.G. "Zack" Taylor poses in his P-40 fighter during World War II. Four of his six aerial victories are marked by the swastikas beside his right knee; the two emblems below them denote bombing missions in the dual-use warbird.

(Courtesy Elizabeth Taylor)

Simanski made it happen. Veteran pilots swear that the air war with Iraq was won in the skies over Nevada.

America had been at war in Vietnam for two years, when Taylor took command of the 4520th Combat Crew Training Wing at Nellis. When pilots would rotate back from combat units in Southeast Asia, some of the best of the best would become Fighter Weapons School instructors at Nellis. There they would teach the best young pilots from other combat units to become experts on the fighter they flew and all the weapons it used.

One of these "best of the best" instructors was Major Jim Abraham, who specialized in the F-4 Phantom, the workhorse of the Vietnam War. Taylor had his choice of aircraft to fly while at Nellis and he naturally chose the Phantom. Abraham was assigned to assess the general's proficiency in handling the hot fighter.

"General Taylor had never been in TAC before," noted Abraham, referring to the Tactical Air Command, which specialized in tactical fighter units. "But the first time we sat down to talk fly-ing, I knew that this guy was a fighter pilot through and through. It made my job very simple."

Soon after arriving at Nellis the general wanted an orientation of the war in Vietnam. "When Taylor learned what we were do-ing he was excited that Nellis was directly in-volved in the war effort and he wanted to find out, first hand, what kinds of problems the pilots over there were facing. So we packed up and went to Vietnam," said Abraham.

Taylor and Abraham visited every major air base in Thailand and Viet-nam. "We would go meet with the wing com-manders and as soon as they realized General Taylor was a real fighter pilot who knew what they were up against, they would gather all the pilots in the wing to talk with us. The general would have me brief them on the latest muni-tions delivery techniques we were developing at Nellis. Then he would ask them what prob-lems they were facing and how could Nellis do a better job of keeping them up with the new techniques.

"We spent three weeks over there and on the way back the general began writing another brief-ing that he would give at 12th Air Force and TAC headquarters about what he learned. He wanted to make sure Air Force knew that Nellis was al-ready making a positive contribution to the war effort and was going to make more," said Abraham.

Abraham's most memorable trip with Taylor though was to the Pentagon, where the concept of a Fighter Weapons Center was being discussed. Leaders realized technology was outpacing the ability of combat units to effectively deal with it.

Taylor's 4520th Combat Crew Training Wing was seen as a core for a fighter-weapons center, but nobody had really stepped forward to sell Nellis as the home for the center.

"Zack said 'Why not Nellis?'" Abraham re-lated. "'We have the Fighter Weapons School, the best flying weather, and the ranges. What could be better than doing it here?' Zack made a point of making sure that Nevada's senators knew how important the center would be and how valuable to Nevada," said Abraham.

Years later, Taylor quipped that his strategy to bring the center to Nevada was simple: "Use a Bible, and if that doesn't work, use a Cannon." Nevada's senators, at the time, were Alan Bible and Howard Cannon.

The senators could take care of the politics, but they couldn't sell Nellis to the Air Force chain of command. That was Taylor's job. "I remember watching him preview his briefing for the base staff in his office. It was masterful. He covered all the bases and he was committed," said Abraham.

By the time Taylor briefed the Air Staff at the Pentagon there were no questions left to ask. On September 1, 1966, the Tactical Fighter Weapons Center was activated and assigned to the 12th Air Force. Before Taylor transferred from Nellis in 1969, the base payroll had nearly tripled with the addition of two wings.

Following his retirement at Scott Air Force Base, Illinois, in 1971, Taylor and his wife Eliza-beth wasted no time in returning to Las Vegas. Frank Scott, former owner of the Union Plaza, re-members giving Taylor his first Las Vegas civilian job there. Later, Scott moved him to First Western Savings, where he retired 20 years later as chairman of the board.

Taylor died on September 17, 1997, after attending one of the events commemorating the 50th Anniversary of the Air Force. ✍

Gen. R.G. "Zack" Taylor (left) and Lt. Col. James Abraham brief a visiting general on Nellis AFB operations.
(Courtesy Dr. Ronald Taylor)

Back in civilian life, Taylor remained deeply involved with Nellis and returned on many ceremonial occasions. From left are Maj. Gen. James Hildreth, who then commanded the base; Sen. Howard Cannon; Taylor; and former Las Vegas Mayor Bill Briare.
(Courtesy Sophia Hesbon)

Robert N. Broadbent (1926–   )

The man who brought McCarran International Airport into the modern age began his political career as a Boulder City councilman and went on to county and federal levels.   BY K.J. EVANS

Commissioner Broadbent is losing touch with reality," concluded *Las Vegas Sun* Publisher Hank Greenspun in a 1976 newspaper column. He referred to an incident the previous day in which a representative of the Salt Lake City-based Skagg's Drugs had come before the Clark County Liquor and Gaming Licensing Board seeking a package liquor license. Quite routine, until Commissioner Robert Broadbent asked the man, "How much money did you give to the United Way last year?"

Unprepared for such a question, the man stood silent. Spectators muttered and whispered. Commissioner Dave Canter declared the question improper and asked Broadbent if he was joking. He wasn't. Broadbent belived that while local entrepreneurs tended to be active, charitable citizens, the chain guys tended toward apathy and stinginess. Broadbent thought it was perfectly reasonable to make philanthropy a requirement for a privileged license. It was a minority view.

"Every major supermarket wanted 25 slot machines, and I voted against them for a long time," he said. "But they just kept coming and getting approved. I finally quit voting on them." It was one of the few fights Broadbent lost in an eclectic 40-year career in public service. He earned a reputation for being thoughtful, innovative and—above all—honest.

A powerful leader in the GOP, Broadbent rode the coattails of Paul Laxalt and Ronald Reagan to Washington in 1980. There, as commissioner of reclamation, he increased Nevada's share of Colorado River water and decreased the amount of money Southern Nevada pays for Hoover Dam power. He came home in 1986 to become Clark County director of aviation, completing the massive McCarran 2000 project, which gave Southern Nevada one of the nation's largest airports.

Robert N. Broadbent was born in Ely on June 19, 1926, to N.E. "Broadie" and Hope Broadbent. Broadie was mayor of Ely for 16 years and also served on the University Board of Regents and the State Pharmacy Board. Young Bob followed his father's career path, graduating from Idaho State University with a degree in pharmacology in 1950.

That year, he was hired by one of his father's former associates, who owned the Boulder City Rexall Drug. Broadbent disliked his new boss and quit after a few months. But the proprietor died not long afterward, and Broadbent's dad bought the pharmacy in 1950. He eventually sold it to his son,

who liked the friendly, chatty ambience of a small-town drug store, as well as the town itself. Here, he and his wife Sue would rear their four children, who remain in Southern Nevada.

In 1950, Boulder City was still a federal reservation, originally built as a temporary community for Hoover Dam workers. By 1955, Congress had decided to sell the many towns that had sprung up around 1930s public-works projects to the people who lived in them.

Broadbent was soon immersed in the Herculean task of converting from a federal autocracy to a small-town democracy. It was decided that the Boulder City Hospital, built and operated by the feds, was too expensive to continue operating and would be closed. Public reaction was unequivocal— keep it open. Broadbent's own business would not be helped by the closure, and he shouldered the responsibilty of finding a stable source of funding for the hospital. A longtime member of the Lion's Club, Broadbent convinced his fellow members, and several other local service clubs, to make the hospital their prime

Broadbent in Southern Nevada

POP.[1]	DECADE
n/a	pre-1900
30	1900
945	1910
2,686	1920
5,952	1930
13,937	1940
45,577	1950
123,667	1960
273,288	1970
463,087	1980
715,587	1990
1,360,000[2]	2000

■ Time spent in Southern Nev.
1 - Population figures are for greater Las Vegas area (*Source: Nevada State Data Center*).
2 - Estimate

Broadbent in the early 1960s
(Review-Journal files)

project.

"That was what really got me into politics," he recalled. "Our goal was to raise $15,000, and we took over that hospital to operate and run with a little over $16,000 in the bank. It's been moved from one location to another, and it's grown a little bit, but it's still run by the same kind of organization."

On January 4, 1960, Boulder City was officially incorporated. The city charter called for an elected five-member council, which picked one of its members as mayor. "I was elected to the first city council, and [it] picked me as the first mayor," said Broadbent. The post entitled him to a seat on the newly formed Las Vegas Convention and Visitors Authority, where he would serve 20 years, eight of those as chairman.

Broadbent remained on the Boulder City Council until 1968. By that time, the pharmacist's addiction to politics had prompted him to run for the Clark County Commission, representing Boulder City, Henderson, and North Las Vegas. He won and served 12 years.

"The county commission at that time was mostly concerned with the management of the unincorporated area of the county," said Broadbent. "They didn't have responsibility for the water district or the sanitation district or the hospital. In the administrative office, there was a county manager and he may have had three or four people, and a budget officer with a couple of people. You had a public-works department and a parks department. That's about all there was to the county government."

Broadbent emerged as a political savant; like most successful politicians, he was tactful yet persuasive. Moreover, he could actually get things done. The Silver Bowl is a good example. From the time it was announced in the summer of 1969, the proposal to build a large outdoor sports stadium incited controversy. Expensive and unneeded was how foes described it.

"There were four or five of us that really pushed to build it," said Broadbent. "We felt we needed it for the university." The stadium was completed in 1981 at a cost of $2 million, according to Broadbent. The site is in Broadbent's commission district. Coincidence? "I had as much to do with it as anybody," he says, grinning.

Just before Christmas of 1975, anonymous late-night phone calls began coming to the Broadbent house. They concerned the pending gaming license application of one Frank "Lefty" Rosenthal, an executive of the Argent Corporation, which operated the Stardust and Fremont hotels. The caller urged Broadbent to look further into Rosenthal's record. With some difficulty, Broadbent recalls, he was able to obtain a copy of the sheriff's investigation of Rosenthal, which showed him to be a convicted felon. Broadbent contacted state gaming authorities with what he thought was new information. But they already knew about Rosenthal's shady past, said Broadbent, and furthermore, they planned to license him anyway. "You can't license him; he's tied to the mob," said an incredulous Broadbent.

Broadbent asked the county to force Rosenthal, on the basis of the information in the sheriff's report, to undergo an investigation and qualify for a county gaming license. Argent Chief Executive Allen Glick publicly denounced Broadbent, who in turn denounced Glick before a meeting of the Republican Men's Club.

"I honestly and sincerely feel that organized crime has gotten into the operation of some of our resort hotels," Broadbent told the group. "If there isn't concern at the state level, there sure ought to be, and there is at the county level." He also chided his colleagues on the County Liquor and Gaming Licensing Board for being "nothing but a rubber stamp," and the sheriff's office for not telling the board what it knew about Rosenthal. All of which was being watched from Carson City.

The Nevada Gaming Control Board, said Broadbent, "got nervous and wrote me a letter and said that if I had any information, I should send it to them, and they would schedule a hearing and bring it up. I wrote a letter back and said, 'You have all the information in your files. Deal with it.'"

The FBI was concerned about Broadbent's safety. "They told me there was talk that they were going to try and get even," said Broadbent. "They issued me a gun and a permit, and I carried it for a couple of days. But if they want to get you, they'll get you."

Rosenthal eventually ended up in Nevada's "Black Book," a short list of people whose very presence in a casino is illegal. And the mob didn't get Broadbent. Paul Laxalt did.

"When he ran for the U.S. Senate in 1974, I was chairman of his campaign in Clark County,"

Robert Broadbent, Clark County director of aviation and master of all he surveyed, 1987
(Review-Journal files)

A meeting of the Reagan administration interior department. Broadbent, commissioner of reclamation, is second from right, next to Interior Secretary James Watt. The man in the foreground is assistant commissioner William Klostermeyer.

(Bureau of Reclamation files)

Bob and Sue Broadbent take a morning stroll.

(Review-Journal files)

said Broadbent. "It was a very tough race." It was not a Republican year. The Watergate affair dominated the news, and voters decimated GOP ranks in Congress. Laxalt also had the problem of Clark County, always a Democratic stronghold, which Harry Reid expected to take easily. But Broadbent's political muscle overcame the odds, and Laxalt beat Reid by a scant 611 votes. Laxalt was deeply impressed by Broadbent's performance.

By 1980, the political pendulum had swung to the right again. Ronald Reagan crushed incumbent Jimmy Carter, and Laxalt beat Democratic challenger Mary Gojack by a generous 88,351-vote margin. Reagan and Laxalt not only were ideologically matched, but also had been personal friends since Reagan was governor of California and Laxalt was governor of Nevada.

Broadbent had just been elected to his fourth term on the county commission when Laxalt invited him to Washington "to interview for a couple of jobs." One was in the commerce department, another in housing and urban development. Both jobs involved the distribution of federal grants and loans.

"I told them that I wasn't really interested in giving money away," said Broadbent. "Even if it's to local governments." Laxalt kept looking for the job that would satisfy his political debt to Broadbent.

"One night Paul called me up, and he had [Secretary of the Interior] Jim Watt on the line, and they said they wanted me to take over as commissioner of the Bureau of Reclamation," Broadbent recalled.

He would command more than 20,000 employees, administer a $1 billion budget, and earn $72,300 per year. He inherited an agency gone

moribund in the four years of the Carter administration, which had stopped work on some 71 Western water projects in progress. Broadbent finished them.

When Hoover Dam was completed in 1935, the states that received its hydroelectric power signed 50-year contracts with the Bureau of Reclamation. Broadbent was at the helm when it came time to renew the contracts. He negotiated a deal wherein the dam's electrical output would be split equally among Nevada, Arizona, and California, and the power would be sold at cost rather than at market value.

Had the bill failed, Southern Nevada power rates would today be much higher. "In some areas, rates would have doubled by now, even tripled," said Broadbent, who also pushed through a $135 million bill to increase Hoover Dam's electrical generating capacity by about 20 percent by installing newer, more efficient generators and adding four new ones.

As the nation's "Water Czar," Broadbent worked out a plan whereby Southern Nevada received credit for treated wastewater returned to Lake Mead. The effect of the return-flow credits was to increase the valley's water allotment from 300,000 acre feet per year to 480,000. "If we didn't have return-flow credits, we would be out of water right now," he said.

By early 1986, Broadbent was approaching age 60 and the Potomac pace was wearing him down. At about the same time, a feud between members of the Clark County Commission and County Aviation Director John Solomon was reaching critical mass. Things were going badly on the airport's $400 million expansion. The $9 million heating and air-conditioning system was

defective, contractors were threatening litigation to collect some $30 million still owed them, and a group of airlines had combined to sue the county over what they regarded as "arbitrary and capricious rates and charges."

County Commissioner Manny Cortez had initially called Broadbent to ask if he would be interested in the job, and Broadbent called other commissioners, as well as County Manager Pat Shalmy, who invited him to apply. Solomon was forced to resign, and Broadbent was unanimously approved.

"The board said they wanted me to end the lawsuits and the claims," recalled Broadbent. "That was the first job, and it took a couple of years to do it."

His own priority was repairing McCarran's deteriorating runways, something that had been shunted aside during the terminal expansion project. Somehow, both problems were solved at once, said Broadbent: "When we settled with the airlines, we also got approval to spend $200 million to rehabilitate and rebuild the old runways. That's when we built the second east-west runway."

Broadbent's solution to the airlines' cost complaints was to rely less on the airlines for revenue and more on peripheral sources such as advertising and concessions.

"We weren't getting hardly any federal grants," said Broadbent, who resigned the post in mid-1997. "The airport now gets $15 [million] to $20 million a year."

Those federal bucks, and the man who obtained and administered them, created the McCarran International Airport that exists today. ◢

Elvis Presley (1935–1977)

Rock 'n' roll's monarch traded his black leather jacket for a white spangled jumpsuit and ascended to the throne via the viva-Las-Vegas rocket, saving both himself and the "Entertainment Capital of the World." **BY K.J. EVANS**

Among the tons of shlocky "memorabilia" marketed after Elvis Presley died in 1977, one of the most interesting was a pair of whiskey bottles, both statues of The King. One depicted him as "The Hillbilly Cat," a knock-kneed teenager wearing pink socks and caressing an old-style microphone. The other was a full-figured man decked out in several pounds of jewelry and a white spangled jumpsuit, his arm outstretched as if throwing a punch.

When the Postal Service decided to issue an Elvis commemorative stamp, there was considerable controversy over whether the stamp should depict the 1950s teen idol or the elder entertainer, whose garish garb and bombastic stage presence would forever identify him as "The Vegas Elvis." Both stamps were ultimately issued.

For Elvis, the transition was abrupt, dramatic, and calculated. He was the first big-name rock 'n' roller to regularly headline in a Las Vegas showroom. Just in time, too, says *Review Journal* entertainment writer Mike Weatherford.

During the late '60s and early '70s, explains Weatherford, Las Vegas had a feeble grip on its claim of being "The Entertainment Capital of the World." The big stars of the '40s and '50s were losing their lustre or were retired or dead. And very few survivors—Frank Sinatra was the exception—had the drawing power to fill the entire town. In his

new, flashier incarnation, Elvis brought the national spotlight once again on Las Vegas and made it a safe place for rock 'n' rollers to recycle themselves.

Two events converged in 1969 to create "The Vegas Elvis." The first was the end of his movie career. In the span of 12 years, he had made 33 of the worst films of all time. In addition to trite scripts and one-dimensional acting, his on-screen songs were penned by some of the least talented (read "cheapest") songwriters available. It is a testament to the loyalty of his fans that all the movies were profitable. However, as a screen star, Elvis was never taken seriously. His theme song, someone joked, was "All Washed Up." By the late '60s, he was hinting to his manager, Colonel Tom Parker, that he would like to go back on the road.

The second crucial event in the evolution of "Vegas Elvis" was the opening in July 1969 of Kirk Kerkorian's 1,500-room International Hotel, the largest in the world at the time. It had three showrooms; the biggest, the Showroom Internationale, was a 2,000-seat monster. Kerkorian's vision for his new property was that of a city in itself, the first megaresort, a place with myriad entertainment choices. The hotel's general manager, Alex Shoofey, a veteran casino man whom Kerkorian had enticed from the Sahara, needed big-name entertainers. He offered to let Elvis open the hotel.

"Absolutely not," declared Parker. "We will not open under any conditions. It's much too risky. Let somebody else stick their neck out." Risky, indeed. Elvis had performed before a live audience only once in 11 years, his 1968 "Comeback Special" for NBC.

He was badly out of practice. But he looked every inch *Elvis*, encased in a skin-tight leather suit. His voice had matured, deeper

Presley in Southern Nevada

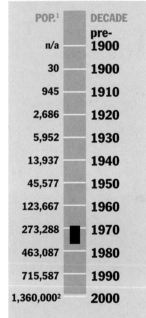

POP.[1]	DECADE
n/a	pre-1900
30	1900
945	1910
2,686	1920
5,952	1930
13,937	1940
45,577	1950
123,667	1960
273,288	1970
463,087	1980
715,587	1990
1,360,000[2]	2000

■ Time spent in Southern Nev.
1 - Population figures are for greater Las Vegas area (*Source: Nevada State Data Center*).
2 - Estimate

Elvis on stage at the International Hotel, 1969. His costume was still conservative compared to what would follow.
(Las Vegas News Bureau/LVCVA)

and more powerful than before. He sang the obligatory hit songs and closed with a new one, "If I Can Dream," his first hit record in years. The critical success of the show was due largely to its producers—Steve Binder, Bones Howe, and particularly Billy Goldenberg, who backed Elvis' vocals with a full-sized orchestra. In Las Vegas and elsewhere, he would never again perform without at least 30-piece orchestra and a legion of backup singers.

He had watched Barbra Streisand, chosen to christen the Showroom Internationale, and had shuddered. She was in fine voice, but she brought no sparkly sets, no high-stepping chorus line, no jokesters, jugglers, or tap-dancing armadillos. Talent wasn't enough.

Parker signed Elvis to a four-week contract with the International at $100,000 per week. The singer knew he had to build a new act from scratch, and he loved the challenge. But he hated being in Las Vegas. Again.

In the spring of 1956, just as Elvis' career was taking off, Parker had booked him at the New Frontier for two weeks. He headlined a program that opened with the soothing strings of the Freddie Martin Orchestra, followed by the Borscht Belt humor of Shecky Greene. Then came Elvis, a 21-year-old punk in a duck-ass hairdo, long sideburns, and eye shadow. The collar of his pink shirt turned up, he slung his guitar forward, and with a sneer began to play, no, to beat on it. He punctuated his vocals with what sounded like hiccups and lurched around the stage in a spastic fervor.

Newsweek magazine likened Elvis' presence in the show to a "jug of corn liquor at a champagne party," and said the stunned audience sat motionless, "as if he were a clinical experiment." Inside of two weeks, Elvis moved from the top to the bottom of the marquee and vowed never again to play nightclubs.

Of course, what Elvis did or did not want was irrelevant. Parker made the decisions. Parker was a showman in the mold of P.T. Barnum, a loutish, greedy, manipulative, cunning scoundrel who rarely concluded a deal without satisfying himself that his adversary had been flim-flammed in some way.

It was the Colonel who insisted that Elvis join the Army. It was the Colonel who for years forbade Elvis to marry for fear he would lose his teenybopper fans. And it was the Colonel who suddenly decided it was time for Elvis to marry his fiancée, Priscilla, with whom he had actually lived for several years. Again, the Colonel wanted to wring every molecule of positive publicity from the event. It would be in Las Vegas. The Colonel conned his old pal, Milton Prell, owner of the Aladdin, into hosting the wedding—that is, picking up the bill. The private ceremony was performed May 1, 1967, by Nevada Supreme Court Justice David Zenoff.

Elvis found the solution to his professional identity crisis in the lounge of the Flamingo Hotel in 1969. He'd been scouting showrooms and lounges, studying entertainers and audiences, looking for the raw material to craft "The Vegas Elvis." In Tom Jones, a then-unknown Welsh singer, he found the prototype. Dressed in a skin-tight tuxedo, Jones would step to the edge of the stage, and lean far, far back, to give fans a good look at the outline of his genitalia. Elvis was impressed with the response this elicited

from the middle-aged female audience. The women screamed, cried, and threw room keys at Jones' feet. Sometimes they would jump up, rip off their panties, and fling them at him. Elvis professed admiration for Jones' vocal skills, telling an aide, "Tom is the only man who has ever come anywhere close to the way I sing." In truth, it was Jone's visceral connection with the audience that wowed Elvis.

Elvis had studied karate for several years and was a second-degree black belt. He replaced the jerky undulations of his old act with the fluid movements of the martial arts. Backing The King was a 35-piece orchestra, his old five-piece rock band, and two soul and gospel groups, the Imperials and the Sweet Inspirations—50 artists in all.

Opening night at the International, July 26, 1969, was a VIP event. The music press had been flown in from New York and the rest of the country on Kirk Kerkorian's private jet. With the band blaring, Elvis took to the stage and launched into the loudest and most elaborate arrangement of "Blue Suede Shoes" ever heard. He sauntered along the stage apron, kissing one woman after another, wisecracking, passing out sweaty handkerchiefs, singing louder, moving faster, driving the energy level of the show to a goose-pimply crescendo. When the show concluded, he had won over the thirty-somethings and the media. For the second time in his life, he was an overnight superstar.

The next day, the Colonel sat down with Alex Shoofey in the showroom. Shoofey wanted Elvis for the long haul. "I'd like to draw up a new agreement with you—for five years," said Shoofey. The

Elvis at the wheel of a Cadillac during his 1956 engagement at the Last Frontier Hotel. He bombed.

(Las Vegas News Bureau/LVCVA)

Elvis and Priscilla cut their wedding cake. The ceremony was a secret one, held at the Aladdin Hotel in May 1967.

(Las Vegas News Bureau/LVCVA)

Colonel feigned disinterest but signed. For the next five years, Elvis would appear for four weeks twice a year at a salary of $125,000 per week.

Shoofey walked away amazed, calling it "the best deal ever made in this town." Even that was an understatement. Showrooms at the time were expected to lose money, which was theoretically recovered in the casino. But by the time Elvis concluded his first month-long engagement, the showroom had generated more than $2 million. It was the first time that a Las Vegas resort ever had profited from an entertainer.

So why did Colonel Tom Parker, known as one of the sharpest and greediest men in show biz, sell his hot "new" act for such a piddling sum? The answer is that Parker, a degenerate gambler, had found a home and planned to settle in. He was housed in luxury, was fed gourmet fare, and traveled in hotel limousines and planes. Best of all, he had unlimited credit in the casino, where he lost $50,000 to $75,000 nearly every night. He was the highest roller in town.

In his first two years at the International, Elvis' enthusiasm for his new career kept him happy and busy, experimenting, tweaking his act. In February 1970, perhaps inspired by fashion tips from Liberace, Elvis came onstage in the famous white jumpsuit. It was adorned with long ropes of pearls, beads, and rhinestones, as well as with a belt buckle of sufficient size to hide his burgeoning belly.

His weight gain was a symptom of a graver problem—boredom. Elvis' antidotes of choice for this malady were teenaged girls, fatty foods, and vast quantities of powerful pharmaceuticals. Dozens of pill bottles bore the names of "The Guys," old redneck pals Elvis kept on the payroll as aides. Each man wore the logo of Elvis' "Memphis Mafia," a necklace with a gold lightning bolt and the acronym "TCB" for "Take Care of Business."

"The image is one thing and the human being is another. … It's very hard to live up to an image, put it that way."
—**Elvis Presley, 1972**

While Elvis was on stage, The Guys would be doing just that, combing the hotel and environs, inviting attractive girls to join Elvis in the penthouse for an after-show party. The handfuls of pills Elvis had taken earlier usually would knock him out in minutes.

Elvis Presley's drug use probably began about the same time as his career in the 1950s. Racing from roadhouse gigs to county fairs for weeks and months on end, surviving on backseat naps, he almost certainly discovered amphetamines. A chronic insomniac plagued by nightmares, Elvis had a legitimate need for sleeping pills. The King liked his medication, as he called it, but feared and despised pot smokers, acid heads, and especially filthy lowlife junkies.

He paid a visit to President Richard Nixon in October 1970 to offer his celebrity as a weapon in the war on drugs. Stoned out of his mind, Elvis was escorted to the Oval Office, where he rambled about the scourge of drug addiction before coming to the point. He wanted the badge of a federal Drug Enforcement Administration officer, and Nixon gave him one. Elvis would always carry and treasure that badge.

Supported by dozens of pliable doctors, Elvis' periods of isolation at Graceland became longer and more frequent. Reviving him and preparing him for his two yearly Las Vegas gigs became a week-long ordeal. Elvis' increased drug use had made him more paranoid than usual. The Sharon Tate-LaBianca murders shook him badly, and he saw attackers everywhere—one night even in the International Showroom.

During a performance, a man draped a jacket across his arm, hopped up on a table, and stepped onto the stage. Security rushed him and others from the audience joined the melee. As a dogpile rose at center stage, Elvis stood safely to one side in a karate fighting stance. "Let 'em go," he yelled.

"Let 'em go." When the stage had been cleared, Elvis assured the audience that had he entered the fray, he would have "kicked their asses." The man turned out to be a porno moviemaker from Lima, Peru, who wanted to present Elvis with a jacket.

Guns, Elvis decided, were the key to security. He figured that if he armed himself and everyone around him, he would be safe. In all, Elvis had more than 250 firearms and probably gave away as many. In 1970 alone, he spent $19,792 on guns, usually on the basis of how they looked. Gold plating fired him up. So did fancy engraving and custom grips.

One night, in a drug-stoked rage, he fished an M-16 rifle from the closet, handed it to security man Red West, and ordered him to go to Los Angeles and kill Mike Stone. A famed karate master, Stone had been having an affair with Priscilla Presley since 1968.

Elvis' wife was profoundly frustrated. Lisa Marie had been conceived almost immediately after their wedding, and Elvis never touched Priscilla again. In the Elvis ethos, women who gave birth were mothers, and Elvis was appalled at the idea of carnality with such exalted creatures.

Elvis rescinded the contract on Stone the next time he got straight, much to Red's relief. But the couple divorced in October 1973. Elvis, the man who never lost, had lost. He became even crazier.

The end came on August 16, 1977, when Elvis was found dead in his bathroom. An autopsy revealed 11 different narcotics in his body, any one of which could have been lethal in a large dose. The official cause of death was listed as cardiac arrythmia. ⌀

Liberace stopped by to ham it up for the camera during Elvis' 1956 Las Vegas engagement.
(Las Vegas News Bureau/LVCVA)

Ray Chesson (1907–1990)

A *Review-Journal* writer found many of his subjects in the saloons and on the streets of town—many were unbelievable, but all were real.   **BY K.J. EVANS**

One morning in 1965, my mother was sipping a cup of coffee at the kitchen table, when she suddenly turned purple, lurched forward as if taken by a seizure, and spewed coffee violently from both nostrils. The seizure became a laughing fit that continued for a couple of minutes.

I later retrieved the soggy sheet, the *Nevadan*, the *Review-Journal*'s Sunday magazine, and read the story myself. I never again started my Sunday paper with the comics and, at age 12, I first became aware of the power of the printed word. Like scores of other young Southern Nevadans, I thus cut my literary teeth on the tales of Ray Chesson.

Dr. John Irsfeld, a UNLV English professor, later recalled, "It didn't take me long to conclude, after I arrived in Las Vegas in 1969, that Ray Chesson was the best writer around." He went on to admit that on one occasion, he "lifted" Chesson's favorite character, Bad Water Bill, and put him in one of his own novels. It didn't work.

"The truth is, I couldn't make him do what Ray Chesson could make him do," said Irsfeld.

Chesson's genius was his clarity. Each word of his prose was carefully considered, agonized over. The images and personalities that emerged were as clear as the Mojave by moonlight, as pungent as smoke from a mesquite fire. His characters, though wildly eccentric, were absolutely real and absolutely hilarious.

Chesson was able to convey a sense of place and time. It was of a place not yet civilized, but moving toward it at a good clip. Every other local writer of the time was obsessed with Southern Nevada's march to the future. Not Chesson.

His settings were the East Mojave and Colorado River country, which were straggling out of the past.

His people were on the fringes of society: drunks, wastrels, the homeless. Chesson saw them simply as free spirits, like himself. In a time when the homeless weren't yet on the political agenda, Chesson gently reminded us of their existence, their need, and their humanity.

He was similarly ahead of his time in writing and illustrating a series of articles on the wildlife of the Mojave and Great Basin deserts. This was a groundbreaking project. Nearly all Southern Nevada residents were from somewhere else, and Chesson's series introduced them to their new furred and feathered neighbors, and did so in the broad forum of a general-circulation newspaper. With his friend and editor Bill Vincent, Chesson fostered respect for the desert environment. It was an idea whose time in the sun arrived only in the late afternoon of Chesson's.

He could have been famous. Maybe even rich. But those things came at a price he wouldn't pay—the loss of his freedom.

"Once, I tried to get him to come into the office and work for the *Nevadan*," recalled former *Review-Journal* Editor Don Digilio in 1990. "He said he'd die if he had to work in the office and especially if he had to wear a necktie."

Mostly, Chesson worked in saloons, fertile fields for the astute student of human nature. When small tape recorders were introduced, he

tried using one on his normally garrulous subjects. They became quiet and wooden, so he tossed it. He even eschewed conventional note-taking, perfecting his own method. As he listened to a story, he would keep a hand in his pants pocket, scribbling notes with a stub pencil. Every so often, he would pick up his beer can and go to the restroom, translate his scratchings into longhand, and dump out about half his beer so as to maintain sobriety — and appearances.

Ray Chesson was born in 1907 in Moyock, North Carolina, and studied art for about a year, then went to work as a freelance pen-and-ink illustrator. After overhearing a couple of fellow artists boasting that they could write as well as any magazine scribe, Chesson bought a typewriter and tried his hand. His words and art appeared in *Colliers*, *Field & Stream*, and numerous other magazines, mostly the outdoor kind.

Despondent over a divorce, Chesson saw "Funeral Mountains" on a map in the 1940s and set out for Death Valley to die. But his health and spirits improved and, in 1954, he met and married Peggy Chesson, with whom he would spend the remaining 36 years of his life. Chesson died in 1990 at the age of 83, and his last *Review-Journal* byline had been 13 years before that. Yet to this day, the *Review-Journal* occasionally gets phone calls asking for one more story by Ray Chesson.

Here is one of those stories — Chesson's own account of his years celebrating characters and a lifestyle already vanishing as he wrote.

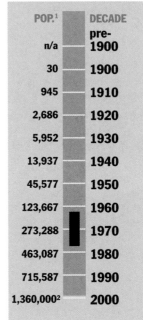

Chesson in Southern Nevada

POP.[1]	DECADE
n/a	pre-1900
30	1900
945	1910
2,686	1920
5,952	1930
13,937	1940
45,577	1950
123,667	1960
273,288	1970
463,087	1980
715,587	1990
1,360,000[2]	2000

■ Time spent in Southern Nev.
1 - Population figures are for greater Las Vegas area (*Source: Nevada State Data Center*).
2 - Estimate

Ray Chesson, 1969
(Review-Journal files)

Desert City. Do you remember that place? It wasn't a city at all. Just a little restaurant and service station, with a few cabins for tourists.

It squatted on the south side of old U.S. 91 on the low east slope of Mountain Pass, Ivanpah Valley. You must have passed it a hundred times on your way to Los Angeles.

Desert City has been dead and buried a good many years. Bulldozed into eternity. It stood squarely in the path of Interstate 15.

We tried to shoot the place down; that seemed a more fitting way for it to go. But all we succeeded in doing was scare the hell out of a flock of customers and cause the owner, George Hopkins, to get hauled into court in San Bernardino.

This was back in 1962, about five months after I went to work for the *Nevadan*. My job was to roam through the boonies and dig up "colorful characters." And illustrate the stories with little pen-and-ink sketches. Some of those sketches were knocked out in about fifteen minutes flat. And they sure looked it. Maybe a thumb six inches from the first knuckle of a forefinger.

Finally I switched to a camera to lend credibility to the stories. Readers thought I was writing fiction. They couldn't believe the characters I stumbled across really existed. Even with the camera I am still called a liar from time to time.

So if you don't mind, let's go back through the years and revisit some of the delightful people I have, in the course of this job, uncovered in various mesquite thickets, saloons, and other homey places. Let's examine them anew, stressing their lovable qualities, the things that should make them believable beyond question.

As a "character" George Hopkins was somewhat on the mild side. He was a pleasant man who had lost a foot in a bulldozer accident. Or at least part of a foot. He still wore both boots and walked around, though limping a bit. His bad foot didn't interfere with his beer drinking.

He was a kindly man with a deep love for Desert City. Sitting there behind his counter while the hired help did the work, he could hear the construction equipment chewing up the side of the Clark Mountains, bringing Interstate 15 ever closer to his door. That's when he took to shooting up the place.

You even shoot a horse when its leg is broken, don't you? So why not shoot Desert City, suffering as it was from a terminal illness known as progress.

I was there the night George really tried to kill the place, to end its suffering. I helped him.

Summertime and hot. Several cars had pulled in and the joint was loaded. Well-dressed residents of California, the customers were — either on their way to Las Vegas or returning home. But a skittish crowd, to be sure.

George and I were sluffing up beer, fighting off dehydration as sensible men do during summer in the Mojave Desert, and I happened to get curious about all the bullet holes in the wall behind the counter.

George said, "Oh, I tried to kill the place, it was the humane thing to do."

"Pretty small holes," I said.

"Twenty-two caliber."

"Takes a lot of lead like that to knock a building like this off its feet," I told him. "You didn't hit it in a vital spot."

We sluffed a while longer and George said, "You know, I think I'll try one more time, I'll shoot it again."

"I'll help you," I said.

George fired from the hip with his .22 and I let one off with my .38. Two more holes in the end wall, and a fearful amount of noise.

Not all of the noise came from the guns; most of it was made by customers dropping their drinks, knocking their plates off the counter, and falling over each other on their way to the door. George and I were suddenly alone.

"I lose a lot of business doing that," he said.

Fortunately for me I was back in Nevada when the cops arrived for George. I don't know what it cost him. I don't know where he went, whatever happened to him. But I'll always remember him as a mighty fine fellow, a man only trying to do his duty as he saw it.

Another of my friends who tried to do his duty as he saw it was Whisker Red. I'd better not give Red's last name. The Vegas police may still be looking for him. I expect durn near every police force in the West has looked for him at one time or another. And at least one of them caught him.

That was down around San Diego. Whisker Red had been working on a construction job at Needles, California, and he happened to go back home unexpectedly.

It's not always a good idea for a married man to to go home unexpectedly. He's liable to run into a surprising situation. Red flushed his surprising situation out of bed, ran the gentleman down in a vacant lot, and killed him.

He was only defending the sanctity of his castle, but damned if the courts didn't send Whisker Red up the river. His relatives pooled their money and reopened the case. It cost plenty. They put Red back out in the air, though. And never spoke to him again. Neither did his wife.

There were a few more little odds and ends of interest in Red's life. Like the time he almost killed a man when he threw him off a bridge in Arizona. And the time when a poor woman in Las Vegas needed money to make up for blowing her husband's paycheck on the slots.

She thought it would be a good idea to burn up her home. The house was insured.

Whisker Red, tender-hearted and always filled with kindness, helped the woman pour kerosene on the place. Maybe he even lit the match; he was a man who would do that much for a friend. But something went wrong. I never knew exactly what happened. Whatever it was, it

Bad Water Bill and mule, Blue Dog, in 1966. Bill, whose real name was Arnold Fryck, made his living posing with tourists. He wandered the West and became a regional character. Ray Chesson's tales of his exploits made him a legend.
(Review-Journal Files)

didn't happen to Red. He left town.

The next time I saw him, he was running from some sheriff in California. I was living in a trailer court in Vegas and Red sneaked in to tell me the sanctity of his castle once more had been invaded.

He had fallen in love with a female horse doctor and they had set up housekeeping in a little town where the deputy sheriff also owned the taxi concession.

I never saw Whisker Red's lady of that particular era, but some of my acquaintances saw her — trustworthy people such as Bad Water Bill, Lester the Terror, Creepy Bob, and Bogdown Munce. Men whose word no one can question. They said the horse doctor had a finer crop of whiskers, even, than Red.

It should have been a lovely match. On the one side there was a tall snake-hipped man with a fiery beard that didn't even need curling, a man steeped in the chivalry of the Old South (he came from Tennessee), and on the other side a woman with a very respectable beard of her own, a stalwart damsel capable of picking up a butcher-knife and chopping the appendix out of a full grown boar. It seemed, Bad Water Bill said, that they were made for each other.

Bad Water gave them, as a wedding gift (although they never really were married), a cracked toilet bowl to help furnish their love nest, a bowl that had been sitting two or three years in the tumbleweeds at Renegade Ranch near Sunrise Mountain east of Las Vegas.

But back there in California a snake reared its head in Whisker Red's Eden. And plucked the fruit.

It was the deputy sheriff with the taxi concession. He lured away the female horse doctor with the magnificent whiskers. But a word should be said in defense of the lady. She had a right to choose a home with an uncracked toilet bowl.

Whisker Red didn't see it that way. In the small hours of a bad black night he took his truck and pushed all of the deputy's taxis over the hump and down into a canyon.

Red got the hell out of California.

He is a good man, wherever he is, always doing what he considers fit and proper, the honorable thing to do at the moment. A man who has been chased unmercifully by law officers who can't seem to understand the necessity of sometimes killing a man, sometimes doing a little arson, sometimes pushing a mess of taxis over a cliff. Hounding him even into the south end of Death Valley where he was forced to hide and grieve over all manner of birds that got trapped by the summer heat and died at his feet.

That's where I first met Whisker Red. Hiding out down there with Bogdown Munce who fled his native Alaska after pirating salmon cannery nets and having his wife take a shot at him through a barroom window in Ketchikan.

Now, Munce was another good friend of mine, a sturdy character I dug out of the boonies. As far as I know Munce was never really arrested for rustling horses, although Clyde Cree, Sr., a Vegan recently deceased, would probably have hung it on Munce could he have caught him. At least that is what Cree once told me.

Cree didn't understand. Bogdown Munce, as he (Munce) has so often said, is only a victim of circumstances. He borrows a horse and someone steals it before he can return it. And then he has to run off and hide. For some people there is simply no justice. Life is filled with disappointments.

Munce once thought he was getting a fair shake, that this world had offered him a bargain. He was camping out on the Tonopah Road just west of Vegas. At least it was west of Vegas at that time. A tall water tank off there in the desert, plenty of old junked automobile bodies for people to live in, and a great stand of arrow weeds where the women in camp could hide to do whatever women do in arrow weeds.

Camping there was a fellow from Mesquite. A real heller with the ladies.

This heller had gone overboard for a crippled waitress in Las Vegas and wanted to shuck his companion, a half-Gypsy girl he had picked up in Northern Nevada. He offered to sell her to Bogdown Munce.

Munce said to the heller, "Shove her in the trailer door so I can see what she looks like."

The man from Mesquite shoved the girl in the door and Munce said, "I'll give you four one-dollar bills and a can of prunes."

Like that he bought the half-Gypsy girl and they were, for a while, a better match even than Whisker Red and the female horse doctor.

They were the happiest two rubber-tramps you ever saw on the Tonopah Road.

They went up to Virginia City and walked the old board sidewalks and looked in the saloons where the dudes were drinking and horsing around and listening to the honky-tonk piano players.

Then one day their money ran short, they were tapped out, and the girl said, "I'll go down to Searchlight and get a job and wait for you to come down."

In those days there were a lot of different kinds of work for a girl to do in Searchlight. Some we won't talk about. But Munce said his girl was working as a waitress. And maybe that is true. Because she ran off with a fry cook from Willie Martello's El Rey Club and Bogdown Munce never saw her again.

Well, knowing these fellows, knowing how they can suffer when mistreated, knowing how low they can feel when their ambitions blow up in their faces, I don't really care to go on. I'd rather not tell you how Bear Claws Stutsman of Phoenix let Bogdown Munce and Bad Water Bill down. But I will.

Bear Claws was a fighter. He said so himself. He was a hell of a handsome fellow, and big as a mountain. Munce brought him into Renegade Ranch, Bad Water's domain, and they damn near starved to death while figuring how to get a match with Sonny Liston, who was heavyweight champion at the time.

I don't know how good a fighter Bear Claws ever was. But he could sure slap the juice out of dog's jowls when the mutt got his snoot in the stewpot. Bear Claws was an eater from way back. He could eat a hindquarter off a steer while it was still running over the ridge. And then he turned out to be a lover. And that did it.

When the women commenced to follow Bear Claws around and feed him, he didn't care to fight anymore.

And that's the way it has gone with all of those wonderful people I have flushed out of the boonies, looking for material for these stories. For many of them nothing has ever turned out quite right. ✍

Pen-and-ink sketch done toward the end of Chesson's association with the **Review-Journal.** *He was anxious to get back to the solitude of the desert.*
Ray Chesson/Review-Journal Files

JERRY VALLEN (1928–)

At a time when no one thought much of "Tumbleweed Tech," an educator found a niche the young university could fill more readily than any other college in the nation—hotel administration. **BY K.J. EVANS**

I believe in matches," says Dr. Jerry Vallen, dean emeritus of the UNLV College of Hotel Administration. He isn't talking about the fiery kind, but about the circumstances under which he founded the UNLV hospitality program and built it into the largest program at the university and one of the most respected in the world.

It was the summer of 1967. The 12-year-old college, then called Nevada Southern, was planning to start a hotel college as a tiny division of the College of Business and Economics. There were 18 students enrolled; there was no laboratory or equipment and a faculty made up mostly of volunteers from local hotels. On the other hand, there was an enthusiastic local resort association, ready and willing to bankroll the start-up, lend employees to serve as faculty, and allow their properties to be used as laboratories. And there was a rapidly growing city, as well as a university, in need of an institution that would train future managers and executives.

Vallen saw a match. But not all the teachers and administrators who came to Las Vegas to interview shared Vallen's vision. Longtime Las Vegas casino executive Leo Lewis, delegated by the resort industry to help in the start-up, recalls that some candidates cut and ran when they got a look

at "Tumbleweed Tech."

"Nobody wanted to come out to the desert," Lewis says. "People didn't want to come to a brand-new school with no reputation and very few research or library facilities." While the ivory-tower types saw a primitive facility in a low-brow town, Vallen, whose background included nearly as much work experience as classroom time, saw that if the school were to flourish, it would have to maintain strong ties to the city's lifeblood industry. This was no problem. He spoke the language.

Jerome J. Vallen was born in Philadelphia in 1928, one of three sons of a restaurateur who owned four restaurants and wanted each of his sons to inherit one. All the boys worked in the family eateries and understood the business before graduating from high school.

Young Vallen was interested in restaurants but more interested in education, so his father sent him to Cornell University. He graduated in 1950 with a bachelor's degree in hotel administration and a plan to teach that discipline. That same year, he married Florence "Flossie" Levinson. The couple had four children, one of whom, Gary, followed in his father's footsteps and is a professor in the hotel college at Northern Arizona University in Flagstaff.

Between 1950 and 1959, Vallen worked toward a master's degree in educational administration from St. Lawrence University, skipping a semester here and there to take hotel management jobs in Atlantic City, Philadelphia, and Miami, and at resorts in New Hampshire and upstate New York. It would be 1976 before he earned his Ph.D. in hotel administration from Cornell.

In 1953, Vallen joined the faculty of the department of food service and hotel management at the junior college of the State University of New York. "I learned from my experience at SUNY," he recalls, "that

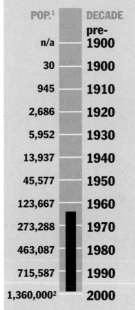

Vallen in Southern Nevada

POP.[1]	DECADE
n/a	pre-1900
30	1900
945	1910
2,686	1920
5,952	1930
13,937	1940
45,577	1950
123,667	1960
273,288	1970
463,087	1980
715,587	1990
1,360,000[2]	2000

■ Time spent in Southern Nev.
1 - Population figures are for greater Las Vegas area (*Source: Nevada State Data Center*).
2 - Estimate

Vallen completed his first textbook on hotel management and posed with it in 1967, the year he was hired to head the new UNLV hotel school.

(Courtesy Jerome Vallen)

Jerome Vallen and Florence Levinson were married in November 1950.
(Courtesy Jerome Vallen)

Vallen at work in the classroom at UNLV, December 1979
(Review-Journal files)

Vallen in his office in the UNLV Humanities Building, early 1970s
(Courtesy Jerome Vallen)

we had a whole bunch of really qualified kids who wanted to go on to a four-year program, but nobody would take them. They [the colleges] didn't have enough space."

Vallen explains that in 1922, Cornell University launched the nation's first four-year degree program in hotel management. By 1967, there were still only 10 major universities offering the program, and the demand for graduates far exceeded the supply. One reason for the dearth of hotel-management baccalaureate programs is that they tend to be equipment-intensive. Expensive laboratory kitchens, faux front desks, and a lot of specialized classroom space must be dedicated to the exclusive use of the hotel college.

In 1966, the Nevada Resort Association offered to take the lead in establishing a hotel school at Nevada Southern, offering $280,000 in start-up money over four years. The NRA appointed Leo Lewis from Binion's Horseshoe Club, as well as Phil Arce from the Sahara and Frank Watts from the Riviera. Together with University President Donald Moyer and Richard Strahlem, acting dean of the fledgling school, they recruited Vallen and Boyce Phillips.

The cozy relationship between the university and the resort industry raised eyebrows back then and still does today. Vallen says that if there is a perception that the gaming curriculum taught at the UNLV College of Hotel Administration was a condition of the hotel industry's support, it is false.

"It was *my* idea," he declares. "It was never one of the prerequisites set by the resort association. As we began to grow, I began to think of ways we could market ourselves differently from the other hotel schools in the country. The answer was right here. We don't teach how to deal cards, fix slot machines, or make change in our classes. Instead, we discuss the various management sys-

tems used in casinos. We teach accounting, marketing, internal gaming control, the impact of new legislation on gaming, and how the changing odds will affect the hotel's revenue."

In 1971, the University Board of Regents split the business and hotel schools. The hotel school was given its own budget, and Vallen was officially named dean of the new, rapidly growing college. From a student body of 18 in 1967, enrollment rose to 120 the following year. In the early 1980s, the Legislature approved $10.8 million for Frank and Estella Beam Hall, completed in late 1982. It would house the business school and the college of hotel administration. Just in time, too. By 1979, enrollment had risen to 790 students. Today, enrollment is about 1,800. Vallen attributes that increase to vigorous recruiting at junior colleges.

The backbone of Vallen's academic program is the internship, something not offered at even the best hotel schools. "I told the resort association that if they're going to be with us, we want internships," says Vallen.

UNLV hotel students must take two internships. In the first, the freshman or sophomore student must find a paying job and hold it for 800 hours, or about two summers. For this, no academic credit is given.

"In the [second] internship, in their senior year, we find the job, they are not paid, and they get three academic credits," says Vallen. Because his interns have quite a bit of experience by their senior year, as well as academic training, Vallen easily places them in hotels around the world.

Attracted by the college's reputation—and, no doubt, by the city—international students are increasingly choosing to study hotel administration at UNLV. "In a typical term," says Vallen, "we would have students from 42 states of the

union and 15 to 25 countries—Greece, Turkey, China, Israel, the Philippines. Practically everywhere."

With success came money, and by the early 1990s the hotel college was doling out more than a quarter of a million dollars a year in scholarships. In 1988, the school received its biggest gift ever, a check for $5 million from Verna Harrah, widow of gaming pioneer William F. Harrah. In his honor, the college was renamed the Harrah College of Hotel Administration.

And while Vallen, who retired from UNLV in 1999, has been a master fundraiser, he is lavish in his praise of hundreds of tourism professionals who have taught, lectured, made donations, or offered a scholarship. "I've never called anyone who failed to respond," he says. "And the industry has had a return on its investment many times over in the manpower supply that we presented to them." ⌀

Mike O'Callaghan (1929–)

> *"He breaks every rule in the book of human relations. He'll yell, curse, ream people out, and he gets away with it because of who he is."*
> —Anonymous source
> On O'Callaghan's management style

A war hero who became a rough-and-tumble politician has not retired into anonymity; he stays in the thick of things with his newspaper column. **BY A.D. HOPKINS**

He might just be the most popular governor Nevada ever had. Donal "Mike" O'Callaghan charged out of obscurity like a Minnesota moose, whipped the anointed candidates, and through two terms of office, set an example of hard-working government responding to the needs of ordinary Nevadans. In the 20 years since, he has pursued a second career as a newspaper executive and an opinionated columnist who has punished many a bureaucrat for failure to meet his high standards of governmental conduct.

O'Callaghan's parents, Neil and Olive, lost their mortgaged farm in the Depression, took up marginal land near Sparta, Wisconsin, and tore subsistence from thin soil. "We had cows and sold cream. We raised our own food, and ate a lot of venison," said O'Callaghan in a 1999 interview in his executive office at the *Las Vegas Sun*.

Were it not for World War II, O'Callaghan might have been a farmer like his dad. When, in order to expand an artillery range, the government condemned the family farm without paying enough to buy another, Neil O'Callaghan returned to his old trade as an operating engineer and young Mike joined the Marine Corps at age 16. But that was a little too late for World War II, and he was assigned to guard prisoners on Guam, where he finished his hitch as a sergeant.

By then his father had relocated to Hanford,

Washington, and his mother taught school over the state line in Idaho, so O'Callaghan joined them, supporting himself as an ironworker and going to Boise Junior College. He kept in shape by boxing. When a group of friends from Boise

decided to join the Air Force, O'Callaghan, attracted by the opportunity to study new technology, joined them. He was trained as an intelligence officer and stationed in Alaska.

To his consternation, the Korean War broke out, leaving him stranded in another military situation in which he was unlikely to see any action. But, because the new war was using up infantry platoon leaders faster than America was training them, a new policy came out authorizing interservice transfers to the Army for military men who could pass a qualifying test. O'Callaghan jumped at the chance. He qualified, signed a waiver releasing the army from its commitment to send him to officer candidate school, and went to Korea as a private.

O'Callaghan explained the decision that put him into an ugly war and his third branch of the military. "I wanted to get into combat. I had been trained for it, and I thought, why send some kid over when I had that training?" As for becoming an officer, he figured he would get a battlefield commission, anyway. He did become a platoon leader, even though he was still a sergeant, because three successive lieutenants were killed or wounded.

O'Callaghan won a Bronze Star with the "V," denoting valor, for an action on December 24, 1952. But on February 13 he paid a high price for his valor. A military document notes: "While his company was being subjected to a barrage of

O'Callaghan in Southern Nevada

POP.[1]	DECADE
n/a	pre-1900
30	1900
945	1910
2,686	1920
5,952	1930
13,937	1940
45,577	1950
123,667	1960
273,288	1970
463,087	1980
715,587	1990
1,360,000[2]	2000

■ Time spent in Southern Nev.
1 - Population figures are for greater Las Vegas area (*Source: Nevada State Data Center*).
2 - Estimate

Former governor Mike O'Callaghan in his present role as executive at the Las Vegas Sun.
Courtesy Mike O'Callaghan

JIM JOYCE

(1937–1993)

"I don't think there's anybody in Nevada who will fill Jim Joyce's shoes. His shoes are retired."

—Mike Sloan
Las Vegas casino executive

A gentle giant in the political world, he roamed the halls of the Legislature for decades, spreading his savvy with ethical arm-twisting. BY K.J. EVANS

Consider the role of the garbage can in Nevada politics. Between 1973 and his death in 1993, Jim Joyce managed campaigns for some 300 candidates, and lost only about 10 percent of them. Having helped elect so many legislators, it is not surprising that he was the most effective lobbyist ever seen in the state Capitol. Victorious politicians and fallen rivals hailed him as a genius. He was certainly imaginative. Which brings us to those garbage cans.

On Election Day, all concerned want to know how voters are leaning. This is determined by an expensive "exit poll," asking people how they voted. In *The Gentle Giant,* Marilee Joyce's tribute to her father, former congressman and client James Bilbray discusses how Jim Joyce made exit polls affordable.

"Jim had a crew of hearty volunteers make the rounds of key districts, emptying the trashcans outside the polling places," Bilbray explained. "Jim theorized that many voters make their ballot decisions at home, marking their choices on their sample ballots and taking those ballots with them to the polls to vote. Once those ballots have been cast, the sample ballot goes in the first trash can they see. It became known as

The Jim Joyce Garbage Can Poll."

Scientific? Hardly. Accurate? Surprisingly so.

Joyce's political acumen and influence was due largely to his natural talent for consensus-building and a reputation for integrity. "I'm sure a lot of his ability as a facilitator came because people enjoyed the sight of him," recalled Renny Ashleman, his attorney and fellow lobbyist.

He was quite a sight, too. At 6-foot-3, Joyce was concerned that his height might intimidate people. So he deliberately walked slowly, with a

stoop, his head and shoulders leading his great gangly frame. His manner was quiet, low-pressure.

James Austin Joyce was born September 23, 1937, in Denver. He and younger sister Peggy were the only children of Austin James Joyce, a Union Pacific Railroad conductor, and Effie Catherine Hart Joyce, a nurse. As a child, Jim Joyce contracted rheumatic fever and the family moved to Las Vegas for his health.

At Las Vegas High School in the early 1950s, Joyce was managing editor of the campus newspaper, the *Desert Breeze,* as well as a sports stringer for the *Las Vegas Review-Journal.* In 1955, he met Richard Bryan, who would go on to become Nevada Governor and a U.S. Senator. In 1956, he enrolled at UNR where he managed Bryan's successful campaign for student body president.

Joyce met Nedra Norton in a UNR journalism class. They married after graduation in 1959, and had two children, Robin and Marilee. Nedra Joyce would make her own mark as a Las Vegas journalist before her death in 1975.

Joyce was a student volunteer on the campaign of Democrat Howard Cannon, writing press releases and setting up interviews. Cannon credits

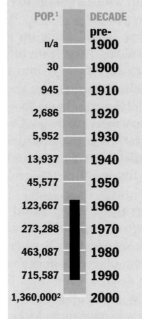

Joyce in Southern Nevada

POP.[1]	DECADE
n/a	pre-1900
30	1900
945	1910
2,686	1920
5,952	1930
13,937	1940
45,577	1950
123,667	1960
273,288	1970
463,087	1980
715,587	1990
1,360,000[2]	2000

■ Time spent in Southern Nev.
1 - Population figures are for greater Las Vegas area (*Source: Nevada State Data Center*).
2 - Estimate

Mr. Joyce goes to work at the Nevada Legislature building, 1981.
(Review-Journal files)

Joyce with helping him get elected to the U.S. Senate in 1958. When he graduated, Joyce became Cannon's press secretary. He was 21. In the mid-1960s, he returned to Las Vegas to head Cannon's local office and, in the early 1970s, he joined May Advertising as a political consultant.

During that time, Joyce made his first big splash as a lobbyist in Carson City. Working on his own time, for no pay, he out-lobbied the American Medical Association, and pushed through legislation legalizing Chinese medicine and acupuncture.

In 1975, Joyce and Marydean Martin founded Joyce and Martin Advertising. Their first client was Sunrise Hospital. At the time, Martin noted, hospitals did not advertise. It was regarded as undignified. Sunrise Administrator David Brandsness thought otherwise, and hired Joyce to design a campaign that wouldn't ruffle too many feathers. Joyce introduced it in small increments. First, there was a Sunrise calendar. Before long, the hospital was advertising free ocean cruises for patients who checked in on weekends.

"Since then, medical advertising has become big business all over the country," said Martin.

Joyce always insisted that he would not champion any candidate or cause he did not believe in himself.

"What set him apart from many was that he would not be a 'hired gun,'" said State Senator William Raggio. He might have drawn that conclusion from watching Joyce deal with a 1981 assembly bill that put a $5 state fee on all marriage licenses, the money to be used for battered women's shelters.

The bill was sponsored by Sue Wagner, R-Reno, and Joyce represented the wedding chapel industry, which opposed the fee. Wagner said Joyce listened intently when she made the case for the fee. "And he agreed that the $5 fee was justified and that the bill should pass," Wagner later recalled. "He promised he would talk to his clients, tell them he personally supported the bill and that they were free to find another lobbyist if they had any problem with the situation." The bill passed easily.

In 1990, Joyce handled Wagner's bid for lieutenant governor. Though she was in a plane crash that left her bedridden between the primary and general elections, and made not a single public appearance, Wagner was elected. She credits Joyce.

In 1992, Joyce found himself uncomfortably in the spotlight. His agency had been awarded a $500,000 contract to produce an on-the-job safety film for the Nevada Department of Industrial Relations. Thirteen other advertising agencies had bid on the project. When Joyce got it, they howled that Joyce juice was responsible.

Common Cause, the citizen watchdog lobby, got into the act when its then-president, James Hulse, a respected author, historian and UNR professor, blasted Joyce for having a conflict of interest. He pointed out that elected officials in the Legislative Counsel Bureau, which awarded the contract, had received more than $140,000 in campaign contributions from casinos and businesses represented by Joyce. Hulse also noted Joyce had landed three other state contracts in 1991, bringing the total to $1 million, and demanded a probe by the Nevada Ethics Commission.

"It seems to us," Hulse said, "that Joyce's special relationship with legislators as fundraiser and lobbyist gives him an unusual advantage in competing for lucrative state contracts."

Joyce argued that his agency had as much right to bid on the contract as anyone. "The perception is that no one can be as successful as I have been lobbying and politically without being corrupt, shady, dishonest, immoral and amoral," Joyce declared. "Nothing is further from the truth."

Legislative Counsel Lorne Malkiewich urged the ethics panel to ignore the matter. It did.

In 1993, Joyce fell ill with emphysema, which had taken all but about 20 percent of his lung capacity. Doctors said he was an "excellent" lung transplant candidate. But Joyce refused.

"Jim said … there was no way in good conscience he could consider a lung transplant," his pulmonologist, Dr. Rachakonda Prabhu, later recalled. "He explained that his lung problems were his own fault—caused by years of smoking and neglect. The lungs he could get through a transplant might be used to save the life of someone who had unwittingly contracted a lung disease."

On March 2, 1993, he died in a Denver hospital. His death precipitated a remarkable public outpouring of grief, and testimonials to his character and effectiveness.

"You can't dust the Nevada Revised Statutes," wrote political observer Jon Ralston, "without finding Jim Joyce's fingerprints." ⌀

Joyce and fellow political operative Sig Rogich make small talk prior to 1982 primary debate between Senator Howard Cannon and challenger Jim Santini, both Democrats. Cannon won.
(Review-Journal files)

First among his peers, Joyce huddles in the hallway of the Nevada Legislature with fellow lobbyists (from left) Sam McMullen, Joyce, Richard Bunker, and Harvey Whittemore.
(Review-Journal files)

Anna Dean Kepper (1938–1983)

"She had this in-the-bones feeling—even 'love' isn't a strong enough word for the passion she brought to her work. It was just part of her makeup, wherever she was, to want to know how people got where they are today."
—Elizabeth Warren
Friend, historian, preservationist

Despite a relatively short stay in the valley, a passionate historian sparked true interest and inspired other preservationists to keep the area's history alive. BY A.D. HOPKINS

Anna Dean Kepper died young and spent only 10 of her 45 years in Las Vegas. But in that decade she taught the community a new respect for its own history. "Without Anna Dean Kepper , there perhaps wouldn't be a state park at the Old Las Vegas Fort," said Frank Wright, curator at the Nevada State Museum and Historical Society in Lorenzi Park.

Without Kepper, fine old houses in the downtown section, now rejuvenated for law offices or moved and faithfully restored at a county museum, would have been torn down. Without Kepper, many of the photos collected from pioneer Las Vegans and now preserved in UNLV Special Collections would have remained in closets and trunks and been lost to history.

"She had this in-the-bones feeling—even 'love' isn't a strong enough word for the passion she brought to her work," said Elizabeth Warren, a historian and preservationist and one of Kepper's closest friends. "It was just part of her makeup, wherever she was, to want to know how people got where they are today."

Kepper was born in Seattle and had dual master's degrees in museology and American folk culture from the State University of New York in Oneonta. She moved to Las Vegas in 1973 with her husband, Jack, who taught geology at UNLV. Years later she told her friend Dorothy Wright

how disappointed she had been to find that so much of Las Vegas' colorful history had already been lost, and that much of the rest was inaccessible to the public. "There was a time she almost cried about it," said Wright. "But she found out what there was, dove in, made the best of it. That was her spirit. And it was infectious."

Kepper soon found work as a curator in the UNLV library's special collections section—where original manuscripts and photos, rare books, oral history tapes, and other irreplaceable research resources are preserved. She wasn't the first curator and she never headed the department, but she made the community more aware of it, which in turn inspired citizens to contribute historically important papers and photos.

"People who remember her, remember the outreach," said Warren. "She would take the material and celebrate the person. For instance, there was Beta Cornwall, who was al-

Anna Dean Kepper digs through the UNLV Special Collections card files, a guide to photos and documents held in the community's archive.

(Review-Journal files)

Kepper in Southern Nevada

POP.[1]	DECADE
n/a	pre-1900
30	1900
945	1910
2,686	1920
5,952	1930
13,937	1940
45,577	1950
123,667	1960
273,288	1970
463,087	1980
715,587	1990
1,360,000[2]	2000

■ Time spent in Southern Nev.
1 - Population figures are for greater Las Vegas area (*Source: Nevada State Data Center*).
2 - Estimate

most single-handedly responsible for getting the city library started. Beta contributed a lot of files that showed her relation to that effort, and if a historian wants to know how libraries developed here, he has to look at this material.

"Well, this is a subject many would have seen as dry, but Anna Dean made it exciting by celebrating Beta Cornwall's life. Beta had been prominent in her time, but by the time Anna Dean came here, she was sort of forgotten outside her own circle of friends. Then Anna Dean put together an exhibit and a reception that showed what she had done and who she was. So people still know who Beta was, even though she's now gone."

Hal Erickson, who was director of the UNLV library when Kepper worked there, shared her enthusiasm for outreach and often traveled with her to gather historic material. "I don't think there was anybody that Anna Dean didn't think had something to contribute," said Erickson at a 1983 memorial service. "Everybody had photographs. They could be of events, street scenes, people. If you were the person she was talking to, she soon had you talking about those pictures, those business records, or those letters, and she was making an appointment to see you."

Kepper became friends with the Lake sisters—Olive, Alice, Ada, and Emily—some of whom came to Las Vegas in a covered wagon before the first railroad trains arrived in 1905. "Olive Lake Eglinton, a member of the first graduating class in 1913 of what was then called Clark County High School, deposited her material and began correspondence with her quickly diminishing circle of Las Vegas classmates to get them to place their material into Special Collections," said Erickson.

Kepper was equally able to get along with the proper Lake sisters and with tough old Harold Stocker, a former bootlegger, who gave unique material about the last days of Prohibition and the first legal casinos.

She enlisted the *Review-Journal's* Sunday magazine to help identify people and puzzling situations depicted in some of these photos. Each Sunday the magazine ran one historic photo, asking readers who might know something about the photo to call UNLV Special Collections and offer the information. Many times the effort was successful, and some callers donated still more historic photos.

Trained as an oral historian, Kepper encouraged history professor Ralph Roske and his students to tape interviews with Clark County pioneers then in their sunset years. The voices and many memories of these founders would have been lost otherwise.

Kepper became the prime motivator behind the effort to preserve the old Las Vegas Mormon Fort, built in 1855 as a religious mission to the Las Vegas Paiute and also to provide protection and services to travelers on the wagon road between Utah and the Pacific Coast. The Daughters of Utah Pioneers had done much to preserve and protect what was left of the fort, but the effort had bogged down.

"The Daughters thought they owned it but they really just had a lease, and she [Kepper] helped us upgrade from that," said Leah Dingle, former Clark County president of DUP. "Of course, all of us in the Daughters are descendants of people who came West in the great migration, and the fort is part of our history. But there were a lot of other people who were interested in preserving it for a lot of other reasons, and she brought in those people."

History professor Roske was one of the founders of the Association for the Preservation of the Las Vegas Fort and became its first president in 1973. Kepper became president the following year and held the job until 1979. She helped obtain funds from the National Bicentennial Commission to restore the fort, as well as city funding to keep it open part time to visitors. Elizabeth Warren picked up the ball by founding Friends of the Fort, a multiorganizational committee. With some help from state Senators Bob Coffin and Ray Rawson, and from Las Vegas military historian James Hinds, Warren and Friends of the Fort finally got the Nevada State Parks system to acquire the site.

Meanwhile, the original Association for the Preservation of the Las Vegas Fort had renamed itself the Preservation Association of Clark County and had moved on to broader efforts. "Anna Dean truly laid the keel of this organization," said Hinds. "But she also had a personal role in the preservation of at least three historic houses." The downtown homes of pioneer businessman Will Beckley and early casino operator P.J. Goumound were moved to the grounds of the Clark County Heritage Museum in Henderson. A Tudor-style home formerly occupied by the influential Houssels and Harmon families was moved to the UNLV campus, where it housed the school of architecture.

Kepper's own home was a tract house near Valley High School, but Kepper individualized it with antiques, most of which were not merely displayed but used. "She collected antique cooking implements and she really cooked with them," remembered Warren.

About 1979, Kepper began urging others to carry the torch in preserving Las Vegas history. Stricken with breast cancer, she underwent surgery and chemotherapy, and continued to work as death loomed, finishing far more than "one last project." She died on December 21, 1983.

On December 2, she had passed her final examination for a master's degree in public administration from UNLV. The degree was bestowed posthumously. ✍

In March 1976 Kepper (left) and Library Director Hal Erickson (right) helped organize a library exhibit celebrating the life and deeds of Maurine Hubbard Wilson (center) a Las Vegas music teacher who collected letters, documents, photos, political literature, and scrapbooks that depicted community history. Erickson holds an early brochure from the Libertarian Party of Nevada.
(UNLV Special Collections)

JOHN SEIBOLD (1934–)

Tapping into the international market, an engineer and pilot gave visitors the grandest view of the Grand Canyon. BY K.J. EVANS

On one side of the hangar sits a wingless airplane fuselage. It has no interior or motors and, to the untrained eye, not much of a future. But to John Seibold, it's a new baby waiting to be born, the latest addition to his family of DeHavilland Twin Otters, the plane upon which his fortune was built.

Seibold is the founder of the modern Scenic Airlines. An aeronautical engineer, he also invented the Twin Otter "Vistaliner," an Otter with oversized windows designed specifically for sightseeing. Seibold's innovation, along with some savvy overseas marketing, turned the Grand Canyon air tour business—initially a handful of one-plane operators—into an industry that generated more than $250 million annually.

Today, Seibold is the part-time vice president of operations for Twin Otter Leasing International, which leases and services the sturdy little planes all over the world.

"This one crashed in the Antarctic," he says, gesturing at the Otter-in-progress. "It belonged to the government of Chile, and we had some long negotiations to get the salvage rights. We'll buy just about anything that's conceivably repairable and repair it, and when it comes out of our shop, it's like a brand-new airplane."

DeHavilland stopped making the Twin Otter in 1988 after turning out about 600. But demand for the planes continues. "There's nearly that many still flying," says Seibold. The reason? The Otter, built in Canada, is a short-takeoff airplane perfectly suited for landing and taking off on crude, backwoods airstrips, even at very high elevations.

"We have a couple leased to the Drug Enforcement Administration," Seibold says. "They needed them for some work they were doing in South America—Bolivia, I think." The planes also are rigged with floats and leased to tour operators in Alaska, where they wend tourists through the misty fjords near Ketchikan. In the Fiji Islands, they are the choice of the local commuter airline. Most of Seibold's customers, however, are his former competitors in the local Grand Canyon air touring business.

Born in New Jersey, Seibold moved to Southern California with his parents at age 16; at 18, he earned his private pilot's wings. After high school, he enrolled in an airframe and powerplant school—a type of trade school that produces aircraft mechanics. But Seibold wasn't especially interested in being a wrench-bender, or even a professional pilot. He just wanted to be able to work on his own plane.

His actual career, he thought, would be in a new and booming field. "At that time, nuclear engineering was the thing," he said. "It was the forefront of technology, and that's where the jobs were."

In particular, Nevada was where the jobs were. After graduating from the California Polytechnical Institute in 1959 with a dual major

John Seibold with a model of the airplane he redesigned for sightseeing, the DeHavilland Twin Otter. His change was to enlarge the windows, normally porthole-sized.
(Review-Journal files)

Seibold in Southern Nevada

POP.[1]	DECADE
n/a	pre-1900
30	1900
945	1910
2,686	1920
5,952	1930
13,937	1940
45,577	1950
123,667	1960
273,288	1970
463,087	1980
715,587	1990
1,360,000[2]	2000

■ Time spent in Southern Nev.
1 - Population figures are for greater Las Vegas area (Source: Nevada State Data Center).
2 - Estimate

in aeronautical engineering and physics, Seibold worked for several California firms doing contract work at the Nevada Test Site.

At first, he maintained his home in San Diego, as did many of his colleagues at the test site. "We would gather a group together and fly down to San Diego on Friday night, then come back again on Monday morning," Seibold recalled. "In the course of doing that, I found out what it cost to operate an aircraft on a regular basis."

Mostly for fun, Seibold occasionally flew charters out of the North Las Vegas Airport for a small firm named Scenic Airlines. It was one of about 40 tiny charter outfits offering air tours. In 1967, Scenic Airlines folded.

"They owed me $300," Seibold said. "And when they bellied up, I said, 'Forget about the $300. Just give me your old reservations and whatever brochures you have, and we'll call it even.'"

He observed that most of his customers were not from California, the city's main market then and now. "The majority of our customers were from overseas, more than half initially," Seibold said. "When we sold the airline, I think it was close to 85 or 90 percent overseas passengers."

The reason is simple. For domestic visitors, the Grand Canyon is something that can be seen on a return trip. For overseas travelers, it may be their only trip, and the Grand Canyon is a must-

see. "They all want to see the canyon, but they don't want to take a week to do it," said Seibold.

One of the early problems with getting foreign visitors aboard his planes was selling the idea that Las Vegas—not Phoenix or Flagstaff—was the logical departure point for tours of the canyon.

In the late 1960s and 1970s, Scenic tried to stir up interest among the rest of the Southern Nevada resort industry in the potential of overseas markets. "At the time we started," recalled Seibold, "the hotel industry in Nevada had absolutely no interest in the international market; they were looking at the Los Angeles crowd. When we tried to talk to them about doing joint promotions and participating in international marketing, their attitude was, 'Who needs it?'

"If you look today at what Las Vegas does to generate international business, it's a far cry from what it was in those days. I like to think that Scenic Airlines played an instrumental part in getting the recreation and resort community in Las Vegas to start looking at the international marketplace."

Initially, the tours were conducted in Cessnas and other small craft. When Seibold borrowed a couple of Otters from another airline, he was impressed with the plane's potential. Its wing was atop the fuselage, giving riders in window seats an unobstructed view below. But the aisle-seat passenger was out of luck. "It [the Otter] had very small windows," Seibold recalled. "We had a lot of complaints that when the person sitting next to the window looked out, his head blocked the whole window."

Seibold borrowed an Otter from a friendly company, took the plane apart, and determined that the windows could be enlarged quite a bit without compromising the plane's structural in-

tegrity. The result was a tool perfectly fitted to the task. So enormous were the windows that passengers could see out both sides of the plane from any seat.

Before selling Scenic to Sky West Airlines in 1993, Seibold purchased an airport at Valle, Arizona, 20 miles south of Grand Canyon National Park, and set about restoring it. He plans a scaled-down air tour operation there, something more easily managed than his previous enterprise. "Running an airline is a 24 hour a day, seven-day-a-week job," says Seibold. "Scenic was an excellent company and did very, very well." But, he adds, he's ready to retire, or at least semi-retire. Scenic had 300 employees. Twin Otter Leasing has 25.

The Valle airport also will have an aviation museum, built by the Planes of Fame Air Museum out of Chino, California. According to Seibold, the museum is intended to be a bit more than another roadside attraction.

"We want to make a very strong statement as far as the value of air tours in the canyon," says Seibold. "They have taken such a beating from the environmentalists and the park service." He refers to the ongoing debate between environmentalists, who are concerned that overflights of the canyon are harming its "natural quiet," and air tour operators, who insist that the flights produce minimal noise in a limited area of the park, don't require trails, and stay only a few hours.

"You'd think they would be begging us to bring more people over by air," says Seibold. "The bottom line is that these are people who hate airplanes. I happen to love airplanes, and anyone who hates them is my enemy." ✍

Because the Ford Tri-Motor was one of the first planes to carry passengers over the Grand Canyon, Seibold acquired two of them. No one was hurt when this one crashed, and it was later restored and donated to an aviation museum in San Diego's Balboa Park. The other plane was totally destroyed in a freak windstorm.
(Review-Journal files)

Scenic Airlines passengers board planes at Grand Canyon Airport. Though he has since sold Scenic, Seibold is regarded as a pioneer in establishing an industry that generates more than $250 million annually.
(Review-Journal files)

Patricia Marchese (1943–)

**Bringing art and recreational opportunities to the desert has been one woman's quest—
a goal she has attained in many different ways at many different venues.** BY A.D. HOPKINS

Patricia Marchese hadn't been in Las Vegas too long when she saw a local guy blowing a trumpet at an informal concert. The Angel Gabriel couldn't have done better, she thought. "That guy's probably got a future," she commented to a bystander.

"I guess he might," came the response. "He's already lead trumpet for 'Blood, Sweat, and Tears.'"

Marchese quickly saw the resources Las Vegas show-business culture offered. She tapped into them to organize most of the city of Las Vegas' present cultural-affairs programs, then did it all over again for Clark County. The two programs became the core of the Las Vegas cultural scene.

Now she's assistant director of the Clark County Parks and Recreation Department, supervising not only cultural affairs but also museums, recreation, sports, aquatics, special facilities, and park maintenance.

In 1972 Marchese moved to Las Vegas with her husband, Lamar, who had taken a job with the Clark County Library District. The following year, she answered an ad seeking a person to start a cultural-affairs program and got the job. "I was in the right place at the right time," she said. She didn't have to talk the Las Vegas City Council into supporting the arts. "It was their idea. ... There was some impetus from the community."

Las Vegas had purchased an outdated Mor-

mon facility to use as a temporary headquarters while its old City Hall was torn down and a new one was built. With city government moved into its new home, the former church facility became Reed Whipple Center, earmarked for recreation and cultural afairs.

The building came equipped with a small stage, so that was one of the first resources Marchese utilized. She hired Jody Johnston, the daughter of entertainer Totie Fields, and a young

local playwright named Brian Strom to build Rainbow Company, a children's theater. The new troupe quickly, and repeatedly, won recognition from the Children's Theater Association of America as best in the United States. Strom became a respected local director; Rainbow-trained kids now have theater careers.

"The premise was the children would learn the discipline of the craft as well as being entertained, and it worked," said Marchese. Rainbow Company has offered classes in acting, playwriting, mime, costuming, makeup, stage combat, and other technical skills.

The Reed Whipple Center also has a gallery to display visual arts and is on the itinerary of important national touring shows.

In 1976 Marchese began working with conductor William Gromko to found the Las Vegas Junior Symphony, pairing student musicians from Las Vegas public schools with professional musicians who played pops in Strip showrooms, but had no outlet to soar into the classics. The organization evolved into the Las Vegas Civic Symphony and continued to combine old pros with the young. It sometimes performed at noon on workdays in Civic Plaza, the courtyard of Las Vegas City Hall. Downtown employees were invited to bring their lunches and eat while listening to excerpts from "Unfinished Symphony."

About the same time, Marchese established the first public arts program and the Las Vegas

Marchese in Southern Nevada

POP.[1]	DECADE
n/a	pre-1900
30	1900
945	1910
2,686	1920
5,952	1930
13,937	1940
45,577	1950
123,667	1960
273,288	1970
463,087	1980
715,587	1990
1,360,000[2]	2000

■ Time spent in Southern Nev.
1 - Population figures are for greater Las Vegas area (*Source: Nevada State Data Center*).
2 - Estimate

Patricia Marchese in Sunset Park.
(Christine H. Wetzel/Review-Journal)

Arts Commission, with a grant from the National Council on the Arts. The commission brought in Bob Beckmann, a Seattle artist who specialized in murals, and established him as artist in residence at Western High School, where he supervised students in designing and painting murals on school walls.

Beckman also painted murals on Dula Recreation Center, Mirabelli Teen Center, and other public buildings. Usually teenagers, from whatever neighborhood the mural would grace, had input into the designs and helped Beckmann paint them. "Some of the murals were in at-risk neighborhoods, and the entire time they were up, they had no problems with graffiti," said Marchese.

Much of Marchese's success came from her skill at working out partnerships between different interest groups and private and public agencies. The Clark County School District, for instance, was an important partner in Beckmann's public-arts projects. Marchese also helped start the Community Schools program, utilizing classrooms after hours for arts and recreation. People have wondered, she said, why these programs are found mainly at middle schools. "It's because high schools tend to be busy after hours, and at elementary schools the chairs are too small," she explained.

She stepped out of public life briefly with the birth of a daughter, Julia, in 1979, then went to work in 1983 as a legislative lobbyist for Clark County and later as an administrator in the county manager's office. She served as director of town services from 1984 to 1986, then went to work for a real estate development company.

But Pat Shalmy, then county manager, looked her up and encouraged her to apply for a new job

"The reason recreation departments are involved in the arts ... a lot of people think of sports as an alternative path for at-risk kids, and it is a valid thought. But not everyone is interested in sports or good at them, and there is a lot of research concluding that the arts and dance are just as good at keeping people on the straight and narrow."
—Patricia Marchese

in a cultural division. "The county had a museum and some other programs already going, but it was basically a ground-up operation, which is always the funnest," Marchese said. "Getting something going from nothing."

The county museums division consisted of the Clark County Heritage Museum, occupying a single building outside of Henderson, when she took over. On her watch the museum became a unique haven for historically important and architecturally interesting buildings.

An aviation museum was added, appropriately located in the terminal at McCarran International Airport. She successfully lobbied for public art in the ultra-modern airport, finding funding for several large contemporary art pieces by nationally known artists. Later additions, she said, featured murals by local artists.

Whenever possible Marchese has pressed for display space for the arts in public buildings. "It's a nice thing to be able to say about Las Vegas that the new county government center has an amphitheater," she added. "A place where people can get together, celebrate, go to something that they all agree is important.

"The building itself shows a lot of allegiance to Native American arts and petroglyphs. For instance, they made sure the petroglyphs were appropriate to the area, that they actually came from the native cultures of the region."

Sunset Park, known to two generations as a green oasis of athletic endeavor, has become an outdoor venue for art shows, an annual Renaissance Faire, and jazz performances.

Today, Marchese is also responsible for sporting events and maintaining parks, but she sees all aspects of the recreational movement as fingers on the same hand.

"The reason recreation departments are involved in the arts ... a lot of people think of sports as an alternative path for at-risk kids, and it is a valid thought," she conceded. "But not everyone is interested in sports or good at them, and there is a lot of research concluding that the arts and dance are just as good at keeping people on the straight and narrow."

While she has spent most of her career advocating public support of the arts, she finds one of the most interesting trends today is in their privatization. "I once made the remark that the arts are not going to make it in this town till the casinos get into the business," Marchese recalled. "And now they have! You have top Broadway shows here, Cézannes here, Russian jewels here, all in casinos. I would hope this would turn into an enlightenment that will lead people to greater support of the local arts." ⌀

Offbeat events like the Renaissance Faire attract some 40,000 each year and give depth to Marchese's park and recreation programs.
(Courtesy Clark County Parks and Recreation)

Don Laughlin

(1931–   )

"I wanted a place on a state line because I have always known that a place on a state line gets much higher play than anywhere else. On a state line, if 10 people come in, you get nine players and maybe all 10, because being able to gamble is the reason they come here."

—Don Laughlin

After leaving high school because he was making a bundle of money gambling, a boy from Minnesota founded a town in Nevada that bears both his name and his luck. **BY A.D. HOPKINS**

The principal was decidedly upset with young Don Laughlin. "He said to get out of the gambling business or get out of high school. I couldn't see what one had to do with the other," said Laughlin. "But I could see that I was making more money than the principal, so I left school."

And that's how Laughlin came to have both an eighth-grade education and enough money to build a small city, which is named for him. In just 30 years, Laughlin, and later other gambling entrepreneurs following his lead, built the town of Laughlin from a bankrupt saloon and motel beside the Colorado River into one of Nevada's most important tourist destinations, attracting 4.2 million visitors a year.

Laughlin was born in Owatonna, 50 miles from Minneapolis, and grew up on a farm seven miles from town. His father was a part-time trucker. "I went to a country school where all eight grades were in one room. I must have graduated from there about 1946, the only school I ever graduated from," he said. Laughlin went to high school only a year, during which time he built up a route of slot machines and punchboards. Then the principal called him in for that chat. "He's long gone and I don't hold it against him," said Laughlin. "He had strong religious convictions and thought he was doing the right thing."

Most of Minnesota, he notes, did not share those convictions. Punchboards and slot machines weren't legal, but nobody enforced the law. "Every little bar and restaurant had a couple of slot machines. If you took your car to get it repaired, the garage had a couple you could play while you waited."

It was not until 1952, after a federal crackdown on illegal gambling, that Minnesota started tightening up. Laughlin went to Las Vegas for a vacation, and liked what he saw. He worked in casinos until about 1954, when he bought a beer-and-wine bar at 412 W. Bonanza Road, and, naturally, put in a few slot machines. After selling the bar at a profit, Laughlin bought the small 101 Club on Salt Lake Highway, expanded it and sold it in 1964 for $165,000.

In 1966 he discovered a bankrupt bar on an unpaved road on the Colorado River, in an area then known generally as South Point because it was in the southern corner of the state.

Across the river was Bullhead City, Arizona, a village that had begun as a supply and support base for construction gangs building Davis Dam on the Colorado River.

"I wanted a place on a state line because I have always known that a place on a state line gets much higher play than anywhere else," Laughlin said. Out of every 10 people who came into his North Las Vegas clubs, he estimated, nine might be there to drink, eat, or hang out, and only one to gamble. "On a state line if 10 people come in, you get nine players and maybe all 10, because

Laughlin in Southern Nevada

POP.[1]	DECADE
n/a	pre-1900
30	1900
945	1910
2,686	1920
5,952	1930
13,937	1940
45,577	1950
123,667	1960
273,288	1970
463,087	1980
715,587	1990
1,360,000[2]	2000

■ Time spent in Southern Nev.
1 - Population figures are for greater Las Vegas area (*Source: Nevada State Data Center*).
2 - Estimate

In the early 1970s, Don Laughlin had already completed the first expansion of the bar and motel at rear, which would eventually become today's Riverside Resort.
(Review-Journal files)

being able to gamble is the reason they come here," he contends.

He got the motel and six riverfront acres for $35,000 down, on a $235,000 total price. Two years later, when the U.S. Postal Service decided to open a post office on the Nevada side of the river, it named the community Laughlin.

There were eight motel rooms when Laughlin bought the Riverside. He and his family lived in four of them, leaving four to rent to the public. Today he has 1,400 plus 800 recreational vehicle spaces. Eight other hotel operators, seven of them also in the casino business, have moved into his backyard. All together there are nearly 11,000 rooms in Laughlin today. Laughlin's phenomenal growth is partly related to the popularity of the nearby Lake Mead National Recreation Area. The National Park Service resisted efforts by private concessionaires to expand its few motels and snack bars, thus directing most recreational business outside the park.

Some of Laughlin's advantages were pure luck, but he also made insightful business deci-

sions. For example many Las Vegas Strip hotels were slow to add amenities for recreational vehicles, assuming that couples who drove a car with a built-in kitchen and bedroom were cheapskates who wouldn't gamble. Laughlin saw them as operators of one-room hotels who handed him all their casino action.

"Anybody who owns an RV is somebody with money. We've found RV customers spend just as much money as people who stay in our rooms," he said. But RV spaces were much cheaper to build, and that helped the city establish itself as a bargain vacation spot. "The prices are cheaper because we're not in the high-rent district. You can still rent a room for $15 or $20 a night, weekdays," said Laughlin.

According to Laughlin, about 20 percent of the summer crowd is directly involved in some water sport. He adds, "We have our own dock and let people tie up boats, jet skis, and even the occasional float plane there. … In the winter the crowd changes. People in [their] 60s, 70s, 80s. We stay packed with them from November to May. They're all gone after 9 or 10 at night, but they're back first thing in the morning."

The town of Laughlin boomed like a kettle drum through the 1980s and early '90s, then went into a four-year decline from 1995 through 1998. Early figures for 1999 show the trend may have been reversed. Don Laughlin blamed the decline on Indian gaming. "There are probably about 18 casinos in Arizona and probably 45 or 50 in California," he said.

The breather has given Clark County and Bullhead City governments a chance to catch up with problems caused by Laughlin's former runaway growth. County Commissioner Bruce Woodbury said one of the main needs is to get the Bureau of Land Management, which controls most land in the area, to release more for private development. "If we can get it, I would hope some would be used for residential development, in-

cluding affordable housing, as well as some general commercial development," said Woodbury. "They don't yet have a lot of the amenities that make it a community." Housing in Laughlin is too expensive for most casino workers, who find what they can in Bullhead City.

Don Laughlin has done his part in solving many of those problems. In one famous incident, he built, at his personal expense, a $4.5 million bridge bypassing the twisting road across Davis Dam, which Laughlin was told had claimed 42 lives in 20 years. "Down here on a state line you've got two fish and game departments, two highway departments, and two of everything else," said Laughlin. "It took four and a half years to get the bridge approved by, I think, 38 different agencies. It only took us four months to build it."

Laughlin founded the town's first bank, but recently sold it. At the age of 68, he explained, he is trying to wind down. However, he still works most of two standard shifts a day in his own casino, starting about 10 a.m., taking a siesta in the early afternoon, then resuming till 3 in the desert morning. "I don't have to do that, but I enjoy working," he said. "I don't play golf or bowl or fish. Don't even go to many movies, although I can do it for free since we have our own theaters here."

Laughlin's oldest son, Dan, 46, is general manager of the Riverside. Another son, Ron, 41, has a restaurant and janitorial supply company headquartered in Bullhead City. His daughter Erin, 38, recently rejoined the Riverside as a parking valet.

Laughlin is separated from his wife, the former Betty Jones, but the two remain friendly.

In 1987 the magazine *Venture*, which specialized in articles on entrepreneurs, ran a long cover piece detailing how Laughlin built his empire, and suggested that the one-man operation would no longer be able to compete against the larger bankrolls of the big corporate competitors from Las Vegas. Twelve years later, he's still there, running the casino that looks the busiest of the nine lining the riverbank. ∅

Ballroom dancing is one of Laughlin's few hobbies, and his casino is one of the few that markets itself by holding dances. In this photo from the 1980s his partner was Carolyn Cox.
(Review-Journal files)

Jerry Tarkanian (1930–)

The man who put UNLV on the map brought both prosperity and notoriety to the university and its basketball program.   BY A.D. HOPKINS

Whatever fame UNLV enjoys nationally rests largely on its Jerry-built basketball program. But so do negative aspects of the university's reputation.

Through nearly two decades at UNLV, Jerry Tarkanian's teams were under almost constant investigation or sanction by the NCAA. He in turn accused the NCAA of singling him out for harassment, and eventually won a large cash settlement, an unheard-of victory over the powerful collegiate athletic watchdog.

Most Las Vegans couldn't have cared less what the National Collegiate Athletic Association thought of UNLV's recruiting practices. They loved Tark the Shark and his teams. Their public image was a metaphor for Las Vegas: a little wicked, a little wild, and all but unbeatable.

Tark's mother was a refugee from the genocide that killed more than two million Armenians over 24 years. In a 1988 autobiography, Tarkanian and his co-author, Terry Pluto, described without emotion the terrible event that sent his mother to America. Tark's grandfather, Mickael Effendi Tarkhanian, was a government official. His oldest son, Mehran, was a medical student. Turkish militiamen arrested Effendi Tarkhanian and forced him to watch while they beheaded his son. Then the elder Tarkhanian was himself killed.

His widow immediately sent her other young son, Levon, and one of her four daughters, Haigouhie, fleeing on horseback. Later, in Lebanon, Haigouhie married a man with a name similar to her father's and returned with him to the United States. Jerry was born in 1930.

Tarkanian won an athletic scholarship to Fresno State University, where he served as a personal aide to football coach Clark van Galder, one of the greatest influences on Tarkanian's life.

"He was an extraordinarily intense individual, and he demanded equal intensity from his players," Tarkanian wrote. "How he got it was

by becoming close with them, by forging an emotional bond. He would take me and my roommate Fred Bistrick, Fresno's quarterback, to the high-school games with him. We spent a lot of time with his family."

Tarkanian adopted the football coach's creed and toted it over to the basketball gym. He was too short and slow for the first string, but he had dedication and a gift for analyzing plays.

When his eligibility ran out, Tarkanian helped coach at a nearby high school. He proved so good he became head coach, in function if not in title, while still in college. (Tarkanian is one of the few college coaches who has never been an assistant.) He coached at four high schools, then in 1961 was hired by Riverside Junior College, which hadn't had a winning season in 11 years. Under Tarkanian, Riverside became the first team to win three consecutive state junior-college championships. Moving to Pasadena City College in 1966, he converted another terrible team to state champions in his first year.

Meanwhile, he had married Lois Huter, whom he'd met while both were students at Fresno State. Lois became an educator and in Las Vegas was elected to the Clark County School Board.

The Tarkanians have four children. Danny played on Tarkanian's first string at UNLV, is currently one of his assistant

Tarkanian in Southern Nevada

POP.[1]	DECADE
n/a	pre-1900
30	1900
945	1910
2,686	1920
5,952	1930
13,937	1940
45,577	1950
123,667	1960
273,288	1970
463,087	1980
715,587	1990
1,360,000[2]	2000

■ Time spent in Southern Nev.
1 - Population figures are for greater Las Vegas area (*Source: Nevada State Data Center*).
2 - Estimate

Tarkanian thought players and coach should share the same level of intensity, and this 1999 photo from a Fresno State game indicates he still subscribes to that principle. (Review-Journal files)

coaches, and has practiced law. George is head basketball coach at College of Sequoias in Visalia, California. Jodie Diamant is a nurse and homemaker. Pamela Tarkanian is a special-education administrator in the Clark County School District.

In 1968, he was asked to repeat his team-building magic at four-year Long Beach State College. Most four-year coaches considered junior-college players second-rate material, but Tarkanian bragged that when he first took a team to the NCAA tournament (from Long Beach in 1970), the entire first-string consisted of former junior-college men.

"Soon Tarkanian's approach provoked complaints that he was running a 'renegade' program built upon less than stellar students," wrote Richard O. Davies, a University of Nevada-Reno history professor, in his book on controversial Nevadans, *The Maverick Spirit.*

Davies also notes Tarkanian was one of the first to ignore an unwritten rule that three of the five starting players had to be white. "This dramatic departure from racial convention established Tarkanian in the black community as a coach who not only talked about equal opportu-

nity, but actually practiced it. This reputation would pay great recruiting dividends later in his career."

UNLV boosters in 1973 were not interested in the color of his players, either. They were interested in a coach who had put obscure Long Beach State College onto the map. When Dr. Donald Baepler, then UNLV's academic vice president, hired Tarkanian, no one else was seriously considered. His first season was 20-6.

Though originally famous for slow methodical play, Tarkanian adopted an entirely new style at UNLV. His second season found him with guys who were short, by basketball standards, but could run like antelope. "I figured that if we got the bigger teams running, it would take away their size advantage," he wrote. "Rather than work the ball around the perimeter, I wanted us to get the ball up the court as fast as possible, and then take a quick jumper before the defense could set up. Speed would be the determining factor in the game."

They lost the first three games they played that way, but came together in the fourth and finished the season 24-5. The Rebels became the Runnin' Rebels.

The 1975 team often scored more than 100 points a game and set a collegiate record of 164 points against Hawaii. It went to the NCAA tournament that year; in 1977 UNLV played in the semifinals, losing 84-83 to North Carolina.

Baepler, by then president of UNLV, said, "Prior to 1977 I had to explain at national meetings, 'Yes, there is a university in Las Vegas.' And after that they knew."

Success also meant being taken seriously in the Nevada Legislature, which had formerly

treated UNLV as a stepchild to the "real" university at Reno. "Before we hired Jerry we had a dream of having a big facility like Thomas and Mack Center, and we knew we had to have a big program to get it," said Baepler. "We thought Jerry could do that, and he did."

Opening in December 1983, the Thomas & Mack multipurpose arena became known as the "Shark Tank," but it also allowed Las Vegas to host the National Finals Rodeo, as well as other events and concerts.

But storms move northeast in the Mojave Desert, and a big one followed Tarkanian from Long Beach. He claimed it all started when he wrote a newspaper column criticizing the NCAA. "It's a crime that Western Kentucky is on probation, but the famous University of Kentucky isn't even investigated," he wrote. "The University of Kentucky basketball program breaks more rules in a day than Western Kentucky does in a year. The NCAA doesn't want to take on the big boys."

Shortly thereafter, the NCAA announced not only an investigation of his Long Beach program, but that it was reopening a dormant investigation of the UNLV program he had just agreed to head up.

In 1976, the NCAA charged UNLV with 10 major infractions of its rules, including one charge that Tarkanian had arranged for player David Vaughan to receive a "B" in a class without even attending it, for a player to get free clothing, and for players to travel free on airplanes chartered by casinos. Tarkanian expressed outrage at the grade-fixing charge and denied the clothing comp. Regarding the junkets, Tarkanian claimed that he pointed out to the junket operators NCAA rules requiring the plane seats be available to other students as well as players, then provided his players with a telephone number for the operators.

UNLV conducted its own investigation and was unable to corroborate the charges. The NCAA found UNLV guilty of all charges anyway, and ordered Tarkanian removed from contact with the UNLV program for two years.

Stacey Augmon snares a rebound in December 1990. Rebels recruited by Tarkanian played with a grace that made it as beautiful as ballet.
(Review-Journal files)

"Before we hired Jerry we had a dream of having a big facility like Thomas and Mack Center, and we knew we had to have a big program to get it. We thought Jerry could do that, and he did."
—**Donald Baepler**
Former UNLV president

Tarkanian sued, and in October 1977 District Court Judge James Brennan granted a permanent injunction prohibiting the suspension.

NCAA investigator David Berst "threatened, coerced, promised immunity, promised rewards to athletes in his effort to obtain derogatory evidence against the plaintiff," Brennan wrote.

Tarkanian had won, but it was only the first round. Each succeeding year brought new allegations, some leveled by the NCAA, some by local media. Players driving luxury cars of cloudy title. Players involved in brawls and petty crimes.

One of the most infamous cases was the recruitment of Lloyd Daniels, a Brooklyn playground legend. A report by the Long Island *Newsday* said this alleged scholar was functionally illiterate and had failed to get a high-school degree from any of five high schools. (Tarkanian said Daniels was dyslexic, not illiterate.)

Someone provided Daniels with a car, which was against NCAA rules; arrangements were made for him to live in Las Vegas rent-free. In what many considered an attempt to circumvent rules limiting the amount of contact coaching staff could spend grooming a prospect, assistant basketball coach Mark Warkentien became Daniels' legal guardian.

In early 1987 Daniels was caught buying cocaine from an undercover police officer. Despite his reputation as "the Father Flanagan of college basketball," Tarkanian at the time said there was such a thing as a player too wild to be on the UNLV team, and Daniels was that player.

Dr. Paul Burns, a retired UNLV history professor and administrator, was faculty athletics representative from 1985 to 1994, in charge of verifying academic eligibility.

"It struck me as odd that he made some of his biggest mistakes when he was at the peak of his career, when he could have his pick of a lot of players," said Burns. "Recruiting Lloyd

The "Hot Tub Photos" ended Jerry Tarkanian's rule at UNLV, proving a link between convicted sports fixer Richard "Richie the Fixer" Perry and three members of the Rebels 1990 championship team. From left are Moses Scurry, Perry, Anderson Hunt, and David Butler.
(Review-Journal files)

Daniels and letting Mark Warkentien become his legal guardian, those things are beyond the pale."

But never once, added Burns, did Tarkanian or his staff exert pressure to bend academic rules.

Enter Dr. Robert Maxson, a president recruited from the University of Houston in 1983 to do for UNLV's academic reputation what Tarkanian had done for its athletic one.

"You can't assess Tarkanian without assessing Bob Maxson," said Michael Green, a history professor at Community College of Southern Nevada. "To their mutual chagrin, they are historically inseparable. ... They became embroiled in this terrible fight where neither man controlled his logic or emotion. In a sense, they destroyed each other."

Maxson tried, initially, to make Tarkanian an ally, escorting important guests to UNLV basketball games, particularly in the 1989-90 season, which culminated in UNLV's first NCAA championship. When an NCAA ban on UNLV post-season play effectively prohibited the champions from defending their title, Maxson helped work out a compromise that delayed the ban until 1992.

The relationship quickly soured, particularly after 1990 when Maxson forced the resignation of Brad Rothermel, the most successful athletic director UNLV ever had, and replaced him with Dennis Finfrock, no fan of Tarkanian.

The reports that most disturbed Maxson involved Richard Perry, a New York gambler who had been convicted in the Boston College basketball point-shaving scandal, who was hanging around the UNLV program. It turned out Perry had helped UNLV land the ill-starred recruit, Daniels.

Tarkanian said he initially knew Perry only as a summer-league coach who spotted great talents. Once Perry was identified as the infamous "Richie The Fixer," Tarkanian warned his players to stay away from Perry, and did so himself.

The 1990-91 team produced the finest record UNLV ever had, 34-0, then lost 79-77 to Duke in the 1991 NCAA semifinals. Duke was the team that UNLV had eaten alive in the 1990 champion-

ship, scoring 103-73.

On May 26, 1991, the *Review-Journal* published photos of Perry sharing his backyard hot tub, and playing basketball on his backyard court, with three members of the 1990 championship team. The photos were believed to have been taken in the fall of 1989, months after Tarkanian said he told his players to stay away from Perry.

On June 7, Tarkanian resigned. His attorneys had worked out an agreement that he would be allowed to coach the team one more year, when it would be banned from post-season play in any case.

Although the FBI issued a curious statement that "neither the University of Nevada-Las Vegas nor its present or former basketball players are subjects or targets of a point-shaving investigation," at least four people were questioned by FBI agents about Perry's relationship to the team and whether points might have been shaved. Nothing came of that investigation, but Perry subsequently was added to Nevada's "Black Book" of people who are not allowed in any gambling establishment.

The 1991-92 Rebels, playing for pride instead of the playoffs, delivered 26 victories and lost but twice. Tark's last game for UNLV, on March 3, 1992, was a 65-53 victory over Utah State. The *Review-Journal* headline next morning said: "Tark Goes Out a Winner."

Maxson was gone two years later. In the spring of 1994 he became president of Long Beach State — the other four-year college Tarkanian had put on the map.

After leaving UNLV in 1992, Tarkanian coached the San Antonio Spurs briefly, didn't get along with the owner and got fired. He resumed college coaching at Fresno State. Meanwhile, he used a $1.3 million settlement from the Spurs to fund a lawsuit against the NCAA.

In April 1998, the NCAA announced it was paying $2.5 million to Tarkanian. It never quite admitted harassing Tarkanian, but vowed "some improvements in the enforcement process ..."

To Tarkanian and those who believed in him, it sounded like vindication. ✍

Jean Ford

(1929–1998)

A driven woman with a knack for organization and a thirst for politics spent her adult life making Nevada a better place to live. **BY A.D. HOPKINS**

"In terms of changing the legislative process, making it more accountable, Jean Ford was more important than anybody else."
—Sue Wagner
Former lieutenant governor

When Jean Ford learned she had terminal cancer, she faced her own death with the same weapons she used to change Nevada. "She organized it," said her daughter, Janet Spelman. Her voice dropping to a whisper, Spelman repeated, "She organized it.

"Of course, she was shocked and angry at first, as anybody would be," Spelman continued. "But then she sat down with my sister and me, took out her calendar, and started crossing off things that weren't important anymore. She showed us what was left and said, 'This is what I want to do. What do you guys want to do?'"

With an estimated year to live, they started scheduling. There were holidays with daughters and grandchildren. There was a tour of Northern Nevada with a play Ford had written and intended to narrate. There was a visit to the Cowboy Poetry Gathering at Elko, with women who had become her allies and friends over some 30 active years in Nevada. She kept her commitments.

Former Lieutenant Governor Sue Wagner, who served with Ford in the Nevada Senate, said, "In terms of changing the legislative process, making it more accountable, Jean Ford was more important than anybody else." Familiar with every small town and crossroad in Nevada, Ford helped create the Nevada Department of Tourism, which spread the bonanza of visitors to smaller cities.

Historian James Hulse of UNR added, "She discovered something about the empowerment of women. She discovered that if you organize and plan your strategy, you can get a lot done. She taught others how to do it. She saw it as her mission to empower others, and particularly women."

Ford established the Nevada Women's Ar-

chives at UNR and UNLV, and the Nevada Women's History Project. Days after word of her terminal diagnosis spread through the academic community, NWHP dispatched an oral historian to record her story, published in a limited edition in 1998 under the title, *Jean Ford: A Nevada Woman Leads The Way.*

Ford was born in 1929 in Miami, Oklahoma, as Imogene Evelyn Young, the daughter of an insurance salesman. In her oral history, Ford described her mother as romantic and fun-loving, but mentally unstable: "One day she ran away and went back to the hospital on her own accord ... and then she never left there for the rest of her life." Ford was 9 years old. Until her father's divorce and remarriage, she helped look after her brother, Byron.

In Joplin, Missouri, Ford became a superior student but developed a stutter, which she never completely overcame. "I don't remember in just one-on-one conversation ever having much of a problem," she recalled. "Reciting in class, reading out loud from fixed words, any of that, I got to where I could not do it." That didn't keep her from becoming valedictorian of her high-school class or from making the required speech. She suggested that her inability to speak eloquently made her strive to excel at all else. Ballet. Tap. Folk dance. Violin in the student orchestra. Even singing with a madrigal group.

She also became active in Girl Scouts. "She

Ford in Southern Nevada

POP.[1]	DECADE
n/a	pre-1900
30	1900
945	1910
2,686	1920
5,952	1930
13,937	1940
45,577	1950
123,667	1960
273,288	1970
463,087	1980
715,587	1990
1,360,000[2]	2000

■ Time spent in Southern Nev.
1 - Population figures are for greater Las Vegas area (*Source: Nevada State Data Center*)
2 - Estimate

Jean Ford about 1980, when she served in the Nevada Senate
(Courtesy Janet Spelman)

earned 55 merit badges, which I believe was all there were to earn at the time," said her daughter, Carla Oberst. Ford majored in sociology at Southern Methodist University and joined the Red Cross as a recreational worker. Assigned to a military hospital in Hawaii, she taught ukulele to a young intern. They were married in 1955. Samuel Ford eventually specialized in dermatology, and the family moved to Las Vegas in 1962. By then they were four, including Janet, born in 1956, and Carla, born in 1958.

The family built a house on the golf course now called National, in Paradise Palms. Accustomed to lusher climes, the Fords began exploring their exotic desert surroundings.

"She would sit down at the typewriter and type an outline of a camping trip," remembered Spelman. "From a packing list to what our first, second, and third stops would be, and on a map she would have a red line drawn. "In her mind, she did it so we would have more fun and nothing would go wrong." But the meticulous organization "used to drive us nuts," Spelman added. "I'm a more spontaneous person. I like to grab stuff and get in the car, and that drove *her* nuts.

"We had a big yellow International Travelall and went all over the state in it. We would be driving along, and she would say, 'Pull over, Sam!' Very excited about seeing some wildflower, and she would bring one back to the car and flip through her wildflower books until she found it. I have some of her old wildflower books, and there are dried flowers between the pages. She has one of nearly every flower in the book."

The Fords' delight in their natural surroundings was not matched by their reaction to local conveniences. They lived in unincorporated Clark County, which had no library. The Fords suggested that their local Unitarian fellowship take on organizing a library. At the time, forming a library district required getting signatures of property owners representing 51 percent of total value in the proposed district. There were many absentee owners, hard to contact and generally uninterested once found.

John Porter, civil deputy in the Clark County District Attorney's Office, suggested looking for a more workable law in some other state. California law required signatures representing only 10 percent of the property, but also required voter approval. Ford journeyed to Carson City and asked that Nevada adopt the same rule, and it did, ultimately resulting in today's Las Vegas-Clark County Library District.

In the early '60s federal legislation mandated that the Bureau of Land Management inventory its lands and determine which should be sold for urban development. Some real estate developers cast avaricious eyes upon scenic Red Rock Canyon. Just the site for condos.

Others, such as the Fords and their buddies in the Sierra Club, thought the canyon should be preserved for public use. Ford signed up with the Clark County League of Women Voters because it was planning to address the parks issue, and one of her first activities for the League was surveying Las Vegans about it. Setting up a booth at the Jaycee State Fair, the women gathered more than 750 responses in two days. Strong community support was used to justify the preserve that eventually became the Red Rock National Conservation Area. Governor Paul Laxalt appointed Ford to the Nevada State Parks Commission, where she served from 1965 until 1972.

During this same period, the League of Women Voters tackled the toughest social issues Las Vegas ever faced, such as school integration. Harriet Trudell, now a Washington lobbyist for a think tank called Feminist Majority, worked on that project.

"The point we made was that the schools attended by black children were separate, but not equal, and we proved it," said Trudell. "We proved they bused white kids right by the black schools, so the neighborhood-schools argument they used was a farce." With this ammunition in hand, added Trudell, "Jean was the one who had the courage to say, 'Let's go.'" The League filed an amicus brief supporting an NAACP lawsuit against the Clark County School District and won the case in federal court.

Ford's work with the League immersed her in the Nevada Legislature, where she became a fixture in the public balcony. One day Senator Carl Dodge asked, "Have you thought about moving down a few rows?"

Instead, in 1972 she ran for the Assembly. In her first term, Ford served with Mary Gojack, D-Reno, on the government affairs committee. They were early advocates of reforms such as an ethics

Ford (left) speaks at the National Women's Conference in Houston, Texas, in November 1977.
(UNLV Special Collections)

bill and registration of lobbyists, which didn't pass at the time, but eventually did. Ford returned to the Legislature in 1975 and pushed through a bill requiring employers to give equal pay, hours, and working conditions regardless of gender.

"At that point Nevada had a law that said an employer could hire a woman at less than the minimum wage for 90 days, and it was called a probationary period," she recalled. "That was only for women, not for men. What was happening in reality is they would hire a woman for 90 days, then fire her and hire another woman for 90 days." Nevada also forbade women to work more than eight hours a day or 40 hours a week. This was originally intended to protect women from the sweatshop system, said Ford, but by 1975 "it really limited the kinds of jobs women could get."

Ford was for equal treatment—even for men. In the 1970s she was one of the first legislators to advocate giving men the same rights as women in custody disputes.

One thing people noticed about Ford was an egalitarian respect for whatever work people chose to do. Ford barely blinked when her daughter, Spelman, became a showgirl. "My sister Carla became a doctor, and of course my mother was very proud of her," said Spelman. "But every time my mother mentioned that to anybody, she also mentioned that I was in *Hallelujah Hollywood*."

In 1976 Ford ran for the Nevada Senate and lost, partly because Republican Party leaders failed to support her. So she became a Democrat and won a seat in 1978.

"She helped me increase marriage license fees to fund domestic violence shelters in the state," remembered Wagner. "She helped me establish Displaced Homemaker Centers, and I think the first was at the community college in Southern Nevada. When women are thrust back into the workforce by death or divorce, after being homemakers for 20 years during which the technology of the workplace has completely changed, they can go there to learn computer skills, for instance."

Ford was an untiring advocate of the Equal Rights Amendment, but the Nevada Legislature did not ratify it.

She did not run for re-election to the Senate, largely because her marriage to Samuel broke up in 1977, and being divorced required her to work full time.

In 1980 Ford and a group of her friends formed Jean Ford Associates, a company capitalizing on skills they had developed in volunteer work. In her oral history Ford said, "What I found is … for the most part the public did not want to pay me to deliver those kinds of skills. They were too used to getting them for free." Jean Ford Associates lasted only a year, but Ford did better as the sole proprietor of Jean Ford Company, offering much the same services. In 1983 she teamed up with Maxine Peterson in Nevada Discovery Tours, which arranged bus tours of Nevada's scenic areas and historic mining towns, largely as daytime amusement for spouses while their mates attended Las Vegas conventions.

Ford served on the tourism commission in the late 1970s and as director of community services from 1985 to 1989, then went to work for a Reno casino.

In 1991 she was hired as acting director of UNR Women's Studies, an interdisciplinary academic program revolving around women's relationship to society. She began teaching courses with names like "Women in Politics" and "Women in Public Leadership." Standard leadership texts were used, but Ford augmented them with guest lectures by 20 prominent Nevada women.

In 1992 she offered a course titled "Nevada Women on the Frontier" and asked UNR's special collections section to give her a list of Nevada women on whom enough information had been gathered for students to research term papers. "They came back to me with a list that was shorter than the number of students I had in the class," said Ford.

It was her first realization that most of women's contributions in Nevada had gone un-

documented. She mounted a campaign to locate letters, diaries, and other documents. The Nevada Women's Archive, as it was named, soon had a branch at UNLV as well. By 1998, Ford estimated the effort had gathered at least 500 collections of papers from women who had played some role in state history. When UNR finally found a permanent director for Women's Studies, Ford was free to throw herself into founding the Nevada Women's History Project, which supports such efforts as researching biographies of women, posting them on the Internet, publishing a newsletter/history magazine, and organizing historical tours.

In the fall of 1997, Ford learned she had pancreatic cancer and that it probably would kill her within a year. She spent much of that time winding up projects already started. She had written a play about a visit to Nevada by Sara Bard Field, the suffragette who crossed the United States in an Overland automobile in 1916. Ford narrated seven performances in five days.

Friends helped her organize 30 years worth of color slides and prints taken in Nevada's back country, and she donated them to the Nevada State Museum. She organized her personal notes chronologically, making her oral history one of the most thorough—and frank—ever gathered in Nevada.

On the last day of her life, daughter Oberst related, "Her friend Kate Butler brought her guitar in, Maya Miller was there … and we sang old campaign songs. One of them goes, 'You can ride on the Jean Machine./Come take a ride, see what we mean./It's all hand-tooled and it's people fueled,/The Jean Machine Mobile." She rarely opened her eyes by then, but she was singing, and she was smiling. Ford died August 26, 1998, at her home in Carson City. ℘

Jean Ford (standing at right) helps volunteers mail out material for her 1976 campaign.
(UNLV Special Collections)

Harry Reid (1939–)

He won some and lost some, but retained the independence of his hard-rock-miner father
and found himself Democratic whip of the U.S. Senate. **BY K.J. EVANS**

The Las Vegas Spaghetti Bowl had been giving drivers heartburn for years, until Senator Harry Reid bathed it in a soothing sauce of $45 million in federal highway funds. Remember that big hole in the ground? Reid spent three years rounding up $98 million to build a new federal courthouse in it.

At the close of the century, Reid has emerged as the successor to Nevada Democrats such as Francis Newlands, Key Pittman, and Pat McCarran, all of whom shared a talent for bringing home the federal bacon.

"His effectiveness for Nevada is his seniority, and the fact that in a relatively short amount of time, he has attained a fairly high profile," says political analyst Jon Ralston, publisher of the *Ralston Report*. "He's only been in the U.S. Senate since 1986, and he's already in its second-highest position [Democratic whip]. That's really saying something.

"He's not the most dynamic personality in the world; what he's been able to do is build relationships. He's willing to take on the grunt work that nobody else really wants, and that earns him chits with the leadership and with members of the other party, too."

Harry Mason Reid was born in Searchlight on December 2, 1939, third of the four sons of Harry and Inez Reid. The elder Reid was a hard-rock underground miner. Underground mining involves dynamite, and miners were frequently pelted by tiny rocks. Reid recalls watching his father sitting backward and shirtless in a chair while his mother scanned his back looking for stony outcroppings. "They would work their way to the surface, and my mother would pick them out as they did," Reid explains.

As a grade-school kid, young Harry, with his own helmet and carbide lamp, would go underground to keep his father company. As he got older, he worked alongside him: "I never did any drilling, but I ran the hoist on a lot of occasions, and I did a lot of mucking." Mucking is the backbreaking job of shoveling rock, shattered by dynamite, into an ore cart.

The senior Reid was a tough independent man possessed of a strong work ethic. By 1972, his health failing, he could no longer work. The reality of never again being productive was more than he could bear, and when his wife stepped out on an errand one day, he fatally shot himself.

Inez Reid taught her boys that despite their humble home life, they were as good as anyone and could reach any station in life if they had the ambition, something that is a "primal instinct" for Reid, according to Larry Werner, a former *Review-Journal* reporter who later worked for Reid as his press secretary.

Reid attended Basic High School in Henderson, where he boarded with a family. It was at Basic that he met Landra Gould. "She was a sophomore and I was a junior," says Reid. "We started dating and we've been together ever since."

In his senior year at Basic, Reid was elected student-body president and met his new history teacher, a big Irishman who had lost a leg in Korea. Donal "Mike" O'Callaghan would loom large

Reid in Southern Nevada

POP.[1]	DECADE
n/a	pre-1900
30	1900
945	1910
2,686	1920
5,952	1930
13,937	1940
45,577	1950
123,667	1960
273,288	1970
463,087	1980
715,587	1990
1,360,000[2]	2000

■ Time spent in Southern Nev.
1 - Population figures are for greater Las Vegas area (*Source: Nevada State Data Center*).
2 - Estimate

Now Nevada's senior senator, Democrat Harry Reid makes a point during an interview, October 1991. He was first elected to the Senate in 1986.

(Review-Journal files)

in Reid's future career.

Reid graduated from Basic High School in 1957 and earned an associate of arts degree from Southern Utah State College in 1959. That year, he married his high-school sweetheart. She was Jewish and Reid was unchurched, but shortly after their marriage, both joined the Church of Jesus Christ of Latter-day Saints. In 1960 and 1961, the first of their five children were born. "She gave up most of her education to put me through school," says Reid. "I'm the one who should have worked and let *her* go to school. She's much smarter than I."

O'Callaghan kept in touch with his former pupil, providing advice, encouragement, money, and the benefit of his burgeoning political power. On a scholarship arranged by O'Callaghan, Reid attended Utah State University in Logan, where he had a dual major in history and political science, graduating in 1961 with a bachelor's degree in both.

That year, O'Callaghan, then chairman of the Clark County Democratic Party, wrote to then Congressman Walter Baring, asking if he could arrange a patronage job in Washington for his young protégé, who was enrolling at the George Washington University School of Law. Baring wrote back, essentially giving O'Callaghan the brush. To make matters worse, he had misspelled O'Callaghan's proud Celtic name.

Reid was present when O'Callaghan received the letter, and watched as he picked up the phone, dialed Baring, and verbally terrorized him for several minutes. "What right do you have to write a letter to me and not even spell my name right?" roared the big man. "This is one of the best kids I've ever had and you're telling me you don't have a place for him?" In short order, Reid was sporting the uniform and badge of a Capitol policeman, and attending law school.

In 1963, with another year of school to go, he petitioned the Nevada Supreme Court to allow him to take the state bar examination, offered only once a year. The court approved Reid's request. He flew home and was met at the airport by O'Callaghan, who pressed a green bill into his hand. "It was the first $50 bill I had ever seen," says Reid. "He is a … disabled veteran, and his pensions have always gone to students. He helped pay my way through law school."

In 1964, when he graduated, Reid was licensed to practice law in Nevada, and the family returned to Henderson where, as the first resident to graduate from law school, he was appointed city attorney. Reid also maintained a private law practice. His first elected office was to the Southern Nevada Memorial Hospital Board of Trustees, which he chaired 1966-68.

Brimming with confidence, Reid decided in 1967 to run for one of Clark County's 18 seats in the assembly. "I picked a fight with the phone company—service was so bad then—and they were dumb enough to respond to me," says Reid. "So I had an issue." Reid was the top vote-getter among the 18 people who won seats in the 1968 assembly and one of only two freshman elected that year. The other was Richard Bryan.

That year, the public got a look at the Reid work ethic. He churned out bills like a mucker being paid by the ton. "I hold the record for introducing more bills in a session than any one person in history," says Reid. "I didn't get many of them passed, though. I think the most important thing I did in that session of the Legislature is pave the way for others to adopt legislation that I introduced."

Reid says he introduced the state's first air pollution bill, and another bill to force utilities to pay interest on the large deposits they levied on ratepayers. Both have since become law.

Reid proved Jimmy Breslin's assertion that politics is "all smoke and mirrors" in the 1970 race for lieutenant governor against Robert Broadbent. "I didn't have organization, and I had very little money, but people didn't realize that," says Reid. "People thought that Howard Hughes was behind my organization, and I never lied to anybody and said he was, but I never said he wasn't, either. It was one of my easier elections."

Surprising, too. His old mentor, Mike O'Callaghan, was the Democratic nominee for governor, facing an "unbeatable" Ed Fike, the outgoing lieutenant governor.

"I was favored to become lieutenant governor; he [O'Callaghan] had no chance when he filed as governor," says Reid. What no one had anticipated, though, was that in the midst of the campaign season, Fike would become embroiled in a conflict-of-interest scandal over his purchase of government land along the Colorado River while in office.

At age 31, Reid was the youngest lieutenant governor in the state's history, and O'Callaghan became governor. "There has never been a governor and lieutenant governor that worked more closely than we did," says Reid. "There was never a meeting he didn't invite me to. I knew everything."

Though O'Callaghan's job was full time and Reid's was part time, the hard-charging governor expected everyone around him to work as hard as he did. "It was a very grueling four years," says

Reid chats with former President Gerald Ford, late 1970s.
(Review-Journal files)

Nevada Gaming Commission Chairman Reid (right) listens to his predecessor, Peter Echeverria, make a point as Commissioner Clair Haycock looks on. This photo was taken in December 1978, during the infamous commission meeting in which Frank "Lefty" Rosenthal was denied a license and subsequently threw a public tantrum.
(Review-Journal files)

Reid receives a dab of makeup prior to going before TV cameras, 1983.
(Review-Journal files)

Reid. "O'Callaghan had no clock in his head; he had no idea what time it was, day or night. He would call me at three in the morning as if it were three in the afternoon."

Veteran Democrat Alan Bible announced he would not seek re-election in the 1974 senatorial race. Reid decided he was ready for national office. His opponent was Paul Laxalt, who had been governor when Howard Hughes came to Las Vegas in 1966. Reid launched an aggressive negative campaign, accusing Laxalt of profiting from his association with Hughes. Laxalt had indeed taken cash donations from the billionaire, but so had Reid, O'Callaghan, and virtually every other politician in the state.

Reid lost to Laxalt by a little over 600 votes. It was the 35-year-old's first such loss, and he didn't handle it well. In a rare public show of petulance, Reid accused the Northern Nevada press of costing him the election. The reply was swift and sharp. "Reid lost because he ran the worst political campaign anyone can recall around here," wrote Warren Lerude, then executive editor of the *Reno Evening Gazette* and *Nevada State Journal*. "All Reid didn't say was that the press won't have Harry Reid to kick around anymore."

"I was young, impetuous, and I had never lost anything," Reid says. "I might as well have blamed Nikita Khrushchev. It was just a sign of my immaturity. But it was one of the most character-building experiences of my life."

Against the advice of all his supporters, Reid filed for the 1975 Las Vegas mayoral race. Still depressed from his senatorial loss, he ran a lackluster campaign, and voters rejected him in favor of Bill Briare.

In mid-1977, O'Callaghan appointed Reid to succeed Peter Echeverria as chairman of the Nevada Gaming Commission. It looked like a political plum, but proved to be a hot potato.

Sometime during the mid-1970s, members of the Chicago and Kansas City mobs began buying into Las Vegas, filling the void created by the departure of Howard Hughes and the retirement of old-line crime bosses such as Meyer Lansky.

The front man was Allen Glick, whose Argent Corp. purchased the Stardust and Fremont hotels. The enforcer was a deadly thug, Anthony "Tony the Ant" Spilotro. Mr. Inside, the guy who actually ran the Stardust and skimmed millions in untaxed dollars for the Chicago and Kansas City bosses, was Frank "Lefty" Rosenthal, a convicted sports fixer. Rosenthal posed variously as Glick's assistant, entertainment director, and food and beverage manager. In 1976, he was forced to apply for a state gaming license, but it was denied based on his criminal background.

Rosenthal decided to fight. On the public-opinion front, the *Las Vegas Sun* and the *Valley Times* abruptly reversed earlier positions favoring strict gambling regulation and began howling about the high-handed tactics of state gaming authorities in general, and the abuse of Rosenthal in particular. On the legal front, Rosenthal hired Oscar Goodman, who eventually took the case to the Nevada Supreme Court, which affirmed the state's broad rights in granting privilege licenses. The U.S. Supreme Court refused to hear the case.

Lefty's last stand came in December 1978, when he came before Reid's five-member Gaming Commission, which unanimously voted to deny Rosenthal's application. Rosenthal pitched an impressive tantrum. He accused Reid of having a complimentary lunch with *Las Vegas Sun* executive Brian Greenspun at the Stardust. Reid recalled the lunch, but pointed out that he wasn't on the Gaming Commission at the time.

"Of all the jobs I've held, that was the most educational," says Reid. "Before that, the words 'organized crime' were nothing but words. When I took over the Gaming Commission, they still didn't mean anything. But that changed when they divulged all the FBI tapes and we found hidden inter-

ests in the Aladdin and at all the Argent properties. They put bombs on my car, there were threatening phone calls at night, people tried to bribe me and went to jail." (The car bombs were simple devices designed to light a spark in the gas tank. They failed.)

Wiseguy Joe Agosto, masquerading as "entertainment director" at the Tropicana, was heard on an FBI wiretap bragging to his bosses in Kansas City that "I've gotta Cleanface in my pocket," which the feds believed to be a reference to Reid. A five-month investigation concluded that Agosto's boast was nothing more than an attempt to show his superiors that he was "connected," and vindicated Reid. Governor Robert List asked Reid to remain chairman, but he declined and left office in April 1981.

By 1982, Nevada was awarded a new congressional seat representing Southern Nevada, and Reid beat Republican Peggy Cavnar to become the first to occupy the seat in 1983. Almost immediately, Reid denounced the high-level nuclear waste repository proposed at Yucca Mountain.

Elected to the U.S. Senate in 1986, Reid concluded the long-unfinished task of creating Great Basin National Park and new wilderness areas. ❧

Alfreda Mitre (1954–)

A woman who grew up as one of the Colony kids helped her Paiute people achieve economic equality without sacrificing their identity. **BY A.D. HOPKINS**

Alfreda Mitre was in the second grade when the differences boiled over. The Colony kids, as children of the Las Vegas Paiute Tribe called themselves, had been redistricted to Washington Elementary School and found the inhabitants hostile.

"The teachers didn't know what to do with us and the other kids didn't like us, and some of the Colony kids were punched around," Mitre said. "Finally, we banded together and had a big knock-down drag-out fight with our tormentors. Boys and girls on both sides, mostly pushing and shoving, and a few sat on others and a few threw blows, and then it was over. We told them ... we don't want to be here ourselves, but we are mandated to be, so leave us alone."

Mitre told the story to illustrate a key fact of life for the Las Vegas Paiutes: "We don't have the choice of moving to some other neighborhood. We're a land-based people; where we are is a big part of who we are."

The long period of poverty endured by the Las Vegas Paiutes, and the economic miracle that lifted them out of it, are both firmly rooted in that fact. For more than 50 years, living on their ancestral tribal lands—the 10-acre fragment that even whites acknowledged as legally theirs—seemed the only way they could hold on to their land and their identity. Yet living there condemned them to a 19th-century lifestyle without running water or electricity, let alone the great cultural leveler of television. City water lines didn't serve the reservation; city equipment didn't pave the streets; city cops didn't patrol the streets.

Mitre, 45, was chairperson of the tribe when some of the most positive changes occurred. "The tribe as a whole can take the credit," she said. "Because we are so small we can do what most reservations can't do, and that is govern almost by consensus." There are only 54 adult members of the tribe.

Las Vegas Paiutes are descendants of a band that used to migrate all over the Las Vegas Valley. They returned to the same spots every year in proper season to harvest wild plants or hunt small game.

But in 1905, a railroad brought settlers by the hundreds, claiming all water sources and all fertile lands. Helen J. Stewart, who had operated the Las Vegas Ranch for years, realized that the Indians who had befriended her would soon be pushed out of their homeland. To prevent that, she sold a 10-acre parcel to the federal government for the

Mitre in Southern Nevada

POP.[1]	DECADE
n/a	pre-1900
30	1900
945	1910
2,686	1920
5,952	1930
13,937	1940
45,577	1950
123,667	1960
273,288	1970
463,087	1980
715,587	1990
1,360,000[2]	2000

■ Time spent in Southern Nev.
1 - Population figures are for greater Las Vegas area (*Source: Nevada State Data Center*).
2 - Estimate

Alfreda Mitre, shown in a 1996 photo, came home to her Las Vegas Paiute Tribe to help a formerly poor people invest their new wealth wisely.

(Review-Journal files)

perpetual use of the Paiutes.

It became known as the Las Vegas Indian Colony. For some 20 years, it was administered—or more accurately, neglected—as a remote part of the Moapa Paiute Reservation. No rations were ever issued there by the Bureau of Indian Affairs.

A school was built at the Colony, but it was soon abandoned. For many years Colony children were sent to boarding schools. By the time Mitre came along, Paiute children attended Clark County schools. But "Colony kids" found themselves different from their classmates in ways that were more than skin deep.

Among American Indians, said Mitre, it is impolite to look another person directly in the face. "So one of my cousins was always in trouble because she wouldn't look at her teacher. The teacher would yell at her, 'Don't you hear me?' And my cousin respected this teacher a lot, liked her, and that was just all the more reason she wouldn't look at her."

The Colony had no electricity, so the children didn't see the TV shows that filled the conversation of their classmates. "We had great imaginations," Mitre says. "We played we were movie stars and put on plays. We had all sorts of competitions. Foot races, or we would race the train that ran along one side of the Paiute land. Some had dirt bikes. We'd see who could throw the farthest, who could hop the highest, who could make up the best stories," remembers Mitre. "On Saturdays we would go uptown and check our mail. We couldn't get our mail delivered because we didn't have defined streets, and therefore no street addresses."

Mitre adds, "Then we would sneak into the library and read as much as we could before they booted us out. We couldn't check out books, again because we didn't have addresses, and you had to have an address to get a library card."

The Las Vegas Paiute Tribe was recognized as an independent body in 1934. The tribe's early leaders, like Raymond and Kenneth Anderson, said Mitre, were heavily involved with the Mor-

mon Church. "They recognized that if you made friends with these people, they would help you."

In the 1960s LDS church leaders helped the tribe get water lines and electricity extended into the tribal land. The 1970s saw the tribe start writing its own building codes and establish a police force.

Curtis Anderson, the current tribal chairman, said the first smokeshop, at North Main Street and Paiute Drive, started about 1983. It quickly developed the reputation of being the cheapest place in town to buy cigarettes.

David A. Colvin, the tribe's attorney, explained that the state cannot collect taxes on sales on Paiute lands. However, the tribe must collect its own tax equal to, or greater than, the amount the state would collect. The tribal tax funds the Colony police department, court, and other social services. Outright profits are divided among tribal members.

Smokeshop money, said Mitre, enabled the tribe to replace substandard houses. "Things moved so quickly that the best thing was to knock down the makeshift dwellings and move in the doublewides," said Mitre. The tribe bought the mobile homes initially and sold them to tribe members on an installment plan.

In the '70s and '80s, Paiute adults saw that the Colony was losing its usefulness as a place to rear children. The location was rural when Helen Stewart sold the property in 1910, but the city had grown up around it and had fallen into urban decay. Tribal members began lobbying Congress to recover additional acreage from their original territory.

In 1983 Congress authorized a new 4,000-acre reservation, straddling the Tonopah Highway north of Kyle Canyon road. Lying at the foot of Mount Charleston, the reservation was given the mountain's Paiute name, translated into English: Snow Mountain.

Mitre, meanwhile, had gone away to Sherman Indian High School in Riverside, California: "It was no longer mandatory, but it was my grandmother's preference that I meet other Indi-

ans." She went to Riverside Community College and then to the University of California-Riverside for a degree and graduate work in sociology. Now she works for the University of California-Santa Cruz in a multidisciplinary program blending history and sociology.

She took leave of her academic career twice to return to Las Vegas and serve as chairperson, from 1990 to 1998, with a break in 1993-1994. "My whole reason for returning home was to assist in diversifying the business," she said. "All we had was the smokeshop."

The tribe's main asset was the 4,000 acres of raw land, and developing it seemed the obvious direction to go. "Deciding what to do was a little scary for us," said Mitre. "We don't feel we're like most businesses in Las Vegas. If they build something and it doesn't work, they can move on. Las Vegas Paiute Tribe doesn't have that option, because they feel the place is what gives them their sense of being."

The decision was to build the Las Vegas Paiute Golf Resort, but to build it in a way that did not violate the desert. "We decided not to import too much vegetation, except the grass. We collected the native seeds and reseeded the disturbed areas, hoping that in five years it would look like somebody had just dropped this golf course into the desert."

There was a water rights lawsuit with the Las Vegas Valley Water District, settled out of court in 1996. The Paiutes got 2,000 acre-feet of water a year, enough to develop two of the four courses, a residential area, and a resort hotel. Two courses, designed by the renowned Pete Dye, are open.

Mitre said the Paiute want to remain good neighbors to the growing city of Las Vegas. "If you look at what has happened in other areas, when human remains are unearthed—under the American Indian Repatriation Act, a tribe can put a stop to almost any kind of development, if they choose. But we don't do that. We have the philosophy to take only what you need, no more and no less." ✍

> "We don't have the choice of moving to some other neighborhood. We're a land-based people; where we are is a big part of who we are."
> —Alfreda Mitre

BOB STUPAK (1942-)

He earned his gift of gab at the heels of his father, then brought his schtick to Las Vegas, bet against the odds, and won. BY JOHN L. SMITH

Leave it to Bob Stupak, perhaps the greatest huckster in Las Vegas history, to defy the odds. Here is a man who took the worst piece of real estate on Las Vegas Boulevard and developed a successful casino there. Here is a man who crashed his Harley Davidson motorcycle going more than 60 mph. He wasn't expected to live, but did.

Finally, here is a man who constructed his dream project—the Stratosphere Tower—and at last won over his many critics. For the first time in his life, it seemed that everyone agreed Bob Stupak had a winner in the 1,049-foot tower with the rooftop roller-coaster and the NASA-like rocket ride. A sure winner, indeed.

So naturally, it went bankrupt. On the way down, Stupak lost more than $100 million in stock value. He lost the trust of hundreds of investors. Somehow, he managed to maintain his sense of humor. It would serve him well throughout his rocky travels.

Bob Stupak was born April 6, 1942, in Pittsburgh to Florence and Chester Stupak. Chester was the reigning king of the South Side gambling rackets at a time when the mob muscled the action and Bob learned early on to appreciate the importance of making friends and influencing people.

After leaving school, Bob Stupak ran his own illegal card games; bought and sold watches; raced motorcycles and nearly killed himself; became a nightclub singer and cut several singles while under a brief recording contract as "Bobby Star"; and started a thriving business selling two-for-one coupon books. "I never had a steady job," he once said. "All the jobs I had were self-inflicted."

The coupon books took him all the way to Australia, where he developed a lucrative telemarketing operation.

Shortly thereafter, with his own cash and some raised from his father's friends, Stupak acquired a homely 1.5-acre parcel, north of Sahara Avenue on Las Vegas Boulevard South, that once was home to a car lot. What rose in its place and opened on March 31, 1974, was a small slot joint named Bob Stupak's World Famous Historic Gambling Museum. "The name was about 10 feet longer than the casino," Stupak recalled years later.

On May 21, an air conditioner caught fire and burned the joint down. Arson was suspected, but the insurance company eventually settled the claim.

In the late '70s, Stupak persuaded Valley Bank legends Ken Sullivan and E. Parry Thomas to part with more than $1 million to build Vegas World, a 20-story tower, on the same site. Vegas World opened on a Friday the 13th in 1979. Stupak suffered not only from a small bankroll and a mediocre location—he was neither downtown nor on the Strip, and construction costs had eaten all his reserve funds—but the only thing his club offered the curious was his unique personality and gift of promotion. His motto was plastered across the building: "The Sky's the Limit."

Stupak developed quirky and interesting

Stupak in Southern Nevada

POP.[1]	DECADE
n/a	pre-1900
30	1900
945	1910
2,686	1920
5,952	1930
13,937	1940
45,577	1950
123,667	1960
273,288	1970
463,087	1980
715,587	1990
1,360,000[2]	2000

■ Time spent in Southern Nev.
1 - Population figures are for greater Las Vegas area (*Source: Nevada State Data Center*).
2 - Estimate

Bob Stupak in a typical promotional pose
(Review-Journal files)

The Titanic hotel, 400 feet long and containing 1,200 rooms, would have been one of the most heavily themed fantasy resorts in Las Vegas. The concept was pure Stupak.
(Review-Journal files)

Bob Stupak's Stratosphere Tower, opened in 1996, became Las Vegas' most conspicuous landmark.
(Craig Moran/Review-Journal)

angles on traditional games, such as blackjack and craps. Among his wagering innovations were Double Exposure 21, Experto, Crapless Craps, and Polish Roulette. He also accepted high-limit wagers at the tables and in his sports book, where he sometimes recklessly shifted the odds in order to generate action.

Stupak constantly promoted himself. He appeared in many movies and TV series, and once starred in a 1987 episode of "Crime Story." He ran for mayor in 1987, surviving the primary with 33 percent of the vote, but losing in the general to incumbent Ron Lurie.

Many of Stupak's wagers appear to have been made as much for promotional reasons as for profit. He played no-limit poker for $500,000 against the ORAC computer on a national television program, made a $1 million bet on Super Bowl XXIII, and made regular appearances at the World Series of Poker. The fact that he won many of his bets was overshadowed by the advertising Vegas World and its owner received.

At its peak, Bob Stupak's Vegas World generated more than $100 million in annual gambling revenues. Ever the gambler, in the late 1980s Stupak began devising a way to make an even bigger mark in Las Vegas. All he had to do was risk everything he owned.

The idea for the Stratosphere Tower began after a heavy windstorm blew down the sign in front of Vegas World. Stupak decided to erect the world's tallest sign. Then, on a trip to Australia, he saw the Sydney Tower and became intrigued. Back in Las Vegas, he researched observation towers and found that throughout history, they had redefined skylines and attracted crowds. But they weren't cheap.

Stupak began building his dream project out of the cash flow at Vegas World, while attempting to round up investors and stage an initial public offering of stock in Stratosphere Corporation. But getting a skeptical public to trust the same Bob Stupak who gave it Vegas World, who gave the voters fits with his outrageous campaigns, and who gave the Gaming Control Board headaches

with his complaint-generating two-for-one coupon vacations, wouldn't be easy.

By late August 1993, the tower was a stumpy but substantial 510 feet high. The offering was similarly situated. With a deadline looming, there were still millions to raise. A fire on August 29 ruined Stupak's chances for a late rally. Although no structural damage was reported, few people were willing to invest in a project that had already been labeled a "towering inferno" in the press.

At the time of the fire, Stupak was in Minnesota attempting to carve out a partnership in the

project with Lyle Berman of Grand Casinos Inc. Berman was on the hottest roll in all of the casino industry, and when he agreed to take on the project, it meant two things: First, Stupak would finally see his dream tower completed; second, he would no longer be in charge of the deal. He would become just an investor, albeit a major one.

And that's the way it went until the night of March 31, 1995, when Bob Stupak and his son, Nevada, were involved in a devastating motorcycle accident on Rancho Drive. "I don't know how anyone could have survived," said Stupak's companion, singer Phyllis McGuire. "Every bone in his face was fragmented. It was worse than anything you could see in a horror movie."

But with daily assistance from doctors and McGuire, Stupak recovered and continued his rehabilitation as Stratosphere moved toward completion. Its costs, however, had skyrocketed. Its debts were mounting.

Although Stupak faced potential fines totaling $2.9 million for gaming violations linked to his vacation programs, the regulatory matters were resolved with a much smaller fine.

When the Stratosphere opened, it was touted as a $550 million project, the third most expen-

sive hotel-casino in the history of Las Vegas. It attracted big crowds of tourists, but few players. Stratosphere's stock price dropped from $17 a share to a few bucks in a matter of weeks. The hotel-casino later went bankrupt, changed management hands, and was eventually purchased by takeover magnate Carl Icahn. Stupak rarely sets foot in the place these days.

In the spring of 1999, the Las Vegas City Council nixed Stupak's plan to build a 280-foot timeshare, shaped like the Titanic ocean liner. As quickly as that plan was rejected, he announced intentions to buy the Moulin Rouge on Bonanza Road. But can he make a comeback in the casino game?

"The big problem Bob has is you can't enter the game as easily as you could in the old days," said author and poker expert David Sklansky. "If you don't have $100 million to throw around, it's hard to get into the game. The sad part about it is Bob had to be almost ruined before he could make a resurgence."

Even Stupak does not sound optimistic about making a comeback. "The days of those characters are gone," Stupak once said. "There's no more Jay Sarnos around. There's no more me's around. It's all over." ⌀

Steve Wynn (1942–)

"Wynn is proactive, and that is his political importance. Also, he has taken an interest in national politics. Howard Hughes quietly gave money to presidential candidates, but Wynn plays golf with them."
—Michael Green
Community College of Southern Nevada history professor

In a bloodless coup with the help of a banker turned mentor, a boy from back East took over a downtown hotel and everything he touched from then on was golden. BY A.D. HOPKINS

Yuppies take a morning stroll in Bellagio's botanical garden, splendid with blooms. They marvel at original paintings they once studied from color slides in school. They dine in French restaurants and buy gowns they'll wear proudly to black-tie fundraisers in Charlotte or Dallas or Boston.

Before the 1990s, the word "elegance" was not used in the same sentence as "Vegas." The reality of an earlier Vegas was excess, not elegance. It was about ogling long-legged cocktail waitresses in Daisy Duke tights. Food was thick steaks, drinks were scotch, and the fashions were furs on the mistress and jackass slacks on the Dunes golf course.

It took a man who understood both worlds to bring about change. Steve Wynn, whose father ran bingo games back East and squandered his profits on the gambling tables of old-time Vegas, has become a tycoon in the business of marketing snob appeal.

He created a new era not only in Nevada resorts, but in Nevada politics as well. Although Nevadans have long worried that casino interests might dominate state politics, Wynn is one of the few to aggressively pursue political agendas. His agendas have included better state colleges, bet-

ter Clark County schools, and a more sensible growth rate for Las Vegas.

Wynn started coming to Las Vegas in 1952. He was 10 years old, and his dad used to go to bed with him and then "sneak out at night and shoot the dice at the Flamingo and the Sands," Wynn told an interviewer in 1983. Some 30 years

earlier, he remembered, Vegas had been a place where one hitched horses on rails at a casino's back door. "It was like stepping back into the frontier," Wynn said. "Casino owners were king; they owned the town. They were glamorous; they had beautiful women and lots of money."

All the observations Wynn made about casino owners in 1952 would be made about Wynn himself in the fullness of time.

Wynn's father opened a bingo parlor in Las Vegas, but he was unable to obtain a gaming license and was forced to close. He returned to Utica, New York, and reared Steve and his brother, Kenneth, who is 10 years younger, in an atmosphere of affluence. Wynn attended a military prep school and the University of Pennsylvania, and also took classes at Wharton Business School. He spent weekends breaking into his father's bingo business.

He met Elaine Paschal, the daughter of one of his father's gambling buddies, a hotel promoter in Miami. Elaine was a blonde beauty who had been selected Miss Miami Beach. They were married in 1963, a couple of months after his father died during open-heart surgery, and a couple of months before Wynn's graduation from the University of Pennsylvania.

The Wynns moved to Las Vegas in 1967 and Wynn invested in the Frontier Hotel,

Wynn in Southern Nevada

POP.[1]	DECADE
n/a	pre-1900
30	1900
945	1910
2,686	1920
5,952	1930
13,937	1940
45,577	1950
123,667	1960
273,288	1970
463,087	1980
715,587	1990
1,360,000[2]	2000

■ Time spent in Southern Nev.
1 - Population figures are for greater Las Vegas area (*Source: Nevada State Data Center*).
2 - Estimate

Steve Wynn, chairman of Mirage Resorts, shows off some of the museum-quality art he put on display at Bellagio, the first ongoing attraction of its kind at a Las Vegas resort.
(Review-Journal files)

Many Nominated for *The First 100*

Time and space considerations required that The First 100 project be limited to profiles of 100 people who contributed to the shaping of Southern Nevada. But more than 300 people were nominated for consideration, forcing editors to make hard choices about which to profile.

A few were rejected because they arrived after the deadline for nominations or because there was no way to verify the accomplishment attributed to them, but most would have made interesting stories. Several important political figures and casino operators, particularly, were passed over to make room for a wider variety of subjects.

Following is a list of other persons who were nominated. In some cases, the Las Vegas Review-Journal was unable to authenticate the information provided about the nominees. But in every case, somebody considered the nominee important enough to become part of the historical record.

Adams, Joanie — 1957 Miss Nevada and the winner of many other beauty titles; also the entertainment coordinator for the Flamingo Hotel.

Adelson, Sheldon — Expanded the convention business in Las Vegas and built the Venetian.

Adler, Wolf — Instrumental in creating the Nevada Chamber Ensemble.

Advent, Mark — Conceptual designer of New York, New York resort.

Agassi, Andre — Champion tennis player and supporter of local charities.

Albanese, Thomas — Founder of the Las Vegas Chili Company.

Allen, Lou — Drove a dynamite truck during the building of Hoover Dam.

Allen, Margaret — A founding member of the Junior League and a lifelong volunteer.

Apcar, Frederick — Major pioneer in defining Las Vegas production shows.

Armijo, Antonio — Brought a trading expedition through this region in January 1830, establishing one version of the "Old Spanish Trail."

Banker, Lem — Professional bettor and sports commentator.

Barrick, Marjorie — Philanthropist, particularly supportive of the arts.

Bartlett, Selma — Pioneered lending and funding for small businesses and schools.

Beam, Tom — A substantial donor to the University of Nevada-Las Vegas and Opportunity Village.

Beckley, Will — Pioneer retailer, whose house is now at the Southern Nevada Heritage Museum.

Beesley, Hal — Land developer and philanthropist.

Bolognini, Enio — Great cellist who lived in Las Vegas and inspired serious music locally.

Borders, Myram — Ran the United Press International Las Vegas bureau for 20 years and served as commissioner of the Nevada Division of Consumer Affairs.

Borsack, Edward W. — Opened El Portal luggage in 1936, one of the city's oldest family-owned businesses.

Boyd, Bill — Golden Nugget poker boss who popularized the game.

Brennan, James — County commissioner and district court judge.

Briare, William H. — Served as Clark County commissioner, 1963-1971, and as mayor of Las Vegas, 1975-1987.

Brookman, Eileen — Represented Clark County in the state assembly, 1967-77.

Brown, Bob — Ran the *Valley Times* newspaper, which briefly challenged the dominance of the *Review-Journal* and the *Sun*.

Brown, Ed — Associated with the African-American newspaper, the *Vegas Voice*.

Brown, Joe W. — Donated 410 acres to Clark County for the convention center site.

Bunker, Richard W. — President of the Nevada Resort Association, Las Vegas city manager, Clark County manager, chairman of the Nevada Gaming Control Board, and chair of the Colorado River Commission.

Burkholder, Lyle — Former superintendent of schools.

Burton, Dave — Strip lounge entertainer during the 1950s.

Call, Anson — Mormon pioneer and the founder of Callville, the head of Colorado River navigation.

Cannon, Helen — Activist member of the Clark County School Board.

Carson, Eileen — Chief clerk at Clark County Justice Court for 22 years.

Christensen, Don — Prominent leader in the Mormon Church.

Christensen, M.J. — Opened one of the city's first jewelry stores; also served in the state legislature and worked with Maude Frazier to start UNLV.

Clark, Donald — Civil rights leader in the 1960s, chair of the Clark County Economic Opportunity Board, and a county commissioner.

Clark, Nina — Purveyor of fine women's fashions.

Clark, Wilbur — Home builder who conceived the Desert Inn and built it with Moe Dalitz' money.

Clyne, Richie — Built the Las Vegas Motor Speedway.

Cohen, Burton — Attorney and resort executive who was an early proponent of special events to stabilize visitor volume through the year.

Cortez, Manny — Current president of the Las Vegas Convention and Visitors Authority.

Crockett, George — Built Alamo Airport, which evolved into McCarran International Airport.

Dickinson, James — First head of the college now known as UNLV.

Di Rocco, Chuck — Publisher of *Gaming Today.*

Diehlman, Jake — Operated a crane at Boulder Dam and founded Jake's Crane and Rigging.

Dingle, Pat and Muffie — Started the city zoo on Rancho Drive.

Dondero, Thalia — Longtime Clark County commissioner.

Doric, Charles — Involved in the development of simulcasts for race and sports books.

Drakulich, Michael "Chub" — Founded the athletic program at what would become UNLV and served as the college's first baseball, basketball, and golf coach.

Ducette, Alice — A beloved first-grade teacher.

Duke, Forrest — Newspaper columnist covering entertainment and Las Vegas booster.

Dula, Sgt. Robert — Motorcycle officer who fought juvenile crime in the 1950s; killed in the line of duty.

Duncan, Ruby — Welfare-rights activist and leader in the black community.

Dungan, Flora — Worked for equal representation of Clark County in state government.

Earl, Ira — First Mormon bishop of Las Vegas; also served on the local school board.

Ellsworth, Elmo — Sales director for the Las Vegas Convention Authority; credited with jump-starting the city's convention business.

Engelstad, Ralph — Resort owner who has an extraordinary automobile collection.

Ernst, Suzanne — Advocate for senior citizens who helped open many of the state's facilities for seniors.

Escobedo, Eddie — Founding publisher of *El Mundo,* a Spanish language newspaper.

Evans, Claude "Blackie" — Prominent state labor leader since the 1950s.

Farnsworth, Frances — Founded the Mesquite Club.

Fleming, Stella — Administrator of Clark County Social Services for 40 years and a founding member of St. Anne's Catholic Church.

Fong, Wing and Lily — Wing Fong was a prominent businessman; his wife, Lily Fong, was a University of Nevada regent.

Frehner, Merle — Involved in establishing the Boulder Dam Area Council, Boy Scouts of America.

Garehime, Jacob — Founder of Las Vegas' first music store in 1924.

Garside, Frank "Scoop" — Publisher of the *Las Vegas Review-Journal* and a Las Vegas postmaster.

Gaughan, Jackie — Operated several downtown casinos.

Gaughan, Michael — Perfected the suburban casino.

George, Lloyd — Federal district judge appointed by President Ronald Reagan.

German, Ray — Las Vegas newspaperman, teacher, and university regent.

Goffstein, Benny — Associated with the Flamingo Hotel and later built the Four Queens Hotel and Casino.

Gohres, William — Developer, builder, and philanthropist.

Goodman, Carolyn — Started the Meadows School, an outstanding private academy.

Goodman, Oscar — Las Vegas' present mayor and an outstanding attorney noted for defending organized crime figures.

Grant, Archie — Chamber of Commerce official who helped Maude Frazier start UNLV.

Gray, R. Guild — First superintendent of the Clark County School District.

Greenbaum, Gus — Brought success to the fledgling Flamingo Hotel after Ben Siegel's death; also largely responsible for creating Paradise Township, thus fending off city annexation of the Strip.

Grier, Dr. Edmund — Physicist and one of the "G's" in EG&G, an early contractor at the Nevada [Nuclear] Test Site.

Gusewell, Francis W. — One of the original Elks; a Clark County commissioner, he helped to establish the tradition of the Elks Helldorado rodeo and parade.

Guzman, Al — Veteran Las Vegas resort publicist.

Hadland, Kenneth — Served as Las Vegas' first park commissioner, beginning in the 1940s.

Hall, Ashley — Las Vegas City Manager, 1983-90; helped the Catholic Charities establish St. Vincent's and Shade Tree homeless shelters.

Ham, Artemus — A Golden Nugget founder and a large donor to UNLV.

Hammes, Romy — Involved in establishing Bishop Gorman High School.

Hannifan, Phil — Longtime chair of the state gaming control board and later chief of operations for Summa Corp.

Harris, Hanshue "Pop" — Figured in the founding of Western Air Express.

Harrison, Sister Mary Carolyn — First administrator of St. Rose de Lima Hospital in Henderson after it was taken over from the government following World War II.

Henry, Hank — Burlesque star and president of the first chapter of the Screen Actor's Guild in Vegas.

Herr, Senator Helen — State senator from Clark County, 1967-1975.

Hess, Dennis — Instrumental in having Red Rock Canyon designated for recreational use.

Hicks, Marion — Partner in the El Cortez and Thunderbird hotels.

Hill, Charlotte — Founder of Friends of Channel 10, United Way president, and Boys and Girls Clubs president.

Hoggard, Mabel — Educator and civil rights leader.

Honn, Betty — Rescuer of stray animals who also assisted homeless people at her shelter.

Houssels, J.K. — Started the Las Vegas Club; also owned the Tropicana and part of the Showboat.

Hudlow, Lloyd — Assistant director of the Boulder Canyon Project.

Hunsberger, Charles — Director of the Las Vegas-Clark County Library District; built several new libraries in the 1980s and 1990s.

Hunt, Leigh — Las Vegas land baron in the 1920s; the Huntridge district is named for him.

Jefferson, P.L. — Built the Brown Derby club in a segregated Las Vegas.

Johns, Albert — UNLV author and political science professor who advocated the establishment of districts for state senators; later, a senior-issues newspaper columnist.

Johnson, Lubertha — Businesswoman and civil rights leader.

Johnson-Cunningham, Anika — Leader in helping African-Americans understand their ancestral culture; also introduced the African holiday of Kwanza to Las Vegas.

Jolley, R.G. "Rube" — One of the founders of Las Vegas' first TV station, KLAS.

Jones, Clifford — Former lieutenant governor and a prominent lawyer involved in dozens of international gaming ventures.

Jones, Glenn — Clark County sheriff in the 1950s.

Jones, Herbert — Lawyer active in state and county bar associations, and founder of the First Presbyterian Church.

Kaye, Mary — Her Mary Kaye Trio was one of the first Las Vegas lounge acts.

Keefer, Milt — FBI agent assigned to watch Bugsy Siegel; later became a respected attorney.

Key, Alice — Entertainer, civil rights activist, and longtime Southern Nevada labor commissioner.

King, Richard — Journalist who was instrumental in getting land donated for the North Las Vegas Civic Center.

Kishner, Irwin — Tourism booster and co-author of the plan that created the Nevada Commission on Tourism; also a co-founder of the Nevada Hotel-Motel Association.

Knudsen, K.O. — Inspiring educator who organized the local system of junior high schools and advocacy groups for the blind and retired.

Kogan, Jack — Early radio and TV personality.

Kozlowski, Mary — Environmental lobbyist and the first woman appointed to the Colorado River Commission.

Kring, Gerald W. — Involved in bringing managed health care to Southern Nevada.

Krolak, Betty — Organized the Women's Council of the Las Vegas Board of Realtors.

Ladd, James — Built the first hotel and later the first resort with a pool.

Lamb, Floyd — Popular and effective legislator, convicted of political corruption.

Laub, Harold Goodspeed — Co-founder of Southwest Gas Corporation.

Laxalt, Paul — Governor, 1966-70; U.S. senator, 1974-1986.

Lenz, Bernie — Started a modeling school in 1949.

Levin, Al and Bonnie — Started Bonnie Springs Ranch in 1952 and built "Old Nevada" in the 1970s.

Levy, Alvin — Former Las Vegas city councilman.

Ley, James — Clark County planner and administrator.

Leypoldt, W.E. "Butch" — Sheriff who closed Clark County's last wide-open brothels.

Lionel, Sam — Founded the state's largest and most influential law firm, Lionel, Sawyer, and Collins.

Lowell, William Jr. — Built Las Vegas' first outdoor theater.

Lynch, Clay — City manager of Henderson and, later, of North Las Vegas.

Lynch, Sister Rosemary — Anti-nuclear activist.

Mack, Jerome "Jerry" — Banker, civic leader, and a co-founder and constant benefactor of UNLV.

Malone, George "Molly" — U.S. senator from Nevada, elected 1946.

Marr, Howard — Involved in creating the county's first school program for handicapped children and a founder of the Clark County Association for Retarded Citizens.

Martin, Anne — Promoted women's suffrage and ran for the U.S. senate in 1918.

Maxson, Dr. Robert — University of Nevada-Las Vegas president during the period when enrollment rose by 10,000 and 17 new buildings were erected.

May, Ernest — First Las Vegas city policeman killed in the line of duty.

McAfee, Guy — Operated several downtown clubs and dubbed U.S. Highway 91 "The Strip."

McCall, Quannah — Local dentist and president of the Clark County School Board.

McClure, Florence — Helped revise Nevada's antiquated rape laws.

McDaniel, James — Architect for several buildings at UNLV.

McDonald, Herb — Promoted Las Vegas as an event city and helped bring the National Finals Rodeo to town.

Mendoza, John — One of the first Hispanic lawyers in Las Vegas; later became a District Court judge.

Michael, Charles B. — Pioneer working man who dug ditches downtown, helped build the road to Mount Charleston, and worked as a high-scaler at Hoover Dam.

Mikulich, Sebastian — Founder of the Las Vegas-Tonopah-Reno bus line.

Miller, Steve — City councilman involved in government-access cable TV and the Citizen Area Transit (CAT) bus system.

Mitchell, A.B. William "Pop" — In an era when Las Vegas was still heavily segregated, ran a resort ranch on the L.A. Highway where blacks could swim and hold picnics and dances.

Moore, R. Julian — Helped the BMI complex become privately owned and operated after World War II.

Moore, William — Co-founder of the Last Frontier resort in 1942.

Morris, "Wildcat" Bill — Archetypical UNLV booster.

Morris, Steve — Lawyer who drafted Nevada Rules for Lawyer Discipline; chair and co-drafter of Nevada Rules of Professional Conduct for Lawyers.

Murray, Trudi — Owner of a fur shop that supplied the wealthy in Las Vegas' era of elegance.

Neal, Joe — First black state legislator.

Newcomer, Leland — Clark County superintendent of schools, 1961-65.

Newlands, Francis — Mississippi senator who created the U.S. Bureau of Reclamation.

Newman, Cy and Evelyn — Started the first black radio station in Las Vegas, KAVA, "The Cool Voice of Vegas."

Newton, Wayne — Entertainer closely identified with Las Vegas.

Oram, Kent — Highly successful political campaign manager.

Pappas, John — Built the White Spot Cafe downtown in 1929.

Park, John S. — Rich Easterner who opened the First State Bank in Las Vegas' earliest years.

Peccole, William — Land developer and city councilman.

Pittman, Key — U.S. senator from Nevada, 1912-1940.

Purcell, Roy — Noted Southern Nevada artist and supporter of the Clark County Heritage Museum.

Pushard, Keith — Veteran worker for Nevada Power Company.

Raizin, Leonard, M.D. — One of the first board-certified anesthesiologists in Las Vegas.

Rasmussen, Charles — Psychology professor at UNLV; served on the pre-professional committee that helped steer qualified applicants to medical schools.

Ralston, Jon — Political observer and writer.

Redd, Si — Head of International Game Technology, the largest slot manufacturing operation in the world.

Reizner, Sonny — Respected oddsmaker who focused national attention on Las Vegas by posting odds on offbeat events, such as "Who shot J.R."

Reynolds, Debbie — Veteran Las Vegas headliner who opened her own hotel-casino.

Reynolds, Donald W. — Bought the Las Vegas Review-Journal in 1949.

Riddle, Major — Owner of the Dunes Hotel, the Silver Nugget casino, and other properties.

Rivera, Rafael — First non-Indian to see the Las Vegas Valley.

Roberts, Eugenia — Active in community concerts, opera, and dance.

Rochelle, Michael — Pastor of Shadow Hills Baptist Church.

Rockwell, Leon — Early land speculator.

Rodman, Kitty — Building contractor and philanthropist.

Ruegg, Eleanor — Started the city's first foreign currency exchange at the Bank of Las Vegas.

Russell, Colonel Bob — Manager of the Apache Hotel, now the Horseshoe, and a city booster.

Ruvo, Angie — The Ruvos brought pizza to Las Vegas by opening the Venetian Pizzeria.

Schneider, Bernadine C. — One of the founders of Las Vegas' first battered women's shelter.

Sakowicz, Sig — Las Vegas radio and TV personality.

Schulman, Bob — Builder of Alexis Park, a major nongaming resort.

Schwartz, Reva — Brought Weight Watchers to Las Vegas.

Scott, Frank — Longtime Las Vegas businessman and the builder of the Union Plaza Hotel.

Searles, Kenneth — Bought Anderson Dairy in 1939.

Seastrand, James — Longtime mayor of North Las Vegas and a founder of Vegas Village, the first all-in-one shopping center in the Valley.

Segerblom, Cliff — Noted local artist, active in Boulder City politics.

Sennes, Frank — Veteran Las Vegas entertainment director and producer.

Shelley, Deecie Kennicott — Citizen activist who helped create a low income mobile home community for seniors.

Shue, Luther — President of Culinary Workers Union Local 226, who helped get its union hall built.

Siegfried and Roy — Popular Las Vegas stage act.

Silvagni, Pietro Otavio — Built the Apache Hotel, which later became the Horseshoe; it was the first Las Vegas hotel with air conditioning and an elevator.

Silver, Jeffrey — Noted gaming law attorney, casino executive, and past member of the Nevada Gaming Control Board.

Simanski, Lt. Col. Donald E. — Established electronic warfare range at Nellis Air Force Base, an important feature of the "Red Flag" air combat games.

Simon, Peter Albert "Pop" — Owned and operated an early airport in Las Vegas, now the site of Nellis Air Force Base; also the founder of Jean, Nevada.

Smith, John L. — Popular local newspaper columnist.

Snow, Robert — Conceived what became the Fremont Street Experience.

Snow, Larry — Popularized baccarat among Las Vegas gamblers; the game now can make or break a hotel's monthly bottom line.

Soss, Fanny — Ladies' fashion retailer.

Soss, Maury — Ladies' fashion retailer and patron of the arts.

Steele, John — Architect of the 1855 Mormon Fort in Las Vegas.

Stuart, John — Created "Legends in Concert," the first hit show built around celebrity impersonators.

Sulich, Vassili — Founder and formerly artistic director of Nevada Dance Theatre for 25 years.

Tabat, Louis — North Las Vegas constable and businessman.

Tam, Richard — Land developer and major UNLV benefactor.

Tecopa — Chief who represented the Southern Paiutes in the late 19th and early 20th centuries.

Tiberti, J.A. — Prolific Las Vegas builder who served on the city planning commission for 25 years.

Tocco, Johnny — Gym owner who helped bring big-time boxing to Las Vegas.

Ullom, George — Founded the Nevada Resort Association.

Underhill, Clarence — Opened the city's first Coca-Cola bottling plant.

Vanda, Charles — Founded KVVU-TV and started the UNLV Master Series and lecture series.

Vandenberg, Joylin J. — Downtown retailer who founded Opportunity Village.

Vega, Rafael E. — Businessman and philanthropist who was appointed honorary consul general by the Mexican government in 1996.

Vincent, Bill — *Review-Journal* writer and editor whose articles jump-started the local environmental movement.

Vitto, G.L. — Eccentric sports commentator.

Warren, Elizabeth — Fought to preserve Las Vegas history and buildings.

Warren, Rose — Established the first maternity home for women and was famed for helping the hungry and homeless.

Wasco, Sister Angelita — Successful fundraiser for St. Rose de Lima, now St. Rose Dominican, with her Angel Bread Foundation.

Weiner, Louis — Attorney, chamber of commerce officer, and city booster.

West, Dr. Charles — Las Vegas' first black physician.

West, Pete — Pioneer Moapa Valley rancher.

White, Juanita Greer — Helped separate Nevada Southern, now UNLV, from the University of Nevada-Reno.

Wiesner, Tom — Businessman, casino owner, and brewer.

Willard, Bill — Writer, artist, and show producer; also the first executive director of the Nevada State Council on the Arts.

Williams, A.G. — Started the first pest-control business in Las Vegas.

Williams, Claudine — Co-founder and head of Harrah's Las Vegas.

Williams, Nancy — Poet who published three books about black experience under the name "Big Mama."

Willis, Vern — Started the first travel agency in Las Vegas.

Wilkerson, William R. "Billy" — Original developer of the Flamingo, muscled out by Benjamin "Bugsy" Siegel.

Woodbury, Claire — Active with the school board and the state board of health.

Wright, Dr. John S. — Taught history at UNLV, 1956-76.

Wyatt, Katie — Involved in developing the Lee Canyon Ski Area.

Young, Brigham — Sent the first Mormon missionaries to Las Vegas.

Zorn, Ann — Citizen activist who advocated strong flood-control measures.

Zunino, Jack — Award-winning landscape architect.

Index